Forensic and Medico-legal Aspects of Sexual Crimes and Unusual Sexual Practices

Forensic and Medico-legal Aspects of Sexual Crimes and Unusual Sexual Practices

Anil Aggrawal

CRC Press
Taylor & Francis Group
Boca Raton London New York

CRC Press is an imprint of the
Taylor & Francis Group, an **informa** business

CRC Press
Taylor & Francis Group
6000 Broken Sound Parkway NW, Suite 300
Boca Raton, FL 33487-2742

International Standard Book Number-13: 978-1-4200-4308-2 (Hardcover)

Library of Congress Cataloging-in-Publication Data

Aggrawal, Anil.
Forensic and medico-legal aspects of sexual crimes and unusual sexual practices / Anil Aggrawal.
p. cm.
Includes bibliographical references and index.
ISBN 978-1-4200-4308-2 (hardcover : alk. paper)
1. Sex crimes. 2. Paraphilias. 3. Psychosexual disorders. 4. Sexual orientation. 5. Sex (Psychology) I. Title.

HQ71.A34 2009
363.25'953--dc22 2008038133

Visit the Taylor & Francis Web site at
http://www.taylorandfrancis.com

and the CRC Press Web site at
http://www.crcpress.com

Dedication

To my friend Sue Black of the University of Dundee,
who has always encouraged me in my scientific endeavors

Contents

Preface

Deviant or abnormal sexual behavior is an exciting field of study. Many professionals including psychologists, psychiatrists, medico-legal professionals, lawyers, law enforcement authorities and criminologists are interested in it. Despite this, no single book seemed to cater to the needs of these professionals. The idea of writing such a book was thus very tempting to me, especially because I have been deeply interested in this field for the last several years.

When I shared this idea with my friend Philippe Lunetta of Finland (Philippe happens to be a worldwide expert on asphyxiophilia), not only was he excited at the proposal, he immediately sent me a bunch of useful papers on strange sexual behaviors. Some were in European languages other than English and I had not seen them earlier. The next stage was to contact the leading publisher in this field, and I was pleasantly surprised when Becky McEldowney Masterman of Taylor & Francis took tremendous interest in the project and asked me to go ahead with this book.

The book deals with all eight major paraphilias mentioned in the latest edition of DSM: pedophilia (302.2), transvestic fetishism (302.3), exhibitionism (302.4), fetishism (302.81), voyeurism (302.82), sexual masochism (302.83), sexual sadism (302.84) and frotteurism (302.89), as well as a ninth group [paraphilias not otherwise specified (302.9)]. A chapter has been devoted to each paraphilia. Seven chapters have been devoted to sexual crimes and other sexually deviant behaviors (rape, bestiality, sexual harassment, necrophilia, incest and telephone scatologia). And finally, one chapter has been devoted to transsexualism, which is neither a paraphilia nor a sexual crime, but has so much in common with transvestism and other seemingly abnormal sexual behaviors that it did warrant a separate treatment in my opinion.

This, to my mind, is the first book that deals with sexually deviant behavior and sexual crimes from a multidisciplinary point of view. Medical, psychological, criminological and legal standpoints have been discussed in detail. Classifications of all major paraphilias have been introduced, many of which were not previously classified. It is hoped that these classifications will shed more light on paraphilias and help us to understand them better.

Although laws relating to major paraphilias and sexual crimes from all major jurisdictions have been included, this is an unfulfilled task and many readers may find laws of their own jurisdictions missing. Some laws were deliberately omitted to keep the size of the book manageable. I would, however, love to hear from readers from different nations with relevant laws in their own countries as well as actual cases decided based on those laws. They will be included in the next edition of the book, with due credit and acknowledgment. Please be kind enough to respond at dr_anil@hotmail.com or anil.aggrawal@gmail.com. The author's mailing address is S-299 Greater Kailash-1, New Delhi-110048, India.

Acknowledgments

At the outset, I must express my deep sense of gratitude to Becky McEldowney Masterman of Taylor & Francis, who found the idea of a book on paraphilias exciting and encouraged me to go ahead. She also gave me a number of valuable ideas. Kari Budyk, also of Taylor & Francis, also helped me in a number of ways in the preparation of this book. And thanks to Becky for coping with my laziness. I know I took much longer to complete this book, than I should have.

During the preparation of this book, I had the benefit of constantly interacting with Ray Blanchard, who advised me on a number of topics. He was also kind enough to send me a CD containing a collection of all his papers on forensic aspects of sex crimes and paraphilias.

I am thankful to my friend Akiyoshi Nishimura, associate professor of forensic medicine, at the Yokohama City University School of Medicine, Japan, who not only sent me a number of valuable and difficult-to-get Japanese papers on paraphilias but even translated them for me.

I am thankful to several colleagues in different parts of the world, who spared no pains in sending me valuable material from their collections. Main among them are Prashant Aggarwal, Department of Forensic Medicine, BHU, India; Philip Lunetta from Finland; Katsuji Nishi from Japan; Ramesh Kaul, Rahul Malhotra and Deepak Kalra from the United States; and Neeraj Gupta from New Zealand. And of course I made good use of the excellent National Medical Library in New Delhi. My son Tarun and nephew Nitin, both currently in the United States, have a vast collection of papers on this subject in their collection, and they freely and ungrudgingly sent me a rare paper whenever I needed one.

Last but not the least, I am thankful to my mother, Kamla Devi, and father-in-law, Satya Pal Gupta Ji, who helped launch my academic career in many ways.

Special Acknowledgment

I wish to extend a very special acknowledgment to my wife and life long passion, Marygold, for her patience, encouragement, understanding, and unflinching support. Needless to say, this book would never have seen the light of the day without her constant presence around me.

About the Author

Anil Aggrawal earned his medical doctorate in forensic medicine and toxicology from All India Institute of Medical Sciences, New Delhi. He moved to Edinburgh—traditionally regarded as the birthplace of forensic medicine—for higher training. As a recipient of a prestigious World Health Organization fellowship, he pursued additional training in Japan and the United States.

Dr. Aggrawal currently teaches forensic medicine at the Maulana Azad Medical College in New Delhi. He also edits a peer-reviewed Internet journal covering forensic medicine. Paraphilias, sexual crimes, and their medico-legal aspects has been his special area of interest for the last 25 years.

Dr. Aggrawal lives in New Delhi with his wife and a personal library of more than 20,000 books.

1 Sexual Crimes and Unusual Sexual Practices: An Overview

INTRODUCTION

Few topics in the realm of human behavior are more fascinating, exciting, or perhaps contentious and controversial than sex. Sex is interesting, intriguing, and sometimes even disturbing. It has stimulated more attention than any other aspect of human behavior. Great curiosity is aroused by sexual practices deemed unusual, deviant, or deplorable. Known variously as sexual perversions, sexual deviations, or more commonly paraphilias, these practices range from the commonly known sadism, masochism, fetishism, and voyeurism to such uncommon and esoteric as homilophilia (sexual arousal from hearing or giving sermons), choreophilia (sexual arousal from dancing), and tripsolagnia (sexual arousal from having hair shampooed)![1]

According to the revised fourth edition of the *Diagnostic and Statistical Manual of Mental Disorders* (DSM-IV-TR),[2] all sexual disorders are divided into three groups. (i) *Sexual dysfunctions,* characterized by inhibitions in sexual desire or dysfunction of the psychophysiological changes that characterize the sexual response cycle are the most common of all sexual disorders.[3] (ii) *Paraphilias* (previously *deviations*) are characterized by arousal in response to sexual objects or situations not part of normal arousal activity patterns, and may interfere with a capacity for reciprocal, affectionate sexual activity. (iii) *Gender identity disorders* are characterized by distinct and continuous identification with the opposite sex and persistent discomfort with one's own.

It is important to realize that these categories are neither totally satisfactory nor mutually exclusive. However, in the absence of any better divisions it is probably inevitable that these categories continue to be used.[4]

Of the three, paraphilias are perhaps unique in the sense that they attract a lot of attention from the general public as well as the legal system. Because they frequently involve victimization and brutality, they are generally considered inappropriate and are frequently illegal.[5]

Paraphilias, according to DSM-IV-TR are diagnosed by two criteria:

> The essential features of a Paraphilia are recurrent, intense sexually arousing fantasies, sexual urges, or behaviors generally involving (1) nonhuman objects, (2) the suffering or humiliation of oneself or one's partner, or (3) children or other nonconsenting persons, that occur over a period of at least 6 months (**Criterion A**). For some individuals, paraphiliac fantasies or stimuli are obligatory for erotic arousal and are always included in sexual activity. In other cases, the paraphiliac preferences occur only episodically (e.g. perhaps during periods of stress), whereas at other times, the person is able to function sexually without paraphiliac fantasies or stimuli. The behavior, sexual urges, or fantasies cause clinically significant distress or impairment in social, occupational, or other important areas of functioning (**Criterion B**).

John William Money (1921–2006),[6] a former professor of pediatrics and medical psychology at Johns Hopkins University, defines paraphilia as follows:

> A condition occurring in men and women of being compulsively responsive to and obligatorily dependent on an unusual and personally or socially unacceptable stimulus, perceived or in the ideation and imagery of fantasy, for optimal initiation and maintenance of sexuoerotic arousal and the facilitation or attainment of orgasm. Paraphilic imagery may be replayed in fantasy during solo masturbation or intercourse with a partner. Its antonym is normophilia.

TABLE 1.1
DSM-IV-TR Codes for Paraphilias

302.2	Pedophilia
302.3	Transvestic fetishism
302.4	Exhibitionism
302.81	Fetishism
302.82	Voyeurism
302.83	Sexual masochism
302.84	Sexual sadism
302.89	Frotteurism
302.9	Paraphilia not otherwise specified

DSM-IV-TR[2] now specifically mentions fifteen paraphilias by name. Of these eight have been allotted specific diagnostic codes (Table 1.1). Seven other paraphilias—telephone scatologia (obscene phone calls), necrophilia (sexual attraction to corpses), partialism (exclusive focus on part of body), zoophilia (sexual attraction to animals), coprophilia (erotic attraction to feces), klismaphilia (enemas), and urophilia (urine)—are grouped in the category "Paraphilia not otherwise specified." It is specifically mentioned that "examples include, but are not limited to" these representative examples.

Paraphilias can be transient, as demonstrated by experimentation during the teenage years, or can remain a life-long problem involving legal, financial, interpersonal, occupational, academic, and other aspects of life.

Aberrant sexual behavior was scientifically studied for the first time by the Austro-German psychiatrist Richard Freiherr von Krafft-Ebing (1840–1902), who mentioned several in his book *Psychopathia Sexualis*[7] (Sexual Psychopathy), published in 1886 (Figure 1.1).

Krafft-Ebing intended the book as a reference tool for academicians, doctors, and judges. So obsessed that only academicians and other educated classes were to read his book, he wrote many sections in Latin—then a language of the educated class. He also deliberately chose a title sounding highly scientific (*Psychopathia Sexualis*), so lay readers would be dissuaded from reading it. The book, however, went on to become highly popular with lay readers and it went through as many as twelve editions in his lifetime and several translations. In fact, due to a high demand when the book was in its second printing, some publishers translated all Latin passages into languages understandable by the general public!

Krafft-Ebing divided sexual deviation into following four categories:

1. *Paradoxia,* sexual desire at the wrong time of life, i.e., childhood or old age.
2. *Anesthesia,* insufficient desire.
3. *Hyperesthesia,* excessive desire.
4. *Paraesthesia,* sexual desire for the wrong goal or object. This included homosexuality (or "contrary sexual desire"), sexual fetishism, sadism, masochism, pederasty, and so on.

The fourth group is roughly equivalent to paraphilias as we know them today.

Krafft-Ebing also shared the ecclesiastical belief that the purpose of sexual desire was procreation, and any form of desire that did not go toward that ultimate goal was a perversion. Thus sexual activities like bestiality, fellation, cunnilingus, lesbianism, and homosexuality were perversions (because pregnancy could not result from them). Rape on the contrary was not a perversion (even though an aberrant act), since pregnancy could result. This belief was seriously challenged later. In fact, it has always been very hard, if not impossible, to formulate a universally acceptable definition of normal and perverted sexual behavior.

FIGURE 1.1 Richard von Krafft-Ebing with his wife Marie Luise. This image was made before 1900.

DEFINITIONS

This highly influential psychiatric text laid the groundwork for the development of further research and treatment in the area of aberrant sexual behavior. The word *paraphilia* was, however, first coined by the Viennese psychotherapist Wilhelm Stekel (1868–1940)in 1924[8] and has been translated as "interest in perversion" or "love of the perverse."[9] Etymologically the word *paraphilia* comes from Greek words *para*, "beside, near or beyond," and *philos*, "love." Thus, literally *paraphilia* refers to a "love of something beyond normal." Politely the term is known as *fringe sex*, *variant sexuality*, *alternate sexuality*, or *sexual variations*. Contemporary slang terms for the term include *bizarre*, *kinky*, *pervy*, or *weird sex*.[10] However, as mentioned earlier, normal sex has never been satisfactorily defined.

What is Normal Sexual Behavior?

Traditionally the definitions of normal sexual behavior have always depended heavily upon who is defining the term, his or her cultural background, and even the era in which the term is defined. Historically the criteria of what is or is not normal have changed time and again. There was a time when any form of sexual expression other than face-to-face copulation (or missionary position) even among legally wedded couples was an offense against canon law and a sin in the eyes of the Christian Church.[11,12] This view, based on the teachings of St. Augustine (d. 430 AD), who taught that sex should be engaged in only for the purpose of procreation, found its adherents in several other religions, such as Buddhism. Masturbation was once considered a perversion, and until recently was even a crime in several jurisdictions such as the State of Nebraska.[13] Leading medical authorities of the nineteenth century were convinced that it led to moral degeneration and insanity.[14] These views even promoted a lucrative trade in mechanical restraints to prevent children from touching their genitals.[15] Today the practice is not only considered normal, but even a healthy "safety valve" for the release of sexual tension. Likewise, oral sex was once considered abnormal, because it could not impregnate a female, but is now considered perfectly normal. The case of homosexuality is perhaps most interesting. In Ancient Greece, homosexual behavior was not only *not* considered abnormal, but was seen as a more elevated and spiritual form of relationship than heterosexual. As time passed, it gradually began to be considered a sexual perversion, and even a criminal behavior. Until 1968, homosexuality was listed as a sexual deviation in the *Diagnostic and Statistical Manual of Mental Disorders*.[16] But once again it came to be considered a normal sexual behavior and removed—about a decade later—from DSM-III (1980).[17] It is, however, not considered an exalted form of sexual relationship yet.

Culture and religion also tend to modify the concept of paraphilia. Although homosexuality has not been included in the *Diagnostic and Statistical Manual of Mental Disorders* since its 3rd edition, it is still considered taboo in many cultures around the world. Currently same-sex marriages are legal only in Belgium and the Netherlands.[18] In many cultures homosexuality even among consenting adults is a crime. In India, for instance, it is a crime punishable under section 377 of the Indian Penal Code (IPC), attracting a maximum penalty of ten years' imprisonment with fine.[19] Adultery is an offense in many countries but not in many others.[13] Premarital or extramarital sex offends some people, but many others consider these acts not worthy of objection as long as they do not bring distress to third parties. Genital stimulation in some societies is a legitimate method of calming and comforting an infant in distress, whereas in other societies it would be viewed as an act of pedophilia, a criminal offense.[20] Cousin marriages are sanctioned—even encouraged—in some societies, while in others they constitute incest. Beating and subjugating a wife into obedience, erotic or otherwise, is socially and legally proper in some societies, whereas in others it may constitute the criminal offense of sadism. Among the tribes of Central Africa, where going topless is the norm for women, such exposure is not likely to be considered an abnormal sexual behavior, while if a girl walked topless on the streets of New Delhi or New York, she would almost certainly be arrested for the offense of indecent exposure. Other sexual behaviors such as fellation, cunnilingus, anal sex, prostitution, and some categories of visual and literary erotica and pornography likewise have been decriminalized in many societies and are better tolerated than in other societies. Paraphilia may thus be conceived more as a social rather than a medical concept. There is, however, a core of extremely deviant behavior (e.g., lust murder) that has always been, and perhaps always will be, considered abnormal.

Sex and Gender

Some sexually odd behaviors such as transsexualism, transvestism, homosexuality, and lesbianism may cause considerable confusion, especially as some behavior patterns in these groups may overlap. To avoid confusion, it is best to define some basic terms as clearly as possible at the outset.

Two terms that are most commonly confused are *sex* and *gender.* While *sex* refers to biological sexuality, *gender* refers to psychosocial sexuality. Sex is defined by six component parts:[21] (i) chromosomes, (ii) gonads, (iii) internal genitalia, (iv) external genitalia, (v) sex hormones, and finally (vi) secondary sexual characteristics. In contrast, *gender* refers to the *psychosocial condition* of being masculine or feminine. To take an example, a person may be born biologically as a male, and have all six components of biological sex seen in males, yet he may show sexual feelings of a woman (i.e., an attraction toward men) and may even dress and behave like women. His *sex* is male, but his *gender* is female. *Transsexual* individuals have opposite sex and gender. Gender identity establishes in a child as soon as he begins to talk (around one year of age). It is usual to refer to genders as man and woman, and to related matching biological sexes as male and female. Individuals having a conflicting sex and gender are included in a broad group known as transgender. *Transphobia*, literally the fear of transsexuals, refers to a prejudicial hatred of transsexuals.

INTERSEXUALITY

Sometimes, even the six biological components may not belong to the same sex. Such condition—occurring in about 0.018% of cases—is known as *intersexuality*, and such a person is called an *intersex* and may have biological characteristics of both the male and female sexes. *Intersexuality* may also be defined as a condition in which chromosomal sex is inconsistent with phenotypic sex, or in which the phenotype is not classifiable as either male or female.

SEXUAL ORIENTATION

Sexual orientation is the experience of or capacity for erotic or sexual attraction to one or both sexes. If a male has an erotic attraction toward members of his own sex, he is said to have a *homosexual* orientation. A person having an erotic attraction toward members of opposite sex has a *heterosexual* orientation. If the erotic attraction is toward both men and women, the orientation is *bisexual*, if on oneself, *autosexual,* and if there is no sexual interest at all, the orientation is *asexual*. Persons whose sexual orientations are not heterosexual form a sexual minority (please see below).

The American biologist and famous sex researcher Alfred Charles Kinsey (1894–1956) realized that sexual orientation did not exist as a discrete entity; instead it existed as a continuum, with many shades and variations.* In 1948, Kinsey[22] advanced a seven-point scale of sexual orientation, often known as the "Heterosexual/ Homosexual Rating Scale" or simply the "Kinsey Scale of Homosexuality " (please see chapter on transsexualism for details of this scale). Eighteen years later, in 1966, the German born American sexologist Harry Benjamin suggested a similar scale for gender identity (please see below).

Pansexuality describes an individual's attraction which is not based on the other person's sex, and includes attraction to transgender and intersex persons. *Queer* is an omnibus term used to describe any non-normative sexuality and gender expression, especially homosexuality, bisexuality, transgenderism, and intersexuality, but also sometimes BDSM and fetishism. *Asexuality* is a sexual orientation describing individuals who do not experience sexual attraction at all. Asexuality is not the same as celibacy, which is the deliberate abstention from sexual activity. Many asexuals do have biological sex.

Nonstandard Genders

Some cultures identify and recognize a *third sex* or *third gender*.[24] These are individuals who behave or dress differently from their socially assigned sex. Same-sex activity is often associated with third-gendered individuals. The term has been used to describe *hijras* of India and Pakistan, *fa'afafine* of Polynesia, *sworn virgins* of the Balkans, *waria* of Indonesia, *mahu* of Tahiti, *xanith* of Middle Eastern Oman, and *washoga* of Muslim Mombasa. Some cultures and societies, such as several Native American Indian societies, have reported a fourth gender[23] and some (e.g., bugis of Sulawesi) even a fifth gender.[24] In Native American Indian societies, the third gender is referred to as *berdache*† (anatomical males) and fourth as *amazons* (anatomical females). Bugis call them calabai ("false woman") and calalai ("false man"), respectively. calabai are anatomical males, while calalai are anatomical females. The fifth gender of bugis is the bissu, a meta-gender group. *Bissu* tends to be translated as "transvestite priest," but this term is not entirely satisfactory.

---

* The term *continuum* is often used in psychology to describe a gradual transition from one condition to a different condition without any abrupt changes or "discontinuities." Many concepts in the psychology of sex, most notably sexual orientation, gender identity and paraphilias are believed to exist on a continuum, rather than as discrete entities.

† For more on berdache, please see chapter on transvestic fetishism.

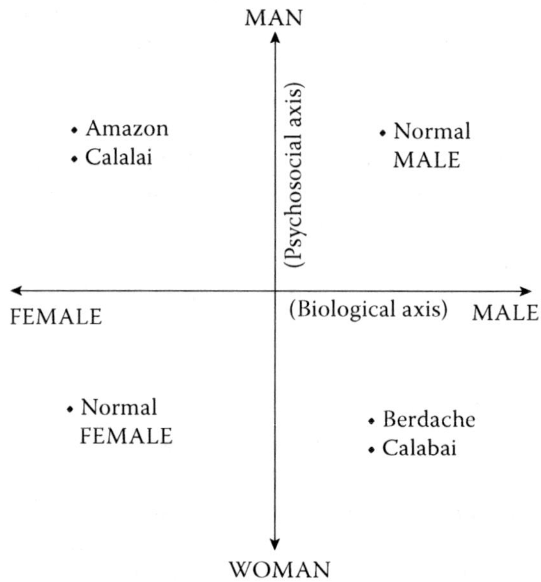

FIGURE 1.2 A proposed *gender spectrum*, locating normal males and females and third and fourth genders. Most conditions involving a conflict between sex and gender can be conveniently located on this graph.

Transvestite implies cross-dressing, but bissu have their own distinctive clothing. Moreover, bissu constitute a combination of all other genders. To become a bissu, one must be born a hermaphrodite, having gonads of both sexes. When such an individual dons the distinctive clothing of a priest, he becomes a bissu. The five genders of the bugis can best be conceptualized by imagining them as constituting a pyramid, with the bissu at the apex, and men, women, calabai, and calalai located at the four base corners (Figure 1.2).

The extra genders are sometimes referred to as "nonstandard genders," and the affected individuals as *androgyne*, *genderqueer*, *bigender*, *multigender*, *intergender* or *two-spirited people*.[23] Cultures recognizing and accepting more than two genders do not adhere to the concept of *gender binary*, the idea that human gender exists in only two forms, male and female.

Various paraphilias may also be seen as disturbed sexual orientations. Generally, however, the paraphilias are considered orthogonal (unrelated) to the sex-based categories of sexual orientation, and are seen as existing *in addition* to such orientations. For example, a male having a homosexual orientation may also *additionally* have a fetishistic orientation. In some cases, a deviant stimulus may be a *more significant* focus of an individual's sexuality than the sex of his partners. Such paraphilias include sexual fetishes, sexual exhibitionism, zoophilia, and even pedophilia.[25]

Gender Role and Gender Identity

Gender roles are those social behaviors, life styles, and personality characteristics that men and women are expected (by the society) to exhibit. For instance, while a man is normally expected to mow the lawn, a woman is expected to stay indoors and look after young children. If a biological male exhibits more interest in staying indoors, looking after young children, his gender role is inverted. *Gender identity*, on the other hand, is one's *own* personal view of himself or herself as male or female. It is the sense of knowing to which sex one belongs, that is, the awareness that "I am a male" or "I am a female." This assumes significance, when it is inconsistent with an individual's biological sex. If a biological male thinks he is a female, he is a *transgender*; he is biologically a male, but his gender identity is female. He is a person who was assigned a gender at birth based

TABLE 1.2
Three Components of Sexual Identity

	Male to Female Transsexual	Male Homosexual	Male Transvestite
Sexual orientation	Same as that of female, i.e., attraction to males	Same as that of female, i.e., attraction to males	Same as that of male, i.e., attraction to females
Gender role	Male	Male	Male
Gender identity	Female	Male	Female

on his genitals, but who feels that this is a false or incomplete description (*cisgender* refers to non-transgender people, i.e., those who identify with the gender assigned at birth. Most people are cisgender). *Gender fluid* is a gender identity which is a dynamic mix of boy and girl. A person who is gender fluid may always feel like a mix of the two traditional genders, but may feel more boy some days and more girl other days. If a person is not content with his biological sex, and would prefer to change it, he is said to have *gender dysphoria.*

The term *analloerotic* (Greek, *an-*, "lacking," and *alloerotic*, "sexual feeling or activity finding its object in another person") has been used to designate gender dysphorics who report no erotic attraction to other persons, male or female. Two types of analloerotics are distinguished; *automonosexuals,** who are erotically aroused by the thought or image of themselves as the opposite sex but not by other persons, and *asexuals* who deny sexual drive or erotic interests of *any* kind.[26] Ray Blanchard introduced the term *autogynephilia* to refer to erotic arousal of a male at the idea of being a woman.[26]Although Blanchard never used the word *autoandrophilia* in his writings, this word would be a logical counterpart, meaning erotic arousal of a female at the idea of being a man.

The American sexologist Harry Benjamin (1885–1986) realized that gender identity (much like sexual orientation) did not exist as a discrete entity, but rather as a continuum, with many shades and variations. In 1966, he proposed a seven-point scale of gender identity,[26] much like the seven-point sexual orientation scale proposed by Alfred Kinsey, 18 years earlier (please see chapter on transsexualism for details of this scale).

Sexual Identity

The sexual identity of a person is composed of three components discussed above, namely, sexual orientation, gender role, and gender identity.[28] The three components may or may not be congruous in every person. If they are incongruous, the person would be seen as afflicted with one or the other sexual disorders, or paraphilias. Table 1.2 shows the three components of sexual identity in a male-to-female transsexual, male homosexual, and a male transvestite.

Sexual Minority

A sexual minority is a group whose sexual identity, orientation, or practices differ from the majority of the surrounding society. Like ethnic minorities, people belonging to sexual minorities may face discrimination and prejudice. Initially, when the term was coined in the late 1960s, it referred primarily to lesbians and gays. Now it has come to include bisexuals and transgender people. These four categories (lesbian, gay, bisexual, and transgender) are often grouped together under the LGBT

* In a strict sense *automonosexuals* should be different from *autosexuals*, a term encountered earlier. Automonosexuals are attracted towards self, imagining themselves to be of opposite sex. This is not necessarily the case with autosexuals, who may be excited by their own bodies as they are.

rubric. Also included under sexual minorities are fetishists, practitioners of bondage and discipline, domination and submission, and/or sadomasochism (collectively referred to as BDSM), and others who engage in less commonly followed sexual practices, but in a completely consensual manner, e.g., wife swapping or swinging. Rapists and child molesters would generally not fall under this term because they do not engage in consensual sex.

Sex Addiction

This term does not appear in any diagnostic classifications, but lately has been used increasingly by the media, lay people, and even some professionals. The term is generally used to describe any form of sexual behavior which is out of control of the patient. The sexual behavior may take the form of seeing pornographic movies, visiting lap dancing clubs, repeated masturbation (several times a day), telephone sex dependence, cyber sex "chat rooms," visiting prostitutes, or having extramarital affairs. The behavior is quite compulsive in nature. Typically the patient experiences an increasing urge to indulge in the desired behavior, which he is able to resist initially to some extent, partly because of the guilt feelings, and partly because he knows that the behavior is self-damaging. However, the pitch of the temptation grows so high, that ultimately his resistance breaks, and he indulges in that behavior (visiting prostitutes, etc.). Immediately after his sex binge is over, there is relief from psychological tension. And as he is relieved of psychological tension, there is a surge of guilt, self-reproach, and promises to change. The cycle of events, which is not unlike that seen with alcohol addiction and food binges, however, keeps on repeating. In some cases it is a true obsessive–compulsive disorder. The behavior is variously known as *sex addiction, sexual addiction, sexual compulsivity, sexual impulsivity*, and *compulsive sexual behavior.* In the past, other labels such as *nymphomania, satyriasis*, and *hypersexuality* have been used for this disorder.[29] It has been argued that the term *impulse control disorder* be used for its description, since it is consistent with the DSM criteria.[30] However, it has little explanatory value beyond inferring a problem of self-control. Paraphilic men frequently report concomitant sexual addiction.[31] This observation has an interesting bearing not only on formulating an etiological model of paraphilia, but also on treatment. Sexual impulsivity alone has often been designated as a paraphilia-related disorder (PRD).[32,33] Simply stated, while paraphilias represent a situation where the stimulus is deviant in nature (e.g., a shoe, a corpse, or a beast), paraphilia-related disorders (or sexual addictions) represent a situation where the stimulus is normal (e.g., a person of the opposite sex), or socially accepted, but the sexual drive is excessive. If a paraphile displays concomitant sexual addiction, as noted above, he suffers from both qualitatively and quantitatively abnormal sexual drives.

It is not entirely clear why some persons go on to become sex addicts, but research in this area is promising. A study conducted on a group of patients with sexual disorders documented that endogenously produced opiates are released in specific brain areas during sexual arousal.[34] Pathological release of such opiates may be a possible etiological factor of sexual addiction.

Objective Criteria of Sexual Deviation

We have seen above that most definitions of *normal* sex are subjective in nature. Holmes,[35] however, tried to determine *objectively* what is or is not normal sex. He devised four criteria which can be used to determine *sexual normalcy*. The list of objective standards suggested by Holmes is as below:

(i) Statistical—what most people do
(ii) Religious—what religion permits or prohibits
(iii) Cultural—what culture encourages or discourages
(iv) Subjective—one's own judgment about behavior

It is clear that using different criteria can develop different definitions of sexual normalcy.

During the early days of the development of the concept of abnormal sexual behavior, the terms *sexual deviation* and *sexual perversion* were common in medical terminology. *Sexual deviation* was the preferred term, because while *deviation* denoted a digression or divergence, *perversion* implied a *willful choice of a wrong course.*[36] However, today both terms are seen as judgmental as they presume an absolute standard of sexual behavior, while there is none. The term "perversion" is considered particularly pernicious, as it carries with it an immoral tone, which can produce in the patient a profound feeling of guilt, which his conduct may not necessarily deserve.[37] In medical literature, these terms have now been replaced almost completely by *paraphilia*, although *perversion* continues to be used in the law and criminal justice systems of many jurisdictions. *Paraphilia* is less judgmental and is therefore scientifically preferable and is used in the latest edition of DSM. Many workers however think that *paraphilia* is not a correct term to describe abnormal sexual behavior. Charles Moser thinks that since the Greek prefix *para* means "other" or "beyond" (as in *paranormal*) or "demented" (as in *paranoia*), and *philia* means "fond" or "loving," the word *paraphilia* translates as "other love" or "demented love." This, he thinks, is a misnomer since abnormal sexual behavior is "demented lust"; the correct term according to him should have been *paralagnia,* from the Greek root *lagnia* or "lust."[38]

HISTORICAL PERSPECTIVES

During the earliest days of the evolution of human culture, any sexual activity which was not procreative was seen as an act against the wishes of God and hence unnatural. It was the Greek philosopher Plato (427–347 BC), who was the first to contend in his *Laws* that masturbation and male–male sexual activity were unnatural because they were not procreative.[39] St. Thomas Aquinas (c. 1225–1274) argued along on the same lines. For him some vices of lechery were contrary to nature, because they were not procreative. On the other hand, some other vices were not contrary to nature, because they were procreative. Among the former group, which were the gravest offenses, were bestiality, masturbation, and homosexuality. Among the latter, which were less grave, were such offenses as heterosexual adultery, rape, seduction, and incest.[40]

One of most sexually perverse men in history was Caligula (AD 12–41), the third Roman Emperor, who reigned from AD 37 to AD 41. It is said that he was a transvestite, committed incest, and even prostituted his sisters to other men. It is alleged that he made his palace into a literal brothel. He was perhaps a zoophile too, because he tried to make his horse, Incitatus, a consul and a priest.[41]

Legendary stories claim that the Frankish king Charlemagne (742–814) displayed many sexual perversions. The main bases of these legends are a wide range of texts from the ninth century onwards which allude to Charlemagne refusing for a long time to confess some serious but unspecified sin, but finally acknowledging it and receiving absolution.[43] Many workers have wondered what this "unspeakable sin " could be. It is said that the standards of sexual behavior at Charlemagne's court were so notoriously loose that the secret sin cannot have been mere adultery. Most now believe that this sin was Charlemagne's deliberate incest with his sister Gillen, resulting in the birth of Roland.[42] Hafner[43] believes this "unspeakable sin" could indeed be incest, but also talks about the possibilities of necrophilia, sodomy, bestiality, and pedophilia (which incidentally she spells as "paludiphilia").

The first physician to study alternative forms of sexual expression was Carl Westphal (1833–1890), who in 1869 published the case study of a young woman who was drawn to her own gender and had historically dressed as a boy.[44]

By the second half of the 19th century, sexual deviations were discussed extensively in the clinical literature. Richard von Krafft-Ebing's *Psychopathia Sexualis*, first published in 1886, discussed such terms as fetishism, flagellation, sadism, necrophilia, sadistic acts with animals, masochism, exhibitionism, bondage, pedophilia, bestiality, and incest.[45]

DSM CLASSIFICATION OF PARAPHILIAS

The *Diagnostic and Statistical Manual* (DSM), published regularly by the American Psychiatric Association, has become the definitive resource for defining psychiatric abnormalities and disorders and for designating the criteria necessary to make specific psychiatric diagnoses. This manual is used by mental health practitioners and also by divorce courts and the criminal justice system to determine what is or is not a mental abnormality. DSM classification of paraphilia is one of the most widely followed among clinicians today. A survey of the evolution of DSM classification gives us some interesting and useful insights into the growth of this concept. Behaviors which were considered paraphiliac or sexually deviant at one point in time were considered quite normal at another.

Prior to the publication of the first DSM (DSM-I), paraphilias were classified as cases of "psychopathic personality with pathologic sexuality." The first edition, which was published in 1952, also did not mention the term *paraphilia*. Instead it mentioned *sexual deviation* under the code number 000-x63. It was included as a subtype of sociopathic personality disturbance within the broad category of personality disorders. The term included such behaviors as homosexuality, rape, and sexual assault. It said:

> This diagnosis is reserved for deviant sexuality which is not symptomatic of more extensive syndromes, such as schizophrenic and obsessional reactions. The term includes most of the cases formerly classed as "psychopathic personality with pathologic sexuality." The diagnosis will specify the type of the pathological behavior, such as homosexuality, transvestitism, pedophilia, fetishism, and sexual sadism (including, rape, sexual assault, mutilation).[46]

The DSM-II, published 16 years later, continued to use the term *sexual deviation* for nonstandard paraphiliac behaviors. It stated:

> This category is for individuals whose sexual interests are directed primarily toward objects other than people of the opposite sex, toward sexual acts not usually associated with coitus, or toward coitus performed under bizarre circumstances as in necrophilia, pedophilia, sexual sadism, and fetishism. Even though many find their practices distasteful, they remain unable to substitute normal sexual behavior for them. This diagnosis is not appropriate for individuals who perform deviant sexual acts because normal sexual objects are not available to them.[47]

In the DSM-II, behaviors listed as sexually deviant were homosexuality, fetishism, pedophilia, transvestism, exhibitionism, voyeurism, sadism, masochism, other sexual deviation, and unspecified sexual deviation. Interestingly, while rape was no longer considered an act of sexual deviation, homosexuality still was.

Homosexuality was eventually dropped as a sexually deviant behavior in DSM-III,[48] but a new term *ego-dystonic homosexuality* was added in the general category of psychosexual disorders. This category was characterized by a feeling of dysphoria or shame over homosexual feelings, fantasies, or behavior.[48,49] In DSM III-R,[50] even this term was dropped.

In DSM-III-R, the criteria sets for the paraphilias included a clinical significance criterion, i.e., "the person has acted on these urges, or is markedly distressed by them." This was done because the mere presence of paraphilic sexual urges or fantasies does not necessarily warrant diagnosis of a paraphilia. During the preparation of DSM-IV, it was felt that there should be uniform wording for the clinical significance criterion across the disorders. In order to do so, the wording of this criterion was adjusted: "The fantasies, sexual urges, or behaviors cause clinically significant distress or impairment in social, occupational, or other important areas of functioning." The mention of *having acted* on the urges was deleted.

However, an unintentional and unforeseen fallout of this rephrasing was considerable confusion regarding the DSM-IV definition of pedophilia. Specifically, the replacement of the DSM-III-R phrase "acts on these urges" with "causes clinically significant distress or impairment in social, occupational, or other important areas of functioning" was misconstrued to represent a fundamental change in the definition of pedophilia. Many workers misunderstood this new wording as greatly restricting the number of individuals who would be diagnosed with pedophilia by requiring that they be distressed by their behavior in order to qualify for the diagnosis. Quite clearly this was never intended, since it is well recognized that a number of individuals with pedophilia are *not distressed* by their pedophilic urges, fantasies, and behaviors. In fact, rather than restricting the diagnosis of pedophilia to fewer individuals, the original purpose of the change was to potentially broaden the diagnosis to include individuals whose pedophilic urges interfered with functioning in a variety of ways (e.g., causing impairment in occupational functioning because of a preoccupation with pedophilic thoughts and images at work). There was never any intention to exclude individuals who acted on their urges.

To remove any possible ambiguity regarding whether acting out pedophilic urges with others was sufficient for a diagnosis of pedophilia, the original DSM-III-R wording was reinstated in DSM-IV-TR. Furthermore, the original DSM-III-R wording was reinstated for other paraphilias that inevitably harm their victims (i.e., voyeurism, exhibitionism, and frotteurism). Because some cases of sexual sadism may not involve harm to a victim such as beating or inflicting humiliation on a consenting partner, the wording for sexual sadism involved a hybrid of the DSM-III-R and DSM-IV wording: The person has acted on these urges with a non-consenting person, or the urges, sexual fantasies, or behaviors cause marked distress or interpersonal difficulty.[51]

Paraphilias, as classified in DSM-IV-TR[2] are given in Table 1.1. For detailed criteria of each paraphilia, respective chapters should be consulted.

It is important to note that for five paraphilias, namely exhibitionism, frotteurism, pedophilia, sexual sadism, and voyeurism, the criterion of "having acted upon the sexual urges" has been added in DSM-IV-TR, i.e., the individual could be diagnosed with these paraphilias if the sexual urges or fantasies cause marked distress or interpersonal difficulty or if the person has actually acted on these urges. In other words, these five paraphilias can now be diagnosed if they are acted upon, even though they may not cause the person whose behavior is in question distress or impaired functioning as a result. For three remaining paraphilias, namely fetishism, sexual masochism, and transvestic fetishism, it is not necessary for an individual to have acted upon his urges; merely the presence of marked distress would enable a diagnosis to be made. It may not be out of place to mention here that a clear victim (i.e., a non-consenting person) is harmed in the first five paraphilias. In the latter three paraphilias there is no victim or a victim is not clearly defined.

Interestingly, the editors of DSM-IV-TR stated unequivocally in their introduction that "All proposed changes were limited to the text sections (e.g. Associated Features and Disorders, Prevalence). No substantive changes in the criteria sets were considered." Changes had indeed been made in criterion B for many paraphilias involving a non-consenting person. Hilliard and Spitzer[52] pointed out this discrepancy and wondered if it would not have been better if DSM-IV-TR editors had explicitly acknowledged that they indeed had made a few substantive changes in the criteria and "that they had corrected a mistake made in DSM-IV for the paraphilias."

INTERNATIONAL CLASSIFICATION OF DISEASES (ICD)

Paraphilias are included in the International Classification of Diseases (ICD), regularly published by the World Health Organization (WHO). ICD has its origins in 1900, when the French government convoked in Paris the first International Conference for drawing up an "International List of Causes of Death."[53] Delegates from 26 countries attended this conference. Since the first ICD, used strictly for the coding of causes of death, revisions have been made about every ten years. The ICD did not provide a separate section for mental disorders until the fifth revision in 1938.[54] The ninth revision of ICD (ICD-9) was published in 1977. As with the previous editions, the main intention was to report and compile *mortality* data. However, the National Center for Health Statistics (NCHS) and the Centers for Medicare and Medicaid Services (CMS) in the United States made some modifications in ICD-9 to report *morbidity* data. This modification—adopted in 1979 in the U.S.—came to be known as ICD-9-CM (Clinical Modification).[55] ICD-9-CM is now required by the U.S. government and most insurance carriers for reporting health care data in the United States. ICD-10[56] (*without* clinical modifications) was adopted for reporting *mortality* after January 1, 1999, but ICD-9-CM is still used for reporting *morbidity*. (At the time of writing this book, although the draft of ICD-10-CM is available for public viewing, the codes are not currently valid. Furthermore, there is not yet an anticipated implementation date for the ICD-10-CM. Updates to this draft are anticipated prior to implementation of ICD-10-CM.) Because of close collaboration of agencies (WHO, NCHS, and CMS), ICD-9-CM codes and terms are fully compatible with those of the DSM-IV.[54]

ICD-9-CM classifies paraphilias under sexual and gender and identity disorders (see Table 1.3).[57] The code assigned to this group is 302, same as that in DSM-IV-TR.

ICD-10[58] classifies paraphilias under the title "Disorders of Sexual Preference." Table 1.4 gives classification of paraphilias under ICD-10. Note that the numerals assigned to these disorders are different from those assigned by DSM-IV-TR and ICD-9-CM.

Table 1.5 compares and contrasts the paraphilias as enumerated in DSM-IV-TR, ICD-9-CM, and ICD-10.

A few interesting features may stand out. Note that while both DSM-IV-TR and ICD-9-CM use the term *transvestic fetishism*, ICD-10 uses *fetishistic transvestism*. Also *transsexualism* does not appear in DSM-IV-TR. It places three former DSM-III-R categories (Gender Identity Disorders of Childhood, Gender Identity Disorders of Adolescence and Adulthood, Nontranssexual Type [GIDAANT], and Transsexualism) under two categories: 302.6, Gender Identity Disorder in Children, and 302.85, Gender Identity Disorder in Adolescents or Adults. While DSM-IV-TR quite clearly separates transsexualism from traditional paraphilias, this differentiation is not so transparent in ICD-9-CM, which groups both paraphilias and transsexualism under one banner "Sexual and Gender Identity Disorders," which is assigned to group 302. Another interesting feature is that while both DSM-IV-TR and ICD-9-CM keep sadism and masochism separate, ICD-10 merges them in one disorder, sadomasochism, implying sadism and masochism as two opposite poles within a single disorder. ICD-10 also mentions a special category "Multiple Disorders of Sexual Preference" (F65.6), which is not seen in other two classifications. It specifically states, "Sometimes more than one abnormal sexual preference occurs in one person and there is none of first rank. The most common combination is fetishism, transvestism and sadomasochism." Perhaps the editors of DSM-V would keep this fact in mind.

Frotteurism does not appear in ICD-10 as a separate category, but is lumped in the last "miscellaneous" or "residual" category, named "Other Disorders of Sexual Preference." The residual category is variously named as "Paraphilia Not Otherwise Specified (NOS)" by DSM-IV-TR, "Unspecified Psychosexual Disorder" by ICD-9-CM, and "Other Disorders of Sexual Preference" by ICD-10. While some representative examples are given by both DSM-IV-TR and ICD-10, ICD-9-CM does not give any representative examples. Both DSM-IV-TR and ICD-10 make clear that the given examples are only representative and there could be other disorders too which could fall under this category. The examples that are common to both are obscene telephone calls, necrophilia, and zoophilia. The terms coprophilia, klismaphilia, urophilia, and partialism find a mention only in DSM-IV-TR. Asphyxiophilia, or the use of strangulation or anoxia for intensifying sexual excitement, finds mention only in ICD-10. Lastly, while zoophilia is classified as a separate disorder in ICD-9-CM, it is lumped in the residual category by both DSM-IV-TR and ICD-10.

OTHER CLASSIFICATIONS

DSM and ICD classifications are mainly numerical in nature, making it easy to collect, collate, and correlate data coming from several sources. However, there are other useful classifications of paraphilias, which are useful from different points of view. A good and useful classification of any group of disorders provides valuable insights into their etiological, management, or perhaps even

TABLE 1.3
ICD-9-CM Classification of Paraphilias

NEUROTIC DISORDERS, PERSONALITY DISORDERS, AND OTHER NONPSYCHOTIC MENTAL DISORDERS (300–316)

302 Sexual and gender identity disorders

Excludes:

sexual disorder manifest in organic brain syndrome (290.0–294.9, 310.0–310.9) and psychosis (295.0–298.9)

302.0 Ego-dystonic sexual orientation

Ego-dystonic lesbianism

Sexual orientation conflict disorder

Excludes:

homosexual pedophilia (302.2)

302.1 Zoophilia

Bestiality

302.2 Pedophilia

302.3 Transvestic fetishism

Excludes:

trans-sexualism (302.5)

302.4 Exhibitionism

302.5 Trans-sexualism

Excludes:

transvestism (302.3)

302.50 With unspecified sexual history

302.51 With asexual history

302.52 With homosexual history

302.53 With heterosexual history

302.6 Gender identity disorder in children

Feminism in boys

Gender identity disorder NOS

Excludes:

gender identity disorder in adult (302.85)

trans-sexualism (302.50–302.53)

transvestism (302.3)

302.7 Psychosexual dysfunction

Excludes:

decreased sexual desire NOS (799.81)

impotence of organic origin (607.84)

normal transient symptoms from ruptured hymen

transient or occasional failures of erection due to fatigue, anxiety, alcohol, or drugs

302.8 Other specified psychosexual disorders

302.81 Fetishism

302.82 Voyeurism

302.83 Sexual masochism

302.84 Sexual sadism

TABLE 1.3 (continued)
ICD-9-CM Classification of Paraphilias

302.85 Gender identity disorder in adolescents or adults		
	Excludes:	
		gender identity disorder NOS (302.6)
		gender identity disorder in children (302.6)
302.89 Other		
		Frotteurism
		Nymphomania
		Satyriasis
302.9 Unspecified psychosexual disorder		
		Paraphilia NOS
		Pathologic sexuality NOS
		Sexual deviation NOS
		Sexual disorder NOS

legal aspects. Unfortunately, no single classification serves that purpose well. There are a number of classifications though which may be examined here.

Sadoff's Classification

In one of the earliest classifications, Sadoff[60] divided all paraphilias in two broad groups—"aggressive" deviations such as rape, pedophilia, and sadomasochism; and "anonymous" deviations such as voyeurism and telephone scatologia. He further asserts that the paraphilias in the second group tend to occur on a continuum, at one end of which the offender maintains a complete anonymity with the victim (such as fetishism, where the offender may simply steal, say, a bra of the victim and use it to masturbate at his home), to the other end, where the offender does maintain anonymity, but is physically present very near to the victim (e.g., frotteurism). Between these two poles lie several paraphilias in which the offender maintains a variable degree of anonymity with the victim. The sequence from greatest anonymity to least may be something like this: Fetishism (absolutely no contact with the victim) → Obscene telephone calling (verbal contact only) → Voyeurism (goes near the victim, but is hidden from victim's view) → Exhibitionism (comes in full view of the victim, but no physical contact) → Frotteurism (goes on to establish physical contact with the victim, but in a crowd, thus maintaining his anonymity). Exhibitionism is not exactly an anonymous deviation, as the victim sees (and recognizes) the offender, but Sadoff remains silent on this issue. He, however, suggests that anonymous deviations do help the offender to save himself from the anxiety which he may experience when he comes in direct contact with the desired sexual object. In Sadoff's view, these anonymous sex deviates may fantasize having sexual intercourse but are too anxious about it to be able to really go through the process of accomplishing it. It is important to realize that Saddoff's anonymous deviations tally very greatly with Freund's courtship disorders (please see chapter on exhibitionism).

Rosenham and Seligman's Classification

Rosenham and Seligman[61] divide paraphilias into three categories. The first is sexual arousal and preference for *nonconsenting partners*. This category includes paraphilias such as exhibitionism, voyeurism, and child molestation. In the second category, there is sexual arousal and preference for *nonhuman objects*. These paraphilias include fetishism and transvestism. In the final category,

TABLE 1.4
ICD-10 Classification of Paraphilias[59]

F65 Disorders of sexual preference

Includes paraphilias

F65.0 Fetishism

Reliance on some non-living object as a stimulus for sexual arousal and sexual gratification. Many fetishes are extensions of the human body, such as articles of clothing or footwear. Other common examples are characterized by some particular texture such as rubber, plastic or leather. Fetish objects vary in their importance to the individual. In some cases they simply serve to enhance sexual excitement achieved in ordinary ways (e.g., having the partner wear a particular garment).

F65.1 Fetishistic transvestism

The wearing of clothes of the opposite sex principally to obtain sexual excitement and to create the appearance of a person of the opposite sex. Fetishistic transvestism is distinguished from transsexual transvestism by its clear association with sexual arousal and the strong desire to remove the clothing once orgasm occurs and sexual arousal declines. It can occur as an earlier phase in the development of transsexualism.

F65.2 Exhibitionism

A recurrent or persistent tendency to expose the genitalia to strangers (usually of the opposite sex) or to people in public places, without inviting or intending closer contact. There is usually, but not invariably, sexual excitement at the time of the exposure and the act is commonly followed by masturbation.

F65.3 Voyeurism

A recurrent or persistent tendency to look at people engaging in sexual or intimate behavior such as undressing. This is carried out without the observed people being aware, and usually leads to sexual excitement and masturbation.

F65.4 Pedophilia

A sexual preference for children, boys or girls or both, usually of prepubertal or early pubertal age.

F65.5 Sadomasochism

A preference for sexual activity which involves the infliction of pain or humiliation, or bondage. If the subject prefers to be the recipient of such stimulation this is called masochism; if the provider, sadism. Often an individual obtains sexual excitement from both sadistic and masochistic activities.

F65.6 Multiple disorders of sexual preference

Sometimes more than one abnormal sexual preference occurs in one person and there is none of first rank. The most common combination involves fetishism, transvestism and sadomasochism.

F65.8 Other disorders of sexual preference

A variety of other patterns of sexual preference and activity, including making obscene telephone calls, rubbing against people for sexual stimulation in crowded public places, sexual activity with animals, and use of strangulation or anoxia for intensifying sexual excitement. (e.g., frotteurism, necrophilia)

F65.9 Disorder of sexual preference, unspecified

Sexual deviation NOS (not otherwise specified)

instead of a human or non-human object, the preference is for certain *situations*. In sadism and masochism, for example, the preference is for situations that involve suffering and humiliation, in pyromania for situations that include fire, and so on.

Freund, Seto, and Kuban's Classification

Freund, Seto, and Kuban [60] divide paraphilias into two broad types—pathological erotic *target* preferences and pathological erotic *activity* preferences. In the former, the preferred targets of activities are *objects* other than physically mature persons (children, animals, dead people). In the latter, the preferred target is a physically mature person, but the preferred erotic *activity* is highly atypical (frotteurism, coprophilia, urophilia).

TABLE 1.5
Comparisons of Paraphilias As Enumerated in DSM-IV-TR, ICD-9-CM, and ICD-10

DSM-IV-TR	ICD-9-CM	ICD-10
	Zoophilia (302.1)	
Pedophilia (302.2)	Pedophilia (302.2)	Pedophilia (F65.4)
Transvestic fetishism (302.3)	Transvestic fetishism (302.3)	Fetishistic transvestism (F65.1)
Exhibitionism (302.4)	Exhibitionism (302.4)	Exhibitionism (F65.2)
	Trans-sexualism (302.5)	
Fetishism (302.81)	Fetishism (302.81)	Fetishism (F65.0)
Voyeurism (302.82)	Voyeurism (302.82)	Voyeurism (F65.3)
Sexual masochism (302.83)	Sexual masochism (302.83)	Sadomasochism (F65.5)
Sexual sadism (302.84)	Sexual sadism (302.84)	
Frotteurism (302.89)	302.89 Other • Frotteurism • Nymphomania • Satyriasis	
		Multiple disorders of sexual preference (F65.6)
Paraphilia not otherwise specified (NOS) (302.9) Examples include, but are not limited to, telephone scatologia (obscene telephone calls), necrophilia (corpses), partialism (exclusive focus on parts of body), zoophilia (animals), coprophilia (feces), klismaphilia (enemas), and urophilia (urine)	302.9 Unspecified psychosexual disorder • Paraphilia NOS • Pathologic sexuality NOS • Sexual deviation NOS • Sexual disorder NOS	Other disorders of sexual preference (F65.8) A variety of other patterns of sexual preference and activity, including making obscene telephone calls, rubbing up against people for sexual stimulation in crowded public places, sexual activity with animals, and use of strangulation or anoxia for intensifying sexual excitement. (e.g., frotteurism, necrophilia)

John Money's Paraphilia Classifications

John Money classified paraphilias, based on his theory of lovemaps (please see below under the heading *Etiology*). According to this theory, all paraphilias can be seen as a reaction to a split or dichotomy between love and lust. All paraphilias attempt to turn the tragedy of lovemap distortion into a triumph of lust without compromising the sanctity of saintly love in any way. The paraphiliac wants to remain a saint, at the same time wishing to enjoy the sinful lust. To resolve this seemingly insoluble paradox, he develops a number of paraphilic strategies. Based on this almost Freudian kind of concept, Money classifies all paraphilias into six categories as below:

Sacrificial Paraphilias

Also sometimes known as expiatory paraphilias or sacrificial/expiatory type paraphilias. These paraphilias can be conceived as a strategy that incorporates sinful lust into the lovemap on the condition that reparation or atonement is achieved by way of penance, sacrifice, and putting one's life in danger. Penance and sacrifice are required since the lust irrevocably defiles saintly love. According to Money's theory, this type of behavior occurs in individuals who feel they must atone for their erotic behavior, thus pairing pleasure with threat or punishment.[61] Autoassassinophilia (arousal from putting oneself in a position to be killed) and symphorophilia (arousal by accidents or catastrophes) are paraphilias of the sacrificial type. Autoerotic asphyxiation is another paraphilia of this type. Money views autoerotic asphyxiation in terms of an eroticization of helplessness, weakness, and a threat to life, which is overcome through survival, thus creating a sense of success.

Predatory Paraphilias

Also sometimes known as marauding paraphilias or predatory/marauding type paraphilias. These are the paraphilias in which the wicked and degenerate ecstasy of the sinful act of lust is so defiling that it can be indulged in only if it is taken from the saint by force, abducted, stolen or robbed. The person experiencing these paraphilias may have the fantasy of being either predator or prey. Examples include biastophilia (arousal from raping someone), somnophilia (arousal from having sex when partner is asleep, "sleeping-princess syndrome").

Mercantile Paraphilias

Also sometimes known as venal paraphilias or mercantile/venal type paraphilias. The strategy is not to use the saint for lust. A wife or a regular partner is a saint, and he dare not use her for sinful lust. But what if he bought the sinful lust? Then the saint would not be defiled. And the paraphiliac does just that. He pays for, purchases, trades, or barters for the sinful lust or at least creates an illusion to that effect. Examples are coprolalia, in which he speaks dirty language to his partner, as someone speaks to a whore, or troilism, in which the paraphiliac invites another man to have intercourse with his wife, as if she were a whore, and watches them to get an arousal. In autagonistophilia, the person becomes a whore; sexual arousal becomes contingent upon displaying one's self in a live show.

Fetishistic Paraphilias

Also sometimes known as talismanic paraphilias or fetishistic/talismanic type paraphilias. In this case, the paraphiliac, in order to protect the saint, uses a fetish for his sinful lust. In other words, he substitutes a fetish, say, a shoe, for the saintly lover, so she may not be defiled with his sinful lust.

Eligibility Paraphilias

Also sometimes known as stigmatic paraphilias or eligibility/stigmatic type paraphilias. The strategy adopted by the paraphilic to protect the saintly love from sinful lust is to chose his partner who is so base, so unqualified, so depraved that he or she is simply unable or ineligible to compete with the saint. The partner must become a pagan infidel or an erotic heathen. The partner must not appear to be a proper or likeable person. This is done by choosing a partner who is very diminutive or towering in stature, fat or skinny, very young (pedophilia) or very old (gerontophilia), disfigured, deformed (dysmorphophilia), crippled, stigmatized (stigmatophilia), even an amputee (acrotomophilia). In extreme cases, the paraphilic wants his partner to be from a different species (zoophilia) or dead (necrophilia), or even a dead specimen of a different species (necrozoophilia).

Sometimes, the paraphilic may want even himself to be deformed (he is also one of the partners in love making). This desire is reflected in paraphilias like apotemnophilia in which the paraphiliac desires to have his own healthy appendages (limb, digit, or genitals) amputated.

Allurement Paraphilias

Also sometimes known as solicitational paraphilias or allurement/solicitational type paraphilias. Allurement paraphilias are *displacement paraphilias*, whereas those in the foregoing five categories are *inclusion paraphilias*. In these paraphilias, some more or less extraneous ritual (such as exhibitionism or making erotic telephone calls) replaces genital intercourse. Thus the pleasure of sinful lust is obtained by not employing the saint at all. Instead, the pleasure is displaced to some other activity, which in normal persons is only a small segment of the preparatory phase of an erotic and sexual activity, before actual genital intercourse begins. It is generally seen as a phase of courtship in animals. In many ways, Money echoes the theory of Freund here (please see *Freund's courtship disorder theory* in the chapter on exhibitionism).

Freeman's Classification

Michael Freeman,[62] leaning heavily on an earlier classification proposed by James,[63] classifies deviant sexual behaviors strongly from a legal point of view. As he points out, in this classification, words such as "normal," "perverted," "homosexuality," etc. are intended to indicate the overt behavior problems *as seen by the court*, and not based on underlying clinical factors. Law is not as much interested in underlying clinical factors (as, for example, how a paraphiliac behavior developed from a distortion of infantile sexuality), as in understanding, how much deteriorating impact the behavior may have on society as a whole. His classification is given in Table 1.6.

To this classification another group, 3(l), may be added with the title "miscellaneous offenses," as several behaviors such as frotteurism have been inexplicably left out. Some other disorders perhaps not widely perceived as perverted in Freeman's time (e.g., cybersex and stalking) are viewed so now.

It might be noted that several patterns of behavior, e.g., sadism and masochism have not been included here, while several others such as bigamy, incest, rape, etc. have been included as sexually deviant (the latter are not listed as paraphilias in DSM-IV-TR). This is a paradox we may have to live with, as the definitions of paraphilias are far from consistent, especially when viewed from different standpoints, e.g., medical and legal. Freeman's classification as noted earlier is strongly from a legal standpoint.

Shaffer and Penn's Classification

Shaffer and Penn[1] classify paraphilias based on two parameters or dimensions: (i) whether the paraphiliac behavior involves violence or not, and (ii) whether the behavior is carried out in the general vicinity of another person (physical) or not (nonphysical). Based on these criteria, they divide all paraphilias in five broad categories: (i) nonviolent physical paraphilia (e.g., swinging, exhibitionism, voyeurism), (ii) nonviolent nonphysical paraphilia (e.g., telephone scatologia, technophilia), (iii) sadistic paraphilia (e.g., sadism, pyromania), (iv) masochistic paraphilia (masochism, autoerotic asphyxiation), and (iv) sadomasochistic paraphilia (aichmophilia, dystychiphilia).

This classification, although useful to some extent in understanding behavioral patterns, especially in relation to violence, does not shed much light on etiological or legal aspects.

Miscellaneous Classifications

Precontact and Contact Paraphilias

Similar to Sadoff's classification is that which stems from the courtship disorder theory of Freund, Scher, and Hucker (although nowhere in their writings do they explicitly mention it). These are the precontact (sometimes called non-contact) and contact paraphilias (for details, please see chapter on exhibitionism).

TABLE 1.6
Michael Freeman's Classification of Deviant Sexual Behavior from a Legal Standpoint

1. Offenses against accepted standards of family life:

(a) Bigamy
(b) Incest
(c) Adultery
(d) Fornication

2. Offenses that display normal sexual drive in a distorted or unacceptable manner:

(a) Rape
(b) Indecent assault on a woman
(c) Unlawful sexual intercourse
(d) Sexual murder
(e) Pedophilia
(f) Prostitution by females to males

3. Offenses that display what is considered a perverted sexual drive:

(a) Homosexuality (including indecent assault by males on males and importuning)
(b) Lesbianism
(c) Transvestism
(d) Fetishism
(e) Voyeurism
(f) Exhibitionism
(g) Bestiality
(h) Sodomy with a woman
(i) Necrophilia
(j) Sadomasochism
(k) Making obscene telephone calls

Consensual and Nonconsensual Paraphilias

This classification would group consensual paraphilias like sadomasochism from other paraphilias. Certain other acts which used to be considered deviant (e.g., homosexuality and lesbianism) could also be included in this group. At first sight, the classification appears useful from a legal angle because it would appear that consensual paraphilias would draw lesser or no punishment. However, this has not been the case. Courts have punished even consensual paraphilias such as sadomasochism severely (for details, please see chapter on masochism).

ETIOLOGY

Paraphilias and sex offenses are complex problems, and no single theory or paradigm (a scientific thought pattern or school) explains these behavior patterns fully. Several workers have aimed to explain them in their own ways, based on their own clinical and research experiences. The truth lies perhaps within a judicious mix of all of them.

In the 19th century, the most widespread opinion as to the etiology of sexual deviation was the idea of degeneration. Italian criminologist Cesare Lombroso (1835–1909) stated, "Certain crimes, such as pederasty and infanticide, can be explained by atavism."[64] This view is obviously flawed. We now know that mentally ill persons do not show a higher incidence of sexual deviation than the rest of the population. Furthermore, many persons who manifest sexual deviations have attained high positions in society.

Some of the more plausible theories may be examined here.

Voluntary Choice

This is the simplest and most straightforward of all theories of paraphilia. It maintains that paraphilia is a matter of voluntary decision and nothing else. Just as one chooses what to eat, drink, or wear, one also chooses how to have sex. This view seems to explain well why paraphilias are more common in males (males are more adventurous sexually). However, this is too simplistic an explanation for a complex phenomenon. Money[65] asserts that this view can misrepresent a case in a court of law.

Freud's Libido Theory

One of the first attempts to explain paraphilias was made by Sigmund Freud (1856–1939) in 1905, when he developed his libido theory.[66] Freud believed that some part of all our energy is directed toward—or attached to—the so-called "sex instinct." There is no way we can measure this energy—certainly no method has been devised so far to do so—but we can ordinarily conceive it quite clearly. For instance, a hypersexed individual, who needs to have sex several times a day, certainly has more energy attached to his libido than a frigid individual, who shies away from sex. Initially Freud regarded sex instinct as it is understood by all of us in the everyday sense (a desire to have sex), but later he applied this term to refer to *any* pleasurable sensation relating to the bodily function, and also, through the process of sublimation, to socially approved forms of behavior such as enjoyment of work and social responsibilities.

> **Sublimation**: In psychology, sublimation is the refocusing of energy away from negative outlets to more positive outlets. For instance, an angry and rageful person who is accustomed to wasting energy on beating others and perhaps risking a jail sentence might instead re-channel that energy—through sublimation—toward combat sports such as boxing and wrestling.

In a way, Freud used the word "libido" as we use the word "desire." Thus a student who is desirous of learning music is attempting to spend part of his libido toward music. Freud believed that the libido could be attached to a variety of objects, and he even outlined a chronological sequence that such attachments follow. This sequence is popularly known as the "stages of psychosexual development." The first is the **oral phase**, which starts at birth and continues for approximately 18 months. During this period, the libido is attached to the mouth, and the infant derives pleasure from such activities as sucking the breast or his thumb, putting things in his mouth, etc. The erogenic zones in such children are the mouth and circumoral structures. The **anal phase** overlaps the oral phase and continues until an infant is 3 years old. During this period the libido is attached to the anus, rectum, and bladder (thus making them the erogenic zones). The child in this phase gets pleasure initially from excretion (defecation and urination) and later from retention of urine and feces.

The **phallic phase** overlaps the anal phase and continues to develop until a child is 7 years old. During this phase the libido is concentrated around the genitalia, and the child begins exploring and enjoying his genitals. The male child discovers that he has a penis, while the girl child finds out she doesn't. The penis becomes the organ of principal interest to both sexes at this stage. Both set great value on the penis (it becomes a symbol of power for them), and their discovery that some human beings do not possess these organs leads to important psychical consequences.

Although Freud did not attempt any distinction between the *phallus* and the *penis*, later psychoanalysts did differentiate. The term *penis* was reserved for the actual biological organ, while *phallus* was a *signifier* of the sexual difference between boys and girls. It also referred to the symbolic functions of the biological organ and the role it played in fantasy and imagery. At this stage, infants of both sexes are dominated by the question of who possesses a penis and the related issue of its masturbatory *jouissance* (gratification). Also up to this point, the mother is imagined as having a penis, and the discovery that she lacks a penis precipitates the *castration complex* (or castration anxiety) in the male child, after an initial denial. He begins to think that his father would cut away his penis, too. He develops a hostile attitude toward his father because he sees his father as a rival and starts drifting toward his mother (Oedipus complex).

The female child desires a penis and the power it represents. She sees the solution in obtaining her father's penis and gradually develops a sexual desire for her father (Electra complex). She also sees her "castration" as inflicted by her mother, for the sin she committed by being attracted to her father (penis envy).

Following these three periods there is a **latency period** between the ages of 7 and 12 years, or the onset of puberty. During this period the complexes and anxieties developed earlier are resolved. After the latency period begins the **genital phase**, when the sex interest is strongly re-awakened and the libido is directed towards external sex organs.

Freud theorized that normally a child is able to navigate through these stages of psychosexual development successfully. In other words, the child undergoes a natural transition from being a "polymorphous pervert" during which his sexual interests are relatively undifferentiated, to a more mature genital and heterosexual orientation. If that happens, the child develops into a normal adult who spends his libido in socially approved ways, such as normal sexual intercourse. Sometimes, however, the libido becomes fixated to a particular zone, and the child continues to derive pleasure from that zone throughout his life. In psychoanalytic theory, this results from various kinds of trauma experienced during the childhood. A mother who weans away an infant from her breast too soon would cause the child's libido to become fixated around his mouth, and he would start deriving pleasure from such activities as fellatio and cunnilingus. During the anal phase, when a child wants to retain urine and feces, and his parents are too strict about toilet training, he may become fixated toward the urethral and anal zones, and may start deriving pleasure in expelling urine and feces during adulthood, when there is no control of parents. In other words, he would become a urophiliac, coprophiliac, or someone interested in anal eroticism. A child whose castration anxiety is not resolved adequately during the latency period may want to reassure himself (and others) that his penis is still intact and may go on to become an exhibitionist. Pedophiles choose children as partners because children elicit less castration anxiety than do adults.[67] Freud even developed psychoanalytic techniques, by which such conflicts during adulthood could be resolved, and he was indeed able to successfully treat a number of such patients, indicating some truth in these theories. However, not all kinds of paraphilias can be satisfactorily explained by this theory. It is difficult, for example, to explain by this theory how a person becomes a fetishist or a zoophiliac. In the 21st century, Freud's libido theory remains somewhat controversial. Credit, however, has to be given to Freud to make everyone look at sexuality in unconventional ways.

Biological Theories

In many cases of paraphilias, biological factors seem to play a role and attempts have been made to co-relate them.

Frontal and Temporal Lobe Lesions

As early as 1937, Heinrich Klüver and Paul Bucy had shown that removal of temporal lobe bilaterally in rhesus monkeys resulted in striking and specific effects on sexual behavior. Known as *Klüver–Bucy syndrome* (KBS), it was later observed in humans too in a variety of neurodegenerative disorders and after traumatic, nontraumatic, and infectious brain injury.[68,69] Hypersexuality is one of its most common manifestations.[70,71]

Taking a lead from this, Kolárský and associates[72] proposed that some paraphilic behavior may be caused by early lesions or similar abnormalities of the left temporal lobe. Patients with lesions in the left temporal lobe were more likely to exhibit paraphilic behavior than those patients who were not brain damaged or whose lesions were in different areas of brain. Also if the lesions occurred early in life, the patient was more likely to exhibit paraphilias. These views have been substantiated by several other workers.

Hypersexuality and fetishism were found in patients with multiple sclerosis showing frontal and temporal lesions.[73] Joyal and associates[74] reviewed the existing data derived from neuropsychiatry, neuroimaging, and neuropsychology and found basal fronto-temporal anomalies in many sexual offenders. Importantly, pedophiles were more consistently and severely impaired than rapists of adults. Joyal et al., however, concluded that this basal fronto-temporal profile was not characteristic of sexual deviance, as it was also found in association with delinquency and criminality in general.

Graber and associates[75] studied six sex offenders using several techniques, one of which was ^{133}Xe radionuclide inhalation to measure cerebral blood flow. They found that in at least three of them, the cerebral blood flow was much lower than that usually observed in normal individuals. One offender exhibited a large difference in blood flow in the right and left hemispheres, which is not seen in normal individuals. The authors conclude that frontal and temporal lobes are in some way involved in inhibitory control of sexual behavior, and when their functioning is compromised, it may lead to paraphilic behavior and sexual offenses. EEG abnormalities too have been found in paraphiliacs, pointing to brain pathology.[76,77]

Hippocampal Pathology

Mendez and associates[78] have reported bilateral hippocampal sclerosis in a patient with homosexual pedophilia. Casanova and associates[79] made a computerized search for deviant sexual behavior on all available medical and autopsy records of St. Elizabeth's Hospital, Washington, DC, a large urban hospital, and identified two cases in which neuropathological examination revealed simple cell atrophy of pyramidal cells confined to different hippocampal subfields. Reactive astrocytosis, indicating a reactive, ongoing process, was present in the outer strata of the affected regions. The pathological changes in the hippocampus resembled those reported after persistent stress or long-term chronic glucocorticoid administration. This is a relatively new etiopathological line that needs to be investigated further.

Neurodevelopmental or Environmental Stressors

Individuals with paraphilia-like behavior are significantly more likely to have concurrent mental disorders. This suggests that common neurodevelopmental or environmental stressors may contribute to paraphilias.[80]

Monoamine Hypothesis

Kafka[81] has put forward a monoamine hypothesis for the pathophysiology of paraphilic disorders. He starts with the well-accepted presumption that sexual behavior in animals (and humans) consists of two chief components, which occur in sequence—*appetitive sexual behavior* or ASB (consisting of detection of a suitable mate, approach to it, and establishment of initial contact; sexual drive builds up during this phase) and *consummatory sexual behavior* or CSB (consisting of actual copulation; sexual drive is satisfied and thus reduced during this phase).[82] The second well-accepted presumption that he starts with is that paraphilias can be conceptualized as disorders that include increased sexual appetite.

The central monoamines (norepinephrine, dopamine, and serotonin [5-hydroxytryptamine, 5-HT]) are synthesized and released by a relatively small number of neurons whose cell bodies lie in the brain stem, but whose projections extend throughout the brain. Kafka considers the following data coming from animal experiments:

(i) An increase in norepinephrine activity enhances sexual behavior, while certain noradrenergic antagonists can have an inhibitory effect on sexual arousal (directly proportional).
(ii) A decrease in central dopaminergic neurotransmission decreases male sexual appetitive behavior. Conversely, pharmacological enhancement of dopaminergic neurotransmission can augment male sexual behavior, including sexual appetite (directly proportional). For instance, it is well known that patients of Parkinsonism treated with levodopa (metabolic precursor of dopamine) show an abnormal increase in sexual drive.[83–90]
(iii) A decrease in brain serotonin (5-HT) is associated with increases in appetitive sexual behavior, and vice versa (inversely proportional).

Kafka also notes that: (i) all three monoaminergic neurotransmitters (i.e., norepinephrine, dopamine, and serotonin) are significantly associated with human and animal sexual appetite and motivation;[91,92] (ii) commonly prescribed pharmacological agents that affect monoamine neurotransmitters (e.g., antidepressants, psychostimulants, neuroleptics) have significant effects on both sexual motivation and consummatory behaviors;[93] and (iii) paraphilic disorders seem to have co-morbidity with other Axis I disorders (e.g., antisocial impulsivity, anxiety, depression, hypersexuality) that too are associated with monoaminergic dysregulation. Depression is known to increase the frequency and intensity of a paraphilic behavior.[94]

From these data, Kafka concludes that paraphilic disorders my be, at least in part, mediated by perturbations in central monoamine neurotransmitters, and can even be ameliorated by pharmacological agents that affect norepinephrine, dopamine, and serotonin levels in the brain. He asserts that the functional role of norepinephrine and dopamine in paraphilias is less clear than that of serotonin. That is why pharmacological agents that increase serotonin levels in the brain (serotonergic agents) may well be used in the treatment of paraphilias.

Although Kafka does not mention as much, this theory could be used to explain seemingly confusing paraphilic behaviors such as masochism. It has always been something of an enigma, how something that induces pain may be used as a sexually provoking stimulus. With monoamine theory this could be easily explained. It is well known that sensations such as pain and violence (as those produced by, say, whipping), and emotions such as sex and love are associated with the release of epinephrine, which in turn leads to the production of other neurotransmitters. The brain interprets the increase in monoamine transmitters, according to what is present in the environment. If the circumstances are hostile, the increase could be perceived as pain and fear. If, on the other hand, the circumstances are favorable, the same increase could be perceived as feelings of love and sex. In certain circumstances which are not well understood, the brain may make mistakes, and may perceive a painful stimulus as sexual as happens in masochism. Some other paraphilias such as arachnephilia (arousal from spiders), formicophilia (arousal from ants or insects), and hybristophilia (sexual arousal following the knowledge that one's partner has committed an act of violence) could also be explained in the same way. John Money[95] calls it "opponent process learning " in which the negative is converted into positive, tragedy into triumph, and aversion into addiction. He even cites two recreational examples of opponent process reversals—bungee jumping and roller coaster riding. Why should these potentially fearful experiences be actively sought after could easily be explained by the monoamine hypothesis.

Head Injury

Head injury as a cause of paraphilias and sex offending has been overlooked by researchers and needs a more in-depth examination. Money[67] presents a case of serial rape and serial lust murder where the precipitating causes were childhood head injuries and adult head injury at age 20. Simpson and colleagues[96] reviewed admissions to the Brain Injury Rehabilitation Unit (New South Wales, Australia) during a period of 5 years. A total of 445 patients were admitted with traumatic brain injury (TBI) during this period. Of these, 29 males (6.5% of all admissions) were identified as having committed some form of sexual offense *after* the injury. Together, they were involved in 128 incidents of sex offending. Significantly, only two patients had a history of sexual offending *prior* to head injury. The most common offenses were touching followed by exhibitionism and overt sexual aggression. Staff members were the most common targets of the offenses, followed by members of the general public, other people with TBI, and family members.

Conditioning and Imprinting

Classical Conditioning

Classical conditioning theories of paraphilias assert that the paraphilic becomes "wrongly" *conditioned* to respond sexually to an inappropriate stimulus, such as a shoe, just as in the classical conditioning experiments by the Russian physiologist, Ivan Pavlov (1849–1936), a dog "learned" to salivate to abnormal stimuli such as a buzzer. To recapitulate briefly, Pavlov first showed a hungry dog some food, and quite appropriately it responded with salivation. In this case food was the unconditioned stimulus (US), and salivation was the unconditioned response (UR). Pavlov then rang a buzzer and saw whether the dog salivated. Naturally it did not. Subsequently Pavlov showed food to the hungry dog (US), but rang the buzzer simultaneously. The dog did salivate again (presumably because of the food, and not because of the buzzer). After the dog had been exposed to several pairings of food and the buzzer, Pavlov just rang the buzzer (without showing the food). The dog salivated and the buzzer became the conditioned stimulus (CS) and salivation became the conditioned response (CR). This phenomenon is termed *classical conditioning* or *Pavlovian conditioning.*

Attempts have been made to explain some paraphilias as a conditioned response. Normally a male would get turned on by the sight of a nude woman. The woman would be the unconditioned stimulus (US, food in Pavlov's experiment) and erection and ejaculation the unconditioned response (UR, salivation in Pavlov's experiment). If a person repeatedly saw a picture of a nude woman wearing high heeled shoes, high heeled shoes would, at some stage, begin to serve the same function as the buzzer did for the dog in the Pavlov's experiment. The shoes would become the conditioned stimulus (CS) or fetish, and would begin to act as sexual objects in their own right. Sexual excitement, erection, and ejaculation upon seeing the high heeled shoe would become a conditioned response (CR).

An interesting observation is that after classical conditioning has occurred, it will not remain persistent forever if CS is not paired with US constantly and regularly. If the conditioned stimulus (buzzer) is presented several times without simultaneous pairing of the unconditioned stimulus (food), salivation would continue to decrease until it finally ceased altogether. This is known as *extinction.* Classical conditioning theories of fetishism do not explain why extinction of behavior does not occur in fetishists. According to classical conditioning theory, after conditioning has occurred, if the high heeled shoe (conditioned stimulus) is seen again and again *without* the nude woman

TABLE 1.7
Comparison of Classical and Operant Conditioning

Similarities

- Both depend on associations.
- Both involve extinction, spontaneous recovery, generalization, and discrimination.
- Both affected by number of repetitions, timing, etc..
- Both are affected by biological factors (neural mechanisms, fatigue, drugs, etc.).

Differences

- Classical conditioning starts with a reflex, operant conditioning does not.
- The response in classical conditioning is a reflex that is *elicited*, whereas the response in operant conditioning is *voluntary* and is *emitted.*
- Classical conditioning involves learning a pairing between two events, CS and US, whereas operant conditioning involves learning a pairing between an action and a consequence.
- Classical conditioning involves learning what stimulus is associated with another stimulus (food is associated with buzzer) whereas operant conditioning involves learning which response is followed by the "desired" stimulus (food follows pressing the right lever; electrical shock follows pressing the wrong lever).

(unconditioned stimulus), the excitement would decrease gradually until it would finally abate altogether. This does not occur in fetishists.

Operant Conditioning

Some paraphilias are explained by operant conditioning as well. Operant conditioning is the use of *consequences* to modify the occurrence and form of behavior. It is distinguished from classical conditioning in that operant conditioning deals with the modification of voluntary behavior through the use of consequences, while Pavlovian conditioning deals with the conditioning of behavior so that it occurs under new antecedent conditions (see Table 1.7). One of the best illustrations of operant conditioning is the teaching of a dog to do a trick. If a dog is given meat when he jumps through a ring, and an electric shock when he does not (or fails), sooner or later he learns to jump through the ring. Similarly, if a rat is allowed a choice to press any of the two levers, one of which delivers food on pressing and another which delivers electric current, the rat would soon learn to press the "right" lever.

Most animal teaching is through process of operant conditioning only. Where jumping through the ring becomes the desired action, the meat becomes the *reinforcement*, and electric shock the *punishment*. These processes are followed in modification of human behavior too, albeit at a subconscious level. A teacher who gives a medal to a student achieving better marks and punishment to a student doing poorly is modifying the behavior of students through operant conditioning.

Masturbation is thought to assume the role of a reinforcer in many paraphilias.[97] When a deviant fantasy or act is followed by an orgasm (the reinforcer), the deviation begins to occur at a greater frequency. More specifically, if a person masturbated after a sadistic act (e.g., after whipping a woman), he would tend to whip a woman with a greater frequency because the act is followed by the joy of orgasm. Attempts have been made to explain Jeffrey Dahmer 's lust murders in this way.[98]

The opponents of this theory have argued that the massive guilt most paraphiliacs experience after their deviant acts should extinguish the behavior (massive guilt would serve as a punishment, just as electric shock does in animal teaching). However, the proponents explain that the behavior does not extinguish, because the sexual pleasure from the masturbation (or the positive reinforcer) comes at a more effective moment, from a conditioning point of view, than the later guilt (the punishment), no matter how intense or long-lasting this may be.

The theory is promising, especially as it is able to explain several associated phenomena. Coexistence of several paraphilias, often found clinically, is easily explained by this theory. A deviant who masturbates to one fantasy as his main sexual outlet, quite possibly masturbates to several other fantasies too, making him a polyparaphiliac. Furthermore, since females masturbate to orgasm much less frequently than males, they should be less likely to develop sexual deviations, which is actually observed too.

McGuire and colleagues have attempted to explain several paraphilias including pedophilia, exhibitionism, homosexuality, voyeurism, and fetishism through masturbation as a reinforcer.[99] More spectacularly, chimpanzee males, trained operantly to insert coins into a food dispenser have been shown to trade coins to equally trained female chimpanzees for sex. Stoller[99] explains convincingly how a mother can use operant conditioning, albeit at a subconscious level, to produce a transsexual male.*

IRMs and Imprinting

Ethologists Lorenz and Tinbergen observed a variety of species from birds to primates, and their studies point to the conclusion that sexual attachments are arrived at by two major instinctual mechanisms. First, the range of potential erotic objects is restricted to certain broad classes of stimuli by inborn neural circuits called *innate releasing mechanisms* (IRMs). Most animals have an innate ability to recognize and respond sexuoerotically to adult members of the opposite sex of their own species. If a male chimpanzee is reared in isolation, so he has no chance to "learn" any behavior from others, he would still be sexuoerotically aroused if the rear side of a female chimpanzee were shown to him. Of course, he would not know what to do about his feelings, and the appropriate action might involve some trial and error (chimpanzees reared in groups would have learned the correct sexual behavior by observation).

The second instinctual mechanism, which fine-tunes the IRMs, is *imprinting*, which is a special form of conditioning† that occurs during a critical period of development. Imprinting can best be defined as any kind of phase-sensitive learning (learning occurring at a particular age or a life stage), that is rapid (needs only one exposure of conditioned and unconditioned stimuli together), and apparently independent of the consequences of behavior.

Lorenz demonstrated how incubator-hatched geese would imprint on the first suitable moving stimulus they saw within the critical period of about 36 hours after hatching. Known as *filial imprinting*, this is a process in which a young animal learns the characteristics of its parent. In his perhaps most famous experiment on filial imprinting, the goslings would imprint on Lorenz (more specifically, on his wading boots). Pictures of Lorenz being followed by a gaggle of geese who had imprinted on him are commonly seen in psychology books. The geese thought Lorenz was their mother.

It has been theorized that almost in a similar way, a kind of *sexual imprinting* can also occur in which animals learn the characteristics of a sexual partner.‡ At what stage of life does this imprinting occur has not been explicitly stated; but it appears to occur at a very early stage of life. It is well known that zookeepers may become the sexual targets of a wide variety of animals in their care if these animals do not have sufficient exposure to members of their own species at the sensitive period of development. Several owners of pet cats and dogs know of the same effect.

If IRMs or imprinting or both go wrong, sexual responses can be attached to peculiar and socially unacceptable stimuli, such as a member of the same sex, an animal, a shoe, perhaps even a dead individual. The beauty of this theory is that it can explain virtually any paraphilia. It only requires that imprinting with the object of attraction occur at a particular period of development (the

---

* Please see chapter on transsexualism for details.

† For details on conditioning, and how it too could produce paraphilias, please see chapter on fetishism.

‡ Opponents have raised the objection that the behavior of birds cannot be extrapolated onto humans because there are marked differences in the central nervous systems of birds and mammals.

so-called critical period for sexual imprinting). Although the theoretical foundations of this theory are strong, its true vindication would be testing in humans. However, as is true with all experiments in psychology, this task is laden with enormous ethical dilemmas, and one would have to rely on interviewing paraphiliacs and eliciting whether they had been exposed to similar stimuli during some early period of life. Some instances of vomerophilia, or erotic vomiting, do seem to suggest that imprinting does play a part in its development (please see chapter on miscellaneous sexual crimes and perversions).

John Money's Lovemap theory

John Money (1921–2006)[100,101] has forwarded a novel theory based on a new concept of lovemaps. Money asserts that there is a lovemap—a kind of template—imprinted in the mind of each one of us. A lovemap is a group of messages encoded in our brains that describes our likes and dislikes regarding an ideal lover with whom we would preferentially like to build a relationship and copulate. It shows things like our preferences in hair and eye color, in voice, smell, body build, even education and mannerisms. It records the kind of personality that appeals to us, whether the warm and friendly type or the strong, silent type. It also includes the preferred sexual scenarios that would be carried out with the ideal lover. Although the individual may never enact these preferred scenarios with actual partners, his masturbatory fantasies or wet dreams will contain explicit representations of lovemaps.[102] The lovemap of a person dictates which sexual partner to take. Some people's lovemaps may say, "If she is a brunette with shoulder-length hair, I'll go for her. A blonde or a redhead just won't do." Some other person's lovemap may dictate that "Adult females are no good. If it is a prepubescent child, I would go for her." A good way to know the contours of one's own lovemap is to go a large gathering, say a party, and notice where the eyes are drifting again and again. The characteristics of the target person represent the programming ingrained within one's lovemap. With men, the lovemap tends to be much more visual than with women, who use information beyond their eyes to determine a male's attractiveness. This also tends to explain why paraphilias are more common in men as we shall see later.

How are Lovemaps Formed?

Money offers a coherent theory. Each of us is born with a basic genetic predisposition, a basic template, that is progressively modified by experience and environment over the course of a lifetime. Just as all of us develop language during the initial years of life, we also formulate a lovemap during the same period. Sexual rehearsal play, engaged in by most children, has a great role to play in formulating this lovemap. Parental influences also tend to play a role, most of us developing an image of an ideal lover around our parents. Our mother's characteristics, for example, leave an indelible impression on us, and we are forever after attracted to people with her facial features, body type, personality, even sense of humor. If she was warm and giving, as adults we tend to be attracted to people who are warm and giving. If our mother was strong and even-tempered, we are going to be attracted to a fair-minded strength in our mates.

By age eight, the pattern for our ideal mate has already formed. When we grow up into adults, we fall for and pursue people who most clearly fit our lovemaps. Once a lovemap is formed, it is extremely resistant to change, but it does change in certain circumstances. For example, in cases of couples living together for long periods, the lovemap of each partner transforms gradually in order to accommodate and integrate the partner's personality into the lovemap. This happens as each partner recognizes the other's sexual needs, likes, and dislikes.

Vandalized Lovemaps

It has been noted earlier that native lovemaps are acquired during children's sexual rehearsal play. Money asserts that if their play is not punished or interfered with (as happens in tribals), the basic geography of the lovemap develops typically as heterosexual. He even cites research[103,104] on the aboriginal culture in Arnhem Land in support of this position. A normal lovemap formed under this scenario has three characteristics in common: (i) it favors heterosexual partners; (ii) it includes penile–vaginal sexual intercourse as the preferred scenario; and finally, and most importantly, (iii) it embodies a view of love and eroticism as mutually compatible. If, according to Money, children's sexual rehearsal play is hampered by too much prohibition, prevention, and punishment, the standard heterosexual lovemap does not develop properly and the individual may respond to this situation in one of three ways:[105]

(i) *The Hypophilic Solution*: The lovemap becomes defaced in such a way that parts are missing. This impairs the sexual functioning of the individual in adulthood, causing difficulty in normal genital intercourse. This may result in hypoactive sexual desire disorder. The individual may become anorgasmic or sexually disinterested.
(ii) *The Hyperphilic Solution*: The lovemap not only defies defacement, but becomes exaggerated, so that the sex organs in adulthood are used with exaggerated defiance, frequency, and compulsiveness, and/or with great multiplicity of partners, in pairs or in groups. This results in what is commonly known as *sexual addiction*. The individual may become satyriacal or nymphomaniacal.
(iii) *The Paraphilic Solution*: It is *this* response which is of interest to us here. The lovemap is not completely defaced, but redesigned with detours that include new elements or relocations of original ones. The new elements or relocations may derive from other childhood encounters in which sexual organs become stimulated, for instance, receiving an enema or a whipping. If, for example, a boy is cuddled and pressed to her bosom by his mother after being whipped or punished in order to demonstrate repentance or forgiveness, he may become sexually aroused and his lovemap may become redefined. Whatever the reason, overt or covert, the further development of the lovemap becomes compromised and distorted, perhaps to the extent of being changed almost beyond recognition. Each paraphilia has its own specific lovemap, which generally unfolds at puberty.

Money further asserts that by punishing a child's sexual rehearsal play, parents and other elders ingrain the widespread view that the world of love and the world of lust must be two separate worlds—the world of love being saintly, pure, and undefiled; that of lust being sinful, dirty, and degrading. For a child who internalizes this view, the notion of sexuality as expression of love becomes an impossibility, a contradiction in terms. The child's developing lovemap will reflect this split: love belongs with the Madonna and the provider, sexuality with the whore and the profligate; love is undefiled and saintly, lust defiling and sinful. The sinful act of lust, therefore, defiles those who participate in it. It turns a saint into a sinner—the Madonna into a whore, and the provider into a playboy.

Since lust and love become two separate worlds for the paraphiliac, now he must learn to achieve the gratification of lust without getting involved in the saintly love in any way (if he did that, he would be defiling the saintly love; a saint cannot be used for a devilish objective, the lust). The paraphiliac achieves this seemingly impossible goal (this may perhaps be likened to quenching thirst without the use of water) by devising a number of strategies. To use Money's terminology, the child's lovemap is defaced, redesigned, or vandalized (for details of this redesigning, please see Money's classification of paraphilias above). A child's lovemap may be "vandalized" by a number of other factors, too, such as an incestuous or pedophilic relationship. In addition, lovemaps can be gender transposed to create a disjunction between the sexual dimorphism of the body and gender behavior; bisexuality, transsexuality, and transvestism are examples of this.

Money's lovemap theory satisfactorily explains a number of features associated with paraphilia. For example, most theories are not able to explain satisfactorily why paraphilias are more common in males. Money's lovemap theory explains it like this. It is well-known that nature has designed males to be dependent more on their eyes for erotic turn-on, and females to be more dependent on other inputs, such as touch, hearing, symbols of power such as physical size, signs of resources, clothing, and property, etc. In a way, a female tries to determine whether her sexual partner has enough strength and resources to provide for a family.

Money asserts that in children, just as language enters the brain through the ears, lovemaps arrive through the eyes. It is well known that more boys than girls have difficulty with their native language because boys rely less on the ears. The same goes for lovemaps. Boys also have more difficulty in getting their lovemaps. It is also easier for misprints to occur in males, giving rise to a greater incidence of paraphilias in men.

Miscellaneous Theories

A number of other theories tend to explain paraphilias, but perhaps not so comprehensively. One asserts that such a wide variation among sexual preferences is an evolutionary trait that offers some adaptive advantage to the species. For example, if people have divergent sexual tastes, no one will be deemed undesirable and left out in the cold.[106] No matter how physically repulsive one is, someone thinks him sexually desirable, and this provides everyone a fair chance to pass on genes to the subsequent generation. This theory tends to explain some select paraphilias, say, acrotomophilia (sexual preference for amputees) or rhytiphilia (arousal from facial wrinkles). It fails completely, for example, to explain why a person should have a fetish for shoes.

As noted above, it has been seen that endogenously produced opiates are released in specific brain areas during sexual arousal in some patients with sexual disorders.[34] It is possible that the patterns of opiate release in various brain areas differ in normal and paraphilic persons. This is a promising area where further research is needed.

EPIDEMIOLOGY

Prevalence and Incidence

Prevalence of paraphilias and sex offenses in society may be much more than imagined. The reason why the incidence appears less is that most victims choose not to report incidents to the police. Similarly, most paraphiliacs do not seek treatment. However, the large commercial market for paraphiliac paraphernalia, books, and magazines would suggest that the prevalence of paraphilia is high.

Prevalence versus Incidence: In epidemiology, the ***prevalence*** of a condition or disease in a statistical population is defined as the total number of cases of the condition or disease in the population at a given time, or the total number of cases in the population divided by the number of individuals in the population.

Prevalence is useful because it is a measure of the commonality of a condition. It helps physicians with the probability of certain diagnoses and is routinely used by epidemiologists, health care providers, government agencies, and insurance companies.

Prevalence is distinct from ***incidence***, which is a measure of the number of *new cases*. Prevalence involves *all* affected individuals, regardless of the date of contraction. Incidence only involves individuals who contracted a disease during a specified time interval. In this book, available data for both prevalence and incidence are provided.

Some reasonable estimates can be obtained by examining related studies. In 1986, the U.S. Commission on Pornography reviewed 3,050 magazine and book titles sold in "adults only" pornographic outlets in several cities. Of these, 746 titles could be assigned to a DSM III-R paraphilia category (513 titles if the partialism category was excluded). Thus, 24.4% of the titles could be assigned to a paraphilia category (16.8% if partialism was excluded as a category).[107] This seems to indicate that paraphilic interests may be widespread.

Sweden established a toll-free telephone help line for impotence and other sexual problems in 1999. In a survey published by Fugl-Meyer[108] and associates, it was found that during the 5 year period from 1999–2003, about 3% of men (n = 2,047) and 2% of women (n = 770) contacted the counselors for paraphilia. Interestingly, both men and women contacted not for their own, but for their partners' paraphilia. It must, however, be noted that this percentage reflects only persons *who contacted the helpline*, and not the percentage among the general population.

Kar and Koola[109] studied sexual preferences in a sample of English-speaking adults in a small town in South India, where responses were obtained through a postal questionnaire method. Sixty-one subjects of 200 persons who were contacted returned the questionnaires. Paraphilias reported were as follows: voyeurism (41.0%), fetishism (18.0%), frotteurism (11.5%), homosexuality (11.5%), telephone scatology (9.8%), and incest (8.2%). In a small minority, telephone scatology (3.3%), voyeurism (1.6%), and fetishism (1.6%) were reported to be the *only* methods of sexual gratification.

The incidence of sex offenses appears much higher. Herold and colleagues[110] conducted a survey in which data were obtained from 103 females in two university classes. Although as many as 84% of the respondents reported having been victims of a sexual offense, very few of these were reported to the police or even discussed with parents or social workers. Most offenses were only discussed with friends.

Paraphilias have a high co-morbidity with other Axis I conditions, such as mood disorders, psychoactive substance abuse, especially alcohol abuse, and anxiety disorders, especially social phobia.[32]

Combinations

It is not unusual for an individual to pursue more than one sexual variation. Multiple paraphilias in an affected individual may be seen simultaneously or sometimes serially.[111,112] ICD-10 assigns code F65.6 to multiple disorders of sexual preference (Table 1.4). These individuals are often referred to as polymorphous perverse.[123] Usually about two or three concurrent paraphilias are found although cases of up to ten paraphilias simultaneously have been reported in about 5% of paraphiliacs.

The most common combination is fetishism, transvestism, sadism, and masochism.[116,117] Fetishism is often seen with pedophilia, too.[113] Transvestic fetishism is usually associated with bondage[114,115] and autoerotic asphyxia.[116] Paraphilic themes may also change from time to time. It is not certain whether the change is a move to another paraphilia or if it is an expanded expression of an existing scenario. Changes between sadism and masochism and between voyeurism and exhibitionism are common and have been known for some time.[117] Other associations have been identified, such as voyeurism to pedophilia and pedophilia to rape. In some paraphilics the most important switch is from thinking about an erotic scenario to an actual sexual behavior.[107] In 1996, Långström and Seto randomly selected 2,450 individuals between the ages of 18 and 60 years from the general population of Sweden and interviewed them in a broad survey of sexuality and health. They found that respondents who reported exhibitionistic or voyeuristic behavior had substantially greater odds of reporting other atypical sexual behavior—sadomasochism or transvestism—as well.[82]

Age

Onset tends to begin during early puberty, reaching full development by the age of 20. Most patients of paraphilias are aged between 15–25 years. Paraphilias are rarely seen in individuals older than 50 years.[118]

Sex

Paraphilias are found with a strong preponderance in males; females represent only a minuscule proportion of all paraphiliacs.[21] Fedoroff and colleagues studied clinical records of 15 years and identified individuals referred to them for suspected paraphilic disorders. The clinics were located in different countries (Canada, the United States, and Great Britain), and all were affiliated with universities. A total of 132 paraphilics were identified, of whom 14 (11%) were women.[119] Within the total female sample, the most common diagnoses were pedophilia (36%), sexual sadism (29%), and exhibitionism (29%). The authors, however, emphasize that this is not a study of the frequency or prevalence of paraphilias in the female population, nor can the findings be used to draw such inferences.

Person[21] asserts that except for sadism and masochism, almost all of the reported cases are in males. Even among these two disorders, the maximum proportion of females is found in masochism; about 5% or about 1 in 20 of all masochists are female.[120] Both Gayford[121] and Sharma[10] assert that according to some surveys, this ratio is about 1 in 5, i.e., for every five masochists, one is a female. But neither quotes such surveys. Hunt[122] conducted a study of sadomasochism in the general population of U.S. and found that while the incidence of sadism was twice in males as compared to females, for masochism it was twice as frequent in females as compared to males. He asserts that since the replies to his questionnaire were anonymous, it is unlikely that the answers—and thus the incidences reported—were fake or spurious.

About the only paraphilia that is seen more commonly in females than in males is hybristophilia, or sexual arousal by criminals.[123] Some studies, such as that of Hunt,[124] report masochism as more common in females than in males; this, however, is not a universal conclusion of all researchers.

Race

Paraphilics have been reported from almost every race, culture, and socioeconomic group throughout history.[124] Brannon asserts that most patients of paraphilias are white,[120] but this could be because most research on paraphilias has been conducted on white persons. Very few studies of paraphilias have been published for other cultures and races.

Mortality and Morbidity

When the paraphilic behavior involved is inherently dangerous, e.g., autoerotic asphyxia, the mortality and morbidity are higher than the normal group and are dependent upon co-morbidity involved and the patient's co-operation with the therapist. No significant differences are noted if the paraphilic behavior is not associated with other morbid conditions (such as alcoholism), or if it is not in itself dangerous.

Relationship with Alcohol and Drugs

The relationship between paraphilias, sexual offenses, and alcohol is well documented in the literature.[125] The incidence of alcoholism among sexual offenders ranges from 28% to 52% depending on the stringency of the criteria used for diagnosing alcoholism.[126] Alcohol use has been implicated prior to the commission of up to 80% of rapes.[127,129] Other sexual crimes are also strongly associated with alcohol. As many as 66% of sexual sadists, 28%–65% of pedophiles, and 8%–72% of incest offenders have been found to have a history of alcohol abuse.[128] Langevin and associates[128] assert that over half of the sex offenders are heavy drinkers, a third chronic alcoholics, and up to three quarters abuse non-medical drugs. This suggests a strong relationship between alcohol and drugs and sexual offenses. However, the debate continues whether alcohol has a direct or indirect influence on sexual crimes.

Co-existence with Other Disorders

Paraphilic behavior has been described in association with a number of disorders. Main among them are temporal lobe epilepsy,[129] postencephalitic states,[130] Tourette's disorder (Gilles de la Tourette's syndrome),[131] frontal lobe disorders, Huntington's disease,[132] brainstem tumors, bilateral temporal injury, septal injury, and multiple sclerosis.[133] As noted earlier, paraphilic behavior has also been seen with dopaminergic therapy of Parkinson's disease.

Traumatic head injuries are associated with sex offenses. Langevin[134] studied a sample of 476 male sexual offenders and found that as many as 49.3% of them had sustained head injuries (mainly as a result of motor vehicle accidents) that led to unconsciousness; of these 22.5% had sustained significant neurological insults.

Other Significant Features

So compelling are sexual urges in paraphilics that they may choose occupations or avocations to increase their access to the objects or people needed to carry out their paraphilia. For example, an individual suffering from necrophilia may choose a profession where he can be near dead bodies (as, for example, a mortuary attendant), a bestialist may want to work with animals (animal attendants in laboratories), a voyeur may choose to work in rental properties so as to have opportunities to "peep" on unsuspecting people who may be nude or engaged in sexual activity, and an individual with pedophilia may volunteer to work with Boy Scouts or at a summer camp to increase access to children of the preferred age. Even if the paraphilia involves consenting partners (sadomasochism) or inanimate objects (fetishism), much time and energy may be spent locating potential partners or locating and viewing pornography that depicts the individual's paraphilia.[126]

Amberson and colleagues[135] studied 200 sex offenders at the University of Minnesota Sex Offender Treatment Program and found that 90% of them were white males, 58% had current partners, 49% had some college or were college graduates. Their mean age was 34.7 years. Forty-nine percent of them had an income of over $15,000, with 20% in the $20,000–$50,000 range. Alcohol was a problem for only one third of offenders, and these were by and large incest perpetrators.

SEX OFFENDERS

There is no universally fixed or agreeable definition of a sex crime or a sex offender. The definitions keep changing with evolving societal values and cultural norms. Sex crimes are defined differently by different cultures, nations, even different states of the same nation, depending on the nature of the act, kinship, age of the perpetrators and victims, degree of consent, sex of the partner, and the intent of the offender. Thus, the same act may be seen as a normal act or a predatory crime depending on these modifiers. However, in general, a *sex crime* may be defined as "behavior that is illegal in a given jurisdiction, that is explicitly sexual, or that has been declared criminal because it exploits, caters to, makes possible, or is dependent upon explicit sexual behavior."[136] A useful definition of sex offenders was offered in 1965 by the Kinsey group: "A *sex offender* is a person who has been legally convicted as a result of an overt act, committed by him for his own immediate sexual gratification, which is contrary to the prevailing sexual mores of the society in which he lives and/or is legally punishable."[137] Definitions provided by most workers are similar. Some authors include specific crimes such as pedophilia or incest within the general definition above, signifying, perhaps, a "personal weightage" given by them to a specific sex crime. Glass,[138] for instance, includes pedophilia in the above definition, and in her modified definition states that a sex offender is "someone who has committed or attempted to commit any type of illegal or nonconsensual sexual act and/or any sexual behavior involving children under the legal age of consent, based upon the laws governing the location where the sexual behavior occurred."

All paraphiliacs are not sex offenders, and conversely all sex offenders may not be paraphiliacs. Shaffer and Penn[1] talk about a number of paraphilias which are completely innocuous, such as acarophilia (arousal from scratching), capnolagnia (arousal from watching others smoke), and titillagnia (arousal from tickling). Some other paraphiliacs—in the more commonly understood meaning of the term—may act against law, but may not necessarily be *sex* offenders. Chan et al.[139] use the term *parasexual offenses* for minor sexual offenses such as exhibitionism, frotteurism, and its variants in which actual sexual acts are not committed.

Some examples may be cited here to clarify this concept. Transvestic fetishism is simply the wearing of clothes of the opposite sex for sexual arousal. This is a paraphilia, but not necessarily a sex offense. Similarly a fetishist who masturbates using the stolen bra of his neighbor may at most be convicted of theft, but cannot be considered a sex offender in a true sense. Conversely a rapist, a confirmed and undisputed sex offender, may not necessarily be a paraphiliac. Quite commonly, however, the two—paraphilias and sex offenses—are exhibited by the same individual. Sexual sadism that involves violence to a nonconsenting victim and pedophilia that manifests itself in child molestation are examples of paraphilias and sex offenses occurring simultaneously.

Paraphiliacs and sex offenders should in fact be construed as forming a gradual continuum, spectrum, or matrix, instead of as two discrete categories (Figure 1.3). At one pole of this continuum, we see pure paraphiliacs, with no vestige of any offense (as in, say, capnolagnia), and at the other pole, pure sex offenders with no vestige of any paraphilias (e.g., rapists). Most paraphilias and sex offenses would lie somewhere in the middle of this continuum.

OFFENDER CHARACTERISTICS

There are important differences between sex and non-sex offenders in personality and offense characteristics. Gudjonsson and Sigurdsson found that sexual offenders were significantly more introverted than violent offenders and tended to assault relatives and friends while violent offenders assaulted strangers.[140] Sex offenders obtained higher social desirability scores than the other groups. Fazel and colleagues found that sex offenders exhibited more schizoid, obsessive–compulsive, and avoidant traits, and fewer antisocial traits, compared with violent offenders.[141] Sexual offenders tend to be more passive, and lacking in initiative than other offender groups, while aggressive offenders display more ego-centered, grandiose, and narcissistic traits than do sexual offenders.[142]

CLINICAL AND LABORATORY ASSESSMENT OF PARAPHILIACS AND SEX OFFENDERS

Assessment of paraphiliacs and sex offenders usually includes the following components:

Clinical Interview

Clinical interview is done to assess the frequency and chronology of the behavior.[145] The possibility of multiple paraphilias must be considered.

Behavioral Assessment and Measurement

Major areas of behavior assessment are: (i) obtaining background and environmental information, (ii) learning, (iii) sensori- and perceptual motor activity, (iv) language and verbal behavior, (v) attention and motivation, (vi) emotional behavior, and (vii) social behavior.

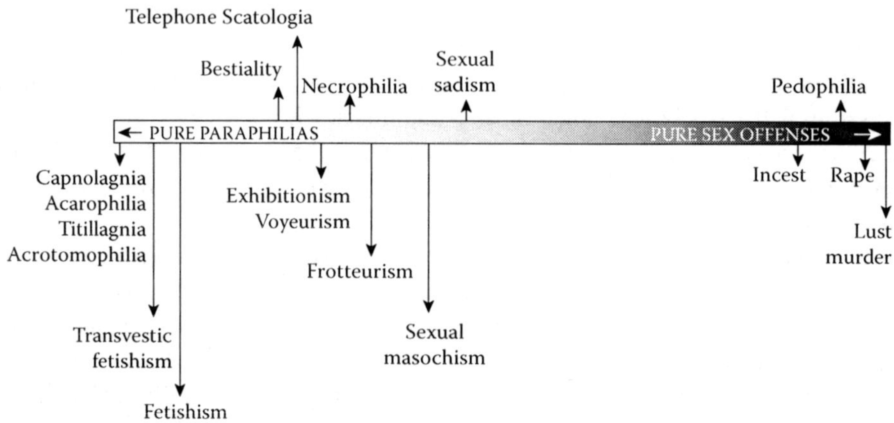

FIGURE 1.3 Paraphilias and sex offenses lie on a gradual continuum. Relative positions of various sex offenses have been determined keeping in mind the associated sentences in major jurisdictions.

Psycho-physiological Assessment

Penile Plethysmography or Phallometry

An objective, physiologic assessment of aberrant sexual behavior may be necessary before labeling a person as a paraphiliac or sex offender and sending him for treatment or criminally prosecuting him. The most widely used physiological assessment of sexual behavior—albeit controversial—is phallometry, penile plethysmography, or phalloplethysmography. The technique relies on the fact that sexual arousal causes penile erection. Thus any technique that could measure and quantify penile erection could in turn—in theory at least—quantify the levels of sexual arousal. The technique also tacitly assumes that while a normal person would not be aroused, or at most very minimally aroused, if shown aberrant sexual stimuli, say, pictures of nude young children. If a comparison were made of the levels of sexual arousal elicited by normal erotic stimuli (e.g., pictures of nude adult women) and aberrant erotic stimuli (e.g., pictures of nude young children), a normal person would show a very high ratio in favor of normal erotic stimuli. A pedophile on the other hand would be much more intensely aroused by seeing pictures of nude young children than by similar pictures of nude adult women. Such arousals can be detected by phallometry.

Theoretically speaking, this technique could objectively diagnose any paraphiliac or sex offender. Thus while a pedophile would be strongly aroused upon seeing pictures of nude young children, a homosexual would be aroused upon seeing pictures of nude persons of the same sex, a fetishist, upon seeing pictures of a fetish (say a shoe), a necrophiliac, upon seeing pictures of nude dead, a zoophiliac, upon seeing pictures of animals, and so on. The technique, however, has been most frequently used on pedophiles, homosexuals, and exhibitionists. Tichy,[144] for example, used this technique with pedophiles and exhibitionists and found it useful in differentiating this group from normal people.

There are two general methods for measuring changes in penis size—measuring the change in penile volume or measuring the change in penile circumference. Both are satisfactory.

Polygraph Assessments

Individuals accused and convicted of sexual offenses have every reason to deny the allegations against them or to provide incorrect information regarding their offense, even if they have to admit it. The polygraph has increasingly been utilized to verify information provided by sex offenders regarding the details of the alleged offense, conduct, and past sexual history. The polygraph is also used to monitor the veracity of reports of a convicted offender's compliance with treatment plans or terms of probation. Various studies have demonstrated that polygraph testing can be an effective means of obtaining a comprehensive sexual offense history and increasing the number of disclosures made by offenders.[145,146]

Polygraph assessment is not without its drawbacks. The results are highly dependent on the examiner's expertise, and results are usually not admissible in court.[147–149] Moreover, like other psychophysiological measures, polygraph testing is criticized for its lack of standardization and the generalizability of research findings. Ethics of administering polygraph tests has also been under scrutiny.[150]

Visual Reaction Time

Visual reaction time (VRT), or the amount of viewing time spent looking at a particular image, has been hypothesized as a less costly and less invasive method of measuring sexual interest.[151] Also known as "viewing time tests, " they are based upon the notion that visual reaction time, or the time spent looking at a particular picture, is an indicator of the sexual interest of the person in the object of that picture. For instance, if a person is shown pictures of a nude adult female, a nude adult male, a nude female child, or other deviant stimuli (say, a shoe with a high heel, an animal, or a corpse), theoretically speaking a normal man would spend maximum time looking at the nude adult female, a pedophile would spend maximum time looking at nude female child, a necrophile, at corpse, and so on. Viewing time tests are, however, used most commonly to assess pedophiles only.

Visual reaction time measurements are based on the work of Rosenzweig,[152] who first employed the quantitative observation and measurement of the amount of time a participant spent looking at sexual and non-sexual stimuli. Visual reaction time has also been used as a measure of sexual preference by Wright and Adams,[153] and as a measure of interest in erotica by several workers.[154–157]

The methodology of administering the test is, however, complex. One representative test, known as Abel Assessment for Sexual Interest (AASI), developed by Dr. Gene Abel of Abel Screening, Inc., Atlanta may give a general idea as to how these tests are administered. The subject is seated in front of a computer that is linked to a slide projector. He is shown how to advance slides (showing pictures of deviant stimuli, such as nude children) by pressing a key on the computer keyboard. The subject is asked also to simultaneously rate his sexual arousal to each slide on a 7-point scale ranging from 1 (highly sexually disgusting) to 7 (highly sexually arousing). The computer measures visual reaction time (VRT), the time the subject takes to rate the slide and press the key to advance the slide. The test if done properly is resistant to faking. However, it still must go through more empirical scrutiny. A drawback of this test is that once offenders learn the protocol the test will be ineffective.

Pupillometry

Pupillometric assessment of sexual preference was first demonstrated by reports of pupil dilation in participants when presented with sexually preferred images and constriction when presented with nonpreferred stimuli.[158] Subsequent research has shown some pupillary response in nonoffenders to preferred sexual stimuli, but large intragroup variation is observed.[159–161] Pupillometry, however, could not be demonstrated to reliably discern sexual preference by several workers.[162,163] Much more research is needed before pupillometry becomes an important tool in investigation in psycho-physiological assessment of paraphilias.

In summary, psycho-physiological testing can play a useful, but limited, role in the assessment of paraphilias and sex offenders. Physiologic test results should be used only in conjunction with a thorough psychiatric evaluation, comprehensive sexual history, and clinical expertise. Great care should also be taken not to overgeneralize test results. The results should not be used in determining the truth of allegations. Significantly, the use of psychophysiological tests to predict recidivism accurately has not been demonstrated in controlled studies.

MANAGEMENT

Mostly paraphilics do not seek treatment on their own. Treatment seeking is generally precipitated by interpersonal or legal pressure, and the individual is more or less forced to undergo treatment because he or she has been caught. Also, the paraphilic forced to seek treatment is likely to experience strongly conflicting feelings over the prospect of "losing" his paraphilia. He may realize that his life would be easier, and the threat of discovery or prosecution would abate, but at the same time he equates his loss of the paraphilia to losing his sexuality.[126]

PHARMACOLOGICAL TREATMENT

Treatment of paraphilias with pharmacological agents has been called chemical castration.[164,165] Currently two distinct classes of psychopharmacological agents, antiandrogens, and serotonergic antidepressants have been found useful in the treatment of paraphilias and paraphilia-related disorders.

Antiandrogens

Medroxyprogesterone Acetate (MPA)

Medroxyprogesterone acetate has been found to be very useful in treatment programs of paraphiliacs and sex offenders.[166–168] Significantly, some jurisdictions tend to enforce treatment by law. For instance, Florida Statute 794.0235 specifies that a court may order MPA treatment as a sentence for sexual battery and *must* order MPA treatment if an offender is convicted of sexual battery for a second offense. The offender may opt for castration in cases where MPA treatment is ordered. Similarly, Section 645 of the California Penal Code says that any person guilty of a first conviction of any sex offense may, upon parole, undergo medroxyprogesterone acetate treatment or its chemical equivalent, in addition to any other punishment prescribed for that offense or any other provision of law, at the discretion of the court. Upon second conviction the treatment is required.

Cyproterone Acetate

Cyproterone acetate (Androcur, Cyprostat) acts by blocking androgen receptors. It has also been found useful for treating paraphilias and sex offenders, especially in pedophilia.[169,170,171]

Leuprolide Acetate

Leuprolide acetate, a gonadotropin-releasing hormone agonist (GnRH agonist), is useful for paraphilias.[172,173] By causing constant stimulation of the pituitary GnRH receptors, it initially causes stimulation, but thereafter decreases pituitary secretion of luteinizing hormone (LH) and follicle-stimulating hormone (FSH) gonadotropins. It has been found useful in a patient with multiple paraphilias who had earlier been treated unsuccessfully for several years with cyproterone acetate and medroxyprogesterone acetate.[174]

Miscellaneous Drugs

Antimanic mood stabilizing agents (e.g., lithium) and antidepressants (imipramine, fluoxetine) have been used in paraphilias with some success. One of the earliest proponents of this treatment was Ward,[175] who successfully used lithium to treat a case of transvestism in a 24 year old manic-depressive man. Ward's reasoning was immaculate. He assumed that the transvestism was perpetuated by mood-dependent motives, which could be eliminated by lithium. Since this was a case of associated mania, another assumption was that the manic state became an intermittent reinforcer for the transvestism, and lithium, by eliminating the mania, treated the condition. Cesnik and Coleman[176] reported the successful use of lithium carbonate in a case of a 26 year old male who repeatedly displayed the life-threatening behavior of autoerotic asphyxia.

Kafka[177] successfully used lithium and also imipramine (Tofranil, a tricyclic antidepressant) and fluoxetine (Prozac, a selective serotonic reuptake inhibitor or SSRI) to treat cases of nonparaphilic sexual addictions and paraphilias. Buresová and co-workers[178] from Czechoslovakia have found oxyprothepine decanoate (a long-acting antipsychotic of Czechoslovak provenance) fairly useful in the treatment of paraphilias. Most recently Alexandra Žourková[179] from Czechoslovakia has found lithium to be fairly useful in the treatment of paraphilias. Levitsky and Owens[180] conducted a Medline search for 20 years, and from various case reports retrieved during this period found that antiandrogens, estrogens, GnRH analogues, and serotonergic medications may be useful in treating hypersexuality and paraphilias when other methods have failed.

However, this is not the experience of all workers. Balon[181] reviewed the role of several drugs in the treatment of paraphilias. Among them were antiandrogen hormones, phenothiazines, lithium, buspirone hydrochloride, and serotonergic drugs such as fluoxetine, clomipramine, sertraline, and fluvoxamine. He concluded that lithium was a rather ineffective, or at best weakly effective, treatment modality for paraphilias. He, however, found it useful in the management of paraphilias with comorbid mood disorders. In a more recent publication, he reiterates his view and suggests that the use of lithium should be confined to cases where all other treatments have failed, or as a last line of treatment.[182]

Buspirone hydrochloride,[183] divalproex sodium,[184] luteinizing hormone-releasing hormone (LHRH) agonists,[185] and naltrexone[186] have been found to be useful in paraphilias by other workers.

PARAPHILIC PREVENTION

Prevention of paraphilias is the Holy Grail of community psychiatry. Three paraphilic prevention models exist: *primary prevention models* that represent efforts directed at the general population with no effort at differential selection of target group; *secondary prevention models* that strive to focus energies on populations of individuals believed to be significantly at risk of paraphilia, but who do not currently manifest paraphilic behavior; and *tertiary prevention models*, directed at overt paraphiliacs to restore them to a state of functioning that existed before the emergence of paraphilias.[187]

REFERENCES

1. Shaffer, L. and Penn J., A Comprehensive Paraphilia Classification System, in *Sex Crimes and Paraphilia*, 1st ed. Hicky, E.W., Pearson, Prentice Hall, New Jersey, 2006, chapter 8, pages 69-93.
2. American Psychiatric Association. *Diagnostic and Statistical Manual of Mental Disorders*, 4th ed. Washington DC, 2000.
3. Watson, J.P., Davies, T. ABC of mental health: Psychosexual problems (clinical review). BMJ 1997;315:239-242
4. Crowe, M. Sexual problems: introduction, description and classification. *Psychiatry*. 2007;6(3):87-89.
5. Johnson, B.R., Becker, J.V., Sexual wickedness. *Psychiatric Annals*. 1997;27:634-7.
6. Money, J. Gay, *Straight, and In-Between: The Sexology of Erotic Orientation*, Oxford University Press, New York, 1988.
7. Krafft-Ebing, R.F. *Psychopathia Sexualis*, 1st ed. F.A. Davis, Philadelphia, 1886 [reprinted by Bloat Books, 1999]
8. Stekel, W. *Peculiarities of behavior: Wandering mania, dipsomania, cleptomania, pyromania, and allied impulsive acts* (2 vols). English translation of *Impulshandlungen* (1922) by J.S. Van Teslaar. Liveright, New York.
9. Rosario, V.A., II. *The erotic imagination: French histories of perversity*. Oxford University Press, New York, 1997.
10. Sharma, B.R. Disorders of sexual preference and medico legal issues thereof. *American Journal of Forensic Medicine and Pathology*, 24(3):277-282, 2003.

11. Westermarck, E., *Christianity and Morals*, Kegal Paul, London, 1939.
12. Taylor, G.R., *Sex in History*, Thames and Hudson, London, 1953.
13. West, D.J. *Sexual Crimes and Confrontations: A Study of Victims and Offenders*, Gower Publishing Company Ltd, Hants, England, 1987, page 1.
14. Hare, E.H., Masturbatory insanity: The history of an idea, *Journal of Mental Science*, 108, 2, 1962.
15. Mountjoy, P.T., Some early attempts to modify penile erection in horse and human: an introductory analysis. *Psychological Record*, 24, 291, 1974.
16. American Psychiatric Association. Diagnostic and Statistical Manual of Mental Disorders, 2nd ed. Washington DC, 1968.
17. Lamberg, L., Gay Is Okay With APA. *Journal of the American Medical Association*, 280, 497, 1998.
18. Drescher, J., Stein, T.S. and Byne, W.M. Homosexuality, Gay and Lesbian Identities, and Homosexual Behavior, in *Kaplan & Sadock's Comprehensive Textbook of Psychiatry*, 8th edition, Sadock, B.J. and Sadock, V.A., Eds., Lippincott, Wilkins and Williams, Philadelphia, 2005, page 1936.
19. The Indian Penal Code, (Act No. 45 of 1860) [6th October, 1860].
20. Money, J., Paraphilias, in *Handbook of Sexology*, Money J. and Musaph H., Eds., Elsevier/North-Holland Biomedical Press, 1977, page 922.
21. Person, E.S, Paraphilias, in *Kaplan & Sadock's Comprehensive Textbook of Psychiatry*, 8th edition, Sadock, B.J. and Sadock, V.A., Eds., Lippincott, Wilkins and Williams, Philadelphia, 2005, chap. 18.2.
22. Kinsey, A.C., Pomeroy, W.B., Martin, C.E. *Sexual Behavior in the Human Male*, W.B. Saunders, Philadelphia, 1948.
23. Kauth, M.R. Sexual Orientation and Identity, in *Sex and Sexuality* (3 vols), McAnulty, R.D. and Burnette, M.M., Eds., Praeger, Westport, Connecticut, 2006, vol 1, chapter 7, pages 153-184.
24. Graham, S., Sulawesi's fifth gender. *Inside Indonesia*, Apr - Jun 2001. Available at: http://www.insideindonesia.org/edit66/bissu2.htm. Accessed September 22, 2007.
25. Berlin, F.S. Treatments to change sexual orientation. *Am J Psychiatry*. 2000;157(5):838.
26. Blanchard, R. The classification and labeling of nonhomosexual gender dysphorias. *Arch Sex Behav.* 1989 Aug;**18(4)**:315-34.
27. Benjamin, H., *The Transsexual Phenomenon*, The Julian Press, New York, 1966.
28. Green, R. Sexual identity: research strategies. *Arch. Sex. Behav.* 1975; 4: 357-362.
29. Rinehart, N.J., and McCabe, M. P. Hypersexuality: Psychopathology or normal variant of sexuality? *Sexual and Marital Therapy*. 1997;12:45-60.
30. Barth, R. J., and Kinder, B. N. The mislabeling of sexual impulsivity. *Journal of Sex and Marital Therapy*. 1987;13: 15—23.
31. Kafka, M.P. Hypersexual desire in males: an operational definition and clinical implications for males with paraphilias and paraphilia-related disorders. *Arch Sex Behav.* 1997 Oct;26(5):505-26.
32. Kafka, M.P., Prentky, R.A. Preliminary observations of DSM-III-R axis I comorbidity in men with paraphilias and paraphilia-related disorders. *J Clin Psychiatry*. 1994;55(11):481-7.
33. Kafka, M.P., Hennen, J. A DSM-IV Axis I comorbidity study of males (n = 120) with paraphilias and paraphilia-related disorders. *Sex Abuse*. 2002;14(4):349-66.
34. Frost, J.J., Mayberg, H.S., Berlin, F., et al. Alteration in brain opiate receptor binding in man following sexual arousal using C-11 carfentinil and positron emission tomography [Proceedings of the 33rd Annual Meeting of the Society of Nuclear Medicine]. *J. Nucl. Med.* 1986;**27**:1027.
35. Holmes, R.M., *Sex Crimes*. Sage, Newbury Park, CA, 1991.
36. Thomson, P.G. Sexual Deviation. *Canadian Med Assoc J.* 1959 Mar 1; 80(5): 381-389.
37. Sim, M. *Guide to Psychiatry*, 3rd ed. Churchill Livingstone, London, 1974, page 397.
38. Moser, C. Paraphilia: A Critique of a Confused Concept, in *New Directions in Sex Therapy—Innovations and Alternatives*, Kleinplatz, P.J., Ed., Taylor & Francis, 2001, pages 91-108.
39. Plato. (ca 355-347 BCE) *Laws*, Trans. Saunders T.J. , in *Plato: Complete Works*, Cooper J (ed) and Hutchinson, D.S. (assoc ed), Hackett, Indianapolis, 1977.
40. Aquinas, T. *Summa Theologica* (translated by Fathers of the English Dominican Province) 5 Volume Set. Christian Classics, MI, 1981.
41. Suetonius, Robert Graves (Translator). *The Lives of Twelve Caesars, Life of Caligula*, Penguin Classics, England, 2003.
42. Archibald, E. *Incest and the Medieval Imagination*. Oxford University Press, Oxford, 2001.
43. Hafner, S. Charlemagne's Unspeakable Sin. *Modern Language Studies*. 2002;32(2):1-14.

44. Ridinger, R.B. Negotiating limits: the legal status of S/M in the United States. *J Homosex.* 2006;**50(2-3)**:189-216.
45. de Silva, W.P. ABC of sexual health. Sexual variations. BMJ. 1999;318(7184):654-6.
46. American Psychiatric Association. *Diagnostic and Statistical Manual of Mental Disorders*, 1st ed. American Psychiatric Association, Washington DC, 1952, pp 38-9.
47. American Psychiatric Association. *Diagnostic and Statistical Manual of Mental Disorders*, 2nd ed. American Psychiatric Association, Washington DC, 1968, p 44.
48. American Psychiatric Association. *Diagnostic and Statistical Manual of Mental Disorders*, 3rd ed. American Psychiatric Association, Washington DC, 1980.
49. Lief, H.I. and Kaplan, H.S. Ego-dystonic homosexuality. *J Sex Marital Ther.* 12, 259, 1986.
50. American Psychiatric Association. *Diagnostic and Statistical Manual of Mental Disorders*, 3rd ed. rev. American Psychiatric Association, Washington DC, 1987.
51. Summary of Practice-Relevant changes to the DSM-IV-TR. Available from: http://www.dsmivtr.org/2-3changes.cfm.
52. Hilliard, R.B., Spitzer, R.L. Change in criterion for paraphilias in DSM-IV-TR. *Am J Psychiatry.* 2002 Jul;159(7):1249.
53. History of the development of the ICD. Available from: http://www.who.int/classifications/icd/en/HistoryOfICD.pdf.
54. Reid, W.H., Wise, M.G. *DSM-IV Training Guide*, Brunner/Mazel, New York, 1995, page 6.
55. Hart, A.C., Schmidt, K.M., Aaran, W.S. *St. Anthony's ICD-9-CM Code Book.* St. Anthony's Publishing, Reston, Va, 1999.
56. World Health Organization. *The ICD-10 Classification of Mental and Behavioral Disorders: Clinical Descriptions and Diagnostic Guidelines.* Geneva, 1992.
57. ICD-9-CM diagnostic codes for paraphilias. Available from: http://icd9cm.chrisendres.com/2007/index.php?action=child&recordid=2342.
58. World Health Organization. *International Statistical Classification of Diseases and Health Related Problems (The) ICD-10*, 2nd Edition. World Health Organization, Geneva, 2004.
59. Sadoff, D.H., Other Sexual Deviations, in *The Sexual Experience*, Sadock, B.J., Kaplan, H.I. and Freedman, A.M., Eds., Williams and Wilkins Company, Baltimore, 1976.
60. Rosenhan, D.L. and Seligman, M.E.P., *Abnormal Psychology*, W. W. Norton and Company, New York, 1984.
61. Freund, K., Seto, M.C. and Kuban, M. Frotteurism and the Theory of Courtship Disorder. In *Sexual Deviance—Theory, Assessment, and Treatment*, 1st ed. Laws, D.R. and O'Donohue, W., (Eds.), The Guilford Press, New York, 1997, chapter 6, pages 111-130.
62. Money, J., Lamacz, M. *Vandalized love maps.* Prometheus Books, Buffalo, New York, 1989.
63. Freeman, M. Sexual Deviance and the Law, in *Sexual Deviation*, 3rd edition, Rosen I., Ed., Oxford University Press, Oxford, 1996, chap. 17.
64. James, T.E. Law and the sexual offender, in *The pathology and treatment of sexual deviation*, Rosen I., Ed., Oxford University Press, Oxford, 1964.
65. Lombroso, C. *Crime, its causes and remedies*, William Heinemann Ltd. London, 1911.
66. Money, J. Forensic sexology: paraphilic serial rape (biastophilia) and lust murder (erotophonophilia). *Am J Psychother.* 1990 Jan;44(1):26-36.
67. Freud, Sigmund (1962). *Three Essays on the Theory of Sexuality* [*Drei Abhandlungen zur Sexualtheorie*], trans. James Strachey. New York: Basic Books [Original edition - 1905].
68. Fenichel, O. *The psychoanalytical theory of neurosis*, Norton, New York, 1945.
69. Terzian, H., Dalle Ore G: Syndrome of Kluver and Bucy reproduced in man by bilateral removal of temporal lobes. *Neurology.* 1955; **5**:373–80.
70. Lilly, R., Cummings, J.L., Benson, D.F., Frankel, M.: The human Kluver-Bucy syndrome. *Neurology.* 1983;**33**:1141–5.
71. Gaul, C., Jordan, B., Wustmann, T., Preuss, U.W. [Klüver-Bucy syndrome in humans] [Article in German]. *Nervenarzt.* 2007 Jul;78(7):821-3.
72. Carroll, B.T., Goforth, H.W., Raimonde, L.A. Partial Klüver-Bucy syndrome: two cases. *CNS Spectr.* 2001 Apr;**6(4)**:329-32.
73. Kolárský, A., Freund, K., Machek, J., Polák, O. Male sexual deviation. Association with early temporal lobe damage. *Arch Gen Psychiatry.* 1967 Dec;17(6):735-43.
74. Huws, R., Shubsachs, A.P., Taylor, P.J. Hypersexuality, fetishism and multiple sclerosis. *Br J Psychiatry.* 1991 Feb;158:280-1.

75. Joyal, C.C., Black, D.N., Dassylva, B. The neuropsychology and neurology of sexual deviance: a review and pilot study. *Sex Abuse.* 2007 Jun;19(2):155-73.
76. Graber, B., Hartmann, K., Coffman, J.A., Huey, C.J., Golden, C.J. Brain damage among mentally disordered sex offenders. *J Forensic Sci.* 1982 Jan;**27(1)**:125-34.
77. Ivashchenko, O.I., Eliseev, A.V., Tkachenko, A.A., Petina, T.V. [Interhemispheric EEG coherence in men with abnormal sexual behavior] [Article in Russian]. *Zh Nevrol Psikhiatr Im S S Korsakova.* 1997;**97(7)**:46-51.
78. Waismann, R., Fenwick, P.B., Wilson, G.D., Hewett, T.D., Lumsden, J. EEG responses to visual erotic stimuli in men with normal and paraphilic interests. *Arch Sex Behav.* 2003 Apr;**32(2)**:135-44.
79. Mendez, M.F., Chow, T., Ringman, J., Twitchell, G., Hinkin, C.H. Pedophilia and temporal lobe disturbances. *J Neuropsychiatry Clin Neurosci.* 2000 Winter;12(1):71-6.
80. Casanova, M.F., Mannheim, G., Kruesi, M. Hippocampal pathology in two mentally ill paraphiliacs. *Psychiatry Res.* 2002 Aug 20;115(1-2):79-89.
81. Långström, N., Seto, M.C. Exhibitionistic and voyeuristic behavior in a Swedish national population survey. *Arch Sex Behav.* 2006 Aug;35(4):427-35.
82. Kafka, M.P. A monoamine hypothesis for the pathophysiology of paraphilic disorders. *Arch Sex Behav.* 1997 Aug;26(4):343-58.
83. Balthazart, J., Absil, P., Gerard, M., Appeltants, D., Ball, G.F. Appetitive and consummatory male sexual behavior in Japanese quail are differentially regulated by subregions of the preoptic medial nucleus. *J Neurosci.* 1998;18(16):6512-27.
84. Quinn, N.P., Toone, B., Lang, A.E., Marsden, C.D., Parkes, J.D. Dopa dose-dependent sexual deviation. *Br J Psychiatry.* 1983 Mar;142:296-8.
85. Vogel, H.P., Schiffter, R. Hypersexuality - a complication of dopaminergic therapy in Parkinson's disease. *Pharmacopsychiatria.* 1983 Jul;16(4):107-10.
86. Uitti, R.J., Tanner, C.M., Rajput, A.H., Goetz, C.G., Klawans, H.L., Thiessen, B. Hypersexuality with antiparkinsonian therapy. *Clin Neuropharmacol.* 1989 Oct;12(5):375-83.
87. Factor, S.A., Molho, E.S., Podskalny, G.D., Brown, D. Parkinson's disease: drug-induced psychiatric states. *Adv Neurol.* 1995;65:115-38.
88. van Deelen, R.A., Rommers, M.K., Eerenberg, J.G., Egberts, A.C. Hypersexuality during use of levodopa [Article in Dutch]. *Ned Tijdschr Geneeskd.* 2002 Nov 2;146(44):2095-8.
89. Both, S., Everaerd, W., Laan, E., Gooren L. Effect of a single dose of levodopa on sexual response in men and women. *Neuropsychopharmacology.* 2005 Jan;30(1):173-83.
90. Klos, K.J., Bower, J.H., Josephs, K.A., Matsumoto, J.Y., Ahlskog, J.E. Pathological hypersexuality predominantly linked to adjuvant dopamine agonist therapy in Parkinson's disease and multiple system atrophy. *Parkinsonism Relat Disord.* 2005 Sep;11(6):381-6.
91. Ivanco, L.S., Bohnen, N.I. Effects of donepezil on compulsive hypersexual behavior in Parkinson disease: a single case study. *Am J Ther.* 2005 Sep-Oct;12(5):467-8.
92. Kogan, B.M., Tkachenko, A.A., Drozdov, A.Z., Andrianova, E.P., Filatova, T.S., Man'kovskaia, I.V., Kovaleva, I.A. [Monoamine metabolism in different forms of paraphilias] [Article in Russian]. *Zh Nevropatol Psikhiatr Im S S Korsakova.* 1995;95(6):52-6.
93. Meston, C.M., Frohlich, P.F. The neurobiology of sexual function. *Arch Gen Psychiatry.* 2000 Nov;57(11):1012-30.
94. Crenshaw, T.L. and Goldberg, J.P., *Sexual pharmacology: Drugs that affect sexual function.*, W.W.Norton, New York, 1996.
95. Rossi, R. Diagnostic of sexual perversions. *J Endocrinol Invest.* 2003;**26(3 Suppl)**:109-11.
96. Money, J. *The Lovemap Guidebook: A Definitive Statement.* Continuum, New York, 1999.
97. Simpson, G., Blaszczynski, A., Hodgkinson, A. Sex offending as a psychosocial sequela of traumatic brain injury. *J Head Trauma Rehabil.* 1999 Dec;**14(6)**:567-80.
98. McGuire, R.J., Carlisle, J.M., Young, B.G. Sexual Deviations As Conditioned Behaviour: A Hypothesis. *Behav Res Ther.* 1965 Jan;**3**:185-90.
99. Purcell, C.E., and Arrigo, B.A. *The Psychology of Lust Murder: Paraphilia, Sexual Killing, and Serial Homicide*, Elsevier Academic Press, MA, 2006, chapter 6.
100. Stoller, R.J., The Gender Disorders, in *Sexual Deviation*, 3rd edition, Rosen I., Ed., Oxford University Press, Oxford, 1996, chap. 5.
101. Money, J. *Lovemaps.* Irvington Publishers, Inc., New York, 1986.
102. Money, J., *Lovemaps: Clinical Concepts of sexual/erotic health and pathology.* Prometheus Books, Buffalo, New York, 1989.

103. Bergner, R. M., Money's "lovemap" account of the paraphilias: a critique and reformulation. *American Journal of Psychotherapy.* 1988;42(2): 254-262.
104. Malinowski, B. *The Sexual Life of Savages in North-Western Melanesia.* Halcyon House, New York, 1929.
105. Marshall, D., and Suggs, R. (Eds). *Human Sexual Behavior. Variations in the Ethnographic Spectrum.* Basic Books, New York, 1971.
106. Money, J., Paraphilias: Phenomenology and Classification. *American Journal of Psychotherapy.* 1984; XXXVIII(2):164-179.
107. Achenbach, J. The Spice of Life? Variety, Pal. *The Washington Post.* Washington, D.C.: Mar 27, 1992. page. b.05.
108. Lebegue B. Paraphilias in U.S. pornography titles: "pornography made me do it" (Ted Bundy). *Bull Am Acad Psychiatry Law.* 1991;**19(1)**:43-8.
109. Fugl-Meyer, K.S. et al. A Swedish telephone help-line for sexual problems: a 5-year survey. *J Sex Med.* 1, 278, 2004.
110. Kar, N., Koola, M.M. A pilot survey of sexual functioning and preferences in a sample of english-speaking adults from a small South Indian town. *J Sex Med.* 2007 Sep;4(5):1254-61.
111. Herold, E.S., Mantle, D., Zemitis, O. A study of sexual offenses against females. *Adolescence.* 14, 65, 1979.
112. Abel, G.G., Becker, J.V., Cunningham-Rathner, J., Mittelman, M., Rouleau, J.L. Multiple paraphilic diagnoses among sex offenders. *Bull Am Acad Psychiatry Law.* 1988;16(2):153-68.
113. Bradford, J.M., Boulet. J., Pawlak, A. The paraphilias: a multiplicity of deviant behaviours. *Can J Psychiatry.* 1992 Mar;37(2):104-8.
114. Abel, G.G. and Osborn, C. The paraphilias: the extent and nature of sexually deviant and criminal behavior. *Psychiatr Clin North America.* 1992; 15: 675–687.
115. Taylor-Buckner, H. The transvestic careeer path. *Psychiatry.* 1970; **33**: 381-389.
116. Buhrich, N., Beaumont, T. Comparison of transvestism in Australia and America. *Arch Sex Behav.* 1981 Jun;**10(3)**:269-79.
117. Blanchard, R., Hucker, S.J. Age, transvestism, bondage, and concurrent paraphilic activities in 117 fatal cases of autoerotic asphyxia. *Br J Psychiatry.* 1991;**159**:371-7.
118. Philpot, C.D. Paraphilia and aging. *Clin Geriatr Med.* 2003 Aug;19(3):629-36.
119. Brannon, G.E., Paraphilias, 2005. Available from : http://www.emedicine.com/med/topic3127.htm.
120. Fedoroff, J. P., Fishell, A., Fedoroff, B., A case series of women evaluated for paraphilic sexual disorders. *Canadian Journal of Human Sexuality.* 1999; 8(2): 127-140.
121. Paraphilias, in *Gale Encyclopedia of Mental Disorders*, Thackery, E. and Harris M., Eds, Thomson Gale, Farmington Hills, MI, 2002, pages 729-30.
122. Gayford, J.J. Disorders of sexual preference, or paraphilias: a review of the literature. *Med Sci Law.* 1997 Oct;37(4):303-15.
123. Hunt, M., *Sexual Behaviour in the 1970s*, Dell, New York, 1974.
124. Vitello, C., Hybristophilia—The Love of Criminals. In "*Sex crimes and paraphilia*", 1st ed. Hickey, E.W., (Ed.), Pearson Prentice Hall, New Jersey, 2006, chapter 22, pages 197-206.
125. Wiederman, M.W. Paraphilia and Fetishism. *The Family Journal.* 2003;11:315 - 321.
126. Rada, R.T. Alcoholism and forcible rape. *Am J Psychiatr.* 1975;132(4):444-46.
127. Allnutt, S.H., Bradford, J.M., Greenberg, D.M., Curry, S. Co-morbidity of alcoholism and the paraphilias. *J Forensic Sci.* 1996 Mar;41(2):234-9.
128. Norris, J., Kerr, K.L. Alcohol and violent pornography: responses to permissive and non-permissive cues. *J Studies Alcohol.* 1993;11:118-27.
129. Langevin, R., Bain, J., Wortzman, G., Hucker, S., Dickey, R., Wright, P. Sexual sadism: brain, blood, and behavior. *Ann N Y Acad Sci.* 1988;528:163-71.
130. Kolarsky, A., Freund, K., Machek, J., Polak, O. Male sexual deviation. Association with early temporal lobe damage. *Arch Gen Psychiatry.* 1967 Dec;**17(6)**:735-43.
131. Thomas, P.R., DeAlwis, K. Transvestism in a person with learning disabilities presenting with behavioural problems. *J Intellect Disabil Res.* 1995 Oct;**39(Pt 5)**:454-6.
132. McDougle, C.J., Southwick, S.M., Rohrbaugh, R.M. Tourette's disorder and associated complex behaviors: a case report. *Yale J Biol Med.* 1990 May-Jun;**63(3)**:209-14.
133. Fedoroff, J.P., Peyser, C., Franz, M.L., Folstein, S.E. Sexual disorders in Huntington's disease. *J Neuropsychiatry Clin Neurosci.* 1994 Spring;**6(2)**:147-53.

134. Frohman, E.M., Frohman, T.C., Moreault, A.M. Acquired sexual paraphilia in patients with multiple sclerosis. *Arch Neurol.* 2002 Jun;**59(6)**:1006-10.
135. Langevin, R. Sexual offenses and traumatic brain injury. *Brain Cogn.* 2006 Mar;**60(2)**:206-7.
136. Amberson, I.J., Dwyer, S.M. and Tenley, J. Bem Test Comparisons: Normals with Sex Offenders. Unpublished paper presented at NIMH meeting, Tampa, FL, 1986.
137. MacNamara, D.E.J. and Sagarin, E. *Sex, Crime, and the Law.* Free Press, New York, 1977.
138. Gebhard, P.H. et al., *Sex Offenders: An Analysis of Types.* Bantam, New York, 1967, 9.
139. Glass, B.J., Sex Offenders. In *Encylcopedia of Rape*, Smith, M.D. (ed), Greenwood Press, Westport, 2004, pages 222-4.
140. Chan, A.O., Lim, L.E., Ong, S.H. A review of outrage of modesty offenders remanded in a state mental hospital. *Med Sci Law.* 1997 Oct;37(4):349-52.
141. Gudjonsson, G.H., Sigurdsson, J.F. Differences and similarities between violent offenders and sex offenders. *Child Abuse and Neglect.* 2000; **24**: 363-372.
142. Fazel, S., Hope, T., O'Donnell, I., Jacoby, R. Psychiatric demographic and personality characteristics of elderly sex offenders. *Psychological Medicine.* 2002; **32**: 219-226.
143. Chantry, K., Craig, R.J. Psychological screening of sexually violent offenders with the MCMI. *Journal of Clinical Psychology.* 1994; **50**: 30-435.
144. Cronch, L.E., Viljoen, J.L., and Hansen, D.J., Forensic interviewing in child sexual abuse cases: Current techniques and future directions. *Aggression and Violent Behavior.* 2006;11(3):195-207.
145. Tichy, P., Phalloplethysmography findings in pedophilia and exhibitionism offenders, *Cas Lek Cesk.*, 135, 521-4, 1996.
146. Ahlmeyer, S., Heil, P., McKee, B., English, K. The impact of polygraphy on admissions of victims and offenses in adult sexual offenders. *Sexual Abuse: A Journal of Research and Treatment* 2000;12(2):123-38.
147. Emerick, R.L., Dutton, W.A. The effect of polygraphy on the self-report of adolescent sex offenders: Implications for risk assessment. *Ann Sex Res* 1993;6:83-103.
148. Anon. Court denies summary judgment to hospital in Employee Polygraph Protection Act suit. Lyle v. Mercy Hospital Anderson. *Hosp Law Newsl.* 1996 Mar;13(5):6-8.
149. Ben-Shakhar, G., Bar-Hillel, M., Kremnitzer, M. Trial by polygraph: reconsidering the use of the guilty knowledge technique in court. *Law Hum Behav.* 2002 Oct;26(5):527-41.
150. Perry, C. Admissibility and per se exclusion of hypnotically elicited recall in American courts of law. *Int J Clin Exp Hypn.* 1997 Jul;45(3):266-79.
151. Cross, T.P., Saxe, L. Polygraph testing and sexual abuse: the lure of the magic lasso. *Child Maltreat.* 2001 Aug;6(3):195-206.
152. Abel, G.G., Huffman, J., Warberg, B., Holland, C.L. Visual reaction time and plethysmography as measures of sexual interest in child molesters. *Sexual Abuse: A Journal of Research and Treatment.* 1998;10:81-96.
153. Rosenzweig, S. The photoscope as an objective device for evaluating sexual interest. *Psychosomatic Medicine.* 1942;4:150-8.
154. Wright, L.W., & Adams, H.E. Assessment and sexual preference using a choice reaction time task. *Journal of Psychopathology and Behavioral Assessment.* 1994;16:221–231.
155. Brown, M., Amoroso, D., Ware, E., Pruesse, M., & Pilkey, D. Factors affecting viewing time of pornography. *Journal of Social Psychology.* 1973;90:125–135.
156. Love, R.E., Sloan, L.R., and Schmidt, M.J. Viewing pornography and sex guilt: the priggish, the prudent, and the profligate. *Journal of Consulting and Clinical Psychology.* 1976;76:624–629.
157. Wright, L.W., and Adams, H.E. (1994). Assessment and sexual preference using a choice reaction time task. *Journal of Psychopathology and Behavioral Assessment.* 1994;16:221–231.
158. Zamansky, H.S. A technique for measuring homosexual tendencies. *Journal of Personality.* 1956;24:436–448.
159. Hess, E.H., and Polt, J.M. Pupil size as related to the interest value of visual stimuli. *Science.* 1960;**132**: 349–350.
160. Bernick, N., Kling, A., & Borowitz, G. Physiologic differentiation of sexual arousal and anxiety. *Psychosomatic Medicine.* 1971;**33**:341–352.
161. Hamel, R.F. Female subjective and pupillary reaction to nude male and female figures. *Journal of Psychology.* 1974;**87**:171–175.
162. Schnelle, J.F., Kennedy, M., Rutledge, A.W., & Golden, S.B. Pupillary response as indication of sexual preference in a juvenile correctional institution. *Journal of Clinical Psychology.* 1974;**30**:146–150.

163. Garrett, J.C., Harrison, D.W., & Kelly, P.L. Pupillometric assessment of arousal to sexual stimuli: Novelty effects or preference? *Archives of Sexual Behavior.* 1989;**18**:191–201.
164. Peavler, W.S., & McLaughlin, J.P. The question of stimulus content and pupil size. *Psychonomic Science.* 1967;**8**:505–506.
165. Berlin, F.S. "Chemical castration" for sex offenders. *N Engl J Med.* 1997 Apr 3;**336(14)**:1030.
166. Bund, J.M. Did you say chemical castration? *Univ Pittsbg Law Rev.* 1997 Fall;*59(1)*:157-92.
167. Kravitz, H.M., Haywood, T.W., Kelly, J., Wahlstrom, C., Liles, S., Cavanaugh, J.L. Jr. Medroxyprogesterone treatment for paraphiliacs. *Bull Am Acad Psychiatry Law.* 1995;**23(1)**:19-33.
168. Gottesman, H.G., Schubert, D.S. Low-dose oral medroxyprogesterone acetate in the management of the paraphilias. *J Clin Psychiatry.* 1993 May;**54(5)**:182-8.
169. Cooper, A.J., Sandhu, S., Losztyn, S., Cernovsky, Z. A double-blind placebo controlled trial of medroxyprogesterone acetate and cyproterone acetate with seven pedophiles. *Can J Psychiatry.* 1992 Dec;**37(10)**:687-93.
170. Reilly, D.R., Delva, N.J., Hudson, R.W. Protocols for the use of cyproterone, medroxyprogesterone, and leuprolide in the treatment of paraphilia. *Can J Psychiatry.* 2000 Aug;**45(6)**:559-63.
171. Cooper, A.J., Cernovovsky, Z. The effects of cyproterone acetate on sleeping and waking penile erections in pedophiles: possible implications for treatment. *Can J Psychiatry.* 1992 Feb;**37(1)**:33-9.
172. Berner, W., Brownstone, G., Sluga, W. The cyproteronacetate treatment of sexual offenders. *Neurosci Biobehav Rev.* 1983 Fall;**7(3)**:441-3.
173. Krueger, R.B., Kaplan, M.S. Leuprolide acetate for treatment of paraphilias: a report of twelve cases. *Arch Sex Behav.* 2001 Aug;**30(4)**:409-22.
174. Saleh, F. A hypersexual paraphilic patient treated with leuprolide acetate: a single case report. *J Sex Marital Ther.* 2005 Oct-Dec;**31(5)**:433-44.
175. Dickey, R. The management of a case of treatment-resistant paraphilia with a long-acting LHRH agonist. *Can J Psychiatry.* 1992 Oct;**37(8)**:567-9.
176. Ward, N.G. Successful lithium treatment of transvestism associated with manic-depression. *J Nerv Ment Dis.* 1975 Sep;161(3):204-6.
177. Cesnik, J.A., Coleman, E. Use of lithium carbonate in the treatment of autoerotic asphyxia. *Am J Psychother.* 1989 Apr;43(2):277-86.
178. Kafka, M.P. Successful antidepressant treatment of nonparaphilic sexual addictions and paraphilias in men. *J Clin Psychiatry.* 1991 Feb;52(2):60-5.
179. Buresová, A., Bártová, D., Hajnová, R., Náhunek, K., and ⊠vestka, J. Oxyprothepin decanoate equals hormonal inhibilory treatment in sexual deviants. *Activ. Ner.* 1986; 28: 37–38.
180. Žourková, A. Use of lithium and depot neuroleptics in the treatment of paraphilias. *Journal of Sex and Marital Therapy.* 2000 Oct-Dec;26(4):359-60.
181. Levitsky, A.M., Owens, N.J. Pharmacologic treatment of hypersexuality and paraphilias in nursing home residents. *J Am Geriatr Soc.* 1999 Feb;**47(2)**:231-4.
182. Balon, R. Pharmacological treatment of paraphilias with a focus on antidepressants. *Journal of Sex and Marital Therapy.* 1998;24 (4):241-54.
183. Balon, R. Lithium for paraphilias? Probably not. *Journal of Sex and Marital Therapy.* 2000 Oct-Dec;26(4):361-3.
184. Fedoroff, J.P. Buspirone hydrochloride in the treatment of an atypical paraphilia. *Arch Sex Behav.* 1992 Aug;**21(4)**:401-6.
185. Nelson, E., Brusman, L., Holcomb, J., Soutullo, C., Beckman, D., Welge, J.A., Kuppili, N., McElroy, S.L. Divalproex sodium in sex offenders with bipolar disorders and comorbid paraphilias: an open retrospective study. *J Affect Disord.* 2001 May;**64(2-3)**:249-55.
186. Briken, P., Hill, A., Berner, W. Pharmacotherapy of paraphilias with long-acting agonists of luteinizing hormone-releasing hormone: a systematic review. *J Clin Psychiatry.* 2003 Aug;**64(8)**:890-7.
187. Ryback, R.S. Naltrexone in the treatment of adolescent sexual offenders. *J Clin Psychiatry.* 2004 Jul;**65(7)**:982-6.
188. Krivacska, J.J., Paraphilic Prevention: Social and Legal Implications, in *The Handbook of Forensic Sexology—Biomedical and Criminological Perspectives*, Krivacska, JJ and Money J., Eds., Prometheus Books, New York, 1994, chapter 17, pages 397-421.
189. ICD-10 diagnostic codes for paraphilias. Available from: http://www.who.int/classifications/apps/icd/icd10online/?gf60.htm+f65

2 Pedophilia and Child Sexual Abuse

INTRODUCTION

Pedophilia (from Greek, *philia*, "love," *pedeiktos*, "child"), in a most general sense, is a paraphilia involving sexual attraction of an adult toward children that may lead to adult–child sex. Different workers have offered different definitions. Freund et al.[1] use a number of Latinized words to classify sexual attraction along a wide spectrum of ages. The following terms are most relevant:

Gynephilia	Sexual interest in adult women
Androphilia	Sexual interest in adult males
Nepiophilia	Sexual arousal by infants of the opposite sex; also known as infantophilia
Pedophilia	Long-term sexual interest in children with the typical body shape of an under 11 year old
Hebephilia	A preference for pubescent children between 11 and 14 years for females and 11-16 years for males. Hebephilia is also known as ephebophilia, hebophilia, phebophilia, or Lolita Syndrome (After Vladimir Nabokov's 1955 novel *Lolita*, in which the protagonist Humbert Humbert becomes sexually obsessed with a twelve year old girl named Dolores Haze). The words *hebephilia* and its variations come from Greek *ephebos*, "one arrived at puberty."
Pedohebephilia	Sexual interest in persons with the body shape of under 11 year olds as well as pubescent children between 11 and 14 years for females and 11-16 years for males.
Teleiophilia	A neologism coined by Ray Blanchard and associates[2] to denote an erotic preference for physically mature persons (from Greek *teleios*, "full grown"). This should not be considered a paraphilia.

There are differences of opinion regarding the age below which a person should be regarded as a child. As noted above, Freund and co-workers believe that a sexual interest in children *below 11 years* should be regarded as true pedophilia. A sexual interest in girls *below 14* and boys *below 16* should be termed pedohebephilia according to them.

As is evident from the above, the sheer number of terminologies used to describe sexual relations with children can be quite confusing. This could be disastrous if clear and unambiguous definitions are not included in relevant statutes preventing pedophilia and child sexual abuse (CSA). In fact, it has been recommended time and again that specific definitions be provided both in statutes governing intervention and in research about prevalence or treatment effectiveness.[3]

DSM-IV-TR, [4] however, recommends the age of 13 years. It assigns code 302.2 to pedophilia , and sets forth criteria for diagnosing it (Table 2.1).

Criteria sets for pedophilia underwent an interesting evolution from DSM-III-R to DSM-IV-TR. In DSM-III-R, if a pedophile had acted upon his sexual urges, he could be diagnosed as a pedophile. However, in an ambitious attempt to bring a uniform wording across all paraphilic disorders, the wording of this criterion was adjusted in DSM-IV to read, "the fantasies, sexual urges, or behaviors

TABLE 2.1
DSM-IV-TR Criteria for Pedophilia (302.2)

A. Over a period of at least 6 months, recurrent, intense sexually arousing fantasies, sexual urges, or behaviors involving sexual activity with a prepubescent child or children (generally age 13 years or younger);

B. The person has acted on these sexual urges, or the sexual urges or fantasies cause marked distress or interpersonal difficulty;

C. The person is at least age 16 years and at least 5 years older than the child or children in Criterion A.

Note: Do not include an individual in late adolescence involved in an ongoing sexual relationship with a 12- or 13- year-old.

Specify if:
- Sexually attracted to males
- Sexually attracted to females
- Sexually attracted to both

Specify if:
- Limited to incest

Specify if:
- Exclusive type (attracted only to children)
- Nonexclusive type

cause clinically significant distress or impairment in social, occupational, or other important areas of functioning." The mention of *having acted* on the urges was deleted. As mentioned in chapter 1, this engendered a huge controversy because most pedophiles do not feel distressed by their fantasies, nor are they significantly impaired in any area of their functioning. To address this concern, the original wordings as mentioned in DSM-III-R were reinstated in DSM-IV-TR.[5]

Pedophilia is the most commonly studied[6] and perhaps the most discussed paraphilia in clinical and forensic literature.[7] The sexual behaviors involved in pedophilia cover a range of activities and may or may not involve the use of force. Some pedophiles limit their behaviors to exposing themselves or masturbating in front of the child, or fondling or undressing the child, but without genital contact. Others, however, compel the child to participate in oral sex or full genital intercourse.

Proponents of Pedophilia

Interestingly, there are advocates and proponents of pedophilia also. They assert that it is nothing but another example of cross-generational sex or intergenerational sex, which is so easily accepted by our society. According to them, sex between a 45-year old and a 10-year old (difference in ages 35, or about a generation) should be as acceptable as that between, say, a 60-year old and a 25-year old (again a difference of 35 years). This is, however, specious reasoning as in the former—a case of pedophilia—the child may be left with permanent psychological damage. This does not happen in the latter case, as the person of the younger generation is also an adult and psychologically mature.

Proponents of pedophilia also argue that the activity is natural—after all the ancient Greeks engaged in it. They assert that our repugnance for it is merely a cultural artifact, a product of repressive patriarchal Christianity, and that our conception of age of consent is purely arbitrary. A boy of, say, 10 is human, has civil rights, and should be allowed to choose. It is also asserted that pedophilia is harmful only because the children are taught that it is shameful; they should instead be taught that it is a natural celebration of life and love. They assert that children who have tried pedophilia have regarded the experience as warm and loving. Scientific studies, however, confirm that victims of pedophilia are left with severe and sometimes permanent psychological damage.

The North American Man/Boy Love Association (NAMBLA) is a New York City and San Francisco-based unincorporated organization that advocates the legalization of sexual relations between adult males and underaged boys.

HISTORICAL PERSPECTIVES

Pedophilia is the most hated of all sex perversions. Contrary to the claims of some authors who see the issue of childhood sexual abuse as an invention of late 20th century feminism, sexual abuse of children is not a recent phenomenon. It is described and proscribed in the book of Leviticus in the Old Testament. Charcot, Janet, and Freud all reported it occurring to their patients; Freud, however, rejected these reports later as neurotic fantasy.[8]

The first scientist to use the term *pedophilia* was the Austro-German psychiatrist Richard Freiherr von Krafft-Ebing (1840–1902). In his book *Psychopathia Sexualis* [9] (Sexual Psychopathy), published in 1886, pedophilia was defined as a psychosexual perversion and was a curable condition. He thought that pedophilia could be caused by senility or as a result of other mental deficiencies. However, his British contemporary Henry Havelock Ellis (1859–1939) believed that pedophilia was nothing but an extreme or exaggerated version of normal masculine sexuality.

It is increasingly becoming clear that child sexual abuse (CSA) is a much more prevalent phenomenon than has been understood till now. Even celebrities have been sexually abused by their parents and other relatives. When the American actress Clara Bow (1905–1965) was diagnosed with schizophrenia in 1949, doctors found out that she had been raped by her father at a young age.

Significantly, famous people have been known to be pedophiles. Lewis Carroll (1832–1898), the author of *Alice's Adventures in Wonderland* and its sequel *Through the Looking-Glass* was a known pedophile. More recently Daniel Carleton Gajdusek (1923–), an American physician and 1976 Nobel Prize winner in physiology or medicine (for his work on kuru, the first prion disease ever described), has been criminally charged with child molestation.[10]

PEDOPHILIA, CHILD MOLESTATION AND CHILD SEXUAL ABUSE

Terms used to describe pedophilia and child sexual abuse can often be confusing and can even be misleading. The terms *pedophilia* and *child molestation* are used in different ways, even by professionals. There are important differences between a pedophile and a child molester. In the case of a pedophile, the sexual interest of the offender is *fixated* on underage people. The offender has no or minimal sexual interest in adults of opposite sex.[11] A child molester on the other hand prefers adult partners, but some inviting circumstances (e.g., finding a girl child alone) may lead him to sexuo-erotic activity with the child.

Another important difference is that pedophilia refers merely to *psychological propensities.* There is indeed a sexuo-erotic preference for prepubescent children; this preference, however, may or may not be acted upon. In contrast, child molestation and child sexual abuse are used to describe *actual* sexual contact between an adult and someone who has not reached the legal age of consent. In this context, the latter individual is referred to as a child, even though he or she may be a teenager. Putting it another way, not all child sexual abuse is perpetrated by pedophiles, and not all pedophiles actually commit child sexual abuse.

Finally, pedophilia is a diagnostic label specifically mentioned in DSM-IV-TR. Child sexual abuse, since it does not represent a mental disorder, is not cited in DSM-IV-TR. The accompanying table summarizes important differences between pedophilia and child sexual abuse (Table 2.2).

TABLE 2.2
Important Differences between Pedophilia and Child Sexual Abuse

Pedophilia	Child Sexual Abuse and Child Molestation
Pedophilia represents a mental disorder, mentioned in DSM-IV-TR	Child sexual abuse and child molestation do not represent mental disorders. These terms are not cited in DSM-IV-TR
Interest of the pedophile is fixated on prepubescent children; he shows no or minimal sexuo-erotic interest in adults	Sexuo-erotic interest primarily in adults, but molests children, if given an opportunity
Refers to psychological propensities only; his psychological propensity may or may not have been acted upon; not all pedophiles actually molest children	Refers to actual sexual contact
Pedophile has an ongoing pattern of sexual attraction to children	Child sexual abuse is situational; may be a one-time incident; does not manifest an ongoing pattern of sexual attraction to children

These differences are, however, not accepted universally. Levin and Stava, for example, regard child molestation as a synonym for pedophilia.[12] Their position is perhaps strengthened by the fact that both pedophiles and child molesters share the same psychological profile.[13]

According to Rada, while a pedophile is an individual whose "sexual interests lie exclusively or almost exclusively in sexual behavior or fantasies involving children," a child molester, on the other hand, is an individual who has been *charged and convicted* of "a crime because of sexual behavior with a minor."[14] He adds that a pedophile is not necessarily a child molester because a pedophile "may never act out on his tendencies; or if he does, he may not come into conflict with the law."

A useful definition of child sexual abuse has been provided by Doek.[15] According to him, child sexual abuse can be defined as including all kinds of sexual activities committed by an adult with or in the presence of minors; these are activities which are detrimental to normal development of the sexuality of the child or which curtail or inhibit his or her sexual self-determination. According to Mulhern, the most prevalent and the most devastating form of child sexual abuse is incestuous rape.[16]

ETIOLOGY

No single factor seems to be at work in the development of pedophilia. Most likely it develops as a result of an interplay of multiple factors. Among the factors implicated are biological (abnormal testosterone levels), psychological, and social.

Biological Theories

The Role of Hormones

There is some evidence that hormonal and serotonergic alterations may play a role in the pathophysiology of pedophilia. Maes and associates[17] intensively studied 8 pedophiles and compared them to 11 normal controls in two neurobiological studies. A series of differences between controls and pedophiles were reported. Pedophiles showed significantly *lower* baseline plasma cortisol and prolactin concentrations and *higher* body temperatures than normal volunteers. Pedophiles also showed a more exaggerated response to pharmacological provocation of serum cortisol and epinephrine with meta-chlorophenylpiperazine (mCPP), a pharmacological probe with affinity for CNS serotonergic receptors. The mCPP-induced cortisol responses were significantly greater in pedophiles than in normal volunteers. In normal volunteers, mCPP-induced a hyperthermic response, whereas in pedophiles no such response was observed. mCPP induced different behavioral responses in pedophiles than in normal men. In pedophiles—but not in normal men—mCPP increased the sensations "feeling dizzy," "restless," and "strange" and decreased "feeling hungry." The results suggest several serotonergic disturbances in pedophiles. The authors hypothesized that pedophiles have a decreased presynaptic serotonergic activity, accompanied by a compensatory up-regulation of postsynaptic 5-HT(2A/2C) receptors.

Recent studies suggest that the pituitaries of pedophilic men may be more sensitive to the hypothalamic hormone LHRH (luteinising-hormone releasing hormone ; also known as gonadotropin releasing hormone, or GnRH), indicating a hypothalamic–pituitary-gonadal dysfunction in pedophiles. Gaffney and Berlin[18] injected 100 micrograms of synthetic luteinising hormone-releasing hormone (LHRH) in three groups: men with pedophilia, men with non-pedophilic paraphilia, and normal male controls. The pituitaries in all responded by releasing the luteinising hormone (LH) as they normally should. However, there was a significant difference between the pedophilic group and the other two groups. The pedophiles responded with a marked elevation of LH, when compared with the non-pedophilic paraphiliacs and controls (it is noteworthy that LH stimulates testosterone production and release from the Leydig cells of the testes).

Fronto-temporal Disorders

Mendez and associates[19] reported two patients with late-life homosexual pedophilia. One met criteria for frontotemporal dementia; the other had bilateral hippocampal sclerosis. Both were professional men with recent increases in sexual behavior. In both, 18-fluorodeoxyglucose positron emission tomography revealed prominent right temporal lobe hypometabolism. These cases suggest that bilateral anterior temporal disease, more so on the right side, can increase sexual interest. It is further suggested that a predisposition to pedophilia may be unmasked by hypersexuality from these brain disorders. Joyal and associates[20] reviewed the existing data derived from neuropsychiatry, neuroimaging, and neuropsychology and found that basal fronto-temporal anomalies were common in pedophiles, suggesting that this could be an etiological factor. They, however, concluded that basal fronto-temporal anomalies were also common in other sexual offenders and were also found in association with delinquency and criminality in general.

Regestein and Reich[21] have reported four cases of pedophilia that emerged after brain insults had produced cognitive impairment. All of these individuals had previously led normal lives without psychiatric disability and had shown no sexual deviation until after the events that resulted in the cognitive disability. In one case, pedophilia, personality change, and declining job performance developed after the removal of a meningioma through a right frontal craniotomy. Psychological testing tended to confirm the existence of a right frontal lobe deficit. Two cases illustrated development of pedophilia, sexual behavior changes, and alterations in personality after multiple cardiac resuscitations and presumed episodes of cerebral hypoxia. The fourth individual who had demonstrable cognitive deficits developed pedophilic behavior only when he was treated or self-medicated with a central nervous system depressant.

Burns and Swerdlow report a case of acquired pedophilia. This patient had a right orbitofrontal tumor. He became unable to inhibit sexual urges despite preserved moral knowledge. Still more significantly, the behavior disappeared following tumor resection.[22]

Flor-Henry and colleagues[23] from Canada studied 96 pedophiles, whose sexual orientation was confirmed by phallometric response to sexual stimuli. Quantitative EEG was performed and compared to age- and sex-matched healthy controls. The EEG analysis showed a pattern of increased frontal delta, theta, and alpha power (especially during verbal processing) and a pattern of reduced interhemispheric and increased intrahemispheric–interhemispheric coherence. These findings suggest that pedophilia may relate to altered dominant hemispheric functions with disruption of frontal interhemispheric relationships.

Neurodevelopmental Perturbations

Recent data from sexual history as well as neuropsychological, plethysmography, and neuroimaging investigations seem to suggest that pedophilia is linked to early neurodevelopmental disturbances.[24,25]

Miscellaneous Brain Anomalies

A definitive and concrete biological etiological factor for pedophilia remains elusive as new research keeps shedding more light in hitherto unexplored areas. Among the various ongoing studies, an fMRI case study of one homosexual pedophile has suggested abnormalities in the fusiform gyrus and the right orbitofrontal cortex during visual sexual stimulation.[26] Recent morphometric studies using structural MRI have found decreased grey matter volume in the ventral striatum, nucleus accumbens, the orbitofrontal cortex, and the cerebellum in pedophiles. These findings may underline an association between frontostriatal abnormalities and pedophilia. They support the hypothesis that there may be a shared etiopathological mechanism with obsessive compulsive (OC) spectrum disorders, especially as OC disorders also display similar structural deficiencies in the brain.[27] In a recent study, Schiffer and colleagues[28] demonstrated that pedophiles may show significant activation of several key regions of brain (comprising the large parts of "reward areas") during their pedophilic activities. They chose 11 known homosexual pedophiles, and 12 healthy homosexual volunteers, and while showing them sexually neutral and sexually arousing pictures, recorded their fMRI, to know which areas of their brains were stimulated. They showed pictures of (i) dressed boys, (ii) dressed men, (iii) nude boys, and (iv) nude men. While the pictures of dressed boys and men were supposed to be neutral stimuli, pictures of nude boys were supposed to be stimulating to pedophiles (and not to the other group), and pictures of nude men were supposed to be stimulating to the healthy homosexual group (again not to the other group).

The results of this study are interesting. Quite understandably, both pedophiles and homosexuals rated their respective sexual stimuli (i.e., nude boys for pedophiles and nude men for homosexuals) as equivalently sexually arousing. Also both groups reported the stimuli of their respective preference to be more arousing than the opposite stimuli. Another expected finding was that in contrast to sexually neutral stimuli, the presentation of respective sexually arousing pictures led—in both groups—to activation of brain areas known to be involved in processing visual stimuli with emotional content. These areas included occipitotemporal and prefrontal cortices. However, compared with pedophiles, homosexual control subjects generally showed less activation during presentation of the respective stimuli.

The most significant finding was that during the presentation of the respective sexual stimuli, the thalamus, globus pallidus, caudate nucleus, substantia nigra, and striatum, corresponding to key areas mediating sexual arousal and behavior, showed significant activation in pedophiles, but not in control subjects. Most of these areas constitute the so-called "reward areas" of the brain. This may partly explain the behavior of pedophiles. However, the authors fail to address the issue, why, in the first place, the reward areas of the brain are stimulated in pedophiles during their pedophilic activities. If this question could be answered, maybe by future research, it may open up promising areas in prevention and treatment.

Unfulfilled Sexual Needs

Many studies have found that fathers engaging in sexual activity with their daughters often have unfulfilled sexual needs. They often find their children sexually attractive and use a variety of strategies both to deal with their own inhibitions against sexual involvement with the child and to overcome the child's own potential resistance. Furthermore, these parents often find themselves in situations which provide a special opportunity for undetected abuse, and they also strive to arrange such circumstances.[29] This view of sexual abuse as primarily fulfilling sexual needs could well lead to a significant change in the management of cases in which sexual abuse has already occurred or is seen as likely to occur.

Conditioning

McGuire and colleagues[30] propose that pedophilia can be explained by conditioning (please see Chapter 1 for details of classical and operant conditioning). To illustrate their theory, they cite the case of one of their actual patients, a 40-year old male who had become a pedophile. The patient had normal sexual interests until age 20 but had been impotent when casual intercourse was attempted. While on military service in Asia during the Second World War, he accompanied other servicemen to the brothels where, through fear of venereal disease, he refused intercourse but allowed the prostitutes to masturbate him. This was his first orgasmic sexual experience with a partner, and the memory of it served as later self-masturbatory fantasies. When he was moved from the town into the jungle, prostitutes were no longer available. He had scruples about having relations with the native married women and finally resorted to native children of both sexes who would masturbate him, and this remained his only sexual outlet till he was discharged home three years later.

In Britain his self-masturbatory fantasies continued to be of masturbation by children, and eventually he succumbed and found young boys to masturbate him. He married 5 years after this, but found that he had no interest in sexual intercourse although he was now potent in the heterosexual situation. Self-masturbation continued to his previous fantasies, and intercourse was only possible to these fantasies or to fantasies that his wife was a prostitute. So strong did his pedophile tendencies become that he even induced his son (between the ages of 4 and 6) to masturbate him. Thus by simple operant conditioning, the patient became a pedophile. Initially his behavior was substitutive, but it gained dominance by frequent positive sexual reinforcement.

Miscellaneous Causes

Lalor[31] studied child sexual abuse in sub-Saharan Africa (SSA) and found that the most frequent explanations for the sexual abuse of children in SSA were rapid social change, AIDS/HIV avoidance strategies, and the patriarchal nature of society. It is widely perceived that the abuse may be increasing as a result of AIDS sufferers' attempts to "cleanse" themselves.[32,33] There is a widespread belief that one can get rid of sexually transmitted diseases by engaging in sexual intercourse with a virgin. To ensure that the girl is a virgin, as young girl as is possible is chosen for sexual intercourse. Other causes were breakdown of traditional childcare systems, foreign influences, poverty, and the lowly position of girls in society.[32]

Some other proposed factors are (i) offenders' faulty interactions with their parents during early years of life; (ii) arrested emotional development, that is, the pedophile is attracted to children because he or she has never matured psychologically; and (iii) a distorted need to dominate a sexual partner. Since children are smaller and usually weaker than adults, they may be regarded as non-threatening potential partners. This drive for domination is sometimes thought to explain why most pedophiles are males.

PREVALENCE AND INCIDENCE

Prevalence and incidence figures are highly variable, with different groups reporting different figures. For the United States, the estimates are reported to be as high as 500,000 cases annually.[34] According to the estimates of the German authorities, the incidence of child sexual abuse in Germany is as high as 550 cases daily (200,000 annually), though only every 20th case is recorded.[28]

Feierman[35] maintains that "the prevalence, or population frequency, of pedophilia is not known." He says this presumably because the only pedophiles we know are those who either report to health care facilities for treatment or are caught by law enforcement officials. There must be a large number of cases which would remain hidden from any epidemiological study aimed at finding prevalence. This is true not only of pedophilia but of all other paraphilias.

Mrazek,[36] for similar reasons, argues that the best incidence data on pedophilia may be provided by epidemiological studies of "normal" populations. From the study of sexual offenders, some "guesstimates" may be made, however. In a nationwide study of over 28,000 American men suspected of sexual offenses, Abel and Harlow[37] found child molestation to be most common at 33% (incidentally, the percentages of other paraphilias were: voyeurism, 17%; exhibitionism, 14%; public masturbation, 11%; all other possible deviant interests, less than 10%).

Several workers have reported that of every 10 children, 1 or 2 have been sexually approached and abused by an adult.[38,39] Lalor[31] studied all English-language literature (papers cited in Social Sciences Citation Index, reports from international and local NGOs and UN agencies) on child sexual abuse in sub-Saharan Africa (SSA), and concluded that there was nothing to support the widely held view that child sexual abuse is very rare in SSA. He found that approximately 0.6–1.8% of all children in high HIV incidence countries in Southern Africa experienced penetrative sexual abuse by an AIDS/HIV infected perpetrator before 18 years of age. Approximately 5% of the sample reported penetrative sexual abuse during their childhood. These prevalence levels were comparable with studies reported from other regions.

Fritz and Wagner[40] administered a questionnaire to 952 college students enquiring whether they had been molested as children and found that while the male molestation rate was 4.8% with a 3:2 ratio of heterosexual homosexual molestation, the female molestation rate was higher at 7.7%.

In Zimbabwe, child sexual abuse cases represent 40 to 60% of the rape cases brought to the attention of hospitals, police, and court, while many more are believed to remain unreported.[33]

According to Gustafson and colleagues,[41] childhood sexual abuse is remarkably common and affects up to one third of women and one eighth of men.

Apparently, even many so-called normal men harbor pedophilic fantasies. Crépault and Couture[42] interviewed 94 men about their erotic fantasies occurring during heterosexual activity. The majority of these men were married, and their average duration of cohabitation with a woman was 6.5 years. As many as 61.7% reported having had erotic fantasies in which they sexually initiated a young girl, and 3.2% reported fantasies in which they sexually initiated a young boy.

Pedophilia is seen among females, too. Fedoroff and colleagues studied Fedoroff's clinical records over 15 years and identified individuals referred to them for suspected paraphilic disorders. The clinics were located in different countries (Canada, the United States, and Great Britain), and all were affiliated with universities. A total of 132 paraphilics were identified, of which 14 (11%) were women.[43] Within the total female sample, the most common diagnoses were pedophilia (36%), sexual sadism (29%), and exhibitionism (29%). The authors, however, emphasize that this is not a study of the frequency or prevalence of paraphilias in the female population, nor can the findings be used to draw such inferences.

SATANISM AND RITUAL SEX ABUSE

Satanic ritual abuse (SRA) refers to the sexual abuse of children in a ritualistic context.[44] The term *sadistic ritual abuse* is sometimes used or suggested as a more descriptive synonym that makes no assumption of whether Satanism is involved.* The term gained currency after the publication of *Michelle Remembers* in 1980, co-written by Michelle Smith and her Canadian psychiatrist Dr.

* *Satanism* is not a desirable term as it may wrongly be construed to refer to "the worship of Satan or the powers of evil." In the context of sexual abuse of children, the term refers to sexual abuse in association with several distinct spiritual practices that may be bizarre.

Lawrence Pazder (eventually her husband).[45] A best-seller, *Michelle Remembers* was the first book written on the subject of Satanic ritual abuse and is an important part of the controversies beginning in the 1980s regarding Satanic ritual abuse and repressed memory.

The book chronicles Pazder's therapy in the late 1970s with Michelle, who allegedly recovered memories of Satanic ritual abuse that occurred when she was 5 in 1954 at the hands of her mother and others in Victoria, British Columbia. Michelle recovered memories of several bizarre incidents such as being placed with a corpse in a car that was then deliberately crashed, being kept locked in a cage with snakes without sleep or sustenance for weeks, being forced to ingest poison and other noxious substances, taking part in bizarre ceremonies in a round room, ritual sexual sacrifice of stillborn babies, and her being forced to undergo surgery to have tails and a horn attached to her body.[46]

OFFENDER CHARACTERISTICS

There is no typical pedophile. Pedophiles may be young or old, male or female, although the great majority are males. Quite possibly hebephilic preferences too are exclusively found in males.[13,47] Their gender identity profiles are not different from those of non-sexual offenders or of normal people.[48] Murray[13] did thorough research on the psychological profile of pedophiles and child molesters. He found that mostly the offenders were family members or acquaintances of the victims, especially if the victim was a girl. They could be heterosexual, homosexual, or bisexual. Some preferred adult sex partners but chose children because they were available and vulnerable (these are the ones classified as child molesters). The sexual abuse perpetrated was sometimes just a one-time incident and consisted only of fondling. Penetration was unlikely with young children.

The ages of the perpetrators ranged from teens to midlife. In case of female victims the perpetrator usually was a relative, friend, or neighbor, and the setting for the incident was the home. In case of boys as victims, there were more instances of perpetrators being strangers, and there was more likelihood of incidents taking place outside of the home. Perpetrators of sexual abuse of children often claimed that they themselves were victims of childhood sexual abuse.

Vernon and Rich[49] have presented an interesting study of 22 deaf pedophiles (including 2 females) and found that primitive personality disorder was much more common in deaf pedophiles than in hearing pedophiles. Other significant differences included a high rate of brain damage, illiteracy, poor communication skills, and other psychiatric illnesses. This presented challenging legal problems, especially competence to stand trial.

The fact that child sexual abuse is perpetrated most frequently by family members, relatives, neighbors, or others known to the victims is brought out by many studies.[13,31]

Some pedophiles are professionals who are entrusted with educating or maintaining the health and well-being of young persons, while others are entrusted with children to whom they are related by blood or marriage.[50]

Regardless of their claimed preferences, the attraction of pedophiles is to the child's immature body type or lack of secondary sex characteristics rather than the child's gender.[51] Contrary to the popular belief, the adult male who sexually molests young boys is not likely to be homosexual.[52,53]

Saunders and colleagues[54] conducted a study in which they divided a group of male adolescent sexual offenders into three groups: Courtship Disorders (Exhibitionism, Toucherism and Obscene Phone Calls), Sexual Assaults, and Pedophilic Offenses. Group III offenders (Pedophilic Offenses) were Canadian born, had witnessed physical violence between their parents, were described as having been infants who did not enjoy being cuddled, and had siblings who were truant.

VICTIM CHARACTERISTICS

Although different studies cite different data, Kristensen and Lau's study from Denmark is quite representative.[55] They studied data related to 385 women with histories of childhood sexual abuse

(CSA) who were referred to them for psychotherapy over a period of 2.5 years. Their mean age at the time of referral was 33 years. Three hundred and forty (or more than 88%) of these victims had experienced intrafamilial CSA. The average age at first abuse was 6.8 years, and it lasted for a mean of 6 years. The women had been abused by more than one perpetrator (a mean of 1.5 perpetrators). A quarter of the women had been subjected to violence in connection with the sexual abuse. The likelihood of violence was significantly higher, if there was more than one perpetrator and/or if penetration had been part of the sexual abuse. Violence was less common if the perpetrator was a brother. The women suffered from a broad spectrum of psychiatric symptoms and illnesses. Compared to a random sample of the general female population, these women were less advantaged with regard to education, financial circumstances, and cohabitation.

SEQUELAE

A history of childhood sexual abuse is associated with numerous psychological sequelae, including depression, anxiety, substance abuse, somatization, and eating disorders.[41] Eating disorders (anorexia nervosa, bulimia nervosa, or binge-eating disorder) have been reported among the most common psychiatric disorders among women who were sexually abused as children. In an extensive study, Rayworth and colleagues[56] found that compared with women who reported no abuse, women who reported childhood physical abuse had twice the odds of suffering from subclinical eating disorder symptoms. Women who reported both physical and sexual abuse during childhood had three times the odds of developing eating disorder symptoms. Childhood sexual abuse also appears to be a risk factor for the development of obesity in later life.[57] Gustafson and colleagues[58] found that a significant number of bariatric surgery candidates reported a history of sexual abuse. However, this relationship has been challenged by some, and currently a direct relationship between sexual abuse and eating disorders remains controversial.[59]

Van Dorn and associates[60] investigated the relationship between sexual abuse of children with severe mental illness (N = 609) and their likelihood of developing risky sexual behaviors (such as trading sex for drugs or money or having unprotected sex) in adult life, and concluded that the two were closely associated. Interestingly, development of similar risky behaviors (e.g., higher lifetime number of sexual partners) have been reported in adolescent and young adult women who also had coercive sexual experiences.[61] Female survivors of child sexual abuse also experience a higher risk of sexual assaults as adults. Urquiza and Goodlin-Jones[62] interviewed 243 women from a multiethnic (white, African-American, Latina, and Asian-American) background and found that nearly two thirds of the women who reported rape as adults had histories of child sexual abuse. On the contrary, only about one third of the non-victimized women had child sexual abuse histories. They even discovered that different ethnic groups suffered differently. Significant differences (i.e., higher rates of rape associated with a prior history of child sexual abuse) were found for white women, African-American women, and Latinas, but not for Asian-American women. The authors conclude that sexual victimization must be viewed in a broader cultural context.

Felitti[63] examined 131 patients of childhood sexual abuse and found that chronic depression , morbid obesity, marital instability, high utilization of medical care, and psychosomatic symptoms, particularly chronic gastrointestinal distress and recurrent headaches, were more common than in the control group. He goes on to suggest that if a physician comes across refractory cases with these symptoms, questions about childhood sexual abuse must be asked.

Self-injurious and self-destructive behavior, high levels of dissociation, and self-criticism are also common sequelae of sexual abuse.[64]

DIAGNOSIS AND INVESTIGATION

Perhaps the most important aspect in investigation of child sexual abuse is interview with the child. However, if the child is very young, it may be difficult for him or her to comprehend the questions properly and even point out the body areas that were improperly touched, or the acts performed. This need to establish clearer communication between the interviewer and the child suspected of being sexually abused led, in 1976, to the design of dolls with genitalia, now known as anatomical dolls (ADs),[65] also sometimes known as anatomically precise dolls or anatomically correct dolls.

Anatomical dolls are usually made of soft cloth with painted facial features, yarn hair, and, most importantly, external genitalia. Female child and adult dolls include vaginal, oral, and anal orifices; male dolls include penis and testicles. Pubic hair is included on all of the adult dolls. Some dolls have penetrable openings for the mouth with an extending tongue. Some dolls are made with separated fingers and toes and different skin tones and may represent three generations (child, adult, and grandparent). The clothing is removable and includes day and night clothing. The adult dolls are approximately 20 inches, and the child dolls are 16 inches, in height generally. The dolls are designed as simple replicas of the human body, and there is no empirical evidence to suggest that one design of doll is better than another. However, studies suggest that the child's story will be more spontaneous, and identification of the offender more accurate when the dolls closely match the real characteristics of the child and offender.[66]

However, the use of ADs is not without controversies: (i) because of their anatomical explicitness, the ADs are suggestible and overly stimulating to young children, and therefore may lead to false positives; (ii) based on the child's behavior with the dolls and the potential for misinterpretations, conclusions are not possible regarding sexual abuse history; and finally, (iii) evidence tendered by ADs does not meet the rigorous *Kelly-Frye* and *Daubert* standards now required for the admissibility of all scientific evidence. In *re Amber B.*, 191 Cal. App. 3d 682, 236 Cal. Rptr. 623 (1987), a psychologist testified that the child was molested by her father. Testimony was based on the child's statements and her play with an anatomical doll. It was held that such testimony is subject to the *Kelly-Frye* standard.

Medical Examination

An urgent medical examination as soon as sexual abuse is reported is a must in all cases. In recent years, the role of a trained *sexual assault nurse examiner* (SANE) in collection of evidence, especially in pediatric cases, has increasingly been appreciated.[67] This is especially important as a frightened child may feel much more comfortable in the presence of a female.

Palusci and associates[68] stress the need for an immediate medical examination and report that children seen within 72 hours of alleged sexual contact have higher rates of disclosure and positive physical examination findings than children seen non-urgently. In their study involving 955 children, no child younger than 10 years of age had positive forensic tests if examined 24 hours or longer after contact (most often due to bathing).

Colposcopic examination is considered the gold standard in child sexual abuse evaluations.[69] The presence of posterior fourchette lacerations in a pediatric patient is strongly suggestive of sexual abuse. Application of toluidine blue (1% aqueous solution) increases detection rate. In one study, it increased the detection rate of posterior fourchette lacerations from 16.5% to 33% in pediatric sexually abused patients and from 4% to 28% in adolescent sexually abused patients.[70]

MANAGEMENT

Pedophilia is a chronic psychiatric disorder, but is treatable in terms of developing strategies for preventing behavioral expression. Treatment goals focus on stopping the behavior and achieving long-term behavioral control in the community. Common treatment methods are cognitive–behavioral, group therapy, and, when appropriate, medications such as androgen-lowering agents that can act as sexual appetite suppressants.[38,71]

Antiandrogens such as cyproterone acetate (CPA) and medroxyprogesterone acetate (MPA) seem to have very little value in the treatment of pedophiles. Cooper et al.[72] completed a double-blind, placebo-controlled two-dose comparison of cyproterone acetate and medroxyprogesterone acetate in seven pedophiles (they screened 28 pedophiles, but only 10 agreed to take part in the study and just 7 completed the study) at a psychiatric hospital in St. Thomas, Ontario. The study lasted 28 weeks.

The drugs inhibited sexual thoughts, fantasies, and sexual frustration, reduced the frequency of early morning erections on awakening, the frequency and pleasure of masturbation, reduced the percentage of erection to a small extent, and led to a decline in serum levels of testosterone, follicle stimulating hormone, and luteinising hormone. However, by the end of the third placebo phase, almost all serum levels returned to or exceeded predrug levels. Both drugs performed similarly. Their effects appeared to depend on dose (e.g., 200 mg had a greater effect than 100 mg). The authors concluded that CPA or MPA use may provide modest short-term improvement in the behavior of pedophiles, but this improvement was largely limited to psychologic responses. The study also showed that very few pedophiles (only 25%) voluntarily agreed to take an antiandrogen, suggesting the need for more research identifying more acceptable treatments.

Leuprolide acetate (LA), a gonadotropin-releasing hormone agonist (GnRH agonist), has been found useful in the management of pedophilia.[73,74] It produces a paradoxical effect on the pituitary, with initial stimulation of the release of luteinising hormone (LH) and follicle-stimulating hormone (FSH), followed by inhibition after repeated administration. These effects are accompanied by a reduction in androgenic hormone release (a decrease in testicular steroidogenesis) that is probably secondary to a primary reduction in LH levels. Rösler and Witztum assert that long-acting GnRH analogues, together with psychotherapy, are highly effective in the management of pedophilia.[75] Selective serotonin reuptake inhibitors (SSRIs) such as sertraline have also been found useful.[76]

LEGAL ASPECTS

HIV/STDs and Child Sexual Abuse

The issue of HIV transmitted through rape and other rape/HIV- related issues have been dealt with more fully in the chapter on rape. HIV-positive offenders have sexually assaulted children, too, and in all cases, courts have taken a serious view of this, sentencing the HIV positive offenders under additional charges. In one case, Angel Cabrera, an HIV-positive man, was successfully prosecuted for three counts of statutory rape, and additionally for reckless conduct, for engaging in unprotected sex with a 14-year old girl.[77] Under New Hampshire law, reckless conduct involves the use of a deadly weapon, defined as an object or substance capable of producing death or serious bodily injury. The HIV status of the offender was taken as a deadly weapon. The crime is a felony, and the judge imposed the maximum sentence allowed by the plea agreement.

In another case, the North Carolina Court of Appeals upheld the conviction of Andrew Lee Monk, convicted of raping a 12-year old girl.[78] Because of Monk's HIV infection, indictments were made against him for attempted murder and assault with a deadly weapon. The defense claimed—unsuccessfully—that in admitting testimony about Monk's AIDS diagnosis, the court prejudiced the jury against Monk. Monk was sentenced to 35 to 42.75 years in prison on the rape charge, and 22 to 32 months for an indecent liberties charge. The girl involved in the case received AZT prophylaxis following the rape and did not test positive.

In Zimbabwe, half of the sexual abuse in children is detected through STDs (including HIV infections).[33]

Recovered Memory

Memories of childhood sexual abuse, recovered through hypnotism, often aided by the use of psychotropic and hypnotic drugs, has raised a lot of controversy lately, especially since many parents have alleged that their children were coaxed to suggest, under the influence of drugs, that they were sexually abused by their parents. This raises important legal issues, and many parents have alleged that they have been falsely convicted. It has been suggested that recovered memory amounts to gathering evidence by improper and unscientific means and should not be admitted in a court of law.[79] The case of Gary Ramona brought this issue to the forefront (See Sidebar 2.1).

Sidebar 2.1: Ramona Case, Recovered Memories and the Rights of the Accused

Gary Ramona, a 50-year old wine company executive, married for more than 20 years to his wife Stephanie, had three daughters. Holly, the eldest of these, developed major depression and bulimia nervosa, during the summer after her first year of college. In 1989, she began therapy with a California marriage, family, and child counselor (MFCC), who allegedly told her that 70–80% of bulimic women had been sexually abused as children.

Holly initially reported no memory of sexual abuse and apparently had no such recollections during her first several months of therapy. But after about 4 months in treatment, she began to develop brief mental images of her father sexually abusing her, perhaps because of repeated suggestions made to her. She came to believe that these images were "flashbacks" of childhood sexual abuse occurring between the ages of 5 and 8.

After 6 months of therapy, Holly was referred to a local psychiatric unit, where a physician began interview sessions with her after sedating her with sodium amytal. On March 15, 1990, Ramona was invited to a family meeting at the hospital, where Holly, apparently under the influence of the hypnotic, confronted him with the allegation, "you raped me." When he responded that this was untrue, both the therapist and his wife forced him to "confess" to the allegations, telling him that the "memories" had been confirmed by amytal, the so-called "truth serum," and that it was almost impossible for anyone to lie under its influence.

Ramona obviously was devastated by these totally unexpected—and according to him untrue—accusations. Despite his protestations that he was innocent, his wife promptly divorced him, and he was not allowed to see either Holly or his other two daughters again. Within a year, he lost his lucrative job as the vice president of marketing and sales for Robert Mondavi wineries, an event which was directly attributable to allegations of sexual abuse. Within that same year, Holly filed suit against him for allegedly having raped her. In order to clear his name, Ramona, in turn, decided to sue the psychiatrist, therapist and the hospital, alleging that his daughter had been tutored, under the influence of hypnosis and drugs, to falsely incriminate him.

The case was unusual in that Ramona included a third party in the suit—his daughter, legally an adult, and the therapist were the two parties involved in therapy. His right to sue the therapist as a third party was challenged by the defense attorneys, but the trial court judge ruled that Ramona, by being brought into the therapy session, had been made a *de facto* client of the therapist, and that she consequently owed him a duty of care. The case went to trial in March 1994.

During the 7-week trial, a series of experts testifying for Ramona argued that there was no adequate scientific evidence that childhood sexual abuse occurred in 70–80% of bulimic patients; that amytal was not a "truth serum"; that memories of years of rape by one's father could not be repressed and recovered years later; and that Holly's "memories" were almost certainly false.

The defendants presented testimony from Holly herself, who not only continued to maintain that her "recovered memories" were accurate, but added further damning statements. She testified that she had recovered several new incest memories extending all the way to age 16 and that her father had forced her to have oral sex with the family's dog. Experts for the defense argued that the conduct of the therapists was reasonable on the basis of present medical opinion; that it was indeed possible for someone to endure years of sexual abuse yet repress the memories from consciousness; that Holly's present symptoms were evidence that she had in fact been sexually abused.

At the conclusion of the case, the jury was instructed to determine specifically whether "the defendants had committed malpractice by implanting or reinforcing false memories of childhood sexual abuse in Holly, while she was being treated for bulimia and major depression." The jury found all three defendants negligent and awarded Ramona $500,000. The case (*Ramona v. Isabella,* No. 61898 Napa Cty Cal Sup Ct [1994]), which received wide publicity throughout the world, started a new, and fierce, debate on the legal validity of "recovered memories" and whether they could be used to prosecute under the strict *Daubert* standards. It also established, for the first time, a parent's right—as a third party—to sue therapists for planting false memories of sexual abuse in a child's mind. Malpractice lawsuits alleging that a psychologist implanted false memories in his patients have now become commonplace.

A *repressed memory*, according to some theories of psychology, is often traumatic, of an event or environment which is stored by the unconscious mind but outside the awareness of the conscious mind. Proponents of recovered memory theorize that these memories may be recovered, i.e., integrated into consciousness, years or even decades after the event, often via therapy or in dreams. They allege that recovered memory may also recur in dreams.

While proponents call it "recovered memory," opponents call it the "false memory syndrome." This phrase has been coined by the False Memory Syndrome Foundation (FMSF), a network of parents and relatives, founded in 1992 in Philadelphia. It soon had a membership of 18,000 families. The British False Memory Society set up the next year had 900 families as members. The members claim that their adult children falsely accused them of earlier sexual abuse.

LEGAL PROVISIONS IN SELECT JURISDICTIONS

A few relevant legal provisions in various countries relating to sexual offenses against children are cited below:

Australia

Western Australia

Section 320 of the Criminal Code of Western Australia defines sexual offenses against children under the age of 13. It states:

320. Child under 13: Sexual offenses against

(1) In this section "child" means a child under the age of 13 years.
(2) A person who sexually penetrates a child is guilty of a crime and is liable to imprisonment for 20 years.
(3) A person who procures, incites, or encourages a child to engage in sexual behavior is guilty of a crime and is liable to imprisonment for 20 years.
(4) A person who indecently deals with a child is guilty of a crime and is liable to imprisonment for 10 years.
(5) A person who procures, incites, or encourages a child to do an indecent act is guilty of a crime and is liable to imprisonment for 10 years.
(6) A person who indecently records a child is guilty of a crime and is liable to imprisonment for 10 years.[80]

Section 321 prescribes punishments to an offender who sexually penetrates a child between 13 and 16 years of age. The penalties are somewhat less severe than in the earlier case.

321. Child of or over 13 and under 16: Sexual offenses against

(1) In this section, "child" means a child of or over the age of 13 years and under the age of 16 years.

(2) A person who sexually penetrates a child is guilty of a crime and is liable to the punishment in subsection (7).

(3) A person who procures, incites, or encourages a child to engage in sexual behavior is guilty of a crime and is liable to the punishment in subsection (7).

(4) A person who indecently deals with a child is guilty of a crime and is liable to the punishment in subsection (8).

(5) A person who procures, incites, or encourages a child to do an indecent act, other than an indecent act that is committed in the presence of or viewed by the spouse of that child, is guilty of a crime and is liable to the punishment in subsection (8).

(6) A person who indecently records a child is guilty of a crime and is liable to the punishment in subsection (8).

(7) A person who is guilty of a crime under subsection (2) or (3) is liable to imprisonment for—
 (a) 14 years;
 (b) where the child is under the care, supervision, or authority of the offender, 20 years; or
 (c) where the offender is under the age of 18 years and the child is not under the care, supervision, or authority of the offender, 7 years.

(8) A person who is guilty of a crime under subsection (4), (5) or (6) is liable to imprisonment for—
 (a) 7 years;
 (b) where the child is under the care, supervision, or authority of the offender, 10 years; or
 (c) where the offender is under the age of 18 years and the child is not under the care, supervision, or authority of the offender, 4 years.

(9) Subject to subsection (9a) it is a defense to a charge under this section to prove the accused person—
 (a) believed on reasonable grounds that the child was of or over the age of 16 years; and
 (b) was not more than 3 years older than the child.

(9a) Where the child is under the care, supervision, or authority of the accused person it is immaterial that the accused person—
 (a) believed on reasonable grounds that the child was of or over the age of 16 years; and
 (b) was not more than 3 years older than the child.

(10) It is a defense to a charge under subsection (2), (3), (4) or (6) to prove the accused person was lawfully married to the child.[81]

While the above sections prescribe punishments for single, isolated instances of sexual penetration, Section 321A deals with cases in which the offender forms a long and continuous sexual relationship with the child. It states:

321. A. Child under 16: Sexual relationship with

(1) For the purposes of this section a person has a sexual relationship with a child under the age of 16 years if that person, on three or more occasions each of which is on a different day, does an act in relation to the child which would constitute a prescribed offense.

(2) In subsection (1) the act referred to need not be the same act, or constitute the same offense on each of the three or more occasions.

(3) A person who has a sexual relationship with a child under the age of 16 years is guilty of a crime and is liable to imprisonment for 20 years.

(4) An indictment under subsection (3) shall specify the period during which it is alleged that the sexual relationship occurred and the accused shall not be charged in the same indictment with any other offense under this chapter alleged to have been committed against the child during that period.

(5) In proceedings on an indictment charging an offense under subsection (3) it is not necessary to specify the dates, or in any other way to particularize the circumstances, of the alleged acts.

(6) An indictment for an offense under this section is to be signed by the Director of Public Prosecutions or the Deputy Director of Public Prosecutions.

(7) It is a defense to a charge under subsection (3) to prove the accused person—
   (a) believed on reasonable grounds that the child was of or over the age of 16 years; and
   (b) was not more than 3 years older than the child.

(8) It is a defense to a charge under subsection (3) to prove the accused person was lawfully married to the child.

(9) Upon an indictment charging a person with an offense under subsection (3), if the jury is not satisfied the accused person is guilty of that offense, the accused person may be convicted of one or more prescribed offenses if the offense or offenses are established by the evidence.

(10) If a person has been tried and convicted or acquitted on an indictment alleging the commission of an offense under subsection (3), that fact is a defense to any charge of an offense under this chapter alleged to have been committed against the same child during the period when it was alleged the sexual relationship with the child occurred.

(11) In this section, "prescribed offense" means—
   (a) an offense under section 320(2) or (4) or 321(2) or (4); or
   (b) an offense under section 320(3) or 321(3) where the child in fact engages in sexual behavior.[82]

The Northern Territory

According to Section 127 of the Criminal Code of the Northern Territory (for details please see chapter on exhibitionism), pedophilia is a crime and attracts a punishment of imprisonment up to 25 years. Section 127 states:

Section 127. Sexual intercourse or gross indecency involving child under 16 years

(1) Any person who—
   (a) has sexual intercourse with; or
   (b) commits any act of gross indecency upon,

   a child who is under the age of 16 years is guilty of a crime and is liable to imprisonment for 16 years.

(2) If the child is of or over the age of 10 years and under the age of 16 years and the crime is committed in any of the following circumstances, the offender is liable to imprisonment for 20 years:
   (a) the offender is in the company of another person;
   (b) the child is (whether generally or at the time of the commission of the offense) under the care of the offender;
   (c) the child has a serious physical disability;
   (d) the child has a serious intellectual disability;
   (e) the offender took advantage of the child being under the influence of alcohol or a drug in order to commit the offense.

(3) If the child is under the age of 10 years, the offender is liable to imprisonment for 25 years.

(4) It is a defense to a charge of a crime defined by this section to prove—
  (a) the child was of or above the age of 14 years; and
  (b) the accused person believed on reasonable grounds that the child was of or above the age of 16 years.
(5) Section 12 does not apply to the child with respect to whom an offense against this section is committed.

For details of Section 12, please see chapter on incest.

New South Wales

The criminal law of New South Wales is governed by the Crimes Act 1900 (for details, please see chapter on frotteurism). Sexual intercourse with children especially under 10 years of age is considered a serious offense. Section 66A states:

66A. Sexual intercourse—child under 10
Any person who has sexual intercourse with another person who is under the age of 10 years shall be liable to imprisonment for 25 years.

Even an attempt to have sexual intercourse with such a child is punishable. Section 66 B states:

66B. Attempting, or assaulting with intent, to have sexual intercourse with child under 10
Any person who attempts to have sexual intercourse with another person who is under the age of 10 years, or assaults any such person with intent to have sexual intercourse, shall be liable to imprisonment for 25 years.

Canada

Sexual offenses are described in Part V (Sections 150 through 182) of the Criminal Code of Canada. Sections 151 and 152[83,84] address the issues of pedophilia and child sexual abuse. According to Section 151, even sexual touching of a person under the age of 14 years is punishable (Table 2.3).

Section 152 prescribes punishments to those offenders who invite a child under the age of fourteen years to touch them or any other person for a sexual purpose (Table 2.4).[14]

TABLE 2.3
Punishment for Sexual Interference with a Child under 14 Years of Age, under Section 151 of the Criminal Code of Canada

Sexual interference	151. Every person who, for a sexual purpose, touches, directly or indirectly, with a part of the body or with an object, any part of the body of a person under the age of 14 years
	(a) is guilty of an indictable offense and liable to imprisonment for a term not exceeding 10 years and to a minimum punishment of imprisonment for a term of 45 days; or
	(b) is guilty of an offense punishable on summary conviction and liable to imprisonment for a term not exceeding 18 months and to a minimum punishment of imprisonment for a term of 14 days.

TABLE 2.4
Punishment for Invitation to Sexual Touching, under Section 152 of the Criminal Code of Canada

Invitation to sexual touching	152. Every person who, for a sexual purpose, invites, counsels or incites a person under the age of 14 years to touch, directly or indirectly, with a part of the body or with an object, the body of any person, including the body of the person who so invites, counsels or incites and the body of the person under the age of 14 years,
	(a) is guilty of an indictable offense and liable to imprisonment for a term not exceeding 10 years and to a minimum punishment of imprisonment for a term of 45 days; or
	(b) is guilty of an offense punishable on summary conviction and liable to imprisonment for a term not exceeding 18 months and to a minimum punishment of imprisonment for a term of 14 days.

If the offender is in a position of trust or authority toward the child, and commits similar crimes as mentioned above, the acts are referred to as sexual exploitation. Section 153 defines the crime of sexual exploitation and prescribes punishment for it (Table 2.5).[85]

Germany

German law has several sections addressing the problems of pedophilia and child sexual abuse. Section 174 of the German Criminal Code (Strafgesetzbuch, StGB) deals with sexual abuse of wards. It states as follows:[86]

Section 174. Sexual Abuse of Wards

(1) Whoever commits sexual acts:

1. on a person under 16 years of age who is entrusted to him for upbringing, education or care in leading his life;
2. on a person under 18 years of age who is entrusted to him for upbringing, education or care in leading his life or who is a subordinate within the framework of an employment or a work relationship, by abusing the dependence associated with the upbringing, educational, care, employment or work relationship; or
3. on his natural or adopted child who is not yet 18 years of age, or allows them to be committed on himself by the ward, shall be punished with imprisonment for not more than five years or a fine.

(2) Whoever, under the prerequisites of subsection (1), numbers 1 to 3:

1. commits sexual acts in front of the ward; or
2. induces the ward to commit sexual acts in front of him, in order to thereby sexually arouse himself or the ward, shall be punished with imprisonment for not more than 3 years or a fine.

(3) An attempt shall be punishable.

(4) In cases under subsection (1), number 1 or subsection (2) in conjunction with subsection (1), number 1, the court may dispense with punishment pursuant to this provision, if, taking into consideration the conduct of the ward, the wrongfulness of the act is slight.

Section 176 aims at a pedophile who commits sexual acts on a child below 14 years of age. It states:[87]

TABLE 2.5
Definition and Punishment of Sexual Exploitation of a Young Person under Section 153 of the Criminal Code of Canada

Sexual exploitation	153. (1) Every person commits an offense who is in a position of trust or authority towards a young person, who is a person with whom the young person is in a relationship of dependency or who is in a relationship with a young person that is exploitative of the young person, and who
	(a) for a sexual purpose, touches, directly or indirectly, with a part of the body or with an object, any part of the body of the young person; or
	(b) for a sexual purpose, invites, counsels or incites a young person to touch, directly or indirectly, with a part of the body or with an object, the body of any person, including the body of the person who so invites, counsels or incites and the body of the young person.
Punishment	(1.1) Every person who commits an offense under subsection (1)
	(a) is guilty of an indictable offense and liable to imprisonment for a term not exceeding 10 years and to a minimum punishment of imprisonment for a term of 45 days; or
	(b) is guilty of an offense punishable on summary conviction and liable to imprisonment for a term not exceeding 18 months and to a minimum punishment of imprisonment for a term of 14 days.
Inference of sexual exploitation	(1.2) A judge may infer that a person is in a relationship with a young person that is exploitative of the young person from the nature and circumstances of the relationship, including
	(a) the age of the young person;
	(b) the age difference between the person and the young person;
	(c) the evolution of the relationship; and
	(d) the degree of control or influence by the person over the young person.
Definition of "young person"	(2) In this section, "young person" means a person 14 years of age or more but under the age of 18 years.

Section 176. Sexual Abuse of Children

(1) Whoever commits sexual acts on a person under 14 years of age (a child), or allows them to be committed on himself by the child, shall be punished with imprisonment from 6 months to 10 years, and in less serious cases with imprisonment for not more than 5 years or a fine.

(2) Whoever induces a child to commit sexual acts on a third person, or to have them committed on the child by a third person, shall be similarly punished.

(3) Whoever:

1. commits sexual acts in front of a child;
2. induces the child to commit sexual acts on his own body; or
3. exerts influence on a child by showing him pornographic illustrations or images, by playing him audio recording media with pornographic content or by corresponding speech, shall be punished with imprisonment for not more than 5 years or a fine.

(4) An attempt shall be punishable; this shall not apply for acts under subsection (3), number 3.

If the sexual abuse was committed by more than one person, or the child suffered serious health damage or if the perpetrator had been convicted of a similar crime within the last 5 years, this is termed "Serious Sexual Abuse of Children." Section 176a states:[88]

Section 176a. Serious Sexual Abuse of Children

(1) The sexual abuse of children shall be punished with imprisonment for no less than one year in cases under Section 176 subsections (1) and (2), if:
   1. a person over 18 years of age completes an act of sexual intercourse or similar sexual acts with the child, which are combined with a penetration of the body, or allows them to be committed on himself by the child;
   2. the act is committed jointly by more than one person;
   3. the perpetrator by the act places the child in danger of serious health damage or substantial impairment of his physical or emotional development; or
   4. the perpetrator has undergone a final judgment of conviction for such a crime within the previous 5 years.

(2) Whoever, in cases under Section 176 subsections (1) to (4), acts as a perpetrator or other participant with the intent of making the act the object of a pornographic writing (Section 11, subsection (3)),* which is to be disseminated pursuant to Section 184, subsections (3) or (4),† shall be punished with imprisonment for not less than 2 years.

(3) In less serious cases under subsection (1), imprisonment from 3 months to 5 years shall be imposed, in less serious cases under subsection (2), imprisonment from 1 year to 10 years.

(4) Whoever, in cases under Section 176, subsections (1) and (2):
   1. by the act seriously physically maltreats the child; or
   2. by the act places the child in danger of death, shall be punished with imprisonment for not less than 5 years.

(5) The time in which the perpetrator is in custody in an institution pursuant to order of a public authority shall not be credited to the term indicated in subsection (1), number 4. An act as to which judgment was rendered abroad shall be deemed equivalent in cases under subsection (1), number 4, to an act as to which judgment was rendered domestically, if under German criminal law it would have been such an act under Section 176, subsections (1) or (2).

If the sexual abuse results in the death of child, the crime is far more serious. Section 176b states:[89]

Section 176b. Sexual Abuse of Children Resulting in Death

If by the sexual abuse (Sections 176 and 176a) the perpetrator recklessly causes the death of the child, then the punishment shall be imprisonment for life or for not less than 10 years.

United Kingdom

The *Sexual Offenses Act 2003*[90] is one of the most comprehensive acts relating to sexual offenses against children and child sexual abuse. Sections 5 through 19 address various sex offenses com-

---

* Section 11 (3) asserts that audio and visual recording media, data storage media, illustrations, and other images shall be the equivalent of writings.

† Section 184, subsections (3) and (4) deals with pornographic writings, that have as their object acts of violence, the sexual abuse of children, or sexual acts of human beings with animals.

TABLE 2.6
Child Sex Offenses Defined in the *Sexual Offenses Act 2003* of UK

Section	Rape and Other Offenses against Children under 13
5	Rape of a child under 13
6	Assault of a child under 13 by penetration
7	Sexual assault of a child under 13
8	Causing or inciting a child under 13 to engage in sexual activity
	Child Sex Offenses
9	Sexual activity with a child
10	Causing or inciting a child to engage in sexual activity
11	Engaging in sexual activity in the presence of a child
12	Causing a child to watch a sexual act
13	Child sex offenses committed by children or young persons
14	Arranging or facilitating commission of a child sex offense
15	Meeting a child following sexual grooming etc.
	Abuse of Position of Trust
16	Abuse of position of trust: sexual activity with a child
17	Abuse of position of trust: causing or inciting a child to engage in sexual activity
18	Abuse of position of trust: sexual activity in the presence of a child
19	Abuse of position of trust: causing a child to watch a sexual act

mitted against children (Table 2.6). Sections 25 through 29 deal with familial child sex offenses, that will be dealt with in the chapter on incest.

It would be useful to refer to the original act for details of each section. As an illustration, it might be pertinent to have a detailed look at Section 9 (Table 2.7).

United States

Each state has different laws regarding child sexual abuse. While it would be useful to refer to the criminal codes of each state to know the details of child sexual offenses, it might be pertinent to have a detailed look at the relevant laws in some representative states.

Arkansas

Arkansas laws cover the crimes of sexual activity against children within the definitions of rape. For details of these laws, please refer to the chapter on rape. One section specifically addresses sexual crimes against children. Section 5-14-110 defines sexual indecency with a child. It states:[91]

5-14-110. Sexual indecency with a child

(a) A person commits sexual indecency with a child if:

(1) Being eighteen (18) years of age or older, the person solicits another person who is less than fifteen (15) years of age or who is represented to be less than fifteen (15) years of age to engage in:

(A) Sexual intercourse;

(B) Deviant sexual activity; or

(C) Sexual contact;

TABLE 2.7
Section 9 of the Sexual Offenses Act 2003 of the United Kingdom

Sexual activity with a child

(1) A person aged 18 or over (A) commits an offense if—
  (a) he intentionally touches another person (B),
  (b) the touching is sexual, and
  (c) either—
    (i) B is under 16 and A does not reasonably believe that B is 16 or over, or
    (ii) B is under 13.
(2) A person guilty of an offense under this section, if the touching involved—
  (a) penetration of B's anus or vagina with a part of A's body or anything else,
  (b) penetration of B's mouth with A's penis,
  (c) penetration of A's anus or vagina with a part of B's body, or
  (d) penetration of A's mouth with B's penis, is liable, on conviction on indictment, to imprisonment for a term not exceeding 14 years.
(3) Unless subsection (2) applies, a person guilty of an offense under this section is liable—
  (a) on summary conviction, to imprisonment for a term not exceeding 6 months or to a fine not exceeding the statutory maximum or both;
  (b) on conviction on indictment, to imprisonment for a term not exceeding 14 years.

(2) (A) With the purpose to arouse or gratify a sexual desire of himself or herself or a sexual desire of any other person, the person purposely exposes his or her sex organs to another person who is less than fifteen (15) years of age.
(B) It is an affirmative defense to a prosecution under subdivision (a)(2)(A) of this section if the person is within three (3) years of age of the victim; or
(3) Being eighteen (18) years of age or older, the person causes or coerces another person who is less than fourteen (14) years of age to expose his or her sex organs or the breast of a female with the purpose to arouse or gratify a sexual desire of himself, herself, or another person.
(b) Sexual indecency with a child is a Class D felony.

California

California has detailed provisions regarding pedophilia and child sexual abuse, but what is more significant is that on September 17, 1996, it became the first state to enact a law subjecting child molesters to chemical castration, an invasive chemical treatment designed to reduce sex drive in males. California's law mandates that twice-convicted child molesters receive weekly injections of medroxyprogesterone acetate (Depo-Provera) as a condition of parole.[92,93] Although California became the first state to introduce this controversial law, more states soon followed suit, among them Georgia,[94] Montana,[95] and Louisiana.[96]

REFERENCES

1. Freund, K.et al. Pedophilia and heterosexuality vs. homosexuality, *Journal of Sex and Marital Therapy*, 10(3), 193, 1984.
2. Blanchard, R., Klassen, P., Dickey, R., Kuban, M.E., Blak, T. Sensitivity and specificity of the phallometric test for pedophilia in nonadmitting sex offenders. *Psychol Assess.* 2001 Mar;**13(1)**:118-26.
3. Larson, C., Terman, D.L., Gomby, D.S., Quinn, L.S., Behrman, R.E. Sexual abuse of children: recommendations and analysis. *Future Child.* 1994;4(2):4-30.

4. American Psychiatric Association. *Diagnostic and Statistical Manual of Mental Disorders*, 4th ed. Text rev. American Psychiatric Association, Washington DC, 2000.
5. Hilliard, R.B., Spitzer, R.L. Change in criterion for paraphilias in DSM-IV-TR. *Am J Psychiatry.* 2002 Jul;159(7):1249.
6. Långström, N., Seto, M.C. Exhibitionistic and voyeuristic behavior in a Swedish national population survey. *Arch Sex Behav.* 2006 Aug;35(4):427-35.
7. Seto, M.C. Pedophilia and sexual offenses against children. *Annu Rev Sex Res.* 2004;15:321-61.
8. Brown, L.S. Memories of Childhood Abuse - Recovered, Discovered, and Otherwise, in *Sexualized Violence Against Women and Children: A Psychology and Law Perspective*, Cling, B.J., Ed, The Guilford Press, NY,2004, chapter 8.
9. Krafft-Ebing , R.F. *Psychopathia Sexualis,* 1st ed. (1886) reprinted by Bloat Books, 1999.
10. McCarthy, M. Nobel prize winner Gajdusek admits child abuse. *Lancet.* 1997 Mar 1;**349(9052)**:623.
11. McConaghy, N. Pedophilia: A review of the evidence. *Australian and New Zealand Journal of Psychiatry.* 1998;32(2):252-265.
12. Levin, S.M. and Stava, L. Personality characteristics of sex offenders: a review, *Archives of Sexual Behavior*, 16(1), 57, 1987.
13. Murray, J.B. Psychological profile of pedophiles and child molesters. *J Psychol.* 2000 Mar;134(2):211-24.
14. Rada, R.T. Sexual Psychopathology: Historical Survey and Basic Concepts, in *Clinical Aspects of the Rapist (Seminars in psychiatry)*, Rada, R.T. (ed), Grune & Stratton, New York, 1978.
15. Doek, J.E., Sexual abuse of children: An Examination of European Criminal Law, in *Sexually Abused Children and their Families,* 1st edition, Mrazek, P.B., and Kempe, C.H., (Eds)., Pergamon Press, Oxford, 1981, chap. 6, pages 75-84.
16. Mulhern S. Incest: a laughing matter. *Child Abuse Negl.* 1990;**14(2)**:265-71.
17. Maes, M., van West, D., De Vos, N., Westenberg, H., Van Hunsel, F., Hendriks, D., Cosyns, P., Scharpé, S. Lower baseline plasma cortisol and prolactin together with increased body temperature and higher mCPP-induced cortisol responses in men with pedophilia. *Neuropsychopharmacology.* 2001 Jan;24(1):37-46.
18. Gaffney, G.R., Berlin, F.S. Is there hypothalamic–pituitary–gonadal dysfunction in pedophilia? A pilot study. *Br J Psychiatry.* 1984 Dec;**145**:657-60.
19. Mendez, M.F., Chow, T., Ringman, J., Twitchell, G., Hinkin, C.H. Pedophilia and temporal lobe disturbances. *J Neuropsychiatry Clin Neurosci.* 2000 Winter;12(1):71-6.
20. Joyal, C.C., Black, D.N., Dassylva, B. The neuropsychology and neurology of sexual deviance: a review and pilot study. *Sex Abuse.* 2007 Jun;19(2):155-73.
21. Regestein, Q.R., Reich, P. Pedophilia occurring after onset of cognitive impairment. *J Nerv Ment Dis.* 1978 Nov;166(11):794-8.
22. Burns, J.M., Swerdlow, R.H. Right orbitofrontal tumor with pedophilia symptom and constructional apraxia sign. *Arch Neurol.* 2003;**60**:437-40.
23. Flor-Henry, P., Lang, R.A., Koles, Z.J., Frenzel, R.R. Quantitative EEG studies of pedophilia. *Int J Psychophysiol.* 1991 Jan;**10(3)**:253-8.
24. Cantor, J.M., Blanchard, R., Christensen, B.K., et al. Intelligence, memory, and handedness in pedophilia. *Neuropsychology.* 2004;**18**:3-14.
25. Cohen, L.J., Nikiforov, K., Gans, S., et al. Heterosexual male perpetrators of childhood sexual abuse: a preliminary neuropsychiatric model. *Psychiatr Q.* 2002;**73**:313-36.
26. Dressing, H., Obergriesser, T., Tost, H., et al. [Homosexual pedophilia and functional networks—An fMRI case report and literature review] [Article in German]. *Fortschr Neurol Psychiatr.* 2001;**69**:539-44.
27. Schiffer, B., Peschel, T., Paul, T., Gizewski, E., Forsting, M., Leygraf, N., Schedlowski, M., Krueger, T.H. Structural brain abnormalities in the frontostriatal system and cerebellum in pedophilia. *J Psychiatr Res.* 2007 Nov;**41(9)**:753-62.
28. Schiffer, B., Krueger, T., Paul, T., de Greiff, A., Forsting, M., Leygraf, N., Schedlowski, M., Gizewski, E. Brain response to visual sexual stimuli in homosexual pedophiles. *J Psychiatry Neurosci.* 2008 Jan;**33(1)**:23-33.
29. Frude, N. The sexual nature of sexual abuse. A review of the literature. *Child Abuse Negl.* 1982;6(2):211-23.
30. McGuire, R.J., Carlisle, J.M., Young, B.G. Sexual Deviations As Conditioned Behaviour: A Hypothesis. *Behav Res Ther.* 1965 Jan;**3**:185-90.

31. Lalor, K. Child sexual abuse in sub-Saharan Africa: a literature review. *Child Abuse Negl.* 2004 Apr;28(4):439-60.
32. Lalor, K. Child sexual abuse in Tanzania and Kenya. *Child Abuse Negl.* 2004 Aug;28(8):833-44.
33. Meursing, K., Vos, T., Coutinho, O., Moyo, M., Mpofu, S., Oneko, O., Mundy, V., Dube, S., Mahlangu, T., Sibindi, F.. Child sexual abuse in Matabeleland, Zimbabwe. *Soc Sci Med.* 1995 Dec;**41(12)**:1693-704.
34. Fuller, A.K. Child molestation and pedophilia. An overview for the physician. *JAMA.* 1989;**261**:602-6.
35. Feierman, J.R., Pedophilia: Paraphilic Attraction to Children, in *The Handbook of Forensic Sexology—Biomedical & Criminological Perspectives*, Krivacska, J.J., and Money J., Eds., Prometheus Books, New York, 1994, chapter 2, page 59.
36. Mrazek, P.J. Sexual abuse of children. *Advances in Child Clinical Psychology.* 1984;6:199-215.
37. Abel, G.G. and Harlow, N., *Stop child molestation.* Xlibris, Philadelphia, PA, 2001.
38. Fagan, P.J., Wise, T.N., Schmidt, C.W. Jr., Berlin, F.S., Pedophilia. *JAMA.* 2002; 288: 2458–2465.
39. Freyd, J.J., Putnam, F.W., Lyon, T.D., Becker-Blease, K.A., Cheit, R.E., Siegel, N.B., Pezdek, K., Psychology. The science of child sexual abuse. *Science.* 2005; 308:501.
40. Fritz, G.S., Wagner, N.N. A comparison of males and females who were sexually molested as children. *J Sex Marital Ther.* 1981 Spring;**7(1)**:54-9.
41. Gustafson, T.B., Sarwer, D.B. Childhood sexual abuse and obesity. *Obes Rev.* 2004 Aug;*5(3)*:129-35.
42. Crépault, C., Couture, M. Men's erotic fantasies. *Arch Sex Behav.* 1980 Dec;**9(6)**:565-81.
43. Fedoroff, J. P., Fishell, A., Fedoroff, B., A case series of women evaluated for paraphilic sexual disorders. *Canadian Journal of Human Sexuality.* 1999; 8(2): 127-140.
44. Victor, J.S. Allegations of Satanism and Ritual Sex Abuse, in *The Handbook of Forensic Sexology—Biomedical & Criminological Perspectives*, Krivacska, J.J. and Money, J., Eds., Prometheus Books, New York, 1994, chapter 13, pages 307-32.
45. Smith, M. and Pazder, L. *Michelle Remembers*, Congdon & Lattes, Inc. New York, 1980.
46. Tully, B., Recovered Memory, In *Encyclopedia of Forensic and Legal Medicine*, *Vol. 3*, Payne-James, J.J., Byard, R.W., Corey, T.S., Henderson, C. (Eds.), Elsevier Academic Press, London Pp. 509-14.
47. Freund, K., Blanchard, R. Phallometric diagnosis of pedophilia. *J Consult Clin Psychol.* 1989 Feb;**57(1)**:100-5.
48. Tardif, M., Van Gijseghem, H. The gender identity of pedophiles: what does the outcome data tell us? *J Child Sex Abus.* 2005;14(1):57-74.
49. Vernon, M., Rich, S. Pedophilia and deafness. *Am Ann Deaf.* 1997 Oct;142(4):300-11.
50. Fallon, L.F., Pedophilia. In *The Gale Encyclopedia Of Mental Disorders*, Thackery, E. and Harris, M., (Eds), Thomson Gale, MI, 2003, pages 740-3
51. Freund, K. Erotic preference in pedophilia. *Behavioral Research and Theory.* 1965;3:229-234.
52. Groth, A. N., & Gary, T. S. Heterosexuality, homosexuality, and pedophilia: Sexual offenses against children and adult sexual orientation, in *Male rape: A casebook of sexual aggression*, Scacco, A.M. (Ed.), AMS Press, New York, 1982, pp. 143-152.
53. Jenny, C., Roesler, T. A., & Poyer, K. L. Are children at risk for sexual abuse by homosexuals? *Pediatrics.* 1994;94(1): 41-44.
54. Saunders, E., Awad, G.A., White, G. Male adolescent sexual offenders: the offender and the offense. *Can J Psychiatry.* 1986 Aug;**31(6)**:542-9.
55. Kristensen, E., Lau, M. Women with a history of childhood sexual abuse. Long-term social and psychiatric aspects. *Nord J Psychiatry.* 2007;61(2):115-20.
56. Rayworth, B.B., Wise, L.A., Harlow, B.L. Childhood abuse and risk of eating disorders in women. *Epidemiology.* 2004 May;**15(3)**:271-8.
57. Gustafson, T.B., Sarwer, D.B. Childhood sexual abuse and obesity. *Obes Rev.* 2004 Aug;*5(3)*:129-35.
58. Gustafson, T.B., Gibbons, L.M., Sarwer, D.B., Crerand, C.E., Fabricatore, A.N., Wadden, T.A., Raper, S.E., Williams, N.N. History of sexual abuse among bariatric surgery candidates. *Surg Obes Relat Dis.* 2006 May-Jun;**2(3)**:369-76.
59. Preti, A., Incani, E., Camboni, M.V., Petretto, D.R., Masala, C. Sexual abuse and eating disorder symptoms: the mediator role of bodily dissatisfaction. *Compr Psychiatry.* 2006 Nov-Dec;**47(6)**:475-81.
60. Van Dorn, R.A., Mustillo, S., Elbogen, E.B., Dorsey, S., Swanson, J.W., Swartz, M.S. The effects of early sexual abuse on adult risky sexual behaviors among persons with severe mental illness. *Child Abuse Negl.* 2005 Nov;29(11):1265-79.
61. Kahn, J.A., Huang, B., Rosenthal, S.L., Tissot, A.M., Burk, R.D. Coercive sexual experiences and subsequent human papillomavirus infection and squamous intraepithelial lesions in adolescent and young adult women. *J Adolesc Health.* 2005 May;36(5):363-71.

62. Urquiza, A.J., Goodlin-Jones, B.L. Child sexual abuse and adult revictimization with women of color. *Violence Vict.* 1994 Fall;**9(3)**:223-32.
63. Felitti, V.J. Long-term medical consequences of incest, rape, and molestation. *South Med J.* 1991 Mar;**84(3)**:328-31.
64. Claes, L., Vandereycken, W. Is there a link between traumatic experiences and self-injurious behaviors in eating-disordered patients? *Eat Disord.* 2007 Jul-Sep;**15(4)**:305-15.
65. Aldridge, N.C., Strengths and Limitations of Forensic Child Sexual Abuse Interviews with Anatomical Dolls: An Empirical Review. *Journal of Psychopathology and Behavioral Assessment.* 1998;**20(1)**: 1-41.
66. Walker, L.E.A. *Handbook on sexual abuse of children: Assessment and treatment issues*, Springer, New York, 1988
67. O'Brien, C. Medical and forensic examination by a sexual assault nurse examiner of a 7-year-old victim of sexual assault. *J Emerg Nurs.* 1992 Jun;18(3):199-204.
68. Palusci, V.J., Cox, E.O., Shatz, E.M., Schultze, J.M. Urgent medical assessment after child sexual abuse. *Child Abuse Negl.* 2006 Apr;30(4):367-80.
69. Templeton, D.J., Williams, A. Current issues in the use of colposcopy for examination of sexual assault victims. *Sex Health.* 2006 Mar;3(1):5-10.
70. McCauley, J., Gorman, R.L., Guzinski, G. Toluidine blue in the detection of perineal lacerations in pediatric and adolescent sexual abuse victims. *Pediatrics.* 1986 Dec;78(6):1039-43.
71. Macready, N. Chemical castration for paedophiles approved. *BMJ.* 1996 Sep 21;**313(7059)**:707.
72. Cooper, A.J. et al. A double-blind placebo controlled trial of medroxyprogesterone acetate and cyproterone acetate with seven pedophiles. *Can J Psychiatry.* 37, 687, 1992.
73. Schober, J.M., Kuhn, P.J., Kovacs, P.G., Earle, J.H., Byrne, P.M., Fries, R.A. Leuprolide acetate suppresses pedophilic urges and arousability. *Arch Sex Behav.* 2005 Dec;**34(6)**:691-705.
74. Saleh, F.M., Niel, T., Fishman, M.J. Treatment of paraphilia in young adults with leuprolide acetate: a preliminary case report series. *J Forensic Sci.* 2004 Nov;**49(6)**:1343-8.
75. Rösler, A., Witztum, E. Pharmacotherapy of paraphilias in the next millennium. *Behav Sci Law.* 2000;**18(1)**:43-56.
76. Prahlada, Rao N., Chand, P.K., Murthy, P. A case of late-onset pedophilia and response to sertraline. *Prim Care Companion J Clin Psychiatry.* 2007;**9(3)**:235-6.
77. Anon. Reckless conduct charge used to jail man for assault. *AIDS Policy Law.* 1999 Sep 3;14(16):10.
78. Anon. North Carolina court affirms conviction of HIV-positive rapist. *AIDS Policy Law.* 1999 Mar 5;14(4):9.
79. Brahams, D. "Repressed memories" and the law. *Lancet.* 2000 Jul 29;356(9227):358.
80. Criminal Code of Western Australia. Section 320 inserted by No. 14 of 1992 s. 6(1).
81. Criminal Code of Western Australia. Section 321 inserted by No. 14 of 1992 s. 6(1); amended by No. 3 of 2002 s. 38.
82. Criminal Code of Western Australia. Section 321A inserted by No. 14 of 1992 s. 6(1); amended by No. 3 of 2002 s. 39.
83. Section 151, Criminal Code of Canada (R.S.C., 1985, c. C-46).
84. Section 152, Criminal Code of Canada (R.S.C., 1985, c. C-46).
85. Section 153, Criminal Code of Canada (R.S.C., 1985, c. C-46).
86. Section 174, German Criminal Code (Strafgesetzbuch, StGB) as promulgated on 13 November 1998 (Federal Law Gazette I, p. 945, p. 3322).
87. Section 176, German Criminal Code (Strafgesetzbuch, StGB) as promulgated on 13 November 1998 (Federal Law Gazette I, p. 945, p. 3322).
88. Section 176a, German Criminal Code (Strafgesetzbuch, StGB) as promulgated on 13 November 1998 (Federal Law Gazette I, p. 945, p. 3322).
89. Section 176b, German Criminal Code (Strafgesetzbuch, StGB) as promulgated on 13 November 1998 (Federal Law Gazette I, p. 945, p. 3322).
90. Sexual Offenses Act 2003 [20th November 2003].
91. Arkansas Code Ann. §5-14-110 (enacted 1975).
92. Cal. Penal Code §645 (West Supp. 1997).
93. Lesher, D. Molester Castration Measure Signed Law: California Becomes the First State to Require that Offenders Get Periodic Injections to Suppress Sex Drive, *L.A. Times*, Sept. 18, 1996.
94. Ga. Code Ann. §16-6-4(d)(2) (Supp. 1998).
95. Mont. Code Ann. §45-5-512 (1997).
96. La. Rev. Stat. Ann. §15:538(C) (West Supp. 1999).

3 Transvestic Fetishism

INTRODUCTION

Transvestic fetishism, fetishistic transvestism, or simply transvestism (from Latin *trans-*, "across, over" and *vestere*, "to dress or to wear"), typically refers to an unusual sexual behavior whereby patients derive sexual gratification from wearing clothes usually worn by the opposite sex. In lay terminology it is referred to as "cross-dressing." The patients typically are heterosexual married males.

Many features of transvestism overlap with transsexualism, causing confusion at times. Oakley[1] even defined transvestism as a "mild form of sex change called transsexuality." Some terms that have been used in the literature for transvestism, especially to differentiate it from transsexualism, are *sexoaesthetic inversion*, *symptomatic transvestism*, and *true transvestism*.[2] Prince, a transvestite himself, has proposed the term *femmiphilia*.[3]

DSM-IV-TR[4] assigns code 302.3 to transvestic fetishism and sets forth criteria for diagnosing it (Table 3.1).

It is important to appreciate that some men may be comorbid and may meet criteria for both transvestic fetishism and gender identity disorder. The specifier "with gender dysphoria" is used, if gender dysphoria* is present in an individual with transvestic fetishism, but full criteria for Gender Identity Disorder are not met.[5]

ICD-9-CM assigns the code 302.3 to transvestic fetishism[6]—same as that assigned by DSM-IV-TR. ICD-10 calls it fetishistic transvestism, and assigns the code F65.1 to it.[7] Fetishistic transvestism according to ICD-10 is defined as:

> The wearing of clothes of the opposite sex principally to obtain sexual excitement and to create the appearance of a person of the opposite sex. Fetishistic transvestism is distinguished from transsexual transvestism by its clear association with sexual arousal and the strong desire to remove the clothing once orgasm occurs and sexual arousal declines. It can occur as an earlier phase in the development of transsexualism.

The term *homeovestism* is sometimes used to denote sexual attraction towards the clothing of one's *own* gender. In a variation of transvestism, known colloquially as petticoat punishment, a male paraphiliac, afflicted with transvestism and masochism, derives pleasure in getting spanked when he is dressed like a school girl or servant girl.

CLASSIFICATION

It is important to note that ICD-10 makes a very clear distinction between *fetishistic transvestism* (also sometimes called nuclear, stable, or periodic transvestism) and *dual-role transvestism* (also sometimes called transsexual transvestism or marginal transvestism). In fetishistic transvestism, which may be referred to as *true transvestism*, there is a feeling of sexual arousal associated with cross-dressing, while in dual-role transvestism, the individual dons the clothes of the opposite sex, simply because he identifies himself with the opposite sex. Such individuals wear clothes of the

---

* Please see Chapter 1 for the definition of gender dysphoria.

TABLE 3.1
DSM-IV-TR Criteria for Transvestic Fetishism (302.3)

A. Over a period of at least 6 months, in a heterosexual male, recurrent, intense, sexually arousing fantasies, sexual urges, or behaviors involving cross-dressing

B. The fantasies, sexual urges, or behaviors cause clinically significant distress or impairment in social, occupational, or other important areas of functioning

Specify if:

With Gender Dysphoria: if the person has persistent discomfort with gender role or identity

opposite sex more to be at ease with themselves and to achieve mental relaxation than to achieve any sexual satisfaction. Hamburger and associates[8] call this condition *genuine transvestism*, *psychic hermaphroditism*, or *eonism* (assigning the term *genuine transvestism* to dual-role transvestism may actually be rather confusing, and is no longer recommended. It is clear that the criteria set out by DSM-IV-TR are met more closely by fetishistic transvestites, and thus they are the ones who must be referred to as "true" or "genuine" transvestites. It is noteworthy that Hamburger and associates' paper dates back to 1953). These transvestites report a lower sexual arousal to cross-dressing, and a stronger interest in same-sex sex than their "true transvestite" counterparts.[9] They often desire feminization (sex change) by hormonal treatment or reconstructive genital surgery. Some of them are full-time transvestites, and live entirely as women.[9] Fetishistic transvestites, on the other hand, are not typically worried about sex change and are satisfied with cross-dressing only.

These two groups have been mentioned by several workers. Stoller[10] interviewed eleven transvestites who showed fetishistic arousal to women's clothes, and described the same two categories. The first was sexually excited by a "single garment or a few garments." The second group began to cross-dress in the same manner as the first, but, with aging, cross-dressing became more complete. Fetishistic arousal persisted in both groups, but subjects in the second increasingly felt like members of the opposite sex. Bancroft,[11] too, described two groups. While a "transvestite" group was satisfied simply with cross-dressing, another group, called the "transsexual" group, desired estrogen therapy or sex-change surgery.

Fetishistic transvestism and dual-role transvestism have also been called *group 1* and *group 2* transvestism, respectively.[9] Grouping like this makes the classification somewhat more appropriate, because it becomes devoid of any semantic interpretations.

Other cross-dressers do not fit in any of the above two groups, and this warrants a fresh classification. This fresh classification proposed in this book is based loosely on the strength of psychological compulsion the transvestite feels to cross-dress, with class I transvestites experiencing the least compulsion (they cross-dress almost at will, with almost no compulsion at all), and class V, the greatest. This scheme of classification is in line followed throughout this book, where individuals belonging to earlier classes are least affected psychologically, and those belonging to latter classes are most affected.

For long it has been known that there are homosexuals, too, who cross-dress. However, very little information is available on such homosexuals.[12] This could perhaps be a reason why this group was never included in any classification of transvestites proposed so far (another strong reason is that the DSM-IV-TR criteria specifically mention a heterosexual male and not homosexuals). As we see in the chapter on transsexualism, Green and colleagues[13] have found an association between some cross-dressers and homosexuality. Person and Ovesey[14] distinguished homosexual cross-dressing from both transsexualism and transvestism. Within homosexual cross-dressers, too, they distinguished two categories—those in whom cross-dressing played a central role in their psychological life and those who cross-dressed rarely for a lark (e.g., to attend a masquerade party, or to see how it felt). Based on the psychological compulsion they experienced, we can group them in two additional classes (please see below).

There is a fifth group of transvestites who are neither sexually aroused by cross-dressing (as are group 1 transvestites of Docter and Prince[9]), nor display any transgender behavior (as group 2 transvestites of Docter and Prince[9]). Instead, they wear clothes of the opposite sex for a number of reasons (please see classification below). Since they do not report any fetishistic feelings associated with cross-dressing, their behavior is simply referred to as transvestism, as contrasted to transvestic fetishism. Since they are normal people in all respects, they do not identify themselves with any of the other classes. Indeed they tend to distance themselves from them. They are also referred to simply as *cross-dressers*, a term that fairly accurately describes their behavior.

The following proposed classification is based on the pattern followed throughout the book, with least affected individuals grouped as the first class and the most affected individuals grouped as the last class. Classes I through III do not meet DSM-IV-TR criteria, and thus may not be true transvestic fetishists as defined by DSM-IV-TR. However, they are included here because they do seem to form part of the continuum along which all cross-dressers can be placed.

Class I Transvestites

These people have little psychological compulsion to cross-dress. They cross-dress almost at will, for a variety of reasons, some of which may be (i) to conceal their identity, e.g., from police or to escape from mandatory military service, also called impersonators, (ii) to act as prostitutes, as *hijras* of India,[15] (iii) to challenge social norms, (iv) to shock others, (v) to look different, (vi) to imitate the other sex, because they admire them, (vii) as a matter of comfort or style (viii), as members of single-sex theatrical troupes, who have to play roles written for members of the opposite sex, (ix) as shamans who cross-dress during religious or spiritual ceremonies, and finally (x) for plain enjoyment. This group has been called *pseudotransvestites.*[16]

Class II Transvestites

These are homosexuals who cross-dress rarely for a lark (e.g., to attend a masquerade party). They do not feel any sexual urge to dress so.

Class III Transvestites

These individuals are homosexuals at the extremely effeminate end of a gradient of sex-role behavior. Cross-dressing plays a central role in their psychological life. Many of them are known to have exhibited extensive cross-gender behavior as children. Class I through class III transvestites do not fulfill DSM-IV-TR criteria for transvestic fetishism, and thus are not true transvestic fetishists.

Class IV Transvestites

Individuals belonging to class IV and class V seem to fulfill the DSM-IV-TR criteria, and it is useful to compare and contrast them. In comparison with class V transvestites, the individuals belonging to this group are characterized by (i) a lower sexual arousal associated with cross-dressing, (ii) a stronger cross-gender identity, (iii) a higher propensity for homosexual sex, (iv) a higher propensity for a sex change, and (v) a higher motivation to live entirely as the other sex. This condition has been called *dual-role transvestism* in ICD-10 (please see below). This class is equivalent to the group 2 transvestites proposed by Docter and Prince.[9]

TABLE 3.2
Fetishistic Transvestism versus Dual-role Transvestism as Classified in ICD-10

	F64 Gender Identity Disorders
F64.0	Transsexualism
F64.1	Dual-role transvestism
F64.2	Gender identity disorder of childhood
F64.8	Other gender identity disorders
F64.9	Gender identity disorder, unspecified
	F65 Disorders of Sexual Preference
F65.0	Fetishism
F65.1	Fetishistic transvestism
F65.2	Exhibitionism
F65.3	Voyeurism
F65.4	Paedophilia
F65.4	Sadomasochism
F65.6	Multiple disorders of sexual preference
F65.8	Other disorders of sexual preference
F65.9	Disorder of sexual preference, unspecified

Class V Transvestites

In comparison with class IV transvestites, these individuals are characterized by (i) a higher sexual arousal associated with cross-dressing, (ii) a weaker cross-gender identity, (iii) a higher propensity for heterosexual sex, (iv) a lower propensity for a sex change, (v) a lower motivation to live entirely as the other sex, and (vi) some may engage in autoerotic asphyxial behaviors to further heighten their sexual arousal and achieve more intense orgasms. This condition has been called *fetishistic transvestism* in ICD-10 (please see Table 3.2). This class is equivalent to the group 1 transvestites proposed by Docter and Prince.[9] It is important and illustrative to go through the relevant codes of ICD-10 to understand the differences among class IV and V transvestites (see Table 3.2).

Dual role transvestism (F64.1) is classified as a *gender identity disorder* (F64), while fetishistic transvestism (F65.1) is classified as a *disorder of sexual preference*. The important differences are:

(i) Fetishistic transvestism is a disorder of sexual preference, while dual role transvestism is a gender identity disorder.
(ii) In fetishistic transvestism, wearing clothes of the opposite sex is accompanied by sexual arousal. No such sexual arousal occurs in dual role transvestism (or the arousal is of a low intensity), where the individual wears such clothes in order to experience temporary membership of the opposite sex.
(iii) In fetishistic transvestism, once orgasm occurs and sexual arousal declines, there is a strong desire to remove the clothing. No such sequence of events occurs in dual role transvestism.
(iv) Fetishistic transvestites are more likely to cross-dress in secret (say in a closed room, with no one around), while dual role transvestites cross-dress and go out in daylight, shopping, meeting friends, etc.

Although nosologically the two disorders (dual role transvestism and fetishistic transvestism) differ, in actual clinical practice the differences often blur, with one disorder often transmorphing into the

TABLE 3.3
Select Transvestism Vocabulary

Berdache—A transvestite Native American anatomical male, accorded some higher degree of respect for his spiritual significance, and allowed to live with the women as a quasi-woman, even when warriors depart camp. The berdache is sometimes treated in all respects as a woman, even in the bestowal of dowry.

Drag—In its broadest sense, the term refers to a costume or outfit that carries symbolic significance, but usually refers to the clothing associated with one gender role when worn by a person of the other gender. To "do drag" is for a person of one sex to wear clothes of the other. It is falsely believed that the term is an acronym for "**d**ressed **a**s **g**irl," and believers would tend to use this term *only* for a male wearing the clothes of a female, reserving *drab* (**d**ressed **a**s a **b**oy) for a female wearing clothes of a male. The term actually arose in the 1870s as theatre slang, when males acting as females were required to wear long skirts. The sensation of long skirts trailing behind on the floor gave a sensation of "dragging," and hence the term.

Drag king—A woman who dresses to look like a man, usually for performance. Drag kings are often lesbian, but not always.

Drag queen—A man who dresses (or "drags") in female clothes and make-up for special occasions and usually because he is performing or entertaining as a hostess, stage artist, or at an event. He does not have any fetishistic feelings associated with cross-dressing. Drag queens are sometimes scorned by members of the transgender community—especially, but not exclusively, by many transsexual women—because of fears that they may be stereotyped as drag queens. Nevertheless, there are transgender or transsexual people who perform as drag queens.

En travesti—Literally "cross-dressed." Conventional theatrical portrayal of women by male actors in *drag*. Up to the late 17th century this was necessary because the law considered performance on stage by women to engender immorality.

Petticoat discipline—Also known as petticoating, pinaforing or pinafore eroticism, it refers to a kind of roleplay or fantasy that revolves around a male being dressed as a girl in front of his mother, sisters, or in some cases, girls of his own age whom he had offended by his boorish behavior. Many mothers who discipline their sons in this fashion have either wanted daughters for long or find it erotic to feminize their sons. This type of punishment is also found in the history of some people who eventually develop transvestic fetishism.

Transvestophilia—Arousal from cross-dressing. Since both class IV and class V transvestites report arousal from cross-dressing, they may be referred to as transvestophiliacs, but not the transvestites belonging to other classes, who don clothes of opposite sex for a variety of other reasons.

Underdressing—Wearing female undergarments under male clothes by a male and vice versa. The famous low-budget filmmaker Edward D. Wood, Jr., said he often wore women's underwear under his military uniform during World War II. Benjamin's type II and type III transsexuals engage in this activity (please see chapter on transsexualism).

other. For instance, some adolescent boys initially develop a transvestic fetishism; they masturbate while wearing female clothing, but they seem to lose interest in this activity in their twenties or thirties and become typical dual role transvestites. Some people who are dual role transvestites gradually begin showing signs of true transsexualism, as they seek surgery for sex change. See Table 3.3 for select transvestism vocabulary.

HISTORICAL PERSPECTIVES

Transvestism was prohibited in the Bible. Deuteronomy, the Fifth Book of Moses (c. 1400 BC) says:

The woman shall not wear that which pertaineth unto a man, neither shall a man put on a woman's garment: for all that do so are abomination unto the Lord thy God.[17]

Transvestism in Prehistory, Legend, and Mythology

Buhrich gives a comprehensive account of transvestic fetishism in history.[18] The origins of transvestic fetishism can be traced to tradition and mythology. In Indian tradition, *Bahuchara Mata* is a Hindu goddess and patroness of the *hijra* (intersex) community. She is worshipped by the *hijras* in India.[15] In one of the many folk stories associated with *Bahuchara Mata,* she was once a princess whose husband used to "behave as a woman" and preferred to go to the forest instead of coming to her bridal bed. To punish him, the *Mata* castrated him. In another story, a man who attempted to molest *Bahuchara Mata* was cursed with impotence. He was forgiven only after he gave up his masculinity, dressed as a woman, and worshipped the goddess.

Transvestite legends occur in many other cultures, showing perhaps their fascination or at least acquaintance with this phenomenon. In Greek mythology, when Heracles (identified by the later Romans as Hercules) "inadvertently" murdered Iphitus, he was remanded, by the Oracle's command, as a slave to Queen Omphale for one year. During this period, he was forced not only to do women's work but also wear women's clothing.[19]

Women tended to wear men's clothes, too. In *The Voyage of the Argo*, Apollonius of Rhodes describes that when the Argonauts reached the island of Lemnos, they saw women donning a suit of bronze (men's wear), looking after a cattle and ploughing the earth for corn.[20]

Greco-Roman Era

Greek historian Herodotus (484–425 BC) reported a disease of Scythians on the northern shores of the Black Sea in which men dressed and worked as women.[18] He referred to the disease as the "mysterious Skythian illness."[21] The Roman Emperors Caligula (AD 12–41), Nero (AD 37–68), Commodus (161–192), and Elagabalus (or Heliogabalus, ca. 203–222) were all transvestites.[18] Caligula appeared publicly in women's shoes or in silk, which men were forbidden by law to wear, and even in women's robes. Nero is reported to have participated as a bride in a formal wedding ceremony. Elagalabus is said to have appalled his army by his effeminacy and cross-dressing behavior. He appeared cross-dressed in public wearing silks, painted eyes, and rouged cheeks.[22]

At least one Roman Pope, Pope Joan, was a transvestite. Legend has it that Pope Joan—a transvestite—reigned for around 2 years between the reigns of Leo IV and Benedict III, in the ninth century. Since a woman cannot become a pope, the only reason she could become a pope was that she was a transvestite and dressed as a man.[23] Her deception was unearthed only because she collapsed in childbirth during a papal procession through Rome. According to one version, the angry crowd then stoned her and her newborn child to death.*

Jeanne d'Arc (more commonly known as Joan of Arc, c. 1412–1431) was supposed to be a transvestite. In fact, transvestism was a major charge against her in her trial by the Catholic Church in 1431 at Rouen and her execution. She was accused of breaking both scriptural and secular law by her male attire. While in the ecclesiastic prison she was lodged in a common dungeon, and was guarded day and night, not by women, but by five English soldiers. While lodged there, she insisted that she needed her male dress and armor for bodily protection. Her later submission to donning female dress was quickly followed by resumption of male attire. This "relapse" is said to have precipitated the judges' verdict; she was pronounced a heretic and handed over to civil justice.[24]

---

* Interestingly, all subsequent popes were supposedly subjected to an examination whereby, having sat on a dung chair containing a hole called *sedia stercoraria*, a cardinal had to reach up and establish that the new pope had testicles, before solemnly announcing *Testiculos habet et bene pendentes* ("He has testicles, and they dangle nicely").

The Case of Chevalier d'Eon

FIGURE 3.1 Chevalier d'Eon.

One of the most famous and best-documented transvestites of history was the Frenchman Chevalier D'Eon de Beaumont (1728–1810). He had been dressed as a girl during his childhood and retained a taste for female clothes throughout his life. When his appearance as a lady at a masquerade ball was noticed by the Prince de Conti and King Louis XV, they formed the idea of hiring him as a spy to engage in secret diplomacy while disguised as a woman. In 1756 he was sent to Russia disguised as Mademoiselle Lia de Beaumont, where he became a confidant and a maid of honor to Empress Elizabeth. He returned to France in 1761.

He continued working for the secret service, and as a member of the French Embassy in London from 1763 was involved in many political intrigues. From this period, numerous rumors spread to the effect that the Chevalier D'Eon really was a woman. Chevalier d'Eon died in London. Doctors who examined him after death discovered that his body was anatomically male. Quite possibly d'Eon was a transsexual (class IV transvestite); he is, however, most often remembered not for his transsexualism, but for his transvestic behavior. The eponymous term *eonism*, referring to transvestism, was first coined by Havelock Ellis[25] (1859–1939) in analogy with sadism and masochism,* but is now used very sparingly.[24] It is best to avoid this term, as different workers have referred to this term in different ways. Hamburger and associates,[8] for instance, prefer not to use it as an omnibus term for *all* transvestites, reserving it *only* for cases of dual-role transvestism (to use their own phraseology, "Eonists are persons with a fundamental feeling of being victims of a cruel mistake—a consequence of the female personality in a male body").

Modern Era

Although the donning of garments of another gender has had a long recorded history, it was only in the late 19th and early 20th centuries that the practice came to be viewed specifically as a psychosexual disorder. The first physician to describe a case of transvestism (in fact to describe *any* alternative form of sexual expression) was Carl Westphal (1833–1890), who in 1869 described two cases of cross-dressing in *Archiv für Psychiatrie und Nervenkrankheiten*.[26,27] One was the case of a young woman who enjoyed dressing like a boy and engaging in boy's games from her earliest years. She was also sexually attracted only to women. The second case described a man who wanted to wear women's clothing and live as a woman all the time. The case study does not clarify his sexual orientation. Westphal, using a neologism, categorized both cases as those of *konträre Sexualempfindung* (contrary sexual feeling). Bullough,[28] however, thinks that these cases include some aspects

* Like *eonism*, both *sadism* and *masochism* have been derived after real people afflicted with the paraphilia, the terms denote.

FIGURE 3.2 Magnus Hirschfeld.

of transsexualism. Perhaps because of this reason, Bowman and Engle assert that the first scientific discussion of transvestism was made by Krafft-Ebing (1840–1902).[24]

The term *transvestism*, however, was first used by the German sexologist and sexual rights activist Magnus Hirschfeld in his study, *Die Transvestiten: eine Untersuchung über den erotischen Verkleidungstrieb* (*The Transvestites: An Investigation of the Erotic Urge to Cross-Dress*), published in 1910.[24,29] He is generally regarded as the first serious student of transvestism (interestingly, he was an avowed homosexual himself).[30] In this study he reviewed the cases of sixteen men and one woman, most of whom were patients, and included cases of both true transvestism and transsexual transvestism.

One of the most notable transvestites of modern times was Friedrich "Fritz" Haarmann (1879–1925), a notorious serial killer from Germany. Throughout his school life, he enjoyed dressing up as a girl, although this tendency later vanished. A sexual psychopath, he committed at least 24 murders from 1919 to 1924, and to acquired the epithet "The Butcher of Hanover." He was beheaded in 1925.

ETIOLOGY

Psychoanalytic Theories

Stoller[31] summed up much of the current thinking on the subject. He felt there was as yet no genetic, constitutional, or biochemical evidence to explain the phenomenon. Male transvestites, however, seem to have several etiological factors in common. (1) The mother has an unconscious wish to feminize her little boy, perhaps as an unconscious expression of her own homosexuality. (2) In such cases the father is either a co-conspirator by being silent and passive about the matter or is altogether absent.* (3) Transvestites themselves suffer from castration anxiety, for which they compensate by making themselves into phallic women. (4) Transvestism actually is an efficient way of handling very strong feminine identification without having to succumb to the feeling that one's masculinity is being submerged by feminine wishes. In effect it allows a man to channel these feelings through his feminine dress and still be acutely aware of the insignia of his maleness, a penis. Noteworthy of almost all studies of transvestism is the fact that it is defined as psychopathological only in terms of male cross-dressing. There is a curious and significant lack of literature on female cross-dressing, implying either that the phenomenon does not exist or, if it does, it is not a problem that can be explained in terms of psychopathology.

Biological Theories

Transvestism is frequently associated with postencephalitic states. Thomas and DeAlwis[32] describe a case of transvestism in a 47-year old man who had developed encephalitis in childhood, resulting in moderate learning disabilities and epilepsy. He had been living in institutions from the age of 6, and did not have any chance to express his sexual desire. This frustration manifested as aggressive behavior. His deviant sexual behavior became apparent when he moved to a community home.

There are many case reports and studies which indicate that temporal lobe lesions may be responsible for transvestic fetishism. Pettit and Barr[33] describe the case of a 24-year old right-handed man, who suffered grand-mal seizures due to temporal lobe lesions since he was 18 months old. During childhood he preferred girls' games and company. At 10 years of age he began to dress in female clothes and wished to live as a woman. Gautier-Smith[34] has described 11 cases which indicate that temporal lobe lesions may be associated with transvestite and transsexual behavior and true hypersexuality.

Iatrogenesis

Riley[35] has described a case where transvestic fetishism arose as a result of treatment with Selegiline. A 72-year old man with a 37-year history of Parkinson's disease was treated with a right thalamotomy and was later treated with levodopa for more than 20 years. Selegiline (5 mg twice daily) was added for motor fluctuations. He developed a frequent impulse to wear women's clothing but did not act on this impulse until his wife died over a year later. He then began to dress in women's clothing an average of once per week. He stated he had never thought of cross-dressing previously. The selegiline was stopped, and his urge to wear women's clothing ceased.

EPIDEMIOLOGY

Prevalence and Incidence

Transvestic fetishism appears to be much more prevalent in biological males than females. Stoller[36] knew of only three cases of female transvestism from his personal cases, one of which he knew only through letters. He made an extensive search of literature and could find just one other case of female transvestism. The outstanding common feature was a powerful masculinity present since childhood.[37]

Not many formal epidemiological studies have been done on prevalence and incidence of this paraphilia. Bullough and Bullough[27] cite a prevalence figure of 1%, but Zucker and Blanchard[38] feel that this figure is based on sheer speculation and not on any serious epidemiological investigation.

Serious epidemiological studies have become available (one in which the critic of the earlier figure Zucker himself was involved!). Långström and Zucker[39] used a random sample of 2,450 18-

* It is interesting to compare this criteria with the proposed etiological factors of transsexualism, which are very similar (please see chapter on transsexualism).

to 60-year-olds in the general population of Sweden to study the prevalence as well as the social, sexual, and health correlates of transvestic fetishism. Almost three percent (2.8%) of men and 0.4% of women reported at least one episode of transvestic fetishism. Separation from parents, same-sex sexual experiences, being easily sexually aroused, pornography use, and higher masturbation frequency were significantly associated with transvestic fetishism.

Other Significant Characteristics

Buhrich and Beaumont[40] studied 222 male subjects of transvestism in Australia (86) and the U.S. (136) by mailing questionnaires to transvestite club members. They found that characteristics of transvestism were remarkably similar across countries. Almost half of the subjects first cross-dressed in prepuberty, and a majority reported established cross-dressing by late adolescence. Over one third of the subjects reported co-existing fantasies of bondage, usually of themselves while cross-dressed. Transvestic fetishism has been found to be associated with bondage,[41] and also with autoerotic asphyxia.[21,42,43]

Two major epidemiological studies on transvestites conducted 25 years apart have produced almost identical results (with few exceptions).[44,9] In the latter study (by Docter and Prince), 87% of respondents described themselves as heterosexual. All except 17% had married, and 60% were married at the time of the survey. An important difference was that in the latter study, 45% reported seeking counseling compared to 24% of the 1972 survey. Furthermore, those reporting strong transsexual inclinations were up by 5% in the latter study. Docter and Prince concluded that although the transvestites of the present generation described themselves much as did similar subjects 25 years earlier, the percentage migrating toward living full-time as women was greater.

MANAGEMENT

Lithium has been used in the management of transvestic fetishism with some success. Ward[45] successfully used lithium to treat a case of transvestism in a 24-year old manic-depressive man. Ward reasoned that the transvestism in general was perpetuated by mood-dependent motives, which could be eliminated by lithium. Additionally, since his was a case of associated mania, another assumption was that the manic state became an intermittent reinforcer for the transvestism, and lithium, by eliminating the mania, treated the condition.

Buspirone has been shown to be useful in the management of transvestic fetishism.[46] Fedoroff[47] describes a 46-year old man with generalized anxiety disorder and transvestic fetishism who responded favorably to treatment with buspirone hydrochloride. The patient stopped cross-dressing while taking buspirone. Alprazolam had had no effect on the frequency of cross-dressing. Sertraline[48] has also been found useful in the management of transvestic fetishism.

LEGAL ASPECTS

Cross-dressing is not listed as a crime in most countries. However, cross-dressing in public can cause breach of peace as curious onlookers gaze at the cross-dresser.

Minor problems may occur concerning the use of rest rooms. Law does not provide any guidelines in this matter. In more conservative societies a male cross-dresser wearing the clothes of a female may find himself in great problems if he uses a female restroom. Conversely, if he used a male restroom, he would raise some eyebrows, but no significant problems are likely to occur. A male cross-dresser is likely to face similar situations in other instances, for example, if he tried to board a female compartment of a train, tried to occupy a seat meant for females in a bus, or tried to use a queue meant exclusively for females. This is more likely to happen in societies where males and females are traditionally segregated and different public facilities exist for men and women.

In sports, however, a transvestite would be expected to take part in activities of his biological sex. For instance, a male transvestite would be expected to swim in the male category rather than the female.

Hate crimes, derisions, and cat calls have occurred. However, most police forces now have transgender policies, codes of conduct, and liaison officers. All hate crime should be reported to the police, who should log the report.

Suicide by Transvestites

The combination of transvestism and autoerotic asphyxia is all too common and cases of transvestite suicide may appear like cases of accidental hangings occurring during autoerotic asphyxial activity. This may have legal implications, especially where an insurance policy will pay no money in cases of suicide. Bhardwaj and colleagues[49] report such a case, where a 22-year old married male, a transvestite, committed suicide, and to the uninitiated it appeared to be a case of autoerotic asphyxial death. He was found hanging by his neck in his bedroom, which was locked from the inside. He was suspended by a *lungi* (male wrap-around cloth commonly worn in India) from the ceiling fan hook in his room, with his feet touching the ground. He was dressed in a brassiere, panties, and silver anklets. However, the similarities with an autoerotic scene ended here. There was no evidence of paraphernalia usually associated with autoerotic deaths, such as protective padding between the neck and ligature, pornographic literature, mirrors, photographic equipment, masochism, genital exposure, ejaculation, or attempts to conceal the act. There was no evidence of previous perverse behavior, and investigation disclosed no evidence of previous autoerotic sexual activity, homosexual behavior, or drug abuse. The deceased did not have cordial relations with his wife, who had left him a month earlier, citing impotency as the cause. He had become depressed after this incident. Keeping all facts in mind, the manner of death was given as suicide, rather than accident. The case illustrates the fact that a forensic pathologist has to be very alert in arriving at an opinion in such cases, only after taking all facts into account.

The issue of transvestism is by and large not addressed by civil and criminal codes of most jurisdictions. However, in United States law the *transvestism* term is cited in disability law.

United States

Transvestism and Disability Law

The Americans with Disabilities Act of 1990,[50] Titles I and V, was enacted to provide a clear and comprehensive national mandate for the elimination of discrimination against individuals with disabilities. The Act does not include transvestism as a disability, i.e., persons suffering from transvestism are *not* entitled to the benefits granted by this Act. These titles appear in volume 42 of the United States Code, beginning at section 12101. A detailed enumeration of relevant sections defining disability (and various exclusions) appears in the chapter on voyeurism. Although section 12211 of the United States Code[51] excludes transvestism as a disability, section 12208 is solely and specifically aimed at excluding transvestites. It states[52]:

> For the purposes of this chapter, the term "disabled" or "disability" shall not apply to an individual solely because that individual is a transvestite.

Chapter 126 is entitled "Equal Opportunity For Individuals With Disabilities." Chapter 126 aims to provide relief to persons with disabilities.

REFERENCES

1. Oakley, C., *Sex Change and Dress Deviation*, Morntide, London, 1970.

2. Buhrich, N., McConaghy, N. The discrete syndromes of transvestism and transsexualism. *Arch Sex Behav.* 1977 Nov;**6(6)**:483-95.
3. Prince, V., Bentler, P.M. Survey of 504 cases of transvestism. *Psychol Rep.* 1972 Dec;**31(3)**:903-17.
4. American Psychiatric Association. *Diagnostic and Statistical Manual of Mental Disorders*, 4th ed. Text rev. American Psychiatric Association, Washington DC, 2000.
5. American Psychiatric Association. Diagnostic and Statistical Manual of Mental Disorders, 4th ed. American Psychiatric Association, Washington DC, 1994, page 536-7.
6. American Medical Association. ICD-9-CM 2007 Physician: Physician, International Classification of Diseases : Clinical Modification (AMA Physician ICD-9-CM), 9th Revised edition, American Medical Association Press, Chicago, IL, 2006.
7. World Health Organization. International Statistical Classification of Diseases and Health Related Problems (The) ICD-10, 2nd Edition, WHO, Geneva, 2004.
8. Hamburger, C., Stürup, G.K., Dahl-Iversen, E. Transvestism—Hormonal, Psychiatric and Surgical Treatment. *JAMA.* 1953;**152(5)**:391-6.
9. Docter, R.F., Prince, V. Transvestism: a survey of 1032 cross-dressers. *Arch Sex Behav.* 1997 Dec;**26(6)**:589-605.
10. Stoller, R.J. The term "transvestism". *Arch Gen Psychiatry.* 1971 Mar;**24(3)**:230-7.
11. Bancroft, J., The relationships between gender identity and sexual behavior: Some clinical aspects. In *Gender Differences: Their Ontogeny and Significance*, Ounsted, C., and Taylor, D.C. (eds.), Churchill Livingstone, London, 1972.
12. McConaghy, N., *Sexual Behavior—Problems and Management*, 1st ed. Plenum Press, New York, 1993, Chapter 4 (Transvestism and Transsexualism—Sex identity disorders, pages 143-181).
13. Green, R., Roberts, C.W., Williams, K., Goodman, M., Mixon, A. Specific cross-gender behavior in boyhood and later homosexual orientation. *Br J Psychiatry.* 1987 Jul;**151**:84-8.
14. Person, E.S., Ovesey, L. Homosexual cross-dressers. *J Am Acad Psychoanal.* 1984 Apr;**12(2)**:167-86.
15. Nanda, S. The hijras of India: cultural and individual dimensions of an institutionalized third gender role. *J Homosex.* 1985 Summer;**11(3-4)**:35-54.
16. Kahn, A.P. and Holt, L.H., *The A-Z of Women's Sexuality.* Facts on File Inc, NY, 1990, page 303.
17. Deuteronomy 22:5. The Holy Bible. Authorized King James version. Oxford Univ. Press, New York, 1972.
18. Buhrich, N. Transvestism in history (Brief communication). *J Nerv Ment Dis.* 1977 Jul;**165(1)**:64-6.
19. Kirkwood, G.M., *A Short Guide to Classical Mythology*, Holt, Rinehart and Winston, New York, 1959
20. Apollonius of Rhodes (translator, Rieu E.V.), *The Voyage of the Argo*, Penguin Books, England, 1959 (written originally c. 300 BC).
21. Walsh, F.M., Stahl, C.J. 3rd, Unger HT, Lilienstern OC, Stephens RG 3rd. Autoerotic asphyxial deaths: a medicolegal analysis of forty-three cases. *Leg Med Annu.* 1977:155-82.
22. Karlen, A. *Sexuality and Homosexuality*, Macdonald, London, 1971.
23. Stanford, P., *The Legend of Pope Joan: In Search of the Truth*, Berkley Trade, NY,2000.
24. Bowman, K.M. and Engle, B., Medicolegal aspects of transvestism. *Am J Psychiatry.* 1957; **113**: 583 - 588.
25. Ellis, H., *Eonism and other Supplementary Studies*, Vol. VII, F.A. Davis, Philadelphia, 1928.
26. Ridinger, R.B. Negotiating limits: the legal status of S/M in the United States. *J Homosex.* 2006;**50(2-3)**:189-216.
27. Bullough, V.L. and Bullough, B., *Cross dressing, sex and gender.* University of Pennsylvania Press, Philadelphia, 1993.
28. Bullough, V.L. Transsexualism in history. *Arch Sex Behav.* 1975 Sep;**4(5)**:561-71.
29. Valentine, D. and Kulick, D. Transsexuality, Transvestism, and Transgender, In: Smelser, N.J., Baltes, P.B. (Eds). *International Encyclopedia of the Social & Behavioral Sciences*, Pergamon, 2001, Pp. 15888-93.
30. Bullough, B., Bullough, V. Are transvestites necessarily heterosexual? *Arch Sex Behav.* 1997 Feb;**26(1)**:1-12.
31. Stoller, R.J. *Sex and Gender.* Science House, New York, 1968.
32. Thomas, P.R., DeAlwis, K. Transvestism in a person with learning disabilities presenting with behavioral problems. *J Intellect Disabil Res.* 1995 Oct;**39(Pt 5)**:454-6.
33. Pettit, I., Barr, R. Temporal lobe epilepsy with diaper fetishism and gender dysphoria. *Med J Aust.* 1980 Aug 23;**2(4)**:208-9.

34. Gautier-Smith, P.C. Cerebral dysfunction and disorders of sexual behavior (author's transl) [Article in French]. *Rev Neurol (Paris).* 1980;**136(4)**:311-9.
35. Riley, D.E. Reversible transvestic fetishism in a man with Parkinson's disease treated with selegiline. *Clin Neuropharmacol.* 2002 Jul-Aug;**25(4)**:234-7.
36. Stoller, R.J., The Gender Disorders, in *Sexual Deviation*, 3rd edition, Rosen I., Ed., Oxford University Press, Oxford, 1996, chap. 5.
37. Stoller, R.J. Transvestism in women. *Arch Sex Behav.* 1982 Apr;**11(2)**:99-115.
38. Zucker, K.J., and Blanchard, R., Transvestic Fetishism—Psychopathology and Theory. In "*Sexual Deviance—Theory, Assessment, and Treatment*", 1st ed. Laws, D.R. and O'Donohue, W., (Eds.), The Guilford Press, New York, 1997, chapter 14, pages 253-279.
39. Långström, N., Zucker, K.J. Transvestic fetishism in the general population: prevalence and correlates. *J Sex Marital Ther.* 2005 Mar-Apr;31(2):87-95.
40. Buhrich, N., Beaumont, T. Comparison of transvestism in Australia and America. *Arch Sex Behav.* 1981 Jun;**10(3)**:269-79.
41. Taylor-Buckner, H. The transvestic career path. *Psychiatry.* 1970; **33**: 381-389.
42. Blanchard, R., Hucker, S.J. Age, transvestism, bondage, and concurrent paraphilic activities in 117 fatal cases of autoerotic asphyxia. *Br J Psychiatry.* 1991;**159**:371-7.
43. O'Halloran, R.L., Dietz, P.E. Autoerotic fatalities with power hydraulics. *J Forensic Sci.* 1993 Mar;**38(2)**:359-64.
44. Prince, V., Bentler, P.M. Survey of 504 cases of transvestism. *Psychol Rep.* 1972 Dec;**31(3)**:903-17.
45. Ward, N.G. Successful lithium treatment of transvestism associated with manic-depression. *J Nerv Ment Dis.* 1975 Sep;**161(3)**:204-6.
46. Fishbain, D.A. Buspirone and transvestic fetishism. *J Clin Psychiatry.* 1989 Nov;**50(11)**:436-7.
47. Fedoroff, J.P. Buspirone hydrochloride in the treatment of transvestic fetishism. *J Clin Psychiatry.* 1988 Oct;**49(10)**:408-9.
48. Rubenstein, E.B., Engel, N.L. Successful treatment of transvestic fetishism with sertraline and lithium. *J Clin Psychiatry.* 1996 Feb;**57(2)**:92.
49. Bhardwaj, D.N., Rautji, R., Sharma, R.K., Dogra, T.D. Suicide by a transvestite or sexual asphyxia? A case report. *Med Sci Law.* 2004 Apr;**44(2)**:173-5.
50. Americans with Disabilities Act of 1990 (Pub. L. 101-336).
51. 42 U.S.C. §12211.
52. 42 U.S.C. §12208.

4 Exhibitionism

INTRODUCTION

Exhibitionism is an uncontrollable urge to exhibit one's genitals to an unsuspecting stranger. It is an obsessive-compulsive paraphilic disorder, which typically involves men exposing themselves to women.* According to most surveys, it is the most common of the paraphilias and the behavior most frequently seen by clinicians.[1,2,3] According to Rooth[4] and Kahr,[5] exhibitionism constitutes about one third of all sexual offenses committed. Freeman[6] cites almost similar figures, 20–35%. This is not a consistent finding, though. Different surveys have reported other paraphilias as being most prevalent. Among the mental health facilities in England, it was found by Bancroft to be the second most common sexual deviation.[7] Some surveys show obscene telephone calls to be the most common paraphilia.[8] Yet others show child molestation to be most common.[9] In a review of 3,050 separate magazine and book titles sold in "adults only" pornographic outlets in 1986, the U.S. Commission on Pornography found that as many as 49.9% of the reviewed titles were devoted to the theme of sadomasochism, making it the most common paraphilia (if prevalence of thematic magazines and books is taken to accurately reflect the corresponding prevalence of a particular paraphilia).[10] By and large, the consensus of opinion, however, is that exhibitionism is the *most common* of all paraphilias, comprising about one third of all paraphilias and sex offenses.

Known in slang as "flashers," exhibitionists are a heterogeneous group closely matching the general population in intelligence, education, and vocations.[11] The most common image of an exhibitionist in popular perception is that of a middle-aged man in a dirty raincoat "flashing." Typically, however, exhibitionists are mostly post pubescent males up to the age of 40 who obtain high levels of sexual gratification and excitement from exposing their genitals to females, usually strangers, and who may masturbate at the same time.[2]

DSM-IV-TR[12] assigns code 302.4 to exhibitionism and states the following criteria for diagnosing it:

A. Over a period of at least 6 months, recurrent, intense, sexually arousing fantasies, sexual urges, or behaviors involving the exposure of one's genitals to an unsuspecting stranger.
B. The person has acted on these sexual urges, or the sexual urges or fantasies cause marked distress or interpersonal difficulty.

The phrases "sexual urges" and "unsuspecting stranger" are important, as they would exclude many similar looking acts from the definition. Thus, such acts as public urination (not a sexual urge) and exposure of genitals during mutual sexual intimacy, cabaret dancing, strip acts, medical examinations, dwelling in primitive tribes or in formal nudist colonies (no unsuspecting strangers in these cases) are excluded. Controversies continue to prevail, many for instance, insisting that at least some people in nudist colonies may indeed be suffering from exhibitionism and scopophilia.[13]

Gymnophobia, a fear or anxiety of being seen naked, even in situations where it is socially acceptable, is the logical opposite of exhibitionism. Gymnophobes may experience their fear of

* The term *peiodeiktophilia* is sometimes used specifically for a male displaying an erect penis to unsuspecting females.

nudity before all people, or only certain people. This phobia often arises from a feeling of inadequacy because their bodies are physically inferior, particularly due to comparison with idealized images portrayed in the media. The fear may also stem from anxiety about sexuality in general, or from a persistent feeling of vulnerability associated with the thought that those who have seen the gymnophobe naked will continue to see the gymnophobe as a nude in his mind.

HISTORICAL PERSPECTIVES

Exhibitionism as a disorder was first described in a scientific journal in 1877 by French physician and psychiatrist Charles Lasègue (1809–1883).[14] Although first described in 1877, instances of this could be found in ancient scriptures. The Holy Bible mentions perhaps the very first case of exhibitionism, where a jubilant David engages in this activity.

The incident appears in the Bible like this. When David heard that the Lord had blessed Obed-edom the Gittite, because of the presence of the Ark of the Covenant in his house, he decided to bring it home to the land of Zion. Since this was a festive occasion, David girded himself with a linen ephod (a garment, quite meager in size, commonly worn by priests in ancient Israelite culture), and "danced before the Lord with all his might." This garment was so scanty in size (David was not wearing underwear, either) that when priests approached the altar during religious ceremonies in the temple, they were warned not to ascend the steps of the altar, lest they would see his nakedness. Yet David, clad only in his ephod, leaped and danced so wildly that his wife Michal (daughter of Saul), who was watching from her window, could see his nakedness and despised him for his blatant exhibitionism.

> And it was told king David, saying, The Lord hath blessed the house of Obed-edom, and all that pertaineth unto him, because of the ark of God. So David went and brought up the ark of God from the house of Obed-edom into the city of David with gladness. And it was so, that when they that bare the ark of the Lord had gone six paces, he sacrificed oxen and fatlings. And David danced before the Lord with all his might; and David was girded with a linen ephod. So David and all the house of Israel brought up the ark of the Lord with shouting, and with the sound of the trumpet. And as the ark of the Lord came into the city of David, Michal Saul's daughter looked through a window, and saw king David leaping and dancing before the Lord; and she despised him in her heart.[15]

As soon as David came home, Michal, his wife accused him of exposing himself like a common pervert or flasher, because maidens of the city had also lined the road of the royal procession.

> Then David returned to bless his household. And Michal the daughter of Saul came out to meet David, and said, How glorious was the king of Israel today, who uncovered himself today in the eyes of the handmaids of his servants, as one of the vain fellows shamelessly uncovereth himself.[16]

However, David, like a true exhibitionist, did not take her remarks kindly, and never again had sexual relations with her, so Michal remained childless.

Jehovah also objected to the frequent acts of exhibitionism which accompanied the pagan ceremonies. He wanted to be sure that his priests were always properly attired and that no exposure of the genitals would be possible as it was with the pagan priests. In Biblical times, a short skirt was the usual attire for a Hebrew priest, and it was possible that if the priest was careless, his genitals would become visible to others. In Exodus, God specifically prohibits the priests from engaging in this form of exhibitionism.

> Neither shalt thou go up by steps unto mine altar, that thy nakedness be not discovered thereon.[17]

FIGURE 4.1 The famous Sheela na Gig at Kilpeck, England.

When the Israelites later worshipped in a tent, where there were no steps at the entrance, God gave specific instructions for the priests to properly cover themselves, so no exhibitionistic acts could occur.

> And thou shalt make them linen breeches to cover their nakedness; from the loins even unto the thighs they shall reach.[18]

Medieval Examples

Bold examples of female exhibitionism can be seen in Sheela-na-Gigs, or simply Sheelas, figurative carvings of naked women displaying exaggerated vulvas, found on churches, castles, and other buildings, particularly in Ireland and Britain dating from the 12th century. Among the explanations for these rather odd carvings is that they served as a religious warning against the sins of the flesh.[19] It is possible that they were influenced by cases of female exhibitionism occurring in those times (Figure 4.1).

The first reported case (in English law) occurred in 1663 and involved a celebrity. Sir Charles Sedley (1639–1701), English wit and dramatist, and an intimate of King Charles II engaged in a drinking spree at The Cock, a local tavern. He and two companions became drunk, stripped off their clothes, climbed a balcony overlooking Covent Garden, and hurled both profanities and bottles filled with an "offensive liquor"—that is, urine—at the public below. A minor riot ensued, ultimately resulting in the arrest and prosecution of Sedley. He was fined 2000 marks, committed without bail for a week, and bound to his good behavior for a year, on his confession of information against him, for showing himself naked on a balcony, and throwing down bottles containing urine.[20] However, as Rooth[4] explains, this incident should more properly be regarded as an example of aristocratic bravado than of exhibitionism in the medical sense.

After the scientific description of exhibitionism by Lasègue in the modern era, early scientific studies were published by East[21] and Ellis[22] and have continued to appear at regular intervals since then.

BEHAVIORS MIMICKING EXHIBITIONISM

The following behaviors mimic exhibitionism in many ways, although not all strictly meet the DSM-IV-TR criteria for exhibitionism. These behaviors must be differentiated from exhibitionism.

ANASYRMA

Anasyrma or "the gesture of lifting up the skirt or kilt" is not truly an exhibitionistic act, as it is *not* associated with arousal of the person exhibiting genitals. It is rather a ritual exposing of one's genitals, used in connection with certain religious rituals, eroticism, and lewd jokes. The practice can be traced to Greek mythology, where Iambe, goddess of verse, made Demeter smile when she (Demeter) was mourning the loss of her daughter, Persephone. Iambe accomplished this by creating an elaborate ritualized exhibition of herself. She exposed herself completely, and Demeter could not help but be amused by her brazen display. This act of humor and courage lifted Demeter from her grief, and the Earth became fertile once more. In some versions, a similar act is ascribed to Baubo, an old woman.

CANDAULISM

In this variation of exhibitionism, persons do not exhibit themselves but their spouses—usually a male exhibiting his wife. Known as *candaulism* or *candaulesism*, it involves getting sadomasochistic pleasure when the husband exposes his wife, or pictures of her, to other voyeurist people.[23] The term derives its name from Candaules, king of the ancient kingdom of Lydia from 735 to 718 BC, who was so proud of the beauty of his wife, and so much did he want to impress others, that he made a plot to show his unaware naked wife to his bodyguard Gyges of Lydia. Discovering Gyges while he was watching her naked, Candaules' wife obviously became enraged and ordered him to choose between killing himself or her husband in order to repair the vicious mischief. Gyges chose to kill the king. The queen married Gyges subsequently and fathered the Mermnad Dynasty.

Often the husband takes this paraphilia to the extreme and enjoys other people having sex with his wife. This practice can take the form of swinging, in which husbands exchange wives for sexual intercourse and watch each other. In certain cases the relation evolves into a stable union of three persons, known as *troilism*.

MOONING

Mooning, not truly an act of exhibitionism (it does not meet DSM-IV-TR criteria and is not associated with masturbation usually), nevertheless can result in legal consequences primarily aimed at exhibitionists. Mooning, an act to express protest, scorn, disrespect, or provocation, involves displaying one's bare buttocks by removing clothing, e.g., by lowering the back side of one's trousers and underpants, usually bending over. Mooning may also be done for shock value or fun. The practice is known as "shooting a moon. " While in flashing, genitals are displayed; in mooning, buttocks are displayed.

NUDISM

Nudism or naturism —practicing, advocating and defending social nudity in private and public spaces—is not true exhibitionism. In Germany, it is known as Freikörperkultur (free body culture). Nudism endorses a naturistic approach to sports and community living.

Nudists believe that the naked human body is to be accepted, respected, cherished, and enjoyed. They believe it is not inherently shameful, corrupting, degrading, or dangerous. They reject the view that being naked with other people is morally wrong, indecent, erotic, or pornographic. They argue that nakedness is a healthy, natural state. However, nudism may only be practiced at places especially earmarked for this activity. Otherwise, it may attract the same legal consequences as those meant for exhibitionists.

Streaking

Streaking —the non-sexual act of taking off one's clothes and running naked through a public place—is also not true exhibitionism for similar reasons as above. Yet it may be pertinent to discuss this phenomenon here as it shares many characteristics with exhibitionism. Also in many jurisdictions both offenses are covered by the same laws. However, the important difference between the two is that while in exhibitionism the intent is generally to shock or traumatize the victim, in streaking it is generally to make a public statement.

Streaking in India, especially by women, is considered a peculiar phenomenon, given that women in India traditionally are very conservative, and go about fully clothed, sometimes even covering their face. Two most notable instances of streaking by women in India are by the film star Protima Bedi in 1974 and by Pooja Chauhan in 2007. While Protima Bedi, who ran completely naked on Juhu Beach, Mumbai, ostensibly did it as a publicity stunt, Pooja Chauhan, who walked semi-naked on the streets of Rajkot, Gujarat, did it to bring the attention of authorities to the ill treatment she was getting from her husband and in-laws.[24]

Zoophilic Exhibitionism

McNally and Lukach describe a curious case of zoophilic exhibitionism (exposure of genitals in front of animals with concomitant masturbation), zoophilic frotteurism (rubbing one's genitals on the furs of live animals), and zoophilic voyeurism (peeping through windows to gaze at animals), all practiced by one person.[25] The patient, whom they refer to as one Mr. Z, was a 33-year old white, mildly mentally retarded man who was referred to them for behavioral treatment of "compulsive sexually deviant behavior." He had been apprehended by police when a neighbor discovered him in her backyard masturbating in front of her dog. He had also been arrested the previous year when he broke into another neighbor's house to masturbate in front of the neighbor's two dogs. Mr Z's parents had separated 4 months after his birth. He was the only child of an alcoholic father and an apparently schizophrenic mother who also had epilepsy. His paraphilic behavior began at the age of 4 when a 4-year old male cousin told him that it was "fun" to rub one's penis on the fur of a dog's back.

When he was 20-years old, Mr. Z was caught rubbing his penis on the back of his neighbor's dog. This episode of zoophilic frotteurism resulted in a brief psychiatric hospitalization during which another male patient taught him to masturbate. Upon his discharge from the hospital, he ceased frotteurism and began masturbating in front of dogs (zoophilic exhibitionism). He used food to attract stray dogs or to lure them from the backyards of his neighborhood. If his grandmother was not home, Mr. Z would take the dog to his house. Otherwise, he would lure the dog to a nearby wooded area or simply expose himself to the dog without removing it from its backyard. He masturbated to orgasm while the dog watched, and usually persuaded it to lick his penis after he ejaculated. He then released it without returning it to its owner. Interestingly, he never attempted sexual intercourse with a dog, nor did he fantasize about doing so. He, however, did engage in zoophilic voyeurism (peeping through windows to gaze at dogs). He was uncertain about how the dogs felt about watching him masturbate, but suspected that they probably enjoyed it. He based this conclusion on an incident in which a dog began to rub its penis on his leg after having watching him masturbate for a few minutes. His paraphilia was responsive to a behavioral program comprising of masturbatory satiation, covert sensitization, and stimulus control procedures.

EXHIBITIONISM OR INDECENT EXPOSURE?

The terms *exhibitionism* and *indecent exposure* are used quite interchangeably, especially in lay literature and media. Activities like strip shows, mothers feeding their children in public, women wearing highly revealing clothes in full view of public, nude sunbathing on beaches and swimming, etc. have been termed as both acts of *exhibitionism* and *indecent exposure* in the lay media. It is important to appreciate that an important difference exists between the two. While exhibitionism is *pathological*, indecent exposure is not. When a professional girl is performing a strip-tease, she may be committing an indecent exposure, but she is certainly not an exhibitionist. Exhibitionism is a pathological condition, where—as DSM-IV-TR criteria suggest—the sufferer is having recurrent, intense, sexually arousing fantasies, sexual urges, or behaviors involving the exposure of one's genitals to an unsuspecting stranger. Furthermore, these urges must cause him or her marked distress or interpersonal difficulty. A striptease dancer, a woman wearing highly revealing clothes in public, or a nude sunbather may not necessarily be acting from "recurrent, intense, sexually arousing fantasies or sexual urges." Such acts may at best be termed of indecent exposure.

Instances of mothers nursing babies in public may not even be termed as acts of indecent exposure, as many jurisdictions now allow mothers to do so publicly. Out of concern that not enough women are breast-feeding, a growing number of nations and states are passing protective laws and policies. Today 38 U.S. states give women the explicit right to nurse in public, and 23 states exempt it from public-indecency laws.[26] A minor controversy arose in 2007, when actress Maggie Gyllenhaal visited a public park in New York and breast-fed her 8 month old daughter. Many newspapers, magazines, and other media outlets variously reported it as indecent exposure and even exhibitionism. This activity should not have been labeled either way, although admittedly it is a controversial area, and the last word on this has not been said.

ETIOLOGY

COURTSHIP DISORDER THEORY

A number of paraphilias, including exhibitionism, are explained quite neatly by the so-called courtship disorder theory, first propounded by Freund, Scher, and Hucker.[27,28] These paraphilias are voyeurism, exhibitionism, frotteurism, toucherism, obscene telephone calling, and biastophilia (an erotic preference for coercing a female stranger, by threats or physical force, to submit to intercourse or carry out fellatio, but without a preference for inflicting physical pain or injury on the victim).

The theory is based on some very sound empirical grounds. Firstly, two or more of the six paraphilias mentioned above tend to occur together in many offenders, indicating that they may have a common etiology. Among the several examples of concurrence available in literature, exhibitionism, toucherism, and frotteurism have been seen to occur together;[29,30] voyeurism, exhibitionism, and rape have been seen to occur concomitantly;[31] and among subjects arrested for indecent exposure, it has been found that about 12% have committed other sexual offenses as well, particularly rape.[32] About one in ten of all exhibitionists have attempted or seriously contemplated rape.[33] A number of other clinical reports mention the occurrence of these paraphilias together.[34,35]

The second argument in favor of courtship disorder theory is equally—if not more—convincing. And this argument has been copiously borrowed from ethology. Freund and his colleagues noted that the courtship ritual of many birds occurs in four main stages: (i) search for a partner, (ii) pretactile interaction, (iii) tactile interaction, and finally (iv) copulation or genital union (please see Table 4.1).

TABLE 4.1
Courtship Stages and Corresponding Normal and Paraphilic Behaviors

	Normal courtship stage	Normal behavior	Abnormal (paraphilic) behavior
Pre-contact stage of courtship	1. Search for a partner	A suitable partner is searched for and selected by viewing a number of prospective partners	Voyeurism. The voyeur spends all energies and attains orgasm at this stage. He masturbates while he surreptitiously views his partner.
	2. Pretactile interaction	Looking, smiling, posturing, and talking to a prospective partner	Exhibitionism. The exhibitionist masturbates while showing his genital organs, and an obscene telephone caller masturbates while (talking to) his prospective partner. The orgasm is attained. The other three stages are short-circuited.
Contact stage of courtship	3. Tactile interaction	Petting, touching, kissing	A toucher grabs the intimate parts of his prospective partner (breasts) and a frotteur rubs his penis against buttocks, etc., achieving orgasm.
	4. Genital union	Normal penile–vaginal copulation	A biastophile or preferential rapist prefers to rape his prospective partner immediately and achieve orgasm. He short-circuits all the previous three stages.

In the first stage, the bird looks for a prospective mate. When a prospective mate has been located, the second stage starts in which the bird displays its most attractive parts. The male peacock, for example, displays its resplendently phallic tail. These two are the so-called "pre-contact stages" of courtship. The third and fourth stages are the "contact stages" of courtship. In the third stage, when the male bird is confident that its partner is interested, it engages in tactile interaction. This is finally climaxed in genital union. Similar behaviors are seen in many other animal species such as baboons, chimpanzees, gorillas, and orangutans.[36]

Human courtship ritual tends to follow exactly the same pattern, and if it is not as explicitly seen as in birds and other animal species, it is only because of overwhelming cultural and societal influences.

A normal human being tends to spend roughly equal amounts of time, resources, and energy in each of these four courtship stages. However, in paraphiliacs, for some reason, almost all the energy is spent in only one stage, and all the other three stages tend to get "short-circuited."

This gives rise to "pre-contact paraphilias " and "contact paraphilias " corresponding to "pre-contact" and "contact" stages of courtship. Thus a voyeur spends all his energy in locating a partner, short-circuiting the other three stages (seeing surreptitiously and masturbating); an exhibitionist and obscene telephone caller spends his energies in pretactile interaction; a frotteur in tactile interaction; and a compulsive rapist in genital union. The other three stages in all these paraphiliacs are either completely absent or present only in very vestigial amounts (Table 4.1).

The beauty of this theory is that it appeals rather intuitively, since it relates in a neat and orderly way normal and abnormal sexual behavior. Interestingly, Money's concept of allurement paraphilias echoes the same philosophy (please see Money's classification of paraphilias in Chapter 1).

Biological Factors

Biological factors, which appear so prominent in other paraphilias such as pedophilia and fetishism, are doubtful as etiological factors of exhibitionism. Tkachenko studied 61 men showing signs of exhibitionism and found that biological causes were doubtful as etiological factors.[37] However, there is some evidence that monoamines, especially dopamine, may play a part in exhibitionism. Quinn and associates[38] describe two interesting cases which lend support to this view. In the first case, they treated a patient suffering from Parkinson's disease with Sinemet (carbidopa/levodopa —a metabolic precursor of dopamine) and bromocriptine (a dopamine receptor agonist). One month later, the patient felt a compulsion to undress and exhibit in public, but was able to resist it. He also manifested overt signs of masochism, which he could not control. In the second case, a 47-year old patient of Parkinsonism was prescribed pergolide (a direct dopamine agonist). Soon afterward he started showing exhibitionistic tendencies. On discontinuing pergolide, his urges subsided. (For full description of both these cases, please see chapter on sexual masochism.)

Conditioning

McGuire and colleagues[39] propose that exhibitionism can be explained by conditioning (please see chapter 1 for details of classical and operant conditioning). To illustrate their theory, they cite the case of two of their patients who became exhibitionistic through conditioning. The patients reported separately that they had on one occasion been urinating in semi-public places when they were surprised by passing women. At the time each had felt embarrassed and left hurriedly. It was only later that the sexual significance of the encounter was appreciated, and each of them had then masturbated frequently to the memory of the incident till the thought of self-exposure had acquired, by conditioning, such strong sexual stimulus value that each had in the end taken to public exposure. Neither patient had had the slightest interest in such behavior prior to the incident.

Psychoanalytical Theories

Psychoanalysts have advanced different reasons for exhibitionism. According to the most common explanation, exhibitionism is a crude attempt to alleviate overwhelming fears of castration.[40] In other words, it is a reaction to unresolved castration anxiety which all male children experience during their psychosexual growth (for more on castration anxiety, please see introductory chapter). By displaying his sexual organs, he announces to the world—with a visual proof—that he has not been castrated by his father, that he has not been humiliated, and that he still retains his virility. This approach, however, does not explain genital exhibitionism in women easily. Zavitzianos,[41] however, asserts that female exhibitionists, by revealing their "mutilated" genitalia, convey the threat of castration to each male viewer.

Psychoanalysts have also argued that some people who were sexually victimized in childhood tend to sexualize the trauma of fear and violence through publicly exposing themselves, fantasizing, and masturbating about the encounters. They seek attention to overcome feelings of low self-esteem, shame, and inadequacy. Exposing genitals thus becomes a sexualized form of countershame that tends to create feelings of power, control, and sexual arousal.[42]

According to another psychoanalytical theory, subconscious homosexuality may act as a motive in many exhibitionists. It has been suggested that the exhibitionist is basically a homosexual, albeit in some cases an "unconscious homosexual."[43] Like most psychoanalytic postulates, this hypothesis is difficult to test. However, from this hypothesis, one might expect that homosexual behavior would exist with some preponderance in exhibitionists and vice versa. Interestingly, many males with homoerotic preferences do expose in public places, albeit to other males, and share with heterosexual exhibitionists the practice of outdoor masturbation with no one around. It is also significant that both homosexual males and exhibitionists often display automonosexualism, a phenomenon in which a person is sexually excited to his own body or by simply being nude.

As is dictated by the courtship disorder theory, exhibitionism and telephone scatologia appear to co-exist in some offenders. For some contributory factors, responsible for both these conditions, please refer to the chapter on telephone scatologia.

CLASSIFICATION

All cases of exhibitionism that have been described in the literature seem to fall in two broad groups—pure exhibitionists and exhibitionistic criminals. Kenworthy and Bloem[44] have mentioned this classification already, without formally mentioning the classes. However, based on the *theory of paraphilic equivalence,* proposed in this book (please see chapter on frotteurism), more classes do seem to exist in society, and it is hypothesized that they will be discovered and described as we learn more about this paraphilia.

The following classification of exhibitionists is proposed to include all reported cases, as well as those that have been extrapolated from the *theory of paraphilic equivalence.* In line with the classification of other paraphilias, it groups all exhibitionists along a continuum, with the most innocuous at one end and the most dangerous at the other.

Class I Exhibitionists: Fantasizing Exhibitionists

These people fantasize about exhibiting their genitals to unsuspecting persons, but are too timid to actually carry out their fantasies. They tend to remain happy merely with their exhibitionistic fantasies. They may turn to zoophilic exhibitionism (please see chapter on zoophilia) to fulfill their fantasies, since it apparently is a safer activity.

Class II Exhibitionists: Pure Exhibitionists

These people are cowardly and docile, and they are content with just showing off their genitals from a distance and masturbating. They do not touch their victims or actually do them any harm.

Class III Exhibitionists: Exhibitionistic Criminals

These offenders are primarily exhibitionists, but they also engage in other sexual crimes, especially pedophilia and child molesting. Upon finding a child alone, their sexual behavior may start with exhibitionism, but may progress to child molestation. These are more dangerous to the society and obviously need more attention.

Class IV Exhibitionists: Exclusive Exhibitionists

These offenders cannot form normal romantic relationships with persons of the opposite sex and cannot engage in normal sexual intercourse. For them, exhibitionism is the *sole* outlet for sexual gratification. Such exhibitionists do not seem to have been reported in literature so far, but based on the *theory of paraphilic equivalence,* it can be predicted that these exhibitionists do exist in society and they will be reported sometime in the future. Behaviorally, they lie on the extreme end of the paraphilic continuum since they cannot form normal romantic relationships with other individuals. However, in a legal sense, class III exhibitionists may be more dangerous as they also resort to criminal activities.

PREVALENCE

In 1996, Långström and Seto randomly selected 2,450 individuals between the ages of 18 and 60 years from the general population of Sweden, and interviewed them in a broad survey of sexuality and health. A total of 76 respondents (3.1%) reported at least one incident of being sexually aroused by exposing their genitals to a stranger.[45]

Exhibitionism is seen among females, too. Fedoroff and colleagues studied the clinical records (of the first author) of 15 years, and identified individuals referred to them for suspected paraphilic disorders. The clinics were located in different countries (Canada, the United States, and Great

Britain), and all were affiliated with universities. A total of 132 paraphilics were identified, of which 14 (11%) were women.[46] Within the total female sample, the most common diagnoses were pedophilia (36%), sexual sadism (29%), and exhibitionism (29%). The authors, however, emphasize that this is not a study into the frequency or prevalence of paraphilias in the female population, nor can the findings be used to draw such inferences.

Hidden desires of showing oneself naked to others may be common. Crépault and Couture[47] interviewed 94 men about their erotic fantasies occurring during heterosexual activity. The majority of these men were married, and their average duration of cohabitation with a woman was 6.5 years. From that group, 30.9% reported harboring erotic fantasies about scenes where they had sexual activity in a public place.

OFFENDER CHARACTERISTICS

Exhibitionists do not form a homogenous population, and in every parameter studied, be it personality structure, attitude to women, erotic gratification from the act, or other deviant behavior, there is no single unifying characteristic which is always to be found in exhibitionists.[3] Radzinowicz,[48] however, found some common characteristics. According to him 80% of exhibitionists were first offenders. The other 20% had been convicted of previous sexual offenses, but 78% of these offenses were also for indecent exposure. This seems to indicate that there is a high rate of recidivism in exhibitionists. Most exhibitionists are non-violent, and as many as 50% of their victims are under 16 years of age. Sexual assault generally does not occur; if it does take place, it is of a minor nature and no physical injury is done to the child.[49]

Rooth classifies all exhibitionists into two main categories based on their personality characteristics—*primary* and *secondary*.[4] The great majority of cases fall into the category of primary exhibitionism. These are committed by persons who are of good character and apparently normal personality. This group appears to coincide well with Radzinowicz's "first offenders." In a few cases, the exhibitionism is secondary to a major mental disorder such as a psychotic illness or dementia; these are the cases of so-called secondary exhibitionism.

It is well-known that exhibitionism and voyeurism often co-exist. Paraphilic themes between these two disorders may change from time to time. Just like the change between sadism and masochism, the switch between exhibitionism and voyeurism is also quite common and has been known for some time.[50]

ONSET

The onset usually occurs before age 18, although it can begin at a later age. Few arrests are made in the older age groups, which may suggest that the condition becomes less severe after the age of 40.[12]

ASSOCIATION WITH GILLES DE LA TOURETTE'S SYNDROME

Exhibitionism is also sometimes seen in patients of Gilles de la Tourette's syndrome. Comings and Comings[51] describe a 32-year old man with Gilles de la Tourette's syndrome whose most severe symptom was exhibitionism. Treatment with low doses of haloperidol eliminated all exhibitionistic urges. This patient's oldest son had multiple tics, and his nephew had Tourette's syndrome with mild exhibitionism. The authors suggest that all patients with compulsive-type exhibitionism should be carefully questioned about symptoms of Tourette's syndrome and, if positive, be given a trial regimen of haloperidol. Even patients showing no associated symptoms of Tourette's syndrome respond favorably to haloperidol.

Family Background

Saunders and colleagues[52] divided a group of male adolescent sexual offenders into three groups: Courtship Disorders (Exhibitionism, Toucherism, and Obscene Phone Calls), Sexual Assaults, and Pedophilic Offenses. Group I offenders (Courtship Disorders) tended to come from a less disorganized family background, were better adjusted to school and in the community, and were seen by clinicians as less seriously disturbed than the adolescents in the other two groups. In addition, these adolescents did not experience the offense as a sexual act.

Female Exhibitionists

Exhibitionists are primarily male, although there are a few reports of female exhibitionists too.[40,53,54,55] Hermann and Schroder[56] describe the case of genital exhibitionism in a woman, whose behavior perhaps resulted from her schizophrenic psychosis. Zavitzianos[41] describes the case of an adolescent girl who briefly engaged in exhibitionistic activity. Grob[40] describes a very interesting case of a 43-year old divorced female, whom he calls M. She had an emotionally deprived and manipulated childhood and gradually came to feel rejected. Two years before she saw her psychiatrist, she had been dismissed from a prominent position in a male-dominated profession, where she had received much public attention. She was unable to find a similar job. Six months before her first visit, M. began a romantic liaison with a male co-worker, who would sometimes give her as many as "50 orgasms in a single night." Shortly after the onset of this relationship, she began to engage in exhibitionistic behavior. Her first act of exhibitionism was when she was engaged in solitary nude sunbathing, and a low-flying aircraft began circling over her. She realized that instead of feeling embarrassed and running for cover, she became tremendously excited and aroused. Having experienced the joy of exhibitionism, she now actively began seeking people to whom she could expose. She would go out driving, looking for large trucks, and would drive alongside them. If there were no other cars in the immediate area, she would disrobe from an easily removable garment, first revealing her breasts, and then, if the evoked response was appreciative, exposing her genital area. These acts of flashing occurred preferentially at night and during weekends. On an average weekend, she would drive 600 miles in pursuit of such adventures, and when she did find a suitable truck, it was not uncommon for her to spend as much as 30 minutes with it, playing a cat-and-mouse exhibitionistic teasing game, before suddenly turning off on an exit ramp where trucks were not permitted. She reported marked sexual arousal and occasional orgasm during these exhibitionistic ventures.

Exhibitionism and Pedophilia

Exhibitionistic behavior can often be focused on children, usually girls. It has been suggested that exhibitionists may share some characteristics with pedophiles, in that at least some of them respond erotically to physically immature children.[57] In fact, it may be difficult in practice to distinguish the pedophile from the exhibitionist. While the pedophile is interested in physical contact with the child, the exhibitionist only wants to be seen, with no physical contact.[58] Even those exhibitionists who appear to prefer mature females do act out with female children. It is, however, not clearly known whether these exhibitionists respond erotically to the body shape of the female child more than normal males do or to some other facet of the child's behavior.

Tichý[59] conducted phallometric (for details of phallometry, please see chapter 1) tests on 50 known pedophilic exhibitionists (offenders who committed exhibitionistic activities in the presence of girls under 12 years). The results were compared with those obtained from fifty healthy male volunteers of similar age and social background. It was found that the men in the control group responded more frequently and more markedly by positive vasomotor reactions to adult heterosexual objects than subjects who committed pedophile exhibitionist offenses. The latter reacted significantly more often to child objects of both sexes.

MANAGEMENT

Management of exhibitionism has traditionally included medications and psychotherapy such as group therapy. Rich and Ovsiew[60] describe the case of a patient with Huntington's disease and exhibitionism, whom they treated successfully with the gonadotropin-releasing hormone agonist, leuprolide acetate. The treatment resulted in the elimination of his deviant sexual behavior with few side effects. They suggest that this regimen may be a safe and effective pharmacological treatment for exhibitionism and also of other paraphilias. Selective serotonin reuptake inhibitors such as fluvoxamine (Luvox, Faverin)[61] and paroxetine (Seroxat, Paxil)[62] have also been found useful in its management. Rösler and Witztum[63] found that long-acting GnRH analogues, together with psychotherapy, are highly effective in controlling exhibitionism (also in controlling pedophilia and voyeurism). They feel that this forms the most promising mode of therapy of exhibitionism in this millennium.

LEGAL ASPECTS

Australia

The Northern Territory

The Criminal Code of the Northern Territory is a comprehensive document comprising of 444 sections divided into 11 parts. Part V entitled "Acts Injurious to the Public in General" is further subdivided into four divisions. Of these, Division 2 entitled "Offenses Against Morality" (sections 125A through 140) deals with most sexual offenses. Section 133 makes exhibitionism an offense and provides a punishment of 2 years. It states:

> **Section 133—Gross indecency in public**
> Any person who in public and in a public place knowingly commits any act of gross indecency is guilty of a crime and is liable to imprisonment for 2 years.

Queensland

Queensland criminal law is governed by Criminal Code 1899. It is divided into 80 chapters. Many sexual offenses are defined in chapter 22, entitled "Offenses against Morality." It includes sections 207A through 229B. Section 227 defines indecent acts, which includes exhibitionism. It states:

> **Section 227—Indecent acts**
> (1) Any person who—
> (a) willfully and without lawful excuse does any indecent act in any place to which the public are permitted to have access, whether on payment of a charge for admission or not; or
> (b) willfully does any indecent act in any place with intent to insult or offend any person;
> is guilty of a misdemeanor, and is liable to imprisonment for 2 years.
> (2) The offender may be arrested without warrant.
> (3) Subsection (1) does not apply to a person who does an indecent act under the authority of an adult entertainment permit.

Canada

The Criminal Code of Canada is a very comprehensive document containing 849 sections divided in 28 parts. Of these, Part V (s150–s182) deals with sexual offenses, public morals, and disorderly conduct. According to section 173 of the Criminal Code of Canada,[64] exhibitionism is an offense. Section 174 bans nudity in public places, which also can apply to exhibitionists.

Indecent acts

173. (1) Every one who willfully does an indecent act

(a) in a public place in the presence of one or more persons, or

(b) in any place, with intent thereby to insult or offend any person, is guilty of an offense punishable on summary conviction.

Exposure

(2) Every person who, in any place, for a sexual purpose, exposes his or her genital organs to a person who is under the age of 14 years is guilty of an offense punishable on summary conviction.

Nudity

174. (1) Every one who, without lawful excuse,

(a) is nude in a public place, or

(b) is nude and exposed to public view while on private property, whether or not the property is his own, is guilty of an offense punishable on summary conviction.

Nude

(2) For the purposes of this section, a person is nude who is so clad as to offend against public decency or order.

Consent of Attorney General

(3) No proceedings shall be commenced under this section without the consent of the Attorney General.

As is common Canadian practice, Parliament leaves the exact definition of these terms up to courts to decide. Various provincial courts have decided that simple nude sunbathing is not indecent exposure and that streaking is not prohibited under the law. However, two places which despite seemingly being private places could be construed as public places are (i) the inside of a car if it is viewable from the street and (ii) the doorway of a home. Thus anybody exhibiting his genitals standing at the doorway of his home or in his car may be prosecuted under the above sections.

Section 174 prohibits being "so clad as to offend against public decency or order" while exposed to public view. Courts have decided that nude swimming is not within the range of this law. This section seems to have been used mainly against nude and semi-nude performances in commercial establishments.

CHINA

According to the Criminal Law of the People's Republic of China (adopted at the Second Session of the Fifth National People's Congress on July 1, 1979, and Revised at the Fifth Session of the Eighth National People's Congress on March 14, 1997), most crimes of a sexual nature are covered in chapter IV, entitled "Crimes of Infringement upon Citizens' Rights and Democratic Rights." This chapter includes articles 232 through 262. Article 237 of this Code includes the crimes of both exhibitionism and frotteurism. It states:

Article 237

Whoever acts indecently against or insults a woman by violence, coercion or any other forcible means shall be sentenced to fixed-term imprisonment of not more than 5 years or criminal detention.

Whoever gathers a number of people to commit the crime mentioned in the preceding paragraph or commits the crime before the public in a public place shall be sentenced to fixed-term imprisonment of not less than 5 years.

Whoever acts indecently against a child shall be given a heavier punishment in accordance with the provisions of the preceding two paragraphs.

Germany

Under section 183 of The German Criminal Code (Strafgesetzbuch, StGB), exhibitionistic acts are punishable. Section 183 entitled "Exhibitionist Acts " states:[65]

(1) A man who annoys another person by an exhibitionist act shall be punished with imprisonment for not more than one year or a fine.
(2) The act shall only be prosecuted upon complaint, unless the prosecuting authority considers ex officio that it is required to enter the case because of the special public interest therein.
(3) The court may suspend the execution of imprisonment and impose probation if it can be expected that the perpetrator will only cease to commit exhibitionist acts after lengthy curative treatment.
(4) Subsection (3) shall also apply if a man or a woman is punished because of an exhibitionist act:
   1. under another provision, which is punishable by a maximum term of imprisonment of no more than one year; or
   2. under Sections 174, subsection (2), no. 1, or 176, subsection (3), no. 1.

German law on exhibitionism is unique in the sense that it treats the act more as a psychiatric disease than as a criminal act, and in as much as this, this law appears far more advanced. It clearly states that if the offender can be cured after a treatment, the court may suspend imprisonment. Sections 174 (2) and 176 (3), as mentioned in the last clause above, refer to committing sexual acts in front of a ward or child. For details of these sections, please refer to the chapter on pedophilia.

Hungary

The Hungarian Criminal Code of 1978 is a comprehensive document comprising of 368 sections divided into 20 chapters.[66] Of these, Chapter XIV (sections 192–210) dealing with "Crimes Against Marriage, Family, Youth and Sexual Morals" mentions most crimes of a sexual nature. Exhibitionism is a misdemeanor attracting a punishment of up to 2 years. Section 208 dealing exhibitionism states:

Obscenity
Section 208
A person who exposes himself before another person in an indecent way for the satisfaction of his or her sexual desire, commits a misdemeanor, and shall be punishable with imprisonment of up to 2 years, labor in the public interest, or a fine.

Iceland

According to the Article 209 of the General Penal Code of Iceland, "Any person who, through lewd conduct, offends people's sense of decency or causes a public scandal, shall be imprisoned for up to 4 years, or shall be sentenced to up to six months' imprisonment or a fine if the offense is minor."

Since "lewd conduct" that "offends people's sense of decency or causes a public scandal" would include both exhibitionism as well as frotteurism, the latter would also be covered under the same law.

India

In India, there is no explicit law on mentioning the world "exhibitionism " in its statutes. However, exhibitionists may be prosecuted under Section 509 of the Indian Penal Code (IPC).[67] It states:

> ***509. Word, gesture or act intended to insult the modesty of a woman***
> Whoever, intending to insult the modesty of any woman, utters any word, makes any sound or gesture, or exhibits any object, intending that such word or sound shall be heard, or that such gesture or object shall be seen, by such woman, or intrudes upon the privacy of such woman, shall be punished with simple imprisonment for a term which may extend to one year, or with fine, or with both.

As can be easily appreciated, this section encompasses the crimes of both exhibitionism and voyeurism (the relevant phrase in the section reads *intrudes upon the privacy of such woman*). The punishment is simple imprisonment for a term up to one year or with fine or both.

Since the title of the section suggests that the offense *must* be committed with an intention to insult the modesty of a *woman*, prosecution may face difficulties especially since (i) they have to prove the *intent* of the offending exhibitionist, and (ii) the victim *must* be a woman. Thus it is conceivable that the prosecution would run into problems if the exhibitionist acted from a compulsive behavior (which would make it difficult to prove intent) or if he did this act before a group of males (say, a pedophile exhibitionist exposing his genitals before a group of male children). It would also be difficult to prosecute a female exhibitionist under this section.

Sections of the Indian Penal Code which take care of these problems, and could be invoked to punish exhibitionists in above circumstances, are 268, 294 and 290. Section 268 states:

> ***268. Public nuisance***
> A person is guilty of a public nuisance who does any act or is guilty of an illegal omission which causes any common injury, danger or annoyance to the public or to the people in general who dwell or occupy property in the vicinity, or which must necessarily cause injury, obstruction, danger or annoyance to persons who may have occasion to use any public right.
>
> A common nuisance is not excused on the ground that it causes some convenience or advantage.

A careful perusal of the wordings suggests that categories of exhibitionists omitted under Section 509 (compulsive behaviors, displaying genitals before males and female exhibitionists) are covered under this section.

Indian law has been very circumspect in this regard and has framed Section 290, which covers almost every conceivable exhibitionistic act, even those behaviors which may not be covered in the previous 2 sections. Section 290 states:

> ***290. Punishment for public nuisance in cases not otherwise provided for***
> Whoever commits a public nuisance in any case not otherwise punishable by this Code, shall be punished with fine which may extend to 200 rupees.

Finally there is Section 294, which not only covers exhibitionism, but also other related acts such as coprolalia (using obscene language or writing). Section 294 states:

> ***294. Obscene acts and songs***
> Whoever, to the annoyance of others—
> (a) does any obscene act in any public place, or
> (b) sings, recites or utters any obscene song, ballad or words, in or near any public place, shall be punished with imprisonment of either description for a term which may extend to 3 months, or with fine, or with both.

It is conceivable that genital exhibitionism would be covered by clause (a) of this section. The maximum punishment is 3 months, or fine, or both. Clause (b) would cover cases of coprolalia.

Japan

According to the Penal Code of Japan, exhibitionism is punishable under Article 174. It states:[68]

> ***Article 174. (Public Indecency)***
> A person who commits an indecent act in public shall be punished by imprisonment with work for not more than 6 months, a fine of not more than 300,000 yen, misdemeanor imprisonment without work or a petty fine.

This article is currently most often used against sleazy strip-tease theaters, but is also commonly used to deal with paraphilic behaviors such as flashing and voyeurism.[69]

New Zealand

Exhibitionism is punishable under Sections 125 and 126 of the Crimes Act 1961 of New Zealand. Section 125 states:[70]

> ***125. Indecent act in public place***
> (1) Every one is liable to imprisonment for a term not exceeding 2 years who willfully does any indecent act in any place to which the public have or are permitted to have access, or within view of any such place.
> (2) It is a defense to a charge under this section if the person charged proves that he had reasonable grounds for believing that he would not be observed.
> (3) For the purposes of this section, the term place includes any railway carriage, and also includes any ship, aircraft, or vehicle used for the carriage of passengers for hire or reward.

If the indecent act, or the act of exhibitionism was done with intent to insult or offend, Section 126 would apply. It states:[71]

> ***126. Indecent act with intent to insult or offend***
> Every one is liable to imprisonment for a term not exceeding 2 years who with intent to insult or offend any person does any indecent act in any place.

Romania

Chapter VII of the Criminal Code of the Republic of Romania is entitled "Crimes against sexual freedom "and lists most crimes of a sexual nature. It contains Articles 217 through Article 224. Article 220 specifically punishes acts of sexual perversion, without specifically defining them.

Using commonly accepted definitions, crimes such as exhibitionism and frotteurism would be covered by Article 220. It states:

> ***Sexual perversion***
>
> Art.220—(1) Acts of sexual perversion committed in public shall be punished by strict imprisonment from 1 to 5 years.
>
> (2) Acts of sexual perversion involving a person under the age of 15 shall be punished by strict imprisonment from 3 to 10 years and the prohibition of certain rights.
>
> (3) The same penalty shall sanction also acts of sexual perversion involving a person aged 15 to 18, if the act is committed by the guardian or curator, or by the person charged with his/her supervision or care, by the physician, teacher/professor or educator, using his/her quality, or if the perpetrator abused the victim's confidence or his/her authority or influence over him/her.
>
> (4) If the acts of sexual perversion with a person under the age of 18 were determined by the perpetrator's offering or giving the victim money or other benefits, directly or indirectly, the penalty shall be strict imprisonment from 3 to 12 years and the prohibition of certain rights.
>
> (5) If the acts in paragraphs (2), (3) and (4) were committed for the production of pornographic material, the penalty shall be strict imprisonment from 5 to 15 years and the prohibition of certain rights, and if for this purpose coercion was used, the penalty shall be severe detention from 15 to 20 years and the prohibition of certain rights.
>
> (6) Acts of sexual perversion involving a person unable to defend him/herself or to express will or by coercion, shall be punished by strict imprisonment from 3 to 10 years and the prohibition of certain rights.
>
> (7) If the acts in paragraphs (1)–(6) have resulted in the victim's death or suicide the penalty shall be severe detention from 15 to 25 years and the prohibition of certain rights.

Sweden

The Swedish Penal Code was adopted in 1962 and became effective on 1 January 1965. The Code has 38 chapters. Of these, chapter 6, having 13 sections, deals with sexual crimes. Section 7 within this chapter deals with exhibitionism (in its last para) and also with frotteurism. It states:

> ***Chapter 6, Section 7***
>
> If a person sexually touches a child under fifteen years of age otherwise than as previously provided in this Chapter, or induces the child to undertake or participate in an act with sexual implication, a fine or imprisonment for at most 2 years shall be imposed for sexual molestation.
>
> A sentence for sexual molestation shall also be imposed on a person who by coercion, seduction or other improper influence induces a person who has attained the age of 15 but not 18 to undertake or participate in an act with sexual implication if the act is an element in the production of pornographic pictures or constitutes pornographic posing in circumstances other than those relating to the production of a picture.
>
> This shall also apply if a person exposes himself or herself in such a manner that the nature thereof gives offense or otherwise manifestly behaves indecently by word or deed towards the latter in a way that flagrantly violates a sense of propriety.

United Kingdom

Traditionally, exhibitionists were booked under Section 4 of the Vagrancy Act 1824.According to Section 66 of the Sexual Offenses Act 2003 of UK,[72] exhibitionism is an offense.

66. Exposure

(1) A person commits an offense if—

(a) he intentionally exposes his genitals, and

(b) he intends that someone will see them and be caused alarm or distress.

(2) A person guilty of an offense under this section is liable—

(a) on summary conviction, to imprisonment for a term not exceeding 6 months or a fine not exceeding the statutory maximum or both;

(b) on conviction on indictment, to imprisonment for a term not exceeding 2 years.

United States

No U.S. federal law either allows or prohibits exhibitionism. Thus, the legality of various forms of undress is currently left to the individual states and localities to decide. Nudity is generally allowed in some areas of some national parks, unless local laws have overriding jurisdiction. It may be useful to have a detailed look at the relevant laws in some representative states.

Alabama

Indecent exposure in Alabama Code is defined as below.[73]

Indecent exposure

(a) A person commits the crime of indecent exposure if, with intent to arouse or gratify sexual desire of himself or of any person other than his spouse, he exposes his genitals under circumstances in which he knows his conduct is likely to cause affront or alarm in any public place or on the private premises of another or so near thereto as to be seen from such private premises.

(b) Indecent exposure is a Class A misdemeanor.

The sentence for Class A misdemeanor is imprisonment of up to 1 year[74] and the fine not more than $6,000.[75] In addition, anyone who makes an obscene gesture in a public place can be prosecuted for *disorderly conduct*.[76] Section 13A-11-7 states:

Disorderly conduct

(a) A person commits the crime of disorderly conduct if, with intent to cause public inconvenience, annoyance or alarm, or recklessly creating a risk thereof, he:

(1) Engages in fighting or in violent tumultuous or threatening behavior; or

(2) Makes unreasonable noise; or

(3) In a public place uses abusive or obscene language or makes an obscene gesture; or

(4) Without lawful authority, disturbs any lawful assembly or meeting of persons; or

(5) Obstructs vehicular or pedestrian traffic, or a transportation facility; or

(6) Congregates with other person in a public place and refuses to comply with a lawful order of the police to disperse.

(b) Disorderly conduct is a Class C misdemeanor.

The sentence for a Class C misdemeanor is imprisonment of up to 3 months.[74] In addition if a person exposes his anus or genitals in a public place, he can be prosecuted for public lewdness.[77] Section 13A-12-130 states:

Public lewdness

(a) A person commits the crime of public lewdness if:

(1) He exposes his anus or genitals in a public place and is reckless about whether another may be present who will be offended or alarmed by his act; or
(2) He does any lewd act in a public place which he knows is likely to be observed by others who would be affronted or alarmed.
(b) Public lewdness is a Class C misdemeanor.

Clause (a) of Section 13A-11-8 of the Alabama Code also addresses the crime of exhibitionism (for details, please see chapter on telephone scatologia).

Alaska

Title 11 of the Alaska Code deals with criminal law. The Alaska Code defines two degrees of indecent exposure —*Indecent Exposure in the First Degree* and *Indecent Exposure in the Second Degree.* Section 11.41.458 of Alaska code defines the former as follows:[78]

AS 11.41.458. Indecent Exposure in the First Degree
(a) An offender commits the crime of indecent exposure in the first degree if
  (1) the offender violates AS 11.41.460 (a);
  (2) while committing the act constituting the offense, the offender knowingly masturbates; and
  (3) the offense occurs within the observation of a person under 16 years of age.
(b) Indecent exposure in the first degree is a class C felony.

Section 11.41.460 defines *Indecent Exposure in the Second Degree.* It states:[79]

AS 11.41.460. Indecent Exposure in the Second Degree
(a) An offender commits the crime of indecent exposure in the second degree if the offender knowingly exposes the offender's genitals in the presence of another person with reckless disregard for the offensive, insulting, or frightening effect the act may have.
(b) Indecent exposure in the second degree before a person under 16 years of age is a class A misdemeanor. Indecent exposure in the second degree before a person 16 years of age or older is a class B misdemeanor.

Arkansas

Title 5 of the Arkansas Code deals with criminal offenses. Chapter 14 of Title 5 deals with sexual offenses. The relevant law on exhibitionism is as follows:

Indecent exposure[80]
(a) A person commits indecent exposure if, with the purpose to arouse or gratify a sexual desire of himself or herself or of any other person, the person exposes his or her sex organs:
  (1) In a public place or in public view; or
  (2) Under circumstances in which the person knows the conduct is likely to cause affront or alarm.
(b) Indecent exposure is a Class A misdemeanor.

It is clear that acts like streaking may not attract the provisions of this law, as a person can commit indecent exposure only when the act is done with the specific purpose to arouse or gratify a sexual desire. Nudism, too, would not attract its provisions for the same reason. But nudism is illegal in Arkansas under obscenity laws. It is a class A misdemeanor. The law on nudism is as follows:

Nudism[81]

(a) As used in this section, "nudism" means the act or acts of a person or persons congregating or gathering with his, her, or their private parts exposed in the presence of one (1) or more persons of the opposite sex as a form of social practice.

(b) The provisions of this section do not apply to the enumerated acts if:
   (1) The purpose of the person committing the act or acts is to render medical or surgical treatment or to determine the need for medical or surgical treatment or to cleanse such sexual part, and the person committing the act:
      (A) Is a licensed physician, as defined by §17-80-101, or any such physician of a sister state making a professional call into Arkansas;
      (B) Committed the act under the professional direction of any physician described in subdivision (b)(1)(A) of this section; or
      (C) Is a nurse duly registered or licensed by the Arkansas State Board of Nursing; or
   (2) The persons are married legally one to another.

(c) It is unlawful for any:
   (1) Person, club, camp, corporation, partnership, association, or organization to advocate, demonstrate, or promote nudism; or
   (2) Person to rent, lease, or otherwise permit his or her land, premises, or buildings to be used for the purpose of advocating, demonstrating, or promoting nudism.

(d) Any person, club, camp, corporation, partnership, association, or organization violating any provision of this section is guilty of a Class A misdemeanor for each offense.

(e) This section does not repeal any existing laws of the State of Arkansas except those in direct conflict with this section but this section is cumulative to the existing laws of the State of Arkansas.

California

According to section 314 of the California Penal Code,[82] exhibitionism is a misdemeanor. It states:

314. Every person who willfully and lewdly, either:

1. Exposes his person, or the private parts thereof, in any public place, or in any place where there are present other persons to be offended or annoyed thereby; or,
2. Procures, counsels, or assists any person so to expose himself or take part in any model artist exhibition, or to make any other exhibition of himself to public view, or the view of any number of persons, such as is offensive to decency, or is adapted to excite to vicious or lewd thoughts or acts, is guilty of a misdemeanor.

Every person who violates subdivision 1 of this section after having entered, without consent, an inhabited dwelling house, or trailer coach as defined in Section 635 of the Vehicle Code, or the inhabited portion of any other building, is punishable by imprisonment in the state prison, or in the county jail not exceeding one year.

Upon the second and each subsequent conviction under subdivision 1 of this section, or upon a first conviction under subdivision 1 of this section after a previous conviction under Section 288, every person so convicted is guilty of a felony, and is punishable by imprisonment in state prison.

Iowa

According to section 709.9 of the Iowa Code,[83] exhibitionism is a misdemeanor. It states:

709.9 Indecent exposure.

A person who exposes the person's genitals or pubes to another not the person's spouse, or who commits a sex act in the presence of or view of a third person, commits a serious misdemeanor, if:

1. The person does so to arouse or satisfy the sexual desires of either party; and
2. The person knows or reasonably should know that the act is offensive to the viewer.

Rhode Island

Section 11-45-1 of R.I. General Laws defines disorderly conduct (both exhibitionism and voyeurism are included under this law). Subsection (a)(8) within this law defines *indecent exposure* as follows:

> **§11-45-1 (a)(8).** A person commits disorderly conduct if he or she intentionally, knowingly, or recklessly: exposes his or her genitals to the view of another person under circumstances in which his or her conduct is likely to cause affront, distress, or alarm to the other person.

The punishment for indecent exposure is defined in subsection c. Subsection f excludes breast feeding in public from the ambit of indecent exposure:

> **§11-45-1 (c)** Any person found guilty of the crime of disorderly conduct shall be imprisoned for a term of not more than six (6) months, or fined not more than five hundred dollars ($500), or both.
> **§11-45-1 (f)** In no event shall the provisions of this section be construed to apply to breast feeding in public.

Significantly, no witness may be required for this offense except the victim herself. In *State v. Magliocco, C.A.* No.: N3/98-0325A (R.I. Super. 1999), the defendant moved to dismiss charge of disorderly conduct, to wit: indecent exposure, arguing that the statute requires more than one witness to an act of indecent exposure. Denying the defendant's motion, the court held "it defies logic to limit this charge to cases where there was more than one person present at the time of the exposure. There are three enumerated elements of indecent exposure: (a) willful or intentional, exposure of a person, (b) in a public place, (c) before others."

Offenders have taken the insanity defense in such cases, but unsuccessfully. In *State v. Supers,* 77 R.I. 251, 75 A.2d 27 (R.I. 1950) the defendant, through counsel, admitted that he had indecently exposed his person to young girls on their way to school while standing in the window of his grocery store. The court held that there was sufficient evidence to sustain the conviction since the jury rejected the defendant's psychiatric defense that "at such times he did not know what he was doing as his mind went blank."

Wisconsin

Chapter 944 of Wisconsin Statutes & Annotations defines crimes against sexual morality. Section 944.20 within this chapter makes both exhibitionism and frotteurism Class A misdemeanors. It states:

944.20 Lewd and lascivious behavior

(1) Whoever does any of the following is guilty of a Class A misdemeanor:
- (a) Commits an indecent act of sexual gratification with another with knowledge that they are in the presence of others; or
- (b) Publicly and indecently exposes genitals or pubic area.

(2) Subsection (1) does not apply to a mother's breastfeeding of her child.

Clearly while subsection 1(a) aims at frotteurism, 1(b) aims at exhibitionism.

REFERENCES

1. Brockman, B. and Bluglass, R., A General Psychiatric Approach to Sexual Deviation, in *Sexual Deviation*, 3rd edition, Rosen I., Ed., Oxford University Press, Oxford, 1996, chap. 1.
2. de Silva, W.P. ABC of sexual health. Sexual variations. *BMJ.* 1999;318(7184):654-6.
3. Snaith, P. Exhibitionism: A Clinical Conundrum. *Br J Psychiatry.* 1983;**143**:231-5.
4. Rooth, F.G. Some historical notes on indecent exposure and exhibitionism. *Med Leg J.* 1970;38(4):135-9.
5. Kahr, B., *Ideas in Psychoanalysis - Exhibitionism*, 1st ed., Icon Books, Cambridge, UK, 2001.
6. Freeman, M., Sexual Deviance and the Law, in *Sexual Deviation*, 3rd edition, Rosen, I., (Ed.), Oxford University Press, Oxford, 1996, chap. 17.
7. Bancroft, H., Behavioral treatments of sexual deviations. In *Handbook of Behavioral Modification and Behavioral Therapy*, Leitenberg, N.H. (ed), Prentice Hall, New York, 1976.
8. Herold, E.S., Mantle, D., Zemitis, O. A study of sexual offenses against females. *Adolescence.* 1979;14(53):65-72.
9. Abel, G.G. and Harlow, N., *Stop child molestation.* Xlibris, Philadelphia, PA, 2001.
10. Lebegue, B. Paraphilias in U.S. pornography titles: "pornography made me do it" (Ted Bundy). *Bull Am Acad Psychiatry Law.* 1991;**19(1)**:43-8.
11. Blair, C.D. and Lanyon, R.I., Exhibitionism: Etiology and treatment. *Psychological Bulletin.* 1981;89:439-463.
12. American Psychiatric Association. *Diagnostic and Statistical Manual of Mental Disorders*, 4th ed. Text rev. American Psychiatric Association, Washington DC, 2000.
13. London, L.S., and Caprio, F.S. *Sexual Deviations.* Linacre Press, London, 1953.
14. Lasègue, C., Les Exhibitionistes. *L'Union Médicale* (Paris), series 3, 23, 709-714, 1877.
15. II Samuel 6:12-16. The Holy Bible. Authorized King James version. Oxford Univ. Press, New York, 1972.
16. II Samuel 6:20. The Holy Bible. Authorized King James version. Oxford Univ. Press, New York, 1972.
17. Exodus 20:26. The Holy Bible. Authorized King James version. Oxford Univ. Press, New York, 1972.
18. Exodus 28:42. The Holy Bible. Authorized King James version. Oxford Univ. Press, New York, 1972.
19. Jerman, J. *Images of Lust : Sexual Carvings on Medieval Churches.* Routledge, New York, 2000.
20. *Le Roy, v. Sir. Charles Sedley*, 1 Keb. 620, 83 Eng. Rep. 1146 (K.B.1663).
21. East, W.N. Observations on Exhibitionism. *The Lancet.* 1924; **204(5269)**: 370-5.
22. Ellis, H. *Psychology of sex.* Heinemann, London, 1933.
23. Marten, Z. Candaulesism - case report [Article in Polish]. *Psychiatr Pol.* 1986 May-Jun;**20(3)**:235-7.
24. Times of India. Rajkot woman stages semi-nude protest against dowry demand. *Times of India.* July 5, 2007, page 11.
25. McNally, R.J., Lukach, B.M. Behavioral treatment of zoophilic exhibitionism. *J Behav Ther Exp Psychiatry.* 1991 Dec;22(4):281-4.
26. Springen, K. Indecent Exposure?; New laws seek to protect breast-feeding in public. *Newsweek.* New York: Jun 11, 2007. Vol.149, Iss. 23; p. 49.
27. Freund, K., Scher, H. and Hucker, S. The courtship disorders. *Arch Sex Behav.* 1983;**12(5)**: 369-379.
28. Freund, K., Scher, H. and Hucker, S. The courtship disorders: a further investigation. *Arch Sex Behav.*1984; **13(2)**: 133-139.
29. Taylor, F. H. Observations on some cases of exhibitionism. *J. Ment. Sci.* 1947;**93**: 681-683.
30. Rooth, G. Exhibitionism, sexual violence and pedophilia. *Brit. J. Psychiat.* 1973; **122**: 705-710.
31. Yalom, I.D. Aggression and forbiddenness in voyeurism. *Arch. Gen. Psychiat.* 1960;**3**:305-319.
32. Grassberger, R. Der Exhibitionismus. *Kriminalistik in Österreich.* 1964; 18: 557-562.
33. Gebhard, P.H., Gagnon, J.H., Pomeroy, W.B., and Christenson, C.V. *Sex Offenders.* Harper & Row, New York, 1965.
34. Macdonald, J., *Indecent Exposure*, Charles C. Thomas, Springfield, Ill, 1973.
35. Rickles, N., *Exhibitionism*, Lippincott, Philadelphia, 1950
36. Maletzky, B.M., Exhibitionism: Assessment and Treatment, in *Sexual Deviance: Theory, Assessment and Treatment*, Laws, D.R. and O'Donohue, W., Eds, Guilford Press, New York, 1997, pages 40-74.
37. Tkachenko, A.A. [Clinico-pathogenetic characteristics of exhibitionism] [Paper in Russian]. *Zh Nevropatol Psikhiatr Im S S Korsakova.* 1991;91(5):65-70.

38. Quinn, N.P., Toone, B., Lang, A.E., Marsden, C.D., Parkes, J.D. Dopa dose-dependent sexual deviation. *Br J Psychiatry.* 1983 Mar;142:296-8.
39. McGuire, R.J., Carlisle, J.M., Young, B.G. Sexual Deviations As Conditioned Behaviour: A Hypothesis. *Behav Res Ther.* 1965 Jan;**3**:185-90.
40. Grob, C.S. Female exhibitionism. *J Nerv Ment Dis.* 1985 Apr;**173(4)**:253-6.
41. Zavitzianos, G. Fetishism and exhibitionism in the female and their relationship to psychopathy and kleptomania. *Int J Psychoanal.* 1971;**52(3)**:297-305.
42. Silverstein, J.L. Exhibitionism as countershame. *Sexual Addiction & Compulsivity.* 1996;**3(1)**:33-42.
43. Karpman, B., *The Sexual Offender and His Offenses*, Julian Press, New York, 1957.
44. Kenworthy, T., Bloem, F., Exhibitionism - Development and Treatment. In *Sex crimes and paraphilia*, 1st ed. Hickey, E.W., (Ed.), Pearson Prentice Hall, New Jersey, 2006, chapter 28, pages 257-265.
45. Långström, N., Seto, M.C. Exhibitionistic and voyeuristic behavior in a Swedish national population survey. *Arch Sex Behav.* 2006 Aug;35(4):427-35.
46. Fedoroff, J. P., Fishell, A., Fedoroff, B., A case series of women evaluated for paraphilic sexual disorders. *Canadian Journal of Human Sexuality.* 1999; 8(2): 127-140.
47. Crépault, C., Couture, M. Men's erotic fantasies. *Arch Sex Behav.* 1980 Dec;**9(6)**:565-81.
48. Radzinowicz, L., Sexual Offenses. *A Report of the Cambridge Department of Criminal Science* (English Studies in Criminal Science). MacMillan, London, 1957.
49. Allen, C.E., *A Textbook of Psychosexual Disorders*, 2nd ed., Oxford University Press, Oxford, 1969.
50. Philpot, C.D. Paraphilia and aging. *Clin Geriatr Med.* 2003 Aug;**19(3)**:629-36.
51. Comings, D.E., Comings BG. A case of familial exhibitionism in Tourette's syndrome successfully treated with haloperidol. *Am J Psychiatry.* 1982 Jul;**139(7)**:913-5.
52. Saunders, E., Awad, G.A., White, G. Male adolescent sexual offenders: the offender and the offense. *Can J Psychiatry.* 1986 Aug;**31(6)**:542-9.
53. Cabanis, D. [Female exhibitionism]. *Z Rechtsmed.* 1972 Nov 28;**71(2)**:126-33.
54. Hollender, M.H., Brown, C.W., Roback, H.B. Genital exhibitionism in women. *Am J Psychiatry.* 1977 Apr;**134(4)**:436-8.
55. Tollison, C.D. and Adams, H.E., *Sexual Disorders: Treatment, Theory and Research*, 1st ed., Gardner Press, Inc., New York, 1979.
56. Hermann, K., Schroder, G.E. Un cas d'exhibitionisme chez une femme. *Acta Psychiatr Neurol.* 1935;**10**:547-564.
57. Langevin, R., *Sexual Strands: Understanding and Treating Sexual Anomalies in Men.* Lawrence Erlbaum Associates, Hillsdale, New Jersey, 1982.
58. Mohr, J.W., Turner, R.E., and Jerry, M.B., *Pedophilia and Exhibitionism*, University of Toronto Press, Toronto, 1964.
59. Tichý, P. Phalloplethysmography findings in pedophilia and exhibitionism offenders. [Article in Czech]. *Cas Lek Cesk.* 1996 Aug 21;**135(16)**:521-4.
60. Rich, S.S., Ovsiew F. Leuprolide acetate for exhibitionism in Huntington's disease. *Mov Disord.* 1994 May;**9(3)**:353-7.
61. Zohar, J., Kaplan, Z., Benjamin, J. Compulsive exhibitionism successfully treated with fluvoxamine: a controlled case study. *J Clin Psychiatry.* 1994 Mar;**55(3)**:86-8.
62. Abouesh, A., Clayton, A. Compulsive voyeurism and exhibitionism: a clinical response to paroxetine. *Arch Sex Behav.* 1999 Feb;**28(1)**:23-30.
63. Rösler, A., Witztum, E. Pharmacotherapy of paraphilias in the next millennium. *Behav Sci Law.* 2000;**18(1)**:43-56.
64. Section 173, Criminal Code of Canada (R.S., 1985, c. C-46).
65. Section 183, German Criminal Code (Strafgesetzbuch, StGB) as promulgated on 13 November 1998 (Federal Law Gazette I, p. 945, p. 3322).
66. The Hungarian Criminal Code, Act IV of 1978.
67. The Indian Penal Code, (Act No. 45 of 1860) [6th October, 1860].
68. Article 174, Penal Code of Japan (Act no. 45 of 1907).
69. Diamond, M. and Uchiyama, A. Pornography, Rape, and Sex Crimes in Japan. *International Journal of Law and Psychiatry.* 1999; 22(1): 1-22.
70. section 125, Crimes Act 1961 of New Zealand.
71. section 126, Crimes Act 1961 of New Zealand.
72. Sexual Offenses Act 2003 [20th November 2003].
73. Alabama Code §13A-6-68 (enacted 1977).

74. Alabama Code §13A-5-7 (enacted 1977).
75. Alabama Code §13A-5-12 (enacted 1977).
76. Alabama Code §13A-11-7 (enacted 1977).
77. Alabama Code §13A-12-130 (enacted 1977).
78. Alaska Statutes §11-41-458 (enacted 1983).
79. Alaska Statutes §11-41-460 (enacted 1983).
80. Arkansas Code Ann. 5-14-112 (enacted 1975).
81. Arkansas Code Ann. §5-68-204 (enacted 1957).
82. California Penal Code, §314-318.6.
83. Iowa Code Ann. §709.9 (enacted 1976).

5 Fetishism

INTRODUCTION

Fetishism, or sexual fetishism, is a form of paraphilia in which the object of erotic interest and affection has been pathologically displaced and is usually a specific inanimate object or part of a person's body, known as the *fetish*. This displacement of erotic interest and satisfaction may continue for the entire life of the patient. Among the more common fetish objects are women's underpants, bras, stockings, shoes, boots, or other wearing apparel. Freud[1] defined *fetishism* as a condition "in which the normal sexual object is replaced by another which, though related to it, is totally unfit for the normal sexual aim."

The word *fetishism* arose from *fetish*, a term used in anthropology for an object believed to have supernatural powers. Early Christians frequently attributed magical and metaphysical powers to such objects as skulls, bones of saints, severed and mummified fingers and arms, etc. These objects were referred to as *fetiches*. When 15th century Portuguese explorers arrived in West Africa and discovered that local people had their own fetiches in the form of religious carvings and other inanimate objects, they began to refer to those inanimate objects as fetiches, too. The French writer Charles de Brosses (1709–1777) coined the term *fetishism* in 1756 (in an anthropological sense) and developed the concept of religious fetishism in his 1760 *Du culte des dieux fétiches*, where he discussed the worship of material objects such as amulets and talismans among ancient and contemporary African populations. De Brosses called this cult *fétichisme* after *fétiche*, derived from the Portuguese trading term *feitiço*, which designated the small objects and charms on which European merchants would take oaths in sealing commercial agreements with Africans.

When early sexologists were searching for a term to describe this paraphilia, they borrowed from the Portuguese term, because in their opinion, like a religious fetish, an erotic fetish, too, possessed magical powers. It had the power to arouse emotions and to inspire sexual ecstasy in a person who was otherwise non-arousable. If a person who could not be aroused by normal erotic stimuli (say, a nude woman) could be aroused by an inanimate object, say, a sandal or a shoe, the object *did* have a kind of magical power on that person, and was thus a fetish. The initial word for this paraphilia, reflecting its true etymology, was *fetichism* (with a "c" in place of "s"), which ultimately was changed to *fetishism*. The obsolete spelling *fetichism* can be seen in many earlier works discussing this phenomenon. Richard Freiherr von Krafft-Ebing (1840–1902), for instance, used the earlier word *fetichism* in his book *Psychopathia Sexualis*. Today religious fetishism and erotic or sexual fetishism are two separate terms having distinct meanings.

DSM-IV-TR[2] assigns code 302.81 to fetishism and states the following criteria for diagnosing it:

DSM-IV-TR criteria for fetishism

A. Over a period of at least 6 months, recurrent, intense, sexually arousing fantasies, sexual urges, or behaviors involving the use of nonliving objects (e.g., female undergarments).

B. The fantasies, sexual urges, or behaviors cause clinically significant distress or impairment in social, occupational, or other important areas of functioning.

C. The fetish objects are not limited to articles of female clothing used in cross-dressing (as in transvestic fetishism) or devices designed for the purpose of tactile genital stimulation (e.g., a vibrator).

ICD-10 assigns code 65.0 to fetishism, and states the following definition:

> Reliance on some nonliving object as a stimulus for sexual arousal and sexual gratification. Many fetishes are extensions of the human body, such as articles of clothing or footwear. Other common examples are characterized by some particular texture such as rubber, plastic or leather. Fetish objects vary in their importance to the individual. In some cases they simply serve to enhance sexual excitement achieved in ordinary ways (e.g., having the partner wear a particular garment).[3]

It has been claimed that fetishism served during the late 19th and early 20th centuries as a model in the scientific analysis of sexual deviation and as a basis for elaborating a general theory of sexuality.[4]

PARTIALISM

Although both DSM-IV-TR as well as ICD-10 insist that a nonliving object (the fetish) be used as a stimulus for a diagnosis of fetishism to be made, in practice cases are seen where there is intense sexual fixation on some specific part of the body, such as the foot, breast, navel, buttock, ear, nose, or long red hair. These are referred to as cases of partialism.[5]

Cases of partialism may often be prosecuted under the rubric of indecent assault. In a case of buttock fetish (*R. v. Court* [1988] 2 All E.R. 221), the defendant, a shop assistant, pulled a 12-year old girl who was in the shop across his knee and spanked her on her clothed bottom. When asked why he did it, he admitted he had a "buttock fetish." He was convicted for indecent assault.[6]

The revised fourth edition of the *Diagnostic and Statistical Manual of Mental Disorders* (DSM-IV-TR)[7] does not assign any specific or unique code to partialism. Instead, along with several other uncommon paraphilias (seven of which are specifically named), it is grouped under the code 302.9 (Paraphilias Not Otherwise Specified—please see chapter on zoophilia for full statement of Code 302.9). It is one of the only seven paraphilias that are specifically mentioned by name in this category.

It is common knowledge that there are men who are turned on by some particular female attributes, say a blonde or a brunette, but it is even possible to be erotically aroused by such individual charms as the color of the eyes or a particular tone of voice. Descartes, for instance, had a partialism for women with a squint![8] He explained that it was because his first love had such an anomaly.[9] Krafft-Ebing designated such cases as *physiological fetishism* and insisted that they were not pathological in nature so long as "the love engendered by it comprises entire mental and physical personality." He also believed that physiological and pathological fetishism (represented by attraction to, say, shoes or corsets) represented opposite ends of a spectrum rather than distinct entities. Physiological fetishes, say, the pubic area, breasts, or buttocks of a female are more *socially acceptable fetishes* than pathological fetishes, such as shoes, handkerchiefs, and corsets.

Partialism may facilitate and even enhance sexual pleasure and may be used as mere adjuncts, as in normal foreplay. In some cases, however, partialism or physiological fetishism may dictate the sufferer to choose a specific partner to the exclusion of all others. It might be at this stage that it may begin to be viewed as a disorder. Thus, an important feature which distinguishes physiological fetishism from pathological is that in the former, the person may be sexually aroused by a particular characteristic of a person (say, a redhead), but he would still be capable to responding sexuoerotically to other individuals not having such a characteristic. In pathological fetishism, the afflicted individual loses all capacity to respond sexuoerotically to any other entity than the fetish.

HISTORICAL PERSPECTIVES

As noted above, fetish is a notion that originally signified magic, fixation, and intense attraction. Anything which was denoted as a fetish automatically meant that it was extremely valuable; it assumed an almost mythical dimension in significance. Derived from this notion, the term *fetishism* has been used in at least three distinct and separate ways—*anthropological fetishism*, *commodity fetishism*, and *psychiatric* or *pathologic fetishism*, more commonly referred to as *sexual fetishism*. *Anthropological fetishism* refers to an attraction to inanimate objects believed by early African tribes to embody magical powers. *Commodity fetishism* is a Marxist term that describes the attribution of excessive value onto products, surpassing their status as articles of utility. *Sexual fetishism* refers to some specific inanimate object (a shoe) or part of a person's body (breasts) that serve to arouse the sexual interest of the fetishist.

The term *fetishism* in a sexual context was first used by Krafft-Ebing.[9] His *Psychopathia sexualis*,[10] first published in 1886, described about 35 cases of fetishism.

He describes one of his cases as follows:[11]

> Z began to masturbate at the age of 12. From that time he could not see a woman's handkerchief without having orgasm and ejaculation. He was irresistibly compelled to possess himself of it. At that time he was a choir boy and used the handkerchiefs to masturbate within the bell tower close to the choir. But he chose only such handkerchiefs as had black and white borders or violet stripes running through them. At age 15, he had coitus. Later on he married. As a rule, he was potent only when he wound such a handkerchief around his penis. Often he preferred coitus between the thighs of a woman where he had placed a handkerchief. Whenever he espied a handkerchief, he did not rest until he was in possession of it. He always had a number of them in his pockets and around his penis.

In 1888, the French psychologist Alfred Binet[12] (1857–1911) borrowed the word from Krafft-Ebing in his own writings. Both Krafft-Ebing and Binet concluded—quite correctly—that fetishism was a pathological entity. In 1905 Sigmund Freud published his psychoanalytic view of fetishism, which reached non-scientific readers also and made the term popular. He wrote:

> A certain degree of fetishism is thus habitually present in [normal] love.... The situation only becomes pathological when the longing for the fetish passes beyond the point of being merely a necessary condition attached to the sexual object and actually takes the place of the normal aim, and, further when the fetish becomes detached from a particular individual and becomes the sole sexual object.[13]

ETIOLOGY

Several theories attempt to explain why fetishism develops in certain people, but none explains the phenomenon completely or in all cases. One of the most logical and popular is the classical conditioning theory.

CLASSIC CONDITIONING

As seen in Chapter 1, many paraphilias including fetishism, can be most easily explained by the classic conditioning theory. To prove this theory in fetishists, Rachman and Hodgson[14] conducted an interesting experiment involving slides of a sexual nature showing women's boots. They found that after several pairings of the stimuli, the subjects experienced an increased sexual arousal when they were shown just the women's boots *without* sexually seductive items (akin to the salivation of dog on hearing just the buzzer in the famous Pavlovian experiment, after several pairings of food and the buzzer—Chapter 1). In other words, the women's boots had become the conditioned stimuli or, as is more commonly known, fetish objects. In normal life such pairings can occur, when a person repeatedly sees, say, a naked woman with high heeled shoes, or a woman with a highly revealing bra. In these cases, the shoes and bra, become fetish objects.

It is known that people who are introverts are more prone to develop conditioned responses.[8] This fact fits in well with the observation that fetishists tend to be mostly lonely, unassertive, and introverted, spending a lot of time in fantasies. However, as seen in Chapter 1, classical conditioning theories do not explain adequately why extinction does not occur in fetishists. They also do not explain why the fetishist displays no interest in the original unconditioned stimulus—the woman. This indicates that more than one factor may be playing a part in the development of fetishism.

It may, however, be said in defense of classical conditioning that shoes, especially those which are black and high-heeled, bear a great similarity in color and shape to the pubic triangles of females, and thus this is a singular conditioned stimulus, which does not need repeated pairings with the unconditioned stimulus. In other words, the shoe itself reminds the fetishist of the pubic triangle, and thus extinction would never occur. However, this is only a conjecture, without any experimental proof.

Operant Conditioning

Fetishism can be explained by operant conditioning also (please see chapter 1 for details of classical and operant conditioning). McGuire and colleagues[15] cite the case of one of their patients to prove this. Their patient, a 17-year old male, once saw a girl dressed only in her underwear through a window. He was sexually stimulated by the sight and later took to masturbating to the memory. However, with the passage of time his memory of the girl became vague whereas advertisements and shop window displays continually reminded him of details of underwear to use in his fantasy, so that the latter became the stronger cue. His interests thereupon changed gradually but consistently, so that when seen 3 years later he no longer had the slightest interest in girls but was sexually stimulated by female underwear which he bought or stole.

Psychoanalytical Theories

According to Freud's libido theory (please see Chapter 1), the child believes that every woman (including his mother) has a phallus and refuses to give up this belief (it is his concept of phallic woman or phallic mother). When he discovers that the females do not possess penises, this discovery comes as a shock to him. He had already begun to think that his father would cut away his penis, and the discovery that he has already done so to his mother sends the child into a denial mode. He constructs for himself a compromise object, the fetish, which to him represents the female phallus. This now absorbs all his erotic interest, and he becomes a fetishist.[16]

Biological Theories

Phylogenetic Considerations

Interestingly, phenomena related to fetishism have been seen in animals. A rubber boot has been observed to evoke penile erection in a baboon (*Papio papio*) and even ejaculation in a chimpanzee (*Pan troglodytes*).[17] A smooth rubbery surface may bear a relationship to primate body parts or markings which have sexual arousal value, as the swollen contour and coloration of the sexual skin of the anogenital area.[18] Thus smoothness and rubberiness are only related sexuals signal emanating from erogenous zones such as breasts and buttocks, which, in fetishistic animals, begins to serve as an erotic stimulus on its own. Wickler asserts that such related sexual signals operate in humans, too. Many fetishes (e.g., wet, shiny, black, pink, or furry objects) have striking visual attributes that are strongly reminiscent of genital signals.

Frontal and Temporal Lobe Lesions

Huws and associates have reported a case of hypersexuality and fetishism in a patient with multiple sclerosis whose MRI scans showed frontal and temporal lesions. This might suggest an etiological factor.[19] It is suggested that hypersexuality may even be the presenting symptom in multiple sclerosis. Many other workers have reported an association of fetishism with temporal lobe lesions.[20,21,22,23]

Neuronal Cross-links

It has been suggested that fetishism may be the result of neuronal cross-links between neighboring regions in the human brain. For instance, the region processing sensory input from the feet lies immediately next to the region processing sexual stimulation.

Genetic Factors

Gorman[24] has reported a case of fetishism in male uniovular twins, supporting the view that genetic factors may be underlying fetishism. The twins (referred to in the paper as E.H. and O.H.) were born in 1920, and examined in 1962. Both displayed rubber fetishism. The age of onset was similar; there was absence of collusion between the twins. O.H., the twin who was examined first, revealed that he had not been in close contact with his twin E.H. for many years. E.H. was then examined and found to have the same fetishism.

Miscellaneous Explanations

It has been suggested that the foot's shape is distinctly phallic and is viewed by the fetishist to replicate the female or male genitals or the shape of a female body. Another view is that the feet and the genitals are in the same visual window, and when looking at one, the other will be in view as well; thus the two (genitals and feet) become associated in the mind. The importance of environment is established by the fact that rubber fetishism was not seen before the advent of rubber.

PREVALENCE

The prevalence of fetishism is largely unknown.[8] Different studies have come up with remarkably different figures. Chalkley and Powell[25] determined the prevalence of fetishism among those seeking treatment for psychiatric disorders at the Bethlem Royal and Maudsley Hospitals during a 20 year period. It turned out to be 0.8%. Gosselin and Wilson,[26] on the other hand, have reported that as many as 18% of healthy individuals (i.e., those who have not sought treatment for sexual disorders) have fetishistic fantasies. This is of course not the same as being a fetishist, according to the DSM-IV criteria. Fetishism often appears with other paraphilias. The most frequently paraphilias associated with fetishism are pedophilia and transvestism.[27]

Scorolli and colleagues[28] have examined 381 discussion groups using the Internet as a data source, in an effort to estimate the relative frequency of fetishes in a large sample of individuals. About 5000 individuals were targeted in all. Preferences for body parts or features (partialism) and for objects usually associated with the body were most common (33 and 30%, respectively), followed by preferences for other people's behavior (18%), self's behavior (7%), social behavior (7%), and objects unrelated to the body (5%). Feet and objects associated with feet were the most common target of preferences.

ANIMAL MODELS OF FETISHISTIC BEHAVIOR

Sexual behaviors similar to fetishism have been observed in animals. Youngi described a male eastern robin that copulated with a clump of earth and a piece of crumpled newspaper. Barraudii reported observing a young male house sparrow copulating with a dandelion. Ficken and Dilgeriii described a woodthrush copulating with a smooth stone, a male Fisher's lovebird copulating with a knot on a wood perch, and an American redstart copulating with a clump of dried droppings. Michaeli described an instance of a male cat copulating with a toy. It is not clear how these seemingly fetishistic behaviors were nitiated in such a vast variety of animals, but it is possible that all these inanimate objects which served as fetishes, were somehow associated with a sexual stimulus such as a female of the same species in the early part of the animals' lives. A frequent association of the unconditioned stimulus (the female of the species), and the conditioned stimulus (the fetish) must have led to a form of conditioning* in these animals. This view is supported by the fact that dogs can actually be experimentally conditioned to modify their sexual behavior. Beachi has shown that dogs masturbated by an experimenter will come to direct their sexual behavior toward that experimenter.

Since animals are known to display fetishistic behavior, fetishism can be studied quite fruitfully in animal models. Such models have other advantages over human subjects as well. These include greater experimental control of the animal's sexual history and the possibility of using copulation as the reinforcer or unconditioned stimulus, which for quite obvious moral, ethical and legal reasons, can not be resorted to in human subjects.

Animals Can Be Conditioned to Become Fetishistic

Köksal and colleagues developed an animal model of the acquisition of sexual fetishism by conducting interesting experiments on Japanese quail (*Coturnix japonica*). Copulation in Japanese quail begins with the male grabbing the back of the female's head, mounting her back with both feet, and then bringing its cloaca in contact with the female's by making the cloacal contact response. They used a replica of a female Japanese quail (a terry cloth object filled with soft polyester fiber) as a conditioned stimulus (CS) and a live Japanese female quail ready for mating as an unconditioned stimulus (US).

They showed the CS to male quails for 30 seconds, followed immediately by access to a live female quail for 5 minutes. Mating usually followed. Thirty such conditioning trials were performed. This was the acquisition phase during which conditioning occurred. Following 30 trials of acquisition, extinction was introduced. Extinction trials consisted of presenting the CS for 30 seconds in the absence of access to a female. Thirty extinction trials were conducted (one per day).

Results of this experiment were interesting. After the acquisition phase, when only the replica of the female bird was shown (not followed by access to a live female quail), half of the males made conditioned copulatory responses (grab, mount, and cloacal contact) to the terry cloth object (now a fetish). The remaining birds approached the CS and pecked it occasionally but did not grab or mount the CS (non-fetishistic males). Still more interestingly, birds that copulated with the CS object (fetishistic males) were much more persistent in approaching the CS during the extinction phase than those that failed to make grab, mount, or cloacal contact responses to the terry cloth CS. These results are analogous to clinical reports indicating that sexual satisfaction achieved through masturbation serves to maintain fetishistic behavior in human males.

The researchers concluded that the male quails' persistent response to the terry cloth object was analogous to a sexual fetish. To prove this, in a subsequent experiment they replaced the US with food, keeping all other parameters exactly the same. This amounted to conditioning the birds without sexual reinforcement. As was expected, this time the conditioned copulatory behavior to the terry cloth CS did not develop.

Why Has Fetishism Persisted during Evolution?

Another intriguing question addressed through animal models is why fetishistic behavior has persisted in humans over centuries. Strictly speaking, fetishistic behavior should be evolutionarily counterproductive because it involves sexual interaction with an inanimate object and does not

* This is true of other paraphilic behaviors including bestiality and necrophilia.

result in the production of viable offspring. Thus, during the course of evolution such a behavior should have been extinguished. To answer this question, Çetinkaya and Domjan (Domjan was a part of the earlier group too) conducted a similar experiment with Japanese quails. The important difference was that at the end of acquisition phase, both fetishistic and non-fetishistic male birds were allowed access to live female quails and allowed to copulate. In the present study, the authors explored the reproductive consequences of fetishistic behavior in a previously developed animal model of sexual fetishism (F.Köksal et al., 2004). Male domesticated quail (*Coturnix japonica*) received sexual conditioning trials in which a terry cloth object (the conditioned stimulus [CS]) was paired with the opportunity to copulate with a female quail (the unconditioned stimulus). Approximately half of the male quail came to copulate with the CS object and were considered to have developed fetishistic behavior.

Each male quail was then tested with a female quail, whose eggs were incubated to determine rates of fertilization. The CS object was present for 30 seconds before and during the copulation test. Fetishistic male quail were slower to achieve cloacal contact with the female quail and showed less efficient copulatory behavior. However, despite this drawback, they fertilized a greater proportion of eggs than their nonfetishistic counterparts. The experiment thus showed that development of fetishism in a male actually improves fertility once an actual female is available. Fetishistic behavior thus seems to be favored by evolutionary forces.

One can only conjecture why this happens. Çetinkaya and Domjan[37] offer two reasons. They observed during the experiments that when the fetishistic males were busy copulating with terry cloth females, and an actual female was presented to them, they showed a fixation or attachment to the terry cloth object. This fixation was not easily disrupted by introduction of a female quail. The fetishistic males took time to dismount from the terry cloth object and approach the female. In contrast, nonfetishistic male quail quickly moved away from the CS object and vigorously pursued the female quail as soon as they saw her. These unexpected results from previous studies of the relationship between reproductive success and copulatory behavior were discussed in terms of how fetishistic behavior directed toward an inanimate object may modify male–female interactions.

Since it has been shown that anticipation of sexual activity elevates the circulating levels of luteinising hormone and testosterone in rats and increases sperm release in quail, it may be that the increased time and attention that fetishistic male quail directed toward the CS object helped prime their reproductive physiology more effectively, which is why they successfully fertilized more eggs.

It was also observed that the fetishistic males were less aggressive towards females than non-fetishistic males. Less aggression in males invites better copulatory cooperation from the female, who lies still during the copulatory process. This, In turn, allows better cloacal contact. If the male is more aggressive, the female is less co-operative which leads to the male slipping off the female's back more frequently. This observation led to the second explanation. Better co-operation from the female results in a better cloacal contact and hence higher rates of fertilization.

Additionally, when the females were presented to fetishistic males, the fetishistic males remained engaged with the terry cloth female for a longer time, thus keeping the female waiting. Çetinkaya and Domjan[37] think that this "waiting period" or not being aggressively pursued may have permitted the female quail to become more sexually receptive and that, in turn, may have increased the rate of egg fertilization.

It is interesting to note that in several animals, including humans, sexual torture acts as an enhancer of fertility (See Chapter 7 on sexual masochism). In fact, this phenomenon has been used to explain the evolutionary persistence of sexual masochism in females. In the current study, aggression resulted in exactly the opposite result—decreased fertility. Lack of aggression, on the other hand, seemed to promote fertility and this has been advanced as an explanation for the evolutionary persistence of another paraphilia—fetishism.

The two observations may not necessarily be contradictory. Sexual torture acts to enhance fertility, perhaps by inducing ovulation. In the current study, sexual aggression decreased fertility via an entirely different mechanism. It resulted in less co-operation from the females which forced males to slip-off their backs.

Animal models are too simplistic to explain the complex behavior patterns in humans, least of all paraphilias; however, in the absence of other experimental avenues, these remain important sources of study of this behavior.

However, they fertilized a greater proportion of eggs than nonfetishistic male quail. These results are unexpected from previous studies of the relationship between reproductive success and copulatory behavior and are discussed in terms of how fetishistic behavior directed toward an inanimate object may modify male–female interactions.

OFFENDER CHARACTERISTICS

The fetishist frequently masturbates while holding, rubbing, or smelling the fetish object or may ask the sexual partner to wear the object during their sexual encounters. The fetish is usually required or strongly preferred for sexual excitement, and in its absence there may even be erectile dysfunction in males. Fetishism is not said to be present when the fetishes are limited to articles of female clothing used in cross-dressing, as in transvestic fetishism, or when the object is genitally stimulating because it has been designed for that purpose (e.g., a vibrator). Fetishism usually begins by adolescence, although the fetish may have been endowed with special significance earlier in childhood. Once established, fetishism tends to be chronic.

CLASSIFICATION

Gebhard has suggested that sexual fetishism can be conceptualized along "a continuum of intensities."[29] Based on this concept, the following classification of fetishists is proposed in this book. The classification is useful since it grades the paraphilias mathematically, and is in line with classification of other paraphiliacs, such as bestialists, necrophiliacs and telephone scatologists.

Class I Fetishists: Desirers

People falling under this class have only a *slight preference* for certain kinds of sex partners (females with large breasts, or blonde hair), sexual stimuli (a female undergarment) or sexual activity (oral sex). But this is not necessary for sexual arousal. Sexual activity can be accomplished with other sex partners, etc., also. This category may not be considered pathological.

Class II Fetishists: Cravers

These people have a *strong preference* for certain kinds of sex partners, sexual stimuli, or sexual activity. The preference is stronger than those in Class I, yet sexual arousal and sexual activity are possible in the absence of preferred sexual stimuli. There is *no* tendency to commit a crime in order to obtain the fetish

Class III Fetishists: Moderate Level Fetishists

Sexual arousal and sexual performance are not possible without the specific stimuli. Persons belonging to this class and Class IV may feel the need to even commit a crime such as theft or burglary in order to obtain the object of their fetishistic desire. They may be convicted for larceny, theft and even assault. In *R. v. George* [1956] Criminal Law Review, 52, the offender stole a shoe belonging to a girl he secretly desired in order to gratify his shoe fetish. He was charged with indecent assault and attempted larceny and was found guilty of assault,[41] but not indecent assault.[6] The court concluded that the hostile act of taking a woman's shoe together with a statement by the accused that he was motivated to perform the act by the sexual gratification he derived from the act could not satisfy a charge of indecent assault because the assault was not accompanied by circumstances of indecency.

Class IV Fetishists: High Level Fetishists

The preferred stimulus (e.g., the high heeled shoe) takes the place of a sex partner. A partner is not necessary and not even desired. Sexual arousal and activity can take place, just with the preferred stimulus, the fetish.

Class V Fetishists: Fetishistic murderers

These fetishists may murder a person in order to obtain a fetishistic object belonging to the victim. In some cases, the fetishist will murder because he is interrupted and startled by someone during the theft. In other instances, the offender may have a fetish for a particular part of the body (breasts, genitals), and the fetish demands expression through his mutilation and destruction of the part that most fascinates him.[42,43]

Case Study

American fetishistic murderer[41] William George Heirens (1928–), widely known as "The Lipstick Killer," belonged to this class. During his interview, he maintained that he killed because he was interrupted during his stealing activities.

William Heirens

William George Heirens was born in Evanston, Illinois on November 15, 1928 to parents of Luxemburg descent. Early in the pregnancy with William, his mother feared she would miscarry. Labor was long (62 hours) and delivery difficult with high forceps employed. At birth, William weighed 8 pounds and 5 ounces and was 24 inches long. Breast feedings were inadequate and extremely painful to the mother and were supplemented by bottle feedings almost from the beginning. Weaning from the breast was completed by the time he was 1 month old. He presented a feeding problem from the beginning; he "vomited in a gush" after every feeding and was sickly and severely underweight for the first 3 months. Thereafter under different care and diet he began to gain weight.

At 9-years old, he became interested in the feeling and color and then the theft of women's underclothing. Initially he took personal items from clotheslines, then from basements, and later from houses where he found the doors open or ajar. Dresses or other articles of women's apparel had no appeal for him. Nor was he interested in the undergarments of his immediate family.

Having secured a pair of women's panties or drawers, he would take it to a basement or home, put it on, experience excitement and sexual completion. Most garments he threw away, some he replaced, and others he hoarded in his grandmother's attic. At a spot he described after an investigation, a cardboard box was recovered, which contained approximately 40 pairs of women's old, used panties or drawers. Most were made of rayon and brightly colored.[44] In the beginning when he stole an undergarment, he would confess to a priest. However, he never confessed to a priest after he committed the later burglaries and murders.

When he was 12 or 13, he secured the desired garments by going into houses through windows. This heightened the excitement and became so closely associated with the sight of open windows that gradually he began to experience sexual excitement and even an erection at the mere sight of an open window at the place he planned to burglarize. Going through the window he often ejaculated. When ejaculation occurred inside the room, it was often accompanied or preceded by defecation and/or urination. It is believed that the emptying of bowel and bladder was due to an overflow of spinal reflex.[44] He either left the products of defecation or urination in the room or found them later in his own clothes. After an emission, he left the entered house without taking anything. This was also the time when he felt he had done something wrong.

Three times he killed during burglaries when he was trying to steal objects of his fetishistic desire. On June 5, 1945, he killed Josephine Ross, a 43-year-old Chicago widow; on December 11, 1945, he murdered Frances Brown; and finally on January 7, 1946, six-year old Suzanne Degnan. It is not clear why he murdered so frequently. Perhaps it was because he had a fetish for certain body parts. However, throughout the entire investigation, he maintained that he murdered because he was startled in the act of burglarizing (He kept changing his statements; later he even maintained that he didn't kill anyone.)

William Heirens was convicted of 25 burglaries, 1 robbery, 3 murders, and 1 assault to commit murder. He received 3 life sentences in addition to various sentences that ran concurrently.

TYPES OF FETISHES

Interestingly a number of attempts have been made to classify the various fetishes. Krafft-Ebing[10] classified his cases into three categories according to the nature of the fetish: (i) a part of the female body, (ii) an article of female attire, and (iii) some special material such as fur or velvet. All his cases were men; he was not able to find any case of pathologic fetishism in women. Epstein[30] noted that objects with certain surface characteristics such as glistening (wetness or rubber), metallic shining, leathery, silky, and velvety, or those objects with unusual accentuation of shape such as high heels, often serve as fetishes. It has been asserted that many fetishes are objects which, like the vagina, can serve as receptacles for the male penis. A shoe as a fetish is explained very well by this theory. In one case, the hollow part of an artificial leg was used as a fetish, which also is easily explained by this theory.

Scorolli and associates[31] studied the fetish preferences of about 5000 individuals by examining 381 discussion groups through the Internet. They found that the most common fetish was a preference for body parts or features (33%). This was followed by objects usually associated with the body (30%), a fetish for other people's behavior (18%), self behavior (7%), social behavior (7%), and objects unrelated to the body (5%). Feet (see Figure 5.1) and shoes were the most common target of preferences.

Some very uncommon and weird fetishes have been described. Epstein[30] describes the case of a 15-year old boy, whose fetish was not just a shoe, but a wet shoe. He would ask all the women in the neighborhood to let him get their shoes and wet them. McGowan and Monteith[32] describe a case—perhaps apocryphal—of a young man, who employed a cow's heart as a masturbatory aid. The youth hooked the dead heart up to an electrical outlet to cause it to beat to stimulate him sexually. This activity resulted in his electrocution. What lends support to the story's being apocryphal is the fact that a dead heart was made to beat by electricity.

Fetish Subculture

Fetish subculture includes people with a broad range of sexual fetishes and other paraphilias. People belonging to this subculture tend to be more tolerant of other fetishists than the general community, even if they do not share the other person's specific fetish. Alternative terms for the fetish subculture include *fetish scene* and *fetish community*. The most common paraphilias seen in the fetish subculture are leather fetishism and rubber fetishism.

Garment Fetishism

Garment fetishes revolve around, or fixate on, a particular type of garment. Common examples are shoes, stockings, diapers, gloves,[33] underwear, and bras. The affected person is fixated on the specific garment to such an extent that it exists as an exclusive or recurrent stimulus for sexual gratification.

FIGURE 5.1 Foot fetishism is graphically displayed In this drawing by French Illustrator Martin van Maële (1863–1926).

Shoes

Shoe fetishism, or *retifism*, refers to a sexual attraction to shoes or other footwear. The term *retifism* comes from the French novelist Nicolas-Edme Rétif (also sometimes referred to as Rétif de la Bretonne, 1734–1806). He not only wrote about retifism (it is simply coincidental that the term rhymes well with its sister term fetishism), but suffered from it as well. In this sense, he resembled his contemporary Marquis de Sâde (1740–1814), who was a sadist and wrote extensively on sadism (incidentally both Rétif and Sâde maintained a mutual hate relationship).

Kunjukrishnan and colleagues[34] describe the case of a 27-year old married male who was a shoe fetishist. He was treated with covert aversive conditioning using self-reports of sexual urges and psychophysiological monitoring as objective measures of therapeutic change. Many other cases of shoe fetishism have been described in the literature.[35,36,37,38,39]

Boot fetishism is closely related to shoe fetishism. In most cases the fetish of the boot is accompanied by a fetish for the material from which it is made. Main examples are leather or latex.

High-heeled boots create the illusion of a longer-legged appearance, which is considered to be more physically attractive.

Diapers

Oguz and Uygur[40] describe a case of diaper fetishism in a twenty-two year old man. His mother was psychologically distant from him. The fetish object—the diaper —was recognized during childhood at around the age of four. The patient exhibited his first perverted behavior when he was six. At twelve, the perverted behavior became sexually arousing. During puberty, the fetish object became sexually attractive. Later, the patient could control this behavior.

Leather and Latex

Leather fetishism refers to a sexual attraction to people wearing leather garments. The smell and the sound of leather are often erotic stimuli for people with a leather fetish. Leather is occasionally finished with a glossy surface and produced in attractive, bright colors, providing visual stimuli for some leather fetishists.

Persons having masochism in addition to fetishism may like wearing tight leather garments. In addition to the smell and feel of leather, the restraint provided by tightness may be experienced by them as a form of sexual bondage. Bondage equipment is often made from leather straps for this reason. The term "leather culture" was applied in the 1960s within the U.S. gay sadomasochistic subculture as an umbrella term for alternate sexual practices. A variant is the pony fetish, which involves the use of equestrian-like gear fitted to humans.

It has been argued that leather fetishism, as well as other fetishistic desires nurtured by male members of the society, have caused the evolution of modern women's wear. In other words, if it is fashionable among women to wear leather garments, it is because several men suffer from leather fetishism and like to see them wearing leather. An analysis of certain comic strips and television serials corroborates this trend.[41]

Second Skin Fetishism

Second skin fetishism includes a range of clothing-related fetishes where the clothing fits so tightly that it gives an illusion of the wearer being naked. This illusion may cause further erotic stimulus. The garments usually included in this umbrella term are soft, stretchy, smooth, and often shiny. Thus there exists nylon fetishism (material stretchy, smooth material, sometimes shiny), spandex fetishism (material shiny, smooth, soft, porous), rubber fetishism (material shiny, smooth, less yielding, waterproof), leather fetishism (material shiny, smooth, waterproof, of animal origins) and fur fetishism (material soft, warm, of animal origins). In rubber fetishism, the association with sex toys and the medical uses of rubber may be significant. In fur fetishism, the fact that the fur was originally an animal's skin and hair, may cater to a latent tendency of zoophilia.

See Table 5.1 for select fetishism vocabulary.

MANAGEMENT

Topiramate, a newer anticonvulsant, has been found to be useful in some cases of fetishism. Shiah and colleagues[42] report the case of a 23-year old male having a fetish for women's feet and shoes, which he used to buy or steal. He would feel sexually excited by seeing or smelling female feet and shoes. When individual psychotherapy was not found to be effective, he was treated with topiramate (200 mg per day). Within 6 months his symptoms of fetishism diminished. There were no significant side effects.

TABLE 5.1
Select Fetishism Vocabulary

Breast expansion fetishism —The process of enlarging breasts, whether by age, pregnancy, weight gain or surgery. The enlarged breasts are sexualized to the extent that they become the sole objects of desire (fetishes), excluding everything else. The entertainment industries in Japan, U.S., and some other countries, the Internet, pornography, and particularly adult comics provide the medium and arena in which this fetish thrives.

Breast fetishism—Also known as mastofact, or breast partialism, it refers to an exclusive or almost exclusive reliance on breasts as a stimulus for sexual arousal. It is such a predominant feature of sexuality in the U.S., that Molly Haskell (1939–), a feminist and author from the USA, went as far as to say that "the mammary fixation is the most infantile and the most American, of the sex fetishes." British zoologist and ethologist Desmond Morris (1928–) sees breast fetishism as a prime example of biosemiotics, by which human sexuality is influenced through signaling.

Daddy's girl fetish —A variation of ageplay (please see chapter on masochism), in which a couple uses their real or imagined age difference as the foundation of their sexual roleplay. Generally practiced by an older man and a younger woman, but also by couples of similar age; the woman intentionally plays the role of a little girl.

Doll fetish —Please see transformation fetish.

Female muscle growth (FMG)—A fantasy genre involving muscular growth. Many men enjoy these fantasies, and are attracted to female bodybuilding and other muscular women. The fantasy is often about a reversal of the power relationship between a man and a woman, and thus may have latent elements of masochism.

Glass fetishism —Fetishistic attraction to people wearing prescription glasses, sunglasses, or cosmetic contact lenses or to the act of wearing glasses or the glasses themselves. Other related activities include wearing glasses during sexual acts and ejaculation on glasses.

Milk fetishism —Also known as lactaphilia, lactophilia, or erotic lactation, it refers to the breastfeeding of an adult partner primarily for erotic reasons. Regular partners are said to be in an *adult nursing relationship* (ANR). Two persons in an exclusive relationship of this kind are called a nursing couple. In a variant, *infantilism*, the non-lactating partner assumes the role of a baby in sexual role play. Other themes that may play a part in this variation are diaper fetishism and mother-son incest. Another variation, *milking*, refers to a BDSM sex play in which the submissive woman is milked by the dominant partner or commanded to give milk to him directly from her breasts. *Lactation prostitution* refers to breastfeeding for a price.

Navel fetishism —A strong attraction to the human navel (often called the belly button). Navel fetishists are sexually aroused by viewing, licking, tickling, sucking, sniffing, or kissing the navel of another person, or by having any of this activity done to their own navel by partner or, to a lesser extent, by themselves. Some navel fetishists engage in outercourse (non-penetrative or dry sex as opposed to intercourse) involving the navel. Navel fetishism often co-exists with stomach fetishism (alvinolagnia). A subcategory of navel fetishism is *navel torture* (please see chapter on sexual masochism).

Robot fetishism —Also known as technosexuality, robot fetishism refers to a fetishistic attraction to humanoid or non-humanoid robots, or to people acting like robots or people dressed in robot costumes. A related fantasy involves transformation into a robot. In some ways this practice is similar to agalmatophilia (attraction to or transformation into statues or mannequins). Robot fetishism can be viewed as a form of erotic anthropomorphism.

Schoolgirl uniform fetishism —A sexual fetish in which the affected person derives sexual pleasure from viewing others dressed like schoolgirls or enjoys dressing himself in the typical uniform of a schoolgirl (school skirt or culottes).

TABLE 5.1 (continued)
Select Fetishism Vocabulary

Stocking fetishism —A condition where the affected person finds sexual partners clothed in sheer nylon or silk stockings to be sexually stimulating, or finds the act of a person donning or removing a pair of stockings arousing. Some fetishistic men collect and wear stockings, sometimes hidden under a pair of trousers. This may be related to transvestic fetishism. Preferences may vary, with different people preferring fishnet stockings, fully-fashioned (seamed) stockings, seamless stockings, designer stockings, luxury stockings, reinforced heel and toe stockings (RHT) and stay-ups, etc.

Transformation fetishism —A form of sexual fetishism where a person becomes sexually aroused by descriptions or depictions of transformations, usually the transformations of people into other beings or objects. Examples are *animal transformation, fantasies*, and *doll fetish*. The former include fantasies in which human beings change to animals, or behave as animals (e.g., lycanthropy, vampires). Animal transformation fantasies are popular among those who participate in pony play (please see chapter on zoophilia). *Doll fetish* is a transformation fetish of being transformed into a doll, or transforming someone else into a doll. It is often played out as role play between two or more people. One partner—often the female—is dressed to look like a Barbie doll in shape, with bold hair, enhanced breasts, small waist, high heels, and a very revealing outfit made from rubber, latex, or spandex.

LEGAL ASPECTS

In most nations and jurisdictions, there is no explicit law against fetishism. The word is certainly not mentioned in any statute. In most jurisdictions, the fetishist can at most be convicted of theft or burglary if he has stolen the fetish object. Most often stolen are intimate articles of clothing from a clothes line, basement, dwelling, lockers at bathing establishments, and other similar locations. In rare cases, a fetishist may resort to violence to obtain some article of clothing and may face even assault and robbery charges. In 1849, a printer named Sprague was arrested in Brooklyn on a robbery charge when he attacked a young woman on a public street, threw her on the pavement and decamped with one of her shoes (not both!). He also did not attempt to steal any of her valuables.[43]

More recently Noguchi and Kato[44] describe the case of a 22-year old male who had a fetish for gloves. He became interested in gloves after watching a television program in which the heroine fought her enemies while wearing gloves. Watching pornographic movies allowed him to attach strong sexual significance to gloves when he was 19-years old. Since that time, he was reported to have assaulted women as many as four times in order to rob them of their gloves. Timothy Hodges, a 43-year old male, primarily a voyeur and frotteur, was also a fetishist. He frequently stole women's underwear from clotheslines and laundromats, for which he was arrested also (for details of this case, please see chapter on frotteurism).

Ebing[10] has described several cases where hair fetishists were caught and imprisoned because they tried to cut off women's hair. Most notable are his cases 100 and 101. Case 100 describes a hair-despoiler P., aged 40. He was single, well developed, and intelligent He used to have coitus with prostitutes but was disgusted with this activity. On August 28, 1889, he was arrested at the Trocadero, in Paris, *in flagrante*, as he forcibly cut off a young girl's hair. He was arrested with the hair in his hand and a pair of scissors in his pocket.

Case 101 describes a 25-year old hair-despoiler, E. At the age of 15 he had an erotic feeling of pleasure, with erection, at the sight of one of the village beauties combing her hair. Until that time persons of the opposite sex had never made any impression on him. Two months later, in Paris, the sight of young girls with their hair flowing down over their shoulders excited him intensely. One day he could not resist an opportunity to twist a young girl's hair in his fingers. For this he was arrested and sentenced to imprisonment for 3 months.

After that he served 5 years in the army. Gradually his sexual excitement due to this fetish became so intense that he had to resort to masturbation. The idea of touching female hair, or, better, of possessing it to masturbate while handling it, grew more and more powerful. When he had

TABLE 5.2
Fetishism: Definition and Punishment under Section 62 of the Sexual Offenses Act 2003 of United Kingdom

62 Committing an offense with intent to commit a sexual offense

(1) A person commits an offense under this section if he commits any offense with the intention of committing a relevant sexual offense.

(2) In this section, "relevant sexual offense" means any offense under this Part (including an offense of aiding, abetting, counseling or procuring such an offense).

(3) A person guilty of an offense under this section is liable on conviction on indictment, where the offense is committed by kidnapping or false imprisonment, to imprisonment for life.

(4) Unless subsection (3) applies, a person guilty of an offense under this section is liable—

(a) on summary conviction, to imprisonment for a term not exceeding 6 months or a fine not exceeding the statutory maximum or both;

(b) on conviction on indictment, to imprisonment for a term not exceeding 10 years.

female hair in his fingers, ejaculation was induced. One day he succeeded in cutting hair, about 25 centimeters long, from three little girls in the street and keeping it in his possession. He was arrested when he made a fourth attempt. He was not sentenced this time, but sent to an asylum.

Canada

The Criminal Code of Canada,[45] despite comprehensively dealing with sexual offenses (part V [s 150–s 182]), does not mention fetishism directly or indirectly. It would appear that a fetishist could only be convicted under section 334 (punishment for theft). According to this section, if the value of the property stolen exceeds $5,000, the punishment is imprisonment up to 10 years, and if the value is less than $5,000, the punishment is imprisonment up to 2 years.

India

In India, there is no explicit law against fetishists. A fetishist could perhaps only be convicted of theft if he had stolen an article to be used as a fetish. According to section 379 of IPC,[46] if a person has committed theft, he can be imprisoned for up to three years, or with fine, or with both.

United Kingdom

The Sexual Offenses Act 2003,[47] one of the most comprehensive legislations in the world on sexual offenses, fails to mention the word "fetishism" explicitly. However, section 62 addresses this paraphilia to a great extent. (Table 5.2).

Since a fetishist often steals female clothing (such as bra, panties, handkerchiefs, etc.) from clotheslines or laundromats, it may be construed (not with much stretch of imagination), that a fetishist commits an offense (theft) with intent to commit a sexual offense (fetishism). It is, however, disputable whether fetishism is construed by this Act as a sexual offense, since the word *fetishism* does not find mention anywhere in the Act. However, what is or is not "sexual" is provided for by Section 78 of the same Act, which states:

> For the purposes of this Part (except section 71), penetration, touching or any other activity is sexual if a reasonable person would consider that—
>
> (a) whatever its circumstances or any person's purpose in relation to it, it is because of its nature sexual, or

(b) because of its nature it may be sexual and because of its circumstances or the purpose of any person in relation to it (or both) it is sexual.

It might be argued by some that it might be simpler and easier to prosecute a fetishist under plain theft rather than invoking the Sexual Offenses Act, 2003.

REFERENCES

1. Freud, S. *Basic Writings.* Modern Library, New York, 1938.
2. American Psychiatric Association. *Diagnostic and Statistical Manual of Mental Disorders,* 4th ed. Text rev. American Psychiatric Association, Washington DC, 2000.
3. ICD-10 diagnostic code for fetishism. Available from: http://www.who.int/classifications/apps/icd/icd10online/?gf60.htm+f65
4. Foucault, M. *La volonté de savoir* (Vol. 1 of *Histoire de la sexualité.* 3 vols. 1976–84). Gallimard, Paris, 1976, pages 203-4.
5. Webster, L., Disorders of sexual preference and gender identity, in *Psychosexual Medicine - An Introduction,* Skrine, R. and Montford, H., Eds., Arnold, London, 2001, chap. 15.
6. Raymond, M.J. Case of Fetishism Treated by Aversion Therapy. *Br Med J.* 1956 October 13; **2(4997)**: 854–857.
7. Pitcher, D., Fetishism, in *Principles and Practice of Forensic Psychiatry,* Bluglass, R. and Bowden, P., Eds., Churchill Livingstone, Edinburgh, 1990, chap. VIII.3
8. Gamman L and Makinen M., *Female Fetishism – A new look,* 1st ed., Lawrence & Wishart, London, 1994, page 15.
9. Krafft-Ebing , RF. *Psychopathia Sexualis,* 1st ed. (1886) reprinted by Bloat Books, 1999.
10. de Silva WP. ABC of sexual health. Sexual variations. *BMJ.* 1999 Mar 6;**318(7184)**:654-6.
11. Binet, A. Le fétichisme dans l'amour, in *Etude de Psychologie Experimentale,* Octave Doin, Paris, 1888, pages 1-85.
12. Freud, S. Three Essays on the Theory of Sexuality, Basic Books, New York, NY, 2000 [originally published in Rachman, S.J., and Hodgson, R.J. Experimentally induced "sexual fetishism": Replication and Development. *Psychological Record.* 1968;**18**;25-7.
13. McGuire RJ, Carlisle JM, Young BG. Sexual Deviations As Conditioned Behavior: A Hypothesis. *Behav Res Ther.* 1965 Jan;**3**:185-90.
14. Freud, S. Fetishism. *Standard Edition.* 1927: 21: 147-157 (Hogarth Press, London, 1961).
15. Epstein, A.W. Fetishism: A Comprehensive view, in *Science and Psychoanalysis, vol. 15,* Masserman, J.H., Ed., Grune and Stratton, New York, 1969, pp 81-87.
16. Wickler, W., Socio-sexual signals and their intra-specific imitation among primates, in *Primate Ethology,* Morris, D. Ed, Aldine, Chicago, 1967, pp. 69-147.
17. Huws R, Shubsachs AP, Taylor PJ. Hypersexuality, fetishism and multiple sclerosis. *Br J Psychiatry.* 1991 Feb;**158**:280-1.
18. Hunter R, Logue V, McMenemy WH. Temporal lobe epilepsy supervening on longstandinglonstanding transvestism and fetishism. A case report. *Epilepsia.* 1963 Mar;**4**:60-5.
19. Epstein AW. Relationship of fetishism and transvestism to brain and particularly to temporal lobe dysfunction. *J Nerv Ment Dis.* 1961 Sep;**133**:247-53.
20. Epstein AW. Fetishism: a study of its psychopathology with particular reference to a proposed disorder in brain mechanisms as an etiological factor. *J Nerv Ment Dis.* 1960 Feb;**130**:107-19.
21. Mitchell W, Falconer MA, Hill D. Epilepsy with fetishism relieved by temporal lobectomy. *Lancet.* 1954 Sep 25;**267(6839)**:626-30.
22. Gorman, G.F. Fetishism Occurring in Identical Twins. *Br J Psychiatry.*1964 Mar; **110**: 255 - 256.
23. Chalkley A.J., Powell GE. The clinical description of fortyfourty-eight cases of sexual fetishism. *Br J Psychiatry.* 1983;**142**:292–5.
24. Gosselin, C. and Wilson, G. *Sexual variations,* Faber and Faber, London, 1980.
25. Abel, G.G. and Osborn, C. The paraphilias: the extent and nature of sexually deviant and criminal behavior. *Psychiatr Clin North America.* 1992; 15: 675–687.
26. Scorolli C., Ghirlanda S., Enquist M., Zattoni S, Jannini EA. Relative prevalence of different fetishes. *Int J Impot Res.* 2007 Jul-Aug;**19(4)**:432-7.
27. Young, H. Atypical copulatory behavior of a robin. *Auk.* 1949: **66**:94.

28. Barraud E.M. Sexual behavior occurring as overflow activity in juvenile house sparrow. *British Birds.* 1953: **36**:382.
29. Ficken, MS, Dilger, WC. Comments on redirection with examples of avian copulations with substitute objects. *Animal Behavior,* 1960: **8**:219–22.
30. Michael RP. "Hypersexuality" in male cats without brain damage. *Science,* 1961: **134**:553–4.
31. Beach FA. Sexual behavior in animals and man. The Harvey Lectures. 1950: **43**:259–79.
32. Köksal F, Domian M, Kurt A, Sertel O, Orüng S, Bowers R, Kumru G. An animal model of fetishism. *Behav. Res. Ther.* 2004 Dec: **42**:1421–34.
33. Weinberg MS, Williams CJ, Calhan, C. "If the Shoe Fits…" Exploring Male Homosexual Foot Fetishism. *The Journal of Sex Research,* 1995: **32(1):** 17–27.
34. Cetinkava H, Domian M. Sexual fetishism in a quail (*Coturnix japonica*) model system: test of reproductive success. *J Comp Psychol.* 2006 Nov **120(4):**427–33.
35. Graham JM, Deshardins C. Classical conditioning: induction of lutenizing hormone and testosterone secretion in anticipation of sexual activity. *Science,* 1980 Nov 28:**210(4473):**1039–41.
36. Domian M, Blesbois E & Williams J. The adaptive significance of sexual conditioning: Pavlovian control of sperm release. *Psychological Science,* 1998**:9**:411–15.
37. Gebhard, P. Fetishism and sadomasochism. *Science and Psychoanalysis.* 1969; **15**: 71-80.
38. Freeman M. Sexual Deviance and the Law, in *Sexual Deviation,* 3rd edition. Rosen I., Ed. Oxford University Press, Oxford, 1996, chap. 17, page 433.
39. DeRiver JP. *Crime and the sexual psychopath.* Charles C. Thomas, Springfield, IL, 1958, page 41.
40. Schlesinger LB. *Sexual Murder, Carathymic and Compulsive Homicides.* CRC Press, Boca Raton, 2004.
42. Kennedy F, Hoffman HR & Haines WH. A Study of William Heirens. *American Journal of Psychiatry.* 1947:**104**:113–21.
43. Wilson C and Pitman P. *Encyclopedia of Murder,* Pan, London, 1984, pp. 316–18.
44. Bowman KM, Engle B. Sex Offenses: *The Medical and Legal Implications of Sex Variations.* Law and Contemporary Problems. 1960:**25(2):292**–308.
45. Epstein AW. The fetish object: phylogenetic considerations. *Arch Sex Behav.* 1975 May;**4(3)**:303-8.
46. Scorolli C, Ghirlanda S, Enquist M, Zattoni S, Jannini EA. Relative prevalence of different fetishes. *Int J Impot Res.* 2007 Jul-Aug;**19(4)**:432-7.
47. McGowan, M.G., and Monteith, D. Hypoxyphilia, asphyxiophilia and autoerotic asphyxia. In *Sex crimes and paraphilia,* 1st ed. Hickey, E.W., (Ed.), Pearson Prentice Hall, New Jersey, 2006, chapter 20, page 185
48. Guillemin J. [The fetishism of gloves in the last Bourbons] [Article in French]. *Sem Hop.* 1969 Dec 20;**45(52)**:3411-4.
49. Kunjukrishnan R, Pawlak A, Varan LR. The clinical and forensic psychiatric issues of retifism. *Can J Psychiatry.* 1988 Dec;**33(9)**:819-25.
50. Weinberg MS, Williams CJ, Calhan C. Homosexual foot fetishism. *Arch Sex Behav.* 1994 Dec;**23(6)**:611-26.
51. Richards AK. Female fetishes and female perversions: Hermine Hug-Hellmuth's "a case of female foot or more properly boot fetishism" reconsidered. *Psychoanal Rev.* 1990 Spring;**77(1)**:11-23.
52. Hamilton JW. The evolution of a shoe fetish. *Int J Psychoanal Psychother.* 1977;**6**:323-37.
53. Chambers WM, Janzen WB. The eclectic and multiple therapy of a shoe fetishist. *Am J Psychother.* 1976 Apr;**30(2)**:317-26.
54. McCully RS. A Jungian commentary on Epstein's case wet-shoe fetish. *Arch Sex Behav.* 1976 Mar;**5(2)**:185-8.
55. Oguz N, Uygur N. [A case of diaper fetishism]. *Turk Psikiyatri Derg.* 2005 Summer;**16(2)**:133-8.
56. Bader A. [Modern images of womanhood and their relationship to fetishism][Article in German]. *Schweiz Arch Neurol Neurochir Psychiatr.* 1976;**119(1)**:49-72.
57. Shiah IS, Chao CY, Mao WC, Chuang YJ. Treatment of paraphilic sexual disorder: the use of topiramate in fetishism. *Int Clin Psychopharmacol.* 2006 Jul;**21(4)**:241-3.
58. Fetishism. In "*Sex Crimes and their legal aspects*" by Drzazga J., Charles C. Thomas, Illinois, 1960, (pages 164-170).
59. Noguchi M, Kato S. [A case of Williams syndrome who exhibited fetishism] [Article in Japanese]. *Seishin Shinkeigaku Zasshi.* 2004;**106(10)**:1232-41.
60. Canadian Legal Information Institute. Criminal Code of Canada. Available from : http://www.canlii.org/ca/sta/c-46/

61. The Indian Penal Code, (Act No. 45 of 1860) [6th October, 1860].
62. Sexual Offences Act 2003 [20th November 2003].

6 Voyeurism

INTRODUCTION

Voyeurism, or inspectionism, is an aberrant sexual behavior whereby an individual derives sexual pleasure and gratification from observing unsuspecting and non-consenting people who may be in the act of disrobing, partially or completely nude, engaged in sexual intercourse, or dressed in whatever other way the voyeur finds sexually stimulating. Karpman defined voyeurism as a "pathological indulgence in looking at some form of nudity as a source of gratification in place of the normal sex act."[1] The word derives from French verb *voir* (to see) with the suffix *eur* that translates as "-er" in English. A literal translation would then be "seer" or "observer," with pejorative connotations. Usual examples of voyeurism include a voyeur stationing himself outside a person's home and watching through a window, training instruments such as binoculars, telescopes, or perhaps even electronic devices in other people's bedrooms and bathrooms, or peeping through cracks and crevices in bathroom doors. In India, women are often seen to take baths openly in holy rivers during festive occasions, with hardly any cover. It is not uncommon for voyeurs to take advantage of this occasion and peep at women disrobing and subsequently taking a bath. The thrill of a voyeur comes mainly from a constantly impending fear of being caught while watching. That is why a voyeur derives more pleasure in watching unsuspecting and non-consenting people than a paid strip show, where although he would get to see nudity more easily and clearly, there would be no fear of getting caught.

It is important to differentiate between a true and an opportunistic voyeur. It has been said that voyeurism in its broadest sense is almost normative among men in general as witnessed by the popularity of male-targeted magazines such as *Playboy*, *Penthouse*, and *Hustler*, erotic or pornographic movies, tapes, and Internet sites.[2] Undoubtedly most men, if given an opportunity to view such material, or perhaps an opportunity to furtively watch a woman disrobing, would not avert their eyes. However, these are men who engage in an opportunistic "peep." Such men are not voyeurs according to the definition provided by DSM-IV-TR. For a true voyeur, the peeping must be recurrent and the urges to do so intense—so much intense that they cause marked distress or interpersonal difficulty to him.

DSM-IV-TR[3] assigns code 302.82 to voyeurism, and states the following criteria for diagnosing it:

A. Over a period of at least 6 months, intense, sexually arousing fantasies, sexual urges, or behaviors involving the act of observing an unsuspecting person who is naked, in the process of disrobing, or engaging in sexual activity.
B. The person has acted on these sexual urges, or the sexual urges, or fantasies cause marked distress or interpersonal difficulty.

It is important to note that DSM-IV-TR has now included the fact that the person has either acted on his sexual urges, or the fantasies caused marked distress or interpersonal difficulty.

ICD-9-CM assigns the code 302.82 to voyeurism[4]—same as that assigned by DSM-IV-TR. ICD-10 assigns the code F65.3 to voyeurism[5] and defines it as:

> **F65.3 Voyeurism**
> A recurrent or persistent tendency to look at people engaging in sexual or intimate behavior such as undressing. This is carried out without the observed people being aware, and usually leads to sexual excitement and masturbation.

Undoubtedly, there are many people who do not meet DSM-IV-TR criteria of voyeurism, yet they secretly wish to see stealthily someone of the opposite sex disrobing, or perhaps a couple engaged in sex. These people may be called *pseudovoyeurs.* Jacqueline Kennedy Onassis (1929–1994) was stalked by photographers who hoped to photograph her nude. When one of them managed to photograph her nude on a Greek island, *Hustler* publisher Larry Flynt bought the photos and published them in the August 1975 issue, much to her and the Kennedy family's embarrassment. The photographs quite obviously catered to the tastes of a large number of pseudovoyeurs in the general population.

HISTORICAL PERSPECTIVES

Perhaps the earliest instance of voyeurism comes from the Bible. The Book of Genesis mentions that once Noah was lying naked when his son Ham saw him.

> And the sons of Noah, that went forth of the ark, were Shem, and Ham, and Japheth: and Ham is the father of Canaan. These are the three sons of Noah: and of them was the whole earth overspread. And Noah began to be a husbandman, and he planted a vineyard: and he drank of the wine, and was drunken; and he was uncovered within his tent. And Ham, the father of Canaan, saw the nakedness of his father, and told his two brethren without. And Shem and Japheth took a garment, and laid it upon both their shoulders, and went backward, and covered the nakedness of their father; and their faces were backward, and they saw not their father's nakedness. And Noah awoke from his wine, and knew what his younger son had done unto him. and he said, Cursed be Canaan; a servant of servants shall he be unto his brethren. And he said, Blessed be the Lord God of Shem; and Canaan shall be his servant. God shall enlarge Japheth, and he shall dwell in the tents of Shem; and Canaan shall be his servant.[6,7]

Curiously though it is Ham who sees his father naked, it is Canaan, his son, who gets the punishment.

Another instance of voyeurism in the Bible is when David gets up from his bed, walks around the roof of his palace, and sees Bathsheba taking a bath. He gets so sexually aroused that he sends messengers to get her, so he could have sexual intercourse with her:

> In the spring of the year, at the time when kings normally conduct wars, David sent out Joab with his officers and the entire Israelite army. They defeated the Ammonites and besieged Rabbah. But David stayed behind in Jerusalem. One evening David got up from his bed and walked around on the roof of his palace. From the roof he saw a woman bathing. Now this woman was very attractive. So David sent someone to inquire about the woman. The messenger said, "Isn't this Bathsheba, the daughter of Eliam, the wife of Uriah the Hittite?" And David sent messengers, and took her; and she came in unto him, and he lay with her; for she was purified from her uncleanliness (menstruation): and she returned unto her house.[8]

In yet another Biblical instance of voyeurism, Abimelech of Gerar peeps out of his palace window and sees Isaac and Rebekah petting.

> And it came to pass, when he had been there a long time, that Abimelech king of the Philistines looked out at a window, and saw, and, behold, Isaac was sporting with Rebekah his wife.[9]

There are instances similar to voyeurism in Hindu mythology, too. Ravana, the king of demons, abducts Sita, the wife of righteous king Lord Rama, and takes her to his country, now Sri Lanka.

Lord Rama sends the monkey god Hanuman to bring her back. Hanuman had never seen Sita, and thus he has to go to Ravana's harem at night and examine all the sleeping beauties. The text describes how Lord Hanuman minutely examines Ravana's wives and concubines as they sleep, exhausted with drink and sexual exertion, their clothes awry, their bodies exposed, some, in their drunken passion for their great lover, making love to their musical instruments and even to each other.

After examining many beautiful women of Ravana's harem, Hanuman comes upon a woman of uncommon loveliness sleeping apart from the others. Judging from her exquisiteness and the richness of her jewelry, he thinks that she must be Sita, although it turns out later that she was Mandodari, the wife of Ravana.

After gazing on the exposed bodies of all those ravishing women—women who belong to another man—Lord Hanuman is stricken with anxiety at having committed so serious a breach of conduct. Finally he is able to assuage his sense of guilt and transgression by reflecting that, although he has looked on these erotically stimulating scenes, his mind has been in no way aroused or disturbed. He had no choice but to search for a woman in the women's quarters, and he did so with a pure mind.[10]

Another instance, not from the mythology this time, comes from the ancient kingdom of Lydia. Candaules, king of Lydia from 735 BC to 718 BC was so proud of the beauty of his wife, and so much wanted to impress others with his "possession," that he arranged for his favorite bodyguard Gyges to see his naked wife by stealth. To be fair to Gyges, he refused at the first instance as he did not wish to dishonor the Queen. He also feared what the King might do to him if he did accept. However, Candaules was insistent, and Gyges had no choice but to obey his king. Candaules worked out a detailed plan according in which Gyges would hide behind a door in the royal bedroom to observe the Queen disrobing before her bed. And when the queen turned her back, Gyges would leave the room quietly. Everything went according to the plan. But the Queen saw Gyges as he left the room and realized that she had been betrayed and shamed by her own husband. She immediately decided to have her revenge and worked out her own plan.

The next day, the Queen summoned Gyges to her chamber and told him of the previous night's sordid episode. She confronted him with a choice—either Gyges must kill himself or kill her husband Candaules. Gyges chose the latter and stabbed Candaules with a knife provided by the Queen, killing him in his sleep. Gyges then married the Queen and became King, and father to the Mermnad Dynasty. The legend has been narrated by Herodotus.[11] It gives rise to the modern paraphilic terms *candaulism* or *candaulesism*, which involves getting sadomasochistic pleasure when the husband exposes his wife, or pictures of her, to other voyeurist people.[12]

The next major instance of voyeurism also involves a king and his queen. Lady Godiva (c. 990?–1067), an Anglo-Saxon noblewoman, the wife of Leofric (968–1057), Earl of Mercia and Lord of Coventry, was the victim this time. Leofric had imposed heavy taxes on his subjects, who felt deeply oppressed. Lady Godiva took pity on them and pleaded with her husband to reduce taxes. Leofric did not relent, but when his queen appealed to him again and again, he made an outrageous offer which he was sure Godiva would reject. He promised he would grant her request if she would ride naked through the streets of the town. Lady Godiva, determined to have the taxes reduced, decided to do exactly that. However, she took care to issue a proclamation that all persons should keep within doors or shut their windows. Eventually, she rode through the streets of Coventry, albeit covering her body in her long hair. Only one person in the town, a tailor ever afterwards known as Peeping Tom, disobeyed her proclamation and bore a hole in his shutters so that he might see Godiva pass. He was struck blind by the king for his offense. Leofric kept his word and abolished the oppressive taxes. Modern voyeurs are still known in common parlance as Peeping Toms.

FIGURE 6.1 Candaules, King of Lydia, Shews his wife by stealth to Gyges, one of his bodyguards, in the painting "As She Goes to Bed" by William Etty. This image illustrates Herodotus's version of the tale of Gygesa.

ETIOLOGY

Conditioning

McGuire and colleagues[13] propose that voyeurism can be explained by conditioning (see Chapter 1 for details of classical and operant conditioning). To illustrate their theory, they cite the case of one of their patients who acquired voyeurism through conditioning. The patient, a 28-year old male, married at the age of 24, had had normal sexual interests. However, his wife proved to be totally frigid so that the marriage was never consummated. In the early months of his marriage, while sexually frustrated, he observed that a young lady in the opposite flat was in the habit of stripping in a lighted room with the curtains open (his wife confirmed this story). The patient found this sexually stimulating. The marriage had not been consummated when the couple moved to a new home. In his new environment the patient sought opportunities of seeing women undressing and developed the habit of masturbating on these occasions. Interestingly, the patient retained all the circumstances of the early stimulus and had no interest in nudist films or strip-tease shows. He came to the investigators' notice after his fourth conviction for a "Peeping Tom" offense.

CLASSIFICATION

No formal classification of voyeurism has been suggested till now. The following classification is proposed in this book, based on the *theory of paraphilic equivalence* proposed in this book elsewhere (please see chapter on frotteurism for details). Based on this theory, one can attempt a reasonably accurate classification. The classification proposed here lists all voyeurs on a continuum

FIGURE 6.2 "Lady Godiva riding naked through the streets of Coventry" by John Collier, ca 1897.

with the most innocuous voyeur (or the one who takes minimal risks for his activities and tends to break the law to the least possible extent) to the most dangerous (who takes substantial risks, breaks laws, and often harms the victims, too).

Class I Voyeurs: Pseudovoyeurs

These people are not true voyeurs, since they do not fulfill the DSM-IV-TR criteria of voyeurism. They merely have erotic fantasies involving witnessing the sexual performances of other persons. It is best to call them pseudovoyeurs, or voyeurs of Class I (for details, please see below). A true pseudovoyeur is happy with his fantasies. If an opportunity arose, he would not be bold enough to take the risk of peeping. In this, he differs from the next class.

Class II Voyeurs: Opportunistic Voyeurs

These people also do not fulfill the DSM-IV-TR criteria of voyeurism, as they do not have "intense, sexually arousing fantasies, sexual urges, or behaviors involving the act of observing an unsuspecting person who is naked". However they do have a latent desire to look at a naked person, or a personwho is in the process of disrobing, or engaging in sexual activity. If an opportunity arose, they would take some risk of peeping to satisfy their latent desires. These people may be called latent voyeurs or opportunistic voyeurs.

Class III Voyeurs: Computer Voyeurs

These offenders fulfill their voyeuristic fantasies by online sexual activities and may hack into others' computers and try to view their explicit pictures. It also includes seeing pornographic images on the internet. These voyeurs break various laws relating to computers, internet, and information technology, and thus are criminals in the true sense of the world.

Class IV Voyeurs: Video Voyeurs

These offenders set up complicated equipment in bathrooms, bedrooms, or other intimate places of their victims to see them naked or in acts of disrobing or intercourse. They take more risk than class III voyeurs in that they actually visit the homes of victims (during their absence perhaps, or during their presence by trickery such as masquerading as a plumber). Video voyeurism is now an offense in most jurisdictions.

Class V Voyeurs: Classical Voyeurs

These offenders are the true or classical voyeurs as DSM-IV-TR describes them. They have over a period of at least six months intense, sexually arousing fantasies, sexual urges, or behaviors involving the act of observing an unsuspecting person who is naked, in the process of disrobing, or engaging in sexual activity. They also act on these sexual urges, and the sexual urges or fantasies cause marked distress or interpersonal difficulty. They take greater risk than voyeurs of class IV, because they are *physically* present when the victim is disrobing or having sexual intercourse, and thus have a greater chance of getting caught.

Class VI Voyeurs: Criminal Voyeurs

Studies suggest that some voyeurs also engage in serious sex offenses and can become sexually aggressive with women or children. Voyeurs who engage in other serious sex offenses, belong to this category. These are the most dangerous of all voyeurs.

PREVALENCE

Crépault and Couture[14] interviewed 94 men about their erotic fantasies occurring during heterosexual activity. The majority of these men were married, and their average duration of cohabitation with a woman was 6.5 years. As many as 54.3% reported having erotic fantasies involving witnessing the sexual performance of other persons. Such people are not true voyeurs because they do not meet the strict DSM-IV-TR criteria. As noted earlier, these are class I voyeurs or pseudovoyeurs. Furthermore, 40.4% reported having had fantasies of a situation where they were observed by other people during sexual activity.

In 1996, Långström and Seto randomly selected 2,450 individuals between the ages of 18 and 60 years from the general population of Sweden and interviewed them in a broad survey of sexuality and health. A total of 191 respondents (7.7%) reported at least one incident of being sexually aroused by spying on others having sex.[15]

VARIATIONS OF VOYEURISM

Several terms have been used as synonyms of voyeurism, although some writers have constantly pointed out subtle differences. The terms *scopophilia* and *scoptophilia* are taken as synonyms to *voyeurism* by most writers. However, others have pointed out a minor difference. If the victim is unsuspecting and non-consenting, the act is voyeurism, but if the other party is consenting, the act is scopophilia or scoptophilia[16] (cf. frottage and frotteurism). Furthermore if the person watched is in the act of disrobing, or nude, the act is voyeurism, but if the person watched is engaged in sex, the act is either mixoscopia (if the watched person is the voyeur's lover) or allopellia (if the watched persons are complete strangers).

Video Voyeurism

Video voyeurism is an entirely new variant, which has risen with the advent of modern electronics, camera-enabled cell phones, spycams, and other sophisticated miniaturized technology capable of taking pictures of unsuspecting persons. The typical technique employed is this: a spycam-like device is hidden in the bedroom, bathroom, or some other place where the victim (a woman usually) is likely to disrobe or engage in sex. Movies of women disrobing or engaging in sex may then be directly transferred to the offender's PC or other receiving device, electronically.

Video voyeurism first gained worldwide attention in 1998, when Susan Wilson discovered that her neighbor had been secretly videotaping her with cameras hidden in her Louisiana home.[17] At that time, there were no laws to fit the crime. Her case partly inspired the federal law known as the Video Voyeurism Prevention Act of 2004.

Another outrageous case of video voyeurism—the one that spurred most jurisdictions to formulate laws against it—occurred in November 2001, when Stephanie Fuller, a Long Island resident, was secretly videotaped in her bedroom by her landlord, William Schultz. Schultz allegedly hid a tiny video camera in the smoke detector directly above her bed and taped her for a month. He also hid a tiny camera in the bathroom. A line from the camera led into Schultz's apartment, from which he both viewed and recorded the images. His crime was exposed when Stephanie's boyfriend noticed suspicious wires coming out of the smoke-detector. The couple called the police, and Schultz was arrested. Ironically, Schultz could not be charged for voyeurism, because at that time, New York State's "Peeping Tom" laws covered only *direct* peeping through the windows, or at most, the use of a camera or other device to peer through a window. Since Schultz was not "peering through a window" either directly or through his device, he could not be charged with voyeurism. He was, however, charged with trespassing. He pleaded guilty to this charge and received three years' probation as well as 280 hours of community service, and was ordered to pay $1,468 in restitution. Specific laws were later enacted against video voyeurism throughout the United States; they are now commonly known as Stephanie's Laws.

Between April and August 2004, Dr. William Fouche, 59, an Idaho gynecologist surreptitiously videotaped a number of women. His victims included a 17-year old Guatemalan exchange student who lived with him while she attended North Idaho College. She had been invited to travel from Guatemala by Fouche to live with him and attend college. Apparently, like most voyeurs, Fouche was also an exhibitionist. The young Guatemalan student began to feel uncomfortable when she found that Fouche would come into her room dressed only in a towel and ask if she needed help with homework. Sometimes the towel fell open, exposing Fouche. She grew suspicious when Fouche began asking her when she planned to shower. He would get angry if she didn't turn on the bathroom's ventilation fan. This was because if she turned it on, the two-way mirror in her bathroom wouldn't fog and obscure his view. When she continued to leave the fan off, Fouche rewired the bathroom so that the fan was no longer on a separate switch. When she began showering at the gym, Fouche was upset. She eventually went into Fouche's bathroom—which shared a wall with the guest bathroom—and discovered a hole in the wall. She could see through the mirror in the neighboring bathroom. She also discovered cameras that had pictures of her friends from school. One victim was videotaped while she was 7 months pregnant and had used his bathroom to change. Fouche was ordered to serve 4 years in prison on one count of video voyeurism.[18]

Another notable case involved Michael Dorrington, a kindergarten teacher who asked some of his female students to change into swimsuits in a closet at school. A hidden camera recorded the children as they changed.

Video voyeurism by its very nature is far more intrusive and disturbing than mere window peeping. Coupled with the instantaneous distribution capabilities of the Internet, it makes the offense still more grave and serious. There are now specific laws against it in most jurisdictions.

Downblousing

Downblouse is a variant of voyeurism where the voyeur is attracted to women bending downward so he can view their breasts down their shirts or blouse. Viewing a woman's breast while sitting on a higher level than the woman is also downblousing. A good example is a person sitting on first floor of a restaurant, viewing the breasts of an unsuspecting woman sitting on the ground floor. Taking surreptitious photographs, especially with camera-enabled cell phones, is also common among voyeurs. Many times, these photographs are then posted on the Internet for all to see. Many nations and jurisdictions have now outlawed downblousing.

Voyeurists, for their part, have argued that women in public areas can claim only limited privacy expectations if portions of their unclothed anatomy are suddenly visible to onlookers or even to photographers.

Upskirting

Upskirting, another variant of voyeurism, is similar to downblousing, except that here the voyeur sees (and sometimes takes photographs of) women's genitalia and buttocks under her skirt. A common technique is to go near a woman standing in a mall, bend down pretending to pick up a fallen item, and quickly take a photograph up the woman's skirt. Like downblousing, upskirting is now also illegal in many jurisdictions. In Japan, the practice is known as *panchira* (from *panty* and *chira*, the Japanese word for "glance" or "glimpse").

Several celebrities have been accused and convicted of upskirting. On September 24, 2000, Masashi Tashiro (1956–), a Japanese television performer and the founding member of the band *Rats & Star*, was sent to the prosecutor's office for filming up a woman's skirt with a camcorder in Tokyu Toyoko Line Toritsudaigaku Station in Meguro, Tokyo. He was later fined 50,000 yen (430 USD) for this incident. On April 8, 2004, Kazuhide Uekusa (1960–), noted Japanese economist, economic analyst, and a professor at the graduate school of Waseda University, was arrested as he tried to peep under a high school girl's skirt using his hand mirror on the escalator of Shinagawa Station of East Japan Railway Company in Minato, Tokyo. At his trial, which opened at the Tokyo District Court on March 23, 2005, the Chief Justice sentenced him to a fine of 500,000 yen and confiscated of his hand mirror. Uekusa, mostly known as "Mirrorman" today, was later convicted of toucherism, too (please see chapter on frotteurism).

Zoophilic Voyeurism

McNally and Lukach describe a curious case of zoophilic voyeurism (peeping through windows to gaze at animals), zoophilic frotteurism (rubbing one's genitals on the furs of live animals), and zoophilic exhibitionism (exposure of genitals in front of animals with concomitant masturbation) practiced by in one person[19] (please see chapter on exhibitionism for details of this case).

OFFENDER CHARACTERISTICS

As noted in Chapter 1, the chapter on exhibitionism, voyeurism often co-exists with exhibitionism. Furthermore, an individual may often switch between these two themes. The switch between voyeurism and exhibitionism is common and has been known for some time.[20] Voyeurism also co-exists with other "courtship disorder paraphilias," such as frotteurism and rape. Timothy Hodges, a 43-year old male, represents a typical voyeur (for details of this case, please see chapter on frotteurism).

It appears that voyeurs may be males or female. Similarly, the victims may also belong to either sex. Thus there could be a male upon female voyeur (a male who secretly watches a female), a female upon male voyeur, a male upon male voyeur, and a female upon female voyeur. Not many examples of the last three varieties have appeared in the literature, although some examples have started appearing lately. Bickham and colleagues[21] interviewed 417 adult (over the age of 18 years) heterosexual females and found that 31 (7.4%) engaged in voyeuristic behavior, in which the victim was a female (female upon female voyeurs).

MANAGEMENT

Long-acting GnRH analogues, together with psychotherapy, have been found to be highly effective in the treatment of voyeurism.[22] Long-term treatment, relapse prevention, and monitoring are required in order for the treatment to be effective.[23] Psychotherapeutical approaches attempt to exert control over impulsivity, developing interpersonal skills and more adept social relationships, and creating healthier methods of sexual gratification. Pharmacological approaches include administration of selective serotonin reuptake inhibitors (SSRIs) such as paroxetine.[24]

LEGAL ASPECTS

Most countries of the developed world now have specific laws against voyeurism and its variants. These are often known as "Peeping Tom" statutes.

AUSTRALIA

Queensland

Queensland criminal law is governed by Criminal Code 1899 (for details please see chapter on exhibitionism). Most sexual offenses are defined in chapter 22, entitled "Offenses against Morality." Section 227A of this Code defines observations or recordings in breach of privacy, which is equivalent to voyeurism. Under Queensland law, voyeurism is a misdemeanor, and the maximum penalty is imprisonment for up to 2 years. The section also gives some explicit examples of what may be construed as illegal observations (voyeurism) in breach of privacy. It states:

Section 227A —Observations or recordings in breach of privacy

(1) A person who observes or visually records another person, in circumstances where a reasonable adult would expect to be afforded privacy—
 (a) without the other person's consent; and
 (b) when the other person—
  (i) is in a private place; or
  (ii) is engaging in a private act and the observation or visual recording is made for the purpose of observing or visually recording a private act; commits a misdemeanor.

 Maximum penalty—2 years imprisonment.

 Examples of circumstances where a reasonable adult would expect to be afforded privacy—
  1. A person changing in a communal change room at a swimming pool may expect to be observed by another person who is also changing in the room but may not expect to be visually recorded.
  2. A person who needs help to dress or use a toilet may expect to be observed by the person giving the help but may not expect to be observed by another person.

(2) A person who observes or visually records another person's genital or anal region, in circumstances where a reasonable adult would expect to be afforded privacy in relation to that region—
 (a) without the other person's consent; and

(b) when the observation or visual recording is made for the purpose of observing or visually recording the other person's genital or anal region;

commits a misdemeanor.

Maximum penalty—2 years imprisonment.

Example for subsection (2)—using a mobile phone in a public place to take photos of women's underwear under their skirts without their consent

(3) In subsection (2)—genital or anal region, of a person, means the person's genital or anal region when the region is covered by underwear or bare.

CANADA

According to section 162 of the Criminal Code of Canada,[25] voyeurism is an offense:

Voyeurism

(1) Every one commits an offense who, surreptitiously, observes—including by mechanical or electronic means—or makes a visual recording of a person who is in circumstances that give rise to a reasonable expectation of privacy, if

(a) the person is in a place in which a person can reasonably be expected to be nude, to expose his or her genital organs or anal region or her breasts, or to be engaged in explicit sexual activity;

(b) the person is nude, is exposing his or her genital organs or anal region or her breasts, or is engaged in explicit sexual activity, and the observation or recording is done for the purpose of observing or recording a person in such a state or engaged in such an activity; or

(c) the observation or recording is done for a sexual purpose.

Definition of "visual recording"

(2) In this section, "visual recording" includes a photographic, film or video recording made by any means.

Exemption

(3) Paragraphs (1) (a) and (b) do not apply to a peace officer who, under the authority of a warrant issued under section 487.01, is carrying out any activity referred to in those paragraphs.

Printing, publication, etc., of voyeuristic recordings

(4) Every one commits an offense who, knowing that a recording was obtained by the commission of an offense under subsection (1), prints, copies, publishes, distributes, circulates, sells, advertises or makes available the recording, or has the recording in his or her possession for the purpose of printing, copying, publishing, distributing, circulating, selling or advertising it or making it available.

Punishment

(5) Every one who commits an offense under subsection (1) or (4)

(a) is guilty of an indictable offense and liable to imprisonment for a term not exceeding 5 years; or

(b) is guilty of an offense punishable on summary conviction.

Defense

(6) No person shall be convicted of an offense under this section if the acts that are alleged to constitute the offense serve the public good and do not extend beyond what serves the public good.

Question of law, motives

(7) For the purposes of subsection (6),

(a) it is a question of law whether an act serves the public good and whether there is evidence that the act alleged goes beyond what serves the public good, but it is a question of fact whether the act does or does not extend beyond what serves the public good; and

(b) the motives of an accused are irrelevant.

INDIA

In India, there is no explicit law on voyeurism, as in the UK. However, voyeurs may be prosecuted under section 509 of the Indian Penal Code (IPC).[26] It states:

> ***509. Word, gesture or act intended to insult the modesty of a woman***
> Whoever, intending to insult the modesty of any woman, utters any word, makes any sound or gesture, or exhibits any object, intending that such word or sound shall be heard, or that such gesture or object shall be seen, by such woman, or **intrudes upon the privacy of such woman**, shall be punished with simple imprisonment for a term which may extend to one year, or with fine, or with both.

The relevant phrase here is *intrudes upon the privacy of such woman*. A voyeur definitely intrudes upon the privacy of a woman. The section seems to cover the intentional setting up of recording or photographic equipment by a voyeur in, say, a woman's bedroom or bathroom. The punishment is simple imprisonment for a term extending up to 1 year. Interestingly, under this section, a voyeur can only be convicted if he/she were secretly watching a woman or perhaps an act involving a woman (e.g., a heterosexual act between a male and a female or perhaps an act of lesbianism between two women). There is no equivalent provision if the voyeur were secretly watching a male, males, or a homosexual act between two males.

To curb the rising menace of video voyeurism, the Government of India has introduced The Information Technology (Amendment) Bill, 2006, in the Parliament, which—among other things—aims to introduce Section 502A in the Indian Penal Code stating as follows:

CHAPTER XXIA
OF PRIVACY

A. Whoever, intentionally or knowingly captures, publishes or transmits the image of a private area of any person without his or her consent, under circumstances violating the privacy of that person, shall be punished with simple imprisonment for a term which may extend to two years or with fine not exceeding two lakh (two hundred thousand) rupees, or with both.

Explanation.—For the purpose of this section—

(a) "transmit" means to send electronically a visual image with the intent that it be viewed by a person or persons;

(b) "capture", with respect to an image, means to videotape, photograph, film or record by any means;

(c) "private area" means the naked or undergarment clad genitals, pubic area, buttocks or female breast;

(d) "publishes" means reproduction in the printed or electronic form and making it available for public;

(e) "under circumstances violating privacy" means circumstances in which a person can have a reasonable expectation that—

(i) he or she could disrobe in privacy, without being concerned that an image of his private area is being captured; or

(ii) any part of his or her private area would not be visible to the public, regardless of whether that person is in a public or private place.

At the time of writing this book, this bill is being examined by a standing committee of the Indian Parliament.

United Kingdom

Voyeurism is a crime in most nations and jurisdictions. According to Section 67 of the Sexual Offenses Act 2003 of UK,[27] exhibitionism is an offense.

Voyeurism

(1) A person commits an offense if—
- (a) for the purpose of obtaining sexual gratification, he observes another person doing a private act, and
- (b) he knows that the other person does not consent to being observed for his sexual gratification.

(2) A person commits an offense if—
- (a) he operates equipment with the intention of enabling another person to observe, for the purpose of obtaining sexual gratification, a third person (B) doing a private act, and
- (b) he knows that B does not consent to his operating equipment with that intention.

(3) A person commits an offense if—
- (a) he records another person (B) doing a private act,
- (b) he does so with the intention that he or a third person will, for the purpose of obtaining sexual gratification, look at an image of B doing the act, and
- (c) he knows that B does not consent to his recording the act with that intention.

(4) A person commits an offense if he installs equipment, or constructs or adapts a structure or part of a structure, with the intention of enabling himself or another person to commit an offense under subsection (1).

(5) A person guilty of an offense under this section is liable
- (a) on summary conviction, to imprisonment for a term not exceeding 6 months or a fine not exceeding the statutory maximum or both;
- (b) on conviction on indictment, to imprisonment for a term not exceeding 2 years.

The main operative word in section 67 is "private act." Section 68 strives to define what exactly is a private act. It also attempts to explain the meaning of "structure" as mentioned in subsection (4) of section 67. Section 68 states:

Voyeurism: Interpretation

(1) For the purposes of section 67, a person is doing a private act if the person is in a place which, in the circumstances, would reasonably be expected to provide privacy, and—
- (a) the person's genitals, buttocks or breasts are exposed or covered only with underwear,
- (b) the person is using a lavatory, or
- (c) the person is doing a sexual act that is not of a kind ordinarily done in public.

(2) In Section 67, "structure" includes a tent, vehicle or vessel or other temporary or movable structure.

UNITED STATES

Video Voyeurism

In 2004, the U.S. government passed the Video Voyeurism Prevention Act of 2004,[28] in order to amend Title 18 (Crimes and Criminal Procedure) of the United States Code. The amendment aimed to prohibit knowingly videotaping, photographing, filming, recording by any means, or broadcasting an image of a private area of an individual, without that individual's consent, under circumstances in which that individual has a reasonable expectation of privacy. The act also aimed to define a "private area" as the naked or undergarment-clad genitals, pubic area, buttocks, or female breast of an individual.

The act amended Title 18, United States Code, by inserting Chapter 88 entitled "Privacy." It states:

CHAPTER 88—PRIVACY
§1801. Video Voyeurism

(a) Whoever, in the special maritime and territorial jurisdiction of the United States, has the intent to capture an image of a private area of an individual without their consent, and knowingly does so under circumstances in which the individual has a reasonable expectation of privacy, shall be fined under this title or imprisoned not more than one year, or both.
(b) In this section—
  (1) the term 'capture', with respect to an image, means to videotape, photograph, film, record by any means, or broadcast;
  (2) the term 'broadcast' means to electronically transmit a visual image with the intent that it be viewed by a person or persons;
  (3) the term 'a private area of the individual' means the naked or undergarment clad genitals, pubic area, buttocks, or female breast of that individual;
  (4) the term 'female breast' means any portion of the female breast below the top of the areola; and
  (5) the term 'under circumstances in which that individual has a reasonable expectation of privacy' means—
    (A) circumstances in which a reasonable person would believe that he or she could disrobe in privacy, without being concerned that an image of a private area of the individual was being captured; or
    (B) circumstances in which a reasonable person would believe that a private area of the individual would not be visible to the public, regardless of whether that person is in a public or private place.
(c) This section does not prohibit any lawful law enforcement, correctional, or intelligence activity.

Significantly, this act aims to define what exactly is a female breast. It is defined as any portion of the female breast *below the top of the areola*. In contrast, Section 68 (1) (a) of the Sexual Offenses Act 2003 of the United Kingdom leaves the definition of breast wide open to the interpretation of the judiciary. The latter also does not attempt to differentiate between a male and a female breast.

Voyeurism and Disability Law

The Americans with Disabilities Act of 1990,[29] Titles I and V, which were enacted to provide a clear and comprehensive national mandate for the elimination of discrimination against individuals with disabilities, *does not* include voyeurism as a disability, i.e., persons suffering from voyeurism are *not* entitled to the benefits granted by this act. These titles appear in Volume 42 of the United States Code, beginning at Section 12101. Section 12102 (2) of the United States Code[30] defines disability as follows:

Disability. The term "disability" means, with respect to an individual—
- (A) a physical or mental impairment that substantially limits one or more of the major life activities of such individual;
- (B) a record of such an impairment; or
- (C) being regarded as having such an impairment.

However, voyeurism, and most other paraphilias (namely, transvestism, transsexualism, pedophilia, exhibitionism, and gender identity disorders which *do not result from physical impairments*), are not counted as disabilities.

Section 12211 of the United States Code[31] states:

- (a) Homosexuality and bisexuality. For purposes of the definition of "disability" in section 12102 (2) of this title [section 3(2)], homosexuality and bisexuality are not impairments and as such are not disabilities under this chapter.
- (b) Certain conditions. Under this chapter, the term "disability" shall not include—
  - (1) transvestism, transsexualism, pedophilia, exhibitionism, voyeurism, gender identity disorders not resulting from physical impairments, or other sexual behavior disorders;
  - (2) compulsive gambling, kleptomania, or pyromania; or
  - (3) psychoactive substance use disorders resulting from current illegal use of drugs.

Section 1630.3 of the Code of Federal Regulations (CFR) giving exceptions to the definitions of "Disability" and "Qualified Individual with a Disability" also excludes voyeurists (and other paraphiliacs) from the list of disabled persons. Subsection (d) of section 1630.3 states:[32]

- (d) Disability does not include:
  - (1) Transvestism, transsexualism, pedophilia, exhibitionism, voyeurism, gender identity disorders not resulting from physical impairments, or other sexual behavior disorders;
  - (2) Compulsive gambling, kleptomania, or pyromania; or
  - (3) Psychoactive substance use disorders resulting from current illegal use of drugs.
- (e) Homosexuality and bisexuality are not impairments and so are not disabilities as defined in this part.

In addition to federal laws, several states have their own voyeurism laws. Here are some representative laws.

Arkansas

Title 5 of Arkansas Code deals with criminal offenses. Chapter 16 of Title 5 deals with voyeurism offenses. The relevant law on video voyeurism and voyeurism is as follows:

Crime of Video Voyeurism.

- (a) It is unlawful to use any camera, videotape, photo-optical, photoelectric, or any other image recording device for the purpose of secretly observing, viewing, photographing, filming, or videotaping a person present in a residence, place of business, school, or other structure, or any room or particular location within that structure, if that person:
  - (1) Is in a private area out of public view;
  - (2) Has a reasonable expectation of privacy; and

(3) Has not consented to the observation.

(b) A violation of this section is a Class D felony.

(c) The provisions of this section do not apply to any of the following:

(1) Video recording or monitoring conducted pursuant to a court order from a court of competent jurisdiction;

(2) Security monitoring operated by or at the direction of an occupant of a residence;

(3) Security monitoring operated by or at the direction of the owner or administrator of a place of business, school, or other structure;

(4) Security monitoring operated in a motor vehicle used for public transit;

(5) Security monitoring and observation associated with a correctional facility, regardless of the location of the monitoring equipment;

(6) Video recording or monitoring conducted by a law enforcement officer within the official scope of his or her duty; or

(7) Videotaping pursuant to §12-12-508 (b).[33]

It is clear that videotaping such as that ordered by a court, or for security purposes, in most instances is not covered under video voyeurism. Statute 12-12-508, which also is immune to video voyeurism, deals with radiology procedures, photographs, and medical records, whereby in cases of child maltreatment, hospitals and clinics may make videotapes which may be probative as to the existence or extent of child maltreatment.

The Arkansas law on voyeurism is as follows:[34]

Voyeurism.

(a) As used in this section:

(1) "Nude or partially nude" means any person who has less than a fully opaque covering over the genitals, pubic area, or buttocks;

(2) "Private place" means a place where a person may reasonably expect to be safe from being observed without his or her knowledge and consent; and

(3) "Public accommodation" means a business, accommodation, refreshment, entertainment, recreation, or transportation facility where a good, service, facility, privilege, advantage, or accommodation is offered, sold, or otherwise made available to the public.

(b) A person commits the offense of voyeurism if for the purpose of sexual arousal or gratification, he or she knowingly:

(1) Without the consent of each person who is present in the private place, looks into a private place that is, or is part of, a public accommodation and in which a person may reasonably be expected to be nude or partially nude; or

(2) Enters another person's private property without the other person's consent and looks into any person's dwelling unit if all of the following apply:

(A) The person looks into the dwelling with the intent to intrude upon or interfere with a person's privacy;

(B) The person looks into a part of the dwelling in which an individual is present;

(C) The individual present has a reasonable expectation of privacy in that part of the dwelling; and

(D) The individual present does not consent to the person's looking into that part of the dwelling.

(c) (1) Except as provided in subdivision (c)(2) of this section, a violation of this section is a Class A misdemeanor.

(2) A violation of this section is a Class D felony if:

(A) A victim is under seventeen (17) years of age; and

(B) The person who commits the offense holds a position of trust or authority over the victim.

Significantly, in the Arkansas statute the important components of the crime of voyeurism are (i) the offender looks at a nude or partially nude person present in a private place, (ii) the offense is committed for the purpose of sexual arousal, (iii) there is an absence of consent of the person who is looked upon, (iv) the person looked upon has a reasonable expectation of privacy, (v) the offense is graver if the victim is under 17 years of age or the person who commits the offense holds a position of trust or authority over the victim. A person committing a sexual offense who "holds a position of trust or authority" (such as a doctor or teacher [trust] or a jailer or police officer [authority]) is usually seen to commit a much graver offense. Most rape laws reflect the same principle.

Indiana

Indiana Code has 36 titles, of which Title 35 deals with criminal law and procedure. Title 35 has 50 articles, of which two are important and relevant to sex crimes—Article 42, entitled "Offenses Against The Person" and Article 45, entitled "Offenses Against Public Health, Order, And Decency." Article 45 has 18 chapters, of which chapter 4 is entitled "Indecent Acts and Prostitution." Section 5 of this chapter deals with voyeurism. The convention of representing a section is: Title-Article-Chapter-Section. Thus, the section dealing with voyeurism would be IC 35-45-4-5 (Indiana Code, Title 35, Article 45, Chapter 4, Section 1). It states:

Voyeurism; "peep" defined

(a) A person:
  (1) who:
    (A) peeps; or
    (B) goes upon the land of another with the intent to peep; into an occupied dwelling of another person; or
  (2) who peeps into an area where an occupant of the area reasonably can be expected to disrobe, including:
    (A) restrooms;
    (B) baths;
    (C) showers; and
    (D) dressing rooms; without the consent of the other person, commits voyeurism, a Class B misdemeanor.

(b) However, the offense under subsection (a) is a class D felony if:
  (1) it is knowingly or intentionally committed by means of a camera, a video camera, or any other type of video recording device; or
  (2) the person who commits the offense has a prior unrelated conviction:
    (A) under this section; or
    (B) in another jurisdiction, including a military court, for an offense that is substantially similar to an offense described in this section.

(c) "Peep" means any looking of a clandestine, surreptitious, prying, or secretive nature.

Rhode Island

Section 11-45-1 of Rhode Island General Laws defines disorderly conduct (both exhibitionism and voyeurism are included under this law). Subsections (a)(6) and (7) within this law define voyeurism as follows:

(6) A person commits disorderly conduct if he or she intentionally, knowingly, or recklessly: enters upon the property of another and for a lascivious purpose looks into an occupied dwelling or other building on the property through a window or other opening; or

(7) Who without the knowledge or consent of the individual, looks for a lascivious purpose through a window, or any other opening into an area in which another would have a reasonable expectation of privacy, including, but not limited to, a restroom, locker room, shower, changing room, dressing room, bedroom, or any other such private area, not withstanding any property rights the individual may have in the location in which the private area is located.

The punishment is same as for exhibitionism, i.e., imprisonment for 6 months, a fine of not more than $500, or both.

Washington

Chapter 9A.44 of The Revised Code of Washington (RCW) deals with sex offenses. Section 9A.44.115 makes voyeurism a class C felony. It states:

A person commits the crime of voyeurism if, for the purpose of arousing or gratifying the sexual desire of any person, he or she knowingly views, photographs, or films:

(a) Another person without that person's knowledge and consent while the person being viewed, photographed, or filmed is in a place where he or she would have a reasonable expectation of privacy; or

(b) The intimate areas of another person without that person's knowledge and consent and under circumstances where the person has a reasonable expectation of privacy, whether in a public or private place.

(c) Voyeurism is a class C felony.

REFERENCES

1. Karpman, B. The *Sexual Offender and His Offenses*, Julian Press, New York, 1954.
2. Bullough, V.L., Voyeurism. In "*Encyclopedia of Rape*", Smith, M.D. (ed), Greenwood Press, Westport, 2004, pages 266-267.
3. American Psychiatric Association. *Diagnostic and Statistical Manual of Mental Disorders*, 4th ed. Text rev. American Psychiatric Association, Washington DC, 2000.
4. ICD-9-CM diagnostic codes for paraphilias. Available from: http://icd9cm.chrisendres.com/2007/index.php?action=child&recordid=2342.
5. ICD-10 diagnostic codes for paraphilias. Available from: http://www.who.int/classifications/apps/icd/icd10online/?gf60.htm+f65.
6. Genesis 9:18-27. The Holy Bible. Authorized King James Version. Oxford University Press, New York, 1972.
7. Akerley, B.E. *The X-Rated Bible: An Irreverent Survey of Sex in the Scriptures.* Feral House, Los Angeles, 1998.
8. II Samuel 11:1-4. The Holy Bible. Authorized King James Version. Oxford University Press, New York, 1972.
9. Genesis 26:8. The Holy Bible. Authorized King James version. Oxford Univ. Press, New York, 1972.
10. Goldman, R.P. and Goldman, S.S. The Ramayana of Valmiki: An Epic of Ancient India, Volume V: Sundarakanda. Princeton University Press, Princeton, New Jersey, 1996.
11. Herodotus, Cary H. (Translator). *The Histories of Herodotus.* Kessinger Publishing, Whitefish, MT, 2005.
12. Marten, Z. Candaulesism—case report [Article in Polish]. Psychiatr Pol. 1986 May-Jun;20(3):235-7.
13. McGuire, R.J., Carlisle, J.M., Young, B.G. Sexual Deviations As Conditioned Behavior: A Hypothesis. *Behav Res Ther.* 1965 Jan;**3**:185-90.

14. Crépault, C, Couture, M. Men's erotic fantasies. *Arch Sex Behav.* 1980 Dec;**9(6)**:565-81.
15. Långström, N., Seto, M.C.. Exhibitionistic and voyeuristic behavior in a Swedish national population survey. *Arch Sex Behav.* 2006 Aug;35(4):427-35.
16. Love, B. *Encyclopedia of Unusual sex practices.* Barricade Books, New York, 1992.
17. Williams, K. Policing Video Voyeurs. *Newsweek* v. 145 no. 7 (February 14 2005) p. 35.
18. Brodwater, T., Doctor Gets 4 Years For Video Voyeurism; Victims describe system he used to videotape people in bathroom. *Spokesman Review.* Spokane, Washington. Nov 17, 2005. page. A.1.
19. McNally, R.J., Lukach, B.M. Behavioral treatment of zoophilic exhibitionism. *J Behav Ther Exp Psychiatry.* 1991 Dec;22(4):281-4.
20. Philpot, C.D. Paraphilia and aging. *Clin Geriatr Med.* 2003 Aug;19(3):629-36.
21. Bickham, P.J, O'Keefe, S.L., Baker, E., Berhie, G., Kommor, M.J., Harper-Dorton, K.V. Correlates of early overt and covert sexual behaviors in heterosexual women. *Arch Sex Behav.* 2007 Oct;**36(5)**:724-40.
22. Rösler, A, Witztum, E. Pharmacotherapy of paraphilias in the next millennium. *Behav Sci Law.* 2000;**18(1)**:43-56.
23. Seligman, L. and Hardenburg, S.A. Assessment and Treatment of Paraphilias. *Journal of Counseling and Development.* 2000;**78**:107-13.
24. Abouesh, A, Clayton, A. Compulsive voyeurism and exhibitionism: a clinical response to paroxetine. *Arch Sex Behav.* 1999 Feb;**28(1)**:23-30.
25. Section 162, Criminal Code of Canada (R.S., 1985, c. C-46).
26. The Indian Penal Code, (Act No. 45 of 1860) [6th October, 1860].
27. Sexual Offenses Act 2003 [20th November 2003].
28. Video Voyeurism Prevention Act of 2004, Pub. L. 108—495, §1, Dec. 23, 2004, 118 Stat. 3999.
29. Americans with Disabilities Act of 1990 (Pub. L. 101-336).
30. 42 U.S.C. §12102 (2).
31. 42 U.S.C. §12211.
32. Code of Federal Regulations, 29 CFR §1630.3.
33. Arkansas Code Ann. §5-16-101 (enacted 1975).
34. Arkansas Code Ann. §5-16-102 (enacted 1975).

7 Sexual Masochism

INTRODUCTION

Sexual masochism is a paraphilia in which sexual arousal and/or orgasm are achieved by having pain inflicted upon oneself, experiencing embarrassment or humiliation by one's sexual partner, or by being controlled through bondage, regulations, or commands.[1] It is the eroticization of submission. Masochistic acts that may be sought with a partner include paddling, spanking, whipping, beating, cutting, restraint (physical bondage), blindfolding (sensory bondage), electrical shocks, pinning and piercing (infibulation), and humiliation (e.g., being forced to crawl and bark like a dog, or being subjected to verbal abuse). Masochism may sometimes be seen in a curious mix with urophilia (bringing humiliation by being urinated upon) or coprophilia (bringing humiliation by being defecated upon). Forced cross-dressing may be sought for its humiliating associations. In infantilism, a variation of masochism, the individual may have a desire to be treated as a helpless infant and clothed in diapers.

Activities involving sexual masochism can be very dangerous. One particularly dangerous form, called hypoxyphilia or asphyxiophilia, involves sexual arousal by oxygen deprivation to the brain. This is obtained by several methods including application of a noose or a ligature round the neck and partially suspending the body, application of a plastic bag or mask over the face, chest compression, or the use of some chemicals (most commonly a volatile nitrite that produces a temporary decrease in brain oxygenation by peripheral vasodilatation, but also other chemicals such as dichlorodifluoromethane, nitrous oxide, cocaine, or compounds containing 1-1-1-trichloroethane[2]). Oxygen-depriving activities may be engaged in alone or with a partner. Because of equipment malfunction, errors in the placement of the noose or ligature, or other mistakes, accidental deaths sometimes occur.

As seen in Chapter 1, masochism is the only paraphilia in which any noticeable number of women participate—and even here the proportion is quite low; only about 5% of masochists are female.[3,4]

Sharma,[5] however, asserts that according to some reports the incidence of masochism in females is rather high. He quotes a ratio of about 1 in 5, i.e., for every five masochists, one is a female. Many psychologists now view masochism as part of a large cluster of human aberrant sexual behavior termed BDSM (bondage, discipline, sadism, masochism). The major subgroupings of BDSM are:

- Bondage and discipline (B&D)*
- Domination and submission (D&S)†
- Sadism and masochism (or sadomasochism) (S&M)

Each grouping describes behaviors located at two diametrically opposite poles—each the mirror image of the other. BDSM generally involves two mutually consenting partners—colloquially termed "top" and "bottom." While the "top " is a partner who takes the active, dominant role in sexual play (such as flogging, bondage, domination, humiliation, servitude), the "bottom " is the partner, who takes on the submissive role and is on the receiving end of bondage, domination, and

* While *bondage* refers to restraining people, *discipline* refers to some form of erotic punishment, often involving caning or spanking.

† While *dominance* refers to being in charge, *submission* refers to letting someone else be in charge.

sadism. Many people enjoy being both and are said to be "switches." The two active roles of bondage and domination are often referred to as B/D (not to be confused with bondage and discipline, which is referred to as B&D). In B/D there is use of *power play* for sexual pleasure, but not for pain.[6] It is only in sadomasochism (S/M or SM) that *pain* is used for sexual stimulation. The counterpart of masochists—sadists—experience sexual pleasure and arousal from inflicting mild or mock pain on others. The majority of the time, this activity occurs between willing partners. Some common terms—slang and otherwise—used in connection with BDSM activities are given in Table 7.1.

Nosologically, masochism and sadism are seen and classified as different disorders. DSM-IV-TR[7] assigns code 302.83 to sexual masochism and states the following criteria:

A. Over a period of at least 6 months, patients have recurrent, intense, sexually arousing fantasies, sexual urges, or behaviors involving the act of being humiliated, beaten, bound, or otherwise made to suffer.
B. The fantasies, sexual urges, or behaviors cause clinically significant distress or impairment in social, occupational, or other important areas of functioning.

Sadomasochism, or S&M, is fairly common in its less extreme forms. Although both masochism and sadism have been included as psychiatric disorders in DSM-IV-TR, perceptions vary widely, from viewing sadomasochism as "an innocuous sophisticated erotic activity," to others viewing it as more than a psychiatric disorder—a sexual crime.[8]

ICD-9-CM assigns the code 302.83 to sexual masochism[9]—same as that assigned by DSM-IV-TR. ICD-10 conceptualizes both masochism and sadism as a single disorder and assigns the code F65.5 to it.[10] Sadomasochism is defined as:

> A preference for sexual activity which involves the infliction of pain or humiliation, or bondage. If the subject prefers to be the recipient of such stimulation this is called masochism; if the provider, sadism. Often an individual obtains sexual excitement from both sadistic and masochistic activities.

It is now known that sadism and masochism rarely occur as completely isolated entities (although DSM-IV-TR does define them separately). It might be more useful to view pure sadism and pure masochism as two extreme points of a gradual continuum, or spectrum, with all kinds of mixed shades appearing in between. Most afflicted people show both masochistic and sadistic tendencies in different proportions.

Although masochism is seen most often with sadism (sadomasochism), sometimes it is seen with other paraphilias, too. In its combination with transvestism, known colloquially as petticoat punishment, the male paraphiliac derives pleasure in getting spanked only when he is dressed like a school girl or servant girl.

HISTORICAL PERSPECTIVES

Although the term *masochism* is usually associated with Krafft-Ebing, masochistic behavior was known much earlier. As early as the fourth century, the Indian philosopher Mallanaga Vātsyāyana (fl. fourth century AD) described sexual masochism in his *Kama Sutra,* a widely quoted text on sexual behavior (please see chapter on sexual sadism for details). In 1495, the Italian philosopher Giovanni Pico della Mirandola (1463–1494) described a man who needed to be flogged before he could have sex.[11,12] He found it both puzzling and amusing. In 1639, the German physician Johann Heinrich Meibom (1590–1655) introduced the first theory of masochism (quite weird in the background of modern knowledge, though). He postulated that "flogging the back warms the semen in the kidneys, which causes sexual excitement once it reaches the testicles." In 1698, Kristian Frantz Paullini modified the theory somewhat, so that warm blood, and not semen, descended from the

TABLE 7.1
Essential BDSM Vocabulary

Abrasion—Sexual practice that involves sexual arousal from contact with abrasive substances. This can be person-to-person as in a harsh rubbing of the skin or with various substances such as scratchy wool or thistles.

Ageplay—A form of regressive roleplay in which an adult takes on the role of a child. This may be purely regressive (in order to re-experience childhood in a non-sexual sense), or sexual (the roleplaying of a child-adult relationship in sex, which may be a sexual fetish and is often grouped within BDSM). Ageplay is not connected with pedophilia in any way, and most individuals engaged in ageplay may find real child abuse abhorrent. *Daddy's girl fetish* is a variation of ageplay (please see chapter on fetishism).

Anal Torture—Any torture applied to the anus, using such devices as a hot poker. The practice also includes subjecting the anus to cold temperature, or insertion of other painful objects. Generally riskier than other BDSM practices because the body tissues involved are very delicate.

Asymmetric Bondage—Sexual bondage in which the bound person is tied in asymmetric positions. A common technique is to make the person stand on one leg and then bind the ankle of the free leg to the other thigh. This can have a disorienting effect, confusing the body's self-image and sense of balance, and hence increasing the psychological impact of the bondage. Asymmetric bondage is a common technique in Japanese bondage.

Ass Worship—A BDSM practice in which the submissive kisses and licks the buttocks and/or anus of the dominant partner. Face sitting or smothering may be applied in order to emphasize the control of the dominant over the submissive. A queening stool may also be used to facilitate this activity. Ass worship commonly involves a woman in the dominant role (femdom) and a submissive man. However, it is also practiced by homosexuals of both genders.

Birching—A form of abrasion play, where a person is struck or brushed with handfuls of twigs and leaves, sometimes on bare buttocks.

Bondage —The practice of tying up or otherwise restraining people for pleasure. Also known as sexual bondage.

Bottom—The passive partner, or the one receiving punishment in BDSM activities.

Breast Bondage—A technique used in BDSM play. It differs from most bondage techniques in that it is not intended to restrict the mobility of the tied person. Several techniques are employed to do this. In one common technique, ropes are tied around the base of each breast, causing the breasts to bulge outwards. Usually, the same rope is used for both breasts so that the rope harness is automatically held together at the front. The rope may then also be fixed behind the back, to make a kind of bra. Sometimes, nipple clamps are placed on the nipples or other, more involved methods of tit torture are combined with breast bondage for a greater erotic effect.

Dominant —Same as top.

Edgeplay—Types of sexual play that are considered to push the edge of the traditional "safe, sane, and consensual" creed. It may involve increased risk of spreading disease (cutting, bloodplay), psychological danger (humiliation play, incest fantasies, rape roleplay), social taboos (ageplay, scat fetishism, racial slurs), and even permanent harm or death (breathplay, gunplay).

Erotic Spanking—The practice of spanking another for the sexual gratification of either or both parties.

Human Animal Roleplay—In a BDSM context, human animal roleplay refers to an activity where one person may be a "slave," treated or used as an animal by his or her mistress/master. For a masochist, the humiliation meted out by being an animal serves to satisfy his or her erotic craving. In some BDSM parties, one partner may wear a dog collar with a leash attached. Some carry their own leashes; others are carried by their partner. If the partner is reduced to a pony, he or she is often known as a ponyboy or ponygirl (for human animal roleplay in a zoophilic context, please see chapter on zoophilia).

Face Sitting—Also known as kinging or queening, is a BDSM practice in which one partner sits on or over the other's face, typically to allow oral-genital or oral-anal contact, or to practice ass worship or body worship.

Interrogation Scene—A form of BDSM roleplay in which the participants act out the parts of torturer and victim, as in real-life torture chambers. The dominant or the torturer uses threats, humiliation, and physical pain to extract whatever information he believes the submissive or victim possesses. The game is over once the victim has broken and divulged his secret. As in real life, the "victim" is often stripped naked, tied up, mocked, abused, and tortured in several other ways.

TABLE 7.1 (continued)
Essential BDSM Vocabulary

Limits—Activities that a partner feels strongly about, and to which special attention must be paid. Before a BDSM scene, it is common to perform a negotiation to outline what will and will not happen during the play session. During this time, all participants outline what they desire and what they will not tolerate. This is called "discussing the limits." Both dominants and submissives can express limits. They can be spoken or written, and discussing them fully usually results in an improved experience for all involved. Variants of limits include:

Hard Limit —Something that absolutely must not be done. Examples are scat (paraphilia involving sexual pleasure from feces), or striking the back, because the partner suffers from disc problem. Violating a hard limit is often considered just cause for ending a scene or even a relationship.

Soft Limit—Something that a partner would agree to do only under special circumstances or when highly aroused. For instance, a partner may agree to indulge in anal sex only with a very experienced partner.

"Must" Limit —Something that a person will not do the scene without. For example, a partner may agree to be flogged only if adequate aftercare is provided.

Time Limit —The amount of time after which play ceases.

No Limits —The dominant may do anything he or she cares to with the submissive. This is usually seen in new and inexperienced players who do not yet know what their limits are. In reality, even the most hardened and experienced players have limits. Seen mostly in thriller movies, but not in real-life BDSM situations. This is also sometimes used as a term for TPE or total power exchange.

Metal Bondage—Also known as device bondage. Bondage involving the use of metal apparatus to restrain the submissive. The range of devices can vary significantly, from simple handcuffs or chains to specifically designed chairs or complex bar linkages.

Milking—A form of BDSM sex play where the submissive woman is milked by the dominant partner or commanded to give milk to him directly from her breasts (please also see chapter on fetishism).

Mummification—An extreme form of bondage in which the person is wrapped from head to toe, much like a mummy, completely immobilizing him. Materials used may be clingfilm, cloth, bandages, rubber strips, duct tape, plaster bandages, bodybags, or straitjackets. The immobilized person may then be left bound in a state of effective sensory deprivation for a period of time or sensually stimulated in his state of bondage—before being released from his wrappings.

Navel Torture—Infliction of intense sensory stimulation and pain to a person's navel. Examples are sucking or pulling the navel out (often with a syringe), dripping hot oil or wax into the navel, and poking pins into the navel. A subcategory of navel fetishism (please see chapter on fetishism).

Predicament Bondage—The practice of tying the submissive (or the bottom) with rope so that he must choose between two positions, neither of which is a pleasant option. Both are so uncomfortable or painful that the submissive is forced to shift his weight or position over and over again. In general, one position causes muscular exhaustion and the other extreme physical pain. An example is when the submissive is tied so that he is forced to stand on tiptoes. An attempt to stand with feet flat on the ground means that his genitals, which are also tightly bound, will be pulled.

Roleplay, Sexual —Please see *Sexual Roleplay*.

Safeword—A safeword is a codeword or series of codewords sometimes used in BDSM to mean that a submissive (or bottom) is reaching a physical, emotional, or moral boundary, or for the dominant (or top) to stop the sceneplay. Safewords are agreed upon before playing a *scene* by all participants. Many organized BDSM groups have standard safewords that all members agree to use to avoid confusion at organized play events. A common example—green means "okay" or even "harder" or "more"; yellow means "slow down" or "stop doing that" without stopping the scene; and red means "let's stop the scene."

Rope Bondage—Bondage involving the use of rope to tie and wrap the body as part of BDSM activities.

Safe, Sane, and Consensual—A code of conduct developed to ensure the safety of BDSM participants. It includes prior negotiation of the parameters of a scene, and a system of safe words to stop or slow down the action. Far from the masochist, or bottom, being at the mercy of the sadist, or top, it is now widely claimed the bottom controls the scene by defining its limits. Furthermore, the top indulges *not* in a frenzy of violence, as some uninitiated believe, but in consciously and attentively deploying practices, some of which demand considerable skill and dexterity. Sexual activities which appear to push to the edge of the traditional "safe, sane, and consensual" creed are termed *edgeplay*.

TABLE 7.1 (continued)
Essential BDSM Vocabulary

Scene—A complete erotic encounter between the top and bottom. It is the BDSM equivalent of a romantic or erotic encounter between heterosexual couples. It may or may not involve sexual activity.

Self-bondage—The practice of sexual bondage without a partner.

Service Top—A dominant who is dominant because the bottom desires or requests it. A service top does not need to be dominant in general. The bottom, in many cases, sets the rules. Most professional dominatrices and masters are considered service tops.

Sexual Bondage—Please see *bondage*.

Sexual Roleplay—A kind of sexual behavior between two or more people in which they take on erotic roles to carry out a sexual fantasy. The depth and extent of the roleplay may depend on the couple, and the scenario may be anywhere from simple and makeshift to detailed and elaborate, complete with costumes and even a script. Sexual roles can be very general designations of power position, sometimes abstracted to top and bottom, or very specific, detailed fantasies. Nearly any role could become the base material for an erotic experience, and there is no limit to what objects an individual could consider erotic. Most common sexual roleplays involve a power differential. Other examples of sexual roleplay are ageplay, asking a partner to play dead (class I necrophiliacs), or act like a beast (class I zoophiles).

Spanking Bench—A piece of furniture used to position a spankee on (one who receives spanking) for *erotic spanking*, with or without restraints. Also known as a *spanking horse*. The nineteenth century British dominatrix Mrs. Theresa Berkley became famous for her invention of the Berkley Horse, a multi-functional device which combined being a spanking bench with several other functions.

Spanking Horse—Same as *spanking bench*.

Spankophiles—People interested in giving or receiving *erotic spankings*. Notable spankophiles include poet Algernon Swinburne (as implied repeatedly in his poetry) and the philosopher Jean-Jacques Rousseau, as detailed in his autobiography *Confessions*.

Submissive —Same as *bottom*.

Suspension Bondage –A bound person is hung from one or more overhead suspension points. Suspension bondage is considered to carry a higher risk than other forms of sexual bondage. In autoerotic asphyxia, the person undergoes self-induced suspension bondage.

Switch —A person who has both sadistic and masochistic tendencies participates in BDSM activities sometimes as a top and other times as a bottom or (in the case of domination and submission) sometimes as a dominant and other times as a submissive. Switches are very common; partners may switch roles based on mood, desire, or to allow each partner to experience their preferred activity. It is common for people to switch with different partners, such as when a person acts exclusively as a top with one partner and exclusively as a bottom with another. The act of switching may also refer to a spontaneous reversal of roles, initiated by the bottom, who then takes control. A person who engages in self-bondage may be viewed as taking both roles simultaneously.

Tit Torture—Inflicting deliberate physical pain to the breasts, areola, and nipples for sexual gratification. A female masochist may demand it from her partner. Breast-oriented BDSM activities range from relatively safe and benign, such as the use of clothespins on the nipples, light flagellation, or simple breast bondage to activities that can include great risk, such as more severe caning, amateur piercing, or being suspended by the breasts.

Top—The active partner, or the one inflicting punishment in BDSM activities.

Topping from the Bottom —A person who wants to be dominated but simultaneously directs the top to do it according to his/her wishes.

Wax Play –A form of sensual play involving warm or hot wax usually dripped from candles or ladled onto the masochist's naked skin. Wax play may be combined with other BDSM or sexual activity.

kidneys (otherwise one could not explain masochism in females).* In 1788, the French physician François Amédée Doppet (1753–1799) expanded this theory to include women by assuming the same effect on the female genitalia.

During the Middle Ages, Elizabethan and Jacobean drama and poetry included motifs of sexualized violence, for example Cleopatra's allusions to the "lover's pinch, which hurts and is desired." *Venice Preserv'd,* an English Restoration play written by the English dramatist Thomas Otway (1652–1685), and first staged in 1682, depicts a masochistic Venetian senator engaging in what might today be termed "puppy-play" or "kennel-training" with his mistress.

Flagellation as a Masochistic Practice

In the Middle Ages, people's masochistic desires found an outlet through flagellation. England has long been represented as the natural home of flagellation. According to Hurwood, "Perhaps it was the cold climate which originally aroused in Englishmen a desire for whipping. Nowhere in the world do we find such a deep affection for the rod."[13] Bloch observed, "Flagellation mania (the desire to beat and flog) and preference for the use of the rod may be described as a specifically English abuse; it was so widespread among all ranks and ages that it formed one of the most interesting features of their sexual life."[14]

There were many high-class brothels in the 19th century. One of the most famous was run by Mrs. Theresa Berkley (died 1836) of 28 Charlotte Street. She was a "governess," i.e., she specialized in chastisement, whipping, flagellation, and the like. She was even credited with the invention of the Berkley Horse, an ingenious flogging machine that reportedly earned her a fortune from flogging wealthy men and women of the time. There are no artworks depicting what Theresa Berkley looked like, short of occasional descriptions usually depicting that she was attractive, with a strong disposition. An expert with all instruments of torture, her talents became highly sought after by the aristocracy of the day. She was a master of the art of inflicting pain for pleasure, and practiced absolute privacy to protect her clientele. Her clients were said to have been both men and women of wealth, and her career was quite financially lucrative.

Modern Era

The term *masochism* was coined in 1886 by the Austro-German psychiatrist Richard Freiherr von Krafft-Ebing (1840–1902), after a contemporary writer, Leopold von Sacher-Masoch (1836–1895, Figure 7.1), whose partially autobiographical novel *Venus in Furs* (1870) tells of the protagonist Severin von Kusiemski's desire to be whipped and enslaved by a beautiful woman Wanda von Dunajew. Severin describes his feelings during these experiences as *suprasensuality.*

Krafft-Ebing defined masochism as "a peculiar perversion of the psychical sexual life in which the individual affected, in sexual feeling and thought, is controlled by the idea of being completely and unconditionally subject to the will of a person of the opposite sex; of being treated by this person as by a master, humiliated and abused." Sigmund Freud also considered masochism to be a perversion and believed it to be "nothing but a continuation of sadism directed at one's own person in which the latter at first takes the place of the sexual object."

There have been some notable masochistic characters in history. One of the most famous is the 14th century German mystic and ascetic Henry Suso (1300–1366). Suso devised for himself several extremely uncomfortable and even painful devices such as an undergarment studded with 150 brass nails, sharpened and so fixed as to pierce his skin, gloves with sharp tacks in order to discourage him from disturbing the noxious insects on his body, a very uncomfortable door to sleep on, and a cross with 30 protruding needles and nails just under his body. In winter he slept on the bare floor

* The closest modern science comes to this is that flogging the buttocks may increase the blood flow to the contiguous genital areas as a result of inflammation.

FIGURE 7.1 Leopold von Sacher-Masoch, Austro-Ukrainian journalist and BDSM writer.

of his cell and froze. His body was always covered with scars and his throat always parched with thirst. Over a period of 25 years he never took a bath.

ETIOLOGY

The etiology of masochism is not completely understood. It is paradoxical and indeed somewhat of an enigma that a painful stimulus can be perceived as something pleasurable and sexually stimulating. However, some plausible theories have been proposed. Some of these are discussed below.

Biological Theories

Endorphins

It is well known that the feelings of both pain and sex are associated with the release of a variety of hormones and chemicals within the human body. Human beings have been shown to exhibit sympathetic responses in their bodies while watching, hearing, or imagining such experiences. Pain experiences are known to release endorphins, molecules similar to morphine, which many addicts take to induce euphoria. It is thus not difficult to perceive that these endorphins may be perceived by masochists as pleasurable. Release of endorphins and subsequent pleasurable sensations may be psychologically addictive, too. It is through the release of endorphins that people can become addicted to self-harm and masochism.

It is noteworthy that endorphins are released in certain non-sexual pleasurable activities, too, most notably during alternating hot saunas with cold plunges. It is also possible that a proper sexual context helps make a potentially painful situation into an erotic one. It is known that during sexual arousal, sensations which might be considered painful in the non-aroused state are experienced as pleasurable. Certain kinds of pain can also become eroticized through their association with sexual pleasure or in anticipation of it.

Dopamine

Monoamines, especially dopamine, seem to have a strong association with masochism. Monoamines (norepinephrine, dopamine, and serotonin) are released during stressful or painful experiences, and they can cause a pleasurable "rush" (please see Kafka's monoamine hypothesis in Chapter 1). This is one possible explanation why masochists seem to associate pain with pleasure.

Additionally, an excessive monoamine load is known to induce masochistic tendencies. Quinn and associates[15] describe two interesting cases that lend support to this view. In the first case, their patient had masochistic fantasies since childhood, in which he imagined himself being flagellated by a woman (but did not exhibit manifest masochism). At the age of 35, he developed Parkinson's disease. Ten years later he was treated with Sinemet (carbidopa/levodopa—metabolic precursor of dopamine). One year after starting Sinemet, bromocriptine (a dopamine receptor agonist) was also administered. One month later, the patient started manifesting overt signs of masochism. He began beating his back with canes, burning himself with cigarettes, and cutting his buttocks. He also felt a compulsion to undress and exhibit in public, but was able to resist it. In an attempt to control his masochistic behavior, a number of drugs were administered including cyproterone, tiapride, haloperidol, pimozide, metoclopramide, and oxyperamide. These drugs effectively improved his masochistic behavior, but at the expense of worsening Parkinsonism. When these drugs were stopped, the masochistic behavior returned. Finally, only when bromocriptine was completely discontinued, his masochistic behavior disappeared.

Case 2 involved a man who developed Parkinsonism at the age of 44. He had a longstanding attraction to bondage. At the age of 14, once he dressed in his sister's bathing costume and tied himself up with a rope. He did not show any manifest symptoms of masochism apart from this single instance. He started treatment with Sinemet at the age of 45 and by the age of 47, he was taking as much as 4 g of Sinemet per day. His masochistic tendencies became overtly manifest after this, and he began binding his testicles with leather thongs. More importantly, this behavior occurred at the peak of action of each dose, after which it would subside and he would become contrite and repentant. Furthermore, when the Sinemet dosage was reduced, these behavioral disturbances also settled. Eighteen months later, he was given pergolide (a direct dopamine agonist). Soon afterwards he exposed himself in public lavatories and on three occasions arranged to be bound at his home by men he met there. Sessions of bondage became of paramount importance for him, and the choice of men rather than women to inflict it was dictated more by easy availability rather than by any other factor such as homosexual tendencies. On discontinuing pergolide, his urges subsided.

Evolutionary Theories

Masochism can also be explained from an evolutionary standpoint. Observation of animal behavior sheds much light on this. Prior to sexual union, many animals, particularly mammals, engage in a kind of fight or struggle. Often the male will bite the female on the back of the neck to maintain a good hold on her while performing the sex act (Kinsey and colleagues[16] name 24 different mammalian species that bite during coitus). Undoubtedly, this inflicts some pain in the female, yet in some species this pain is known to the instrumental in releasing the ovum, thereby increasing the fertility of the female. This effect is quite probably mediated by her emotions and endocrine system. In a way, the rough treatment that the female receives from her partner (a bite on her neck to keep her steady) is a turn-on for her. There is a distinct evolutionary advantage in this behavior; only assertive males can pass on their genetic material to the next generation.

Thus this pattern of sex combined with brutality offers two distinct advantages to the species: (i) it increases the fertility of the female; (ii) it allows only desirable genetic material to be passed on to the next generation. This pattern may have passed on to humans as a love for masochism.

Sexual Torture as Enhancer of Fertility

There is evidence that indicates that women who have been handled roughly during intercourse show increased fertility. Apparently, women who have been raped are more likely to get pregnant than those having consenting acts of intercourse.[17] In a survey of 405 women, between 12 and 45 who experienced one incident of penile–vaginal rape, Gottschall and Gottschall[18] found that pregnancy rate per-incident rape was 6.42% (after adjustment for the use of oral contraception and IUDs the overall per-incident rape-pregnancy rate climbed to 7.98%). In comparison, the overall per-incident pregnancy rate for reproductive age women engaged in consensual, unprotected penile–vaginal intercourse is only 3.1%.[19] Holmes and colleagues[20] also found a higher figure for rape-related pregnancy. They found that in the US, the national rape-related pregnancy rate was 5.0% per rape among victims of reproductive age (aged 12 to 45). Other studies have found that rates of pregnancy resulting from rape could be as much as 30%.[21] These figures may be an indication that sexual torture (as in rape) may be an enhancer of fertility, perhaps by inducing ovulation.* This explains why masochism is found so frequently in females, but fails to explain why it is found in males at all.

Pain as Enhancer of Immune System

It has been known for some time that pain can influence the immune system favorably. For instance, the role of pain in producing positive changes in the expression of leukocyte cellular adhesion molecules is well known.[22] Although not proposed by any worker so far, it is proposed in this book, that a "love for pain" may be acting as a positive evolutionary force, justifying the existence of so many masochistic individuals.

Psychoanalytical Theories

Sigmund Freud developed the Life–Death Instinct Theory to explain much of human behavior, including masochism. According to this theory, all human beings are driven by two kinds of energy—a constructive energy called *Eros*, life force or life instinct, and a destructive energy called *Thanatos*, death force or death instinct. While Eros tends to sustain life, Thanatos tends to end it, thus bringing to an end life's inevitable tensions. Sexual urges stem from Eros, while feelings like suicide and aggression stem from Thanatos. Eros remains constantly under the threat of Thanatos. The interaction of the two produces all variations of human activity and behavior. Freud considered psychiatric symptoms as the result of misdirection or inadequate discharge of libido. According to him, sexual masochism resulted from transmutation of the death instinct. Karen Horney, another psychoanalyst, explained masochism as an attempt to find safety and satisfaction through dependency.[23] Maslow suggested that masochism developed out of feelings of insecurity.[24]

PREVALENCE

For some reason, SM has not engendered much attention from researchers. All large surveys of sexual behavior have ignored it almost completely. Thus, our estimates of the incidence and prevalence of SM behavior are rudimentary.

If one goes by the number of pornographic magazines and books available in the market, sadomasochism tops the list. In 1986, the U.S. Commission on Pornography reviewed 3,050 mag-

* Before this can be taken as a logical conclusion, it is only fair to add that these figures can be interpreted in several other—perhaps more—logical ways. For instance, it is quite possible that rapes resulting in pregnancy are reported to the law enforcement agencies with overwhelmingly more frequency; men who rape are more potent and fertile at the time of the offense (because of having been in a state of sexual deprivation) or their testosterone levels may be higher (this has been advanced as one explanation, why they became rapists in the first place). It is also possible, that many women falsely reported pregnancies as having resulted from rapes, to save themselves or their parents and husbands of unnecessary embarrassment.

azine and book titles sold in "adults only" pornographic outlets randomly selected in several U.S. cities. Of the 746 titles that could be assigned to a DSM III-R paraphilia category, as many as 49.9% were devoted to sadomasochism, making it the most common paraphilic theme.[25]

Hunt[26] asked a representative sample, whether they had ever obtained sexual pleasure from inflicting or receiving pain, and concluded that the incidence of sadomasochism in the general population was less than 5%. In his sample, twice as many males as females reported as being sadistic, while twice as many females as males reported as being masochistic.

Playboy in 1976 reported that 3% of 3,700 male college students had practiced and enjoyed bondage.[27] More recently Moser and Kleinplatz[28] estimated privately that approximately 10% of the general population is involved in SM, but they are quick to add that there are no studies on which to base that figure; the figure is based simply on their interactions with sexologists, sex educators, sex researchers, sex therapists, and even SM practitioners.* Going by the amount of sadomasochistically oriented material available at an average adult bookstore or sex toy store, this figure sounds reasonable. This abundance of material would not be produced without a market for it.

Crépault and Couture[29] interviewed 94 men about their erotic fantasies occurring during heterosexual activity. The majority of these men were married, and their average duration of cohabitation with a woman was 6.5 years. Many of them reported having had fantasies centered around a masochistic theme. From that group 5.3% reported having had a fantasy of a scene where they were beaten up, 11.7% reported having fantasies of a scene where they were humiliated, 17.1% fantasized a scene where someone was aggressive to them. A total of 26.6% had fantasies where they pretended to fight and to resist before surrendering to a woman's sexual attempts, 36.2% had a fantasy where they were tied up and sexually stimulated by a woman, and 45.8% reported having had erotic fantasies where they were raped by a woman.

CHARACTERISTICS

Masochistic sexual fantasies are likely to have been present in childhood. The age at which masochistic activities with partners begins is variable, but is commonly early adulthood. Self-directed aggression and masochism are frequent in the depressive character (characterized by perpetual and unsuccessful efforts to maintain self-esteem and to avoid a sense of helplessness).[30]

Some individuals are bothered by their masochistic fantasies, which may be invoked during sexual intercourse or masturbation but not otherwise acted on. In such cases, the masochistic fantasies usually involve being raped while being held or bound by others so that there is no possibility of escape. Others act on the masochistic sexual urges by themselves (e.g., binding themselves, sticking themselves with pins, shocking themselves electrically, or self-mutilation) or with a partner.

Some males with sexual masochism also have associated paraphilias such as fetishism, transvestic fetishism, or sexual sadism. Sexual masochism is usually chronic and repetitive. Some individuals with sexual masochism may engage in masochistic acts for many years without increasing the potential injuriousness of their acts. Many increase the severity of the masochistic acts over time or during periods of stress, which may eventually result in injury or even death.

Some individuals can go to dangerous lengths to produce erotic pain. Schmeling and associates describe the case of a 23-year old man who derived sexual pleasure from painful irritation of the peritoneum by sharp force. For this purpose he clamped 2 knife blades into a vise suspended from a rope-pulley construction so that he could lower it to pierce the abdominal skin with the tips of the knives. When one of the ropes broke, the vise with the knives fell onto the man's abdomen, piercing the inferior vena cava and leading to death by hemorrhage.[31]

* Moser claims that he was the first scientific researcher to be invited to an SM party by the participants where he witnessed a female severely beaten to orgasm.

CLASSIFICATION

No formal classification of masochists has been suggested so far. The classification proposed here is based on a review of a vast literature on masochism. Extrapolations have also been made from the theory of paraphilic equivalence (please see chapter on frotteurism for details). In line with the classification of other paraphilias, it groups all masochists along a continuum, with the most innocuous at one end and the most seriously affected at the other (roughly in increasing degree of psychopathology).

Class I Sexual Masochists

These individuals are bothered by their masochistic fantasies, but they do not actively seek to act out their fantasies. They may be preponderantly sadists with minimal masochistic tendencies or normal individuals with minimal masochistic tendencies.

Class II Sexual Masochists

These individuals have a fairly equal mix of sadistic and masochistic tendencies. They like to receive pain, but also like to be dominant partners (sadists) at other times. They are also capable of achieving sexual orgasm in the absence of pain or humiliation.

Class III Sexual Masochists

These the individuals are mainly masochists with minimal or no sadistic tendencies. They prefer to receive pain or humiliation for sexual orgasm (pain or humiliation facilitates sexual orgasm), but are capable of forming romantic relationships with other persons and are capable of achieving orgasm even if no punishment is received.

Class IV Sexual Masochists

These individuals are exclusive masochists, i.e., they cannot form normal romantic relationships with other persons, and cannot achieve sexual orgasm without infliction of pain or humiliation. A satisfactory sexual intercourse resulting in an orgasm is an impossibility, if no pain is inflicted or no humiliation meted out.

LEGAL ASPECTS

Validity of Consent

One of the most hotly debated legal questions in sexual masochism is the validity of consent. So important is consent in criminal law in general that it has been referred to as legal magic by some commentators, turning most horrific crimes into non-crimes. In criminal law, consent can turn a theft into a proper giving of gifts, kidnapping into vacation, grievous hurt into inadvertent playful injury, trespass into hospitality, maiming into therapeutic surgery, criminal abortion into medical termination of pregnancy, and even rape into sexual intercourse! But can consent be given for so-called "illegal acts"? Does a fully informed consent by a masochist to suffer harm by his partner absolve his partner of the guilt of causing hurt to the masochist? Most masochists and their partners would say "yes," going by the legal maxim *Volenti non fit injuria* (Latin: To a willing person, no injury is done). The courts, however, do not appear to agree with this view. Here are a few significant cases which address this issue.

R. v. Coney (1882)

This is one of the earliest cases addressing the question whether harm caused during consensual activity absolves the offender from any legal implications or not. In *R. v. Coney* (1882) 8 QBD 534, an English case, the Court for Crown Cases Reserved* found that despite the consent of the participants, a bare-knuckle fight was an assault occasioning actual bodily harm. The court made the following general statement in relation to consent:

> where the act charged is in itself unlawful, it can never be necessary to prove absence of consent on the part of the person wronged in order to obtain the conviction of the wrongdoer. There are, however, many acts in themselves harmless and lawful which become unlawful only if they are done without the consent of the person affected.

This landmark decision ended the public bare-knuckle contests in England, which were widespread at that time. The case has been referred to widely in several cases of bodily injury involving sadomasochistic activity, most notably in *R v. Brown* (please see below).

R. v. Donovan (1934)

In *R. V. Donovan* (1934) 2 K.B.498, Donovan was charged with indecent assault and common assault upon a 17 year old girl, Miss Harrison. Donovan had taken Harrison to a garage and beaten her with a cane "in circumstances of indecency." The arrangement had been made in advance by telephone, and Miss Harrison was clearly a willing participant. According to the physician who examined her 2 days later, she had marks indicative of a "fairly severe beating." It was held that:

> if an act is unlawful in the sense of being itself a criminal act, it is plain that it cannot be rendered lawful because the person consents to it. No person can license another to commit a crime.

Furthermore, Swift J said, at 507 that: "It is an unlawful act to beat another person with such a degree of violence that the infliction of bodily harm is a probable consequence, and when such an act is proved, consent is immaterial." Donovan's conviction was, however, reversed because of errors by the trial judge.

Reg. v. McCoy (1953)

In the Southern Rhodesian case, *Reg. v. McCoy,* 1953 2 SA 4 (SR), the manager of an airline caned an air hostess, allegedly *with her consent*, as a punishment for failing to secure her seat belt when landing. She was an immigrant on probation, was in financial difficulties, and consequently would have been placed in a very difficult position by losing her job. She consented to being caned when this was offered as an alternative to her being grounded, which would have meant loss of pay and perhaps dismissal. The beating consisted of six cuts with a light cane but was administered in degrading and humiliating circumstances. The manager's appeal was dismissed, and he was convicted of assault. The court held that the prosecution had proved the infliction of bodily harm and the accused's intention to inflict it. But this observation was not vital to the decision since the court also found that the woman had not consented freely. Significantly, the whole tone of the judgment indicates that the court was much influenced in its finding of an intention to cause bodily harm by the degrading circumstances of the caning.

---

* The Court for Crown Cases Reserved was an English appellate court for criminal cases established in 1848 to hear references from trial judges. It did not allow retrials, only judgment on a point of law. Neither did it create a right of appeal, and only a few selected cases were heard every year. It was superseded by the Court of Criminal Appeal in 1907.

People v. Samuels (1967)

In *People v. Samuels,* 58 Cal. Rptr. 439 (Ct. App., 1st Dist. 1967), defendant Dr. Marvin Samuels was a self-confessed sadist, who released his desire to inflict physical pain on others by producing and acting in motion pictures depicting sadomasochistic behavior. One of these films, which showed Dr. Samuels whipping a naked man gagged and suspended from the ceiling, was turned over to the police by the film developer perhaps because he wondered whether some criminal activity was going on in the film. The victim was never located nor formally identified, so there was no complainant. Dr. Samuels testified that the victim was a masochist who consented to the physical abuse depicted in the film. Since there was no complainant, his story seemed genuine. Despite this, Dr. Samuels was convicted of aggravated assault on the basis of the film. Conviction was affirmed on appeal. It was held that "the purpose of the aggravated assault statute is to prohibit one person from severely injuring another and thus, except in cases involving ordinary physical contact or sports, consent of the victim is no defense. Moreover, since it is a matter of common knowledge that a normal person in full possession of his mental faculties does not freely consent to the use, upon himself, of force likely to produce great bodily injury, the alleged consent is legally ineffective."

When is the Consent to Suffer Bodily Harm Legally Valid?

Several interesting points arise as a result of this court ruling. It is common knowledge that consent to suffer voluntary harm is legally valid in several significant situations in day-to-day life, for example in (i) operations performed by a surgeon; (ii) sporting activities, such as rugby or boxing; (iii) ritual circumcision, tattoos, or piercings if they are for ornamental purposes, as in the case of nipple rings, clitoral rings, and tongue studs; and (iv) dangerous exhibitions. One can also use consent as a defense against a charge of what is called common assault. This is an assault which causes no significant injury. In addition, interestingly, in cases of parental chastisement, consent of the child is not even necessary (for beating), and even then, no one seriously thinks it is an offense on the part of parents!

Why is Consent to Suffer Bodily Harm in S/M Activities Not Valid?

The central question that one has to address is where we draw the line beyond which consent is no defense to physical injury? If consent to suffer harm is valid in the areas mentioned above, why not in sadomasochistic activities?

The answer appears to be manifold. Firstly, while the activities mentioned above, especially the operations conducted by a surgeon, have significant *utility* value, sadomasochistic activity appears to have *no social utility.* It only appears to be driven by the pleasure principle. Second, and perhaps more valid reason, is that in the former two activities bodily harm is not the *aim* or *motive* on either side; on the contrary, in SM activities bodily harm is certainly the aim (although perhaps not the motive, which is seeking of pleasure). As Lord Templeman said in *R. v. Brown* (please see below):

> ...there is a difference between violence which is incidental (as occurs in sporting activities or surgery) and violence which is inflicted for the indulgence of cruelty. The violence of sado-masochistic encounters involves the indulgence of cruelty by sadists and the degradation of victims. Such violence is injurious to the participants and unpredictably dangerous. I am not prepared to invent a defense of consent for sado-masochistic encounters which breed and glorify cruelty. Society is entitled and bound to protect itself against a cult of violence. Pleasure derived from the infliction of pain is an evil thing. Cruelty is uncivilized.

A possible consensual activity between two parties in which bodily harm would be the aim and motive on both sides would be the maiming of a beggar by a surgeon, so he could get more alms. Surely no person in his right mind would condider this act acceptable. In sadomasochistic activities, nothing is different in principle, except for the fact that maiming is replaced by less alarming wounding and bodily harm.

A third, and perhaps a weaker line of reasoning, is that while the activities cited above (surgery, sport, tattoos, piercings, and parental chastisement) are carried out without any secrecy, there is a great deal of secrecy surrounding sadomasochism. The very fact secrecy is ensured tends to support the view that the activity is illegal. But obviously this is circular reasoning, because the proponents of SM would immediately claim secrecy is required because the society wrongly considers the activity illegal. In a latter case, *R. v. Brown* (please see below) video tapes were made of secret sadomasochistic activities which were meant for distribution among members. This brings us on a rather slippery wicket. One could argue this case either way. The activities were secret, because they were carried out secretly, but perhaps not so secret, as video tapes were made to be distributed among members. Paradoxically, one of the arguments advanced by the defendants in *R. v. Brown* was that their activities were carried out in secret (thus carrying no danger of the proselytisation and corruption of young men), and one of the judges countered by saying that they were not so secret, because video recordings were being made. He observed:

> Furthermore, the possibility of proselytisation and corruption of young men is a real danger even in the case of these appellants and the taking of video-recordings of such activities suggests that secrecy may not be as strict as the appellants claimed to your Lordships. If the only purpose of the activity is the sexual gratification of one or both of the participants what then is the need of a video-recording?

The recordings, of course, were not being made for advertising their activities or for sale at a profit but for the benefit of those members of the "ring," who had not had the opportunity of witnessing the events in person.

R. v. Brown ([1993] 2 All England Law Reports 75)

This is perhaps the most important and most cited case on the role of consent in sadomasochistic activities. The case began in the UK in 1987, during a raid when the police seized a videotape which showed a number of identifiable men engaging in heavy SM activities. The acts consisted mainly of maltreatment of the genitalia (e.g., with hot wax, sandpaper, fish hooks, and needles) and ritualistic beatings either with the assailant's bare hands or a variety of implements, including stinging nettles, spiked belts and a cat-o'-nine tails. There were instances of branding and infliction of injuries which resulted in the flow of blood and left scarring. Other potentially dangerous activities such as nailing a foreskin or scrotum to a board, insertion of hot wax into one's urethra followed by the burning of his penis with a candle, and incising of scrotum with a scalpel to the extent of effusion of blood were involved.

Operation Spanner

A murder investigation—popularly labeled by the media as *Operation Spanner** —was immediately launched, because the police was convinced that the men in the videotape were being killed. During the investigation—one of the most expensive ever undertaken by Scotland Yard (it supposedly cost £4 million)—the police learned that none of the men in the video had been murdered or even suffered injuries which required medical attention. However, they did arrest 42 gay men (perhaps to justify the expense, as some claim). Most belonged to a group of sadomasochistic homosexuals who over a 10-year period from 1978 had *willingly* participated in sadomasochistic activities.

As happens in consensual S/M activities, the passive partner or victim in each case had consented to the acts being committed and no permanent injury occur to any of them. The activities

* The case became known thus, reportedly because a police detective remarked after watching one video that he felt as though "someone had tightened a spanner (wrench) around his nuts."

TABLE 7.2

Sections 20 and 47 of the Offenses against the Person Act 1861

20. Inflicting bodily injury, with or without weapon.

Whosoever shall unlawfully and maliciously wound or inflict any grievous bodily harm upon any other person, either with or without any weapon or instrument, shall be guilty of a misdemeanor, and being convicted thereof shall be liable to be kept in penal servitude.

47. Assault occasioning bodily harm. Common assault.

Whosoever shall be convicted upon an indictment of any assault occasioning actual bodily harm shall be liable to be kept in penal servitude.

took place in private at a number of different locations, including rooms equipped as torture chambers at the homes of three of those arrested. Video cameras were used to record the activities and the resulting tapes were then copied and distributed among members of the group. The tapes were not sold or used other than for the delectation of members of the group.

Sixteen of those arrested were eventually charged with assault occasioning actual bodily harm, contrary to Section 47 of the *Offenses against the Person Act 1861*, and unlawful wounding, contrary to Section 20 of that Act (see Table 7.2). Even men who participated as bottoms or submissives were charged with aiding and abetting assaults upon themselves.[32]

The evidence against them was largely the video footage that the police had seized earlier and their own statements. When they were questioned by the police, the men were so confident that their activities were lawful (because they had consented to them) that they freely admitted to taking part in the activities on the video. It is widely acknowledged that without these statements and the videotape, the police would have had no evidence to present against the men and would have found it impossible to bring any prosecutions. The defense case was that the consent of those suffering bodily harm immunized them against any legal action.

Rulings by the Lower Courts and House of Lords

The trial judge ruled—on 19 December 1990—that the consent of the victim afforded *no defense* to the charges, and participants received prison sentences of up to four and a half years or fines. A number of defendants appealed against their convictions and sentences. The Court of Appeal, Criminal Division—on 19 February 1992—upheld their convictions, although the sentences were reduced as it was felt the accused might well have been unaware that their activities were illegal. The Appeal Court, however, noted that this exception would not apply to similar cases in the future.

The appellants then appealed to the House of Lords. The central question was, "Where A wounds or assaults B occasioning him actual bodily harm in the course of a sadomasochistic encounter, does the prosecution have to prove lack of consent on the part of B before they can establish A's guilt under section 20 and section 47 of the Offenses against the Person Act, 1861?"

The appellants cited the following reasons why their activities should not be considered criminal: (i) The activities were conducted with fully informed consent; every person has a right to deal with his own body as he chooses; (ii) sexual appetites of sadists and masochists can only be satisfied by the infliction of bodily harm and that the law should not punish the consensual achievement of sexual satisfaction; (iii) their activities were conducted in a well-ordered manner, and that they did not result in any injuries which required medical attention; (iv) the only injuries to which consent would be irrelevant would be those which resulted in actual expense to the public by reason, for example, of the expenses of hospital or other medical treatment, or payment of some benefit. None of the injuries caused in the current case resulted in any burden on public exchequer; (v) one could consent to less serious bodily harm. Public interest intervened only when more serious harming or maiming occurred; and (vi) hostility, an essential element in the offense of assault, was lacking in their case.

The Law Lords heard the case in 1992 and delivered their judgment on 11 March 1993.* They upheld the convictions by a majority of 3:2,† holding that it was indeed not necessary to prove lack of consent on the part of B. Holding the appellants guilty, they reasoned that public policy required society to be protected by criminal sanctions against a cult of violence which contained the danger of the proselytisation and corruption of young men and the potential for the infliction of serious injury. Accordingly, a person could be convicted of unlawful wounding and assault occasioning actual bodily harm, contrary to sections 20 and 47 of the 1861 Act, for committing sadomasochistic acts which inflicted injuries that were neither transient nor trifling, notwithstanding that the acts were committed in private, the person on whom the injuries were inflicted consented to the acts and no permanent injury was sustained by the victim. Lord Templeman, one of the Lordships, hearing the case concluded thus, "Society is entitled and bound to protect itself against a cult of violence. Pleasure derived from the infliction of pain is an evil thing. Cruelty is uncivilized. I would answer the certified question in the negative and dismiss the appeals of the appellants against conviction."

One of the reasonings advanced by Lord Templeman was that if it was an offense for a person to abuse his *own mind and body*, say, by taking drugs, how could he seek exemption for causing harm to others even with their consent. Could a person A administer narcotic drugs to another person B with the latter's consent? Obviously, no. Similarly, a person who assists another to commit suicide is guilty of murder or manslaughter. The aim of the criminal law is to restrain a practice which is regarded as dangerous and injurious to individuals and which if allowed and extended is harmful to society generally. The governments of most civilized nations do tend to control personal injury in many cases by making motorcycle helmets, automobile seatbelts, and vaccinations necessary. A person who does not wear a motorcycle helmet because he wants to suffer self-harm voluntarily cannot be allowed to do so. It was also pointed out that sado-masochistic participants have no way of foretelling the degree of bodily harm which will result from their encounters, and thus this activity should be considered illegal.

Regarding the appellants' contention that the sexual appetites of sadists and masochists can *only* be satisfied by the infliction of bodily harm and that the law should not punish the consensual achievement of sexual satisfaction, Lord Templeman, doubting the consent of the participants, observed:

> There was no evidence to support the assertion that sado-masochist activities are essential to the happiness of the appellants or any other participants but the argument would be acceptable if sado-masochism were only concerned with sex, as the appellants contend. In my opinion sado-masochism is not only concerned with sex. Sado-masochism is also concerned with violence. The evidence discloses that the practices of the appellants were unpredictably dangerous and degrading to body and mind and were developed with increasing barbarity and taught to persons whose consents were dubious or worthless.

Lord Templeman observed further:

> The evidence disclosed that drink and drugs were employed to obtain consent and increase enthusiasm. The victim was usually manacled so that the sadist could enjoy the thrill of power and the victim could enjoy the thrill of helplessness. The victim had no control over the harm which the sadist, also stimulated by drink and drugs might inflict. In one case a victim was branded twice on the thigh and there was some doubt as to whether he consented to or protested against the second branding. The dangers involved in administering violence must have been appreciated by the appellants because, so it was said by their counsel, each victim was given a code word which he could pronounce when excessive harm or pain was caused. The efficiency of this precaution, when taken, depends on the circumstances and on the personalities involved. No one can feel the pain of another.

* Widely referred to as *R. v. Brown* ([1993] 2 All England Law Reports 75).

† Lord Templeman, Lord Jauncey of Tullichettle and Lord Lowry upheld convictions, while Lord Mustill and Lord Slynn of Hadley dissented.

It was also argued by Lord Templeman that since the sadomasochistic activities of the appellants also involved wounding with instruments, branding, bloodletting, and smearing with human blood, there were obvious dangers of serious personal injury, blood infection, and contracting hepatitis or HIV infection. It was observed that two members of the group had died from AIDS, and one other had contracted an HIV infection although not necessarily from the practices of the group. Some activities of the group involved excrement. The appellants asserted that the instruments employed by them were clean and sterilized, but Lord Templeman said that this could not have removed the danger of infection. According to him, the assertion that care was taken demonstrated the possibility of infection.

Dissensions by Lord Mustill and Lord Slynn

Significantly, the decision was not unanimous. Lord Mustill and Lord Slynn of Hadley dissented. In dissent, Lord Mustill held up boxing as an example of one person seriously injuring another with legal impunity. He observed:

> Each boxer aims to end the contest prematurely by infliction of brain injury serious enough to make the opponent unconscious or temporarily by impairing his central nervous system through a blow to the midriff, or cutting his skin to a degree which would ordinarily be well within the scope of the Act of 1861.

He argued against the appropriateness of prosecution under the 1861 Act, pointing to its title, "Offenses Against The Person." He observed that since there was no animosity, aggression, or personal rancor from the assailant and no protest by the victim, the appellants could not be convicted.

Lord Slynn argued undoubtedly the sadomasochistic acts were consensual, and thus the appellants could not be prosecuted. He observed:

> Indeed there was more than mere consent. Astonishing though it might seem, the persons involved positively wanted and asked for the acts to be done to them. [Further] the accused were old enough to know what they were doing, [and] the acts were done in private.

The appellants were, however, convicted by a majority decision. There were many who welcomed this decision. Their contention was that the decision marked a definite shift in judicial attitudes to protect vulnerable people, particularly women, from violence. Others attacked the decision on several grounds including that it was based upon an "undesirable misconception," mistaking a sexual practice for one of violence.[33]

The case did not end here, however. Three defendants, namely, Collin Laskey, Roland Jaggard, and Anthony Brown, appealed the decision in the European Court of Human Rights in Strasbourg immediately.* Their contention was that the decision violated Articles 7 and 8 of the *European Convention for the Protection of Human Rights and Fundamental Freedoms.* The decision of the court, widely referred to as *Laskey, Jaggard, and Brown v. United Kingdom,* 24 Eur. H.R. Rep. 39 (1997), was delivered on 19 February 1997.

Laskey, Jaggard, and Brown v. United Kingdom, 24 Eur. H.R. Rep. 39 (1997)

As seen above, the appellants' main contention was that Articles 7 and 8 of the European Convention for the Protection of Human Rights and Fundamental Freedoms (1953) were violated (see Table 7.3).

* Money for the appeal was raised from SM communities around the world, with a large portion of funds coming from the Bay Area in California.

TABLE 7.3
Articles 7 and 8 of the Convention for the Protection of Human Rights and Fundamental Freedoms

Article 7—No punishment without law

1. No one shall be held guilty of any criminal offense on account of any act or omission which did not constitute a criminal offense under national or international law at the time when it was committed. Nor shall a heavier penalty be imposed than the one that was applicable at the time the criminal offense was committed.
2. This article shall not prejudice the trial and punishment of any person for any act or omission which, at the time when it was committed, was criminal according to the general principles of law recognized by civilized nations.

Article 8—Right to respect for private and family life

1. Everyone has the right to respect for his private and family life, his home and his correspondence.
2. There shall be no interference by a public authority with the exercise of this right except such as is in accordance with the law and is necessary in a democratic society in the interests of national security, public safety or the economic well-being of the country, for the prevention of disorder or crime, for the protection of health or morals, or for the protection of the rights and freedoms of others.

The Commission declared the applications admissible as to the complaint under Article 8 of the Convention on 18 January 1995. Regarding Article 7, it was observed that since at the relevant time it *was* a criminal offense under English law to inflict actual bodily harm, this article could not be invoked by the appellants. Appellants' contention that they reasonably believed that consent was a defense was also dismissed. The court announced its judgment on 19 February 1997.* Holding that there had been no violation of Article 8 of the Convention, it rejected the appeal unanimously at 9–0. The arguments and counterarguments were:

(i) The European Court observed that the interference by the public authority had been "in accordance with the law."

(ii) It also said that the interference pursued the legitimate aim of the "protection of health or morals," within the meaning of the second paragraph of Article 8.

(iii) In the Court's opinion, every sexual activity carried out behind closed doors did not necessarily fall within the scope of Article 8. In the present case, the appellants were involved in consensual sadomasochistic activities for purposes of sexual gratification. Sexual orientation and activity does concern an intimate aspect of private life. However, a considerable number of people were involved in the activities in question which included, *inter alia*, the recruitment of new members, the provision of several specially-equipped chambers, and the shooting of many video-tapes which were distributed among the members. It may thus be open to question whether the sexual activities of the appellants fell entirely within the notion of private life in the particular circumstances of the case.

(iv) The appellants had maintained that the interference at issue could not be regarded as "necessary in a democratic society" as is meant in the second paragraph of Article 8. This submission was contested by the government and by a majority of the commission. The appellants submitted that their case should be viewed as one involving matters of sexual expression, rather than violence.

However, the European Court maintained that one of the roles which every state was unquestionably entitled to undertake was to seek to regulate, through the operation of the criminal law, activities which involved the infliction of physical harm. This was so whether the activities in question occurred in the course of sexual conduct or otherwise.

* One of the appellants, Laskey died on 14 May 1996, before the pronouncement of judgment.

(v) The appellants also contended that, in the circumstances of the case, the behaviour in question formed part of private morality which is not the state's business to regulate. In their submission, the matters for which they were prosecuted and convicted concerned only private sexual behaviour. Previous cases were cited concerning consensual homosexual behaviour in private between adults (*Dudgeon v. the United Kingdom* 1981, *Norris v. Ireland* 1988, and *Modinos v. Cyprus* 1993), in which it was ruled that private sexual behaviour could not be intruded upon.*

The Court, however, was not persuaded by this submission. It observed that there was a material difference between homosexuality and sadomasochism. It was plainly evident that the appellants' sadomasochistic activities involved a significant degree of injury or wounding which could not be characterised as trifling or transient. This feature is significantly absent in consensual homosexual behaviour.

(vi) Another contention of the appellants was that they were singled out partly because of the authorities' bias against homosexuals. They referred to *R. v. Wilson*, 3 Weekly Law Reports, 125 (1996), a judgment which had been delivered only a year earlier (please see below for this case). This case involved a heterosexual married couple, where a husband had branded his wife's buttocks with her consent, (an activity quite similar to the one engaged in by the appellants) and yet was found *not guilty*. It was argued that the only reason Wilson was found not guilty was that he was engaged in a heterosexual relationship. Had the same case occurred between homosexuals, he would have been convicted.

The European Court dismissed this argument also. In this respect it recalled the remark of the trial judge when passing sentence that "the unlawful conduct now before the court would be dealt with equally in the prosecution of heterosexuals or bisexuals if carried out by them." Moreover, it was clear from the judgment of the House of Lords that the opinions of the majority were based on the extreme nature of the practices involved and not the sexual proclivities of the appellants. In any event, the European Court did not consider that the facts in the *Wilson* case were at all comparable in seriousness to those in the present case.

In conclusion, the Court found that the United Kingdom authorities were entitled to consider that the prosecution and conviction of the appellants were necessary in a democratic society for the protection of health within the meaning of Article 8 Para 2 of the Convention. The consenting sadomasochistic sexual activities between adult men were *not* protected by Article 8 of the Convention which guarantees a right to private life.

Aftermath

The Spanner Case triggered a Law Commission consultation paper in 1995. Feeling that perhaps the government went overboard in convicting these men, it recommended a change in the law under which they were convicted. The Commission provisionally proposed that either intentional or reckless causing of injury, other than that which is seriously disabling, even if amounting to "grievous bodily harm" within the meaning of the 1861 Act, not be criminal, if the other person consented. In place of criminal prosecution, the Commission recommended licensing arrangements aimed at ensuring safe and hygienic practices. However, no action has been taken since these proposals were submitted.[34]

* In the early years of the European Commission and Court of Human Rights, gay men were already challenging the legislation banning consensual sex between adult men. At that time the Commission rejected all these applications and stated that such legislation did not breach the European Convention on Human Rights. In the case of *Dudgeon v. the United Kingdom* (1981), the European Court of Human Rights for the first time declared that legislation criminalizing consensual sexual acts between adult men in Northern Ireland was in breach of Convention Article 8 which provides a right to a private life. The Court also confirmed that such legislation contradicted the right to a private life in the cases of *Norris v. Ireland* (1988) and *Modinos v. Cyprus* (1993).

Since the decision, questions have also been asked about the legality of SM prostitution, a large market for which does exist in most countries (prostitution itself is generally legal). Questions have also been asked about the legality of making SM films, which continue being made. No satisfactory answers to these questions have emerged.

Other Illustrative Cases

There are some other interesting cases which need mention. In 1992, a military man used nipple clamps and nipple piercing during bondage with his female partner, an activity quite similar to the one observed in *R. v. Brown*. At trial, his partner testified that she had consented. The judge directed the jury to acquit.[35]

R. v. Wilson (1996)

In another interesting case (*R. v. Wilson,* 3 Weekly Law Reports, 125 [1996]), a man branded his initials with a knife on his wife's buttocks with her consent. He was convicted but on appeal his conviction was overturned. Lord Justice Russell writing for the court stated:

> There is no factual comparison to be made between the instant case and the facts of either Donovan or Brown: Mrs. Wilson not only consented to that which the appellant did, she instigated it. There was no aggressive intent on the part of the appellant. We do not think that we are entitled to assume that the method adopted by the appellant and his wife was any more dangerous or painful than tattooing. Consensual activity between husband and wife, in the privacy of the matrimonial home, is not, in our judgment, a proper matter for criminal investigation, let alone criminal prosecution.

It has been argued (Please see *Laskey, Jaggard, and Brown v. United Kingdom,* 24 Eur. H.R. Rep. 39 [1997] above) that Wilson was acquitted only because he was involved in a heterosexual relationship, which is considered more acceptable to the society than a homosexual relationship. The European Court, however, did not subscribe to this view.

In one instance, Steve Davidson, a conman with masochistic tendencies, used an acting ploy to get women to spank him for sexual gratification. Davidson, who was actually an agent for the Internal Revenue Service, pretended to audition women for a movie role. Since there was no clear existing law under which he could be prosecuted, the state chose to prosecute him rather cleverly for a scheme to defraud, a property crime, rather than a sexual offense! The property was the women's videotaped performances. Davidson pleaded guilty and was sentenced to 5 years of probation; he was also fired.[36]

Not many countries have explicit laws relating to masochism, whereby a person is punished for causing and suffering injury to his own body (with or without conspiring with another person). A few legal provisions in the General Civil Penal Code of Norway[37] can be used against the practice of masochism, although they do not seem to have been legislated specifically with masochists in mind:

Norway

Section 223. Any person who unlawfully deprives another person of his liberty or who aids and abets such deprivation of liberty shall be liable to imprisonment for a term not exceeding 5 years.

If the deprivation of liberty has lasted for more than 1 month or has caused any person abnormal suffering or considerable injury to body or health or has resulted in the death of any person, imprisonment for a term of not less than 1 year shall be imposed.

Any person who conspires with any other person to commit an act referred to in the second paragraph shall be liable to imprisonment for a term not exceeding 10 years.

The relevant clause seems to be "any person who conspires with *any* other person" in the third paragraph. Thus a masochist who conspires with his partner to cause injuries on his own body may perhaps be prosecuted under this law, although no real cases appear to be on record whereby a masochist was punished under this law.

REFERENCES

1. Baumeister, R.F. *Masochism and the self.* Lawrence Erlbaum Associates, Hillsdale, NJ, 1989.
2. Gowitt, G.T., Hanzlick, R.L. Atypical autoerotic deaths. *Am J Forensic Med Pathol.* 1992 Jun;**13(2)**:115–9.
3. Person, E.S., Paraphilias, in *Kaplan & Sadock's Comprehensive Textbook of Psychiatry*, 8th edition, Sadock, B.J. and Sadock, V.A., Eds., Lippincott, Wilkins and Williams, Philadelphia, 2005, chap. 18.2.
4. Paraphilias, in *Gale Encyclopedia of Mental Disorders*, Thackery, E. and Harris, M., Eds, Thomson Gale, Farmington Hills, MI, 2002, pages 729–30.
5. Sharma, B.R. Disorders of sexual preference and medicolegal issues thereof. *American Journal of Forensic Medicine and Pathology*, 24(3): 277–282, 2003.
6. Bell, R. ABC of sexual health: homosexual men and women. *BMJ.* 1999 Feb 13;318(7181):452–5.
7. American Psychiatric Association. *Diagnostic and Statistical Manual of Mental Disorders*, 4th ed. Text rev. American Psychiatric Association, Washington DC, 2000.
8. Santtila, P., Sandnabba, N.K. and Nordling, J. Sadomasochism, in *Sex and Sexuality* (3 vols), McAnulty, RD and Burnette, M.M., Eds., Praeger, Westport, Connecticut, 2006, vol 3, chapter 2, pages 21–45.
9. ICD-9-CM diagnostic codes for paraphilias. Available from: http://icd9cm.chrisendres.com/2007/index.php?action=child&recordid=2342.
10. ICD-10 diagnostic codes for paraphilias. Available from: http://www.who.int/classifications/apps/icd/icd10online/?gf60.htm+f65.
11. Shorter, E. A. *Historical Dictionary of Psychiatry.* Oxford University Press, Oxford, 2005, Pp 168–170.
12. Farin, M., *Lust am Schmerz: Texte und Bilder zur Flagellomanie.* Schneekluth, Munich, 1990.
13. Hurwood, B.J., *The Golden Age of Erotica*, Sherbourne Press, Los Angeles, CA, 1965.
14. Bloch, I. *Sexual Life in England*, Corgi Books, UK, 1965.
15. Quinn, N.P., Toone, B., Lang, A.E., Marsden, C.D., Parkes, J.D. Dopa dose-dependent sexual deviation. *Br J Psychiatry.* 1983 Mar;142:296–8.
16. Kinsey, A.C., Pomeroy, W.B., Martin, C.E. and Gebhard, P.H. *Sexual Behavior in the Human Female*, W.B. Saunders, Philadelphia, 1953.
17. Parkes, A.S., *Patterns of Sexuality and Reproduction*, Oxford University Press, London, 1976.
18. Gottschall, J.A. and Gottschall, T.A. Are Per-Incident Rape-Pregnancy Rates Higher Than Per-Incident Consensual Pregnancy Rates? *Human Nature.* 2003;14(1):1–20.
19. Wilcox, A.J., Dunson, D.B., Weinberg, C.R., Trussell, J., Baird, D.D. Likelihood of conception with a single act of intercourse: providing benchmark rates for assessment of post-coital contraceptives. *Contraception.* 2001 Apr;63(4):211–5.
20. Holmes, M.M., Resnick, H.S., Kilpatrick, D.G., Best, C.L. Rape-related pregnancy: estimates and descriptive characteristics from a national sample of women. *Am J Obstet Gynecol.* 1996 Aug;**175(2)**:320–5.
21. Walker, M. Insult to injury. *New Scientist*, June 23, 2001.
22. Griffis, C.A., Compton, P., Doering, L. The effect of pain on leukocyte cellular adhesion molecules. *Biol Res Nurs.* 2006 Apr;**7(4)**:297–312.
23. Moser, C., Sadomasochism. In *The Sexually Unusual—Guide to Understanding and Helping*, Dailey, D.M., (Ed.), The Harrington Park Press, New York, 1988, pages 43–56.
24. Maslow, A. Self–esteem (dominance-feeling) and sexuality in women. *Journal of Social Psychology.* 1942;16:259–294.
25. Lebegue, B. Paraphilias in U.S. pornography titles: "pornography made me do it" (Ted Bundy). *Bull Am Acad Psychiatry Law.* 1991;**19(1)**:43–8.
26. Hunt, M., *Sexual Behaviour in the 1970s*, Dell, New York, 1974.
27. *Playboy.* What's really happening on campus. 1976;**23**: 128–131.

28. Moser, C., Kleinplatz, P.J. Introduction: the state of our knowledge on SM. *J Homosex.* 2006;**50(2–3)**:1–15.
29. Crépault, C., Couture, M. Men's erotic fantasies. *Arch Sex Behav.* 1980 Dec;**9(6)**:565–81.
30. Kahn, E. The depressive character. *Folia Psychiatr Neurol Jpn.* 1975;**29(4)**:291–303.
31. Schmeling, A., Correns, A., Geserick, G. An unusual autoerotic accident: sexual pleasure from peritoneal pain. [Article in German]. *Arch Kriminol.* 2001 May–Jun;**207(5–6)**:148–53.
32. White, C. The spanner trials and the changing law on sadomasochism in the UK. *J Homosex.* 2006;**50(2–3)**:167–87.
33. Moran, L.J. Laskey v. The United Kingdom: Learning the Limits of Privacy. *The Modern Law Review.* 1998;61(1):77–84.
34. Green, R. (Serious) sadomasochism: a protected right of privacy? *Arch Sex Behav.* 2001 Oct;**30(5)**:543–50.
35. Thompson, B., *Sadomasochism: painful perversion or pleasurable play?* Cassell, London, 1994.
36. Fairstein, L.A., *Sexual Violence: Our War Against Rape*, Berkley Trade, US, 1993, pages 195–97.
37. The General Civil Penal Code of Norway (Straffeloven 1902). Act of 22 May 1902 No. 10, with subsequent amendments, the latest made by Act of 21 December 2005 No. 131.

8 Sexual Sadism

INTRODUCTION

Sexual sadism refers to an aberrant sexual behavior where the person derives *sexual excitement* from inflicting pain—psychological or physical or both—on his sexual partner. Sadistic fantasies or acts may involve activities that indicate the dominance over the victim (e.g., forcing the victim to crawl or keeping the victim in a cage). They may also involve administering electrical shocks, beating, blindfolding, burning, cutting, mutilation, paddling, pinching, rape, restraint, spanking, stabbing, strangulation, torture, whipping, or even killing. It is the eroticization of dominance and control, as opposed to masochism, which is the eroticization of submission. It is the *suffering* of the victim, *not* the infliction of physical or psychological pain, that is sexually arousing.[1,2] For sexual sadists, inflicting pain is just a means to create suffering and to elicit the desired responses of obedience, submission, humiliation, fear, and terror. British sexologist Henry Havelock Ellis (1859–1939) preferred the term "algolagnia," viewing sadomasochism as a love of pain. He noted that "the sadist desires to inflict pain, but in some cases, if not in most, he desires that it should be felt as love."[3]

SADISM AND MASOCHISM

It has been seen that in many cases, both sadism and masochism are found in the same individual; many sadomasochists in fact are able to consciously alter their sexual orientation to adjust to the needs of a potential partner. It is also very common for people who take the dominant role in sadomasochistic interaction to have started out as submissives. Many think that a distinction between sadism and masochism is artificial, and in fact ICD-10 conceptualizes both sadism and masochism as a single disorder called sadomasochism (please see below). DSM-IV-TR, however, assigns different codes to both disorders, and since this book is keyed to DSM-IV-TR codes, it was considered best to deal with the two disorders separately.

SADISM DIRECTED TOWARD SPECIFIC GROUPS

Sometimes, sadistic acts may be directed toward a specific group or population, or a specific part of the body. Kaul and Duffy describe a case of a homosexual gerontophile who derived sadistic pleasure from assaulting only old men (gerontophilic sadism).[4] Cases of pedophilic sadism (where only young children are sexually tortured) have been described. Lachman and colleagues[5] describe a case of a pedophilic sadist who had genetic mental retardation and primary hypogonadism (Klinefelter's syndrome with karyotype 48, XXXY), who sadistically abused a boy aged 13. Cases of perverse sexuality with sadistic elements such as the passage of sticks or objects into the vagina, anus, or penis of young children have been described[6,7] (see also Satanism and Ritual Sex Abuse in chapter on pedophilia). Zoosadism involves deriving sexual pleasure from torturing animals, and necrosadism, mutilation of corpses.

One of the most notable examples of zoosadists is Peter Kürten (1883–1931), a German serial killer dubbed "The Vampire of Düsseldorf" by the contemporary media. He committed a series of sex crimes, assaults, and murders against adults and children, most notoriously from February to November 1929 in Düsseldorf. However, he started his criminal career as a zoosadist. As a youth he was employed by the local dogcatcher, who taught him how to masturbate and torture dogs. He also stabbed sheep while sexually molesting them, and indulged in necrophiliac and vampiristic activities with numerous humans.[8] Later he progressed from torturing animals to attacks on people.

The term *autosadism* is sometimes used for infliction of pain or injury on oneself, although it is the same thing as masochism. *Sapphosadism* denotes sadistic activities among lesbians.

Anal, Oral and Phallic Sadism

In Freudian theory the terms *anal sadism*, *oral sadism*, and *phallic sadism* are frequently used. Although these terms are not related to sadism, as defined in DSM-IV-TR, their definitions may be not out of place here. Anal sadism refers to the cluster of personality traits (e.g., aggressiveness, negativism, destructiveness, and outwardly directed rage) typical of the anal stage of development (please see Freud's libido theory in chapter 1). Oral sadism is a sadistic form of oral eroticism manifested by fantasies of chewing, biting, or otherwise using the mouth, lips, or teeth aggressively or destructively, and phallic sadism is the aggressive and destructive tendency associated with the childhood phallic stage of development, stemming from the child's interpretation of sexual intercourse as aggressive and violent.

Sexual Sadism Contrasted with Sadism

The Work Group to Revise DSM-III and the Joint Ad Hoc Committee believed that there was sufficient research and clinical evidence regarding the existence of sadistic personality disorder (SPD). However, critics believed that not only was adequate evidence of the validity of this category lacking, but it had such a high potential for misuse that it should not be included.

This controversy was resolved by the inclusion of this category (along with two other similarly disputed diagnoses) in Appendix A, "Proposed Diagnostic Categories Needing Further Study." The Work Group did not list SPD in the classification of mental disorders, but included it in the manual simply to facilitate further systematic clinical study and research. Thus DSM-III-R[9] came to use the terms sadistic personality disorder (SPD) and sexual sadism in different senses. Sadistic personality disorder, often termed just sadism, was not supposed to have any sexual component. In other words, while a person afflicted with SPD would derive plain pleasure in inflicting pain, a person afflicted with sexual sadism would derive sexual excitement. The controversy surrounding sadistic personality disorder increased in later years, and thus was excluded from DSM-IV and its successor DSM-IV-TR.[10] The evidence to support its inclusion as a separate diagnostic category in latter editions was thought to be rather insufficient. However, it is well recognized that not all those who engage in cruelty, torture, etc. are sexually aroused while engaging in such behavior, and hence it is best to call them simply sadists rather than sexual sadists. DSM-III-R explained how the two categories differed (Table 8.1).

Sadistic tendencies appear to be inherent in humans and animals alike. Sadism may be linked to our aggressive responses in protecting ourselves and may have had survival value, at least in the past.

DSM-IV-TR[1] assigns code 302.84 to sexual sadism and states the following criteria for diagnosing it:

A. Over a period of at least 6 months, recurrent, intense sexually arousing fantasies, sexual urges, or behaviors involving the act (real, not simulated) in which the psychological or physical suffering (including humiliation) of the victim is sexually exciting to the person.
B. The person has acted on these sexual urges with a nonconsenting person, or the sexual urges or fantasies cause marked distress or interpersonal difficulty.

It may, however, be appreciated that the only person who can know with any degree of certainty that these acts generate sexual arousal is the person himself, and thus it might be very difficult to assign

TABLE 8.1
Diagnostic Criteria for Sadistic Personality Disorder According to DSM-III-R

A. A pervasive pattern of cruel, demeaning, and aggressive behavior, beginning by early adulthood, as indicated by the repeated occurrence of at least four of the following:

(1) has used physical cruelty or violence for the purpose of establishing dominance in a relationship (not merely to achieve some noninterpersonal goal, such as striking someone in order to rob him or her)
(2) humiliates or demeans people in the presence of others
(3) has treated or disciplined someone under his or her control unusually harshly, e.g., a child, student, prisoner, or patient
(4) is amused by, or takes pleasure in, the psychological or physical suffering of others (including animals)
(5) has lied for the purpose of harming or inflicting pain on others (not merely to achieve some other goal)
(6) gets other people to do what he or she wants by frightening them (through intimidation or even terror)
(7) restricts the autonomy of people with whom he or she has a close relationship, e.g., will not let spouse leave the house unaccompanied or permit teen-age daughter to attend social functions
(8) is fascinated by violence, weapons, martial arts, injury, or torture

B. The behavior in A has not been directed toward only one person (e.g., spouse, one child) and has not been solely for the purpose of sexual arousal (as in sexual sadism).

this code. Few sexual offenders who commit violent acts do in fact admit that the violent acts were sexually arousing to them, and researchers are often left to derive this fact from other sources, such as the details of crime scene, reports by victims, or the offender's previous life history.

ICD-9-CM assigns the code 302.84 to sexual sadism[11]—the same as that assigned by DSM-IV-TR. ICD-10 conceptualizes both sadism and masochism as a single disorder, sadomasochism, and assigns the code F65.5 to it.[12] Sadomasochism is defined as:

> A preference for sexual activity which involves the infliction of pain or humiliation, or bondage. If the subject prefers to be the recipient of such stimulation this is called masochism; if the provider, sadism. Often an individual obtains sexual excitement from both sadistic and masochistic activities.

It is well known that multiple paraphilias may exist in a person at the same time, and that paraphilic themes may change from time to time. Changes between sadism and masochism are quite common and have been known for some time.[13]

HISTORICAL PERSPECTIVES

The term *sadism* was coined by the Austro-German psychiatrist Richard Freiherr von Krafft-Ebing (1840–1902) in the 19th century. He was also the first to clearly describe this clinical entity,[14] and his description of the features of sexual sadists has influenced diagnostic criteria ever since. He based this term from the name of the French aristocrat Marquis de Sâde (1740–1814), who allegedly was a sadist and wrote a number of works with sadism as a major theme (in this sense he was similar to his lesser known contemporary Nicolas-Edme Rétif [1734–1806], who suffered from retifism and wrote extensively on this subject. Please see chapter on fetishism for more). In his book, *Les 120 journées de Sodome ou l'école du libertinage* (1785 [*The 120 Days of Sodom or the School of Licentiousness*]), there are dozens of references to sadism. The book relates the story of four wealthy men who enslave twenty-four victims, mostly teenagers, and sexually torture them while listening to stories told by old prostitutes.

FIGURE 8.1 Marquis de Sâde, whose alleged practices and writings, led to the term *sadism*.

Krafft-Ebing defined *sadism* as "the experience of sexually pleasurable sensations (including orgasm) produced by acts of cruelty, bodily punishment afflicted on one's own person or when witnessed in others, be they animals or human beings. It may also consist of an innate desire to humiliate, hurt, wound or even destroy others in order thereby to create sexual pleasure in oneself." Freud asserted that "the roots of … sadism can be readily demonstrable in the normal individual." Both he and Krafft-Ebing believed that sadomasochistic-like activities were readily apparent during normal lovemaking. The sadomasochist, however, goes beyond what they saw as acceptable behavior. Gebhard noted that sadomasochism is embedded in our culture, because our culture is centered on dominance and control in social relationships and aggression is socially valued.[15]

India

Although the term is based on the works of Sâde, the earliest references to sadism can be found much earlier. In the ancient text *Kama Sutra* written by the Indian philosopher Mallanaga Vātsyāyana (4th century AD), one can find references to the practice of pinching, biting, and flogging erotic body parts as long as it was done with consent.[16] The *Kama Sutra* goes so far as to name all the different kinds of bites and scratches, including those focused on the breasts and nipples. Eight kinds of bites are described in the chapter "On Biting, and the Means to be Employed with Regard to Women of Different Countries." These are (i) the hidden bite, (ii) the swollen bite, (iii) the point, (iv) the line of points, (v) the coral and the jewel, (vi) the line of jewels, (vii) the broken cloud, and (viii) the biting of the boar.

China

By contrast, episodes of sexual sadism (and masochism) in China were very rare in handbooks of sex or erotic and pornographic literature, in spite of the pervasiveness of cruelty by modern Western standards.[17]

Rome

Religious floggings were used in the fertility rites of the Roman god Lupercus, and women during the Thessaly (Greek) festival of Aphrodite used flagellation to build their passions in preparation for sexual orgies. Barren Greek women were stripped naked and beaten in the temple of Juno to cure their infertility.

The Roman emperor Elagabalus (or Heliogabalus, ca. 203–222) was a transsexual and a sadomasochist. He married five times, thrice to women and twice to men. In the guise of a woman Elagabalus married Hierocles, a former slave and chariot driver, and he wished to be beaten by him as an adulterous wife.

Middle Ages

During the Middle Ages, Kokkoka in India wrote *The Koka Shastra,*[18] and Muhammad ibn Muhammad al-Nafzawi, in the Arab world, wrote *The Perfumed Garden,*[19] a marriage and sex manual and work of erotic literature. These books, which mainly give advice on sexual technique, also have sections which today would be construed as S/M behavior. Thus it appears that in these parts of the world, S/M behavior was prevalent and was socially sanctioned, at least among consenting couples.

In Europe, Baron Gilles de Rais (1404–1440), a French noble and soldier and a sexual sadist, was accused and ultimately convicted of torturing, raping, and murdering several hundred young children, mainly boys. Another notorious sexual sadist—a female—was Countess Elizabeth Báthory (1560–1614) of Hungary. She was known as the most infamous serial killer in Hungarian and Slovak history and is remembered as the Bloody Lady of Čachtice (after the castle near Trenčín, in Royal Hungary, present-day Slovakia, where she spent most of her life). After her husband's death, she was accused of torturing and killing hundreds of girls and young women. Her extraordinary life inspired innumerable legends, including the now famous story that she bathed in the blood of virginal girls whom she killed in order to retain her youth. These stories have led to the modern nicknames of the Blood Countess and Countess Dracula. She was imprisoned in 1610 in Čachtice Castle, where she remained bricked in her room until her death 4 years later.

It appears that elements of sadism were present in several Western European medieval religious ceremonies involving flagellation. In an early 15th-century Catalan painting, *The Flagellation of Christ*, the floggers certainly appear to be deriving sexual pleasure from their activities.[20] Historians have pointed to connections between sexual sadism and pedagogical punishment in English schools, too. The first overtly pornographic work on the subject of flagellation entitled *A Treatise on the Use of Flogging* was published in the year 1718. With the appearance of this book, flagellation became a passion throughout Europe. The French derided this practice as "*le vice anglais,*" although such a practice did not seem uncommon in their own society. In fact, whipping as a punishment had long been so common in European societies that beating of wives, children, and servants was already an accepted practice. Therefore, devotees of sexual sadism did not need to go far to seek it out and practice it for their own pleasure.

During the Spanish Inquisition, torture was frequently used especially that focusing on the breasts and nipples. Particular attention was paid to these erotic organs, ostensibly in order to extract confessions from alleged witches. But the possibility of perpetrators deriving sexual pleasure from these activities cannot be ruled out. During this time, torture manuals such as the *Malleus Maleficarum* (literally, *The Witch Hammer*, written in 1486 by Heinrich Kramer and Jacob Sprenger, and first published in Germany in 1487)[21] made specific reference to the suitability of breasts as objects of torture. Certain devices, such as the breast ripper (basically a set of tongs with two pairs of big pointed claws, which dug inside the breasts), were actually designed with this torture in mind.

In 1748, English novelist John Cleland (1709–1789) wrote the controversial classic *Memoirs of a Woman of Pleasure*, better known as *Fanny Hill*. Widely considered as the first modern erotic novel in English, it included scenes of sadomasochism, including a detailed description of a mutual flagellation scene between Fanny and an English client.

Modern Era

Many clubs now cater to the interests of sexual sadists. In these clubs, they are able to meet people who volunteer to receive punishment (since the latter are masochists). The culture followed among the members of these clubs is very elaborate and complex and difficult to comprehend even by experts. Charles C. Moser, professor of sexual medicine at the Institute for Advanced Study of Human Sexuality, who has published generously on sadism was once invited to an SM party. He admits that "it was my first such experience and the first time the participants allowed a researcher to observe them 'in action.'" From the description he gives, it is clear that even he could not understand what was going on. While an act of consensual sadomasochism was going on, Moser almost contemplated a complaint to the police. This is how he describes his experience:[22]

> At the beginning of the party, a man began what seemed like an especially savage beating of a woman. I watched uncomfortably, not knowing why the other, seemingly nice guests were not coming to her aid. Obviously, this severe beating could not be pleasurable and this must be violating all the limits and party rules I had studied beforehand. While deliberating about what to tell the police when asked why I sat by and did nothing as this man savagely beat this woman to death, I decided I had to act. Just as I stood up to intercede, the woman had a magnificent orgasm and I sank back into my chair to ponder my miscalculation. At the end of the evening, the woman asked her partner, "Can we stop on the way home for a drink, before we do this again?" It was amazing that she could still walk, but unbelievable that she was eager for a repeat performance. Obviously, there was much to be learned and a neophyte researcher's fascination with the subject was born.

In many schools, colleges and universities, there allegedly are student clubs that specifically cater to their sadomasochistic interests. One such club, Cuffs (from handcuffs), a student group at Iowa State University (ISU), made national headlines after their Nov. 10, 2003, meeting during which the group's president, Duane Long, Jr, flogged a clothed volunteer to demonstrate how to properly and safely perform BDSM. The girl Long allegedly assaulted signed written testimony stating she volunteered, received no marks or injuries and, thus, was not assaulted. Long also said that it was not his intent to cause pain, but to show safe techniques using the least amount of force.

Despite this, in early 2004, Bethany Schuttinga, director of judicial affairs, charged the club with violating university rules, the Student Conduct Code, and Iowa law and imposed a sanction on group activities. Group members appealed to Dean of Students Pete Englin, who upheld her decision. They further appealed to ISU President Gregory Geoffroy, who declined to review the case and recommended to the regents they deny request for an appeal. ISU officials argued the demonstration was an assault based on an earlier Iowa Court of Appeals case—*Iowa v. Collier*, 1985 (please see below)—that had ruled that BDSM activities are not exempt from Iowa's assault statute.

Quite obviously sadism is thriving in our society, and much needs to be learned about it.

ETIOLOGY

Early Speculations

Early speculations regarding the etiology of sadism centered around psychoanalytic theories. Moser[23] dwells on some of the earlier attempts to explain sexual sadism. Krafft-Ebing suggested that sadism could be congenital. Freud explained it as aggression attached to sex (for more on Freud's life–death instinct theory, please see chapter on sexual masochism). Stekel took it to be a kind of psychosexual infantilism. Horney explained it as a neurotic need for superiority. Thorpe and Katz[24] suggested that it stemmed from early condemnation and shaming, and tended to dissipate castration fears. None of these theories, however, has been adequately tested and at best is considered inspired guesswork.

Brain Abnormalities

Modern research tends to explain sadism more in terms of biological factors than psychoanalytical factors. Eliseev and Kunikovskiy[25] of the laboratory of forensic sexology in Moscow researched the EEG patterns of sexual sadists and came up with interesting data on brain abnormalities in sexual sadists. They examined 112 right-handed males, of whom 20 were diagnosed as cases of sexual sadism (according to ICD-10 criteria), 43 displayed abnormal sexual behavior *without* any diagnosis of paraphilia, and 49 were normal. Most sadists showed signs of organic disorders, with 95% showing signs of dysthymia, 85% dysphoria, 60% mental infantility syndrome, and 45% anxiety states. EEG of all subjects revealed that EEGs of sexual sadists compared with that of other groups. Significantly, the EEG patterns of sexual sadists differed from those of other groups. The most typical peculiarities found in the sadists was a significant increase in interhemispheric coherence in all frequency bands in the temporal area. This may represent pathological changes in the cortical-subcortical interactions in the temporal lobes. Furthermore, the sadists showed greater desynchronization of EEG rhythms (theta, alpha, beta) in the central and frontal regions of the right cerebral hemisphere. This may represent the presence of right-hemispheric dysfunction of hyperactivation type. The authors concluded that the pathogenetic mechanism of sadism may be the characteristic neurophysiological pattern of changed cortical-subcortical, regional, and hemispheric interactions, particularly with early brain damage.

Langevin and colleagues[26] examined the brain structure and function in a total of 91 sexual aggressives including 22 sadists, 21 nonsadists and 48 controls. They found right temporal horn dilatation in 41% (about two fifths) of sadists. In comparison, only 11% of nonsadistic sexually aggressives and 13% of controls showed this anomaly. Two isolated findings are also worth mentioning. In one sexual sadist, the CT scan showed a left frontal-temporal lobe glioma and CT of another showed an abnormally gross enlargement of the ventricles.

They also conducted neuropsychological testing on sexual sadists, sexually aggressives who were nonsadists and controls, using Halstead Reitan Battery and the Luria Nebraska Neuropsychological Test Battery. Using these test batteries, they found that impairment on Halstead Reitan Battery was higher in sexual sadists. On the other hand, impairment on Luria Nebraska Neuropsychological Test Battery was higher in nonsadists.

Endocrine Abnormalities

Lagevin[27] studied 15 cases of sexual aggression and 16 controls and suggested that the hypothalamic–pituitary–adrenal axis of the endocrine system might be important in sexual sadists and nonsadistic sexual aggressors. The weak androgen DHEAS (dehydroepiandrosterone sulfate) was found to be *elevated* in sexually aggressive individuals. In addition, prolactin was generally lower and cortisol higher in sexual aggressors. Significantly, cortisol is generally lower among nonsexual aggressors.[28,29] Testosterone was not significantly different in the two groups, although it has been hypothesized to be related to sexual anomalies as well as to aggression in general. The authors feel that the latter could be because of the fact that there is a high incidence of alcohol and substance abuse in aggressors, which may cause testosterone levels to rise.

Langevin and colleagues later expanded their study to include 49 cases of sexual aggression and 31 controls.[26] In the new study they found one sadist whose LH and FSH levels were five times the normal male limits, and in one case testosterone levels were very low. They also encountered some physical abnormalities in sadists. Two cases of hypospadias were found, which were believed to be due to local testosterone insufficiency. This led the authors to conjecture that *low* testosterone levels (perhaps in the brain), may be responsible for sexual sadism (please also see below). In one case there was gynaecomastia and lactation, one case with XYY syndrome, and one of possible XXY or Klinefelters' syndrome. The authors conclude by noting that further research on sex hormones in sexual sadists is warranted.

Levels of free testosterone show a low positive co-relation with sexual aggression. The ratio of five-alpha-dihydrotestosterone to testosterone, however, correlates significantly with sexual aggression.[30]

Other Factors

Langevin and colleagues,[26] who have conducted research in etiological factors of sexual sadism, conclude that although biological factors play a part in sexual sadism, they cannot force an individual to act on his sexual impulses. Other psychological factors playing a part include family background and substance abuse.

PREVALENCE

It might appear that the prevalence of sexual sadism parallels that of masochism because the practice of one paraphilia would require at least one other individual with the opposing paraphilia for the activity to take place. However, since sadistic acts may occur with nonconsenting normal individuals, too, the true prevalence of both conditions may not coincide.

No direct figures of its prevalence are available, but reasonable guesses can be made indirectly by studying related material such as sale of pornographic paraphernalia related to sadistic themes. This is discussed more fully in the chapter on sexual masochism.

The first systematic study on the subject of prevalence of sadism was done by Kinsey and colleagues,[31] and they found that 3–12% of women and 10–20% of men engaged in sadomasochistic activities.

Crépault and Couture[32] interviewed 94 men about their erotic fantasies occurring during heterosexual activity. The majority of these men were married, and their average duration of cohabitation with a woman was 6.5 years. Many of them reported having had fantasies centered around a sadistic theme. Of them 10.7% reported having had a fantasy of a scene where they beat a woman up, 14.9% reported fantasies of humiliating a woman, 26.6% had a fantasy of being aggressive to someone, 39.4% harbored a fantasy where they tied up a woman and stimulated her sexually, and 44.7% had a somewhat sadistic fantasy where the woman that they seduce pretends to resist.

Sexual sadism is seen among females, too. Fedoroff and colleagues studied the clinical records (of the first author) of 15 years, and identified individuals referred to them for suspected paraphilic disorders. The clinics were located in different countries (Canada, the United States, and Great Britain), and all were affiliated with universities. A total of 132 paraphilics were identified, of which 14 (11%) were women.[33] Within the total female sample, the most common diagnoses were pedophilia (36%), sexual sadism (29%), and exhibitionism (29%). The authors, however, emphasize that this is not a study of the frequency or prevalence of paraphilias in the female population, nor can the findings be used to draw such inferences.

OFFENDER CHARACTERISTICS

Sadistic sexual fantasies are likely to have been present in childhood. The age at onset of sadistic activities is variable, but is commonly by early adulthood.[1] Sadomasochistic activity, however, tends to blossom in the fifth decade of life.[34] Offenders are mostly males, but female sadists are also known. A female sadist is usually referred to as a mastix. Sexual sadism is usually chronic.[1]

DSM-IV-TR describes three types of sexual sadists. These are:

(i) Individuals who are simply bothered by their sadistic fantasies, but they do not act out their fantasies. These may be invoked during sexual activity. The victim is terrified by the anticipation of the impending sadistic act.
(ii) Individuals who act on the sadistic sexual urges with a consenting partner (who may have sexual masochism) who willingly suffers pain or humiliation.
(iii) Individuals who act on their sadistic sexual urges with nonconsenting victims.

In all of these cases, it is the suffering of the victim that is sexually arousing. When sexual sadism is practiced with nonconsenting partners, the activity is likely to be repeated until the person with sexual sadism is apprehended. Some individuals with sexual sadism may engage in sadistic acts for many years without a need to increase the potential for inflicting serious physical damage. Usually, however, the severity of the sadistic acts increases over time. When sexual sadism is severe, and especially when it is associated with antisocial personality disorder, individuals with sexual sadism may seriously injure or kill their victims.[1] This has been termed severe sexual sadism.[35] Since *lepto-sadism* is a term already being used for mild forms of sadism (categories (i) and (ii) above), the term *barysadism* (Greek *barys*, heavy) is proposed in this book for severe sexual sadism.

Alcoholism and Drug Abuse

Sadists are similar in many respects to other sexually aggressive people who are not primarily sadistic in their sexual acts.[26] The incidence of alcoholism and drug abuse is high in both groups. The number of crimes including sex crimes committed by both groups is very high. Both show a long history of antisocial behavior, so that approximately 40% of both groups could be labeled as psychopaths or having an antisocial personalities.

Co-existence with Other Paraphilias

Myers and colleagues[36] studied the case records of five serial sexual killers—four from the United States and one from Russia, and found that all five were involved in autoerotic asphyxiation and sexual sadism (100%), two (40%) had concomitant bondage fetishism, and two (40%) had concomitant transvestic fetishism. Overall the group averaged 4.0 lifetime paraphilias. Some possible relationships were observed between the offenders' paraphilic orientation and their modus operandi, e.g., all of these serial killers strangled victims—suggesting an association between their sadistic and asphyxiative paraphilic interests.

Abel and colleagues used self reports to gather data with assured confidentiality from 561 non-incarcerated paraphiliacs and found that of all sadists, 18% also engaged in masochism, 21% in exhibitionism, 25% each in voyeurism and frotteurism, 33% in pedophilia, and 46% in rape.[37]

Disturbances in Gender Identity

The sadists are unique in showing a disturbances in gender identity. Brittain noted an "effeminate tinge" in the sadistic murderer.[38] Langevin and colleagues have reported similar characteristics. They report the case of a sadist who wanted to grow female breasts and showed an interest in sex reassignment surgery.[26]

Narcissism

Many sadists show signs of narcissism or self-love. Some enjoy parading themselves before their terrorized victims, while some others—sex killers particularly—show a childish delight at the attention they generate through their crimes. They enjoy seeing their pictures in the newspapers. They derive as much satisfaction from publicity as from the sexual mutilations and deaths that they cause.

CLASSIFICATION

Any attempt to classify sexual sadists is likely to meet with frustration, because many variables are involved. One classical difficulty has already been mentioned, i.e., it is nearly impossible to determine in most cases whether the acts of violence really generate sexual arousal. Another is that a true sexual sadist has two components in his behavior—a sexual component and a sadistic component. It may be possible in many cases that one or the other component is missing. Based on a comprehensive review of literature, the following classification is proposed (roughly in increasing degree of psychopathology).

Class I Sexual Sadists

These individuals are bothered by their sadistic fantasies, but they do not act out their fantasies.

Class II Sexual Sadists

These individuals act on the sadistic sexual urges with consenting partners (who may have sexual masochism) who willingly suffers pain or humiliation. Class I and class II sadists may be loosely grouped under the category leptosadists. The disorder may be called *leptosadism*.

Class III Sexual Sadists

These individuals act on their sadistic sexual urges with nonconsenting victims, but they do not seriously injure or kill them. This group almost coincides with sex aggression defusion or sadistic sexual type rapists. Please see chapter on rape for more details.

Class IV Sexual Sadists

These individuals not only act on their sadistic sexual urges with nonconsenting victims, but they seriously injure or kill them. The condition is called *severe sexual sadism* or *barysadism*. The difference between class I and class II sexual sadists (leptosadists), on one hand, and class III and class IV sexual sadists (barysadists), on the other, is almost the same as that between those who commit consensual intercourse and those who commit rape. Class III and class IV sexual sadists may loosely be grouped under the *sexual aggressors* category. There indeed are more types of sexual aggressors (please see chapter on rape [rapist typology] for details).

In addition, three more groups of individuals need be considered. While they are not true sexual sadists, they share a number of characteristics with them. These are plain sadists, plain sexual murderers and plain murderers. *Plain sadists* enjoy cruelty and torture, but are not *sexually* aroused by these activities. *Plain sexual murderers* combine sex and homicide, but for a number of reasons *other than* sexual arousal. These reasons could be many. A sexual offender may murder his victim in order to silence his potential accuser, he may become angry and kill in response to her resistance, he may simply panic, death may be accidental, or homicide may be the result of pathological group behavior, such as may occur when an army goes on a rampage in an occupied territory.[39] Finally, the *plain murderer* kills, but has neither the sexual nor the sadistic component to his behavior. He does,

TABLE 8.2
Behavioral Components of Various Classes of Sexual Sadists and Allied Groups

Class of individuals/offenders	Behavioral components present		
	Sexual component	Sadistic component	Homicidal component
Sexual sadists, class I, II and III	Yes	Yes	No
Sexual sadists, class IV (severe sexual sadism)	Yes	Yes	Yes
Nonsadistic sexual offenders who kill	Yes	No	Yes
Nonsadistic sexual offenders, who do not kill (e.g., exhibitionists or voyeurs)	Yes	No	No
Plain sadists (included under SPD in DSM-III-R)	No	Yes	No
Plain sadists who kill	No	Yes	Yes
Plain murderers	No	No	Yes

however, share the propensity to kill with class IV sexual sadists. These and other allied groups are examined in Table 8.2.

TYPES OF SADISTIC BEHAVIOR

Krafft-Ebing[14] subclassified sexual sadism into the following eight categories.

(i) Lust murder —In this category, there is a connection between killing and sexual arousal. It may extend to anthropophagy or cannibalism. Jack the Ripper has been included in this category.
(ii) Necrophilia or mutilation of corpses—Although Krafft-Ebing included it under sadism, according to current DSM-IV-TR classification, this would be a separate category.
(iii) Injury to females (stabbing, flagellation, etc.).
(iv) Defilement of women.
(v) Other kinds of assaults on women. This includes symbolic sadism, where, for example, the offender cuts the hair of his victims rather than causing any serious harm.
(vi) Ideal sadism —This includes sadistic fantasies alone without any actual act of sadism.
(vii) Sadism with other objects—This includes sadistic activities such as whipping boys.
(viii) Sadistic acts with animals.

Rajs and colleagues[40] have described mainly four types of mutilations involving element of sadism (for details, please see chapter on Miscellaneous sexual crimes and perversions, under the subtitle mutilomania).

LEGAL ASPECTS

The legal issues pertaining to whether a hurt caused by a sadist upon his partner (who has voluntarily consented to undergo any harm during S/M activity) make him liable to prosecution or not have been dealt with in the chapter on sexual masochism. Some significant cases involving sadistic activities are as follows.

Commonwealth v. Appleby (1980)

In *Commonwealth v. Appleby* 402 N.E.2d 1051 (Mass. 1980), the Massachusetts court held that for sadistic acts amounting to assault or battery, consent of the victim is *not* a defense. Kenneth Appleby had been engaged in "a homosexual, sadomasochistic relationship for over two years" with Steven Cromer. The two lived together, with Cromer acting as Appleby's servant. Appleby used to beat Cromer frequently as a result of his sexual sadistic tendencies. In October 1975, Appleby had beaten Cromer with a bullwhip and a baseball bat, fracturing Cromer's kneecap, and in February 1976 he again beat Cromer with a bullwhip. Despite these beatings, Cromer continued to live with Appleby after each of these incidents. In August 1976, Appleby hit Cromer lightly with a riding crop. After this incident Cromer left him. Appleby was tried for all three specific instances of assault and battery. At trial, Cromer testified that Appleby was a sadist, but denied that he was involved in a consensual SM relationship with Appleby. He claimed he stayed with Appleby out of fear that "Appleby would harm him or members of his family if he did not continue the relationship." In 1978, a Superior Court jury convicted Appleby of assault and battery with a dangerous weapon (a riding crop).

Appleby appealed, arguing that Cromer had consented to the beatings, and that "as a matter of law Cromer could consent to their sadomasochistic relationship." The court held that even if Cromer had consented, it was not a valid defense to the charge of assault and battery with a dangerous weapon.

Iowa v. Collier (1985)

This important case determined whether consensual sadistic activities of an individual could be called a "social activity." In *Iowa v. Collier, 372 N.W.2d 303, 304 (Iowa Ct. App. 1985),* one Edward Collier was charged with assaulting Leanne Steele, whom he employed as an "out-call model." Steele alleged that Collier blindfolded her, tied her to a bed, and whipped and raped her, responding to her cries to stop by gagging her. Collier was convicted in Polk County District Court for assault resulting in serious injury (also for possession of a firearm). He appealed to the Iowa Supreme Court, asserting that theirs (Collier and Steele's) was a case of consensual S/M sex and that Steele had herself requested that he tie her up and beat her. He asserted that the trial court erred in refusing to instruct the jury on the defense of consent on the charges of assault. He further took the defense that their sadomasochistic activity was a social activity, which would make it exempt from the definition of assault in section 708.1 of the Iowa Code [41] which states:

> A person commits an assault when, without justification, the person does any of the following:
>
> 1. Any act which is intended to cause pain or injury to, or which is intended to result in physical contact which will be insulting or offensive to another, coupled with the apparent ability to execute the act.
> 2. Any act which is intended to place another in fear of immediate physical contact which will be painful, injurious, insulting, or offensive, coupled with the apparent ability to execute the act.
> 3. Intentionally points any firearm toward another, or displays in a threatening manner any dangerous weapon toward another.

Provided, that where the person doing any of the above enumerated acts, and such other person, are voluntary participants in a sport, social or other activity, not in itself criminal, and such act is a reasonably foreseeable incident of such sport or activity, and does not create an unreasonable risk of serious injury or breach of the peace, the act shall not be an assault.

Collier did not deny that sadomasochistic activity occurred. He asserted that it was consensual and that it was *a social activity*, which would make it exempt from the definition of assault in section 708.1 of the Iowa Code.

The Court however did not consider sadomasochism a social activity and observed, "We have found no cases which directly consider the question of whether sadomasochism or other deviant sexual behavior is a 'social or other activity' within the meaning of the statute." Edward Collier was found guilty.

This ruling has been used subsequently to hold similar BDSM activities illegal. Most importantly, the ruling was used in 2003-4, when Cuffs, a student BDSM group at Iowa State University, made public demonstrations of their BDSM activities (please see above).

People v. Jovanovic (1999)

People v. Jovanovic, 700 N.Y.S.2d 156 (N.Y. App. Div. 1999), was a highly publicized criminal case in New York, that involved sadomasochistic activities. Oliver Jovanovic (born 1966) was a doctoral candidate in molecular biology at Columbia University in 1996. In the summer of that year, a Barnard student, Jamie Rzucek, 20, (dubbed "Madame X" by the press during the trial, as she could be the victim of a possible rape, and the law prohibits revealing names of such victims) made a friendship with him in an Internet chat room. They exchanged several email messages about a shared taste for sadomasochistic sex and often talked on telephone. On 22 November, the two met for a dinner date and then went to Jovanovic's apartment, where they watched Peter Jackson's "Meet the Feebles" on video (in the movie, Muppet-like characters engage in sexually violent behavior). After that they spent the night together.

After their date of November 22-23, they continued to exchange emails, and Rzucek never made any specific complaints. However, after waiting 4 days she alleged that Jovanovic had kidnapped her and had kept her in his custody for 20 hours, during which time he tied her up with pieces of cloth, burned her with candle wax, tortured her in various ways, and sexually abused her with a martial arts baton. This late complaint, of itself, meant little because rape victims often wait before acting legally. On December 5, Jovanovic was arrested and accused of kidnapping, sexual abuse, and assault. Linda Fairstein, head of the Sex Crime Division of Manhattan's District Attorney's office, decided to press charges.

During the trial, Jovanovic maintained that the acts were consensual. Justice William A. Wetzel, presiding over the case did not allow the e-mail correspondence between them to be admitted as evidence, ruling that rape shield laws precluded references to her sexual past. Jovanovic was convicted and sentenced to 15 years to life. After having served 20 months in prison, Jovanovic was released in December 1999 when the appeals court ruled that the rape shield law had been improperly applied by the trial judge.

A few countries and jurisdictions have explicit laws allowing sadistic acts. Sections 229 and 235 of the General Civil Penal Code of Norway[42] serve as good illustrations.

Norway

Section 229. Any person who injures another person in body or health or reduces any person to helplessness, unconsciousness or any similar state, or who aids and abets thereto, is guilty of occasioning bodily harm and shall be liable to imprisonment for a term not exceeding 3 years, but exceeding 6 years if any illness or inability to work lasting more than two weeks or any incurable defect or injury is caused, and not exceeding 8 years if death or considerable injury to body or health results.

From this section, it appears that a sadist would be liable to prosecution. However, section 235 states as follows:

Section 235. A penalty pursuant to sections 228 and 229 shall not be imposed when the act is committed against any person who has consented thereto.

If any person is killed or considerably injured in body or health with his own consent, or if any person out of compassion deprives a hopelessly ill person of his life, or aids and abets thereto, the penalty may be reduced below the minimum otherwise prescribed and to a milder form of penalty.

This section seems to completely absolve sadists who cause injuries to their partners with consent.

REFERENCES

1. American Psychiatric Association. *Diagnostic and Statistical Manual of Mental Disorders*, 4th ed. Text rev. American Psychiatric Association, Washington DC, 2000.
2. Hazelwood, R.R., Dietz, P.E., Warren, J. The Criminal Sexual Sadist. *FBI Law Enforcement Bulletin*, February 1992.
3. Ellis, H. Studies in the Psychology of Sex. Vol. 3, *Analysis of the Sexual Impulse, Love, and Pain; the Sexual Impulse in Women*. 2nd. Ed., F.A. Davis, Philadelphia, 1903, 1926.
4. Kaul, A., Duffy, S. Gerontophilia—a case report. *Med Sci Law.* 1991 Apr;**31(2)**:110-4.
5. Lachman, M., Brzek, A., Mellan, J., Hampl R, Starka L, Motlik K. Recidivous offense in sadistic homosexual pedophile with karyotype 48, XXXY after testicular pulpectomy. A case report. *Exp Clin Endocrinol.* 1991;**98(2)**:171-4.
6. Young, W.C., Sachs, R.G., Braun, B.G., & Watkins, R.T. (1991). Patients reporting ritual abuse in childhood: A clinical syndrome. *Child Abuse & Neglect.* 1991;**15**:181-189.
7. Jonker, F., & Jonker-Bakker, P. (1991). Experiences with ritualist child sexual abuse: A case study from the Netherlands. *Child Abuse & Neglect.* 1991;**15**:191-196.
8. Persaud, R. Blood-lust in the clinic. *The Independent (London).* February 2, 1993, Tuesday.
9. American Psychiatric Association. *Diagnostic and Statistical Manual of Mental Disorders*, 3rd ed. rev. American Psychiatric Association, Washington DC, 1987.
10. Myers, W.C., Burket, R.C., Husted, D.S. Sadistic personality disorder and comorbid mental illness in adolescent psychiatric inpatients. *J Am Acad Psychiatry Law.* 2006;**34(1)**:61-71.
11. ICD-9-CM diagnostic codes for paraphilias. Available from: http://icd9cm.chrisendres.com/2007/index.php?action=child&recordid=2342.
12. ICD-10 diagnostic codes for paraphilias. Available from: http://www.who.int/classifications/apps/icd/icd10online/?gf60.htm+f65.
13. Philpot, C.D. Paraphilia and aging. *Clin Geriatr Med.* 2003 Aug;19(3):629-36.
14. Krafft-Ebing , R.F. *Psychopathia Sexualis*, 1st ed. F.A.Davis, Philadelphia, 1886 [reprinted by Bloat Books, 1999].
15. Gebhard, P. Fetishism and Sadomasochism. In *Dynamics of Deviant Sexuality*, Masserman, J.H.(ed.), Grune & Stratton, New York, 1969.
16. Vātsyāyana, M. *Kama Sutra*, Lancer Books, New York, 1964 (originally written 4th Century AD).
17. Van Gulik, R.H. and Goldin, P.R. *Sexual Life in Ancient China*: A Preliminary Survey of Chinese Sex and Society from Ca. 1500 B.C. Till 1644 A.D. Brill Academic Publishers, Leiden, 2003.
18. Kokkoka. *The Koka Shastra* (trans. Comfort, A.), Stein & Day, New York, 1965 (originally written 1150).
19. Nefzawi, S. *The Perfumed Garden* (trans. Burton, R.; ed. Walton, A.H.). G.P. Putnam's Sons, New York, 1964 (origially written 1400 A.D.).
20. Gibson, I. *The English Vice: Beating, Sex and Shame in Victorian England and After.* Duckworth, London, 1978.
21. Mackay, C.S. (Ed. and trans.), *Malleus Maleficarum*. Cambridge University Press, Cambridge, 2006.
22. Moser, C., Kleinplatz, P.J. Introduction: the state of our knowledge on SM. *J Homosex.* 2006;50(2-3):1-15.
23. Moser, C., Sadomasochism. In *The Sexually Unusual—Guide to Understanding and Helping*, Dailey, D.M., (Ed.), The Harrington Park Press, New York, 1988, pages 43-56.
24. Thorpe, L., and Katz, B., *The psychology of abnormal behavior*, Ronald Press, New York, 1948.
25. Eliseev, A.V. and Kunikovskiy, J.E. EEG and clinical peculiarities of sexual sadists. *Biological Psychiatry.* 1997;**42(1, Supp 1)**:45S.

26. Langevin, R., Bain, J., Wortzman, G., Hucker, S., Dickey, R., Wright, P. Sexual sadism: brain, blood, and behavior. *Ann N Y Acad Sci.* 1988;528:163-71.
27. Langevin, R., Bain J., Ben-Aron, M., Coulthard, R., Day, D., Handy, L., Heasman, G., Hucker, S.J., Purins, J.E., Roper, V., Russon, A., Webster, C.D. and Wortzman, G. Sexual aggression: Constructing a prediction equation, in *Erotic Preference, Gender Identity and Aggression in Men*, Langevin, R., Ed., Lawrence Erlbaum Associates, Hillsdale, New Jersey, 1985.
28. McBurnett, K., Lahey, B.B., Rathouz, P.J., Loeber, R. Low salivary cortisol and persistent aggression in boys referred for disruptive behavior. *Arch Gen Psychiatry.* 2000 Jan;**57(1)**:38-43.
29. Anderson, G.S., *Biological Influences on Criminal Behavior*, CRC Press, Boca Raton, 2007, pages 144-6.
30. Christiansen, K., Knussmann, R. Androgen levels and components of aggressive behavior in men. *Horm Behav.* 1987 Jun;**21(2)**:170-80.
31. Kinsey, A.C., Pomeroy, W.B., Martin, C.E and Gebhard, P.H. *Sexual Behavior in the Human Female*, W.B. Saunders, Philadelphia, 1953.
32. Crépault, C., Couture M. Men's erotic fantasies. *Arch Sex Behav.* 1980 Dec;**9(6)**:565-81.
33. Fedoroff, J. P., Fishell, A., Fedoroff, B., A case series of women evaluated for paraphilic sexual disorders. *Canadian Journal of Human Sexuality.* 1999; 8(2): 127-140.
34. Quinn, N.P., Toone, B., Lang, A.E., Marsden, C.D., Parkes, J.D. Dopa dose-dependent sexual deviation. *Br J Psychiatry.* 1983 Mar;142:296-8.
35. Marshall, W.L., and Hucker, S.J. Severe Sexual Sadism: Its Features and Treatment, in *Sex and Sexuality* (3 vols), McAnulty, R.D. and Burnette, M.M., Eds., Praeger, Westport, Connecticut, 2006, vol 3, chapter 10, pages 227-250.
36. Myers, W.C., Bukhanovskiy, A., Justen, E., Morton, R.J., Tilley, J., Adams, K., Vandagriff, V.L., Hazelwood, R.R. The relationship between serial sexual murder and autoerotic asphyxiation. *Forensic Sci Int.* 2007 Oct 31 [Epub ahead of print].
37. Abel, G.G., Becker, J.V., Cunningham-Rathner J, Mittelman M, Rouleau JL. Multiple paraphilic diagnoses among sex offenders. *Bull Am Acad Psychiatry Law.* 1988;*16(2)*:153-68.
38. Brittain, R.P. The sadistic murderer. *Med Sci Law.* 1970 Oct;10(4):198-207.
39. Grubin, D. Sexual murder. *Br J Psychiatry.* 1994 Nov;**165(5)**:624-9.
40. Rajs, J., Lundström, M., Broberg, M., Lidberg, L., Lindquist, O. Criminal mutilation of the human body in Sweden—a thirty-year medico-legal and forensic psychiatric study. *J Forensic Sci.* 1998 May;**43(3)**:563-80.
41. Iowa Code Ann. §708.1 (enacted 1976).
42. The General Civil Penal Code of Norway (Straffeloven 1902). Act of 22 May 1902 No. 10, with subsequent amendments, the latest made by Act of 21 December 2005 No. 131.

CHIKAN

Frotteurism in Japan is known by a special term—*chikan*. The term is used to describe men who take advantage of the crowded conditions of certain places, such as the public transit systems, to touch people sexually. It is seen in other situations as well; a common situation is for the offender to wait in a bicycle parking lot until a woman is bent over unlocking her bicycle lock. The offender then gropes her from behind (toucherism). As part of the effort to combat chikan, some railway companies have designated women-only passenger cars.

The Saikyō Line (an abbreviation for Saitama-Tokyo Line), the railway line between Ōsaki Station (Shinagawa Ward, Tokyo) and Ōmiya Station (Ōmiya Ward, Saitama City, Japan), has a particularly severe problem of overcrowding during rush hours, encouraging incidents of frotteurism. It has had the dubious distinction of reporting the maximum incidents of frotteurism in Tokyo. This problem has now been addressed by installation of women-only passenger cars, as mentioned above.

Celebrities have been accused and convicted of frotteurism and toucherism. On September 13, 2006, in the night at around 10:10 p.m, Kazuhide Uekusa (1960–), noted Japanese economist, economic analyst and a professor at the graduate school of Waseda University, was arrested as he put his hands under a high school girl's skirt while on a Keihin Kyuko Line train near Shinagawa Station. Although he denied having committed toucherism, forensic evidence verified a match between fabric traces found on Uekusa's suit with that of the victim's skirt. The Tokyo District Court sentenced him to 4 months in prison on October 17, 2007.[7] He had earlier been fined ¥50,000 for a similar offense in 1998 and ¥500,000 in 2005 for upskirting (please see chapter on voyeurism).

HISTORICAL PERSPECTIVES

No clear-cut examples of frotteurism appear in ancient historical texts. Frotteurism is either a more recent phenomenon, or more likely, this behavior was not recognized as an illegal behavior in earlier times. Also quite possibly, the victims chose—as they do now—not to report this phenomenon to the law enforcement authorities, the behavior causing only a minor annoyance.

Austro-German psychiatrist Richard Freiherr von Krafft-Ebing (1840–1902) was one of the first to describe frotteurism scientifically.[8] He described four cases of frotteurism (cases 211 to 214), describing the phenomenon as "a forensically important variety of exhibition" (*sic*).

His case 211 described a 44-year old male D., a heavy drinker, who suffered from lead poisoning. Until the previous year he had masturbated much, and often drawn pornographic pictures and shown them to his acquaintances. He had repeatedly dressed himself as a woman in secret (showing signs of transvestic fetishism, too). Gradually he became impotent, and for two years thereafter, he was obsessed with frotteuristic desires while in crowds at dusk. Once, when discovered in the act, he had been sentenced to imprisonment for 4 months.

Case 212 described a 31-year old male M., married for 6 years and father of 4 children. He was badly predisposed and subject to melancholia at times. Three years earlier, he was discovered with a silk dress on by his wife, masturbating (transvestic fetishism). One day he was discovered in a shop committing the act of frottage on a lady. He was very repentant, and asked to be severely punished for his irresistible impulse.

Case 213 described a 33-year old male G., who was badly predisposed hereditarily. At an omnibus station he was discovered in the act of *frottage* with his penis on a lady. He was deeply repentant; but he stated that at the sight of a noticeable *posteriora* of a lady, he was irresistibly impelled to practice *frottage*, and that he became confused and knew not what he did. He was sent to an asylum.

His last case, number 214 described a frotteur Z., who was born in 1850. He had had a blameless life previously, and belonged to a good family. He was well off financially. After a short married life he became a widower, in 1873. For 2 years he had been subject to the unhappy impulse to go in crowds of people—in churches, at box-offices of theatres, etc.—and press up behind females and manipulate the prominent portion of their dresses (bustles), thus producing orgasm and ejaculation. He was watched, and one day he was arrested in the act. He was terribly frightened, and in despair about his situation; and, in making a full confession, he begged for pardon. He stated that he was never given to masturbation, and had never been in any way perverse sexually. Since the early death of his wife, he had gratified his great sexual desire in temporary love affairs, having always had an aversion for prostitutes and brothels. The impulse to *frottage* had suddenly seized him 2 years earlier, while he happened to be in church. Though he was conscious that it was wrong, he could not help yielding to it immediately. Since then he had been excitable to the *posteriora* of females, and had been actually impelled to seek opportunities for frottage. The only thing on women that excited him was the bustle; every other part of the body and attire was a matter of indifference to him; neither did he mind whether the woman was old or young, beautiful or ugly. Since this began, he had had no more inclination for natural gratification. Of late *frottage* scenes had appeared in his dreams, too.

During his acts he was fully conscious of his situation and the act, and tried to perform it in such a way as to attract as little attention as possible. After his act he was always ashamed of what he had done. The medical examination revealed no sign of mental disease or mental weakness, but symptoms of *neurasthenia sexualis—ex abstinentia libidinosa* (?)—which was also proved by the circumstance that even the mere touch of the fetish with the unexposed genitals sufficed to induce ejaculation. Apparently Z., weakened sexually and distrusting his virility, and yet libidinous, had come to practice *frottage* by having the sight of *posteriora feminae* fall together accidentally with sexual excitement.

After describing these 4 cases, Ebing tried to explain the causes of the phenomenon. He thought that frottage was a masturbatorial act of a hypersexual individual who was uncertain about his virility in *corpore feminae* (females). He supported his theory (of a lack of virility in frotteurs), by noting that all frotteurs rubbed their genitals on the women's *posteriors*, and not *anteriors*. He also thought that fetishism played a part to some extent in frotteurism. To support his theory, he cites case 212, which displayed signs of silk-fetishism. He asserts that "very likely the lady in question wore a silk gown, and the indecent attack was directed upon the dress, not the nates." Also in case 214 the act was evidently qualified by the bustle and not by the particular part of the body.

ETIOLOGY

The etiology of frotteurism is best explained by the courtship disorder theory first propounded by Freund, Scher, and Hucker[9,10] (for details, please see chapter on exhibitionism). However, a few other factors seem to play a part, too. Simpson and colleagues[11] from New South Wales, Australia, found that many patients after traumatic brain injury, start indulging in frotteuristic behavior (for details, please see Chapter 1). According to psychoanalytic theory, someone who develops frotteurism may have been touched or rubbed against inappropriately at a younger age. He may react to dealing with this trauma by becoming a frotteur himself.[4]

Horley[12] suggests that frotteur is actually a timid or nonassertive rapist. He describes the case of a 28-year.old individual, whom he calls T.O. He had been diagnosed as a schizophrenic, and during the 10 years that he had lived in Canada, he had engaged in 4 instances of frotteurism (which came to the notice of authorities. One can only guess, how many other similar acts he may have performed). His first assault occurred as a teenager when he fondled a woman's breast as he asked directions from a woman in a public street. His second offense occurred 5 years later, when he stroked a woman's buttocks in an apartment building laundry. Just prior to when Horley saw him, he rubbed up against and caressed a young woman in a shopping mall, which was his third frotteuristic offense. His final act of frotteurism was when he brushed up inappropriately against at 9-year old girl in a crowded store. All victims were unknown to him.

Horley concludes by observing that frotteurs are actually timid or nonassertive rapists. These offenders only need a sufficient dose of "liquid courage" or a very docile victim to go on to the state of rape. This fact is in accordance with courtship disorder theory,[9,10] too, which sees voyeurism, exhibitionism, frotteurism, toucherism, obscene telephone calling, and biastophilia as part of a single disorder, rather than as separate disorders (in fact it is tempting to think of courtship disorder theory much in the same vein as physicists think of unified field theory, where 4 basic forces of nature are construed not as separate forces, but different manifestations of a single unified field. In fact, courtship disorder theory may well be called the *unified field theory of psychosexuality*). Horley even goes to the extent of suggesting that frotteurs may better be construed and classified as a subtype of rapists, and even if such a classification completely eliminates a paraphilia (frotteurism) from the lexicon, so be it.

CLASSIFICATION

No classification of frotteurs has been suggested till now, perhaps because few cases have been reported in the literature, and therefore the size of the sample is too small to allow a reasonable classification.

It appears that all paraphilias are roughly similar to one another, in as far as all of them exist on a continuum of increasing severity (ranging from the most innocuous to the most dangerous). It may tentatively be called the *theory of paraphilic equivalence*. Based on this theory (which enables us to extrapolate classes of one paraphilia by studying classes of other paraphilas), and from existing case reports, the following classifications of frotteurism are proposed.

Class I Frotteurs: Fantasizing Frotteurs

These people fantasize about rubbing their genitals against other persons, or grabbing their sexual organs in a crowd, but are too timid to actually carry out their fantasies. They tend to remain happy merely with their frotteuristic fantasies. They may or may not seek out partners with whom they may carry out consensual frottage.

Class II Frotteurs: Consensual Frotteurs

These people are normal in behavior, but they are abnormal only in that they seem to enjoy rubbing their genitals against their partners more than their normal counterparts. But they do it with consenting partners. This act has been called frottage by several writers. Obviously these people do not fulfill DSM-IV-TR criteria (which requires nonconsenting partners), so they cannot be classified as psychologically abnormal. However, they do form the most innocuous terminal of the frotteuristic continuum.

Class III Frotteurs: Romantic Frotteurs

These offenders fit into DSM-IV-TR criteria. Their behaviors involve touching and rubbing against a nonconsenting person. However, they are able to form a normal romantic relationship with persons of opposite sex, and can get involved in normal sexual intercourse with persons of opposite sex. Frotteurism is merely an additional sexual activity which they enjoy. Most existing case reports belong to this class.

Class IV Frotteurs: Fearless Frotteurs

This group is more fearless than class III frotteurs. Most frotteurs and touchers wish to remain anonymous and take great care to be sure that their victims are not able to identify them. However, class IV frotteurs are fearless and not concerned with anonymity. Typical behavior involves grab-

TABLE 9.1
Age Distribution of Frotteurism Victims in Japan

Age of victim	Percentage
18–21 yrs	49.3%
22–25 yrs	32.1%
26–29 yrs	17.7%
Other age groups	0.9%

TABLE 9.2
Place Distribution of Frotteuristic Actions in Japan

Place where incident occurred	Percentage
Train and bus	76.2%
On a street at night	27.7%
On a street in the daytime	19.3%
At a station	11.9%
In a public building	5.0%

bing potential victims' hands and forcing the victims to rub the offenders' private parts (masturbation byproxy). Cases of class IV frotteuism have been reported (See Dr. Karunasekera's case).

Class V Frotteurs: Exclusive Frotteurs

This is the most severe category as far as psychopathology is concerned. These offenders cannot form a normal romantic relationship with persons of the opposite sex, and cannot engage in normal sexual intercourse. For them, frotteurism is the *sole* outlet for sexual gratification. Such frotteurs do not seem to have been reported in literature so far, but based on the *theory of paraphilic equivalence,* it can be predicted that these frotteurs do exist in society and they would be reported sometime in future, as we learn more about this paraphilia.

EPIDEMIOLOGY

Chan et al.[13] from Singapore present valuable information regarding epidemiology of frotteurism. In Singapore, there is no specific law directed towards frotteurism. Sexual offenses which involve touching, grabbing, kissing or fondling go by the name "outrage of modesty" or "molestation." The authors undertook a five-year retrospective study looking into the profiles of 157 outrage of modesty offenders (these included people committing minor sexual offenses such as exhibitionism, frotteurism and its variant), which were remanded to Woodbridge Hospital, a state mental hospital. They found that schizophrenia was the predominant psychiatric diagnosis among the offenders (45.3%) followed by mental retardation (21.7%). However, the majority of the offenders (94.9%) were of sound mind *at the time* of the offense. Touching, stroking or fondling, i.e., frotteurism was the most frequently reported type of molestation (60.5%). The majority of the offenses took place between 6 am and 6 pm. Only 15.3% had a past history of sexual offenses. There were no statistically significant differences between first time and repeat offenders with regard to age, ethnic group, educational level, marital status, diagnoses, place of offense, time and type of offense, soundness of mind, and fitness to plead.

TABLE 9.3
Age Distribution of Frotteurism Offenders in Japan

Age of Offenders	Percentage
Under-age young male	25.2%
Young adult male	50.0%
Middle aged male	62.4%
Aged male	4.0%
Unidentified	20.3%
Unclear memory	9.9%

Incidence of frotteurism is quite high in Japan. Harima[14] reports that, in 1998, 58.4% adult females reported having been touched by unknown person. In 1999, 69.8% adult female reported having been touched on the body, and 21.4% of adult females reported being touched on the genitals.

A questionnaire was circulated to senior high school and university students in Japan: 1.6% of male students and 30.2% female students reported having had a forced contact on their genitals in trains or buses; 4.3% males and 48.3% females were touched on other parts. Conversely, 7.9% males and 0.4% females very strongly wanted to engage in acts of frotteurism if given a chance; and an additional 30% of males and 2.5% of females had a somewhat "weaker" desire to engage in similar acts.[14] Harima gives some other epidemiological information on frotteurism (see Tables 9.1, 9.2, and 9.3).

Since these data are based on victims' reports and many victims reported being touched upon at more places than one, the total is more than 100% in Table 9.2.

Since most victims do not normally like to report cases of frotteurism to the law enforcement authorities, data on the age of offenders based on prosecutions would be very thin. Instead victims were asked about the apparent ages of the persons who touched them, and since many victims reported having been touched by different people at different times, the total in Table 9.3 is also more than 100%.

Harima[14] has described two main factors for the increasing incidence rate of frotteurism and toucherism in crowded trains in Japan. Firstly in Japan, the trains are too crowded, providing ample opportunities for frotteurs and touchers. Secondly, and perhaps more importantly, not many Japanese take it as an immoral of unethical activity. In the survey conducted by Harima,[14] 18.1% of the male university students replied that they did not have any feeling of repulsion, or had a very mild degree of repulsion regarding frotteurism. Of male university students, 5.0% thought that here was absolutely no ethical problem with toucherism. Of male senior high school and university students, 0.2% replied that frotteurism in crowded train should be allowed at anytime, and 5.5% thought that it should be dealt with on a case by case basis, implying that frotteurism may be perfectly allowed in some cases, but not in others. Regarding toucherism, 0.7% male senior high school and university students answered that it should be allowed anytime in crowded trains, while 8.7% thought that it should be decided on a case by case basis. These epidemiological results show that there are significant groups in Japan who take frotteurism and toucherism to be perfectly legal. Such studies should be undertaken in other parts of the world and the data compared and contrasted, to determine if people in other parts of the world think the same.

OFFENDER CHARACTERISTICS

The typical age distribution of frotteurs is shown in Table 9.3 above. Frotteurs often show co-morbidity with other paraphilias. This is also supported by the courtship disorder theory (for details, please see chapter on exhibitionism). A typical frotteur may engage in 4 or 5 other deviant sexual behaviors while at the same time experiencing the urge to frotteur.[4] There is a co-morbidity between frotteurism, telephone scatologia, exhibitionism, and voyeurism.[15] Bradford and colleagues[16] have demonstrated co-morbidity of frotteurism with voyeurism, exhibitionism, telephone scatologia, pedophilia, hebephilia, and cross-dressing. Some statistics show that frotteurs may have a history of rape.[4] Co-morbidity of these paraphilias can better be understood in the light of the courtship disorder theory.[9,10] The co-morbidity, however, does demonstrate that offenders who are brought to the law enforcement authorities for frotteurism (a relatively less serious crime) must be evaluated for other paraphilias, too. This may have implications for future prevention.

Frotteurs are typically not reported by the victims to the law enforcement authorities, as this is considered merely a minor annoyance. It may well be the *least reported* of all paraphilias. Abel and colleagues[15] assessed the frotteuristic acts of 62 adult males, and reported that a typical frotteur may commit up to 849.5 acts of frotteurism before getting arrested. Horley[12] suggests that three typical features of frotteurs are that (i) they have a large number of victims, (ii) they are often not arrested, and finally (iii) even if arrested, they are unlikely to serve long sentences.

CASE LAW

Dr. Nayan Prasanna Karunasekera's Case (2003)

Dr. Nayan Prasanna Karunasekera arrived in New Zealand on a work visa with his wife and 2 young children in February 2002. During his time at Grey Hospital, Dr. Karunasekera was involved in a conflict with a senior consultant who was critical of his work although the matter was dealt with by the hospital administration.

Toward the end of 2002, Dr. Karunasekera and his family went to Queenstown on holiday. During this period, Dr. Karunasekera was involved in acts of toucherism and other similar behaviors in 3 separate incidents, In the first 2 incidents, Dr. Karunasekera visited a souvenir and gift shop and entered into conversations with the shop assistants. He commented on the assistants' complexions. He persuaded the one assistant to allow him to examine her hands and the other assistant to examine her back. During the physical examinations, Dr. Karunasekera pulled their hands onto the penile region of his trousers.[19]

In the third incident, Dr. Karunasekera approached a shop assistant and inquired about purchasing clothing for his wife. While the assistant was displaying the clothing, Dr. Karunasekera ran his fingers against the shop assistant's breasts, holding them for a period of approximately 2 seconds.

Initially, Dr. Karunasekera denied all allegations, pled not guilty and elected to be tried by a jury. The depositions took place in March 2003 and in the succeeding 6 months, Dr. Karunasekera challenged the joining of the charges. It was only after the Court refused severance of the charges that Dr. Karunasekera pled guilty. On September 19, 2003, he was convicted by the District Court in Invercargill of the three offenses of indecent assault under Section 135(1)(a) on the Crimes Act of 1961, and sentenced to the following punishment: 12 months supervision; and referral for assessment to the adult Straight Thinking On Probation (STOP) program and, if found suitable, to undertake the program as directed and to the satisfaction of his probation officer; and referral for Department of Corrections psychological assessment and treatment as directed by and to the satisfaction of his probation officer; and payment of reparation (emotional harm) of $500 to each of the three complainants.

Earlier, on May 16, 2003, the Medical Council of New Zealand had resolved to cancel Dr. Karunasekera's temporary registration. Dr. Karunasekera had also been convicted by the Medical Practitioners Disciplinary Tribunal (MPDT). Section 109 of the Medical Practitioners Act 1995 of New Zealand prescribes "grounds on which medical practitioners may be disciplined." Section 109(1)(e) states that the medical practitioner may be disciplined if he has been convicted by any court in New Zealand or elsewhere of any offense punishable by imprisonment for a term of 3 months or longer, and the circumstances of that offense reflect adversely on the practitioner's fitness to practice medicine.[20]

Since the offenses Dr. Karunasekera had committed were punishable by imprisonment for a term of 7 years (see Legal Aspects – New Zealand below), the Complaints Assessment Committee (CAC) charged that the circumstances of the offenses reflected adversely on Dr Karunasekera's fitness to practice medicine.

A hearing was held at Wellington on August 2, 2004. On September 15, 2004, the Tribunal finding Dr. Karunasekera guilty issued an order recommending that (a) Dr Karunasekera be censured; (b) publication of these orders be published in the New Zealand Medical Journal; (c) any application to re-register should not occur until completion by Dr Karunasekera of the STOP program; (d) a recommendation be forwarded to the Medical Council that Dr Karunasekera undertake the Sexual Misconduct Assessment Test (SMAT) and that registration and conditions of practice that might be imposed following that process should address matters such as practicing within a team or with a chaperone and issues of supervision; and finally (e) Dr Karunasekera pay 15% of the costs and expenses of the prosecution and hearing of this inquiry.

Iowa v. Timothy Hodges (2004)

Not many cases related solely to frotteurism are available for study, because, as mentioned earlier, this crime is underreported. In a 2004 case, *State Of Iowa, Appellee, v. Timothy Hodges, Appellant (2004)*, Hodges, a frotteur, claimed that his detention violated due process. Timothy Hodges, a 43-year old male, was a typical frotteur, voyeur, fetishist, pedophile, and rapist. After his father sexually molested him at age 10, Hodges began molesting his sister. Around the same time, he began peeping into the girls' locker room at school to watch girls undress and shower. He also peeped into the bathroom at home to watch women or other girls use the rest room. He also peeped through windows in various houses in his community. On one occasion, after mowing a woman's lawn, he asked her if she could take her nightgown off for him. Following this incident, he was placed in the children's unit at Cherokee Mental Health Institute.

Hodges remained at Cherokee for 2 years. He continued his voyeuristic activities even there, and after he was released from there. At 15 years of age, he was placed in a children's home. While there, he would pull down girls' bed covers to look at their naked bodies as they slept. When intervened, he threatened to kill himself. Thereafter, he was returned to the Cherokee Institute.

After his release from Cherokee, Hodges was placed in the Boys and Girls Home in Sioux City until he was 17. While there, he began to engage in frotteurism. Hodges described his frotteuristic impulses and actions, which are quite typical of a frotteur, "I might notice their breasts or their butt and I might grab their breasts for sexual pleasure. Just to grab them. Not really to harm them. Just to grab them for my own gratification." He would randomly grab women inappropriately on the streets of downtown Sioux City. He was arrested and charged with 26 different counts over a 2 to 3 month period. While at the Boys and Girls Home, he continued engaging in voyeuristic activities, clandestinely watching the house counselors take showers. As a result of these activities, Hodges was placed in the State Boys Training School until he was eighteen.

After Hodges was released from the training school, he continued his frotteurism in Creston. He was also convicted of trespassing for peeking under the restroom stalls at the Union County courthouse to watch women using the bathroom. Instead of serving jail time, Hodges went to the Clarinda Mental Health Institute for 30 days. When Hodges was 21, he served 30 days in jail for fondling a woman without her consent. Between the ages of 21 and 24, he frequently took women's underwear from clotheslines and laundromats (possibly for fetishism). He also molested his 12-year-old cousin for 2 to 3 months during this time.

In 1984, Hodges raped a mentally challenged woman on the grounds of Cherokee. He was charged with sexual abuse, but pled guilty to the reduced charge of assault causing bodily harm. He served 87 days in jail.

After his release from jail, Hodges moved to LeMars, where he was arrested for watching women use the restroom at a Laundromat through a hole in the wall.

After Hodges was released from prison, he broke into a woman's house "to feel or fondle her while she was asleep." He also broke into another woman's house for the same purpose on 2 occasions. He was arrested and charged with trespassing and 4 counts of second-degree burglary. He pled guilty to 1 count of second-degree burglary and was sentenced to 10 years in prison.

After Hodges was released from prison, he began a sexual relationship with a mentally challenged woman and engaged in sexual intercourse with the woman in the presence of her 4-year-old daughter. He then sexually molested the child. He was convicted of third-degree sexual abuse in 1998 and discharged his sentence in December 2002.

The State filed a petition seeking to have Hodges deemed a sexually violent predator and civilly committed under Iowa Code chapter 229A. The trial commenced on August 12, 2003, and the jury heard testimony about Hodges' history of sex offending and testimony from psychiatrists. On August 14, 2003, the jury concluded Hodges was a sexually violent predator under Iowa Code section 229A.2(11), and the district court ordered him committed to the Civil Commitment Unit for Sexual Offenders at Oakdale.

The case deals with Hodges' appeal, claiming that a civil commitment under chapter 229A based on a diagnosis of antisocial personality disorder violated due process under the United States and Iowa constitutions. The court opined that Hodges' commitment *did not* violate his due process rights under the United States and Iowa constitutions.

LEGAL ASPECTS

Frotteurism is a criminal act in many jurisdictions. It is usually classified as a misdemeanor. As a result, legal penalties are often minor. It is also not easy to prosecute frotteurs, as intent to touch is difficult to prove. In their defense statements, the accused often claim that the contact was accidental.

Australia

Western Australia

According to the Criminal Code of Western Australia, frotteurism is an act of assault. Section 222 of the Criminal Code of Western Australia defines assault as follows:

> A person who strikes, touches, or moves, or otherwise applies force of any kind to the person of another, either directly or indirectly, without his consent, or with his consent if the consent is obtained by fraud, or who by any bodily act or gesture attempts or threatens to apply force of any kind to the person of another without his consent, under such circumstances that the person making the attempt or threat has actually or apparently a present ability to effect his purpose, is said to assault that other person, and the act is called an assault.
>
> The term "applies force" includes the case of applying heat, light, electrical force, gas, odor, or any other substance or thing whatever if applied in such a degree as to cause injury or personal discomfort.

Since frotteurism involves touching genital region, breasts or buttocks, the act can also be prosecuted as indecent assault. Section 323 of the same code defines indecent assault as follows:[17]

A person who unlawfully and indecently assaults another person is guilty of a crime and liable to imprisonment for 5 years.

Summary conviction penalty: Imprisonment for 2 years or a fine of $8,000.

New South Wales

The criminal law of New South Wales is governed by the Crimes Act 1900. The Act comprises of 582 sections divided into 16 parts. Part 3 of this Act entitled "Offenses Against the Person" is further subdivided into 16 divisions, of which division 10 entitled "Offenses in the nature of rape, offenses relating to other acts of sexual assault, etc." deals with most sexual offenses. It comprises of sections 61H through 80AA. Although frotteurism is not named explicitly in the act, Section 61N entitled "Act of indecency" covers frotteurism. It states:

(1) Any person who commits an act of indecency with or towards a person under the age of 16 years, or incites a person under that age to an act of indecency with or towards that or another person, is liable to imprisonment for 2 years.
(2) Any person who commits an act of indecency with or towards a person of the age of 16 years or above, or incites a person of the age of 16 years or above to an act of indecency with or towards that or another person, is liable to imprisonment for 18 months.

There are similar laws relating to frotteurism in other jurisdictions of Australia, e.g., section 58 of Criminal Law Consolidation Act 1935 (South Australia) addressing acts of gross indecency and Section 227 of the Criminal Code 1899 of Queensland. The latter addresses acts of exhibitionism also (please see chapter on exhibitionism for full text of this law).

China

According to the Criminal Law of the People's Republic of China, frotteurism is prosecuted under Article 237. For details, please see chapter on exhibitionism.

Iceland

Frotteurism is prosecuted under Article 209 of the General Penal Code of Iceland, For details, please see chapter on exhibitionism.

India

In the criminal law of India, there is no specific mention of frotteurism or toucherism. However, in such cases, section 354 (assault or criminal force to woman with intent to outrage her modesty)* can be invoked against the perpetrator. No convictions have been made though under this section; first, because frotteurs are rarely brought to the notice of the law enforcement authority; and second, because the intent is difficult to prove; and, third, because the victim does not consider it worthwhile to follow the case, given the minor nature of the offense.

Malaysia

Frotteurism in Malaysian law is covered under "gross indecency with another person." Section 377D of the Malaysian Penal Code states:

* For full statement of section 354 IPC, please see chapter on sexual harassment.

> Any person who, in public or private, commits, or abets the commission of, or procures or attempts to procure the commission by any person of, any act of gross indecency with another person, shall be punished with imprisonment for a term which may extend to 2 years.

Romania

Article 220 of the Criminal Code of the Republic of Romania outlaws acts of frotteurism. For details, please see chapter on exhibitionism.

United States

Each state has different laws regarding frotteurism. While it would be useful to refer to the criminal codes of each state to know the details of law prevalent there, it might be pertinent to have a detailed look at the relevant laws in some representative states.

Alabama

Frotteurism is mentioned in Alabama Code as sexual abuse. Two degrees are defined—sexual abuse in the first degree and sexual abuse in the second degree. The crimes are committed, when the offender subjects another person to *sexual contact*. Sexual contact is defined in the code as any touching of the sexual or other intimate parts of a person not married to the actor, done for the purpose of gratifying the sexual desire of either party.[18] Sexual abuse in the first degree is defined as below:

Sexual abuse in the first degree.

(a) A person commits the crime of sexual abuse in the first degree if:
  (1) He subjects another person to sexual contact by forcible compulsion; or
  (2) He subjects another person to sexual contact who is incapable of consent by reason of being physically helpless or mentally incapacitated.
(b) Sexual abuse in the first degree is a class C felony.[19]

The punishment for a class C felony is imprisonment of up to ten years, but not less than one year and one day[20] and the fine is up to $15,000.[21]

Sexual abuse in the second degree.

(a) A person commits the crime of sexual abuse in the second degree if:
  (1) He subjects another person to sexual contact who is incapable of consent by reason of some factor other than being less than 16 years old; or
  (2) He, being 19 years old or older, subjects another person to sexual contact who is less than 16 years old, but more than 12 years old.
(b) Sexual abuse in second degree is a class A misdemeanor, except that if a person commits a second or subsequent offense of sexual abuse in the second degree within 1 year of another sexual offense, the offense is a class C felony.[22]

The sentence for class A misdemeanor is imprisonment of up to 1 year[23] and the fine is up to $6,000.[24]

Clause (a) of section 13A-11-8 of Alabama Code also addresses the crime of frotteurism (for details, please see chapter on telephone scatologia).

Arkansas

Although the Arkansas Code does not mention *frotteurism*, a similar act is worded as a "sexual contact." Clause 9 of Section 5-14-101 defines "sexual contact" as:

> "Sexual contact" means any act of sexual gratification involving the touching, directly or through clothing, of the sex organs, buttocks, or anus of a person or the breast of a female.

If the act of sexual contact is without the consent of the other person, the definition is similar to that of frotteurism. Section 5-14-111 considers an act of sexual contact as an act of "public sexual indecency" and classifies it as a class A misdemeanor. It states:[25]

(a) A person commits public sexual indecency if he or she engages in any of the following acts in a public place or public view:
  (1) An act of sexual intercourse;
  (2) An act of deviate sexual activity; or
  (3) An act of sexual contact.
(b) Public sexual indecency is a class A misdemeanor.

However, this section is silent on the "consent" aspect of the other party. A more relevant law on frotteurism —where the act of sexual contact is without the consent of the other party—is Section 5-14-125, which defines *sexual assault in the second degree*. It states:[26]

(a) A person commits sexual assault in the second degree if the person:
  (1) Engages in sexual contact with another person by forcible compulsion;
  (2) Engages in sexual contact with another person who is incapable of consent because he or she is:
    (A) Physically helpless;
    (B) Mentally defective; or
    (C) Mentally incapacitated;
  (3) Being eighteen (18) years of age or older, engages in sexual contact with another person who is:
    (A) Less than fourteen (14) years of age; and
    (B) Not the person's spouse;
  (4) (A) Engages in sexual contact with another person who is less than eighteen (18) years of age and the actor is:
      (i) Employed with the Department of Correction, Department of Community Correction, any city or county jail, or any juvenile detention facility, and the minor is in custody at a facility operated by the agency or contractor employing the actor;
      (ii) A professional under §12-12-507(b) and is in a position of trust or authority over the minor; or
      (iii) The minor's guardian, an employee in the minor's school or school district, a temporary caretaker, or a person in a position of trust or authority over the minor.
    (B) For purposes of subdivision (a)(4)(A) of this section, consent of the minor is not a defense to a prosecution;
  (5) (A) Being less than eighteen (18) years of age, engages in sexual contact with another person who is:
      (i) Less than fourteen (14) years of age; and
      (ii) Not the person's spouse.

(B) It is an affirmative defense to a prosecution under this subdivision (a)(5) that the actor was not more than:
(i) Three (3) years older than the victim if the victim is less than twelve (12) years of age; or
(ii) Four (4) years older than the victim if the victim is twelve (12) years of age or older; or
(6) Is a teacher in a public school in a grade kindergarten through twelve (K–12) and engages in sexual contact with another person who is:
(A) A student enrolled in the public school; and
(B) Less than twenty-one (21) years of age.
(b) (1) Sexual assault in the second degree is a class B felony.
(2) Sexual assault in the second degree is a class D felony if committed by a person less than eighteen (18) years of age with another person who is:
(A) Less than fourteen (14) years of age; and
(B) Not the person's spouse.

This is one of the most exhaustive laws on frotteurism. It prescribes punishment also for acts of frotteurism committed against physically helpless and mentally defective or incapacitated persons. Persons who are in a position of trust or authority (including professionals under §12-12-507[b]) are guilty of this offense even with consent of the victim. For an exhaustive list of professionals listed under §12-12-507(b), please refer to the chapter on rape (under Arkansas law).

Another section in Arkansas Code addresses the crime of frotteurism. Section 5-14-127 defines sexual assault in the fourth degree as follows:[27]

(a) A person commits sexual assault in the fourth degree if the person:
(1) Being twenty (20) years of age or older, engages in sexual intercourse or deviate sexual activity with another person who is:
(A) Less than sixteen (16) years of age; and
(B) Not the person's spouse; or
(2) Engages in sexual contact with another person who is:
(A) Less than sixteen (16) years of age; and
(B) Not the person's spouse.
(b) (1) Sexual assault in the fourth degree under subdivision (a)(1) of this section is a Class D felony.
(2) Sexual assault in the fourth degree under subdivision (a)(2) of this section is a Class A misdemeanor if the person engages only in sexual contact with another person as described in subdivision (a)(2) of this section.

Washington

Chapter 9A.44 of the Revised Code of Washington (RCW) deals with sex offenses. Section 9A.44.010 (2) defines sexual contact as "any touching of the sexual or other intimate parts of a person done for the purpose of gratifying sexual desire of either party or a third party," which in effect is the definition of frotteurism. According to section 9A.44.100, a person is guilty of *indecent liberties* when he or she knowingly causes another person who is not his or her spouse to have sexual contact with him or her or another. Indecent liberties is a class B felony, and if indecent liberties are done by forcible compulsion, it becomes a class A felony.

Wisconsin

In Wisconsin, frotteurism is termed "Sexual contact," which is defined in section 940.225 (5) (b) of Wisconsin statute. It states:[28]

Sexual contact means any of the following:

1. Any of the following types of intentional touching, whether direct or through clothing, if that intentional touching is either for the purpose of sexually degrading; or for the purpose of sexually humiliating the complainant or sexually arousing or gratifying the defendant or if the touching contains the elements of actual or attempted battery under Section 940.19 (1):
   a. Intentional touching by the defendant or, upon the defendant's instruction, by another person, by the use of any body part or object, of the complainant's intimate parts.
   b. Intentional touching by the complainant, by the use of any body part or object, of the defendant's intimate parts or, if done upon the defendant's instructions, the intimate parts of another person.
2. Intentional penile ejaculation of ejaculate or intentional emission of urine or feces by the defendant or, upon the defendant's instruction, by another person upon any part of the body clothed or unclothed of the complainant if that ejaculation or emission is either for the purpose of sexually degrading or sexually humiliating the complainant or for the purpose of sexually arousing or gratifying the defendant.
3. For the purpose of sexually degrading or humiliating the complainant or sexually arousing or gratifying the defendant, intentionally causing the complainant to ejaculate or emit urine or feces on any part of the defendant's body, whether clothed or unclothed.

As can be seen, both frotteurism and toucherism are covered by this statute. Furthermore, urophilia and coprophilia are covered (under clauses 2 and 3). Very few statutes cover these rare paraphilias. Wisconsin sex laws are very progressive. In a significant case pertaining to toucherism, it was ruled that a jury instruction that touching the vaginal area constituted sexual contact was correct (*State v. Morse,* 126 Wis. 2d 1, 374 N.W.2d 388 [Ct. App. 1985]).

Section 944.20 also addresses the crime of frotteurism. For details, please see chapter on exhibitionism.

Colorado

Section 18-7-301 of Colorado Revised Statute prohibits any lewd fondling or caress of the body of another person. This kind of behavior is included in "public decency" and is considered a class 1 petty offense. It states:

(1) Any person who performs any of the following in a public place or where the conduct may reasonably be expected to be viewed by members of the public commits public indecency:
- (a) An act of sexual intercourse; or
- (b) An act of deviate sexual intercourse; or
- (c) A lewd exposure of the body done with intent to arouse or to satisfy the sexual desire of any person; or
- (d) A lewd fondling or caress of the body of another person.

(2) Public indecency is a class 1 petty offense.

Delaware

According to section 11-5-601 of the Delaware Criminal Code, offensive touching is an unclassified misdemeanor. It states:

(a) A person is guilty of offensive touching when the person:

(1) Intentionally touches another person either with a member of his or her body or with any instrument, knowing that the person is thereby likely to cause offense or alarm to such other person; or

(2) Intentionally strikes another person with saliva, urine, feces or any other bodily fluid, knowing that the person is thereby likely to cause offense or alarm to such other person.

(b) When charged with a violation of paragraph (a)(2) of this section, the defendant shall be tested for diseases transmittable through bodily fluids, the cost of such tests to be assessed as costs upon conviction. The results of such tests shall be provided only to the Attorney General, the victim of the offense, the defendant and the Department of Correction's medical care provider.

(c) Any violation of paragraph (a)(1) of this section shall be an unclassified misdemeanor. Notwithstanding the above, any violation of paragraph (a)(1) of this section shall be a class A misdemeanor when the victim is acting in the lawful performance of the victim's duty as one of the following: law-enforcement officer, hospital or nursing home employee, physician, medical professional, ambulance attendant, emergency medical technician, Delaware State Fire Police Officer, correctional officer, volunteer firefighter or full-time firefighter. Any violation of paragraph (a)(2) of this section shall be a class A misdemeanor.

As can be seen, this section includes acts of coprophilia and urophilia against non-consenting persons [subsection (a)(2)].

REFERENCES

1. Freund K. Courtship disorder, in *Handbook of Sexual Assault, Laws,* D.R. and Barbaree, H.E., Eds., Plenum, New York, 1990, pages 195-207.
2. Krueger, R.B. and Kaplan M.S. Frotteurism – Assessment and Treatment. In *Sexual Deviance – Theory, Assessment, and Treatment,* 1st ed. Laws, D.R. and O'Donohue, W., (Eds.), The Guilford Press, New York, 1997, chapter 7, pages 131-151.
3. Lane, S., Assessment of sexually abusive youth. In *Juvenile sexual offending: Causes, consequences, and correction,* 1st ed. G. Ryan & S. Lane, (Eds.), Jossey-Bass, San Francisco, 1997, pages 219–263.
4. Anon. Professional Discipline — Indecent Assault Conviction. *N Z Med J.* 2004 Dec 17;117(1207): U1228.
5. American Psychiatric Association. *Diagnostic and Statistical Manual of Mental Disorders*, 4th ed. Text rev. American Psychiatric Association, Washington DC, 2000.
6. Neumann, S., Alley, D., Paclebar, A.M., Sanchez, C. and Satterthwaite, B., Frotteurism, piquerism, and other related paraphilias. In *Sex crimes and paraphilia*, 1st ed. Hickey, E.W., (Ed.), Pearson Prentice Hall, New Jersey, 2006, chapter 26, pages 237-248.
7. Bonnar J, Lamprecht V, O'Conner E. Alternatives to vaginal intercourse practiced during the fertile time among calendar method users in Ireland. *Adv Contracept.* 1997 Jun-Sep;13(2-3):173-7.
8. McNally RJ, Lukach BM. Behavioral treatment of zoophilic exhibitionism. *J Behav Ther Exp Psychiatry.* 1991 Dec;22(4):281-4.
9. Hongo, J. Groping economist gets four-month prison term. *The Japan Times Online*, Oct. 17, 2007. Available at http://search.japantimes.co.jp/cgi-bin/nn20071017a4.html. Accessed Feb 1, 2008.
10. Krafft-Ebing , RF. *Psychopathia Sexualis*, 1st ed. F.A.Davis, Philadelphia, 1886 [reprinted by Bloat Books, 1999] – pages 522-4.

11. Freund K, Scher H and Hucker S. The courtship disorders. *Arch Sex Behav.* 1983:12(5): 369-379.
12. Freund K, Scher H and Hucker S. The courtship disorders: a further investigation. *Arch Sex Behav.*1984; 13(2): 133-139.
13. Simpson G, Blaszczynski A, Hodgkinson A. Sex offending as a psychosocial sequela of traumatic brain injury. *J Head Trauma Rehabil.* 1999 Dec;14(6):567-80.
14. Horley, J. Frotteurism: A term in search of an underlying disorder? *Journal of Sexual Aggression.* 2001; 7(1): 51-55.
15. Chan AO, Lim LE, Ong SH. A review of outrage of modesty offenders remanded in a state mental hospital. *Med Sci Law.* 1997 Oct;37(4):349-52.
16. Harima K. [Frotteurism] [Article in Japanese]. Ryoikibetsu Shokogun Shirizu. 2003;(39):294-6.
17. Abel GG, Becker JV, Mittelman M, Cunningham-Rathner J, Rouleau JL and Murphy, WD. Self-reported sex crimes of nonincarcerated paraphilics. *Journal of Interpersonal Violence.* 1987:2(1):3-25.
18. Bradford JM, Boulet J, Pawlak A. The paraphilias: a multiplicity of deviant behaviours. *Can J Psychiatry.* 1992 Mar;37(2):104-8.
19. Medical Practitioners Disciplinary Tribunal (New Zealand), Decision No: 299/04/121C. In the matter of the Medical Practitioners Act 1995, and in the matter of a charge laid by a Complaints Assessment Committee pursuant to Section 93(1)(b) of the Act against Nayan Prasanna Karunasekera.
20. Section 109, Medical Practitioners Act 1995 of New Zealand
21. Criminal Code of Western Australia. Section 323 inserted by No. 14 of 1992 s. 6(1); amended by No. 36 of 1996 s. 17
22. section 135, Crimes Act 1961 of New Zealand
23. ALA. CODE §13A-6-60 (enacted 1977)
24. ALA. CODE §13A-6-66 (enacted 1977)
25. ALA. CODE §13A-5-6 (enacted 1977)
26. ALA. CODE §13A-5-11 (enacted 1977)
27. ALA. CODE §13A-6-67 (enacted 1977)
28. ALA. CODE §13A-5-7 (enacted 1977)
29. ALA. CODE §13A-5-12 (enacted 1977)
30. Arkansas Code Ann. §5-14-111 (enacted 1975)
31. Arkansas Code Ann. §5-14-125 (enacted 2001)
32. Arkansas Code Ann. §5-14-127 (enacted 2001)
33. Colo. Rev. Stat. § 18-7-301 (enacted 1971)
34. Del. Code Ann. Tit 11, ch. 5 §601 (enacted 1953)
35. Wis. Stat. Ann. § 940.225 (enacted 1987)

10 Rape

INTRODUCTION

Rape (from Latin *rapio*, "seize, snatch") is defined differently among nations and jurisdictions. It is thus difficult, if not impossible, to give any single definition of rape. However, all definitions, have one requisite element, which must be satisfied in order to constitute the offense of rape, namely *absence of the victim's will and consent*. Consent to sex is important because its absence can transform coitus from a pleasurable activity having no legal concern, to one of the most heinous of criminal offenses.* The consent is said to be absent when it has been taken illegally, such as by force or fraud, by promising or providing illegal gratifications or inducements, by impersonation, under the influence of alcohol or drugs, or by a mentally ill person. The absence of consent may be also be statutory or technical, when the victim is under the age of consent (please see below).

Definitions of rape vary from nation to nation and even in the same nation from jurisdiction to jurisdiction. However, all rape statutes address the following essential components: (i) type of penetration, (ii) genders of the perpetrator and victim, and (iii) the way consent is violated. In many jurisdictions, only penile–vaginal penetration, the most basic type, constitutes rape, while in others, penile penetration of any orifice—anal, oral, etc.—would constitute rape. In still others the penetration need not be by the penis. It may be by any other organ or the body, say a digit or even, a pencil.

Regarding gender, one extreme is where only a male can legally rape a female. On the other side of the spectrum, both the perpetrator as well as victim could be of either gender, and in many modern rape statutes, a gender-neutral language is used, which includes perpetrators and victims of both sexes. Thus it is possible for a person of either gender to rape another person of either gender. Regarding the way the consent is violated, the statutes include at least one of the following five broad themes in order to constitute an offense of rape. Sexual penetration or contact is rape if it is accomplished by (i) plain nonconsent or absence of will, (ii) fraud, (iii) force and coercion, (iv) abuse of trust, and (v) abuse of authority.

The first theme is perhaps the simplest. There is simple nonconsent or absence of will, without reference to force, fraud, or coercion. Drug-facilitated sexual assault, date rape, or acquaintance rape fall under this theme. The second group specifically outlaws the use of fraud or deception in securing sexual compliance. The third involves physical force or coercion. The fourth category addresses groups of potential offenders who abuse positions of trust and have access to vulnerable victims, e.g., medical personnel. Finally the fifth theme prohibits sexual conduct when the criminal actor abuses a position of authority over a victim, e.g., a prison guard.

A special case is the marital exemption (please see "marital rape" below); in many jurisdictions a husband cannot legally rape his wife (or vice versa), even if force was used to accomplish intercourse. However, most states are now removing marital exemptions from their statute books.

---

* For some similar concerns regarding consent, please see chapter on sexual masochism.

HISTORICAL PERSPECTIVES

Rape is mentioned in the ancient scriptures of many religions. Bass[1] is of the opinion that some ancient Hindu scriptures even condone rape. He quotes the following passage from the *Brhadārankyaka Upanishad*, insisting that the language amounts to condoning rape:

> Surely, a woman who has changed her clothes at the end of her menstrual period is the most auspicious of women. When she has changed her clothes at the end of her menstrual period, therefore, one should approach that splendid woman and invite her to have sex. Should she refuse to consent, he should bribe her. If she still refuses, he should beat her with a stick or with his fists and overpower her, saying: "I take away the splendor from you with my virility and splendor" (6.4.9,21).

The Bible clearly states the law of rape. If the woman who was raped was already married, then the penalty was death. If she was unmarried, the ravisher must pay fifty shekels of silver to her as well as marry her.

> And if a man entice a maid that is not betrothed, and lie with her, he shall surely endow her to be his wife. If her father utterly refuse to give her unto him, he shall pay money according to the dowry of virgins.[2]

Deuteronomy also sheds some light on the laws of rape:

> If a damsel that is a virgin be betrothed unto a husband, and a man find her in the city, and lie with her; then ye shall bring them both out unto the gate of that city, and ye shall stone them with stones that they die; the damsel, because she cried not, being in the city; and the man, because he hath humbled his neighbor's wife: so thou shalt put away evil from among you. But if a man find a betrothed damsel in the field, and the man force her, and lie with her; then the man only that lay with her shall die: but unto the damsel thou shalt do nothing; there is in the damsel no sin worthy of death: for as when a man riseth against his neighbor, and slayeth him, even so is this matter: for he found her in the field, and the betrothed damsel cried, and there was none to save her. If a man find a damsel that is a virgin, which is not betrothed, and lay hold on her, and lie with her, and they be found; then the man that lay with her shall give unto the damsel's father fifty shekels of silver, and she shall be his wife; because he hath humbled her, he may not put her away all his days.[3]

The last sentence signifies that such a culprit would never be allowed to divorce his wife.

Despite the punishments prescribed for rape, there are several instances of rape in the Bible. Perhaps the most telling of them all is where Amnon, the son of David and Ahinoam, rapes his half sister Tamar (daughter of David and Maachah).[4] Another notable instance of rape occurs when Dinah, Jacob's only daughter, is raped by Shechem, although he did try to make amends by offering marriage to her afterwards.[5]

ETIOLOGY AND TYPOLOGY

Two main motivations have been seen in rapists—sexual and aggressive. All rape includes both motivational components. For some rapists the aim is primarily aggressive—to humiliate, defile, and injure. For others the aim is primarily sexual with a relative absence of violence and brutality. The dichotomization and crossing of these two motivational components yields five types as shown in Table 10.1.[6,7] All five may together be called *sexual aggressors*.

(i) ***Sexual component—high; aggressive component—high.*** Known as sex-aggression defusion or sadistic sexual type. Sexual and aggressive feelings are synergistically intertwined. There is sadistic quality to the assault, and tendency to eroticize destructive behaviors. The sexual aggression is manifest in the humiliation of the victim and in the infliction of physical harm. There is significant planning and rehearsal preceding the assault. This group

TABLE 10.1
Typology of Rapists Based on their Motivational Components

Aggressive Component	Sexual Component	High	Low
	High	Sex-aggression defusion type. Also known as sadistic sexual type	This group is divided into two types: (i) displaced aggression type, also called pervasively angry type (ii) vindictive type
	Low	Sexual aim/compensatory type. Also known as nonsadistic sexual type	Impulsive, predatory, exploitative, opportunistic type

almost coincides with class III sexual sadists (please see chapter on sexual sadism).

(ii) ***Sexual component—low; aggressive component—high.*** Displaced aggression or pervasively angry type. The aim is primarily aggression, with sexual behavior being used not for sexual satisfaction, but to degrade, defile and physically harm the victim. Other characteristics are impulsivity, poor behavioral control, excessive and gratuitous use of force and violence. Violence occurs even when the victim is fully compliant. Resistance from the victim is likely to exacerbate the violence, and serious physical injury or death may result. Rage is not sexualized, and the assault is not fantasy-driven. Violence is a general lifestyle characteristic that is directed toward males and females alike. The rape is but one feature in a history of unsocialized, aggressive behaviors exhibited across various social contexts.

(iii) ***Sexual component—low; aggressive component—high.*** Vindictive type. While the assaults perpetrated by the vindictive type of rapist share a clear manifestation of anger and aggression with the pervasively angry type, the anger here is not part of a general disposition but is directed specifically toward females only. The aggression evident in the assault behavior ranges from verbal abuse to homicide, and appears intended to degrade and humiliate the victim. There is a low sexual component in the assault behavior. The aggression is not eroticized, suggesting that paraphilic fantasies are not involved. Like the nonsadistic sexual subtype (please see below), the vindictive rapist is a socially isolated individual.

(iv) ***Sexual component—high; aggressive component—low.*** Sexual aim/compensatory type. Also known as nonsadistic sexual type. The motivation in this group is primarily sexual with minimal aggression facilitating the gratification of the sexual fantasy. This type has an enduring sexual preoccupation, and the rape may be just a single manifestation of deviant sexual interest from a range of paraphilias. There is relatively little interpersonal aggression in general social interactions. Typically socially isolated and inadequate individuals, with low masculine self-image and feelings of sexual inadequacy.

(v) ***Sexual component—low; aggressive component—low.*** Impulsive, predatory, exploitative, opportunistic type. The sexual assault is predatory in nature, typically impulsive and shows little or no planning or preparation. Neither sexual nor aggressive motives appear to be important. There is a history of unsocialized behavior, and the rape serves as an illustration of the degree to which the rapist lacks interpersonal awareness. These rapists exhibit no concern for the comfort or welfare of their victims. The actual assault is nonparaphilic, with the goal being immediate sexual gratification rather than the enactment of highly developed or ritualized fantasies. The degree of force used is necessary only to effect the assault, and any anger exhibited is in response to victim resistance rather than an indica-

tion of expressive aggression. If the opportunity to rape is not available, this type of rapist will not attempt to plan an elaborate assault.

For sexual offenders who have both sexual and sadistic components in their behavior, please see chapter on sexual sadism.

INCIDENCE

Approximately one in four women in the United States will be victims of rape or attempted rape at some point during their lives.[8] In a study of 1307 females in the Central African Republic (CAR), as many as 22% reported that their first experience with intercourse was rape.[9]

Many so-called normal people harbor fantasies of raping someone, although they do not do it (biastophilia). Crépault and Couture[10] interviewed 94 men about their erotic fantasies occurring during heterosexual activity. The majority of these men were married, and their average duration of cohabitation with a woman was 6.5 years. From this group, 33.0% reported having had a fantasy of raping a woman. Interestingly 45.8% reported having had erotic fantasies involving a scene where they were raped by a woman.

Michael and Zumpe[11] studied the significance of seasonal changes in assaults, rapes, robberies, and murders committed during 2 to 3 consecutive years in 16 different locations in the U.S. and found that the incidence of rape was significantly higher in 14 of 16 locations between the months of July and September. The authors feel that there may be a relationship between the incidence of rape and ambient temperature.

OFFENDER CHARACTERISTICS

In contrast to some rapists who penetrate their victims vaginally, there are rapists who penetrate their victims—both male and female—anally. Neuwirth and Eher[12] of the Federal Documentation Centre for Sexual Offenders, Austria, studied both types of offenders during their daily assessment routine. They came to the conclusion that anal rapists were more violent and hypersexual and had a more obsessive sex life than vaginal rapists. Oliver and associates[13] from the United Kingdom compared rapists with sexual murderers on background, personality, offense, and victim characteristics. As compared to the sexual murderer group, the rapists were more likely to have been involved in a relationship at the time of their offense, generally attacked younger victims, and had lower self-esteem. They were also found to have more violent previous convictions and scored higher on measures of historical deviance (nonsexual), paranoid suspicion, and resentment.

Saunders and colleagues[14] conducted a study in which they divided a group of male adolescent sexual offenders into three groups: Courtship Disorders (exhibitionism, toucherism, and obscene phone calls), Sexual Assaults, and Pedophilic Offenses. Group II offenders (sexual assaulters) came from a more disturbed family background characterized by a high rate of long-term parent-child separations, committed more violent crimes, and had a higher frequency of intellectual functioning in the borderline range of intelligence.

RAPE INDEX

Phallometry (please see chapter 1 for details) can often distinguish potential rapists from non-rapists. Using this procedure, one can calculate the so-called *rape index*, which is conventionally defined as the average penile response to stimuli depicting rape and brutal sexual assaults, relative to the average penile response to stimuli depicting consenting sex. It can be calculated either as a differential (the difference by subtraction) or a ratio of the average responses to the two stimulus categories.[15] Both approaches are common in the literature, but there is some evidence that using a differential rape index improves criterion-related validity.[16]

There is much data indicating that rape index is a valid criterion for differentiating potential rapists from nonrapists.[17,18,19] There is also data suggesting that the differential rape index is predictive of sexual reoffense.[20]

USE OF COERCION

Coercion to obtain sex can be perceived to occur on a gradual continuum, from the strongest and clearest examples of coercion such as threat to one's life, physical well-being, and livelihood to less clear, and doubtful instances of coercion. A teacher threatening to award lower grades than the candidate deserves, or a boss not gratnting promotions to his secretary, unless she succumbs to sexual intercourse with him, are examples of the weaker and less clear extreme of coercion continuum. An extremely doubtful case of coercion lying on the weaker end of the "coercion continuum" is this: a boy and girl have been dating for some time, but they have not had sex. The girl likes the boy very much and does not want to terminate the relationship. The boy wants sex. He says, "Either we have sex now, or I am not willing to continue dating." The girl is afraid to lose him. She agrees to sexual intercourse.

This brings us to the rather philosophical question: what makes a proposal coercive? What is the point at which there is sufficient coercive pressure to undermine the legitimacy of consent? What are the situations when a "yes" by a victim is not necessarily "yes"? Many rape statutes have struggled—albeit not completely successfully—to address this vital question.

In *Louisiana v. Powell,* 438 So. 2d 1306 (Ct. of App., 1983), the defendant and the victim were both social acquaintances. One evening, when the victim was waiting to get a ride home in the evening, she saw the defendant in a car nearby. She walked up to the car and started talking to the defendant. During the conversation, the defendant offered to drive her home, which she gladly accepted. However, instead of driving her home, the defendant took her to a secluded area where he slapped her several times to intimidate her into acquiescing to sexual intercourse. Rather than try to run, or struggle, the victim went along with his demands by removing her pants, and allowing sexual intercourse.

The defendant was charged with aggravated rape. Under Louisiana law (please see below), a charge of aggravated rape can stand only if the rape is committed under any one or more of the six circumstances. Circumstances 3 to 6 were clearly not met (defendant was not armed with dangerous weapon, victim not under the age of 13 years, two of more offenders did not participate in the act, and the victim did not suffer from any physical or mental infirmity). The charge could only be proved by the presence of either of the first two circumstances—that the victim resisted the act to the utmost or that the victim was prevented from resisting the act by threats of great and immediate bodily harm, accompanied by apparent power of execution. There was no evidence of either of these two circumstances in the case—neither did the defendant resist the act to the utmost, nor was she prevented from doing so by "threats of great and immediate body harm." The victim testified that she did not resist because she was afraid, and the Louisiana Court of Appeal did agree with her that she was afraid. Yet the court reversed the defendant's conviction. According to the court, the repeated slapping by the defendant did not constitute "threats of great and immediate body harm."

USE OF DECEPTION AND FRAUD

Use of fraud to accomplish sexual intercourse, i.e., rape by fraud includes four distinct categories: (i) where sexual intercourse is presented to the victim fraudulently as a genuine method of treatment, (ii) fraud as to the defendant's identity (i.e., impersonation), (iii) sexual scams, and (iv) sexual theft.

Sexual Intercourse Presented as a Treatment

This is a situation where the offender has a sexual intercourse with a patient under the guise of medical treatment. These cases fall in three broad categories: (i) deception as to the nature of the act, e.g., the victim believes that she is having a routine vaginal examination while the offender is actually having sexual intercourse with her; (ii) the offender induces the victim to have sexual intercourse by fraudulently maintaining that the sexual intercourse is necessary for medical treatment; (iii) the offender gets involved in "ambiguously sexual" touching that the patient believes is necessary for medical purposes, but which is only for the offender's sexual gratification.

Deception as to the Nature of the Act

The first category is typified by *McNair v. State,* 825 P.2d 571 (Nev. 1992), where the victims had consented to a gynecological examination, but discovered that they had unwittingly positioned themselves for an anal penile penetration by their physician. The court opined that when a defendant had obtained sexual intercourse by means of fraud, legally recognized consent is negated. The victims had consented to one thing, and the defendant did something materially different.

In *People v. Ogunmola,* 238 Cal. Rptr. 300, 304 (Cal. Ct. App. 1987), the victims consented to a gynecological examination, but instead of a speculum, the doctor inserted his penis into their vaginas. The court concluded the victims had not consented to the nature of the act which was performed.

Two Illinois cases are also instructive. In *People v. Castello,* 586 N.E.2d 742 (Ill. 1992), the defendant posed as a medical doctor and offered the victim a free medical examination, which included touching her breasts and vagina. The court observed, "There is no evidence to suggest that [the victim] would have consented to defendant's acts of sexual penetration if she was aware that defendant was not the doctor he represented himself to be," and concluded, "undoubtedly this deception took away [the victim's] ability to give knowing consent to these acts." In *People v. Quinlan,* 596 N.E.2d 28 (Ill. App. Ct. 1992), the defendant, a respiratory therapist, told the victim she needed a special test, in which he placed his fingers in her rectum and vagina. The court found the victim had consented to an invasive medical procedure, not to sexual acts, and concluded her consent was vitiated because it was received through deceit.

Sexual Intercourse Presented as Treatment

In contrast to opinions involving deception as to the sexual act, courts considering cases in which defendants lied about the purported benefits of sexual intercourse as a therapeutic treatment generally have found that no rape occurred. Courts have advanced two kinds of reasonings for this conclusion: one, that the force requirement was not satisfied, and two, that the consent to the act deprived the conduct of its criminality.

This category is typified by *Boro v. Superior Court,* 210 Cal. Rptr. 122 (Cal. Ct. App. 1985). Boro, whom the press nicknamed "Dr. Feelgood," posed as a doctor and tricked women into sexual intercourse by telling them that such act was necessary to cure their fatal blood disease. Boro explained that the choice was either to undergo a painful and expensive surgery or have sexual intercourse with a donor (Boro himself) who had been injected with a special serum. The state prosecuted Boro for rape after he persuaded at least four women to engage in sexual intercourse, claiming that his actions fell under a statute prohibiting sexual intercourse with a victim who is unconscious of the nature of the act. Boro appealed, arguing that the rape statute did not cover his case. The appellate court agreed and prohibited his prosecution. The court held that there is a distinction between fraud in the factum and fraud in the inducement, and that only the former vitiates consent. The California legislature, in response to *Boro,* had to pass a new statute specifically criminalizing this kind of conduct.[21] Boro was apprehended again in 1987 for the same scam and prosecuted under the new statute specially designed for him.

A similar case is *Don Moran v. People* 25 Mich. 356 (1872), in which a doctor induced a 15-year old girl to have sexual intercourse with him, falsely making her father believe that it was necessary for her treatment and that the alternative was a painful medical procedure that would probably kill her. Believing the doctor, the girl's father authorized the sexual union. The Michigan Supreme Court overturned the conviction because the trial court erred in instructing the jury by omitting the requirement of force. It held that fraud cannot substitute for force in rape.

Ambiguously Sexual Touching

This category lies between the two traditional categories of fraudulent medical treatment cases mentioned above. Here, the patients agreed to various forms of intimate touching, falling short of sexual intercourse, in the mistaken belief that such touching constituted medical treatment.

These cases differ from the first category—deception as to the act—because the patients were aware of the nature of the contact and not caught by surprise. These cases also differed from the second group—sexual intercourse as necessary medical treatment—because unlike the patients in the second group, none of the patients consented to engage in sexual conduct. A brief look at some cases may help illustrate this.

In *State v. Quinlan,* 596 N.E.2d 28 (Ill. App. Ct. 1992), the defendant, working as a respiratory therapist, convinced a twenty-six year old patient to allow him to digitally penetrate her under the guise of performing a cardio-neurological-respiratory exam. The patient believed that Quinlan's conduct was a *legitimate* medical procedure for diagnosing her respiratory problems. Quinlan was convicted because the patient had consented to a medical procedure, not to sexual penetration, and that her consent was vitiated because it was obtained by deceit. In *State v. Tizard,* 897 S.W.2d 732 (Tenn. Crim. App. 1994), Tizard, the offender rubbed his patient's—a seventeen-year-old male—genitals and, on one occasion, masturbated him to climax, under the garb of administering treatment. Tizard was prosecuted under the sexual battery statute that included an explicit fraud provision.

Impersonation

Here the offender obtains sex by impersonating a person, whom the victim may want to have sex with; the person may be her husband, her boyfriend, or some celebrity. In earlier cases, the courts were generally reluctant to prosecute such offenders because the force requirement is not met. In *Lewis v.,* State 30 Ala. 54 (1857), Lewis, a slave, climbed into the bed of his employer—a white woman—and had sexual intercourse with her, who believed Lewis was her husband. The court held that force requirement was not met.

Courts have reached similar decisions in much more recent cases. In *People v. Hough,* 124 Misc.2d 997, 607 N.Y.S.2d 884 (1994), the defendant impersonated his twin brother in order to have sexual intercourse with the brother's girlfriend. The court found that New York's nonconsent statute required either forcible compulsion or incapacity to consent and did not include fraud.

By and large, however, such cases are prosecuted. In *United States v. Booker,* 25 M.J. 114 (CMA 1987), Booker had sexual intercourse with a sleeping woman shortly after she had consensual intercourse with another man, impersonating the woman's voluntary lover. He was convicted. The court held that fraud as to the identity of a sexual partner constitutes fraud in the factum which vitiates consent. In one famous case, the offender Oscar E. Kendall impersonated fashion photographer Richard Avedon in a ruse to persuade women to sleep with him and give him money. In yet another case, Raymond Mitchell, whom the press dubbed the "Fantasy Man" used to telephone women, pretending to be their fiancées or boyfriends. He explained that he had had a fantasy about having sex with a blindfolded woman and persuaded them to leave their doors unlocked and to wait in bed blindfolded. He also instructed his victims not to touch him during sex. Both Kendall and Mitchell were prosecuted.

Sexual Scams

Sexual scams typically involve business settings, in which the defendants deceive the victims into sexual intimacy by false promises of benefit. The offenders mostly belong to the entertainment industry, but they may also come from other professions. This category closely resembles fraudulent commercial transactions. Attempts to prosecute these defendants for sexual crimes, based on exploitation of victims under the guise of the casting couch or similar stratagems, have been largely unsuccessful. Most of these sexual con men have escaped criminal sanction or, more rarely, have been convicted of fraud or property crimes rather than the underlying sexual offense.

In India, a number of cases have reached the courts, where a male engages in frequent acts of consensual sexual intercourse with his fiancée after engagement and then refuses to marry her. The victim then approaches the court alleging rape. Despite Indian law being very comprehensive on rape, courts have found offenders in such cases almost impossible to prosecute.

A typical "casting couch" case occurred in India in 2004 when female actor Preeti Jain filed a police complaint alleging that film director Madhur Bhandarkar had sexually exploited her for many months and made false promises of casting her in a lead role in his next film. She stated that she was never given any role in any of his films. According to her, Bhandarkar repeatedly had sex with Jain from 1999 to 2004 at Natraj Apartment at Yari Road, Hotel Seaside at Juhu, and at Bhandarkar's friend's (Akbar) flat at Mount Mary road, Bandra.[22]

An almost similar situation occurred in *United States v. Condolon,* 600 F.2d 7 (4th Cir. 1979), where the defendant engaged in an elaborate scheme designed to acquire sexual favors from women. He rented an apartment, obtained a business license, and placed newspaper ads offering to find women acting and modeling jobs. Condolon propositioned many of the women who contacted him and a number submitted to his advances. In reality, Condolon had neither the means nor the intention of assisting his clients in obtaining work. He could only be convicted of wire fraud. Without resort to the wire fraud statute, Condolon would likely have gone unpunished.

In *United States v. Altman,* 901 F.2d 1161 (2d Cir. 1990), Altman posed as an owner of a modeling agency and induced women to pay him money to become his models. He then plied the women with the amphetamine Didrex diet pills, had intercourse with them, and took sexually explicit photographs of them. He was convicted of sexual exploitation of a minor, interstate transportation of a minor with intent to engage in illegal sexual activity, and wire fraud.

In an English case, James Finningham posed as a wealthy psychic and pretended to be inhabited by a dead American Indian chief. He persuaded a gullible victim to sleep with him by telling her during a séance that she should give herself to him. Following both sexual and financial exploitation of the woman, Finningham was convicted of fraud and false imprisonment, but could not be charged of rape.[23]

Sexual Theft

This is perhaps the most controversial category, and is mostly comprised of prostitutes as victims. The controversy exists largely because prostitution is illegal in most jurisdictions, and prostitutes are mostly seen unworthy of any sympathy. The typical scenario involves a customer getting sexual favors from a prostitute on promise of payment and then refusing to pay. The term "theft" is used here because the victim herself offers to sell sexual services and then is not paid.

In a recent case from England, *Regina v. Linekar,* Crim LR 320 (C.A. 1994), the defendant approached a part-time prostitute and negotiated a price of twenty-five pounds for sexual intercourse. Afterward, the defendant refused to pay and the woman alleged rape. The trial court returned a guilty verdict, but the appellate court quashed the conviction because the prostitute had consented to the intercourse.

Other Issues Involving Consent

Mens Rea

Among the other issues involved in the issue whether the consent was valid or not is the issue of *mens rea* or whether the accused had a guilty mind or not. One of the most illustrative cases in this regard is the UK case of *R. v. Morgan,* (1975) 2 All E.R. 347 (also sometimes cited as *D.P.P. v. Morgan,* [1975] 2 All E.R. 347, D.P.P. standing for Director of Public Prosecutions). This case involved Morgan, a senior non-commissioned officer in the Royal Air Force, and three men who were the junior members of that service. On the night of the offense, Morgan invited his three juniors home to have intercourse with his wife. Morgan was perhaps aware that his wife would not consent for such an intercourse, so he fabricated a story that his wife—even during normal consensual intercourse—feigned non-consent, and they would perhaps have to use force to have intercourse with her. He further suggested that his wife apparently did so in order to increase her own sexual pleasure. The three men believed this. When they entered the house, they found Mrs. Morgan asleep. They woke her up and took her forcibly to another room, where each of them had forcible intercourse with a fiercely struggling and screaming Mrs. Morgan. She even shouted to her son to call the police, but one the men put a hand over her mouth. All through the act, they sincerely believed that Mrs. Morgan was putting up a show of resistance merely to increase her own sexual pleasure. Each man took turns having intercourse with her, while the others restrained her. Her husband, who was watching, was the last to rape her.* Immediately after they were through, Mrs. Morgan drove to a hospital and complained that she had been raped.

In the trial court, the jury convicted the three accused of rape and Morgan for aiding and abetting rape (he had the "husband immunity" so he could not be prosecuted for rape). Their appeal to the Court of Appeal was dismissed. When the case went to the House of Lords, the main question considered was whether the three rapists had guilty minds or not. It was significant that they had been told by the husband that his wife would resist merely to heighten her own sexual pleasure. So in effect they believed that her "no" meant "yes." Thus they did not appear to have guilty minds. The central question in this case was, "can a man be said to have committed rape if he *sincerely* believed that the woman was consenting, no matter how unreasonable the belief?" Lord Cross of Chelsea, writing the judgment as part of a 3-2 majority opined, "I do not think he can." The *mens rea* or the guilty mind, so necessary for prosecution in all criminal matters, is missing from such cases. Interestingly, the men were still convicted because of a technical point (unrelated to the issue of consent). Such kinds of defense later came to be called "Morgan honest belief defense. " Essentially, they included cases where the defendant was reckless as to whether the victim consents. Such defenses have now been removed from the law by adding a clause that it is the duty of the person committing the act to ensure that the other party consents and that he must take sufficient steps to ascertain this (see Legal aspects, UK below).

Sexual Intercourse with People Having Intellectual Disabilities (ID)

In most legislation sexual intercourse with people of unsound mind is considered rape. However, none *quantify* the degree of unsoundness of mind (e.g., in terms of IQ) below which a person is unable to consent to have sexual intercourse. This is a serious legal question begging immediate attention. Another serious issue is the high rate of rape and sexual abuse against people with intellectual disabilities (ID). This is mainly because they either do not understand the nature of the act itself or the related law. In an interesting and illustrative study, O'Callaghan and Murphy[24] from Kent, UK, studied 60 adults (mean chronological age 37.6 years) with intellectual disabilities and 60 young people aged 16-18 years (deemed in most legislation to be capable of consenting to a sexual

---

* It is possible that Morgan was suffering from troilism, a paraphilia in which a man invites another man to have intercourse with his wife.

relationship). The aim was to investigate their understanding of the law relating to sexuality. Several questions were posed to them, including those on general laws around sexuality and abuse, as well as the law relating to sexual relationships and ID. It was found that adults with IDs had a very limited understanding of the general laws relating to sexuality (e.g., age of consent, sexual abuse), as well as the law relating to sexuality and IDs (e.g., whether they could have sexual relationships, whether they were allowed to marry, what protection they should expect from the law). On the other hand, people much younger in age but without ID showed a better understanding, both for general laws and for those relating specifically to adults with IDs. The authors concluded that there was a need to educate people with ID about the laws relating to sexuality.

Difference between Consent and Submission

Difference between consent and submission have been pointed out by various courts. In *R. v. Olugboja,* (1981) 73 Cr.App.R 344, Stephen Olubunmi Olugboja, a twenty year old Nigerian and his friend Lawal met victim Jayne, 16, and her friend Karen, 17, on March 8, 1979, at a discotheque in Oxford, where they had been dancing. They offered the girls a lift home, but instead drove them to Lawal's bungalow, which was in the opposite direction from where they lived. When they got there, Olugboja went in. However, both Jayne and Karen refused to go in and started walking away. They did not know where they were. Since Olugboja was already in the bungalow, Lawal followed them alone in the car, and after some argument they got in. After a further argument Karen again got out, and, as she was trying to get Jayne out, Lawal drove off, stopped in a lane, and raped Jayne.

Lawal then drove back to the bungalow, picking Karen up on the way, and the 3 of them went inside. Olugboja was lying on the sofa, and saw them arrive. Jayne was the last to come in. Music was put on. Jayne declined to dance. She went to the lavatory and returned to find Lawal dragging Karen into the bedroom. Olugboja switched the sitting room lights off and told Jayne that he was going to fuck her. She told him that Lawal had had her in the car and asked the defendant to leave her alone. He told her to take her trousers off, and she did because she said she was frightened. She was still crying, and the room was in darkness. Olugboja pushed her on the settee and had intercourse with her. It did not last long. She did not struggle; she made no resistance; she did not scream or cry for help. She did struggle when she thought after penetration that the defendant was going to ejaculate inside her, and he withdrew. She put her clothes on and the other two emerged from the bedroom, where Lawal had raped Karen.

In all 3 acts of sexual intercourse, coercion took place: (i) Lawal had sexual intercourse with Jayne in the car, which was quite obviously without Jayne's consent and hence rape; (ii) Lawal had sexual intercourse with Karen in his Bungalow, which again was without Karen's consent; and (iii) Olugboja had sexual intercourse with Jayne, which apparently was with her consent as she did not resist.

Not only this, but when Jayne finally did reach her home, she complained to her mother about Lawal but not about Olugboja (further giving the impression that the act of sexual intercourse was with her consent). Not only did she make no complaint against Olugboja, but she said he had not touched her. Jayne did say later she did not know why she did not complain to her mother about Olugboja. She supposed that she was more upset about the first one, referring to the forced intercourse by Lawal. Based on Jayne's description, the police initially saw Olugboja as a witness to the complaints by both Jayne and Karen with regard to the rapes on each of them by Lawal, rather than as an accused. It was much later that Jayne insisted that Olugboja had had sexual intercourse with her, against her will.

In his defense Olugboja said that Jayne had consented to intercourse, which was apparent from the fact that she removed her trousers herself and that was in itself an open invitation to sex. However, Judge Leo Clark said that the circumstances in which she was consenting were also to be taken into consideration. The circumstances before the act (Lawal raping her in the car, and then almost forcing her inside his bungalow) and just at the time of the act (Lawal dragging her friend Karen into the bedroom), were such that any girl would feel terrorized and submit herself, if only to avoid violence. Olugboja was found guilty of rape by a majority of 11-1 and sentenced to 30 months' imprisonment.

RAPE VARIATIONS

Following specific variations of rape are of special note:

Acquaintance Rape

Acquaintance rape involves someone being forced to have sexual contact against his or her will with a person known to the victim.

Drug Facilitated Sexual Assault

Drug facilitated sexual assault (DFSA) refers to acts of sexual assault, in which the judgment of the victim has been vitiated by surreptitiously spiking her drink with a psychotropic drug. The first instance of drug facilitated sexual assault is found in the Bible. Kutz[25] thinks that the sexual intercourse of Lot with his daughters would today be taken as drug rape (Lot's daughters used wine to drug him, before lying with him to extract his seed. The elder daughter has sexual intercourse with Lot on the first day and the younger on the next day. Lot was drugged with wine on both days). Both liaisons resulted in pregnancies.

The typical drug for DFSA needs to be a sedative, amnesiac, and effective in small doses. Common drugs used are gammahydroxybutyrate (GHB), Rohypnol (flunitrazepam), ketamine, MDMA (Ecstasy), chloral hydrate and alcohol. Recently Gamma Butyrolactone (GBL) and 1,4-butanediol (BD)—two industrial cleaners—have been increasingly used in DFSA. The drugs are given usually in a bar or club setting. Women who have been given these drugs may feel weak or dizzy (with Ecstasy they may actually want to be touched and held by partners, who may have been complete strangers only a few minutes before). The predator then offers to drive the victim home, where he commits sexual assault. The victim will experience an 8 to 24 hour blackout, and on coming around, may not have any memory of the event, or even who drove her home. Attempts at reviving memories through hypnosis have been fruitless.

Recently a drink spike detector (DSD) has been developed, which can test both GHB and Ketamine in drinks.[26] About the size of a credit card, it displays a visible color change when it comes in contact with GHB or Ketamine. Each card can test two drinks. Due to their size and ease of use, the test cards are relatively inconspicuous and can be used discreetly. The test takes only seconds to perform, and is as easy as placing a couple of drops from the drink in question onto the active test spots using a swizzle stick, straw or even one's finger.

Gang Rape

Instances of gang rape can be found in the Bible. In one instance, the act of gang rape kills the victim. A Levite was returning home from his father-in-law's house in Bethlehem, along with his concubine-wife and his servant. They traveled as far as Jebus when the sun set, but they decided against spending the night there since it was not a city of Israel. They continued on to Gibeah, a city of the tribe of Benjamin. Upon their arrival in Gibeah, an old man offered them lodging for the night at his home. Soon many men of the city surrounded the house and demanded that the host hand his male guests over to them so they could sodomize them. Since the old man wanted to protect his guests, he offered them his own virgin daughter, but they rejected her. Finally they agreed to take the Levite's concubine-wife, whom they raped all night long. The next day the Levite found his wife lying dead at his host's doorstep. In grief he loaded her body onto his jackass, and on arrival home dismembered her body into 12 parts, and sent one part each to the twelve tribes of Israel to apprise them of what had happened to his wife at the hands of the Benjaminites of Gibeah.[27]

In a general sense, gang rape is sexualized violence involving two or more assailants. However, the meaning acquires different meanings in different cultures and jurisdictions. Sanday[28] defines it as "a violent act committed by a group of males with a common bond (such as gang, fraternity, or athletic team members) in which each member has sex in turn with a female in the presence of the entire group." According to Indian law, "where a woman is raped by 1 or more in a group of persons acting in furtherance of their common intention, *each* of the persons shall be deemed to have committed gang rape.[29] Thus if out of a group of 5 persons, 4 persons restrained the woman, one person restraining each limb, and *only* the fifth person perpetrated the actual act of sexual intercourse, after the woman was thus restrained, *each* of the 5 persons of the group would be deemed to have committed gang rape.

Incest Rape

Incest rape is *forcible* sexual relationship between near relatives in a family. It must be clearly distinguished from plain incest. While the latter implies full consent of both parties, incest rape implies that the sexual intercourse was done against the wishes of one party, usually the female. Father-daughter incest rape is the commonest. It has been considered the most prevalent and most devastating form of child sexual abuse.[30]

Male Rape

Traditionally rape laws have been gender specific, providing that only women could be victims of rape and only men could be rapists. In recent years an increasing number of states have modified their rape laws to be gender neutral. In these states it is possible for a woman to be charged with raping a man (male rape). For example, in Canada, statutes prohibiting sexual assault apply to both male and female perpetrators and victims.

Another issue involving male rape is homosexual rape, where a male commits forcible anal or oral intercourse on another male. If this is not covered by a state's general rape statute, it may sometimes be covered by statutes that prohibit anal or oral sex between members of the same sex. Although some statutes do not distinguish between forcible and consensual acts, forcible sodomy is generally subject to more severe punishments. Homosexual rape is a notorious problem in prisons. At the time of writing of this book, rape of men—whether by women or other men—is not a highly problematic issue.

Marital Rape

Marital or spousal rape is sex with one's spouse without his or her consent. This may appear paradoxical to some, especially because of the historically held view that a man had an unrestricted sexual access to his legally wedded wife, and could not be charged of rape, even if the wife had not consented to sexual intercourse. In medieval times, in most countries, wives were considered the *sexual property* of their husbands under the legal concept of *coverture*, meaning that a woman was literally "covered" by her husband when she married. She, in fact, ceased to have a separate legal existence after that. As recently as the 1960s, the American Law Institute recommended retaining this historical legal doctrine; the recommendation was based on the theory that it was inappropriate for the law to invade marital privacy. Most jurisdictions, however, abandoned this doctrine and began to allow prosecutions for marital rape, especially if it was committed by force. In India, for example, till 1983, forcible sexual intercourse by a husband, even when his wife was living separately from him under a decree of separation, was not rape, but the law was changed after that (please see below for relevant law). In Canada, if sexual intercourse is done without consent, spouses may be convicted of criminal sexual assault.

Prison Rape

Simply put, rape occurring within a prison setting is prison rape. Prisoners are more liable to be raped, because of their increased vulnerability and helplessness. Prisoners with mental disabilities, those diminutive in size, and new inmates are more likely to be victims. Overcrowding in jails and understaffing in the current prison system increases their vulnerability. Both males and female prisoners are vulnerable; male prisoners perceived as having feminine traits are more vulnerable than other males. Youth of both sexes are more vulnerable, especially when placed along with adult prisoners.

Rape can be committed either by jail staff or by fellow prisoners either singly or in groups. Instances of rape perpetrated by jail staff in collaboration with prisoners are also known. The incidence of male inmate-on-inmate rape could be as high as 7–12% of all incarcerated males.[31] It also exposes tens of thousands of inmates to HIV/AIDS and other sexually transmitted diseases (STDs).

Male custodial rape, especially by fellow prisoners, can be explained better by a quest for dominance and control, rather than by sexual needs. In one study of prison rape, it was reported that 72% of the perpetrators were inmates, 8% were staff and in 12% of cases, staff and inmates collaborated.[32] Among female victims of rape, 47% of the perpetrators were inmates, and 41% were staff. This indicates that the prison staff tends to take advantage of female prisoner vulnerability. Mainly because of this fact, in most countries prison rape invites much harsher punishment than rape occurring otherwise. In the United States, prison rape is recognized as a violation of the prisoner's rights as spelled out in the eighth amendment U.S. constitution, which expressly prohibit cruel and unusual punishment.

Secondary Rape

Secondary rape is used to describe the process that agencies, institutions, or individuals perform when questioning a rape victim during investigations.[33] The process exerts the same power over the victim as that exerted by the initial rapist: it is equally invasive and destructive of privacy and it denies the victim control over his or her body in a similar fashion. Thus secondary rape has the same characteristics as the primary or original rape. The victim is put in the same awkward positios (lithotomy position) that she may have been forced to assume during the actual rape, and the very same penetrative actions are performed (inserting a swab stick in the vagina to take forensic samples).

Being forced to give birth after conceiving from a rape may be termed *tertiary rape*.

Serial Rape

Serial rape as defined by Federal Bureau of Investigation (FBI) involves sexual attacks upon ten or more stranger victims; however, local police forces and the general public frequently use the term after more than two similar rapes have occurred.[34]

PSYCHOLOGICAL SEQUELAE

Sexual assault, rape, and gang rape by family members, acquaintances, and strangers may result in psychological disorders.

Rape Trauma Syndrome

Rape Trauma Syndrome (RTS), first described in 1974 by Ann Wolbert Burgess, an associate professor of nursing, and Lynda Lytle Holmstrom, an associate professor of sociology at the Boston College, Massachusetts, is a set of acute and long-term symptoms resulting from rape or attempted rape.[35] The syndrome is a two-phase reaction, an acute *disorganization phase* lasting about 2 to 3 weeks after the rape, during which time there is a great deal of disorganization in the woman's lifestyle as a result of rape, and the *reorganization phase* lasting for years, during which the victim reorganizes her life. In the acute phase, the victim is apt to appear calm and subdued mainly due to fear, anger, or anxiety. Many women in the acute phase also experience physical symptoms, such as tension headaches, fatigue, and disturbed sleep patterns.[36] In the reorganization phase, the victim develops motor activity changes, nightmares, and phobias related to the circumstances of the rape.

There are differences in opinion regarding the scientific reliability and, therefore, admissibility of RTS evidence. While it *may not* be introduced as proof of the commission of the rape, it may sometimes be used to demonstrate why the victim took time (often days) to report rape to the authorities. A judge or a lay juror, in the absence of RTS evidence, may likely consider this delay as evidence of a false allegation of rape.

Other Sequelae

Groer and colleagues[37] measured serum stress hormones, proinflammatory cytokines, acute phase proteins, functional assays, and lymphocyte subsets in 15 rape victims and compared the levels with those of 16 control participants. They found that rape victims had higher cytotoxic cells, lower B lymphocyte counts, higher proinflammatory biomarkers, and decreased lymphocyte proliferation compared to the control group. The findings suggest that rape produces activation of the innate immunity and suppression of some aspects of adaptive immunity. The authors conclude that if these immune changes persist, they may contribute to the pathophysiology of long-term health sequelae of rape by provoking chronic inflammation and decreased cellular immunocompetence.

Kahn and associates[38] have shown that adolescent and young adult women who experience coercive sexual experiences are more likely than controls to develop risky behaviors such as a higher lifetime number of sexual partners, leading to an increased risk of subsequent human papillomavirus (HPV) infection and squamous intraepithelial lesions (SILs).

Boughn and Holdom[39] have described the development of trichotillomania (an impulse control disorder characterized by the repeated urge to pull out scalp hair and other body hair) in victims of rape, gang rape, and sexual abuse.

INVESTIGATION OF RAPE

Medical Examination of the Victim

A thorough medical examination of an alleged sexual assault victim is required for two main reasons—for collecting evidence and for instituting therapy, directed at both physical as well as emotional consequences of assault.

It has increasingly been felt that many accused of rapists go free because of inadequate examination and collection of evidence done by rather inexperienced medical personnel. This could be because of the minimal importance given to this vital topic during the teaching of medical curricula. Koschorke and colleagues[40] found that only 8 medical schools of the 21 surveyed in the United Kingdom provided any teaching about sexual assault. They concluded that because rape is so common and traumatic, medical schools should seriously consider providing more comprehensive teaching and training in this area. Most others are also of the view that the medical students should be taught about this topic at the level of undergraduate teaching itself, especially the correct procedures of examination and a proper collection of evidence.[41,42,43]

In recent years, the role of a trained *sexual assault nurse examiner* (SANE) in collection of evidence has increasingly been appreciated.[44,45,46,47,48] A sexual assault nurse examiner is a registered

TABLE 10.2
Steps of Examination of Victim in a Suspected Case of Rape

Step 1—Taking a proper informed consent

Step 2—History taking/recording of injuries with sensitivity to the patient and her traumatic condition

Step 3—a. Examination/collection of outer clothing

b. Examination/collection of inner clothing

[outer clothing and inner clothing collected and packaged separately to prevent contamination]

Step 4—Debris collection: Debris collected from web spaces or intertriginous folds of fingers, hair, and from under fingernails. Suspected seminal stains from thighs or other areas collected by dropping a drop of distilled water on the stain, and rolling a collection swab across the area. Debris from each area to be packaged separately.

Step 5—Breast swab

Step 6—Combing pubic hair

Step 7—Clipping public hair

Step 8—Collection of matted pubic hair

Step 9 a. Vaginal secretion collection

b. Cervical mucus collection

Step 10—Culture

Step 11—Washings from vagina

Step 12—Rectal examination

Step 13—Oral swab

Step 14—Victim's saliva sample

Step 15—Blood of victim

Step 16—Urine (for toxicology and pregnancy tests)

Step 17—Medical examination forms

Step 18—Medical examination report

nurse (RN) who is specifically trained not only to show compassion and sensitivity to survivors of sexual assault, but also to provide comprehensive care to them, to conduct a forensic examination including evidence collection, and even to provide effective courtroom testimony if required. Many medico legal centers do have SANEs, who assist doctors in the collection of evidence. The presence of a trained nurse also gives much needed assurance to the victim of rape, and she can confide freely with the medical personnel.

Steps of Examination

A thorough medico-legal examination of the rape victim is vital in collecting evidence that would ultimately lead to the prosecution of the offender. So that an inadvertent omission may not occur, it is useful to conduct the examination in a series of predefined steps. Although in a broad manner the examination remains the same, individual steps may differ from center to center in either their number or sequence. The steps which this author has found most useful are given in Table 10.2.

A few precautions must be taken during the examination. The examiner must wear gloves at all times during the exam to avoid transfering his own DNA onto the evidence. Powderless gloves must be worn during exams, as powder may interfere with the subsequent laboratory examination. The vaginal speculum must be moistened with warm water and not with lubricating jelly, as the jelly may interfere with the forensic tests.

Informed Consent

Informed consent from the victim should be obtained[50] and confidentiality of information maintained[51] in all cases to avoid any legal problems later. There have been cases where informed consent was not taken and the physician sued for invasion of privacy or making an assault. If the victim is below the age of consent (generally 18 years in most jurisdictions), the consent must be taken from accompanying parent or guardian. Informed consent is also necessary if it is felt that emergency contraceptives should be used to avoid pregnancy.[52] Signs of injuries such as abrasions, bruises, and lacerations on cheeks, neck, breasts, thighs, vulva, and other parts of the body must be noted carefully and recorded.

Breast Swab

Analysis of breast swabs cannot be overemphasized. DNA profiling can be done by recovering saliva of the offender from a bite mark. It has been possible to prepare DNA profiles of offenders in this way, even from dead bodies which have been submerged in water for long periods. In one case, in which a female body was recovered after approximately 5.5 hours in a river with slow-moving current, a bite mark was found on the victim's right breast. DNA profile could be successfully prepared from it, and suspects screened.[53] It is thus advisable that investigators routinely swab for salivary DNA in bite mark cases, even when the amount is thought to be minimal.

Colposcopy should always be employed in genital examinations of rape victims, as conventional rape examination protocols have been rather poor in yielding genital findings (10% to 30% typically).[54] In contrast, colposcopy—once reserved for victims of child abuse only—has been shown to identify genital injury in up to 87% of rape victims.[55] Photographic records of colposcopic findings may be essential for courtroom presentations.[56,57]

Microtrauma to the vagina can be demonstrated by colposcopic examination of the vaginal mucosa after staining with toluidine blue (1% aqueous solution) and its subsequent removal from unstained areas by means of a destaining reagent, such as diluted acetic acid or a lubricant.[58,59] Its use has been shown to increase the detection rate of posterior fourchette lacerations from 16% to 40% in adult rape victims.[60] Since it is known that some of the lubricants used for destaining can have a destructive effect on sperm motility, it is feared by some investigators that their use may interfere with subsequent DNA recovery. However, it has been shown that evidentiary material contaminated with these reagents can be successfully typed.[60] It has been suggested that a vaginal speculum should not be used until *after* toluidine dye application, as the use of speculum can introduce fresh injuries, which may be wrongly interpreted as those due to sexual assault.[61] Lugol's solution has also been successfully used for staining and demonstrating genital injuries.[62] Its use in cases of rape has also been justified because of its direct spermicidal effect, especially if applied soon after coitus, thus avoiding the possibility of pregnancy.[63]

Photographic evidence of all injuries is essential for legal purposes.

Reflective and fluorescent ultraviolet photography is essential to record evidence of abrasions, contusions, lacerations[64] and bite marks.[65] Reflective ultraviolet photography has been successfully used to record bite marks in rape victims as late as five months after the assault.[66]

It is important to remember that genital injuries are far more common in women *without* prior experience of sexual intercourse than in those having a prior sexual experience.[67]

Post-Exposure Prophylaxis

With increasing incidence of HIV around the world, it is advisable to institute a course of post-exposure prophylaxis (PEP) immediately, especially if the offender has not been caught.[68] Standard PEP at the time of writing this book is Lamivudine 150 mg combined with Zidovudine 300 mg, twice a day for 28 days. PEP must preferably be started immediately, but not later than 72 hours of exposure.

Rape Kit

Rape kits (prepackaged sterile evidence collection kits, sometimes also referred to as sex crime kit, Sexual Assault Evidence Kit, or SAEK)[69,70] are now available, which ensure that the examining doctor goes through all steps in an orderly manner without missing out on any step. All envelopes in the rape kit are self-sealing and must never be moistened with saliva.

The contents of a typical rape kit are given in Table 10.3.

SAKiTA

Usually, once the physician or SANE sends the evidence in a rape kit to the forensic laboratory, he is almost cut off from any further interaction with it. This means that unless a case goes to trial it is extremely unlikely that he will ever know the results of the evidence collected. If a system existed whereby he could know which samples had been collected properly and which hadn't, which showed positive results and which didn't, he could improve his sample collection techniques in future cases.

To solve this problem, since January 2006, the state of West Virginia has used the Sexual Assault Kit Tracking Application (SAKiTA).[71] In this system, the SANE or medical provider contacts the state coalition for a user name and password to access the SAKiTA system, which is located on a secure Web site. All sex crime kits are assigned tracking numbers when sent to the hospitals from the West Virginia State Police Forensic Laboratory. All sex crime kits include a feedback form, which is filled up by the medical provider at the time of collecting the evidence. This form is submitted to the crime lab either electronically or mailed to them along with the kit. Crime lab personnel post the feedback information on the SAKiTA system. The medical provider can directly access SAKiTA to review the feedback form on the completed kit that he collected. This shows what evidence was found in the kit, which swabs were positive and which were not, whether the evidence was packaged and dried correctly, if sperm was found, if DNA was identified, and if so from which sources. It also provides data for a comparison of sex crime kits collected by SANEs and non-SANEs, including weaknesses in evidence collection procedures if any. The resulting data may show the need for hospitals to support the SANE initiative by training nurses and developing more SANE programs. An additional advantage is that it helps the forensic laboratory determine the location of sex crime kits once they have been sent from the laboratory to hospitals throughout the state, and creates a method to determine the status of a sex crime kit once it is received at the lab.

Medical Examination of the Offender

Medical examination of the offender is done for injuries as well as to determine impotency according to standard protocols. In many jurisdictions, if the offender is arrested, the medical examination can be done *without* consent (e.g., in India, under section 53 of Cr.P.C., the examination of the offender can be done without consent). Examination for impotency is necessary in all cases, as this is a common defense taken by sex offenders in a court of law, many times as an afterthought after consultation with a lawyer. Recovery of trace evidence such as female DNA from the offender's penis is vital for successful prosecution.[72,73,74]

Physical Evidence at the Crime Lab

Detection of Semen

Data have been reported showing that 8 to 10% of the general male population have low or absent sperm counts.[75] In such cases, detection of Prostate Specific Antigen or PSA is a quite useful technique; it is also useful if the offender had undergone a vasectomy operation. PSA, also known variously as prostate antigen (PA), p30 (referring to its molecular weight being 30 kiloDaltons) or

TABLE 10.3
Contents of a Typical Rape Kit, Specimens To Be Collected, and Tests To Be Conducted

	Contents of the kit	What to collect/Test to be conducted
1.	One extra large white paper, large envelope to hold folded paper containing clothes	Ask victim to stand over paper and request to remove outer clothing. Fold paper and send to lab. Trace evidence sticking to outer clothing (hair, fibers, grass leaves, dried seminal fluid, etc.) is not lost this way (step 3a).
2.	Several standard paper clothing bags	Collect inner clothings for trace evidence, especially assailant's pubic hair, dried seminal stains, saliva (step 3b).
3.	Fingernail file or clippers, envelope or tube, distilled water, collection swab, envelopes	Fingernail scrapings; debris and stains from other areas (step 4).
4.	Distilled water, cotton-tipped swabs, envelope	Breast swab for saliva of the offender, if he tried to put his mouth to the breast (step 5).
5.	Plastic comb, large paper towel to comb hair onto, envelope to contain comb and folded paper towel	Pubic hair combing (step 6).
6.	Forceps, scissors, envelopes (for reference pubic hair of victim and for matted public hair, if present)	Pubic hair trimming for reference hair of the victim. Crime lab uses this data to differentiate offender hair from that of victim (step 7). If pubic hair is found matted with offender semen, it can be very valuable evidence (step 8).
7.	Two glass slides (one marked V for vaginal swab and one marked C for cervical swab), two cotton-tipped swabs. Saline tube. Cover slips	Vaginal and cervical swab (step 9a and 9b). After taking samples from vagina (and cervix), roll swabs on the slides, put a drop of saline and cover with a cover slip. The slides are examined for motile spermatozoa immediately after the physical examination (including collection of evidence).
8.	Cotton-tipped swabs, culture media such as Thayer-Martin plates, Transgrow media, chocolate agar plate, Chlamydia Transport Kit, or CVM Transport Kit (for the recovery of chlamydial, viral, and mycoplasmal agents)	Collect material from cervix for culture, and transfer to the lab, according to established protocols (step 10). If the cervix is absent, the collection is done from upper vagina.
9.	10 cc. saline, syringe, catheter	Vaginal washings (step 11) for spermatozoa, protein markers, and DNA.
10.	Glass slides, cover slip, cotton-tipped swabs, saline	Rectal swab and slide (step 12), if anal assault took place. Test for spermatozoa.
11.	Glass slides, cover slip, cotton-tipped swabs, saline	Oral swab and smear (step 13), if oral assault took place. Test for spermatozoa. Cultures also taken.
12.	Filter papers. Envelopes	Saliva for secretor status of victim (step 14). Ask victim to moisten filter paper with saliva. Filter paper dried and preserved. If oral intercourse with ejaculation took place, this step is postponed to avoid cross contamination of the specimen.
13.	Three test tubes, tourniquet, nonalcoholic swab to prep skin, syringe and needle	Blood samples from victim (step 15) for blood type, HIV, hepatitis B screen, RPR (rapid plasma reagin) and pregnancy tests. Also for toxicology screen including alcohol.
14.	Two urine containers	Urine—one for pregnancy test, and the other for drug screen (step 16).

gamma-seminoprotein (gamma-Sm),[76] was first identified as a suitable marker to demonstrate the presence of semen by Sensabaugh[77] of the University of California at Berkeley. It is now increasingly being used in all parts of the world in the investigation of rape. Talthip and associates[78] describe the use of PSA in the investigation of rape and murder of a 30-year old Thai female found dead on the floor at the base of a small monument in Bangkok. The scene investigation and autopsy findings suggested multiple sharp force injuries along with sexual assault. PSA was tested in this case with ELISA with success. The authors suggest and recommend the use of the PSA test kit in addition to conventional sperm smear and acid phosphatase test for sexual assault investigation. Semenogelin (Sg), a protein originating in the seminal vesicles and a substrate for p30, has also been used as a useful marker for the identification of semen.[79]

DNA Profiling

DNA profiling of the recovered samples is done according to standard protocols. Recently it has become possible to conduct DNA profiling even from microscopic slides.[80] This assumes importance if the medical provider prepared microscopic slides for spermatozoa but did not submit samples separately for DNA, or when the samples for DNA profiling were submitted but deteriorated and failed to provide successful profiling. In this technique—laser capture microdissection (LCM)—a laser beam is used to "cut out" and remove spermatozoa from glass slides and low copy number (LCN) PCR used to prepare DNA profiles.

If rape is reported so late that pregnancy has resulted, the offender can still be identified by conducting a paternity test on the child in-utero by DNA typing.[81]

Mitochondrial DNA (mtDNA) has also been used in the investigation of rape.[82] The advantage is that it is present in multiple copies in one cell (an average spermatozoon has 70 to 80 mitochondria with one mtDNA copy per mitochondrion), and thus analyses based on mtDNA are highly sensitive even when working with degraded samples or minute amounts of biological material.

Time since Intercourse

It is difficult, if not impossible, to determine the time since intercourse. Attempts have been made to deduce the time by finding sperms, motile or otherwise, in the vaginal canal.[83] In vaginal samples, motile sperms commonly are not found after a few hours,[84] but nonmotile sperms may persist for up to 17 days.[85] Motile sperm in the endocervix have been found up to 6 days after intercourse in adults.[86] While these may represent the upper limits, the generally accepted *maximum* times for sperm heads to be detected in living persons are 7 days in the vaginal cavity, 2 to 3 days in the anus and rectum, and 24 hours in the mouth.[87] Intact spermatozoa (tail attached) are commonly observed on vaginal swabs taken up to 26 hours after intercourse and are rarely observed in oral, anal, and rectal samples after 5 hours. Survival of sperm in the human genital tract may even be related to the vaginal flora. It has been seen that in menstruating women, spermatozoa survive longer in the vagina with Haemophilus type vaginal flora than with Doderlein type vaginal flora.[88]

The level of acid phosphatase (AP) activity in human semen is 500 to 1000 times higher than in other normal body fluids or secretions. This activity has been shown to decrease logarithmically as a function of time up to 4 days after intercourse, when it reaches nearly normal values.[89] Attempts have been made to extrapolate time of intercourse by determining AP levels in postcoital vaginal samples, albeit with variable success rates.[90,91,92,93,94,95] Levels of gamma-glutamyltransferase have also been used to extrapolate time since intercourse.[96]

Miscellaneous Techniques

Zinc has been found in unusually high concentrations in semen (140 mcg/ml in semen in contrast to 1.2 mcg/ml in normal blood serum). This is perhaps to maintain microbiological sterility of semen. This fact has been exploited for detection of semen in vaginal samples by using reagents which give brightly colored products in the presence of zinc.[75] Even without the deposition of semen, transfer of male epithelial cells from penile shaft to the vaginal tract does occur (Locard's exchange principle), and this fact has been exploited recently in proving penile penetration. Fluorescent in situ hybridization (FISH) has been used in such cases to detect Y chromosome from male epithelial cells, up to 7 days post coitus.[97] If an HIV infected offender has sexually assaulted a non-HIV infected victim, it is possible to detect semen anti-human immunodeficiency virus (HIV) antibodies within the cervicovaginal secretions, since the seminal fluid from all HIV-infected men contains a high titer of IgG antibodies to HIV.[98] If a condom has been used before assault, its use can be proved by detection of Lycopodium spores in the vaginal tract, as they are present in several condom coatings.[99] This proof assumes significance, if no spermatozoa are recovered from the genital tract, and it becomes necessary to show that a condom was used. Detection in the genital tract of lubricants such as polydimethylsiloxane (PDMS) liquid[100] and spermicides such as nonoxynol-9 (nonylphenoxy polyethoxyethanol) serves the same purpose.[101,102] Swabs can be taken from both the internal and external surfaces of the condom, and from both the victim (by DNA from the outer surface of the condom) and the offender (by DNA from the inner surface) identified.[103]

LEGAL ASPECTS

Legal Definitions of Sexual Intercourse and Rape

Traditional Definitions

Initially, almost every jurisdiction defined rape *only* as heterosexual, vaginal intercourse without consent, and only a female could be raped by a male and not vice-versa. As our understanding of human psychology grew, and as law made rapid advances, it began to be argued that sexual acts other than the penetration of a vagina by a penis could be "humiliating and traumatic" and "serious invasions of a person's physical and emotional integrity" when they took place without consent. It was also necessary for nonconsensual sexual acts against men and boys to be legally recognized as rape.

Current Definitions

Many jurisdictions have been quick to change their laws along these arguments. However many others—more traditional jurisdictions—have been rather slow to act. The result is that currently legal definitions of sexual intercourse vary widely from jurisdiction to jurisdiction. They range from the obvious penile-vaginal penetration to penile-oral and penile-anal penetration, with or without emission, to penetration of vagina with even other parts of the body such as a digit or tongue. In some jurisdictions vaginal penetration even with some object other than a body part (such as a stick) is called rape, and in yet some others, penetration of other body openings such as anus with a non-body part is called rape. In many jurisdictions these latter examples are recognized as genuine sexual offenses, but are covered by terms other than rape. Among the myriad of terms that have been legally used are *deviant sexual activity, deviant sexual intercourse, forcible rape, aggravated rape, sexual assault, aggravated sexual assault, sexual aggression, sexual coercion, sexual connection, sexual contact, sexual misconduct, sexual penetration, sexual torture* and *sexual violation.* In many jurisdictions, these sexual offenses are covered under such legal terms as rape in the first degree, rape in the second degree and so on, and also by sexual assault in the first degree, sexual assault in the second degree, etc.

Table 10.4 describes various permutations and combinations that can exist between the orifice penetrated and the object penetrating.

TABLE 10.4
Various Permutations and Combinations that Can Exist Between the Body Orifice Penetrated and the Object Penetrating. While P-V Is Defined As Rape in Almost All Jurisdictions, Legal Situations about Other Combinations Vary from Jurisdiction to Jurisdiction

Penetration of	Vagina	Anus	Mouth
Penetration by **P**enis	P-V	P-A	P-M
Penetration by **O**ther body parts	O-V	O-A	O-M
Penetration by an object, which is not a body part, (**N**on-body part, e.g., a stick)	N-V	N-A	N-M

TABLE 10.5
Classification of Sexual Penetration According to Gender of the Offender and Victim. While M-F Is Defined As Rape in Almost All Jurisdictions, Legal Situation about Other Combinations Vary from Jurisdiction to Jurisdiction

Victim →	Male	Female
Offender is **M**ale	M-M	M-F
Offender is **F**emale	F-M	F-F

Similarly a classification of sexual penetrations according to gender is depicted in the Table 10.5. If the female is the offender, she can only penetrate with an artificial penis, a body part, such as a digit, or by a non-body part such as a stick.

In more traditional jurisdictions, only the M-F part (i.e., when offender is male and the victim is female) is considered rape. All the others fall under other categories mentioned above. In jurisdictions which have been sensitive to such issues, all 4 categories are now considered as rape. A reference to rape laws according to countries (please see below) will clarify these concepts further.

Is Emission Necessary to Constitute an Offense of Rape?

The question whether emission is necessary to constitute an offense of rape is almost settled now. Virtually every jurisdiction (even more traditional ones) now considers that emission is *not necessary* to constitute an offense of rape. What is necessary is *penetration*. However, the very pertinent question here is "would a partial penetration of penis suffice to constitute an offense of rape?" And if yes, how much penetration is sufficient?

The earliest judgment that aimed to solve this question came in 1781. In the English case, *R. v. Hill* (1781) 1 East P.C. 434, it was decided that minimal penetration of the vagina or anus would suffice to constitute an offense of rape. Later a number of other judgments corroborated this view (*R. v. Reekspear* [1832] 1 Mood C.C. 342; *R. v. Allen* [1839] 9 C. & P. 31; *R. v. Nicholls* [1847] 2 Cox C.C. 182; *R. v. M'Rue* [1938] 8 C. & P. 641). In *R. v. Lines* (1844) 1 C. & K. 393, it was held that it was sufficient to constitute an offense of rape, if any part of the defendant's penis entered within the labia of the pudendum of the girl. In other words, it was not even necessary for the penis to enter the vagina. Thus virtually a touching of the penis with the vulva would legally constitute rape, although this might almost be impossible to prove medically.

Since a minimal penetration of vagina by penis is sufficient to constitute the offense of rape, it is not necessary that the hymen be torn or ruptured. Several court decisions have confirmed that if a woman is found to be *virgo intacta* upon medical examination, she may still be a genuine victim of rape (*R. v. Hughes* [1841] 2 Mood 190; *R. v. Killride* [1981] 23 Cr. App. R. 12).

Rape Shield Laws

Rape shield laws are meant to protect rape victims from public scrutiny by prohibiting the media from broadcasting or publishing their names and protect them in court by preventing their previous sexual histories from being revealed.

Age of Consent

Another major legal issue in cases of alleged rape and sexual assault is the issue of the age of the girl. If the age of the girl is below a certain minimum, set by the statute of that country, it is called a statutory rape. This statutory minimum age is commonly known as the "age of consent."

The age of consent is the age at which a young person is *legally* able to understand the nature of the sexual act and agree to it. In most countries, until a person reaches this age it is illegal for somebody to have sex with that person, irrespective of the actual *will* of the person. Sometimes the law is slightly different when the partners are of a similar age, but there is usually still a minimum age below which sex is always illegal. Age of consent laws are intended to protect young people from being sexually exploited by adults. These laws ensure that the young partner (usually the female) has reached sufficient emotional development to deal with sexual intimacies and their consequences and also that she has grown enough to feel confident to say "no" if she does not want to enter into a sexual relationship.

The ages of consent differ based on each country's past history, culture, religion, social mores and codes and sexual freedom (please see Appendix A: Ages of consent for sexual intercourse in different countries). Graupner[104] gave comprehensive tables on ages of consent, but laws have modified since his paper, and in this book an attempt has been made to update and add laws of as many countries as was possible by taking information from many other authentic sources.[105,106]

Mostly the age of consent is sixteen years but there are variations on either side as can be seen in the accompanying table. It is, however, easy to see that the age of consent can neither be set too low (say, nine years), so as to compromise the need of young persons and adolescents to protection from unwanted sex, nor too high (say, twenty-one years), so as to make it appear more like a threat for the sexual self-determination of youngsters. A reasonable and proper balance has to be met.

HIV/STDs and Rape

In many jurisdictions, it is a criminal offense to pass HIV or other sexual transmitted infections through rape. In many others, HIV transmission especially through rape is not addressed properly through legislation, and the offender can only be booked for passing the infection in a more general sense. In India, for example, the offender can only be booked through section 270 of the Indian Penal Code (IPC),[107] a general law *not* specifically aimed at rapists:

> ***Section 270. Malignant act likely to spread infection of disease dangerous to life***
> Whoever malignantly does any act which is, and which he knows or has reason to believe to be, likely to spread the infection of any disease dangerous to life, shall be punished with imprisonment of either description for a term which may extend to two years, or with fine, or with both.

The Supreme Court of India has suggested that the law must be amended to address the issue of HIV spread through rape.[108]

Requiring Blood for HIV Testing Does Not Violate a Rapist's Fourth Amendment Rights

In the United States, The Violence Against Women Act of 1994 (VAWA) makes a blood test of the offender permissible as soon as the accused is charged with sexual assault that poses a risk of HIV transmission, probable cause exists that the accused committed the assault, the victim requests the test, and the test would provide information necessary for the victim's health. In *United States v. Ward,* 131 F.3d 335, 337 (3d Cir. 1997), the U.S. Court of Appeals for the Third Circuit has held that requiring a criminal defendant to provide a blood sample to test for HIV antibodies does not violate the defendant's Fourth Amendment rights.[109] David J. Ward, an interstate truck driver, had kidnapped a 24-year old woman on the evening of December 4, 1995, while she was working at a Marriott Courtyard Hotel in New Jersey. During the next three days, Ward sexually assaulted her on numerous occasions. On December 7, in Indianapolis, she managed to escape after she was left alone in the defendant-appellant's truck.

On January 30, 1996, a grand jury in the United States District Court for the District of New Jersey indicted Ward for violating 18 U.S.C. §1201, a federal kidnapping statute that addresses the sexual assault of a victim. Ward eventually pled guilty to this charge. The court then ordered Ward to submit to a blood test to determine the presence of human immunodeficiency virus (HIV), which causes AIDS. Ward claimed that, regardless of whether the court order resulted from VAWA or a court's inherent power, a compelled HIV test violated his Fourth Amendment protection against unreasonable searches and seizures. The U.S. Court of Appeals for the Third Circuit held that it does not.

Disclosure of HIV Status of a Rapist Does Not Prejudice a Jury

An Ohio appeals court upheld the conviction of an HIV-positive man convicted of kidnapping and raping a 17-year old mentally retarded boy. The defendant had appealed his conviction, claiming that disclosure of his HIV status prejudiced the jury against him. The appeals court found that the statements about his HIV infection were relevant testimony.[110]

Prisoner's HIV Status

Oklahoma Senate Bill 886 requires prison inmates to undergo HIV and hepatitis B testing if they expose other people to body fluids.[111] The bill requires the Department of Corrections to provide the results to the person who was potentially exposed. If the prison already knows that the inmate is HIV-positive, the testing requirement is waived. Prompted by a case involving a Tulsa County rape victim, a second bill, House Bill 2570, was passed to expedite HIV testing of defendants charged with sex offenses.

Miscellaneous Legal Aspects

Among the several defenses against an allegation of rape is the presence of Peyronie's disease. However, this defense may not work in all cases. Mohanty[112] describes two cases where the defendants charged with rape pleaded not guilty on the ground of the presence of Peyronie's disease. They argued that they could not have committed the acts because of the severe bending of the penis. While one was acquitted, the other was found guilty and imprisoned for 6 years for the offense of rape. The reason was the difference in location where the fibrosis had occurred. While in the defendant who was acquitted, the fibrosis was present ventrally, producing a curvature downwards and making it impossible for him to penetrate vagina, in the defendant who was convicted, the fibrosis was present dorsally producing a curvature upwards, which facilitated penile penetration.

Instances of rape understandably increase during times of war or civil conflict. It has been noted that military leaders have actually tolerated and even encouraged rape, either as a reward for soldiers or as part of a campaign of terror. This issue was addressed in The Fourth Geneva Convention (or GCIV) of 1949, where it was resolved (through Article 27) that "women shall be especially protected against any attack on their honor, in particular against rape, enforced prostitution, or any form of indecent assault." Additionally, various human rights organizations have sought to hold those who rape women during wartime accountable.

RAPE LAWS IN VARIOUS COUNTRIES

Australia

Western Australia

The Criminal Code of Western Australia does not make a mention of *rape*. Instead it talks of "sexual penetration without consent." According to Section 325 of the Criminal Code of Western Australia:

> ***325. Sexual penetration without consent***
> A person who sexually penetrates another person without the consent of that person is guilty of a crime and is liable to imprisonment for 14 years.[113]

Section 326 defines "Aggravated sexual penetration without consent":

> A person who sexually penetrates another person without the consent of that person in circumstances of aggravation is guilty of a crime and liable to imprisonment for 20 years.[114]

South Australia

Section 5 of the Criminal Law Consolidation Act 1935 of South Australia provides a very broad definition of sexual intercourse. According to section 5:

> "sexual intercourse" includes any activity (whether of a heterosexual or homosexual nature) consisting of or involving—
> (a) penetration of the labia majora or anus of a person by any part of the body of another person or by any object; or
> (b) fellatio; or
> (c) cunnilingus

Rape is defined in the same statute under section 48:

A person who has sexual intercourse with another person without the consent of that other person—
(a) knowing that that other person does not consent to sexual intercourse with him; or
(b) being recklessly indifferent as to whether that other person consents to sexual intercourse with him, shall (whether or not physical resistance is offered by that other person) be guilty of rape and liable to be imprisoned for life.

This is a typical example of gender neural law of rape. If read with the definition of sexual intercourse, it becomes amply clear that in South Australia, it is legally possible for a person of either sex to rape another person of either sex. In many jurisdictions, only a male can rape a female.

Queensland

Queensland criminal law is governed by the Criminal Code 1899 (for details please see chapter on exhibitionism). Although most sexual offenses are defined in chapter 22, entitled "Offenses against morality," rape is defined under a separate chapter (chapter 32, entitled "Rape and sexual assaults"). It includes sections 347 through 352. Rape is defined under section 349:

(1) Any person who rapes another person is guilty of a crime.
Maximum penalty—life imprisonment.
(2) A person rapes another person if—
(a) the person has carnal knowledge with or of the other person without the other person's consent; or
(b) the person penetrates the vulva, vagina or anus of the other person to any extent with a thing or a part of the person's body that is not a penis without the other person's consent; or
(c) the person penetrates the mouth of the other person to any extent with the person's penis without the other person's consent.
(3) For this section, a child under the age of 12 years is incapable of giving consent.

Carnal knowledge as mentioned in the above section is defined in section 6 of the same code. It states:

(1) If carnal knowledge is used in defining an offense, the offense, so far as regards that element of it, is complete on penetration to any extent.
(2) Carnal knowledge includes sodomy.

AUSTRIA

Rape is a criminal offense, governed by Austrian Penal Code of 1974. Section 201 of Austrian Penal Code defines rape:[115]

1. Whoever coerces a person by serious force directed against this person or by the threat of immediate danger for life and limb to perform or to endure sexual intercourse or a sexual act equated to sexual intercourse shall be punished by imprisonment from one to ten years. Anesthesia has to be regarded as serious force.

Interestingly, sexual intercourse under anesthesia is regarded as serious force. Very few codes make a mention of anesthesia in their rape law. Sexual coercion is defined in section 202:

1. Whoever coerces a person except in the cases referred to in section §201 by force or by dangerous threat to perform or to endure a sexual act shall be punished by imprisonment up to 3 years.

CANADA

There was a general wave of rape law reform during the 1970s and 80s, and many jurisdictions were swept by it. Canada was one of these countries. In 1983, the offenses of rape, attempted rape, and indecent assault (male and female) were replaced by a tripartite classification of sexual assault. The new classification defined 3 levels of seriousness: (i) sexual assault (S. 271); (ii) sexual assault with a weapon, threats to a third party or causing bodily harm (S. 272); and (iii) aggravated sexual assault (S. 273). Some commentators have compared them to 3 increasing levels of sexual assault and have designated them as Sexual Assault I, II, and III respectively. The maximum penalties for the 3 levels are: 10 years, 14 years, and life imprisonment (the minimum penalty is not specified for the offense of S. 271, while for S. 272 and S. 273 it is 4 years).[116]

The sexual assault offenses correspond in structure to the 3 assault offenses created at the same time (assault [S. 266], assault with a weapon or causing bodily harm [S. 267] and aggravated assault [S. 268]). The maximum penalties for the 3 assault offenses are, 5, 10, and 14 years, respectively (no minimum punishment has been prescribed for any of these three offenses).

Significantly, the new offenses of sexual assault were placed in the Offenses Against the Persons Section of the Canadian Criminal Code, while prior to 1983, equivalent offenses were located in the Sexual Offenses section. This signified that these crimes came to be viewed more as assaultive in nature than sexual. Among the other significant changes were the removal of spousal immunity (S. 278). Previously a man could not be charged for rape of his legally wedded wife; now he could be. The law also became gender neutral in the sense that men and women were afforded the same legal protection regarding sexual assault. Some other inconsistencies and idiosyncrasies were removed. For instance, earlier indecent assault carried a higher maximum penalty if the victim was a male. Henceforth, the law treated assaults against male and female victims in the same way.

Sexual assault is also mentioned within the offense of assault, which is defined in section 265 of the code[117] (Table 10.6). Significantly, the code does not define the "sexual" element of a sexual assault anywhere.

In *R. v. Chase* (1987) 2 S.C.R. 293, the Supreme Court of Canada has defined this element as follows:

> Sexual assault is an assault... which is committed in circumstances of a sexual nature, such that the sexual integrity of the victim is violated. The test to be applied in determining whether the impugned conduct has the requisite sexual nature is an objective one: "Viewed in the light of all the circumstances, is the sexual or carnal context of the assault visible to a reasonable observer?"[118]

Thus, according to current law, all forms of intentional, nonconsensual touching that violate the complainant's sexual integrity constitute sexual assault. This is a much stricter law, as many cases which would now be construed as sexual assault would not have amounted to rape or even indecent assault before 1983.

Sections 271 through 273 create the offenses of sexual assault, sexual assault causing bodily harm, and aggravated sexual assault. As mentioned earlier, these offenses are unique in the sense that they are gender-neutral. Unlike most other rape statutes, in Canadian law, both the complainant and the accused can be either male or female (see Tables 10.7–10.10).

China

In the People's Republic of China, any person who rapes a woman faces a minimum sentence of 3 years up to a maximum of 10 years. A girl below 14 years cannot give legal consent for sexual intercourse. Article 236 of the Criminal Law of the People's Republic of China 119 states:

> Whoever rapes a woman by violence, coercion or any other means shall be sentenced to fixed-term imprisonment of not less than 3 years but not more than 10 years.
>
> Whoever has sexual intercourse with a girl under the age of 14 shall be deemed to have committed rape and shall be given a heavier punishment.

TABLE 10.6
Assault Including Sexual Assault As Defined in Section 265 of the Criminal Code of Canada

Assault	265. (1) A person commits an assault when (a) without the consent of another person, he applies force intentionally to that other person, directly or indirectly; (b) he attempts or threatens, by an act or a gesture, to apply force to another person, if he has, or causes that other person to believe on reasonable grounds that he has, present ability to effect his purpose; or (c) while openly wearing or carrying a weapon or an imitation thereof, he accosts or impedes another person or begs.
Application	(2) This section applies to all forms of assault, including sexual assault, sexual assault with a weapon, threats to a third party or causing bodily harm and aggravated sexual assault.
Consent	(3) For the purposes of this section, no consent is obtained where the complainant submits or does not resist by reason of (a) the application of force to the complainant or to a person other than the complainant; (b) threats or fear of the application of force to the complainant or to a person other than the complainant; (c) fraud; or (d) the exercise of authority.
Accused's belief as to consent	(4) Where an accused alleges that he believed that the complainant consented to the conduct that is the subject-matter of the charge, a judge, if satisfied that there is sufficient evidence and that, if believed by the jury, the evidence would constitute a defense, shall instruct the jury, when reviewing all the evidence relating to the determination of the honesty of the accused's belief, to consider the presence or absence of reasonable grounds for that belief.

TABLE 10.7
Sexual Assault As Defined in Section 271 of Canadian Criminal Code

271. (1) Every one who commits a sexual assault is guilty of

(a) an indictable offense and is liable to imprisonment for a term not exceeding ten years; or

(b) an offense punishable on summary conviction and liable to imprisonment for a term not exceeding eighteen months.

TABLE 10.8
Sexual Assault with a Weapon As Defined in Section 272 of Canadian Criminal Code

272. (1) Every person commits an offense who, in committing a sexual assault,

(a) carries, uses or threatens to use a weapon or an imitation of a weapon;

(b) threatens to cause bodily harm to a person other than the complainant;

(c) causes bodily harm to the complainant; or

(d) is a party to the offense with any other person.

(2) Every person who commits an offense under subsection (1) is guilty of an indictable offense and liable

(a) where a firearm is used in the commission of the offense, to imprisonment for a term not exceeding fourteen years and to a minimum punishment of imprisonment for a term of four years; and

(b) in any other case, to imprisonment for a term not exceeding fourteen years.

TABLE 10.9
Aggravated Sexual Assault As Defined in Section 273 of Canadian Criminal Code

273. (1) Every one commits an aggravated sexual assault who, in committing a sexual assault, wounds, maims, disfigures or endangers the life of the complainant.

(2) Every person who commits an aggravated sexual assault is guilty of an indictable offense and liable

(a) where a firearm is used in the commission of the offense, to imprisonment for life and to a minimum punishment of imprisonment for a term of four years; and

(b) in any other case, to imprisonment for life.

TABLE 10.10
Removing Spousal Immunity under Section 273 of Canadian Criminal Code

278. A husband or wife may be charged with an offense under section 271, 272 or 273 in respect of his or her spouse, whether or not the spouses were living together at the time the activity that forms the subject-matter of the charge occurred.

> Whoever rapes a woman or has sexual intercourse with a girl under the age of 14 shall, in any of the following circumstances, be sentenced to fixed-term imprisonment of not less than 10 years, life imprisonment or death:
>
> (1) the circumstances being flagrant;
> (2) raping a number of women or girls under the age of 14;
> (3) raping a woman before the public in a public place;
> (4) raping a woman with one or more persons in succession; or
> (5) causing serious injury or death to the victim or any other serious consequences.

India

Section 375 of the Indian Penal Code (IPC)[107] defines rape. It states:

> **Rape—**A man is said to commit "rape" who, except in the case hereinafter excepted, has sexual intercourse with a woman under circumstances falling under any of the six following descriptions: —
> **Firstly—**Against her will.
> **Secondly—**Without her consent.
> **Thirdly—**With her consent, when her consent has been obtained by putting her or any person in whom she is interested in fear of death or of hurt.
> **Fourthly—**With her consent, when the man knows that he is not her husband, and that her consent is given because she believes that he is another man to whom she is or believes herself to be lawfully married.
> **Fifthly—**With her consent, when, at the time of giving such consent, by reason of unsoundness of mind or intoxication or the administration by him personally or through another of any stupefying or unwholesome substance, she is unable to understand the nature and consequences of that to which she gives consent.
> **Sixthly—**With or without her consent, when she is under 16 years of age.

Explanation—Penetration is sufficient to constitute the sexual intercourse necessary to the offense of rape.

Exception—Sexual intercourse by a man with his own wife, the wife not being under fifteen years of age, is not rape.

STATE AMENDMENT: Manipur

(a) in clause sixthly, for the word "sixteen" substitute the word "fourteen"; and
(b) in the Exception, for- the word "fifteen" substitute the word "thirteen".

A few interesting points need be noted here. Firstly, Indian law is one of the very few statutes in the world which makes a subtle difference between will and consent. Absence of either constitutes rape. While will is more a psychological construct, consent is more legal in nature. In most cases, there will be absence of both, but there can be absence of either in the presence of the other. A person accomplishing a completely consensual sexual intercourse with a woman in exchange for, say, a piece of bread, shelter, or security; money for the treatment of, say, her ailing child; or maybe to give her husband a raise in his company—that person would be accomplishing consenual sexual intercourse with her legal consent, but against her will, and would thus be guilty of rape. On the other hand, a person having sexual intercourse with a woman during, say, her somnambulistic activity, or under some kind of hypnotism, would be accomplishing it perhaps with her will, but without her legal consent (which should be free and fair and without the use of force or fraud).

Other salient features to be noted are that only a male can rape a female and not vice-versa; a female can not rape a female; a male can not be raped, by either a male or a female; a husband can legally rape his wife, *only when she is below 15 years of age and not otherwise,* even if force is used; and in one Indian state, Manipur, the legal age of consent is different.

The "marriage exception" of rape is based on the rather dubious notion that getting married provides *ex ante* consent for the husband to engage in sexual relations at will. This exception, while being deleted from the statute books the world over, continues to remain on Indian statute books.

The punishment of rape is defined in section 376 of the same statute.

(1) Whoever, except in the cases provided for by subsection (2), commits rape shall be punished with imprisonment of either description for a term which shall not be less than seven years but which may be for life or for a term which may extend to ten years and shall also be liable to fine unless the women raped is his own wife and is not under twelve years of age, in which cases, he shall be punished with imprisonment of either description for a term which may extend to two years or with fine or with both:

Provided that the court may, for adequate and special reasons to be mentioned in the judgment, impose a sentence of imprisonment for a term of less than seven years.

(2) Whoever,—
- (a) being a police officer commits rape—
  - (i) within the limits of the police station to which he is appointed; or
  - (ii) in the premises of any station house whether or not situated in the police station to which he is appointed; or
  - (iii) on a woman in his custody or in the custody of a police officer subordinate to him; or
- (b) being, a public servant, takes advantage of his official position and commits rape on a woman in his custody as such public servant or in the custody of a public servant subordinate to him; or
- (c) being on the management or on the staff of a jail, remand home or other place of custody established by or under any law for the time being in force or of a woman's or children's institution takes advantage of his official position and commits rape on any inmate of such jail, remand home, place or institution; or

(d) being, on the management or on the staff of a hospital, takes advantage of his official position and commits rape on a woman in that hospital; or
(e) commits rape on a woman knowing her to be pregnant; or
(f) commits rape on a woman when she is under twelve years of age; or
(g) commits gang rape,
shall be punished with rigorous imprisonment for a term which shall not be less than ten years but which may be for life and shall also be liable to fine:
Provided that the court may, for adequate and special reasons to be mentioned in the judgment, impose a sentence of imprisonment of either description for a term of less than ten years.

Explanation 1—Where a woman is raped by one or more in a group of persons acting in furtherance of their common intention, each of the persons shall be deemed to have committed gang rape within the meaning of this sub-section.
Explanation 2—"Women's or children's institution" means an institution, whether called an orphanage or a home for neglected woman or children or a widows' home or by any other name, which is established and maintained for the reception and care of woman or children.
Explanation 3—"Hospital" means the precincts of the hospital and includes the precincts of any institution for the reception and treatment of persons during convalescence or of persons requiring, medical attention or rehabilitation.

A. Intercourse by a man with his wife during separation
Whoever has sexual intercourse with his own wife, who is living separately from him under a decree of separation or under any custom or usage without her consent shall be punished with imprisonment of either description for a term which may extend to two years and shall also be liable to fine.

B. Intercourse by public servant with woman in his custody
Whoever, being a public servant, takes advantage of his official position and induces or seduces, any woman, who is in his custody as such public servant or in the custody of a public servant subordinate to him, to have sexual intercourse with him, such sexual intercourse not amounting to the offense of rape, shall be punished with imprisonment of either description for a term which may extend to five years and shall also be liable to fine.
C. Intercourse by superintendent of jail, remand home, etc.
Whoever, being the superintendent or manager of a jail, remand home or other place of custody established by or under any law for the time being in force or of a woman's or children's institution takes advantage of his official position and induces or seduces any female inmate of such jail, remand home, place or institution to have sexual intercourse with him, such sexual intercourse not amounting to the offense of rape, shall be punished with imprisonment of either description for a term which may extend to five years and shall also be liable to fine.

Explanation 1—"Superintendent" in relation to jail, remand home or other place of custody or a women's or children's institution includes a person holding any other office in such jail, remand home, place or institution by virtue of which he can exercise any authority or control over its inmates.
Explanation 2—The expression "women's or children's institution" shall have the same meaning as in Explanation 2 to sub-section (2) of section 376.]

D. Intercourse by any member of the management or staff of a hospital with any woman in that hospital

Whoever, being on the management of a hospital or on the staff of a hospital takes advantage of his position and has sexual intercourse with any woman in that hospital, such sexual intercourse not amounting to the offense of rape, shall be punished with imprisonment of either description for a term which may extend to five years and shall also be liable to fine.

Explanation—The expression "hospital" shall have the same meaning as in Explanation 3 to sub-section (2) of section 376.

In India, rape is considered such a serious offense that the minimum sentence is 7 years. There are very few statutes in Indian law in which a *minimum sentence* has been prescribed, i.e., it is difficult, if not impossible, for a judge to award a sentence of less than 7 years. If the judge wants to award a sentence of less than 7 years to the accused, he has to write in his judgment, why a lesser award is being given.

Although a husband can be charged with raping his own wife under 15 years of age, the sentence awarded to him is greatly reduced. Instead of having a *minimum sentence* for the husband, the law provides for a *maximum sentence* of only 2 years. This effectively means that if the judge so desires, the accused can get away with a sentence of just 1 day. In fact even this is not necessary as the law reads that "...[the husband] shall be punished with imprisonment of either description for a term which may extend to 2 years *or* with fine *or* with both." The existence of the word *or* allows the judge to let the husband off with just a fine, and absolutely no imprisonment.

This is done because marriage is considered a great and sacred institution in India, and although a husband may have raped his own underage wife, she is legally wed to him, and he cannot be punished too strongly for having sexual intercourse with her, however unjustified.

It has been noted earlier that in Indian law, only a female can be raped. Interestingly even a female can be raped *only* when her vagina is penetrated, *and only by the penis of a male.* Anal or oral penetration by penis, or vaginal penetration by some other organ such as a finger is not be covered by rape. These forms, and in fact all forms of nonvaginal sexual penetrations and many other unusual sexual practices such as bestiality are covered by Section 377 of the IPC. This section has been described in detail in the chapter on bestiality.

In cases where a male organ was not used to penetrate the vagina, Section 354 (assault or criminal force to woman with intent to outrage her modesty)* has been invoked against the perpetrator. In *State of Punjab v. Major Singh,* AIR 1967 SC 63, where the accused had caused injuries to the vagina of a seven-and-a-half month old child by fingering, the accused could not be convicted under Section 376, but was convicted under section 354. This section is more commonly used against sexual harassment (please see chapter on sexual harassment).

Ireland

Ireland is one of the very few jurisdictions which have separate acts entirely devoted to the offense of rape. In Ireland, the offense of rape is defined and punished under the Criminal Law (Rape) Act, 1981[120] and the Criminal Law (Rape) (Amendment) Act, 1990.[121] The 1990 Act aimed to overcome the shortcomings of the earlier 1981 Act. Among the improvements it made were: (i) a gender neutral, broader definition of rape; (ii) including sexual assault other than penile penetration, and other than vaginally; (iii) including oral and anal sex, and the use of objects to violate the vagina; (iv)

* For full statement of section 354 IPC, please see chapter on sexual harassment.

abolition of marital exemption in relation to rape; (v) the removal of the presumption of incapacity in relation to boys under 14 years, and the removal of a minimum age requirement; (vi) the inadmissibility of past sexual history of the victim as being irrelevant to a rape case; (vii) the failure or omission by the victim to offer resistance to the act does not of itself constitute consent to the act; (viii) the separate legal representation of complainants with state funding; (ix) the holding of trials in camera (without the public); (x) the anonymity of the complainant always being assured; (xi) many offenses at that time being defined as simply indecent assault to come within the board definition of rape; (xii) juries to comprise a balance of the sexes, six women and six men; (xiii) rape cases never to be heard at district court level; and (xiv) finally, the warning no longer to be given automatically to the jury about the danger of convicting the accused on uncorroborated evidence; the judge would determine on a case by case basis whether to include the warning or not.[122]

Section 2 of the Criminal Law (Rape) Act, 1981, defined rape as following:[123]

(1) A man commits rape if—
  (a) he has unlawful sexual intercourse with a woman who at the time of the intercourse does not consent to it, and
  (b) at that time he knows that she does not consent to the intercourse or he is reckless as to whether she does or does not consent to it, and references to rape in this Act and any other enactment shall be construed accordingly.

(2) It is hereby declared that if at a trial for a rape offense the jury has to consider whether a man believed that a woman was consenting to sexual intercourse, the presence or absence of reasonable grounds for such a belief is a matter to which the jury is to have regard, in conjunction with any other relevant matters, in considering whether he so believed.

The Criminal Law (Rape) (Amendment) Act, 1990, aimed to improve upon this definition by adding a section entitled sexual assault (section 2), which made the offense of sexual assault gender neutral, and by introducing a special section (section 4) called *Rape under section 4*. Section 2 of the act, 1990 states as follows:[124]

Sexual assault.

2. —(1) The offense of indecent assault upon any male person and the offense of indecent assault upon any female person shall be known as sexual assault.

(2) A person guilty of sexual assault shall be liable on conviction on indictment to imprisonment for a term not exceeding 5 years.

(3) Sexual assault shall be a felony.

Section 4 of The Criminal Law (Rape) (Amendment) Act, 1990, which aims to classify non-vaginal, nonpenile sexual penetration as rape, states as follows:[125]

(1) In this Act "rape under section 4" means a sexual assault that includes—
  (a) penetration (however slight) of the anus or mouth by the penis, or
  (b) penetration (however slight) of the vagina by any object held or manipulated by another person.

(2) A person guilty of rape under section 4 shall be liable on conviction on indictment to imprisonment for life.

(3) Rape under section 4 shall be a felony.

Besides these major improvements, the 1990 Act aimed to rectify several shortcomings of the earlier act as mentioned earlier.

NAMIBIA

Namibia is one of the few countries which has an entire act addressed to the offense of rape. Entitled *Combating of Rape Act, 2000,* it has 19 sections.[126] The definitions are influenced by the latest statutes from around the world. For instance, the definition of sexual act (section 1) is truly very broad and is not limited to insertion of penis into the vagina. Section 1 (among other things) states:

> "sexual act" means—
> (a) the insertion (to even the slightest degree) of the penis of a person into the vagina or anus or mouth of another person; or
> (b) the insertion of any other part of the body of a person or of any part of the body of an animal or of any object into the vagina or anus of another person, except where such insertion of any part of the body (other than the penis) of a person or of any object into the vagina or anus of another person is, consistent with sound medical practices; carried out for proper medical purposes; or
> (c) cunnilingus or any other form of genital stimulation;

Rape is defined in section 2 of this act:

> (1) Any person (in this Act referred to as a perpetrator) who intentionally under coercive circumstances—
> (a) commits or continues to commit a sexual act with another person; or
> (b) causes another person to commit a sexual act with the perpetrator or with a third person, shall be guilty of the offense of rape;

A number of situations can be construed as "coercive circumstances" mentioned above. These include, but are not limited to, the application of physical force to the complainant, threats (whether verbally or through conduct) of the application of physical force to the complainant, circumstances where the complainant is under the age of 14 years and the perpetrator is more than 3 years older than the complainant, circumstances where the complainant is unlawfully detained, circumstances where the complainant is affected by physical disability, helplessness, mental incapacity or other inability (whether permanent or temporary), intoxicating liquor, any other drug or other substance which mentally incapacitates the complainant or sleep. The punishment varies from 5 to 45 years depending upon the circumstances of the case.

Section 4 of the act states that there will be no presumption or rule of law to the effect that a boy under the age of fourteen years is incapable of sexual intercourse.

NEW ZEALAND

Section 2 of the Crimes Act 1961 of New Zealand defines sexual connection as follows:[127]

> (a) connection effected by the introduction into the genitalia or anus of one person, otherwise than for genuine medical purposes, of
> (i) a part of the body of another person; or
> (ii) an object held or manipulated by another person; or
> (b) connection between the mouth or tongue of one person and a part of another person's genitalia or anus; or
> (c) the continuation of connection of a kind described in paragraph (a) or paragraph (b)

Thus introduction of, a finger, into the anus of another person, or even holding another's genitalia comes within the range of sexual connection.

Most sexual crimes in New Zealand law fall under Part 7 (entitled *Crimes against religion, morality, and public welfare* in Sections 123 through 150) of the Crimes Act 1961. Rape and unlawful sexual connection have been grouped together under the heading *sexual violation*, which is defined in section 128. It states:[128]

(1) Sexual violation is the act of a person who—
 (a) rapes another person; or
 (b) has unlawful sexual connection with another person.
(2) Person A rapes person B if person A has sexual connection with person B, effected by the penetration of person B's genitalia by person A's penis,—
 (a) without person B's consent to the connection; and
 (b) without believing on reasonable grounds that person B consents to the connection.
(3) Person A has unlawful sexual connection with person B if person A has sexual connection with person B—
 (a) without person B's consent to the connection; and
 (b) without believing on reasonable grounds that person B consents to the connection.
(4) One person may be convicted of the sexual violation of another person at a time when they were married to each other.

Significantly, under New Zealand law the husband does not have marital immunity against the rape of his own wife.

Norway

Chapter 19 (Sections 191 through 214) of the General Civil Penal Code of Norway[129] defines sexual offenses. Rape is defined in section 192 as follows:

Any person who
 (a) engages in sexual activity by means of violence or threats, or
 (b) engages in sexual activity with any person who is unconscious or incapable for any other reason of resisting the act, or
 (c) by means of violence or threats compels any person to engage in sexual activity with another person, or to carry out similar acts with himself or herself, shall be guilty of rape and liable to imprisonment for a term not exceeding 10 years. In deciding whether the offender made use of violence or threats or whether the aggrieved person was incapable of resisting the act, importance shall be attached to whether the aggrieved person was under 14 years of age.

A penalty of imprisonment for not less than 2 years shall be imposed if
 (a) the said activity was sexual intercourse, or
 (b) the offender has rendered a person in such a state as is specified in the first paragraph (b) in order to engage in sexual activity.

Imprisonment for a term not exceeding 21 years may be imposed if
 (a) the rape has been committed by two or more persons jointly,
 (b) the rape has been committed in a particularly painful for offensive manner,
 (c) the offender has previously been convicted and sentenced pursuant to this provision or section 195, or
 (d) as a result of the act the aggrieved person dies or sustains considerable injury to body or health. Sexually transmitted diseases and generally infectious diseases, cf. section 1-3, No. 3, cf. No. 1 of the Act relating to control of communication diseases, shall always be deemed to be serious injury to body or health pursuant to this section.

Any person who through gross negligence is guilty of rape pursuant to the first paragraph is liable to imprisonment for a term not exceeding 5 years. If such circumstances as are specified in the third paragraph subsist, the penalty shall be imprisonment for a term not exceeding 8 years.

Section 195 refers to sexual activity with a child who is under 14 years of age. This section is dealt with in the chapter on pedophilia.

Russia

Article 131 of the Criminal Code of the Russian Federation[130] defines rape as:

1. Rape, that is sexual relations with the use of violence or with the threat of its use against a victim or other persons, or in taking advantage of the victim's helpless condition, shall be punishable by deprivation of liberty for a term of 3 to 6 years.
2. Rape:
   a) committed repeatedly or by a person who has earlier committed violent sexual actions;
   b) committed by a group of persons, a group of persons under a preliminary conspiracy, or an organized group;
   c) connected with the threat of murder or the infliction of grave injury, or committed with especial cruelty towards the victim or to other persons;
   d) entailing the infection of the victim with a venereal disease;
   e) of an obvious juvenile,
   shall be punishable by deprivation of liberty for a term of 4 to 10 years.
3. Rape:
   a) entailing, by negligence, the death of the victim;
   b) entailing, by negligence, the infliction of grave injury to the victim, the infection of the victim with HIV, or other grave consequences;
   c) of a victim who obviously has not attained 14 years of age,
   shall be punishable by deprivation of liberty for a term of eight to 15 years.

Spain

According to Act 3/1989, which updated the Spanish Penal Code on June 21, 1989, a person commits the crime of rape, punishable with minor imprisonment, if he has carnal access to another person by vaginal, anal, or oral means using force or intimidation, or when the person lacks full faculties or is in an impaired condition, or when the person is under 12 years of age, despite the absence of the above circumstances.[131] Sexual aggression accomplished under the above circumstances is punished with minor imprisonment and a fine. If the aggression includes the use of objects or brutal, degrading, or harassing means, methods or instruments, the punishment is grand imprisonment. The new law also prohibits public officials from soliciting sex from a person who, independently or through her spouse, spouse-like partner, ascendant, descendant, brother, or person related in the same degree, has business involving that official. A prison official who solicits sex from a person in his custody or any relative of that person is punished with minor imprisonment.

United Kingdom

Rape is defined in section 1 of the Sexual Offenses Act 2003 of the United Kingdom.[132] Section 1 states:

(1) A person (A) commits an offense if—
   (a) he intentionally penetrates the vagina, anus or mouth of another person (B) with his penis,

(b) B does not consent to the penetration, and
(c) A does not reasonably believe that B consents.

(2) Whether a belief is reasonable is to be determined having regard to all the circumstances, including any steps A has taken to ascertain whether B consents.
(3) Sections 75 and 76 apply to an offense under this section.
(4) A person guilty of an offense under this section is liable, on conviction on *indictment, to imprisonment for life.*

Interestingly, under the law of the United Kingdom it is possible to rape a male. A female cannot rape either a male or a female.

United States

Each US state has different laws regarding sexual assault and rape. While it would be useful to refer to the criminal codes of each state to know the details of rape law prevalent there, it might be pertinent to have a detailed look at the relevant laws in some representative states.

Alabama

Rape is defined in Title 13A (Criminal Code), chapter 6 (offenses involving danger to the person) of the Alabama Code. The following general definitions are relevant.[133]

(1) SEXUAL INTERCOURSE. Such term has its ordinary meaning and occurs upon any penetration, however slight; emission is not required.
(2) DEVIATE SEXUAL INTERCOURSE. Any act of sexual gratification between persons not married to each other involving the sex organs of one person and the mouth or anus of another.
(3) SEXUAL CONTACT. Any touching of the sexual or other intimate parts of a person not married to the actor, done for the purpose of gratifying the sexual desire of either party.
(4) FEMALE. Any female person.
(5) MENTALLY DEFECTIVE. Such term means that a person suffers from a mental disease or defect which renders him incapable of appraising the nature of his conduct.
(6) MENTALLY INCAPACITATED. Such term means that a person is rendered temporarily incapable of appraising or controlling his conduct owing to the influence of a narcotic or intoxicating substance administered to him without his consent, or to any other incapacitating act committed upon him without his consent.
(7) PHYSICALLY HELPLESS. Such term means that a person is unconscious or for any other reason is physically unable to communicate unwillingness to an act.
(8) FORCIBLE COMPULSION. Physical force that overcomes earnest resistance or a threat, express or implied, that places a person in fear of immediate death or serious physical injury to himself or another person.

Alabama Code defines rape in the first degree[134] and rape in the second degree.[135] Rape in the first degree is a class A felony and is a *more* serious crime than rape in the second degree.

Rape in the first degree.

(a) A person commits the crime of rape in the first degree if:
  (1) He or she engages in sexual intercourse with a member of the opposite sex by forcible compulsion; or
  (2) He or she engages in sexual intercourse with a member of the opposite sex who is incapable of consent by reason of being physically helpless or mentally incapacitated; or

(3) He or she, being 16 years or older, engages in sexual intercourse with a member of the opposite sex who is less than 12 years old.

(b) Rape in the first degree is a class A felony.

Rape in the second degree (a less serious crime) is defined as below:

Rape in the second degree.

(a) A person commits the crime of rape in the second degree if:

(1) Being 16 years old or older, he or she engages in sexual intercourse with a member of the opposite sex less than 16 and more than 12 years old; provided, however, the actor is at least 2 years older than the member of the opposite sex.

(2) He or she engages in sexual intercourse with a member of the opposite sex who is incapable of consent by reason of being mentally defective.

(b) Rape in the second degree is a class B felony.

For a class A felony, the sentence is for life or for more than 10 years, but less than 99 years, and for a class B felony, for more than 2 years but less than 20 years (imprisonment includes hard labor).[136] Fines for a class A felony are up to $60,000, and for a class B felony up to $30,000.[137]

Two additional crimes listed in Alabama Code related to rape are of interest. These are sexual misconduct[138] and sexual torture.[139] If a female engages in sexual intercourse with a male without his consent, it is *not* classified as rape, but as sexual misconduct. A few other acts also qualify under this heading.

Sexual misconduct.

(a) A person commits the crime of sexual misconduct if:

(1) Being a male, he engages in sexual intercourse with a female without her consent, under circumstances other than those covered by Sections 13A-6-61 and 13A-6-62; or with her consent where consent was obtained by the use of any fraud or artifice; or

(2) Being a female, she engages in sexual intercourse with a male without his consent; or

(3) He or she engages in deviate sexual intercourse with another person under circumstances other than those covered by Sections 13A-6-63 and 13A-6-64. Consent is no defense to a prosecution under this subdivision.

(b) Sexual misconduct is a class A misdemeanor.[138]

The sentence for a class A misdemeanor is imprisonment up to 1 year[140] and the fine is up to $6,000.[141] Thus if a male engages in sexual intercourse with a female without her consent, he faces a much stiffer sentence than a female would face if she engaged in sexual intercourse with a male without his consent.

Sexual torture.

(a) A person commits the crime of sexual torture:

(1) By penetrating the vagina or anus or mouth of another person with an inanimate object by forcible compulsion with the intent to sexually torture or to sexually abuse.

(2) By penetrating the vagina or anus or mouth of a person who is incapable of consent by reason of physical helplessness or mental incapacity with an inanimate object, with the intent to sexually torture or to sexually abuse.

(3) By penetrating the vagina or anus or mouth of a person who is less than 12 years old with an inanimate object, by a person who is 16 years old or older with the intent to sexually torture or to sexually abuse.

(b) The crime of sexual torture is a class A felony.[139]

Alaska

The word *rape* does not appear in Alaska law. Instead what is normally understood as rape appears as "sexual assault in the first degree." Section 11.41.410 of Alaska code defines it as follows:[142]

(a) An offender commits the crime of sexual assault in the first degree if
 (1) the offender engages in sexual penetration with another person without consent of that person;
 (2) the offender attempts to engage in sexual penetration with another person without consent of that person and causes serious physical injury to that person;
 (3) the offender engages in sexual penetration with another person
  (A) who the offender knows is mentally incapable; and
  (B) who is in the offender's care
   (i) by authority of law; or
   (ii) in a facility or program that is required by law to be licensed by the state; or
 (4) the offender engages in sexual penetration with a person who the offender knows is unaware that a sexual act is being committed and
  (A) the offender is a health care worker; and
  (B) the offense takes place during the course of professional treatment of the victim.
(b) Sexual assault in the first degree is an unclassified felony and is punishable as provided in AS 12.55.

The most interesting part of this statute is clause (4), which makes sexual intercourse engaged in as a fraudulent medical treatment an offense.

Arkansas

Section 5-14-101 of the Code of Arkansas[143] gives some important definitions, many of which are significant with respect to rape law. According to this section, "Deviate sexual activity" means any act of sexual gratification involving: (a) the penetration, however slight, of the anus or mouth of a person by the penis of another person; or (b) the penetration, however slight, of the labia majora or anus of a person by any body member or foreign instrument manipulated by another person. "Sexual contact " means any act of sexual gratification involving the touching, directly or through clothing, of the sex organs, buttocks, or anus of a person or the breast of a female; and "Sexual intercourse" means penetration, however slight, of the labia majora by a penis.

Section 5-14-03 of Arkansas law defines rape as follows:[144]

(a) A person commits rape if he or she engages in sexual intercourse or deviate sexual activity with another person:
 (1) By forcible compulsion;
 (2) Who is incapable of consent because he or she is:
  (A) Physically helpless;
  (B) Mentally defective; or
  (C) Mentally incapacitated;
 (3) (A) Who is less than fourteen (14) years of age.
  (B) It is an affirmative defense to a prosecution under subdivision (a)(3)(A) of this section that the actor was not more than three (3) years older than the victim; or
 (4) (A) Who is less than eighteen (18) years of age and the actor is the victim's:
   (i) Guardian;
   (ii) Uncle, aunt, grandparent, step-grandparent, or grandparent by adoption;
   (iii) Brother or sister of the whole or half blood or by adoption; or

(iv) Nephew, niece, or first cousin.

(B) It is an affirmative defense to a prosecution under subdivision (a)(4)(A) of this section that the actor was not more than three (3) years older than the victim.

(b) It is no defense to a prosecution under subdivisions (a)(3) or (4) of this section that the victim consented to the conduct.

(c) (1) Rape is a class Y felony.

(2) Any person who pleads guilty or nolo contendere to or is found guilty of rape involving a victim who is less than fourteen (14) years of age shall be sentenced to a minimum term of imprisonment of twenty-five (25) years.

(d) (1) A court may issue a permanent no contact order when:

(A) A defendant pleads guilty or nolo contendere; or

(B) All of the defendant's appeals have been exhausted and the defendant remains convicted.

(2) If a judicial officer has reason to believe that mental disease or defect of the defendant will or has become an issue in the case, the judicial officer shall enter such orders as are consistent with §5-2-305.

Significant points to note are that (i) Arkansas law of rape is gender neutral, i.e., it is legally possible for a person of either sex to rape another person of either sex; (ii) age of consent is 14 years, but if the offender was less than 3 years older than the victim, then it is a good defense for him; (iii) if the sexual relationship occurs within certain close relationships, then the age of consent is 18 years.

If the offender was suffering from HIV, he may also be charged for exposing the victim to the HIV virus.[145] The relevant law is Section 5-14-123 as below:

(a) A person with acquired immunodeficiency syndrome or who tests positive for the presence of human immunodeficiency virus antigen or antibodies is infectious to another person through the exchange of a body fluid during sexual intercourse and through the parenteral transfer of blood or a blood product and under these circumstances is a danger to the public.

(b) A person commits the offense of exposing another person to human immunodeficiency virus if the person knows he or she has tested positive for human immunodeficiency virus and exposes another person to human immunodeficiency virus infection through the parenteral transfer of blood or a blood product or engages in sexual penetration with another person without first having informed the other person of the presence of human immunodeficiency virus.

(c) (1) As used in this section, "sexual penetration" means sexual intercourse, cunnilingus, fellatio, anal intercourse, or any other intrusion, however slight, of any part of a person's body or of any object into a genital or anal opening of another person's body.

(2) However, emission of semen is not required.

(d) Exposing another person to human immunodeficiency virus is a class A felony.

If the offender was in a position of trust or authority with the victim, it is no defense that the victim consented to the sexual intercourse. The relevant law is as follows:[146]

5-14-124. Sexual assault in the first degree.

(a) A person commits sexual assault in the first degree if the person engages in sexual intercourse or deviate sexual activity with another person who is less than eighteen (18) years of age and is not the actor's spouse and the actor is:

(1) Employed with the Department of Correction, the Department of Community Correction, the Department of Health and Human Services, or any city or county jail or a juvenile detention facility, and the victim is in the custody of the Department of

Correction, the Department of Community Correction, the Department of Health and Human Services, any city or county jail or juvenile detention facility, or their contractors or agents;

(2) A professional under §12-12-507(b) and is in a position of trust or authority over the victim and uses the position of trust or authority to engage in sexual intercourse or deviate sexual activity; or

(3) An employee in the victim's school or school district, a temporary caretaker, or a person in a position of trust or authority over the victim.

(b) It is no defense to a prosecution under this section that the victim consented to the conduct.

(c) It is an affirmative defense to a prosecution under subdivision (a)(3) of this section that the actor was not more than three (3) years older than the victim.

(d) Sexual assault in the first degree is a class A felony.

Offenders under this section include professionals under §12-12-507(b). Several professionals holding positions of trust or authority over the victim are named, e.g., any child care worker or foster care worker, coroner, day care center worker, dentist, dental hygienist, domestic abuse advocate, domestic violence shelter employee, domestic violence shelter volunteer, employee of the Department of Health and Human Services, employee working under contract for the Division of Youth Services of the Department of Health and Human Services, foster parent, judge, law enforcement official, licensed nurse, any medical personnel who may be engaged in the admission, examination, care, or treatment of persons, mental health professional, osteopath, peace officer, physician, prosecuting attorney, resident intern, school counselor, school official, social worker, surgeon, teacher, court-appointed special advocate program staff member or volunteer, juvenile intake or probation officer, or any clergyman, which includes a minister, priest, rabbi, accredited Christian Science practitioner, or other similar functionary of a religious organization, or an individual reasonably believed to be so by the person consulting him or her.

If persons in position of trust or authority engage in sexual intercourse with subjects under their care or supervision, *even with their consent*, the act is regarded as sexual assault in the third degree (for sexual assault in the second degree and fourth degree, please see chapter on frotteurism). Section 5-14-126 states:[147]

Sexual assault in the third degree.

(a) A person commits sexual assault in the third degree if the person:

(1) Engages in sexual intercourse or deviate sexual activity with another person who is not the actor's spouse, and the actor is:

(A) Employed with the Department of Correction, Department of Community Correction, Department of Health and Human Services, or any city or county jail, and the victim is in the custody of the Department of Correction, Department of Community Correction, Department of Health and Human Services, or any city or county jail; or

(B) A professional under §12-12-507(b) or a member of the clergy and is in a position of trust or authority over the victim and uses the position of trust or authority to engage in sexual intercourse or deviate sexual activity; or

(2) (A) Being under eighteen (18) years of age, engages in sexual intercourse or deviate sexual activity with another person who is:

(i) Less than fourteen (14) years of age; and

(ii) Not the person's spouse

(B) It is an affirmative defense under this subdivision (a)(2) that the actor was not more than three (3) years older than the victim.

(b) It is no defense to a prosecution under this section that the victim consented to the conduct.

(c) Sexual assault in the third degree is a class C felony.

Louisiana

Louisiana law has an "all-inclusive" definition of rape, where both male and female can be raped by both male and female. Section 41 defines rape:

A. Rape is the act of anal, oral, or vaginal sexual intercourse with a male or female person committed without the person's lawful consent.

B. Emission is not necessary, and any sexual penetration, when the rape involves vaginal or anal intercourse, however slight, is sufficient to complete the crime.

C. For purposes of this subpart, "oral sexual intercourse" means the intentional engaging in any of the following acts with another person:

(1) The touching of the anus or genitals of the victim by the offender using the mouth or tongue of the offender.

(2) The touching of the anus or genitals of the offender by the victim using the mouth or tongue of the victim.[148]

Oral sexual intercourse without the other person's lawful consent is considered rape. Furthermore, Louisiana differentiates between simple rape, forcible rape, and aggravated rape. While for simple rape, the punishment is up to 25 years, for forcible rape the minimum sentence is 5 years and the maximum can go up to 40. For aggravated rape, the most serious of the rape offenses, the punishment is life imprisonment at hard labor without benefit of parole, probation, or suspension of sentence. Aggravated rape is defined in Section 42:

A. Aggravated rape is a rape committed upon a person sixty-five years of age or older or where the anal, oral, or vaginal sexual intercourse is deemed to be without lawful consent of the victim because it is committed under any one or more of the following circumstances:

(1) When the victim resists the act to the utmost, but whose resistance is overcome by force.

(2) When the victim is prevented from resisting the act by threats of great and immediate bodily harm, accompanied by apparent power of execution.

(3) When the victim is prevented from resisting the act because the offender is armed with a dangerous weapon.

(4) When the victim is under the age of thirteen years. Lack of knowledge of the victim's age shall not be a defense.

(5) When two or more offenders participated in the act.

(6) When the victim is prevented from resisting the act because the victim suffers from a physical or mental infirmity preventing such resistance.

B. For purposes of Paragraph (5), "participate" shall mean:

(1) Commit the act of rape.

(2) Physically assist in the commission of such act.

C. For purposes of this Section, the following words have the following meanings:

(1) "Physical infirmity" means a person who is a quadriplegic or paraplegic.

(2) "Mental infirmity" means a person with an intelligence quotient of 70 or lower.

D. (1) Whoever commits the crime of aggravated rape shall be punished by life imprisonment at hard labor without benefit of parole, probation, or suspension of sentence.

(2) However, if the victim was under the age of 13 years, as provided by Paragraph A(4) of this Section:

(a) And if the district attorney seeks a capital verdict, the offender shall be punished by death or life imprisonment at hard labor without benefit of parole, probation, or suspension of sentence, in accordance with the determination of the jury. The provisions of C.Cr.P. Art. 782 relative to cases in which punishment may be capital shall apply.

(b) And if the district attorney does not seek a capital verdict, the offender shall be punished by life imprisonment at hard labor without benefit of parole, probation, or suspension of sentence. The provisions of C.Cr.P. Art. 782 relative to cases in which punishment is necessarily confinement at hard labor shall apply.[149]

If the age of victim is below 13 years or above 65 years, it is classified as aggravated rape.

Forcible rape is defined in Section 42.1:

A. Forcible rape is rape committed when the anal, oral, or vaginal sexual intercourse is deemed to be without the lawful consent of the victim because it is committed under any one or more of the following circumstances:
 (1) When the victim is prevented from resisting the act by force or threats of physical violence under circumstances where the victim reasonably believes that such resistance would not prevent the rape.
 (2) When the victim is incapable of resisting or of understanding the nature of the act by reason of stupor or abnormal condition of the mind produced by a narcotic or anesthetic agent or other controlled dangerous substance administered by the offender and without the knowledge of the victim.

B. Whoever commits the crime of forcible rape shall be imprisoned at hard labor for not less than 5 nor more than 40 years. At least 2 years of the sentence imposed shall be without benefit of probation, parole, or suspension of sentence.[150]

Simple rape is defined in Section 43:

A. Simple rape is a rape committed when the anal, oral, or vaginal sexual intercourse is deemed to be without the lawful consent of a victim because it is committed under any one or more of the following circumstances:
 (1) When the victim is incapable of resisting or of understanding the nature of the act by reason of a stupor or abnormal condition of mind produced by an intoxicating agent or any cause and the offender knew or should have known of the victim's incapacity.
 (2) When the victim is incapable, through unsoundness of mind, whether temporary or permanent, or understanding the nature of the act and the offender knew or should have known of the victim's incapacity.
 (3) When the female victim submits under the belief that the person committing the act is her husband and such belief is intentionally induced by any artifice, pretense, or concealment practiced by the offender.

B. Whoever commits the crime of simple rape shall be imprisoned, with or without hard labor, without benefit of parole, probation, or suspension of sentence, for not more than 25 years.[151]

REFERENCES

1. Bass, A. An Investigation of Hindu Scripture. Apologetics Press [On-line]. Available from : http://www.apologeticspress.org/articles/2580.

2. Exodus 22:16-17. The Holy Bible. Authorized King James Version. Oxford University Press, New York, 1972.
3. Deuteronomy 22:23-29. The Holy Bible. Authorized King James Version. Oxford University Press, New York, 1972.
4. II Samuel 13:11-19. The Holy Bible. Authorized King James Version. Oxford University Press, New York, 1972.
5. Genesis 34:1-4. The Holy Bible. Authorized King James Version. Oxford University Press, New York, 1972.
6. Prentky, R.A., Knight, R.A., Rosenberg, R. Validation analyses on a taxonomic system for rapists: disconfirmation and reconceptualization. *Ann N Y Acad Sci.* 1988;**528**:21-40.
7. Langton, C.M., Marshall, W.L. Cognition in rapists: Theoretical patterns by typological breakdown. *Aggression and Violent Behavior.* 2001;**6**:499–518.
8. Schmid, S.L. Date rape/Acquaintance rape. In *Encyclopedia of Rape*, Smith, M.D. (ed), Greenwood Press, Westport, 2004, pages 54-6.
9. Chapko, M.K., Somsé, P, Kimball, A.M., Hawkins, R.V., Massanga, M. Predictors of rape in the Central African Republic. *Health Care Women Int.* 1999 Jan-Feb;**20(1)**:71-9.
10. Crépault, C, Couture, M. Men's erotic fantasies. *Arch Sex Behav.* 1980 Dec;**9(6)**:565-81.
11. Michael, R.P., Zumpe, D. Annual rhythms in human violence and sexual aggression in the United States and the role of temperature. *Soc Biol.* 1983 Fall;**30(3)**:263-78.
12. Neuwirth, W., Eher, R. What differentiates anal rapists from vaginal rapists? *Int J Offender Ther Comp Criminol.* 2003 Aug;**47(4)**:482-8.
13. Oliver, C.J., Beech, A.R., Fisher, D., Beckett, R. A comparison of rapists and sexual murderers on demographic and selected psychometric measures. *Int J Offender Ther Comp Criminol.* 2007 Jun;**51(3)**:298-312.
14. Saunders, E, Awad, G.A., White, G. Male adolescent sexual offenders: the offender and the offense. *Can J Psychiatry.* 1986 Aug;**31(6)**:542-9.
15. Seto, M.C., Kuban, M. Criterion-related validity of a phallometric test for paraphilic rape and sadism. *Behav Res Ther.* 1996 Feb;**34(2)**:175-83.
16. Harris, G.T., Rice, M.E., Quinsey, V.L., Chaplin, T.C. and Earls, C.M. Maximizing the discriminant validity of phallometric data. *Psychological Assessment.* 1992;**4**:502-511.
17. Lalumière, M.L., Quinsey, V.L., Harris, G.T., Rice, M.E., Trautrimas, C. Are rapists differentially aroused by coercive sex in phallometric assessments? *Ann N Y Acad Sci.* 2003 Jun;**989**:211-24.
18. Eccles, A., Marshall, W.L., Barbaree, H.E. Differentiating rapists and non-offenders using the rape index. *Behav Res Ther.* 1994 Jun;**32(5)**:539-46.
19. Earls, C.M., Proulx, J. The differentiation of francophone rapists and non-rapists using penile circumferential measures. *Med Law.* 1989;**8(3)**:287-95.
20. Quinsey, V.L., Rice, M.E. and Harris, G.T. Actuarial prediction of sexual recidivism. *Journal of Interpersonal Violence.* 1995;**10**:85-105.
21. Cal. Penal Code §266c (West 1997 & Supp. 1998).
22. Sighal, S. Preeti Jain promises to provide more proof of 16 times sex—Madhur Bhandarkar alleges Preeti did it to many others! *India Daily*, July 28, 2004. Available at http://www.indiadaily.com/editorial/07-28g-04.asp. Accessed Feb 12, 2008.
23. Falk, P.J., Rape by Fraud and Rape by Coercion. *Brooklyn Law Review.* 1998;**64(1)**:39-179.
24. O'Callaghan, A.C., Murphy, G.H. Sexual relationships in adults with intellectual disabilities: understanding the law. *J Intellect Disabil Res.* 2007 Mar;**51(Pt 3)**:197-206.
25. Kutz, I. Revisiting the lot of the first incestuous family: the biblical origins of shifting the blame on to female family members. *BMJ.* 2005 Dec 24;**331(7531)**:1507-8.
26. Quest, D.W., Horsley, J. Field-test of a date-rape drug detection device. *J Anal Toxicol.* 2007 Jul-Aug;**31(6)**:354-7.
27. Judges 19:1-30. The Holy Bible. Authorized King James Version. Oxford University Press, New York, 1972.
28. Sanday, P.R., Fraternity gang rape: Sex brotherhood, and privilege on campus. New York University Press, New York, 1990.
29. Section 376 (g) [Explanation 1]. The Indian Penal Code, (Act No. 45 of 1860) [6th October, 1860].
30. Mulhern, S. Incest: a laughing matter. *Child Abuse Negl.* 1990;**14(2)**:265-71.
31. Robertson, J.E. Rape among incarcerated men: sex, coercion and STDs. *AIDS Patient Care STDS.* 2003 Aug;17(8):423-30.

32. Struckman-Johnson, C., Struckman-Johnson, D. A comparison of sexual coercion experiences reported by men and women in prison. *J Interpers Violence*. 2006 Dec;21(12):1591-615.
33. Thompson, L., Secondary Rape. In *Encyclopedia of Rape*, Smith, M.D. (ed), Greenwood Press, Westport, 2004, pages 217-8.
34. Neumann, C.E., Serial Rape and Serial Rapists. In *Encyclopedia of Rape*, Smith, M.D. (ed), Greenwood Press, Westport, 2004, pages 221-2.
35. Burgess, A.W., Holmstrom, L.L. Rape trauma syndrome. *Am J Psychiatry*. 1974 Sep;131(9):981-6.
36. Caldwell, B.A., Redeker, N. Sleep and trauma: an overview. *Issues Ment Health Nurs*. 2005 Aug-Sep;26(7):721-38.
37. Groer, M.W., Thomas, S.P., Evans, G.W., Helton, S., Weldon, A. Inflammatory effects and immune system correlates of rape. *Violence Vict*. 2006 Dec;21(6):796-808.
38. Kahn, J.A., Huang, B., Rosenthal, S.L., Tissot, A.M., Burk, R.D. Coercive sexual experiences and subsequent human papillomavirus infection and squamous intraepithelial lesions in adolescent and young adult women. *J Adolesc Health*. 2005 May;36(5):363-71.
39. Boughn, S., Holdom, J.J. The relationship of violence and trichotillomania. J Nurs Scholarsh. 2003;35(2):165-70.
40. Koschorke, A., Tilzey, A., Welch, J. Should medical students be taught about rape? A survey of UK medical schools. *BJOG*. 2007;114:224–225.
41. Williams, L., Forster, G., Petrak, J. Rape attitudes amongst British medical students. *Med Educ*. 1999 Jan;33(1):24-7.
42. Anon. (editorial). Medical students should be taught about rape. *Lancet*. 2007;369(9569):1234.
43. Norfolk, G.A., and White, C. Teaching medical students about rape. *Lancet*.2007;369(9578): 1996-1997.
44. Jezierski, M. Sexual assault nurse examiner: a role with lifetime impact. *J Emerg Nurs*. 1992 Apr;18(2):177-9. No abstract available.
45. Ledray, L.E. Sexual assault nurse clinician: an emerging area of nursing expertise. *AWHONNS Clin Issues Perinat Womens Health Nurs*. 1993;4(2):180-90.
46. Ledray, L.E., Arndt, S. Examining the sexual assault victim: a new model for nursing care. *J Psychosoc Nurs Ment Health Serv*. 1994 Feb;32(2):7-12.
47. Aiken, M.M., Speck, P.M. Sexual assault and multiple trauma: a sexual assault nurse examiner (SANE) challenge. *J Emerg Nurs*. 1995 Oct;21(5):466-8.
48. Sheridan, D.J. The role of the battered woman specialist. *J Psychosoc Nurs Ment Health Serv*. 1993 Nov;31(11):31-7.
49. American College of Obstetricians and Gynecologists ACOG. Sexual assault. *ACOG Educ Bull*. 1997 Nov;(242):1-7.
50. Lukic, A., Sassi, M.T., Vecchiotti, C., Vetrano, G. [Alleged sexual assault. The role of the emergency department gynecologist] [Article in Italian]. *Minerva Ginecol*. 2000 Jul-Aug;52(7-8):313-20.
51. English, A. The health of adolescent girls: does the law support it? *Curr Womens Health Rep*. 2002 Dec;2(6):442-9.
52. Smugar, S.S., Spina, B.J., Merz, J.F. Informed consent for emergency contraception: variability in hospital care of rape victims. *Am J Public Health*. 2000 Sep;90(9):1372-6.
53. Sweet, D., Shutler, G.G. Analysis of salivary DNA evidence from a bite mark on a body submerged in water. *J Forensic Sci*. 1999 Sep;44(5):1069-72.
54. Slaughter, L, Brown, C.R. Colposcopy to establish physical findings in rape victims. *Am J Obstet Gynecol*. 1992 Jan;166(1 Pt 1):83-6.
55. Sommers, M.S., Fisher, B.S., Karjane, H.M. Using colposcopy in the rape exam: health care, forensic, and criminal justice issues. *J Forensic Nurs*. 2005 Spring;1(1):28-34.
56. Azzarone, M., Cittadini, E. [The value of colposcopy and colpophotography in the medico legal diagnosis of defloration.] [Paper in Italian] *Sicil Sanit*. 1962 Sep;15:615-21.
57. Slaughter, L., Brown, C.R. Cervical findings in rape victims. *Am J Obstet Gynecol*. 1991 Feb;164(2):528-9.
58. Lauber, A.A., Souma, M.L. Use of toluidine blue for documentation of traumatic intercourse. *Obstet Gynecol*. 1982 Nov;60(5):644-8.
59. McCauley, J., Guzinski, G., Welch, R., Gorman, R., Osmers, F. Toluidine blue in the corroboration of rape in the adult victim. *Am J Emerg Med*. 1987 Mar;5(2):105-8.

60. Hochmeister, M.N., Whelan, M., Borer, U.V., Gehrig, C., Binda, S., Berzlanovich, A., Rauch, E., Dirnhofer, R. Effects of toluidine blue and destaining reagents used in sexual assault examinations on the ability to obtain DNA profiles from postcoital vaginal swabs. *J Forensic Sci.* 1997 Mar;42(2):316-9.
61. Jones, J.S., Dunnuck, C., Rossman, L., Wynn, B.N., Nelson-Horan, C. Significance of toluidine blue positive findings after speculum examination for sexual assault. *Am J Emerg Med.* 2004 May;22(3):201-3.
62. Norvell, M.K., Benrubi, G.I., Thompson, R.J. Investigation of microtrauma after sexual intercourse. *J Reprod Med.* 1984 Apr;29(4):269-71.
63. Lin, T.J., Tanaka, Y., Aznar, R., Lin, S.C., Yamasaki, Y., Hori, S., Brar, H.K., Kirton, K.T., Little, B. Contraceptive effect of intrauterine application of Lugol's solution. *Am J Obstet Gynecol.* 1973 May 15;116(2):167-74.
64. Barsley, R.E., West, M.H., Fair, J.A. Forensic photography. Ultraviolet imaging of wounds on skin. *Am J Forensic Med Pathol.* 1990 Dec;11(4):300-8.
65. Krauss, T.C., Warlen, S.C. The forensic science use of reflective ultraviolet photography. *J Forensic Sci.* 1985 Jan;30(1):262-8.
66. David, T.J., Sobel, M.N. Recapturing a five-month-old bite mark by means of reflective ultraviolet photography. *J Forensic Sci.* 1994 Nov;39(6):1560-7.
67. Biggs, M., Stermac, L.E., Divinsky, M. Genital injuries following sexual assault of women with and without prior sexual intercourse experience. *CMAJ.* 1998 Jul 14;159(1):33-7.
68. Kim, J.C., Martin, L.J., Denny, L. Rape and HIV post-exposure prophylaxis: addressing the dual epidemics in South Africa. *Reprod Health Matters.* 2003 Nov;11(22):101-12.
69. Cryer, L., Mattox, K.L. Rape evidence kit: simplified procedures for the emergency department. *JACEP.* 1976 Nov;5(11):890-3.
70. Parnis, D., Du Mont, J. Examining the standardized application of rape kits: an exploratory study of post-sexual assault professional practices. *Health Care Women Int.* 2002 Dec;23(8):846-53.
71. Lopez-Bonasso, D., Smith, T. Sexual Assault Kit Tracking Application (SAKiTA): technology at work in West Virginia. *J Forensic Nurs.* 2006 Summer;2(2):92-5.
72. Cina, S.J., Collins, K.A., Pettenati MJ, Fitts M. Isolation and identification of female DNA on postcoital penile swabs. *Am J Forensic Med Pathol.* 2000 Jun;21(2):97-100.
73. Drobnic, K. Analysis of DNA evidence recovered from epithelial cells in penile swabs. *Croat Med J.* 2003 Jun;44(3):350-4.
74. Kaarstad, K., Rohde, M., Larsen, J., Eriksen, B., Thomsen, J.L. The detection of female DNA from the penis in sexual assault cases. *J Forensic Leg Med.* 2007 Apr;14(3):159-60.
75. Steinman, G. Rapid spot tests for identifying suspected semen specimens. *Forensic Sci Int.* 1995 Apr 27;72(3):191-7.
76. Hara, M., Kimura, H. Two prostate-specific antigens, gamma-seminoprotein and beta-microseminoprotein. *J Lab Clin Med.* 1989 May;113(5):541-8.
77. Sensabaugh, G.F. Isolation and characterization of a semen-specific protein from human seminal plasma: a potential new marker for semen identification. *J Forensic Sci.* 1978 Jan;23(1):106-15.
78. Talthip, J., Chirachariyavej, T., Peonim, A.V., Atamasirikul, K., Teerakamchai, S. An autopsy report case of rape victim by the application of PSA test kit as a new innovation for sexual assault investigation in Thailand. *J Med Assoc Thai.* 2007 Feb;90(2):348-51.
79. Pang, B.C., Cheung, B.K. Identification of human semenogelin in membrane strip test as an alternative method for the detection of semen. *Forensic Sci Int.* 2007 Jun 14;169(1):27-31.
80. Elliott, K., Hill, D.S., Lambert, C., Burroughes, T.R., Gill, P. Use of laser microdissection greatly improves the recovery of DNA from sperm on microscope slides. *Forensic Sci Int.* 2003 Oct 14;137(1):28-36.
81. Hammond, H.A., Redman, J.B., Caskey, C.T. In utero paternity testing following alleged sexual assault. A comparison of DNA-based methods. *JAMA.* 1995 Jun 14;273(22):1774-7.
82. Hatsch, D., Amory, S., Keyser, C., Hienne, R., Bertrand, L. A rape case solved by mitochondrial DNA mixture analysis. *J Forensic Sci.* 2007 Jul;52(4):891-4.
83. Eungprabhanth, V. Finding of the spermatozoa in the vagina related to elapsed time of coitus. *Z Rechtsmed.* 1974;74(4):301-4.
84. Soules, M.R., Pollard, A.A., Brown, K.M., Verma, M. The forensic laboratory evaluation of evidence in alleged rape. *Am J Obstet Gynecol.* 1978 Jan 15;130(2):142-7.
85. Sharpe, N. The significance of spermatozoa in sexual offenses. *Can Med Assoc J.* 1963;89:513-4.
86. Nicholson, R. Vitality of spermatozoa in the endocervical canal. *Fertil Steril.* 1965;16:758-64.

87. Greenfield, A., and Sloan M.M., Identification of Biological Fluids and Stains, in "*Forensic Science—An Introduction to Scientific and Investigative Techniques*", 1st ed. James, S.H. and Nordby J.J., (Eds.), CRC Press, Boca Raton, 2003, chapter 12, pages 203-220
88. Leppaluoto, P. Vaginal flora and sperm survival. *J Reprod Med.* 1974 Mar;12(3):99-107.
89. Lantz, R.K., Eisenberg, R.B. Preservation of acid phosphatase activity in medico-legal specimens. *Clin Chem.* 1970 Mar;24(3):186-8.
90. Linde, R.E. Survival Time Of Sperm In The Vagina Of Living And Deceased Females, Together With The Rate Of Decay Of Acid Phosphatase. *Med Leg Bull.* 1963 Dec;128:1-8.
91. Schumann, G.B., Badawy, S., Peglow, A., Henry, J.B. Prostatic acid phosphatase. Current assessment in vaginal fluid of alleged rape victims. *Am J Clin Pathol.* 1976 Dec;66(6):944-52.
92. Findley, T.P. Quantitation of vaginal acid phosphatase and its relationship to time of coitus. *Am J Clin Pathol.* 1977 Aug;68(2):238-42.
93. Masood, S., Bernhardt, H.E., Sager, N. Quantitative determination endogenous acid phosphatase activity in vaginal washings. *Obstet Gynecol.* 1978 Jan;51(1):33-6.
94. Rutter, E.R., Kind, S.S., Smalldon, K.W. Estimation of time since intercourse from acid phosphatase/UV270 absorbance ratios. *J Forensic Sci Soc.* 1980 Oct;20(4):271-82.
95. Meira, A.R., Soares-Vieira, J.A., Souza, J.M. A critical appraisal of the value of vaginal acid phosphatase determination for the estimation of post-coital time. *Rev Paul Med.* 1992 Jul-Aug;110(4):173-6.
96. Gohara, W.F. Rate of decrease of glutamyltransferase and acid phosphatase activities in the human vagina after coitus. *Clin Chem.* 1980 Feb;26(2):254-7.
97. Dziegelewski, M., Simich, J.P., Rittenhouse-Olson, K. Use of a Y chromosome probe as an aid in the forensic proof of sexual assault. *J Forensic Sci.* 2002 May;47(3):601-4.
98. Bélec, L., Matta, M., Payan, C., Tévi-Bénissan, C., Meillet, D., Pillot, J. Detection of seminal antibodies to human immunodeficiency virus in vaginal secretions after sexual intercourse: possible means of preventing the risk of human immunodeficiency virus transmission in a rape victim. *J Med Virol.* 1995 Jan;45(1):113-6.
99. Berkefeld, K. [A possibility for verifying condom use in sex offenses] [Article in German]. *Arch Kriminol.* 1993 Jul-Aug;192(1-2):37-42.
100. Blackledge, R.D., Vincenti, M. Identification of polydimethylsiloxane lubricant traces from latex condoms in cases of sexual assault. *J Forensic Sci Soc.* 1994 Oct-Dec;34(4):245-56.
101. Hollenbeck, T.P., Siuzdak, G., Blackledge, R.D. Electrospray and MALDI mass spectrometry in the identification of spermicides in criminal investigations. *J Forensic Sci.* 1999 Jul;44(4):783-8.
102. Shen, Z., Thomas, J.J., Siuzdak, G., Blackledge, R.D. A case study on forensic polymer analysis by DIOS-MS: the suspect who gave us the SLIP. *J Forensic Sci.* 2004 Sep;49(5):1028-35.
103. Cina, M.S., Collinsk, K.A, Fitts, M., Pettenati, M.J. Isolation and identification of male and female DNA on a postcoital condom. *Arch Pathol Lab Med.* 2000 Jul;124(7):1083-6.
104. Graupner, H. Sexual consent: the criminal law in Europe and overseas. *Arch Sex Behav.* 2000 Oct;29(5):415-61.
105. World Wide ages of consent. Available from: http://www.avert.org/aofconsent.htm.
106. Council of Europe. Ages of consent in member states. Available from: http://www.statesassembly.gov.je/documents/propositions/8821-2135-2652006.htm.
107. The Indian Penal Code, (Act No. 45 of 1860) [6th October, 1860].
108. Mohanty, N.K. Rape-law and woman's right--critical analysis vis-a-vis role of attending doctor. *J Indian Med Assoc.* 2002 Dec;100(12):695-7, 699.
109. U.S. Court of Appeals, Third Circuit. United States v. Ward. *Fed Report.* 1997 Nov 13;131:335-43.
110. Anon. Court upholds conviction in rape of mentally retarded boy. *AIDS Policy Law.* 1999 Jun 25;14(12):14.
111. Anon. Oklahoma adopts testing laws for inmates, rape suspects. *AIDS Policy Law.* 1998 May 15;13(9):12.
112. Mohanty, K.C. Medico legal implications of Peyronie's disease: imprisonment or acquittal. *Int J STD AIDS.* 2006 Jul;17(7):488-90.
113. Criminal Code of Western Australia. Section 325 inserted by No. 14 of 1992 s. 6(1).
114. Criminal Code of Western Australia. Section 326 inserted by No. 14 of 1992 s. 6(1).
115. Section 201, Austrian Penal Code, 1974.
116. Criminal Code of Canada (R.S.C., 1985, c. C-46).
117. Section 265, Criminal Code of Canada (R.S.C., 1985, c. C-46).
118. *R. v. Chase*, [1987] 2 S.C.R. 293 at 302.

119. Criminal Law of the People's Republic of China (1997) [March 14, 1997].
120. Criminal Law (Rape) Act, 1981, No. 10/1981, enacted [6th May, 1981].
121. Criminal Law (Rape) (Amendment) Act, 1990, No. 32/1990, enacted [18th December, 1990].
122. Ireland [Corporate Author]. Criminal Law (Rape) (Amendment) Act 1990 [18 December 1990]. *Jinko Mondai Kenkyu.* 1990 Dec 26;(24):32(1)-27). [PMID: 12155046].
123. Section 2, CRIMINAL LAW (RAPE) ACT, 1981.
124. Section 2, The Criminal Law (Rape) (Amendment) Act, 1990.
125. Section 4, The Criminal Law (Rape) (Amendment) Act, 1990.
126. Combating of Rape Act, No. 8 of 2000 (Signed by the President on 19 April 2000).
127. Section 2, Crimes Act 1961 of New Zealand.
128. Section 128, Crimes Act 1961 of New Zealand.
129. The General Civil Penal Code (Act of 22 May 1902 No. 10), with subsequent amendments, the latest made by Act of 21 December 2005, No. 131. Norwegian Ministry of Justice, Legislation Department, 2006.
130. The Criminal Code Of The Russian Federation (1996) [Adopted by the State Duma on May 24, 1996, Adopted by the Federation Council on June 5, 1996].
131. Spain. Organic Act No. 3/1989 updating the Penal Code, 21 June 1989. [Selected provisions]. *Annu Rev Popul Law.* 1989;16:21, 301-4.
132. Sexual Offenses Act 2003 [20th November 2003].
133. Ala. Code §13A-6-60 (enacted 1977).
134. Ala. Code §13A-6-61 (enacted 1977).
135. Ala. Code §13A-6-62 (enacted 1977).
136. Ala. Code §13A-5-6 (enacted 1977).
137. Ala. Code §13A-5-11 (enacted 1977).
138. Ala. Code §13A-6-65 (enacted 1977).
139. Ala. Code §13A-6-65.1 (enacted 1977).
140. Ala. Code §13A-5-7 (enacted 1977).
141. Ala. Code §13A-5-12 (enacted 1977).
142. Alaska Stat. §11-41-410 (enacted 1983).
143. Arkansas Code Ann. §5-14-101 (enacted 1975).
144. Arkansas Code Ann. §5-14-103 (enacted 1975).
145. Arkansas Code Ann. §5-14-123 (enacted 1989).
146. Arkansas Code Ann. §5-14-124 (enacted 2001).
147. Arkansas Code Ann. §5-14-126 (enacted 2001).
148. La. Rev. Stat. Ann. §14:41 (enacted 1978).
149. La. Rev. Stat. Ann. §14:42 (enacted 1978).
150. La. Rev. Stat. Ann. §14:42.1 (enacted 1978).
151. La. Rev. Stat. Ann. §14:43 (enacted 1978).

Appendix 1: Ages of Consent for Sexual Intercourse in Different Countries

(http://www.avert.org/aofconsent.htm)

Country	Male–Female Sex	Male–Male Sex	Female–Female Sex
Albania	14	14/18	14
Algeria	16	Illegal	Illegal
Andorra	16	16	16
Antigua and Barbuda	16	16	16
Argentina	13/16	13/16	13/16
Armenia	16	16	16
Aruba	16	16	16
Australia	16	16	16
Australian Capital Territory	16	16	16
New South Wales and Norfolk Island	16	16	16
Northern Territory	16	16	16
Queensland[1]	16/18	18	16
South Australia	17	17	17
Tasmania	17	17	17
Victoria	16	16	16
Western Australia	16	16	16
Austria[2]	14	14	14
Azerbaijan	16	16	16
Bahamas	16	18	18
Barbados	16	Illegal	Illegal
Belarus	16/18	16	16
Belgium	16	16	16
Belize	16	?	?
Bermuda	16	18	16
Bosnia	16	16	16
Brazil[3]	14/18	14/18	14/18
Brunei	14/16	Illegal	Illegal
Bulgaria	14	14	14
Burkina Faso	13	13	13
Cambodia	16	?	?
Cameroon	?	Illegal	?
Canada[4]	12/14/18	18	12/14
Chile	14	18	18
China	14	14	14
China–Hong Kong	16	16	16
China–Taiwan)	16	16	16

Country	Male–Female Sex	Male–Male Sex	Female–Female Sex
Colombia	14	14	14
Cook Islands	16	Illegal	16
Costa Rica	15	15	15
Cote D'Ivoire	15	15?	15?
Croatia	14	14	14
Cuba	16	16	16
Cyprus	13/17	17 (Illegal in north)	17
Czech Republic	15	15	15
Denmark	15	15	15
Dominica	16	?	?
Dominican Republic	18	18	18
Dutch Antilles	16	16	16
Ecuador	14	14	14
Egypt	18	18/Illegal	18
El Salvador	18	?	?
Equatorial Guinea	?	?	?
Eritrea	18	Illegal	Illegal
Estonia	14	14	14
Ethiopia	15	Illegal	Illegal
Falkland Islands (Malvinas)	16	16	16
Faroe Islands	15	15	15
Fiji	16	16 (unofficial)	16
Finland[5]	16	16	16
France	15	15	15
French Guiana	15	15	15
French Polynesia (Tahiti)	16	16	16
Gabon	18	18	18
Gambia	?	Illegal	?
Georgia	16	16	16
Germany[6]	14/16	14/16	14/16
Ghana	?	?	?
Greece	15	15/17	15
Greenland	?	?	?
Grenada	17	Illegal	17
Guam	16	16	16
Guadeloupe	15	15	15
Guatemala	18	18	18
Guinea	15	Illegal	Illegal
Guyana	16	Illegal	16
Haiti	18	18	18
Honduras	14/17	14	14
Hungary	14	14	14
Iceland	14	14	14
India[7]	15/16	Illegal	Illegal
Indonesia	16f/19m	18	18
Iran	Must be married	Illegal	Illegal

Country	Male–Female Sex	Male–Male Sex	Female–Female Sex
Iraq	18	?	?
Ireland	17	17	17
Israel	14-16	14-16	14-16
Italy	14	14	14
Jamaica	16	Illegal	16
Japan[8]	13-18	13-18	13-18
Jordan	16	16	16
Kazakhstan	?	?	?
Kenya	16	Illegal	16
Kuwait	Must be married?	Illegal	Illegal
Kyrgyzstan	?	?	?
Laos	?	?	?
Latvia	14/16	14/16	14/16
Lebanon	15/18/Married	Illegal	Illegal
Lesotho	?	?	?
Liberia	16	Illegal	Illegal
Liechtenstein	14	14	14
Lithuania	14	14	14
Luxembourg	16	16	16
Macedonia	16	16	16
Madagascar	21?	21	21
Mali	16	?	?
Malta	18	18	18
Malaysia	18/Married	Illegal	18
Marshall Islands	16	16	16
Martinique	15	15	15
Mauritius	15	Illegal	Illegal
Mexico[9]	12-18	12-18	12-18
Moldova	14	14	14
Monaco	15	15	15
Mongolia	?	?	?
Montenegro	14	14	14
Morocco	15	Illegal	Illegal
Mozambique	?	Illegal	?
Namibia	16	Illegal	16
Nepal	16	?	?
Netherlands	16	16	16
Netherlands Antilles	16	16	16
New Caledonia	16	16	16
New Zealand	16	16	16
Nicaragua	?	?	?
Niger	?	21	21
Nigeria	13	Illegal	Illegal
North Korea	Undefined	Undefined	Undefined
Norway[5]	16	16	16
Oman	Must be married	Illegal	Illegal
Pakistan	Must be married	Illegal	Illegal

Country	Male–Female Sex	Male–Male Sex	Female–Female Sex
Panama	12/18?	?	?
Papua New Guinea[10]	14/16/Illegal	Illegal	16
Paraguay[11]	14/16	16	16
Peru	14	14	14
Philippines[12]	12/18	12/18	12/18
Poland	15	15	15
Portugal[13]	14/16	16	16
Puerto Rico	16	16	16
Qatar	Must be married	Illegal	Illegal
Reunion	16	16	16
Romania	15	15	15
Russia	14	14	14
Rwanda	16	18	18
San Marino	14/16	14/16	14/16
Saudi Arabia	Must be married	Illegal	Illegal
Senegal	?	Illegal	Illegal
Serbia	14	14	14
Singapore	16	Illegal	16
Slovakia	15	15	15
Slovenia	15	15	15
Somalia	?	Illegal	Illegal
South Africa	16	19	19
South Korea	13	13	13
Spain	13	13	13
Sri Lanka	16	Illegal	16
St. Kitts and Nevis	14/16	?	?
St. Martin	?	?	?
Sudan	Must be married	Illegal	Illegal
Suriname	16	18	18
Sweden	15	15	15
Swaziland	18	Illegal	Illegal
Switzerland	16	16	16
Syria	13/15	Illegal	Illegal
Tajikistan	?	Illegal	?
Tanzania	15	Illegal	Illegal
Thailand[14]	15/18	15/18	15/18
Togo	14	Illegal	Illegal
Tonga[15]	16/Illegal	Illegal	16
Trinidad & Tobago	16	Illegal	Illegal
Tunisia	20	Illegal	Illegal
Turkey	18	18	18
Turkmenistan	16	Illegal	16
Tuvalu	?	Illegal	?
Uganda	18	Illegal	18
Ukraine	16	16	16
United Arab Emirates	18/Married	Illegal	Illegal
Uzbekistan	16	Illegal	16

Country		Male–Female Sex	Male–Male Sex	Female–Female Sex
Uruguay		15	15	15
Vanuatu		15	18	18
Venezuela		16	16	16
Vietnam		18	18	18
Western Samoa		16	Illegal	Illegal
Yemen		Must be married	Illegal	Illegal
Zaire		?	Illegal	?
Zambia		?	Illegal	?
Zimbabwe		12/16	Illegal	12/16
England, Scotland, Wales, Jersey, Isle of Man		16	16	16
Northern Ireland		17	17	17
Guernsey and Gibraltar		17	17	17
USA	Alabama	16	Law invalidated	Law invalidated
USA	Alaska	16	16	16
USA	Arizona	18	law repealed	law repealed
USA	Arkansas[16]	16	Law invalidated	Law invalidated
USA	California	18	18	18
USA	Colorado[16]	15/17	15/17	15/17
USA	Connecticut	16	16	16
USA	D.C.	16	Law repealed	Law repealed
USA	Delaware[16]	16/18	Law repealed	Law repealed
USA	Florida[16]	16/18	Law invalidated	Law invalidated
USA	Georgia	16	16	16
USA	Hawaii	16	Law repealed	Law repealed
USA	Idaho[16]	16/18	Law invalidated	Law invalidated
USA	Illinois	17	17	17
USA	Indiana[16]	16	16	16
USA	Iowa[16]	14/16	Law repealed	Law repealed
USA	Kansas	16	Law invalidated	Law invalidated
USA	Kentucky	16	Law invalidated	Law invalidated
USA	Louisiana	17	Law invalidated	Law invalidated
USA	Maine	16	16	16
USA	Maryland	16	Law invalidated	Law invalidated
USA	Massachusetts	16	Law invalidated	Law invalidated
USA	Michigan	16	Law invalidated	Law invalidated
USA	Minnesota	16	Law invalidated	Law invalidated
USA	Mississippi	16	Law invalidated	Law invalidated
USA	Missouri[16]	14/17	Law repealed	Law repealed
USA	Montana	16/18	Law invalidated	Law invalidated
USA	Nebraska	17	Law repealed	Law repealed
USA	Nevada	16	Law invalidated	Law invalidated
USA	New Hampshire	16	Law invalidated	Law invalidated
USA	New Jersey	16	16	16
USA	New Mexico	17	17	17
USA	New York[16]	17	17	17
USA	North Carolina	16	Law invalidated	Law invalidated

Country		Male–Female Sex	Male–Male Sex	Female–Female Sex
USA	North Dakota	18	Law repealed	Law repealed
USA	Ohio	16	Law repealed	Law repealed
USA	Oklahoma	16	Law invalidated	Law invalidated
USA	Oregon	18	18	18
USA	Pennsylvania	16	16	16
USA	Rhode Island	16	Law repealed	Law repealed
USA	South Carolina[16]	14/16	Law invalidated	Law invalidated
USA	South Dakota	16	Law repealed	Law repealed
USA	Tennessee	18	Law Invalidated	Law Invalidated
USA	Texas[16]	17	Law invalidated	Law invalidated
USA	Utah[16]	16/18	Law invalidated	Law invalidated
USA	Vermont	16	Law repealed	Law repealed
USA	Virginia	18	Law invalidated	Law invalidated
USA	Washington[16]	16/18	16/18	16/18
USA	West Virginia	16	Law invalidated	Law invalidated
USA	Wisconsin	18	18	18
USA	Wyoming	16/18?	Law repealed	Law repealed
USA	Traveling Citizens	18	18	18
USA	Military personnel[17]	16	Illegal	Illegal
		16	16	Average age* 16

GENERAL NOTES

If more than one age is given, the law within that country or state varies according to region or circumstances. Some countries have regional laws that may overrule the federal law. Also in some cases, the age of consent is lower when partners are of a similar age. The question mark indicates the information is either incomplete or unavailable.

In some countries the age of consent is higher for those taking part in commercial sex. In many countries the age of consent is higher when one partner is in a position of trust with regard to the other, or when one partner takes advantage of the other's immaturity. Age of consent laws often do not apply when the partners are married.

The U.S. military prohibits sex between people of the same gender, and sex with a female aged under 16.

In this table, male–female sex is defined as vaginal or anal sex, and male–male sex is defined as anal sex. Other sexual activities may be legal at a lower age.

* The average age of consent does not include countries where it is illegal.

NOTES ON U.S. LAWS

The U.S. Supreme Court has recently struck down sodomy laws which outlawed consensual, same–sex adult sexual activity. In general this means that the ages of consent for male–male and female–female sex are the same as the age for male–female sex. However in some states it is not entirely clear how the decision will be applied to their laws. If you are unsure about the age of consent in your state, seek clarification from your state government.

"Law invalidated" means that the legislation was struck down in court and is "null and void." It does not mean that the law has been removed. "Law repealed" means that the law was removed and changed.

REFERENCES

1. Queensland has a sodomy law that defines the legal age of consent for anal intercourse as 18 and for vaginal intercourse as 16.
2. Although the Austrian age of consent is basically 14, it is illegal to have sex with someone under 16 by "exploiting their lack of maturity."
3. In Brazil, authorities may not choose to prosecute if the younger partner is aged 14 to 17 and does not lodge a complaint.
4. In Canada, consensual activity with those over 12 may not be an offense if the accused is under 16 and less than 2 years older than the complainant. The exception is anal intercourse, to which unmarried persons under 18 cannot legally consent according to national law, although provincial laws may vary.
5. In Finland, sex with someone under 16 is not deemed sexual abuse of a child if "there is no great difference in the ages or the mental and physical maturity of the persons involved." Similarly in Norway, a prison sentence may not be imposed "if those who have committed the act of indecency are about equal in age and development." In both countries, lesser punishments may nevertheless be imposed.
6. In Germany, sexual intercourse is legal from the age of 14 provided the older partner is aged under 18 and provided they are not "exploiting a coercive situation" or offering compensation. In addition, sex between one partner aged 14-15 and another aged under 21 is legal unless the older partner "exploits the victim's lack of capacity for sexual self-determination."
7. India sets the age of consent at 15 within marriage and 16 outside of marriage.
8. The age of sexual consent in Japan is 13 years of age, although prefecture law usually overrides federal law raising the age to 18.
9. In Mexico, the federal law varies according to the age gap between partners and is often overruled by regional laws.
10. In Papua New Guinea, anal sex is illegal in all cases. The age of consent for vaginal sex is 16 for females and 14 for males.
11. Paraguay sets the age of consent at 14 within marriage and 16 outside of marriage.
12. The age of sexual consent in the Philippines is 12 for all, but contacts with minors (under 18) are an offense if the minor consents to the act for money, gain or any other remuneration or as the result of an influence of any adult person.
13. In Portugal, it is illegal to perform vaginal intercourse with a minor between 14 and 16 years old "by taking advantage of their inexperience."
14. Although Thailand's age of consent is usually said to be 15, the laws can be interpreted to allow prosecution for sex with someone under 18.
15. Anal sex is illegal in Tonga regardless of age and gender.
16. In some U.S. states, a lower age applies when the age gap between partners is small or when the older partner is below a certain age (usually 18 or 21).
17. Under some circumstances it is possible for members of the U.S. military to also be charged under state laws.

11 Zoophilia and Bestiality

INTRODUCTION

Zoophilia, *zooerasty*, *zooerastia*, *bestiality*, and *bestiosexuality* are terms denoting human sexual contact with animals. Zoophilic behaviors include not just coitus with animals, but a whole range of other sexual activities, including fellatio, cunnilingus, masturbation of animals,[1] anal intercourse,[2] exhibitionism, frotteurism, and voyeurism.[3]

Richard Freiherr von Krafft-Ebing (1840–1902) introduced the terms *zoophilia erotica* and *zooerasty* in 1894.[4] Though the terms are often used interchangeably, there is a subtle difference between them. *Zoophilia* or *zoophilism* (Greek, *zoon*, "animal"; *philia*, "love") is the name given to a perversion where the affected individual is both emotionally and sexually attracted to animals. These people—known as zoophiles, or simply zoos —begin to love the animals as their own family members and form a deep emotional bond with them. Sexual union with the animals arises as a part of that emotional bonding. *Bestiality*, on the other hand, refers to sexual contact between a human and animal *without* any kind of emotional bonding with the animal. The animal is used simply as a vehicle for satisfying the lust. A bestialist is more or less an opportunist. He uses the animal for sex, when for instance, normal outlets for sex are not available. *Zooerasty* or *zoorasty* is almost the same as bestiality, with the additional fact that here the offender, the zooerast, has a decidedly pathological component, i.e., he may prefer an animal even when other normal sexual outlets, are available.

A number of other terms have been used for zoophilia, one of the most common being *sodomy*. Originally, the term *sodomy* was used to refer only to male homosexuality or pederasty.[5] However, later it came to include several abnormal sexual acts and perversions, especially bestiality. In fact, the term sodomy came to be used to denote any sexual activity that was non procreative, such as masturbation, oral–genital contact, oral–anal contact, anal intercourse, and bestiality. In most modern jurisdictions, however, the term *sodomy* is reserved for anal intercourse. *Buggery* is another term that has been used in the past, as a synonym for bestiality. The more recent term *zoosexuality* describes the full spectrum of human–animal orientation.

Some variants on the theme of zoophilia (involving another co-existing paraphilia) are necrozoophilia, sexual attraction to dead animals (also known as necrobestiality), and zoosadism, zoophilic sadism or bestialsadism (torture of animal during sexual contact). Zoosadism is partly explained by the hypothesis that some aggressive children and adolescents who get less chance to live out their aggressions in interpersonal relations turn to zoosadism.[6] Sometimes there is a desire to be transformed into the animal the paraphiliac has had contact with.[7] This can be understood as a narcissistic tendency and is not necessarily related to lycanthropy (a mental illness in which a patient believes he or she is, or has transformed into, an animal and behaves accordingly).

ZOOPHILIA AND DSM

Bestiality and zoophilia are not mentioned in the first two editions of *Diagnostic and Statistical Manual* (DSM), published by the American Psychiatric Association. Zoophilia as a paraphilia made its first appearance in DSM-III, and was categorized as mental disorder number 302.10. Under the diagnostic criteria for zoophilia the following description was given, "The act or fantasy of engaging in sexual activity with animals is a repeatedly preferred or exclusive method of achieving sexual excitement." According to the manual, "the animal may be the object of intercourse or may be trained to sexually excite the human partner by licking or rubbing. Usually the preferred animal is one with which the individual had contact during childhood, such as a household pet or farm animal. The animal is preferred no matter what other forms of sexual outlet are available."[8] No information was provided regarding the age of onset. The manual notes that "initially in the course of the disorder there may also be sexual arousal by humans. As time progresses, however, the animal becomes the most powerful sexual stimulus. This usually occurs by early adulthood, and the course then becomes chronic. Nonpathological sexual activity with animals may occur because of the unavailability of suitable human partners or as a form of sexual experimentation. In such instances the use of animals is not the consistently preferred method of achieving sexual excitement."

In the revised, third edition of the DSM (DSM-III-R), zoophilia was removed as a disorder. The diagnostic committee that worked on the paraphilia section of the DSM-III-R concluded that "zoophilia is virtually never a clinically significant problem by itself."[9] They omitted it as a formal diagnosis and listed zoophilia with the diagnostic label of "paraphilia not otherwise specified" (302.90).

Subsequent editions of DSM continued the tradition of not listing zoophilia as a separate disorder. The latest edition, DSM-IV-TR,[10] likewise does not assign any specific or unique code to zoophilia. Instead, along with several other uncommon paraphilias (seven of which are specifically named), zoophilia is grouped under the code 302.9 (paraphilias not otherwise specified):

> This category is included for coding paraphilias that do not meet the criteria for any of the specific categories. Examples include, but are not limited to, telephone scatologia (obscene phone calls), necrophilia (corpses), partialism (exclusive focus on part of body), zoophilia (animals), coprophilia (feces), klismaphilia (enemas), and urophilia (urine).

International Classification of Diseases, Ninth Edition, Clinical Modification (ICD-9-CM) assigns code 302.1 to zoophilia (please see chapter 1, Table 1.3). Shaffer and Penn[11] list at least 16 different types of paraphilia involving animals (see Table 11.1).

HISTORICAL PERSPECTIVES

Throughout recorded history, solitary and isolated shepherds have been known to engage in sexual intercourse with the animals they tended. In fact, syphilis was named for a mythical shepherd, Syphilus, who was the first man to contract the disease. The disease was sent to him by the god Apollo as punishment for his sin of bestiality.

Bestiality in Mythology and Folklore

Bestiality abounds in mythology and folklore. The Greek god Zeus had a great penchant for assuming shapes of various animals and seducing maidens. He became a swan to seduce Leda, a bull to abduct Europa, and an eagle to carry off the beautiful youth Ganymede. Many other cultures have myths of men and particularly women mating with animals. According to the Greenlandic polar explorer and anthropologist Knud Rasmussen (1879–1933) and the "father of Eskimology," the Inuit believe that the white man and the Indian were offspring of an Inuit woman who mated with a dog.[12]

Literary references to bestiality are also widespread. Among some widely known literary works referring to bestiality in one form or the other are the fairy tales *Beauty and the Beast* and *The Frog Prince*, the tale of the ape as lover in *The Book of the Thousand Nights and One Night*, the ballet *Swan Lake*, Shakespeare's *A Midsummer Night's Dream* (the character of Nick Bottom), Balzac's novelette *A Passion in the Desert* (a love affair between a soldier and a female panther), the giant

TABLE 11.1
Different Types of Zoophilia As Listed by Shaffer and Penn

Paraphilia	Arousal from
Aelurophilia	Deriving gratification from cats
Anolingus	Arousal from licking lizards
Arachnephilia	Arousal from spiders
Avisodomy	Breaking the neck of a bird while penetrating it for sex
Batrachophilia	Arousal or attraction to frogs
Bee stings	Use of bees, such as to sting genitalia
Canophilia	Arousal from dogs
Cynophilia	Arousal from sex with dogs
Entomophilia	Arousal from insects or use of insects in sexual activity
Entomocism	Arousal from insects or use of insects in sexual activity
Formicophilia	Enjoyment of the use of ants or insects for sexual purposes
Melissophilia	Arousal from bees
Musophilia	Arousal from mice
Necrobestialism	Arousal from having sex with dead animals
Ophidiophilia	Arousal from snakes
Ornithophilia	Arousal from birds
Phthiriophilia	Attraction to lice

ape King Kong's cinematic infatuation with a human heroine, and Piers Anthony's Xanth fantasy novels portraying interspecies couplings, resulting in such hybrids as flying centaurs.

Bestiality in Hinduism

The Manu Smriti, an important Hindu law code compiled between 200 BC and 200 AD, considers bestiality a crime. Chapter XI deals with sins, major and minor, and their expiations. Law 174 of this chapter states:[13]

> A man who has committed a bestial crime, or an unnatural crime with a female, or has had intercourse in water, or with a menstruating woman, shall perform a Samtapana Krikkhra. (Manu.XI.174)

Manu goes on to explain Samtapana Krikkhra in Law 213:

> [Subsisting on] the urine of cows, cow dung, milk, sour milk, clarified butter, and a decoction of Kusa grass, and fasting during one [day and] night, [that is] called a Samtapana Krikkhra. (Manu.XI.213)

There are several references to bestiality in the ancient Hindu scriptures. Horse sacrifice or *Ashvamedha* was a particularly solemn rite in early Hinduism. In this ritual, a stallion, more than 24, but less than 100 years old, was sacrificed for the acquisition of power and glory, the sovereignty over neighboring provinces, and general prosperity of the kingdom. Before the sacrifice, the animal was driven into water and bathed. It was then anointed with *ghee* (clarified butter) by the chief queen and two other royal consorts. The chief queen anointed the fore-quarters, and the others the barrel and the hind-quarters. After the animal was killed, the queens walked around the dead horse reciting *mantras* (holy verses). The chief queen then had to mimic copulation with the dead horse, while the other queens ritually uttered obscenities. On the next morning, the priests raised the queen from the place where she had spent the night with the horse. Presumably the intercourse with the dead animal was enacted in the belief that the queen would subsequently give birth to princes as strong as the stallion.

There are different versions of how this intercourse was mimicked. In one variation, the severed penis of the stallion was inserted in the vagina of the chief queen. Bass[14] in this interesting commentary on Hindu scripture says:

> Bestiality is likewise advocated [in Hindu religion]. A particularly solemn rite for the early Vedic religion was the horse sacrifice. Though it probably was performed rarely, it is mentioned frequently in the Vedic commentaries. Note one section from the *Śatapatha Brāhmana*: "Then they draw out the penis of the horse and place it in the vagina of the chief queen, while she says, 'May the vigorous virile male, the layer of seed, lay the seed'; this she says for sexual intercourse...." (13.5.2.1-10)

Bestiality in the Bible

The Holy Bible makes several allusions to sex with animals.

> For she doted upon their paramours, whose flesh is as the flesh of asses, and whose issue is like the issue of horses.[15,16]

Reference is made here to Oholibah, the younger sister of Oholah. Both Oholah and Oholibah became prostitutes and became infatuated with their neighbors, the Assyrians. In the verse above, Ezekiel refers to Oholibah becoming so oversexed that she lusted after her lovers "whose flesh [penises] were like those of asses and whose issue [the amount of semen output] was like that of horses." The Bible here appears to be praising the lovers by comparing the size of their penises with that of the asses and the power and speed of their semen emission with that of horses.

At several places, the Bible proscribes sexual contact with animals.

> Neither shalt thou lie with any beast to defile thyself therewith: neither shall any woman stand before a beast to lie down thereto: it is confusion.[17]

The penalty of bestiality is death for both the offender and the beast.

> And if a man lie with a beast, he shall surely be put to death; and ye shall slay the beast.[18]

The beast was to be killed perhaps because it was feared that the sexual union between man and animal could give rise to monsters. A woman committing bestiality is also to be put to death along with the beast.

> And if a woman approach unto any beast, and lie down thereto, thou shalt kill the woman, and the beast: they shall surely be put to death; their blood shall be upon them.[19]

The Old Testament states, "Cursed be he that lieth with any manner of beast" (*Deuteronomy* 27:21) and "Whosoever lieth with a beast shall surely be put to death" (*Exodus* 22:19).

Prehistoric Times

Prehistoric man was not bound by any social or cultural taboos with regard to sexuality, and was likely to have indulged in bestiality quite commonly. Bestiality is supposed to be have been quite common during the Fourth Glacial Age, between 40,000 and 25,000 years ago.[20] The practice can be seen in prehistoric art, too. An engraved bone rod from the cave of La Madeleine, France, dated around 25,000 years ago, depicts a lioness licking a human penis.[21] An open-air rock engraving about 5000 years old in Val Camonica, a valley in the lower Alpine regions of Lombardy, Italy, depicts a man with full erection standing behind a donkey.[22] Quite clearly, the man intends to have sex with the donkey. Such paintings leave no doubt that our prehistoric ancestors enjoyed frequent and pleasurable sexual relations with animals.[23]

Greco-Roman Period

It appears that Caligula (12–41AD), one of most sexually perverse men in history, was a zoophile. This conjecture appears highly likely, given the undisputed fact that he was polymorphous perverse (had multiple sexual perversions simultaneously) and that he loved his horse Incitatus so much that he even tried to make it a consul and a priest.[24]

In ancient Rome, the practice of bestiality was so common that professional people supplied animals for this purpose. The *Belluari* supplied dogs and monkeys, the *Caprarii,* she-goats, and the *Anserarii,* geese. People who engaged in bestiality could do it openly and with impunity by paying a tax of 90 tornesi, 12 ducats, and 6 carlini. Roman women kept snakes as pets and trained them to coil around their thighs, and slide past the lips of their vaginas.[25] Egyptian women may have been involved in similar practices. It is noteworthy that Cleopatra (69–30 BC) poisoned herself by inducing an asp to bite her. Bestiality flourished as a public spectacle in ancient Rome, and the Romans even invented a game where women were raped by animals for the amusement of the audiences at the Coliseum and Circus Maximus.[26]

Other Civilizations

Among the Incas, bestiality was punishable by hanging.[27] Yet so common does the practice of bestiality appear in this culture, that at least 6% of Inca archaeological decorated specimens, dating from before AD 1000, depict bestiality.[28]

David Forbes (1828–1876), British mineralogist, metallurgist, and chemist, who lived for a long time in Peru where he studied geology, stated that in that country the belief was current that syphilis was a malady peculiar to the alpaca and that from this animal it had been passed on to man as the result of vice against nature.[29] According to an ancient Peruvian law, bachelors were prohibited from keeping female alpacas in their homes because of the fear of bestiality committed on alpacas.[30] For the same reason Peruvian men unaccompanied by women were also forbidden from herding llamas.[31] When the Spaniards arrived in Central and South America, they found bestiality to be so prevalent that their priests included the "sin of bestiality" in their confessional protocol.[20]

The Chinese are famous for their love affairs with geese. Just when they are at the point of ejaculation, they wring off the birds' necks, in order that they may get the pleasure of the last spasms of the anal sphincters of the dying geese.[29] Several necrophiliacs engage in anal intercourse with dying soldiers on a battlefield for similar reasons (please see chapter on necrophilia for details).

Middle Ages

In the Middle Ages, it was thought that the devil was a man, wearing either an animal's skin or a mask in the form of an animal's head as a ritual disguise. The animal forms in which the devil most commonly appeared were the bull, cat, dog, goat, horse, and sheep. Curiously, the devil appeared as a goat or a sheep in only in France, where bestiality became punishable with death. Both the accused and the animal had to die. The animals had to be executed for two reasons; one, for fear of bearing monsters and, two, if allowed to live, they would be constant reminders to others of the act, and perhaps fall further prey to bestial activities of others. In a trial in 1453, a priest named Guillaume Edeline was sentenced, executed, and burned at Evreux for having made a pact with the devil in the form of a sheep whom he had kissed under the tail and on the fundament in paying him homage. In 1465, Gillet Soulart was burned alive with a sow. In 1468, a 24 year old laborer Jean Beisse, a native of Greslart, near Châteaudun, was convicted of copulating with a cow and a goat. Jean, the cow, and the goat were all burned at the stake.[32] On May 26, 1546, one Guyot Vuide was hung and burned for having cohabited with a cow; the cow was burned before he was put to death. On January 5, 1556, Jean de la Soille was burned alive with a she ass for bestiality. The animal was, however, slain before being consigned to the flames. It was not only the men who were executed. Female bestials were known and executed, too. At Toulon, a woman was burned who had made love with a dog

Court records available in Europe and the United States, dating back to the 14th century and continuing into the 20th century, nearly always show males, rather than females, as the human parties to bestiality. The animals have typically been mares, pigs, and sheep, and occasionally other domesticated farm animals, such as goats, rabbits, and chickens. Thousands of female witches were accused of having had sex with the devil in animal form, although such accusations do not prove fact. One of the most popular myths (often claimed to have been spawned by the French nobility) attributes the death of the Russian empress Catherine the Great (1729–1796) to a mishap while attempting coitus with a bull (or perhaps a horse).

Modern Era

In the modern era, many zoophiles have attempted to increase awareness of zoophilia, and have advocated the practice. The late Mark Matthews wrote *The Horseman* in which he narrated his love for his female horse.[33] He loved his mare so much that he not only "kept her", but also married her. It was an actual wedding, and he even made pink "hooflets" and lingerie for the ceremony.[34] Dekkers, a Dutch biologist and popular naturalist, assembled a substantial body of evidence in his book to show that throughout human civilization, humans have engaged in sex with animals without harming them and with a proper concern for their welfare.[35] His book includes a wide range of illustrations, going back to a Swedish rock drawing from the Bronze Age of a man copulating with a large quadruped. A Greek vase from 520 BC shows a male figure having sex with a stag; a 17th-century Indian miniature of a deer mounting a woman; an 18th-century European engraving of an ecstatic nun coupling with a donkey, while other nuns smilingly look on; a 19th-century Persian painting of a soldier, also with a donkey; and, from the same period, a Japanese drawing of a woman enveloped by a giant octopus who appears to be licking her private parts, as well as caressing her body with its many limbs.

Females have been penalized for bestiality, too. In the late 1940s, Virginia Tarrant was indicted in Franklin County, Ohio, on the charge that she "unlawfully had carnal copulation against nature with a dog" (*State v. Tarrant,* 80 NE 2d 509, 1948). More specifically, she "took into her mouth the male organ of a dog and engaged in the act of sodomy over some period of time."[36]

Interesting cases of bestiality are still being encountered. On July 2, 2005, a 45-year old man accidentally died in Enumclaw, Washington, when trying to have sex with a horse. Three men were present at the scene when the death occurred, but the police could not charge anyone because bestiality is not a crime in Washington. However, the police charged one of the men, James Michael Tait, 54, with first-degree trespassing, a misdemeanor because the group had apparently entered someone else's farm to have sex with his horse.[37]

A curious case occurred in Sudan in 2006. Around midnight on 13 February 2006, Mr. Alifi, of Hai Malakal in Upper Nile State, Sudan, heard a loud noise. When he got up, he found, Mr. Tombe copulating with his (Alifi's) goat. Alifi was aghast and took Tombe to a council of elders, who ordered Tombe not only to take a goat as his "wife," but even to pay a dowry of 15,000 Sudanese dinars ($50) to Alifi.[38]

ETIOLOGY

Sadomasochistic Theories

It is thought that if the paraphiliac is a sadist, he may derive pleasure from bestiality, because he could derive pleasure from giving them pain simultaneously while having sex. Similarly for a masochistic person, submission to a lower life form may be intensely appealing.

Familial Upbringing

Familial upbringing is an important etiological factor. A dysfunctional home environment is often seen among bestialists. A father who is emotionally distant and uninvolved with family and a mother who is unaffectionate, demanding, intrusive, and belittling may lead to inadequacies, low self-esteem, and problems in social skills, which may ultimately cause the person to find solace in animal sex.

Zoophilia also arises from childhood trauma and physical or sexual abuse. Due to this trauma, zoophiles are not able to form proper emotional attachments with other humans. Since they have never been able to identify with humans, zoophiles then compensate by turning to the only source of love still left: animals. Some turn to bestiality to perpetuate the cycle of physical abuse, choosing animals as their targets.

Triune Brain Theory

Paul MacLean has proposed a triune brain model to explain the traces of evolution existing in the structure of the human brain.[39] In this model, the brain is broken into 3 separate brains that have their own special intelligence, subjectivity, sense of time and space, and memory. These are the R-complex, limbic system, and the neocortex. The first two are remnants of lower animals' brain that have survived evolution. The R-complex, also known as the "reptilian brain," includes the brain stem and cerebellum. The term comes from the fact that a reptile's brain is dominated by the brain stem and cerebellum, which control instinctive survival behavior. The limbic system composed of the amygdala, the hypothalamus, and the hippocampus interacts with the neocortex (cerebral cortex, the third and most advanced part) to process the emotions. MacLean has proposed that since in all of our daily activities, all 3 brains make contributions to our thoughts, behaviors, emotions, and feelings, it is only natural that some people desire to engage in sex with animals.

Complication of Drug Therapy

Jiménez-Jiménez and colleagues[40] report an interesting case of a 74 year old man with advanced Parkinson's disease who developed zoophilia as a possible complication of dopaminergic therapy. He developed hypersexuality with zoophilia 5 days after standard levodopa was substituted for controlled-release levodopa and the dose of bromocriptine was increased. The abnormal sexual behavior disappeared two days after the doses of standard levodopa and of bromocriptine were reduced.

Miscellaneous Causes

Sex with animals may simply arise from opportunity. A farm boy with several sheep around and nobody looking may be tempted to have sexual intercourse with them. Many may resort to this activity for sheer experimentation and the joy of a new experience.

PREVALENCE

Kinsey and colleagues interviewed about 5300 adult white men and 5800 adult white women about their sexual experiences, and found that in rural areas about 40 to 50% of the males had had at least one sexual encounter with an animal, and 17% had experienced an orgasm as a result.[41] If urban areas were included, the overall percentage of American males who had engaged in intercourse with animals decreased to about 8%. In a similar study conducted 5 years later on women, they found a prevalence rate of about 3% for females.[42] Rates were higher among those with lower educational status. The figures appear sizeable, and because bestiality is such a socially sensitive subject, the incidences were perhaps underreported. However, Hunt believes that due to the expansion of sexual opportunities over the last several years, particularly after the so-called "sexual revolution," sex with animals—often considered a substitute sexual activity—has become less prevalent in the U.S. population.[43]

Crépault and Couture[44] interviewed 94 men about their erotic fantasies occurring during heterosexual activity. The majority of these men were married and their average duration of cohabitation with a woman was 6.5 years. From that group, 5.3% reported having had erotic fantasies involving sexual activity with an animal.

Zoophilia is seen among females, too. Fedoroff and colleagues studied the clinical records (of the first author) of 15 years, and identified individuals referred to them for suspected paraphilic disorders. The clinics were located in different countries (Canada, the United States, and Great Britain), and all were affiliated with universities. A total of 132 paraphilics were identified, of which 14 (11%) were women.[45] Within the total female sample, two (cases 7 and 11) were found to have zoophilic tendencies, i.e., 14% of all female paraphiliacs seen by them were zoophiles. The authors, however, emphasize that this is not a study into the frequency or prevalence of paraphilias in the female population, nor can the findings be used to draw such inferences.

Alvarez and colleagues studied the prevalence of bestiality among psychiatric in-patients, medical in-patients, and psychiatric staff and found the prevalence rates to be 55%, 10%, and 15%, respectively.[46] Since the psychiatric patients exhibited a statistically significant higher prevalence rate, the authors recommend that questions exploring this previously ignored topic should be routinely included in any psychiatric history taking.

CLASSIFICATION OF ZOOPHILIC BEHAVIOR

Zoosexuality, as noted above, describes the full spectrum of human–animal orientation. This full spectrum has been described explicitly by Massen, who distinguishes 9 basic forms of zoosexual activity.[47] These forms, which increase gradually in severity on a scale from 1 to 9, and overlap frequently. Several of them may occur in combination. These forms are:

1. Incidental experience and latent zoophilia
2. Zoophilic voyeurism (also called mixoscopic zoophilia or faunoiphilia)
3. Frotteurism (rubbing against animals, physical contact as source of pleasure) [Massen actually uses the term *frottage*, but since frottage is generally taken to mean consensual rubbing, and frotteurism taken to mean nonconsensual rubbing, the latter term is preferable here]
4. The animal as a tool for masturbatory activities
5. The animal as a surrogate for a behavioral fetishism (sadomasochistic practices, sexual murder, zoosadism, etc.)
6. The animal as fetish (fixation on one specific kind, breed, or individual)
7. Physical contact and affection
8. The animal as a surrogate for a human sex partner
9. The animal as deliberately and voluntarily chosen sex partner

Of course, a number of other zoophilic behaviors could be added here, such as zoophilic exhibitionism (please see below).

Bartmann and Wohlsein describe traumatic injuries of 193 horses over a 4 year period, out of which at least 10 cases were due to acts of zoophilism and zoosadism. The injuries were caused by gunshots, spear-like instruments, or knives. Only 7 could be saved by surgical or medical treatment.[48] Wochner and Klosinski[6] studied 1502 aggressive children and adolescents treated at the Department of Child and Adolescent Psychiatry at the University of Tübingen, and found that 25 had been zoosadists. These were exclusively boys (23 out of 25). The age distribution of the zoosadists showed an increased incidence in 13-, 17-, and 18-year olds which could be connected with problems of puberty, group constraints, and proving virility. Compared with a control group of "only aggressive" patients, organic brain damage owing to complications of pregnancy or delivery, difficult and harsh upbringing by the parents and absence of a positive father figure could be demonstrated in the zoosadists. One third of the zoosadists showed additional disorders of sexual behavior, and the sexual-sadistic component was manifested in the zoosadistic action.

CLASSIFICATION OF ZOOSEXUALS

Zoosexuality involves a vast spectrum of sexual interaction between humans and animals, ranging from the most innocuous where the human only needs his normal human partner to act as an animal during sex (role-player), to the most gruesome, where the offender kills an animal in order to have sex with its carcass (necrobestial). From the study of vast literature available on zoosexuality, it is clear that all zoosexuals fall into clear categories. The following classifications proposed in this book, roughly increasing in order of pathologic degeneracy, seems to accommodate all cases reported in the literature.

Class I Zoosexuals: Human Animal Role-players

These people do not use animals for sex, but rather want their human partners to act as animals during sex, because the thought of having sex with animals excites them. Also known as pet play, pony play, ponyism, or pup play, human animal role play thus involves one participant taking on the role of a real or imaginary animal in character, including appropriate mannerisms and behavior. Thus it is a kind of s*exual role play* (please see "Essential BDSM vocabulary" in chapter on masochism).

The principal theme of human–animal role play is usually the voluntary or involuntary reduction (or transformation) of a human being to animal status, and focus on the altered mind-space created. The most common examples of "conversion" are canids (pup, dog, wolf), felines (cat, kitten, lion) and equines (pony, horse). The activity is common among people with t*ransformation fetish*es (please see chapter on fetishism for details). Human-animal role-play is also used in a BDSM context, where the partner is reduced to the status of an animal as a symbol of authority and dominance (please see chapter on masochism for details).

Class II Zoosexuals: Romantic Zoophiles

These people love the company of animals, and the mere sight of them gives them erotic pleasure, even ejaculation. Some may also show various other paraphilias mixed with zoophilia. McNally and Lukach describe a curious case of zoophilic voyeurism (peeping through windows to gaze at animals), zoophilic frotteurism (rubbing one's genitals on the furs of live animals), and zoophilic exhibitionism (exposure of genitals in front of animals with concomitant masturbation) all seen together in one person[3] (please see chapter on exhibitionism for details of this case).

Class III Zoosexuals: Animal Fetishists

These people can get sexual excitement by touching, stroking, or fondling an animal. The touch of soft and silky fur of animals may act as an erotic stimulus, just as ordinary fur does for a fetishist. Some may use part of an animal body, such as a fur or skin, to masturbate. Randall and associates[49] narrate an interesting case where the tongue of a deer was used as a masturbatory tool. These people may be called animal fetishists. They use animals for sexual excitement, *without* actually engaging in intercourse with them.

Class IV Zoosexuals: True Zoophiles

These people love animals at an emotional level and express their love through sexual intercourse. They have sex with animals, as one would normally have with human partners. People in classes I through IV tend to love animals and by and large do not hurt or harm animals.

Class V Zoosexuals: Opportunistic Bestials

Pathogenicity starts with this class. People belonging to this class do not love animals at an emotional level, nor would they normally have sex with them. However, when starved of a normal human sexual partner (e.g., incarcerated or stranded persons), or when they see an opportunity (e.g., a shepherd taking cattle away for grazing on a lonely farmland), they engage in sexual intercourse with animals. Normally, however, they are content to have a sexual intercourse with human partners. Pathogenicity is minimal in this class.

Class VI Zoosexuals: Exclusive Bestials

These people have sex only with animals, even if normal human partners are available. This group is truly pathological. They are called zooerasts by some writers (please see above).

Class VII Zoosexuals: Necrobestials and Zoosadists

These people are also pathological. Zoosadism has been dealt with above. Necrobestiality, the act of having sex with dead animals, may not be as rare as was imagined previously. The reason for its apparent rarity is that the crime is never reported, given the nature of the victim. The infamous killer Jeffrey Dahmer (1960–1994) is reported to have collected animal carcasses from the road, dissected them, and masturbated, as he found the glistening viscera of animals sexually arousing.[50] In November 2006, Bryan James Hathaway, 20-years of age, of Douglas County, Minnesota, was arrested for having sex with a deer carcass he found on the side of the road while bicycling. He was charged with violating a law against "sexual gratification with an animal." He was placed on probation, and sentenced to be evaluated, as a sex offender and treated at the Institute for Psychological and Sexual Health in Duluth.

SOME ILLUSTRATIVE CASES

Rex v. Cozins

In *Rex v. Cozins,* 6 C&P 351, 25 ECL 469, 172 Reprint 1272 (March 5, 1834), the central issue was whether penetration was sufficient to constitute the crime of bestiality or emission was necessary. The accused Cozins was trying bestiality with a ewe when he was interrupted by one of the witnesses calling to him. He withdrew himself from the animal, being then in a state of erection (indicating emission had not occurred). Justice Park, summing up, observed, "In the former state of law, the prisoner would have been entitled to an acquittal; but, as the law is now, if there was penetration, the capital offense is completed, although there has been no emission; however, as the proof is less than was formerly required, it behooves judges and juries to see that the proof now required is satisfactory." A guilty verdict was passed against Cozins.

Ausman v. Veal

In *Ausman v. Veal,* American Decisions, 331, 10 Indiana, 355 (Indiana, May, 1858), the issue was whether pups could be borne by a woman if she engaged in bestiality. Eli Ausman and his wife Mary filed a suit for slander against their neighbor Veal, who on June 27, 1857, made allegations that Mary had had sexual connection with a dog. Veal, the defendant, was supposed to have defamed Mary by saying, "She [Mary] is out gathering news. She has run all over the neighborhood telling tales on my family. She can talk as much as she pleases. Thank God if my daughters did have bastards, they never had pups. Mary had two pups by a haystack." Mary and her husband filed a case against Veal.

Veal, who seemed to have been chastised by the action of the Ausmans, asserted in his defense that his "words charge an impossible crime and an impossible fact, and thus carry upon their face their own refutation." Among other things, Justice Perkins said in his decision, "Whether the words in the case at bar imply an impossible fact or impute an impossible crime, we are not able to say. Whether it is physically impossible for sexual connection to take place between a dog and a woman, and whether, could such a connection take place, it is a physical impossibility that conception should follow, we are not advised. If such be the case, we do not think it is generally known to the people. They are presumed—bound, indeed—to know the law, but not philosophic or scientific facts and principles. Hence we think the injury to the plaintiff may not be affected by the truth of falsity of such facts and principles, and that this action may well lie."

Khandu v. Emperor

In *Khandu v. Emperor (*1934) 35 Cr LJ 1096: 150 IC 320: Lah. 261, a case from British India, the accused Khandu committed intercourse by placing his penis into the nostril of a bullock. The question was whether Khandu was guilty of bestiality under section 377 of the Indian Penal Code or not. It was held that his act amounted to bestiality, and thus he was guilty.

MEDICAL ASPECTS

The health practitioner must remember that a number of medical problems may arise from engaging in bestiality. A proper history must be elicited with tact and caution, if bestiality is suspected to be the cause of the medical condition.

Zoonoses

Zoonoses are infections that are transmitted from animals to humans. Some of these are transferred through casual contact, but others are much more readily transferred by activities that expose humans to the semen, vaginal fluids, urine, saliva, feces, and blood of animals, implying that sexual activity with animals may not be a risk-free activity. Some diseases that can be transmitted sexually to humans are brucellosis, leptospirosis (Weil's disease), Q fever, rabies, flea tapeworm, echinococcosis (hydatid disease), Campylobacter, Cryptosporidium, Cysticercosis (pork tapeworm), Giardia, Salmonella, and toxocariasis (dog roundworm).

Other Medical Conditions and Injuries

Reactive arthritis, defined as joint inflammation triggered by a distant infection with no cultivable microbes in the joints, seen after a zoophilic (canine) sexual intercourse.[51] In 1976, a 46-year old French farmer underwent surgery for peritonitis after sex with a boar.[52] In 2002, a 62-year old farmer in Bulgaria was treated for a torn rectum after sex with a male pig.[53] In 2005, Kenneth Pinyan, a resident of Washington state died from internal injury after being anally penetrated by a stallion. In an extremely unusual case, allergy to dog sperm has been reported. In October 1971, a 42-year old divorced woman having 4 children and pregnant for the fifth time by her boyfriend reported dizziness and syncope. Her attending physician found her hypotensive. She admitted to having had sexual contact with her German shepherd dog 20 minutes prior to her arrival. A scratch test with dog sperm was found to be positive.[54,55] Bites and abrasions through paws may also occur during zoophilic sexual intercourse.

LEGAL ASPECTS

Zoosexuality is permitted in a few countries such as Sweden, Denmark, Hungary, and the Netherlands, although ordinary animal treatment laws apply. In other countries, such as Germany and Russia, zoosexuality is legal, but zoosexual pornography is illegal.

Australia

Northern Territory

According to section 138 of the Criminal Code of Northern Territory (for details of this Code, please see chapter on exhibitionism), bestiality is a crime and attracts a punishment of imprisonment up to 3 years. Section 138 states:

> Any person who inserts, to any extent, the person's penis into the genital passage or anus of an animal or permits an animal to insert its penis into the person's vagina or anus is guilty of a crime and is liable to imprisonment for 3 years.

South Australia

Section 69 of the Criminal Law Consolidation Act 1935 of South Australia deals with the offense of bestiality. It states as follows:

> Any person who commits buggery with an animal shall be guilty of an offense and liable to be imprisoned for a term not exceeding 10 years.

Queensland

Queensland criminal law is governed by Criminal Code 1899 (for details please see chapter on exhibitionism). Most sexual offenses are defined in chapter 22, entitled "offenses against morality." Bestiality is defined in this chapter under Section 211:

> Any person who has carnal knowledge with or of an animal is guilty of a crime and is liable to imprisonment for 7 years.

Carnal knowledge as mentioned in the above section is defined in section 6 of the same code (for details, please see chapter on rape).

New South Wales

The criminal law of New South Wales is governed by the Crimes Act 1900 (for details, please see chapter on frotteurism). Bestiality is punished under Section 79:

> Any person who commits an act of bestiality with any animal shall be liable to imprisonment for 14 years.

Crimes Act 1900 is also one of the few statutes in the world which punishes anyone who even *attempts* to commit bestiality. Section 80 states:

> Any person who attempts to commit an act of bestiality with any animal shall be liable to imprisonment for 5 years.

Tasmania

According to the Tasmanian Criminal Code Act 1924, bestiality is a crime. The charge leveled against the offender is of unnatural sexual intercourse. Section 122 (included in chapter XIV entitled "Crimes Against Morality") states:[56]

> ***Unnatural crimes***
> Any person who has sexual intercourse with an animal is guilty of a crime.

Victoria

According to section 59 of the Crimes Act 1958 of Victoria, bestiality is an offense. The law even explicitly states the acts included within the meaning of bestiality:[57]

> (1) A person must not commit an act of bestiality.
> Penalty: Level 6 imprisonment (5 years maximum).
> (2) An act of bestiality is any of the following—
> (a) buggery committed by a man on an animal of either sex;
> (b) buggery committed by an animal on a man or woman;
> (c) penetration of the vagina of an animal by the penis of a man;
> (d) penetration of the vagina of a woman by the penis of an animal.
> (3) The law relating to buggery is as set out in this Act and no prosecution shall be instituted for an offense of buggery unless it is for an offense under this section.

Canada

According to section 160 of the Criminal Code of Canada,[58] bestiality is an offense:

> (1) Every person who commits bestiality is guilty of an indictable offense and liable to imprisonment for a term not exceeding 10 years or is guilty of an offense punishable on summary conviction.
>
> ***Compelling the commission of bestiality***
> (2) Every person who compels another to commit bestiality is guilty of an indictable offense and liable to imprisonment for a term not exceeding 10 years or is guilty of an offense punishable on summary conviction.
>
> ***Bestiality in presence of or by child***
> (3) Notwithstanding subsection (1), every person who, in the presence of a person under the age of 14 years, commits bestiality or who incites a person under the age of 14 years to commit bestiality is guilty of an indictable offense and liable to imprisonment for a term not exceeding 10 years or is guilty of an offense punishable on summary conviction.

Interestingly, in Canada, there are provisions for punishing offenders who compel others to commit bestiality and also if a child below 14 years of age is incited to commit bestiality or commits bestiality himself in the presence of such a child. These provisions are not included in the laws of most other countries.

China

Criminal law of the People's Republic of China (for details, please see chapter on exhibitionism) does not specifically outlaw bestiality. However, the crime is covered under general animal welfare law contained within the criminal law. Under Article 276, if injury results to an animal as a result of bestiality, then the person may be liable. Article 276 states:

> Anyone who, for purposes of giving vent to spite or retaliating or out of other personal motives, destroys or damages machines or equipment, cruelly injures or slaughters farm animals or sabotages production and business operation by other means, shall be sentenced to fixed-term imprisonment of not more than three years, criminal detention or public surveillance; if the circumstances are serious, he shall be sentenced to fixed-term imprisonment of not less than three years but not more than seven years.

Germany

The German Criminal Code (Strafgesetzbuch, StGB) cites no specific punishment for having sex with animals (for details of the code, please see chapter on necrophilia). Before 1969, section 175b made bestiality a crime, but in that year, this section was removed. However, according to section 184 (3), pornography showing sexual acts of human beings with animals is still prohibited.

Dittert and colleagues believe that zoophilia in Germany is no longer considered a severe mental disorder, and in clinical practice is rarely seen, particularly since it was decriminalized.[7]

Hungary

The Hungarian Penal Code of May 28, 1878, carried a maximum penalty of one year imprisonment for sexual relations with animals,[32] but the modern Hungarian Criminal Code of 1978 makes no mention of bestiality as a crime (for more on modern Hungarian Criminal Code of 1978, please see chapter on exhibitionism). So for all intents and purposes, bestiality appears legal in modern Hungary.

India

Criminal Law

In India, bestiality is defined under section 377 of the Indian Penal Code as an unatural offense:[59]

> Whoever voluntarily has carnal intercourse against the order of nature with any man, woman or *animal*, shall be punished with *imprisonment for life*, or with imprisonment of either description for a term *which may extend to 10 years*, and *shall also be liable to fine*.
>
> Explanation—Penetration is sufficient to constitute the carnal intercourse necessary to the offense described in this section.

Surprisingly, the only law in India relevant to the welfare of animals, The Prevention of Cruelty to Animals Act, 1960 (amended in 1982), does not explicitly talk about any offense related to sexual activity with animals. The closest it comes to is in section 11(1)(a), which states:

> If any person beats, kicks, over-rides, over-drives, over-loads, tortures or otherwise treats any animal so as to *subject it to unnecessary pain or suffering* or causes, or being the owner permits, any animal to be so treated shall be punishable (in the case of a first offense, with fine which shall not be less than 10 rupees but which may extend to 50 rupees and in the case of a second or subsequent offense committed within 3 years of the previous offense, with fine which shall not be less than 25 rupees but which may extend, to 100 rupees or with imprisonment for a term which may extend, to 3 months, or with both.

If sexual activity with an animal can be construed by some courts as amounting to subjecting the animal to unnecessary pain or suffering, then the provisions of this section may be applicable. But the punishment prescribed is abysmally small. For the first offense the punishment extents to only 50 rupees (equivalent to about $1) and for the second offense, the punishment is not much. Obviously the lawmakers, at the time of framing this law, were aware that any sexual activity with animals was already punishable under section 377 of the IPC.

Civil Law

In India, bestiality is relevant for civil suits also. According to section 13 (2) (ii) of The Hindu Marriage Act 1955, a wife may present a petition for dissolution of her marriage by a degree of divorce on the ground that the husband has, since the solemnization of the marriage, been guilty of rape, sodomy, or bestiality.[60] Interestingly, the husband cannot present a similar petition if the wife is guilty of bestiality.

United Kingdom

According to section 69 of the Sexual Offenses Act 2003 of UK,[61] intercourse with an animal is an offense:

(1) A person commits an offense if—
  (a) he intentionally performs an act of penetration with his penis,
  (b) what is penetrated is the vagina or anus of a living animal, and
  (c) he knows that, or is reckless as to whether, that is what is penetrated.
(2) A person (A) commits an offense if—
  (a) A intentionally causes, or allows, A's vagina or anus to be penetrated,
  (b) the penetration is by the penis of a living animal, and
  (c) A knows that, or is reckless as to whether, that is what A is being penetrated by.
(3 A person guilty of an offense under this section is liable—
  (a) on summary conviction, to imprisonment for a term not exceeding 6 months or a fine not exceeding the statutory maximum or both;
  (b) on conviction on indictment, to imprisonment for a term not exceeding 2 years.

United States

Only eight US states lack bestiality laws.[37] The rest all have specific laws prohibiting bestiality. Here are some representative laws.

Arkansas

Chapter 14 of the Arkansas Code deals with sexual offenses. The relevant law on bestiality[62] is as follows:

(a) As used in this section, "animal" means any dead or alive nonhuman vertebrate.
(b) A person commits bestiality if he or she performs or submits to any act of sexual gratification with an animal involving the sex organs of the one and the mouth, anus, penis, or vagina of the other.
(c) Bestiality is a class A misdemeanor.

Interestingly, the law defines as animal a vertebrate. This includes fishes, amphibians, reptiles, birds, and mammals. Dead animals are also included in the law. The crime is known as necrozoophilia or necrobestiality.

California

The California Penal Code is divided into 5 parts; Part 1 ("Of Crimes and Punishments") deals with most crimes and punishments. It has 17 titles. Title 9 (entitled "Of Crimes against the Person Involving Sexual Assault, and Crimes Against Public Decency and Good Morals") deals with many crimes of a sexual nature. This Title has 12 chapters. Of these, Chapter 5 ("Bigamy, Incest, and the Crime Against Nature") is composed of Sections 281-289.6. Section 286.5 deals with bestiality. It states:[63]

> **286.** Any person who sexually assaults any animal protected by Section 597f for the purpose of arousing or gratifying the sexual desire of the person is guilty of a misdemeanor.

Section 597f includes "all animals lawfully seized and impounded."

Indiana

Bestiality is a class D felony in the state of Indiana. It is defined in Title 35, Article 46 ("Miscellaneous Offenses"), Chapter 3 ("Offenses Relating to Animals"), Section 14 of Indiana Code (for details of the Indiana Code, please see chapter on voyeurism). It states:

35-46-3-14—Bestiality

A person who knowingly or intentionally performs an act involving:

(1) a sex organ of a person and the mouth or anus of an animal;
(2) a sex organ of an animal and the mouth or anus of a person;
(3) any penetration of the human female sex organ by an animal's sex organ; or
(4) any penetration of an animal's sex organ by the human male sex organ; commits bestiality, a class D felony.

Wisconsin

Chapter 944 of Wisconsin statutes defines crimes against sexual morality. Section 944.17 makes bestiality a Class A misdemeanor. It states:

Sexual gratification

(1) In this section, "in public" means in a place where or in a manner such that the person knows or has reason to know that his or her conduct is observable by or in the presence of persons other than the person with whom he or she is having sexual gratification.
(2) Whoever does any of the following is guilty of a Class A misdemeanor:
   (a) Commits an act of sexual gratification in public involving the sex organ of one person and the mouth or anus of another.
   (c) Commits an act of sexual gratification involving his or her sex organ and the sex organ, mouth or anus of an animal.
   (d) Commits an act of sexual gratification involving his or her sex organ, mouth or anus and the sex organ of an animal.
(3) Subsection (2) does not apply to a mother's breast-feeding of her child.

Subsections 2(c) and 2(d) address the crime of bestiality (subsection 2[b] has been deleted).

REFERENCES

1. London, L.S. and Caprio, F.S., *Sexual Deviations*, Linacre Press, Washington DC, 1950.
2. Peretti, P.O., Rowan, M. Zoophilia: factors related to its sustained practice. *Panminerva Med.* 1983 Apr-Jun;25(2):127-31.
3. McNally, R.J., Lukach, B.M. Behavioral treatment of zoophilic exhibitionism. *J Behav Ther Exp Psychiatry.* 1991 Dec;22(4):281-4.
4. Oosterhuis, H. *Stepchildren of Nature: Krafft-Ebing, Psychiatry, and the Making of Sexual Identity.* (The Chicago Series on Sexuality, History, and Society). University Of Chicago Press, Chicago, IL, 2000.
5. Karpman, B. *The Sexual Offender and His Offenses*, 7th Ed., Julian Press, Inc., New York, NY. 1962.
6. Wochner, M., Klosinski, G. Child and adolescent psychiatry aspects of animal abuse (a comparison with aggressive patients in child and adolescent psychiatry) [Article in German]. *Schweiz Arch Neurol Psychiatr.* 1988;**139(3)**:59-67.
7. Dittert, S., Seidl, O., Soyka, M. Zoophilia between pathology and normality. Presentation of 3 case reports and an internet survey [Article in German]. *Nervenarzt.* 2005 Jan;76(1):61-7.
8. American Psychiatric Association. *Diagnostic and Statistical Manual of Mental Disorders*, 3rd ed. American Psychiatric Association, Washington DC, 1980.
9. American Psychiatric Association. *Diagnostic and Statistical Manual of Mental Disorders*, 3rd ed. rev. American Psychiatric Association, Washington DC, 1987, page 405.
10. American Psychiatric Association. *Diagnostic and Statistical Manual of Mental Disorders*, 4th ed. Text rev. American Psychiatric Association, Washington DC, 2000.
11. Shaffer L and Penn J., A Comprehensive paraphilia classification system, in *Sex Crimes and Paraphilia*, Hickey E.W., Pearson Prentice Hall, New Jersey, 2006, chap.8.
12. Moss, J.G. (Ed). *Echoing Silence: Essays on Arctic Narrative*, University of Ottawa Press, Ottawa, Ontario, 1997, page 200.
13. Manu (tr. Buhler, G.). *The Laws of Manu,* Cosmo Publications, India, 2004.
14. Bass, A. An Investigation of Hindu Scripture. Apologetics Press [On-line]. Available from : http://www.apologeticspress.org/articles/2580.
15. Ezekiel 23:20. The Holy Bible. Authorized King James Version. Oxford University Press, New York, 1972.
16. Akerley, B.E. *The X-Rated Bible: An Irreverent Survey of Sex in the Scriptures.* Feral House, Los Angeles, 1998.
17. Leviticus 18:23. The Holy Bible. Authorized King James Version. Oxford University Press, New York, 1972.
18. Leviticus 20:15. The Holy Bible. Authorized King James Version. Oxford University Press, New York, 1972.
19. Leviticus 20:16. The Holy Bible. Authorized King James Version. Oxford University Press, New York, 1972.
20. Rosenberger, J.R. *Bestiality*, Medco Books, Los Angeles, CA, 1968.
21. Taylor, T. *The Prehistory of Sex*, Bantam Books, New York, 1996.
22. Gregersen, E. *Sexual Practices: The Story of Human Sexuality*, Franklin Watts, New York, 1983.
23. Waine, W.W. *Canine Sexualis*, Publishers' Exxport Co. Inc., San Diego, CA, 1968.
24. Suetonius, Robert Graves (Translator). *The Lives of Twelve Caesars, Life of Caligula*, Penguin Classics, England, 2003.
25. Davis, P., *Sex Perversion and the Law, Volume One*, 5th ed., Mental Health Press, New York, 1954.
26. Bledsoe, R.J. *Male Sexual Deviations and Bizarre Practices*, 2nd ed., Sherbourne Press, Inc., Los Angeles, CA, 1965.
27. Miletski, H. A history of bestiality, in *Bestiality and Zoophilia—Sexual Relations with Animals*, 1st edition, Beetz, A.M. and Podberscek, A.L., Eds., Purdue University Press, West Lafayette, Indiana, 2005, chap. 1, Pp 1-22.
28. Bullough, V.L. *Sexual Variance in Society and History*, The University of Chicago Press, Chicago, IL, 1976.
29. Mantegazza, P. *The Sexual Relations of Mankind*, University Press of the Pacific, Honolulu, Hawaii, 2001.

30. Mantegazza, P. *Anthropological Studies of Sexual Relations of Mankind.* Anthropological Press, New York, 1932.
31. Menninger, K.A. Totemic Aspects of contemporary attitudes toward animals, in *Psychoanalysis and Culture: Essays in Honor of Geza Roheim*, Wilbur, G.B., and Muensterberger, W., Eds., International Universities Press, New York, NY, 1951, Pp 42-74.
32. Dubois-Desaulle, G. Bestiality—*An Historical, Medical, Legal and Literary Study*, University Press of the Pacific, Honolulu, Hawaii, 2003.
33. Matthews, M. *The Horseman*, Prometheus Books, Amherst, NY, 1994.
34. Garbage, G., *That's Disgusting : An Adult Guide to What's Gross, Tasteless, Rude, Crude, and Lewd*, Ten Speed Press, Berkeley, CA, 1999.
35. Dekkers, M. *Dearest pet*, Verso, New York, 2000.
36. Delaney, D. *Law and Nature (Cambridge Studies in Law and Society).* Cambridge University Press, New York, 2003, page 262.
37. Anderson, R. Closing the Barn Door. *Seattle Weekly*, Wednesday, 9 November 2005. Available at http://www.seattleweekly.com/2005-11-09/news/closing-the-barn-door.php. Accessed, Jan 21, 2008.
38. BBC News. Sudan man forced to 'marry' goat. Available at http://news.bbc.co.uk/1/hi/world/africa/4748292.stm. Retrieved Jan 18, 2008.
39. MacLean, P. *The Triune Brain in Evolution*, Plenum Press, New York, 1990.
40. Jiménez-Jiménez, F.J., Sayed, Y., García-Soldevilla, M.A., Barcenilla, B. Possible zoophilia associated with dopaminergic therapy in Parkinson disease. *Ann Pharmacother.* 2002 Jul-Aug;36(7-8):1178-9.
41. Kinsey, A.C., Pomeroy, W.B., and Martin, C.E., *Sexual Behavior in the Human Male*, Saunders, Philadelphia, 1948.
42. Kinsey, A.C., Pomeroy, W.B., Martin, C.E. and Gebhart, P.H., *Sexual Behavior in the Human Female*, Saunders, Philadelphia, 1953.
43. Hunt, M.M. *Sexual behavior in the 1970's.* Playboy Press, Chicago, 1974.
44. Crépault, C., Couture, M. Men's erotic fantasies. *Arch Sex Behav.* 1980 Dec;**9(6)**:565-81.
45. Fedoroff, J.P., Fishell, A., Fedoroff, B., A case series of women evaluated for paraphilic sexual disorders. *Canadian Journal of Human Sexuality.* 1999; 8(2): 127-140.
46. Alvarez, W.A., Freinhar, J.P. A prevalence study of bestiality (zoophilia) in psychiatric in-patients, medical in-patients, and psychiatric staff. *Int J Psychosom.* 1991;**38(1-4)**:45-7.
47. Massen, J., Zoophilie—*Die sexuelle Liebe zu Tieren (Zoophilia—the sexual love for animals)*, Pinto Press Verlag, Köln, 1994, page 57.
48. Bartmann, C.P., Wohlsein, P. Injuries caused by outside violence with forensic importance in horses. [Article in German]. *Dtsch Tierarztl Wochenschr.* 2002 Mar;**109(3)**:112-5.
49. Randall, M.B., Vance, R.P., McCalmont, T.H. Xenolingual autoeroticism. *Am J Forensic Med Pathol.* 1990 Mar;11(1):89-92.
50. Hickey, E.W. Paraphilia and Signatures in Crime Scene Investigation. In *Sex Crimes and Paraphilia*, 1st ed. Hickey, E.W., (Ed.), Pearson Prentice Hall, New Jersey, 2006, chapter 9, pages 95-107.
51. Ergun, U.G., Celik, M., Ozer, H.T. Reactive arthritis due to zoophilic (canine) sexual intercourse. *Int J STD AIDS.* 2007 Apr;**18(4)**:285-6.
52. Blondel, P.H. [Digestive perforation of unusual origin. 2 cases] [Article in French]. *Nouv Presse Med.* 1976 Apr 3;**5(14)**:915-6.
53. Kirov, G.K., Losanoff, J.E., Kjossev, K.T. Zoophilia: a rare cause of traumatic injury to the rectum. *Injury.* 2002 May;**33(4)**:367-8.
54. Holden, T.E., Sherline, D.M. Bestiality, with sensitization and anaphylactic reaction. *Obstet Gynecol.* 1973;**42(1)**:138-40.
55. Aggrawal, A. Allergies, in *Encyclopedia of Forensic and Legal Medicine (Vol. 1)*, Payne-James JJ, Byard RW, Corey TS, Henderson C., Eds., Elsevier Academic Press, London, 2005, Pp. 58-68.
56. Section 122, Criminal Code Act 1924 (No. 69 of 1924).
57. Section 59, Crimes Act 1958 (No. 6231 of 1958).
58. Section 160, Criminal Code of Canada (R.S., 1985, c. C-46).
59. The Indian Penal Code, (Act No. 45 of 1860) [6th October, 1860].
60. The Hindu Marriage Act, 1955, (Act No. 25 of 1955) [May 18, 1955] as amended by The Marriage Laws (Amendment) Act, 2003 (50 of 2003).
61. Sexual Offenses Act 2003 [20th November 2003].
62. Arkansas Code Ann. §5-14-122 (enacted 1977).
63. Cal. Penal Code §286.5 (enacted 1975).

12 Sexual Harassment

INTRODUCTION

Sexual harassment (SH) has become one of the most controversial issues of our time. It is a sex crime, which can be defined as "the making of sexually offensive remarks or acts, or unwanted, unwelcome, and offensive sexual advances, often intimidating in nature, especially by one in a superior or supervisory position." The American Psychological Association (APA) defines sexual harassment as "deliberate or repeated comments, gestures, or physical contacts of a sexual nature that are unwanted by the recipient."[1] Acquiescence to such behavior is often a condition of continued employment, promotion, or satisfactory evaluation. It also carries threats of employment reprisals if such advances are refused. According to the Equal Employment Opportunity Commission's (EEOC) 1980 regulations:

> Unwelcome sexual advances, requests for sexual favors, and other verbal or physical conduct of a sexual nature constitute sexual harassment when this conduct explicitly or implicitly affects an individual's employment, unreasonably interferes with an individual's work performance, or creates an intimidating, hostile, or offensive work environment.[2]

In general, the following types of conduct are considered to be illegal sexual harassment:

(1) repeated sexual innuendo, obscene or off-color jokes, slurs, lewd remarks and language, and other offensive sexual comments;
(2) content in letters and notes, facsimiles, e-mail, graffiti that is of a sexual nature or sexually abusive;
(3) sexual propositions, insults, and threats;
(4) sexually-oriented demeaning names;
(5) persistent unwanted sexual or romantic overtures or attention;
(6) leering, whistling, or other sexually suggestive sounds or gestures;
(7) displaying pornographic pictures, calendars, cartoons, or other sexual material in the workplace;
(8) coerced or unwelcome touching, patting, brushing up against, pinching, kissing, stroking, massaging, squeezing, fondling, or tickling;
(9) subtle or overt pressure for sexual favors;
(10) coerced sexual intercourse (e.g., as a condition of employment or academic status).

Significantly, the victim of sexual harassment does not have to be of the opposite sex. The victim as well as the harasser may be a woman or a man. The harasser may be a victim's supervisor, employer's agent, co-worker, or even a non-employee. Also the victim does not have to be the person harassed but may be anyone affected by the offensive conduct.

FIGURE 12.1 Joseph and the Wife of Potiphar, by the German Romantic painter Philipp Veit..

HISTORICAL PERSPECTIVES

It is said that the first case of sexual harassment occurred in Biblical times, when sexual advances were made on Joseph by his employer Potiphar's wife Zuleika. Joseph had been taken from the Promised Land to Egypt by Ishmaelite traders, where Potiphar, a senior officer in Pharaoh's court, bought him. Joseph began to make large sums of money for his master, so much so that Potiphar turned over the running of his estate to him.

One day, as Potiphar was away, his wife looked at Joseph with desire, and said, "Lie with me." But he refused and told her, "Behold, with me around, my master does not concern himself with anything in the house, and he has put all that he owns in my charge. There is no one greater in this house than I, and he has withheld nothing from me except you, because you are his wife. How then could I do this great evil, and sin against God?"

But such refusals had little effect on her, and she requested Joseph day after day to lie with her. Seeing that her requests had little effect on Joseph, one day she caught him by his garment and said again, "Lie with me!" Joseph left his garment in her hand and fled outside. Stung by his refusal, she complained to her husband that Joseph had wanted to sleep with her, and when she raised her voice, left his garment and fled outside. Potiphar believed his wife's story and had Joseph thrown into jail.[3]

One of the earliest cases on record that could classify as a case of sexual harassment by today's standards occurred in 1734 when a group of female servants published a notice in the *New York Weekly Journal* that said, "We think it reasonable we should not be beat by our mistresses' husbands, they being too strong and perhaps may do tender women mischief."[4]

However, despite these early cases, the issue of sexual harassment really began occupying a general consciousness in the 1060s when: (i) women began entering jobs in large numbers; (ii) in the U.S., the Civil Rights Bill was passed in 1964, Title VII of which covered sex discrimination, and which was interpreted by courts as including sexual harassment; and finally (iii) the advent of the birth control pill, the women's movement, and the sexual revolution, which suddenly changed society's view of men, women, and how they interacted at work.

Early Cases of Sexual Harassment

The first cases with substantial sexual harassment issues came before the U.S. courts in the 1970s. In several of these cases, the courts tended to take the view that sexual harassment was a "personal matter" between the two individuals, *not* seen as amounting to sex discrimination at the workplace, which was illegal under Title VII of the Civil Rights Act, 1964. In 1974, for instance, a case was dismissed where a female employee claimed that she was retaliated against for rejecting her boss's sexual advances (*Barnes v. Train,* 13 FEP Cases 123 [D.D.C.]). The trial court decided that there was no sex discrimination. The male supervisor, according to the court, merely solicited his subordinate because he found her "attractive" and then retaliated because he felt "rejected." A year later, in *Corne v. Bausch & Lomb, Inc.* 1975. 390 F.Supp. 161, two female employees, Jane Corne and Geneva DeVane resigned because of repeated verbal and physical advances by their supervisor. The district court viewed the supervisor's conduct as "a personal proclivity, peculiarity or mannerism," without holding the company liable. The court observed:

> An outgrowth of holding such activity to be actionable under Title VII would be a potential federal lawsuit every time any employee made amorous or sexually oriented advances towards another. The only sure way an employer could avoid such charges would be to have employees who were asexual.

In another case, *Miller v. Bank of America,* 418 F. Supp. 233 (1976), where Margaret Miller's supervisor wondered what it would be like to have sex with a "black chick," and fired her when she refused his advances, the trial court dismissed Miller's complaint. In this case the court advanced biological reasons for sexual harassment, and once again regarded it as a personal problem between the two parties, rather than a systematic social problem. The court observed:

> [I]t would not be difficult to foresee a federal challenge based on alleged sex motivated considerations of the complainant's superior in every case of a lost promotion, transfer, demotion or dismissal. And who is to say what degree of sexual cooperation would found a Title VII claim? It is conceivable, under plaintiff's theory, that flirtations of the smallest order would give rise to liability. The attraction of males to females and females to males is a natural sex phenomenon and it is probable that this attraction plays at least a subtle part in most personnel decisions. Such being the case, it would seem wise for the Courts to refrain from delving into these matters....

Williams v. Saxbe

However, in 1976, in *Williams v. Saxbe,* 413 F.Supp. 654 (1976), in a landmark decision, a district court recognized, for the first time, quid pro quo harassment as a form of sex discrimination. The court observed that such kind of behavior created an "artificial barrier to employment that was placed before one gender and not the other, even though both genders were similarly situated." In a way, this behavior created conditions of employment that were applied differently to men and women. Therefore sexual harassment was forbidden under Title VII as sex discrimination.

Meritor Savings Bank v. Vinson

The hostile environment sexual harassment was first recognized in 1986 in *Meritor Savings Bank v. Vinson,* 477 U.S. 57 (1986). Sidney Taylor of the Meritor Savings Bank hired Mechelle Vinson in September 1974 as a teller trainee. She subsequently progressed to teller, head teller, and finally to assistant branch manager. All these promotions were based on merit. In September 1978, she took sick leave, but was fired on November 1, 1978, for "excessive use of that leave." Vinson sued Meritor Savings Bank under Title VII, claiming that Taylor made repeated demands upon her for sexual favors, usually at the branch, both during and after business hours. She claimed that Taylor had had sex with her about 40 to 50 times during the four years she was at the bank and that she agreed only because she feared that she would lose her job. She also claimed that Taylor fondled her in front of others, followed her into the ladies' room, and exposed himself to her. This in effect created a hostile environment for Vinson, entitling her to relief under Title VII. The district court denied the relief based upon three observations: (i) that the sexual relationship was voluntary; (ii) that it did not affect her job, and no economic loss was suffered by Vinson; and (iii) that the alleged sexual harassment was never made known to the bank. The court of appeals reversed the decision. Finally, the U.S. Supreme Court granted *certiorari* and heard the case on March 25, 1986.

The Supreme Court, granting relief to Vinson, answered each of the three questions raised earlier: (i) the defense that the sexual relationship was voluntary was not enough. What was sufficient was that the relationship was "unwelcome" and this in effect created a hostile environment; (ii) while formulating the law, it was never the intention of the Congress to limit the loss of the harassed person only to "economic loss." If merely a hostile environment was created, the sufferer was liable for relief; and finally (iii) the Supreme Court made employers strictly liable if sexual harassment occurred at the workplace. It observed that "absence of notice to an employer does not necessarily insulate that employer from liability."

EEOC v. Mitsubishi Motor Manufacturing

In 1998, in *EEOC v. Mitsubishi Motor Manufacturing*, 990 F. Supp. 1059 (C.D. Ill 1998),[67] the Mitsubishi Motor company paid an astounding $34 million in a sexual harassment case.[5] About 350 female workers of the company complained of being fondled, targeted with air guns, and taunted as "bitches" and with even cruder, sexually explicit names.[6] Phalluses and pornographic drawings were painted on bathroom walls, and some of the victims were explicitly propositioned by male workers, managers, and even union officials to provide sexual services.

Sexual Harassment Involving Public Figures

Anita Hill and Justice Clarence Thomas

Celebrities have faced sexual harassment cases, too. One of the most famous is the controversy surrounding Justice Clarence Thomas and Anita Hill occurring in 1991. On July 8, 1991, President George Bush nominated Thomas to replace Thurgood Marshall who had recently announced his retirement. At the time of his nomination, Anita Hill, an Oklahoma law school professor, accused Thomas of sexually harassing her when the two had worked together at the DOE and EEOC. Among other things, her testimony stated, "Thomas was drinking a Coke in his office. He got up from the table at which we were working, went over to his desk to get the Coke, looked at the can and asked, 'Who has put pubic hair on my Coke?'" The confirmation hearings were notable for their explicit content, particularly Senator Orrin Hatch's questions "Did you ever say in words or substance something like there is a pubic hair in my Coke?" and "Did you ever use the term Long Dong Silver in conversation with Professor Hill?" Thomas denied all allegations, describing them as a "high tech lynching." After an extensive debate, on October 15, 1991, the US Senate narrowly confirmed Thomas by a vote of 52-48, making it the closest confirmation vote for a Justice in the 20th century. Justice Thomas took his seat on October 23, 1991.

Paula Corbin Jones and Bill Clinton

On May 6, 1994, 2 days prior to the 3 year statute of limitations, Paula Corbin Jones filed a sexual harassment and eschewal suit against President Bill Clinton. She alleged that on the afternoon of May 8, 1991, Clinton, then governor of Arkansas, had summoned her to his suite at the Excelsior Hotel in Little Rock, Arkansas. Jones at that time was a state employee with the Arkansas Industrial Development Commission (AIDC). Thinking that it was an honor to be asked to meet the Governor and that it might lead to an enhanced employment opportunity, she agreed to meet him. When she was in his room, it was alleged that Clinton "unexpectedly reached over to [her], took her hand, and pulled her toward him, so that their bodies were close to each other. The Governor then said, 'I love your curves' and attempted to kiss her on the neck without her consent. Among her other allegations was that the governor 'lowered his trousers and underwear, exposed his penis (which was erect) and told her to kiss it.' When Corbin said, she had to go, the Governor, 'while fondling his penis,' said, 'Well, I don't want to make you do anything you don't want to do,' and then pulled up his pants and said, 'If you get in trouble for leaving work, have Dave (Dave Harrington, Corbin's ultimate superior within the AIDC) call me immediately and I'll take care of it.' Finally before she left his room, Clinton said, 'You are smart. Let's keep this between ourselves.'"[7]

Judge Susan Webber Wright of the U.S. Court of Appeals for the Eighth Circuit dismissed the case, because even if Jones' allegations were correct, she could not demonstrate any tangible job detriment or adverse employment action for her refusal to submit to Clinton's alleged advances. However, while the dismissal was on appeal, Clinton entered into an out-of-court settlement by agreeing to pay Jones $850,000.

Anna Richardson and Arnold Schwarzenegger

In August 2006, Californian Governor Arnold Schwarzenegger settled a sexual harassment case by British television personality Anna Richardson. She claimed that the California governor had groped her breast during a 2000 interview in London, to promote *The Sixth Day*, in which he had starred as an actor.

Moshe Katsav

In 2006, sexual harassment charges were made by as many as 10 women against the then President of Israel, Moshe Katsav (1945–). Since many cases had problems of proof and evidence, and in some, the statute of limitations had expired, the final indictment focused on 4 cases. Katsav, pled guilty to lesser offenses of committing indecent acts without consent, sexual harassment of 2 women, and harassing a witness, in exchange for Israeli government dropping much graver rape charges against him. He admitted to "hugging a woman and touching her leg," and "touching of hips, an attempt at a kiss, and a kiss" of the other. Katsav received a suspended sentence and paid an equivalent of about $11,695 in compensation to the two women. One of them had worked for Mr. Katsav when he was tourism minister in the late 1990s; the other worked in his office in 2003 and 2004.

Other highly influential people in Israel have continuously been accused of sexual harassment charges. In March 2006, an Israeli court sentenced former Justice Minister Haim Ramon to 120 days of community service for forcibly kissing a female soldier. In yet another case Ofer Glazer, the husband of billionaire Shari Arison, served 4 months of a 6-month term for sexual harassment. Glazer was convicted of committing indecent acts against 2 women: one whom he met in Eilat when she sought to rent an apartment, the other was a nurse who looked after his wife after an operation.

Same-Sex Sexual Harassment

By the 1990s, the issue of sexual harassment of women by men—their colleagues or superiors—was fairly well settled. But could a male employer sexually harass a male employee? Or for that matter could a female employer sexually harass a female employee? These questions—whether same-sex sexual harassment was possible—were not settled till 1997. In that year, a landmark judgment—*Fredette v. BVP Management Associates,* 112 F.3d 1503 (1997)—seemed to settle this question. Robert Fredette, a male waiter at a restaurant owned by BVP Management Association, was sexually harassed by Dana Sunshine, the male manager of the restaurant. Sunshine asked Fredette repeatedly for sexual favors, and offered to give him employment benefits in exchange for these sexual favors. Fredette brought a suit against BVP Management Associates, claiming that these repeated sexual advances constituted both a *quid pro quo* and hostile work environment sexual harassment under Title VII. The district court rejected his claim. It observed that Fredette was discriminated against *not because of his gender, but because of his sexual orientation.* Thus he was not entitled to relief under Title VII. Fredette appealed, and the U.S. Court of Appeals for the Eleventh Circuit reversed the judgment of the trial court. The court observed that it is immaterial whether the harassed employee is of same sex or of different sex. It stated:

> We think [this reasoning] is equally applicable to the situation where a homosexual male propositions another male. The reasonably inferred motives of the homosexual harasser are identical to those of the heterosexual harasser—i.e., the harasser makes advances towards the victim because the victim is a member of the gender the harasser prefers.

CLASSIFICATION OF SEXUAL HARASSMENT

LEGAL CLASSIFICATION

The courts generally recognize two basic types of sexual harassment. These types naturally flow from the EEOC regulations mentioned above:

(1) ***Quid pro quo* sexual harassment**: (Latin *Quid pro quo*, "this for that") It occurs when an employer or other decision-maker either promises some type of benefit (e.g., higher grades in school, better work conditions, promotion, or job security) in exchange for sexual favors or threatens to take away an employment benefit if the employee does not give in. In behavioral terms (please see the classification below), promise of better work conditions, etc. would be taken as sexual bribery, while threat to take away some employment benefit would be sexual coercion. Generally speaking, *quid pro quo* cases are brought against employees with the authority to impact a tangible employment benefit, such as hiring, firing, promoting, reassigning to another position with different responsibilities, or monetary benefits. *Quid pro quo* sexual harassment was first recognized by the U.S. courts in *Williams v. Saxbe,* 413 F.Supp. 654 (1976).

(2) **Hostile environment sexual harassment**: In this type of sexual harassment, there is no reward of any type in return for granting sexual favors, nor is there any threat to take away something if sexual favors are not granted. It occurs simply when sexual conduct by *anyone* in the work environment, such as supervisors, co-employees, or even customers and vendors, creates an offensive and unpleasant working environment. Whether a hostile working environment has been created is measured in most jurisdictions by the reasonable person standard, i.e., the courts ask whether a reasonable person would consider the work environment to be hostile. It can consist of sexual language, the presence of sexual materials, or unwelcome physical contact. Cartoons or posters of a sexual nature, vulgar or lewd comments or jokes, or unwanted touching or fondling all fall into this category. Hostile environment sexual harassment, as a violation of Title VII of the Civil Rights Act of 1964, was first recognized by the U.S. courts in *Meritor Savings Bank v. Vinson,* 477 U.S. 57 (1986).

Interestingly, while in *quid pro quo* cases, a single sexual advance can be considered actionable harassment, in hostile environment cases, generally, a single incident does not constitute an actionable offense as a single incident does not create a hostile environment. A hostile environment claim usually requires a showing of a regular pattern of offensive conduct. However, the more egregious the conduct, the less the need to show a repetitive series of incidents.

In an unanimous decision of the U.S. Supreme Court in April, 2001, a supervisor's isolated single crude remark was not enough to trigger a sexual harassment case under the federal civil rights law (*Clark County School District v. Breeden*). The justices stated that, based on the reasoning in previous cases, sexual harassment refers to a pattern of "severe or pervasive" abuse; the supervisor's offhand, one remark was not the type of behavior that supported a sexual harassment claim, though the employee might think it was unlawful harassment.

Behavioral Classification

On the basis of behavior, sexual harassment falls into the following 5 classifications, ranging from simple to heinous:

(1) **Gender Harassment** consists of generalized sexist statements and behavior that convey insulting or degrading attitudes about women. Examples include offensive graffiti, insulting remarks, obscene jokes, or humor about sex or women in general. This is by far the most common type of sexual harassment.
(2) **Seductive Behavior** can be considered a grade above gender harassment and consists of unwanted, inappropriate, and offensive sexual advances. Examples include repeated unwanted sexual invitations, insistent requests for dinners, drinks or dates, persistent letters, phone calls, and other invitations. This is the second most common type of sexual harassment after gender harassment. Both behaviors roughly overlap with hostile environment type sexual harassment noted above.
(3) **Sexual Bribery** roughly overlaps the *quid pro quo* sexual harassment noted in the previous classification. Sexual bribery involves solicitation of sexual activity or other sex-linked behavior by promise of reward. The proposition may be either overt or subtle.
(4) **Sexual Coercion** also overlaps the *quid pro quo* sexual harassment. However, in this case, instead of a reward for sexual favor (as in sexual bribery above), there is a threat of punishment, etc. if sexual favors are not granted. Examples include negative performance evaluations, withholding of promotions, threat of termination, etc. if sexual favors are not granted. Both sexual bribery and sexual coercion constitute the classic forms of sexual harassment.
(5) **Sexual Imposition** is the most severe form of sexual harassment. It involves gross sexual imposition such as forceful touching, feeling, grabbing, or even sexual assault. The most notable example of this form of sexual harassment occurred in India in 1992 (please see below).

Other classifications exist and overlap with earlier classifications. DiVasto et al.[8] consider sexual harassment as a type of a sexually stressful event. According to them, all sexually stressful events may be classified into two categories—noninvasive (harassment, obscene calls, exposures, "peepers") and invasive (fondling, attempted rape, rape). Clearly they limit the word *harassment* to a noninvasive event, while most classifications would include invasive events, such as rape, under the term *sexual harassment.*

PREVALENCE AND INCIDENCE

Sexual harassment is prevalent in hospital setups. Pennington and associates[9] studied the prevalence and details of sexual harassment of female dental hygienists by distributing a questionnaire to 540 randomly selected registered Virginia dental hygienists; 285 surveys (53%) were returned. As many as 54% of the responding dental hygienists experienced sexual harassment. Of these, 50% experienced sexual harassment 4 or more years earlier, 23% 1 to 3 years, and 28% within the last year; these categories were mutually exclusive. The perpetrators of the harassment were reported to be either male dentists (73%) or male clients (45%). Less than 10% reported being harassed by women. While 70% of the sexually harassed respondents indicated that filing formal complaints was an effective strategy for managing sexual harassment, less than 1% actually did so.

McKenna and associates[10] studied the problem in New Zealand hospitals by a similar method. They sent anonymous questionnaires to 1169 registered nurses in their first year of practice, of which 551 were returned (47%). Verbal sexual harassment was reported in 30% cases (n = 167).

Hibino and associates[11] studied the prevalence and details of sexual harassment of female nurses by patients in Japanese hospitals by distributing similar questionnaires to hospital nurses. Of 600 nurses to whom the questionnaires were given, 473 (78.8%) were returned. It was discovered that sexual harassment was prevalent in the hospital environment. As many as 55.8% of nurses had been sexually harassed by patients. Nurses, on their part, tended to react passively and moderately and, in many cases, they did not attempt to stop the patients. Relatively few incidents were reported to the appropriate supervisors. The researchers concluded that administrators tended to underestimate the problem, and effective policies to combat this situation did not exist in Japanese hospitals.

Chaudhuri[12] conducted a study in 2005-2006 among 135 female doctors, nurses, health care attendants, administrative and other non-medical staff working in 2 government and 2 private hospitals in Kolkata, West Bengal, India. Four types of experiences were reported by the 77 women who had experienced 128 incidents of sexual harassment: verbal harassment (41), psychological harassment (45), sexual gestures and exposure (15), and unwanted touch (27). None of the women reported rape, attempted rape, or forced sex, but a number of them knew of other women health workers who had experienced these. The women who experienced harassment were reluctant to complain, fearing for their jobs or being stigmatized, and most were not aware of formal channels for redress. The latter problem has been mentioned by Pennington and associates[9] as well, who went to the extent of suggesting that information about managing sexual harassment (including the process of filing a formal complaint) needed to be incorporated into the curricula of professionals.

A similar survey conducted among nurses in Turkey (n = 622) revealed that 37.1% had been harassed sexually. Physicians were identified as the primary instigators of sexual harassment. About 80% of sexually harassed nurses did not report the incidents to hospital administration.[13]

OFFENDER CHARACTERISTICS

Levine and associates[14] studied the psychiatric histories of 31 professionals accused of sexually inappropriate behaviors within their work context. Eight types of professionals were evaluated; the majority were clergy, physicians, and teachers. Paraphilia was diagnosed in 26%, a nonparaphilic sexual compulsive syndrome in another 29%, and some form of character disorder in 58%. Seven professionals had offended six or more times. The ethical failures of the professionals were diverse and could not be explained by psychiatric diagnoses. Approximately half of the professionals were thought to be safe to return to work, often with a recommendation for psychotherapy and monitoring of their professional activities. A recommendation to no longer practice their professional roles was given for 47% of those evaluated, and the referring agency followed through with the recommendation. Outpatient psychotherapy was recommended for 84% of the sample.

ACTIONS HELD TO BE SEXUAL HARASSMENT

Instances of sexual harassment can be subjective at times. What is sexual harassment to the victim or the person harassed may genuinely not appear to be so to the offender. Thus in attempting to identify—and thereby eliminate—sexual harassment, there is no simple list of behaviors that constitute sexual harassment. However, a number of actual cases have tried to define it. Case law illustrates some behaviors that have been classified as sexual harassment (see Table 12.1).

In developing its 1993 survey of sexual harassment in schools, the American Association of University Women (AAUW) categorized 14 distinct forms of sexual harassment that students experience in schools. This list includes "flashing" or "mooning," being called gay or lesbian, being shown or given sexual messages, pictures, or notes, being spied on while dressing or showering, being touched, grabbed, or pinched in a sexual way, clothing pulled at, off, or down in a sexual

TABLE 12.1
Behaviors Classified as Sexual Harassment

Attempted kissing	*Carrero v. NYC Housing Authority*, 690 F2d 569 (2d Cir. 1989)
Behavior that can be shown would be different if the victim were the opposite sex	*Delgado v. Lehman*, 665 F.Supp 460 (E.D. Va. 1987)
Intercourse or invitations for such behavior	*Meritor Savings Bank v. Vinson*, 477 U.S. 57 (1986)
Love letters and repeated requests for a date	*Ellison v. Brady*, 924 F.2d 872 (9th Cir. 1991)
Nude or suggestive pictures and posters	*Hall v. Gus Construction Co.*, 842 F2d 1010 (5th Cir. 1988)
Sexual jokes and cartoons	*Broderick v. Ruder*, 685 F.Supp. 1269 (D.C. Cir. 1988)
Sexual remarks, insults, or innuendoes	*Jew v. Univ. of Iowa*, 749 F.Supp 957 (S.D. Iowa 1990); *Katz v. Dole*, 709 F.2d 251 (4th Cir. 1983)
Unequal facilities	*Harrington v. Vandalia-Butler Board of Education*, 585 F2d 192 (6th Cir. 1978)

way, forced kissing, forced to do something sexual other than kissing, passing sexual comments, gestures, jokes, or looks and spreading sexual rumors.

LEGAL ASPECTS

It is important to examine international laws against sexual harassment, if only to compare and contrast, so that important insights may be gained. In 1992, a study indicated that only 9 of 23 countries examined had specific laws against sexual harassment. In 2000, 31 countries that had statutes against sexual harassment were identified.[15] However, punishment and liability for the behavior vary due to different legal systems and conceptualizations of the issue.

India

Currently India has no explicit law on sexual harassment although sexual harassment at the workplace has remained one of the central concerns of the women's movement in India since the early 1980s.[16] Classically the problem has been addressed by the Indian Penal Code in Sections 354* and 509:

> ***354. Assault or criminal force to woman with intent to outrage her modesty***
>
> Whoever assaults or uses criminal force to any woman, intending to outrage or knowing it to be likely that he will thereby outrage her modesty, shall be punished with imprisonment of either description for a term which may extend to two years, or with fine, or with both.
>
> ***509. Word, gesture or act intended to insult the modesty of a woman***
>
> Whoever, intending to insult the modesty of any woman, utters any word, makes any sound or gesture, or exhibits any object, intending that such word or sound shall be heard, or that such gesture or object shall be seen, by such woman, or intrudes upon the privacy of such woman, shall be punished with simple imprisonment for a term which may extend to one year, or with fine, or with both.

* Section 354 has also been invoked in some cases of non-penile vaginal penetration (please see chapter on rape for details).

Vishaka v. State of Rajasthan

In India, the first major case of sexual harassment which hit media headlines occurred in the state of Rajasthan in September 1992. A female social worker, 41-years old, tried to stop the wedding of an infant girl, less than a year old in her village, Bhateri, about 45 km from Jaipur. Outraged by the audacity of this woman—who incidentally happened to be of low caste—who challenged their traditions, 5 men from the upper-caste family of the infant decided to "teach her a lesson" and gang-raped her repeatedly in the presence of her husband. After an extremely humiliating legal battle in the Rajasthan High Court when the rape survivor did not get justice and the rapists—educated and upper caste affluent men—were allowed to go free, a women's rights group called Vishaka filed a public interest litigation in the Supreme Court of India. In its landmark judgment, *Vishaka v. State of Rajasthan,* A.I.R. 1997 S.C. 3011, the Supreme Court of India for the first time laid down guidelines defining what exactly is sexual harassment at the work place, and what should be done to deal with it (Table 12.2).[17] The judgment was delivered by a three judge bench headed by the then chief justice of India, Justice J.S. Verma, and Justices Mrs. Sujata V. Manohar and B.N. Kirpal.

Following this decision, many states and territories of India acted upon the guidelines, but many others did not. Several institutions did not set up complaints committees (CCs) as envisaged in the Supreme Court guidelines. Aggrieved by this apathy, a woman activist, Medha Kotwal Lele, filed a writ petition in the Supreme Court.[18] Subsequent to this, in its order dated April 26, 2004, the Supreme Court issued notices to several parties including the governments concerned. It also directed further that the complaints committee as envisaged by the Supreme Court in its *Vishaka* judgment be deemed to be an inquiry authority and that the report of the complaints committee shall be deemed an inquiry report (not just a preliminary report). In pursuance of this direction, the Central Government, in its order dated July 1, 2004, amended sub-rule (2) of rule 14 of the Central Civil Services (Classification, Control and Appeal) Rules, 1965, to incorporate the necessary provision.[19]

Bajaj v. Gill

Another significant case which involved sexual harassment is *Rupan Deol Bajaj v. Kanwar Pal Singh Gill,* AIR (1996) SC 309. At a dinner party on July 18, 1988, K.P.S. Gill, the then director general of police of the state of Punjab came and stood in front of Mrs. Rupan Deol Bajaj, a senior Indian Administrative Service (IAS) officer. Allegedly he stood so close that his legs were just about 4 inches from her knees. He then asked her "to get up immediately" and come along with him. When she objected, Gill slapped her on the posterior in the full presence of all guests. Mrs. Bajaj immediately lodged a first information report (FIR) with the police. Because, Gill was an influential person in the police, it did not initiate any action. When the case reached the High Court of Punjab and Haryana, Gill petitioned the court for quashing of FIR on the ground that the matter was too trivial (section 95 IPC, "Act causing slight harm. Nothing is an offense by reason that it causes, or that it is intended to cause, or that it is known to be likely to cause, any harm, if that harm is so slight that no person of ordinary sense and temper would complain of such harm.") The High Court agreed with Gill and allowed the petition.

The case finally reached the Supreme Court of India. It held that slapping Mrs. Bajaj on her posterior amounted to "outraging her modesty" within the meanings of sections 354 and 509 of IPC. The act was not only an affront (disrespect) to the normal sense of feminine decency, but also an affront to her dignity. The Supreme Court also disallowed the defense taking shelter behind 95 IPC, stating that the offense was related to a woman's modesty and thus not trivial. Mr. Gill was slapped with a fine of Indian Rupees 250,000 (around US $6,250.00)

TABLE 12.2
Guidelines Set by the Supreme Court of India in 1997 To Ensure Prevention of Sexual Harassment of Women

1. Duty of the employer or other responsible persons in work places and other institutions:

It shall be the duty of the employer or other responsible persons in work places or other institutions to prevent or deter the commission of acts of sexual harassment and to provide the procedures for the resolution, settlement or prosecution of acts of sexual harassment by taking all steps required.

2. Definition:

For this purpose, sexual harassment includes such unwelcome sexually determined behavior (whether directly or by implication) as:

a) physical contact and advances;

b) a demand or request for sexual favors;

c) sexually colored remarks;

d) showing pornography;

e) any other unwelcome physical, verbal or non-verbal conduct of sexual nature.

Where any of these acts is committed in circumstances whereunder the victim of such conduct has a reasonable apprehension that in relation to the victim's employment or work whether she is drawing salary, or honorarium or voluntary, whether in government, public or private enterprise such conduct can be humiliating and may constitute a health and safety problem. It is discriminatory for instance when the woman has reasonable grounds to believe that her objection would disadvantage her in connection with her employment or work including recruiting or promotion or when it creates a hostile work environment. Adverse consequences might by visited if the victim does not consent to the conduct in question or raises any objection thereto.

3. Preventive Steps:

All employers or persons in charge of work place whether in the public or private sector should take appropriate steps to prevent sexual harassment. Without prejudice to the generality of this obligation they should take the following steps:

(a) Express prohibition of sexual harassment as defined above at the work place should be notified, published and circulated in appropriate ways.

(b) The rules/regulations of government and public sector bodies relating to conduct and discipline should include rules/regulations prohibiting sexual harassment and provide for appropriate penalties in such rules against the offender.

(c) As regards private employers steps should be taken to include the aforesaid prohibitions in the standing orders under the Industrial Employment (Standing Orders) Act, 1946.

(d) Appropriate work conditions should be provided in respect of work, leisure, health and hygiene to further ensure that there is no hostile environment towards women at work places and no employee woman should have reasonable grounds to believe that she is disadvantaged in connection with her employment.

4. Criminal proceedings:

Where such conduct amounts to a specific offense under the Indian Penal Code or under any other law, the employer shall initiate appropriate action in accordance with law by making a complaint with the appropriate authority.

In particular, it should ensure that victims, or witnesses are not victimized or discriminated against while dealing with complaints of sexual harassment. The victims of sexual harassment should have the option to seek transfer of the perpetrator or their own transfer.

5. Disciplinary action:

Where such conduct amounts to misconduct in employment as defined by the relevant service rules, appropriate disciplinary action should be initiated by the employer in accordance with those rules.

6. Complaint mechanism:

Whether or not such conduct constitutions an offense under law or a breach of the service rules, an appropriate complaint mechanism should be created in the employer's organization for redress of the complaint made by the victim. Such complaint mechanism should ensure time bound treatment of complaints.

TABLE 12.2 (continued)
Guidelines Set by the Supreme Court of India in 1997 To Ensure Prevention of Sexual Harassment of Women

7. Complaints committee:

The complaint mechanism, referred to in (6) above, should be adequate to provide, where necessary, complaints committee, a special counselor or other support service, including the maintenance of confidentiality.

The complaints committee should be headed by a woman and not less than half of its member should be women. Further, to prevent the possibility of any undue pressure or influence from senior levels, such complaints committee should involve a third party, either NGO or other body who is familiar with the issue of sexual harassment.

The complaints committee must make an annual report to the Government department concerned of the complaints and action taken by them.

The employers and person in charge will also report on the compliance with the aforesaid guidelines including on the reports of the complaints committee to the Government department.

8. Workers' initiative:

Employees should be allowed to raise issues sexual harassment at workers' meeting and in other appropriate forum and it should be affirmatively discussed in employer-employee meetings.

9. Awareness:

Awareness of the rights of female employees in this regard should be created in particular by prominently notifying the guidelines (and appropriate legislation when enacted on the subject) in a suitable manner.

10. Third party harassment:

Where sexual harassment occurs as a result of an act or omission by any third party or outsider, the employer and person in charge will take all steps necessary and reasonable to assist the affected person in terms of support and preventive action.

Apparel Export Promotion Council v. A.K.Chopra

The first true case of sexual harassment at a workplace in India was the celebrated *Apparel Export Promotion Council v. A.K. Chopra*, AIR 1999 Supreme Court 625. The case was so sensitive that it was fought under a pseudonym—Miss X—for the harassed girl. A.K. Chopra was working as a private secretary to the chairman of the Apparel Export Promotion Council. It was alleged that on August 12, 1988, he tried to molest Miss X, an employee of the Council, who at the relevant time was working as a clerk–typist. She was not competent or trained to take dictation. The respondent, however, insisted that she go with him to Taj Palace Hotel to take dictation from the chairman and then transcribe the material. Reluctantly, she went. While she was waiting for the director in the room, Chopra tried to sit too close to her and despite her objection did not cease his objectionable behavior. When she took dictation from the director, Chopra told her to type it at the business center which was located in the basement of the hotel. He volunteered to show her the business centre for getting the matter typed and, taking advantage of the isolated place, tried to sit too close to her and touch her despite her objections.

The typed material was corrected by the director (finance) who asked Miss X to retype the same material. Chopra again went with her to the business center and repeated his overtures. Although Miss X told Chopra that she would "leave the place if he continued to behave like that," he did not stop. He also tried to molest her physically in the lift while coming to the basement, but she saved herself by pressing the emergency button, which made the door of the lift to open. On August 16, 1988, Miss X went to meet the director (personnel) to lodge a complaint against Chopra, but was unable to meet him. However, she succeeded in meeting him on August 17, 1988. She narrated the whole incident to him orally and also submitted a written complaint. Chopra was placed under suspension via an order dated August 18, 1988. A charge-sheet was served on him to which he replied denying the allegations and asserting that "the allegations were imaginary and motivated." J.D. Giri, a director of the council, was appointed as an enquiry officer to enquire into the charges framed against the respondent. On behalf of the management with a view to prove the charges, as many as 6 witness were examined including Miss X. The respondent also examined 7 witnesses. The enquiry officer, after considering the documentary and oral evidence and the circumstances of the case, arrived at the conclusion that the respondent had acted against morality and modesty. He, therefore, held the charges leveled against the respondent had been proved. The disciplinary authority agreed with the enquiry officer, and removed Chopra from service effective June 28, 1989. Chopra moved the Delhi High Court to set aside this order. The High Court while entertaining the petition noted that the petitioner did indeed "try to molest," but "had not molested her." It disposed of the petition with a direction to reinstate Chopra without the benefit of back wages. The court also directed that Chopra be posted in an office outside Delhi for at least 2 years. The Apparel Export Promotion Council went to the Supreme Court in appeal. A two judge bench of the Supreme Court composed of the then Chief Justice of India, Dr. A.S. Anand, and Justice V. N. Khare allowed the appeal, ruling that the High Court had erred in saying that the respondent did not "actually molest" Miss X. The Court observed:

> The observations made by the High Court to the effect that since the respondent did not "actually molest" Miss X but only "tried to molest" her and therefore, his removal from service was not warranted rebel against realism and lose their sanctity and credibility. In the instant case, the behavior of the respondent did not cease to be outrageous for want of an sexual harassment or attempt to sexually molest. The Courts are required to examine the broader probabilities of a case and not get swayed away by insignificant discrepancies or narrow technicalities or dictionary meaning of the expression "molestation,". They must examine the entire materials to determine the genuineness of the complaint. The statement of the victim must be appreciated in the background of the entire case. Where the evidence of the victim inspires confidence, as is the position in the instant case, the Courts are obliged to rely on it. Such cases are required to be dealt with great sensitivity. Sympathy in such cases in favor of the superior officer is wholly misplaced and mercy has no relevance. The High Court overlooked the ground realities and ignored the fact that the conduct of the respondent against the junior female employee, Miss X was wholly against moral sanctions and decency.

The court also referred to a number of international conventions prohibiting sexual harassment at the workplace, and indicated that the spirit of those conventions should be implemented. The Court observed that in 1993 at the ILO Seminar held at Manila, it was recognized that sexual harassment of women in the workplace was a form of "gender discrimination." It also referred to the Convention on the Elimination of All Forms of Discrimination Against Women, 1979 (CEDAW) and the Beijing Declaration which directs all State parties to take appropriate measures to prevent discrimination of all forms against women besides taking steps to protect the honor and dignity of women. The International Covenant on Economic, Social and Cultural Rights contains several provisions particularly important for women. Article 7 recognizes their right to fair conditions of work and reflects that women shall not be subjected to sexual harassment at the place of work which may vitiate working environment. Referring to these international instruments, the court observed:

> These international instruments cast an obligation on the Indian State to gender sensitize its laws and the Courts are under an obligation to see that the message of the international instruments is not allowed to be drowned. This Court has in numerous cases emphasized that while discussing constitutional requirements, Court and counsel must never forget the core principle embodied in the international conventions and Instruments and as far as possible give effects to the principles contained in those international instruments. The courts are under an obligation to give due regard to International Conventions and Norms for construing domestic laws more so when there is no inconsistency between them and there is a void in domestic law.

The court also observed that the fundamental rights guaranteed in Indian Constitution were of sufficient amplitude to encompass all facets of gender equality, including prevention of sexual harassment and abuse, and that the courts are under a constitutional obligation to protect and preserve those fundamental rights.

Summing up the judgment, the court said that the respondent did not deserve any mercy or leniency. It observed:

> The act of the respondent was unbecoming of good conduct and behavior expected from a superior officer and undoubtedly amounted to sexual harassment of Miss X and the punishment imposed by the appellant, was thus commensurate with the gravity of his objectionable behavior and did not warrant any interference by the High Court in exercise of its power of judicial review. At the conclusion of the hearing, learned counsel for the respondent submitted that the respondent was repentant of his actions and that he tenders an unqualified apology and that he was willing to also go to apologize to Miss X. We are afraid, it is too late in the day to show any sympathy to the respondent in such a case. Any lenient action in such a case is bound to have demoralizing effect on working women. Sympathy in such cases in uncalled for and mercy is misplaced. Thus, for what we have said above, the impugned order of the High Court is set aside and the punishment as imposed by the Disciplinary Authority and upheld by the Department Appellate of removal of the respondent from service is upheld and restored. The appeals thus succeed and are allowed. We, however, make no order as to costs.

Sexual Harassment of Women at Work Place Bill, 2006

As stated earlier, currently there is no law which caters specifically to the sexual harassment of women. However, the Indian Government is actively considering the The Sexual Harassment of Women at Work Place (Prevention, Prohibition and Redressal) Bill, 2006. Section 2 (m) of this bill defines sexual harassment as follows:[20]

> "Sexual Harassment" is such unwelcome sexually determined behavior such as physical contact, advances, sexually colored remarks, showing pornography or making sexual demands, whether verbal, textual, graphic or electronic or by any other actions, which may contain—
>
> (i) Implied or overt promise of preferential treatment in that employee's employment or
> (ii) An implied or overt threat of detrimental treatment in that employee's employment or an implied or overt threat about the present or future employment status of that employee and includes the creation of a hostile working environment.
> (iii) The conduct interferes with an employee's work or creates an intimidating, hostile or offensive work environment or
> (iv) Such conduct can be humiliating and may constitute a health and safety problem
>
> **Explanation 1**: Hostile Environment: A work environment is "hostile" when unwelcome verbal, non-verbal or physical behavior focusing on sexuality is severe and pervasive enough to interfere with the victim's work performance or be intimidating or offensive to a reasonable person.
>
> **Explanation 2**: It is clarified that it is the reasonable perception of the woman that would be relevant in determining whether any conduct was sexually colored and, if so, whether such conduct was unwelcome or not and that her objection would disadvantage her in connection with her employment, including recruitment or promotion, or when it creates a hostile working environment.

Poland

In October 2003, the lower house of the Polish parliament approved a set of amendments to the Labour Code, which included new provisions, in line with EU law, aimed at ensuring equal treatment and preventing discrimination at work. A notable change was the recognition of the issue of sexual harassment, which was defined, made illegal, and expressly prohibited. Article 18(3)(a)(6) states:

> Discrimination in reference to gender shall also comprise all unaccepted behavior of a sexual character or behavior referring to the gender of the employee whose objective or effect comprises transgression against the dignity, or insult or humiliation, of an employee; such behavior may comprise physical, verbal, or non-verbal elements (sexual harassment).

Sexual harassment can also be prosecuted under Article 199 of The Polish Penal Code, which states:

> Whosoever, using the relation of dependence or critical situation of another person, forces that person to have sexual intercourse or any other form of sexual activity or forces a person to perform such an activity, shall be punished by three years of imprisonment.

Romania

Article 223 of the Criminal Code of the Republic of Romania (for details, please see chapter on exhibitionism) outlaws sexual harassment. Interestingly, it is a gender neutral law, i.e., both males and females may be punished under its provisions:

(1) act of harassing a person by threat or coercion in order to obtain sexual satisfaction, committed by a person abusing his/her quality or the influence provided by the office held at the workplace, shall be punished by imprisonment from 3 months to 1 year or by days/fine.
(2) Criminal action is initiated upon prior complaint from the injured person. Reconciliation of parties removes criminal liability.

United States

In the United States, sexual harassment violates Title VII of the Civil Rights Act of 1964. Title VII applies to employers with 15 or more employees, including state and local governments. It also applies to employment agencies and to labor organizations, as well as to the federal government.[2] Sexual harassment in schools and universities is illegal under Title IX of the Education Act Amendments of 1972, which prohibits sex discrimination in schools receiving federal funds.[21] This law applies to all school-sponsored activities—athletics, field trips, extracurricular programs, and transportation.

Franklin v. Gwinnett county public schools, 503 U.S. 60 (1992)

This is a landmark case highlighting the issue of sexual harassment in schools. Events in the case date back to 1986. According to Christine Franklin, then a student at the North Gwinnett High School in suburban Atlanta, Andrew Hill, an economics teacher at the school, began approaching her with sexually suggestive remarks. The harassment continued over a period of 15 months, and included sexually-oriented conversations in the teacher's office, forced kisses, and phone calls. Ultimately the teacher pressured her into having sex with him 3 times at various places on the school campus and during school hours. The administrators were aware of her complaints but were slow to take action, and the school's band director even suggested that she drop her allegations in order to avoid embarrassment.

At the time, the district had no formal policy for reporting or investigating sexual harassment, although eventually an investigation was conducted that led to the resignation of the teacher, who resigned on the condition that all matters pending against him be dropped. The school thereupon closed its investigation.

In 1988 Franklin filed a formal complaint with the U.S. Department of Education's Office for Civil Rights, which after its investigation concluded that the teacher and school district had indeed violated Title IX. Later Franklin filed a federal suit asking for $11 million in compensatory damages.

Two lower courts dismissed Franklin's suit, holding that individuals cannot collect monetary damages under Title IX. But in 1992 the U.S. Supreme Court, by a 9-to-0 vote, reversed those rulings, noting that "absent clear direction to the contrary by Congress, the federal courts have the power to award any appropriate relief" to individuals suing under federal statutes. The school district and the Bush administration argued that Title IX authorized suits only for backpay or for an injunction ordering an end to the illegal activity. However, the Supreme Court reasoned that these remedies were useless to most students, who received no pay in the first place and who would have typically graduated and cut their ties to a school by the time a lawsuit can result in an injunction.

REFERENCES

1. Musaph, H., Sexual Harassment in the workplace and in psychotherapeutic relationships, in *The Handbook of Forensic sexology*, Krivacska JJ and Money J., Eds., Prometheus Books, New York, 1994, chapter 9.
2. The U.S. Equal Employment Opportunity Commission. Sexual Harassment. Available at: http://www.eeoc.gov/types/sexual_harassment.html.
3. Genesis 39:1-23. The Holy Bible. Authorized King James Version. Oxford University Press, New York, 1972.
4. Webb, S.L. The History of Sexual Harassment on the job, in *Sexual harassment—Issues and Answers*, LeMoncheck, L. and Sterba, J.P., Eds., Oxford University Press, Oxford, 2001, Chapter 17, Pp 136-45.
5. EEOC v. Mitsubishi Motor Manufacturing, 990 F. Supp. 1059 (C.D. Ill 1998), 67.
6. Braun, S., Mitsubishi to Pay $34 Million in Sex Harassment Case, in *Sexual Harassment—Issues and Answers*, LeMoncheck, L. and Sterba, J.P., Eds., Oxford University Press, Oxford, 2001, chap. 26, Pp 184-7.
7. *Jones v. Clinton*, U.S. District Court, Arkansas, Western Division, in *Sexual Harassment—Issues and Answers*, LeMoncheck, L. and Sterba, J.P., Eds., Oxford University Press, Oxford, 2001, chap. 24, Pp 172-180.
8. DiVasto P.V., Kaufman, A., Rosner, L., Jackson, R., Christy, J., Pearson, S., Burgett, T. The prevalence of sexually stressful events among females in the general population. Arch Sex Behav. 1984;13(1):59-67.
9. Pennington, A., Darby, M., Bauman, D., Plichta, S., Schnuth, M.L. Sexual harassment in dentistry: experiences of Virginia dental hygienists. *J Dent Hyg.* 2000 Fall;**74(4)**:288-95.
10. McKenna, B.G., Poole, S.J., Smith, N.A., Coverdale, J.H., Gale, C.K. A survey of threats and violent behavior by patients against registered nurses in their first year of practice. *Int J Ment Health Nurs.* 2003 Mar;**12(1)**:56-63.
11. Hibino, Y., Ogino, K., Inagaki, M. Sexual harassment of female nurses by patients in Japan. *J Nurs Scholarsh.* 2006;**38(4)**:400-5.
12. Chaudhuri, P. Experiences of sexual harassment of women health workers in four hospitals in kolkata, India. *Reprod Health Matters.* 2007 Nov;**15(30)**:221-9.
13. Celik, Y., Celik, S.S. Sexual harassment against nurses in Turkey. *J Nurs Scholarsh.* 2007;**39(2)**:200-6.
14. Levine, S.B., Risen, C.B., Althof, S.E. Professionals who sexually offend: evaluation procedures and preliminary findings. *J Sex Marital Ther.* 1994 Winter;**20(4)**:288-302.
15. Sigal, J., Sexual harassment, in *Encyclopedia of Applied Psychology*, Spielberger C., Ed., Academic Press. San Diego, CA, 2004, pages 393–403.

16. Patel, V., *Women's Challenges of the New Millennium*, Gyan Publications, Delhi, 2002.
17. *Vishaka v. State of Rajasthan*, A.I.R. 1997 S.C. 3011.
18. *Medha Kotwal Lele & Others v. Union of India and others* (Writ Petition (Crl.) No. 173-177/1999).
19. Report of the Complaints Committee constituted for prevention of sexual harassment of women at work places—follow up action. Government of India. Ministry of Personnel, Public Grievances & Pensions. Available at: http://persmin.nic.in/estt/CCSRules_1964/ccs_conduct_rules_1964_details.htm.
20. The Sexual Harassment of Women at Work Place (Prevention, Prohibition and Redressal) Bill, 2006. Available from: http://ncw.nic.in/sexualharassmentatworkplacebill2005.pdf.
21. Title IX of The Education Amendments of 1972. 20 U.S.C. §1681.

13 Necrophilia

INTRODUCTION

Necrophilia, sexual gratification by having sex with the dead, is one of the weirdest, most bizarre, and revolting practices of abnormal and perverse sensuality. Also known as necrophilism, necrolagnia, necrocoitus, necrochlesis, and thanatophilia, it may be seen alone or in association with other paraphilias, namely sadism, cannibalism, vampirism (the practice of drinking blood from a person or animal), necrophagia (eating the flesh of the dead), necropedophilia (sexual attraction to the corpses of children), and necrozoophilia (sexual attraction to the corpses of or killings of animals—also known as necrobestiality).

Very often the corpses used for sexual purposes are not fresh but rather dug up from graves in a putrefied or mummified condition. Some necrophiliaes prefer only the bones. A variation, referred to as necrophagists, feed on decaying dead bodies. These are different from cannibals, who prefer fresh meat or who consume deceased loved ones for spiritual purposes. A vast spectrum of necrophagists is seen, from those who merely want to lick the genitals or breasts of a dead person, to persons who want to devour specific parts* to necrophiles who would eat the entire body. Necrophilia is mostly seen in males. It is possible for a necrophiliac to have normal sexual relations with living beings.

DSM-IV-TR[1] does not assign any specific or unique code to necrophilia. Instead along with several other uncommon paraphilias (7 of which are specifically named), necrophilia is grouped under the code 302.9 (paraphilias not otherwise specified; please see chapter on Zoophilia for full statement of Code 302.9).

NECROSADISM

When seen in association with sadism, the paraphilia is termed *necrosadism*. This paraphilia involves deliberate assaults on dead bodies, subjecting them to considerable indignities, and wanton mutilations. Some necrosadists may present with strange propensities. Langevin and associates[2] describe the case of Mr. A, who murdered a woman and had intercourse with the corpse. He then removed the genitals and was contemplating eating them when he was interrupted by a third party and he ran away from the scene. He then attempted to rape and murder a second woman, but was apprehended. Upon examination, he presented as a very narcissistic individual, and expressed an interest in sex reassignment surgery. He was particularly eager to have hormones so that he might grow female breasts.

Necromania is an obsession with having intercourse with the dead to such an extreme extent that dead bodies may be embalmed and preserved for long periods, with repeated acts of sexual intercourse perpetrated on the corpses daily.

* A case is known where a man merely wanted to eat the nail trimmings from a corpse. One woman whose family members had died, went into the family crypt to devour the genitals of her male relatives.

Necrophilia in Gravediggers and Mortuary Attendants

Gravediggers and mortuary attendants, who are most often found practicing necrophilia, engage in this activity perhaps because of their loneliness, coupled with easy access to corpses. It is also possible that they chose this profession because they were necrophiles. It is known that necrophiles often choose professions that allow them free and unhindered access to dead bodies.

In ancient times, when dead bodies were transported by sea for last funeral rites (as in cases of deaths occurring in foreign countries), sailors were often accused of necrophilia. Long transportation periods coupled with loneliness and the absence of witnesses allowed, and even encouraged, sailors to commit acts of necrophilia with dead bodies.

In his seminal work, *Psychopathia Sexualis*, Richard von Krafft-Ebing called necrophilia a horrible manifestation of sadism.[3] Abraham A. Brill, who published one of the earliest detailed studies of necrophilia in 1941, characterized necrophiles as mentally deficient, psychotic, and incapable of obtaining a consenting partner. Necrophilia has frequently been associated with necrophagia and vampirism (drinking blood of humans), as all are considered perversions.

Necrophilia may be explained—in some cases, at least—by the simple fact that the dead can't refuse, reject, or resist; they also don't tell tales or talk back. Necrophagia may represent a "hangover" from our evolutionary past when carrion-eating was common.

HISTORICAL PERSPECTIVES

A necrophile may be seen as the very opposite of the vampire. While the term *vampire* generally refers to a dead person disturbing the living, the necrophile is a living person disturbing the dead. The practice of necrophilia has a long and rich history, perhaps as old as civilization itself. Mythology abounds with instances where a queen or goddess succeeded in getting herself impregnated by a deceased husband. The Egyptian goddess Isis was said to have conceived her son Horus after her consort Osiris had been murdered and cut to pieces—simply by using his severed member as a dildo while reciting ritual incantations.

Necrophilia in Greek Mythology

Necrophilia can be found in Greek mythology, too. One such instance is given by Parthenius of Nicaea (first century BC), a Greek grammarian and poet, and tutor of the poet Virgil. His only surviving work is a collection of Love Stories (*Erotica Pathemata*), sourced from a variety of classical and Hellenistic writers. Some are myth-themed, while others are historical or pseudo-historical tales. In this book, he mentions the curious story of Dimoetes who married his brother Troezen's daughter, Euopis. Euopis, however, was besieged with love for her own brother and was even consorting with him. This enraged Dimoetes, who informed Troezen accordingly. Not able to bear the shame, Euopis hung herself, but not without having cursed her husband, who was the cause of her fate. Perhaps because of the curse, it was not long before Dimoetes came upon the dead body of a beautiful woman thrown up by the sea and tossed about by the waves. He immediately fell in love with her dead body and hatched a plan so he could enjoy her privately. He kept the body and had sexual intercourse with her repeatedly. Soon, however, the body began to decay and became useless for intercourse. Dimoetes built a magnificent tomb for her body but could not withstand the grief of losing her. Unable to bear the separation any longer, he committed suicide with his sword at her tomb. Curiously, the grief which led to suicide in this case was not due to the loss of a living being, as is usually the case; it was the loss of a dead body. Dimoetes, a true necrophile, had fallen in love with a girl he had never met in life.[4,5,6]

Necrophilia in Ancient Cultures

Necrophilia was practiced in some ancient cultures as a spiritual means of communicating with the dead, while others employed it as an attempt to revive the recently departed. There is evidence that necrophilia was practiced by the Moche civilization of South America. Remains of their pottery depict skeletal figures (presumably the dead) engaged in coitus with living human beings. The Greek historian Herodotus (484–425 BC) noted that sexual interference with the dead was known and abhorred by the Egyptians:

> Wives of notable men, and women of great beauty and reputation, are not at once given to the embalmers, but only after they have been dead for three or four days; this is done to deter the embalmers from having intercourse with the women. For it is said that one was caught having intercourse with the fresh corpse of a woman, and was denounced by his fellow-workman.[7]

It has been suggested that the curse of pharaoh's tomb myth was deliberately created to discourage people from engaging in necrophilia. It appears that one of the reasons for burning bodies after death in some cultures (most notably Hindus), or burying them deeply or in solid granite and marble tombs, was to prevent their violation by necrophiliacs. At one time a curious necrophilic custom prevailed in India. If a female who was engaged died before marriage, her fiancé had to deflower her before she could be cremated. This ritual had to be carried out in front of the village priest.[8]

Greco-Roman Period

Periander (625–585 BC), the second tyrant of Corinth, Greece, was a known necrophiliac. He learned his "savagery" from Thrasybulus, the tyrant of Miletus, who instructed Periander to get rid of anyone who could conceivably take power from him. Among his cruel acts were sending young boys from Corcyra to be castrated in Lydia (who were reputed to have escaped and be rescued by the Samians). He also murdered his wife Melissa and then had sexual intercourse with her dead body. Referring to his act of necrophilia, the Greek historian Herodotus (484 BC–ca. 425 BC) commented that he was "putting his loaves into a cold oven."[9] His son Lycophron discovered that Periander was the murderer, so Periander exiled him from Corinth and forbade any of his subjects to shelter him.

About the murder of Melissa, Herodotus writes:

> For after killing his own wife Melissa, Periander suffered yet another calamity on top of what he had already suffered. He had two sons by Melissa, one seventeen and one eighteen years old. Their mother's father, Procles, the sovereign of Epidaurus, sent for the boys and treated them affectionately, as was natural, seeing that they were his own daughter's sons. When they left him, he said as he sent them forth: "Do you know, boys, who killed your mother?" The elder of them paid no attention to these words; but the younger, whose name was Lycophron, was struck with such horror when he heard them that when he came to Corinth he would not speak to his father, his mother's murderer, nor would he answer him when addressed nor reply to his questions. At last Periander was so angry that he drove the boy from his house.[10]

About the alleged necrophilia, he writes:

> Periander, however, understood what had been done, and perceived that Thrasybulus had counseled him to slay those of his townsmen who were outstanding in influence or ability; with that he began to deal with his citizens in an evil manner. Whatever act of slaughter or banishment Cypselus had left undone, that Periander brought to accomplishment. In a single day he stripped all the women of Corinth naked, because of his own wife Melissa. Periander had sent messengers to the Oracle of the Dead on the river Acheron in Thesprotia to enquire concerning a deposit that a friend had left, but Melissa, in an apparition, said that she would tell him nothing, nor reveal where the deposit lay, for she was cold and naked. The garments, she said, with which Periander had buried with her had never been burnt,

> and were of no use to her. Then, as evidence for her husband that she spoke the truth, she added that Periander had put his loaves into a cold oven. When this message was brought back to Periander (for he had had intercourse with the dead body of Melissa and knew her token for true), immediately after the message he made a proclamation that all the Corinthian women should come out into the temple of Hera. They then came out as to a festival, wearing their most beautiful garments, and Periander set his guards there and stripped them all alike, ladies and serving-women, and heaped all the clothes in a pit, where, as he prayed to Melissa, he burnt them. When he had done this and sent a second message, the ghost of Melissa told him where the deposit of the friend had been laid. "This, then, Lacedaimonians, is the nature of tyranny, and such are its deeds. We Corinthians marveled greatly when we saw that you were sending for Hippias, and now we marvel yet more at your words to us. We entreat you earnestly in the name of the gods of Hellas not to establish tyranny in the cities, but if you do not cease from so doing and unrighteously attempt to bring Hippias back, be assured that you are proceeding without the Corinthians' consent."[11]

The death of a loved one can sometimes lead to this practice. Herod the Great (c. 74–4 BC) had 10 wives, but he loved his second wife Mariamne 1 (54 BC–29 BC) the most. Although he had her executed on charges of adultery, so much did he love her, that—according to a legend—he had her preserved in honey and had regular intercourse with her for 7 years.[12,13]

The Frankish king Charlemagne (742–814) is believed to have suffered from necrophilia. Many legends of the ninth century state that Charlemagne committed some "unspeakable sin," for which he was eventually pardoned directly by God without benefit of confession or priestly mediation. What that unspeakable sin was has remained largely conjectural. Most now believe that it was some form of sexual perversion, most probably incest. But several workers believe that it could be necrophilia.[31]

Middle Ages

In 1533, King Henry VIII (1491–1547) promulgated the Buggery Act 1533.[14] Mainly an anti-sodomy law, the act also made buggery with beasts punishable by hanging. Undoubtedly, bestiality was specifically included because of the widely prevalent fear of hybrid births following the union of man and animal, e.g., the centaur (the body of a horse with a man's torso). Mythical and legendary beasts such as satyr (an animal with the torso of a man, the legs and feet of a goat), mermaids and mermen (half fish, half human), minotaur (a beast with the body of a man and the head of a bull), and manticore (a beast having the face of a man, the body of a lion, and the tail of a scorpion) were supposed to have been created from such unions.

Necrophilia was a frequent theme in the writings of the Marquis de Sade. Two well-known necrophiliacs of 19th century France are Henri Blot and Victor Ardisson. In 1886, Blot, 26-years old, exhumed and fornicated with the dead body of a recently buried dancer. After the sexual act, Blot lapsed into a deep sleep that was only interrupted when the cemetery's groundskeeper physically shook him awake.[15] At his trial, Blot is supposed to have commented, "Every man to his taste. Mine is for corpses."[16]

Victor Ardisson, a mortician in his tiny town, supposedly had sex with over 100 corpses. According to his confession, Victor regularly spoke to his cadaverous lovers, feeling genuine shock and hurt when they would not respond. When police raided his home (after a tip from suspicious neighbors), they found the decaying remains of a three-and-a-half year old girl whom Ardisson had used for oral sex. He also kept a 13-year old girl's head as his bed mate, with whom he supposedly had oral sex.

In an 18th century case, Sir John Pryce embalmed his first wife when she died and kept her in bed with him, even after he married a second time. When his second wife died, she too was embalmed and placed in the same bed. His third wife, however, wanted no part of his gruesome hobbies and brought the facts before the world.[17]

While many grave robberies in the Middle Ages were connected with acquiring dead bodies for anatomical dissections, at least some were connected to necrophiliac activities. In this connection the legend of Jean Baptiste in 19th century Utah is most notable. John Baptiste was one of the first gravediggers ever employed in Salt Lake City in the late 1800s. He was believed to be well-off and lived comfortably. He was a quiet person and had few friends, so most people never paid much attention to him as he went about his work.

About 3 years after Baptiste came to work for the city, a man died in Salt Lake City and was buried by the gravedigger in the local cemetery. A short time later, the man's brother came to Utah from the east. He was not familiar with the Mormon religion and wished to have his sibling returned to the east to be buried in the family plot. His wish was granted, and the grave was uncovered. When the casket was pried open, the corpse inside was discovered to be nude and lying in the coffin face-down, as though somebody had practiced sodomy on him.

City officials began an immediate investigation, focusing on John Baptiste, and several men were assigned to keep him and the cemetery under surveillance. Soon after another burial, Baptiste was seen pushing a wheelbarrow from a nearby storage shed to a freshly opened grave. Authorities stopped him and found a pile of clothing hidden in the bushes. The corpse had been removed from the grave, his clothing removed, and was being moved from the storage shed in the wheelbarrow.

Baptiste was arrested, and his home was searched. His house was filled with clothing. He had used some of it for drapes and furniture covers, and in the cellar was a large vat for boiling the clothing of the dead.

The news spread, and local citizens descended on the cemetery to check on their deceased loved ones. Authorities believed that he had stolen clothing and jewelry from more than 350 corpses. All of the clothing from Baptiste's home was taken to City Hall for identification by relatives. Authorities also went to local second-hand stores, where they learned that the gravedigger had sold large amounts of stolen jewelry for cash.

Baptiste was tried and convicted of grave robbery, branded with a hot iron, and exiled to an island in the Great Salt Lake, northwest of the city. It is believed now that he may have done more than just steal clothes and jewelry from the dead bodies. He was perhaps a necrophiliac, who used the dead bodies for necrophiliac activities.[17]

Bloch[18] describes some remarkable cases of necrophilia. In one case, a porter in a Paris morgue was arraigned after being caught having intercourse with the body of a girl drowned in the Seine. The second case is more interesting. In the town of Schonau, 30-year old Mrs. Maschke was buried in the morning in a local cemetery, but the grave was not sealed. In the afternoon, a female resident visiting the cemetery observed that Mrs. Maschke's coffin was moving. She immediately notified the caretaker, who hurried to the grave accompanied by some local men. They were surprised to find that a poorhouse inmate named Wokatsch was engaged in sexual intercourse with Mrs. Maschke's dead body. He was captured and turned over to the court in Hainspach.

Some notorious cases of necrophilia have come from France. In 1827, a Frenchman named Leger mutilated the genitals of a young girl and drank her blood after necrophilia.[19] One of the most famous necrophiles was François Bertrand (1824–1850), a sergeant in the French army, who during the years 1847–9 dug up corpses from Montparnasse, a Paris cemetery, to have sex with them. Widely known as "the Vampire of Montparnasse, " the sergeant showed a strange fascination with the dead early in life, when he developed a habit of dissecting dead cats and dogs. When he grew up, he began exhuming dead bodies to perform sexual intercourse with them. He also eviscerated and dismembered the bodies after intercourse. Bodies of both men and women were retrieved from graveyards. He even chewed some of the bodies, thus showing signs of necrophagia as well.

The youngest of his victims was 7-year old. On one occasion, he dug out a grave with his bare hands on a rainy night, and when the lower part of the body was exposed, he tore out pieces of the body and closed the grave. In November 1847, he disinterred the body of a 16-year old girl and performed coitus on her dead body. In March 1848, he had coitus with 4 dead women and subsequently mutilated their bodies.

When Sergeant Bertrand was eventually captured (as a result of being wounded by a police bullet in Montparnasse Cemetery), during a stay at a military hospital, he offered neither denials nor regrets to the police investigators. He claimed he could not explain why he committed these crimes. He could only explain that he often felt compelled to exhume the recently deceased and cut into their flesh with his sword and teeth. He violated dozens of graves before being caught. He was convicted on 15 counts. Dr. Lunier, the state psychiatrist of the time, opined that the sergeant did not have all his mental faculties and should be confined and treated in a psychiatric asylum, rather than being imprisoned. It was a new thought at that time. The famed McNaughton case, which introduced the concept of insanity as a defense in criminal cases, had occurred just 6 years earlier—in 1843.

Nevertheless, Bertrand was awarded a sentence of 1 year and was imprisoned (the prosecution could not prove rape, as it could only be committed on live people). He proved a model prisoner, served his sentence, and left in 1850. He committed suicide soon afterwards. Nobus[20] suggests that his case may not be that of a true necrophile, since what was central to his offense was mutilation of corpses, and not sexual gratification since gratification was only secondary. This does not, however, appear to be the case, if his records are studied in detail.

It is known that at the time of violent death, the victim suffers from spasms of the anal sphincter. Many potential necrophiliacs have sought to take advantage of this fact by engaging in anal intercourse with dying soldiers on a battlefield. Soldiers during the Russo-Turkish war of 1877–8 and Moroccan campaigns of 1919–26 were violated in this way on the battlefield.[8,21] The practice has been termed "warm necrophilia," although the term is more suitably applied elsewhere (please see below). The Chinese are known to engage in sexual intercourse with geese and killing them intentionally at the point of ejaculation for similar reasons (please see chapter on bestiality for details).

Modern Era

The *Aghoris*, a small Hindu sect in India, have been known to live in graveyards, sit on corpses, wear ash from the pyre, drink urine from skulls, use human bones from graveyards for rituals, and desecrate corpses including various acts of necrophilia. Some reputedly even eat parts of the corpse. *Aghori* means "non-terrifying" in Sanskrit, and may refer to how members of the sect view death.

It has been alleged by the prosecution that in the infamous 1994 Megan Kanka case, Jesse Timmendequas committed acts of necrophilia on 7-year old Megan Kanka in his car, after raping and murdering her (for details please see chapter on pedophilia).

In September 1994, Chinese police arrested a 39-year old a minivan driver from Canton, capital of the southern province of Guangdong. He was suspected of serial necrophilia and the rape, murder, and dismemberment of 13 or 14 women since 1990. The police came to know about him by the discovery of parts of dismembered corpses in rubbish bins. All victims were prostitutes. They had been raped, murdered, and cut up. Some parts had been kept, preserved in antiseptic, "so that he could continue to use them during his fantasies." He was arrested after a prostitute from the northwestern region of Xinjiang recovered consciousness after an assault, escaped, and went to the police. There was no doubt regarding his necrophiliac activities because the police confiscated videos recording of the acts of rape, murder, and necrophilia, as well as a diary listing the personal details of those killed. They also found mannequins to which the skin and sexual organs of some of the victims had been glued. The suspect's wife had left him several years earlier because of his cruelty.[22]

Two most notable necrophiles of modern times were Surendra Koli and Moninder Singh Pandher, who allegedly committed several acts of necrophilia on dead bodies of young children (please see below).

NECROPHILIA IN ANIMALS

Sometimes peculiar human behaviors can be understood better by studying similar behaviors in other species. Curiously, necrophilia is seen in the animal world, too. Male cane toads (*Bufo marinus*) have been documented engaging in copulation with dead toads and even inanimate objects.[23] Heterosexual necrophilia has been known in the drake mallard (*Anas platyrhynchos*).[24] Kees Moeliker of the Rotterdam Natural History Museum, Netherlands, has described a curious case of even homosexual necrophilia among drake mallards, in which a drake engaged in copulation with a dead drake for almost 75 minutes, with 2 short breaks in between.[25]

NECROPHILIA AND INTELLIGENCE

Bernardi and Ponti[26] describe a strange case from Italy. A 15-year old boy had a sexual intercourse with a 7-month old stillborn female baby by inserting his penis between her thighs. The crime occurred in the mortuary of the hospital. To conceal his crime, he threw the body in a well afterward. The boy was in the hospital for the treatment of tuberculosis of the knee. On examination, he was found to have the mental age of an 8-year old and no moral sense. He was not prosecuted. The authors conclude that necrophilia is generally associated with a low intelligence level, and this is the reason for the relative absence of prosecutions. The exceptionality of the case is the age of the victim (stillborn 7-months).

VARIATIONS OF NECROPHILIA

Some variations are *autonecrophilia* (imagining oneself as a corpse or becoming sexually aroused by simulated corpses) and *pseudonecrophilia*. The term *pseudonecrophilia* has been used differently by different authors. Some take it to mean arousal from having sex with someone pretending to be dead,[27] while others use the term to describe erotic fantasies of a person to have sexual relations with a dead body, and masturbation (but not actual contact).[28,29,30] Still others use it to refer to a person who has a transient attraction to a corpse, but corpses are not the main object of his sexual fantasies.[31] According to the latter definition, the preferable sexual contacts of pseudonecrophiles are with living persons. Because of the multitude of meanings the term *pseudonecrophilia* has acquired, it is preferable to do away with this term entirely and follow the classification system suggested below.

ETIOLOGY

The etiology of necrophilia is not clear. One difficulty is the existence of a vast spectrum of necrophiles—from role players (Class I necrophiles) to those who kill (Class VIII necrophiles). Obviously, a single explanation cannot account for the behavior of all. Etiological theories of necrophilia can broadly be divided in two groups—biological and psychoanalytical.

BIOLOGICAL THEORIES

The genetic basis of necrophilia has been proposed by many authors.[32,33] It is noteworthy that in the literature certain instances of "necrophiliac rampages" have been described following heavy alcohol intoxication.[34] Fugue states or severe headaches prior to or after overt necrophiliac behavior have also been reported. Coupled with the fact that alcohol can induce temporal lobe abnormalities,[35] and that temporal lobe abnormalities are associated with a number of other paraphilias, it may be reasonable to deduce that temporal lobe anomalies may be responsible for some instances of necrophilia.

Psychoanalytical Theories

German psychiatrist Albert Moll* (1862–1939) believed that "congenital degeneracy " was responsible for necrophilia.[36] Krafft-Ebing blamed it on "acquired mental weakness."[37] After Freud, psychoanalytic interpretations of necrophilia became more fashionable. Some common interpretations are:

- (i) Unconscious suppressed hostility toward parental figures and sadistic impulses to explore the mother's body. A deep-seated thirst for revenge displaced from the dominating mother onto the dominating spouse, resulting in a compulsive and ecstatic association between love or admiration on one hand, and pain or humiliation on the other.[38] The offender takes revenge from a "female figure" (the dead female, symbolizing mother or spouse), by ravishing her.
- (ii) Several psychoanalysts have emphasized the central role of the victim's "helplessness and resistlessness".[28,39,40] Castration anxiety, feelings of male inadequacy, and fear of women may be at work here. As a result of these factors, the offender feels a need to prove his strength by inflicting humiliation on a totally subservient victim.
- (iii) It is theorized by some psychoanalysts that a necrophile's concept of sexuality is somewhat infantile. Psychologically healthy people participate in human relationships by receiving and giving pleasure. With a corpse, one only gets pleasure, with no need to give, indicating an immature and narcissistic ego of the necrophile.
- (iv) Other theorists focus on the necrophile's unconscious internalization of the parental attitude that sex is dirty and unnatural. This may lead to compulsion of having sex with the dead. Since sex with the dead is not true sex, it cannot be dirty.

Miscellaneous Causes

According to Stekel,[33] Hellwig reports that a mother, in order to cure her hermaphroditic son, opened the grave of a virgin. The son had to follow the counsel of his mother and lie naked upon the corpse "in order to bring his sex in order." It must, however, be remembered that acts like this, although simulating necrophilia, are not necrophilic acts in the true sense of the word. According to DSM-IV-TR, the "essential features of a paraphilia are recurrent, intense sexually arousing fantasies, sexual urges, or behaviors" (please see chapter 1 for details). A single act of lying naked upon a corpse based on a superstitious belief is *not* necrophilia in the true sense.

CLASSIFICATION

Wulffen[41] divided necrophilia into lust murder or necrosadism, necrostuprum, and necrophagy. In *lust murder*, the offender kills first and then goes ahead with sexual intercourse with the corpse; in *necrostuprum*, he steals the corpse; and in *necrophagy*, he mutilates and eats parts of the corpse.

Rosman and Resnick[31] classify all necrophilias into two groups—genuine necrophilia and pseudonecrophilia. Genuine necrophilia is further subdivided into necrophilic homicide (equivalent to Wulffen's lust murder), regular necrophilia (equivalent to Wulffen's necrostuprum) and necrophilic fantasy (roughly equivalent to Wulffen's necrophagy). However, a newer classification is more appropriate because it tends to end an enormous confusion currently centering around the term *pseudonecrophilia*. According to various authors, pseudonecrophilia currently finds a place in as many as 3 proposed classes—Class I, III, and VI. From the least innocuous to the most dangerous, all necrophiles may be categorized in following nine categories:

* Albert Moll was the founder with Iwan Bloch and Magnus Hirschfeld of modern sexology.

Class I Necrophiliacs: Role Players

These people are only mildly pathological, since they seem to enjoy a kind of role playing. They do not have sex with a dead body, but get intense arousal from having sex with a living person *pretending* to be dead. It is a kind of *sexual roleplay* (please see BDSM vocabulary in chapter on masochism). Some authors have called this practice pseudonecrophilia.[27] Some others have used the terms *simulated necrophilia* and *symbolic necrophilia*.[42] A more appropriate term appears to be *necrobiophilia* (from Greek *nekros*, "dead," and *bios*, "living"). Certain Parisian brothels cater to this perversion; the prostitute is made up like a corpse with a pallid appearance, dressed in a shroud, and lies in a coffin (often known as casket sex).[43] A person may want his sexual partner to cover her body with a whitish cosmetic to simulate the blood-drained skin of a corpse, cover her in a plastic sheet, and even add a toe tag before starting sexual intercourse. Some may utilize a resurrection fantasy where the lover brings the "dead" partner to life through sexual activity. The lover who pretends to be brought back to life may turn the tables on the other, dominating him, and even acting out a zombie fantasy.

Sometimes a vampire fantasy is involved where the lover simulates a killing by biting the neck. A case is recorded of a woman who imagined herself to be a vampire. She would ask her husband to pretend he was dead and then stimulate his organ with her mouth. She would then pretend that the resulting erection was rigor mortis, and this would give her erotic pleasure.

Class II Necrophiliacs: Romantic Necrophiles

These people show only very mild necrophilic tendencies. These are the normal bereaved people, who cannot bear separation from their loved ones and cannot accept their deaths. They mummify their loved one's dead body (or parts of them) and continue relate sexually to them much as they did in life. Their psychopathology transient and they normally recover as time passes. From a legal standpoint, Class I and II necrophiliacs are innocuous. There are no cases on record where they have been prosecuted; Class II necrophiles may be in need of psychiatric help.

Class III Necrophiliacs: People Having a Necrophilic Fantasy

Class III necrophiliacs are somewhat less innocuous from a legal standpoint. Psychosocially, they show aberrant behavior and are thus abnormal. These necrophiles do not engage in sexual intercourse with the dead. They are content simply with fantasizing intercourse with the dead. They visit cemeteries and funeral parlors often for this purpose, and merely the sight of dead bodies may give them erotic pleasure.[44]

Some like to have a sexual intercourse in the presence of a coffin because it increases their orgasmic intensity. Some may be seen masturbating during funeral sermons or dirges as they sit in a crowd of mourners. These incidents occurred at the Paris morgue several years ago, when a number of individuals were discovered, on different occasions, in the act of masturbating in front of the glass case where the cadavers were exposed. These incidents ultimately necessitated a surveillance system to prevent repetitions.[45]

Some enjoy touching, stroking or licking parts of the dead body, such as genitalia or breasts. Some even take jobs as mortuary attendants because they want to be near dead bodies. They insist that attendance at funeral homes (during visiting hours, of course) should be encouraged as an outlet for them. Medical students who get erections while dissecting cadavers also fall in this group. Indeed, Stekel mentions the case of a student who would have a sudden erection when dissecting a corpse during anatomy classes.[46]

These cases may be termed latent necrophilia or fantasy necrophilia. As seen earlier, many authors have called this pseudonecrophilia.[28,29,30] Taphophilia is the name given to people who are aroused by funerals.

Most paraphiliacs in the first three classes never touch a dead body. Those who never touch the dead but find sexual gratification merely from looking at them have been labeled *platonic necrophilisists* or *platonic necrophiles*.[45]

Class IV Necrophiliacs: People Having Fetishistic Necrophilia

These necrophiliacs are a shade more abnormal than Class III necrophiliacs, but they still do not engage in any copulatory activity with the dead. Instead, if they come across a dead body and if the chance arises, they cut up some portion of the body—perhaps a breast—for later fetishistic activities. They may even keep some portion of the dead body—pubic hair or a finger perhaps—in the pocket for continuous erotic stimulation, or wear it as an amulet for similar pleasure. Some remove clothes, especially panties or even tampons, from corpses to keep as fetish objects. These perverts are necrofetishists, and their paraphilia is known as necrofetishism.

Martin Schurig (1656–1733) in his *Spermatologia*, describes the case of a Belgian woman who secretly cut off the penis of her husband when he died and treasured it as a sacred relic in a silver casket.[47] She eventually powdered it and found it an efficacious medicine for herself and others. Havelock Ellis[48] cites an earlier example of a lady at the French court who embalmed and perfumed the genital organs of her dead husband, always preserving them in a gold casket.

Class V Necrophiliacs: People Having Necromutilomania

These are more severe cases than earlier classes. Rosman and Resnick[31] described this category as "necrophilic fantasy." Wulffen[41] describes it as necrophagy. These individuals also do not engage in sexual intercourse with the dead. However, their erotic pleasure comes from mutilating the dead body and masturbating simultaneously. In some cases, the offender may eat parts of corpse as part of sexual gratification. Rajs and colleagues[49] have described 4 types of mutilations, of which *necromanic mutilation* is one (for details of this and other types of mutilations, please see chapter on miscellaneous sexual crimes and perversions, under the subtitle mutilomania).

Rosman and Resnick[31] describe the case of a 40-year old, single white male, who fantasized killing a woman, cutting her up, removing her organs, and then masturbating while immersing his hands in the blood of the corpse. His erotic pleasure came mainly from the mutilation of warm bodies. He obtained a job in a morgue for the sole purpose of being near dead bodies and being able to cut them up. His case represents a typical Class V necrophile. Many mortuary attendants and technicians belong to this category.

Class VI Necrophiliacs: Opportunistic Necrophiliacs

Rosman and Resnick[31] describe this category as *pseudonecrophilia*. These individuals are content having intercourse with the living and would not think of engaging in sexual intercourse with the dead. However, if an opportunity arose, they would. Rosman and Resnick describe an interesting case in which a 37-year old, single white male was dating a 49-year old woman and having normal sexual relations with her. One day he accidentally shot her under the influence of alcohol. He panicked and tried to hide the dead body. When he was hiding her body, he became sexually excited and had anal intercourse with the corpse and then disposed it of. He was aware of necrophilia and necrophiliacs, as he had read about them in pornography magazines.

Mortuary attendants, funeral workers, and sailors who resort to sexual intercourse with the dead, because they have easy access to them, fall into this category.

Sometimes a person may murder his consort for other reasons (say, jealousy) and then have sexual intercourse with the dead body. Setia and Tabin[50] describe a rare case where the accused killed his wife and then had sexual intercourse with her. The reason he gave in his testimony was that she had not consented to have intercourse with him for last few years because she was having an extramarital affair with someone else. Sometimes, she would have physical relations with her boyfriend in the presence of her husband, which frustrated him very much. There was no previous history of any psychiatric illness in the accused. The authors see the behavior of the accused as being a result of jealousy resulting from his wife's extramarital affair, as well as frustration for not getting sexual gratification.

Class VII Necrophiliacs: Regular Necrophiliacs

These are the classic necrophiliacs. Wulffen[41] describes this class as necrostuprum, and Rosman and Resnick[31] as their sub-class "regular necrophilia." Such Class VII necrophiliacs do not enjoy sexual intercourse with the living, even if this choice is available to them. Instead they seek out a dead body for sexual intercourse because they get more pleasure in from sex with a dead body. They resort to stealing dead bodies from mortuaries or graveyards for this purpose. A mortuary attendant who has intercourse with the dead *only* because a dead body is easily available to him would not fall under this category. However, if he prefers a dead body to the complete exclusion of living partners, he comes under this category.

Necrophiliacs are mostly males, but Rosman and Resnick[31] describe the case of 21-year old, separated white woman who was employed as an apprentice embalmer for 4 months. She had been sexually molested at the age of 8, and raped by a teacher at the age of 14. At the age of 20—perhaps as a result of repeated childhood trauma—she came to regard herself as having "died in spirit," started drinking heavily, avoided living beings, and enjoyed only the company of the dead. She had very low self-esteem. During the short period she was employed as apprentice embalmer, she had sexual intercourse with as many as 20 to 40 male corpses. Her case is typical of Class VII necrophilia.

Class VIII Necrophiliacs: Homicidal Necrophiliacs

This is the most dangerous category. These need to have sex with a dead body to such an extent that they resort to killing. They are also known as violent necrophiles or lagnonectors (persons who kill in order to have sex with the corpse), and the practice is often known as homicidophilia. The term "warm necrophilia" may be applied to these cases, since intercourse is attempted on fresh bodies.

This is the class to which Wulffen's[41] lust murderers or necrosadists belong. Many cases of lust murder belong to this category. Rosman and Resnick[31] include this in their sub-class "necrophilic homicide." They describe the case of a 25-year old, single white male, who had a very strong sex drive. He masturbated at least 7 times a day, had a large collection of pornography, and had committed acts of bestiality, urophilia, coprophilia, necrophilia with animals (necrozoophilia) and dead bodies in the morgue of the hospital where he worked as an orderly. He murdered an 8-year old neighborhood girl in order to carry out his sexual fantasy.

Many murders of the American serial killer Jeffrey Dahmer (1960–1994) are believed to be of this category. He was believed to be aroused merely by pieces of the bodies of his victims (he was also aroused by dead animals. Please see chapter on zoophilia for more on this behavior).

Another offender who could be listed among this category is Gary Leon Ridgway (1949–), also known as the Green River Killer. He claimed an addiction to prostitutes and most of his victims were either prostitutes or female teenage runaways. He would return to places where he had dumped his victims' bodies and have sexual intercourse with their corpses. It has been suggested that on one instance he left his son in a vehicle while he went into the woods and preformed sexual activities with the dead body of one of his victims.

Class IX Necrophiliacs: Exclusive Necrophiles

This group, perhaps the rarest of all, is not necessarily the most dangerous. However, this is listed last, because these offenders must have dead bodies for intercourse. They are unable to perform intercourse with the living. Since dead bodies are an absolute necessity, they may go to any length to acquire them. In this way, they may be more dangerous than the rest. If a given necrophile is able to perform sex with a living person of either sex or of any age, he is not be listed among this class. In Rosman and Resnick's[31] series of 122 cases, the authors could find only 6 which could be listed among this class.

PREVALENCE

Necrophilia is generally presumed to be rare.[51] However, it has been argued that it may be more prevalent than statistics imply. Because that the act is carried out in secret with a victim unable to complain, only those cases in which offenders are caught come to light.[52] Even among those, not all cases are reported in medical journals or textbooks. Despite these drawbacks, the fact that Rosman and Resnick[31] could compile 122 cases of necrophilia (88 from world literature and 34 unpublished case reports from colleagues) implies that necrophilia may be far commoner than has been believed till now.

OFFENDER CHARACTERISTICS

Perhaps the best source to study the offender's characteristics is Rosman and Resnick's[31] series (please see above), wherein they describe these characteristics in a sample of 122 necrophiles. Hucker[38] also describes offender characteristics in some detail.

AGE

According to Hucker,[38] the youngest offender described in literature was 16 years, and the oldest 58 (the ages typically denote the age at which the offenders committed the necrophilic acts, or in case of fantasizers, when their fantasies were revealed). According to him, most cases fall between 20 and 50 years of age. In Rosman and Resnick's[31] series of 122 cases, they could explicitly determine ages of offenders in 68 cases (n = 68). The range was 16 to 65 years. The mean age was 34 years.

SEX

Like most other sexual deviations, necrophilia appears to be almost the exclusive domain of males, although a few authors have described necrophilia in females, too.[31,53,54] Sex of offenders could be gleaned from 115 cases out of 122 in Rosman and Resnick's[31] series. Of these 95% (n = 109) were males and 5% (n = 6) were females. Of the 14 necrophiles who committed homicide to obtain corpses for intercourse (homicidal or Class VIII necrophiles according to proposed classification), none was a female. Of the 6 female necrophiles described, 3 were regular necrophiles (Class VII necrophiles according to proposed classification), one was a fantasizer (Class V necrophile according to proposed classifications), and 2 were of undetermined class.

INTELLIGENCE

Case reports do not always mention the intellectual capacity of the offenders, but from the reports that do, offenders' intellectual capacity seems to range from the mentally retarded[55] to those with exceptionally high intelligence.[56] According to Hucker,[38] the offenders mostly appear to be of average intelligence. In Rosman and Resnick's[31] series, the IQ could be gathered or gleaned only from 13 case reports (n = 13). All 13 had an IQ above 80. Of these, 69% had an IQ above 100.

SEXUAL ORIENTATION

In Rosman and Resnick's[31] series of 122 cases, the sexual orientation of necrophiles could be determined in 71 cases (n = 71), and it was quite comparable to what prevails in the general population: 79% (n = 56) were heterosexual, 13% (n = 9) were bisexual, and 9% (n = 6) were homosexual.

Sex of the Corpses

Interestingly, not all necrophiles choose the corpse of the opposite sex for sexual intercourse. In Rosman and Resnick's[31] series, the sex of the corpse in relation to the sex of the offender could be gleaned from 91 case reports (n = 91). Of these 85% (n = 77) used corpses of the opposite sex. But significantly 10% (n = 9) used same-sex corpses (the authors do not mention if all of these nine cases belonged to males choosing male corpses for sex, but it appears so. One would imagine that if there were any case of a female necrophile choosing a female corpse for necrophilia, the act would be so bizarre that the authors would have mentioned it). Five percent (n = 5) used corpses of both sexes. The highest percentage of same-sex corpses was among the necrophilic killers (n = 14). Fifty percent of these (n = 7) used same-sex corpses.

Marital Status

Marital status could be determined in 78 cases of Rosman and Resnick's[31] series (n = 78). Sixty percent of these (n = 47) were single, 26% (n = 20) were married, and 14% (n = 11) were either divorced or widowed.

History of Sadistic Acts

In Rosman and Resnick's[31] series, histories of prior acts to were available in 42 cases (n = 42), out of which 29 were true necrophiles, 11 were pseudonecrophiles, and 2 were undeterminable. Out of all 42 cases, a total of 64% (n = 27) had a history of prior sadistic acts. All 11 pseudonecrophilic killers had a history of sadistic acts. Among the true necrophiles, the rate was 52% (n = 15). The highest rate of sadistic acts among the true necrophiles was in the necrophilic homicide group, where as many as 78% showed a history of prior sadistic acts (total offenders in necrophilic homicide group were 9, of which 7 showed a history of prior sadistic acts).

Nonnecrophilic Intercourse

A significant question is whether necrophiles engage in nonnecrophilic intercourse (i.e., intercourse with regular living partners) or not. Among Rosman and Resnick's[31] series, this fact was determinable in 56 cases (n = 56). Of these 36 were true necrophiles and 20 were pseudonecrophiles. Of the 36 true necrophiles, 31 had had a history of nonnecrophilic intercourse (i.e., 5 were exclusive necrophiles or Class IX necrophiliacs according to the proposed classification). Of the 20 pseudonecrophiles, 19 had a history of nonnecrophilic intercourse, and only one was an exclusive necrophile.

CASE STUDIES

Many necrophiles have attracted lay attention in the past. Most notable among them are Carl Tanzler, Douglas Clark, Ed Gein, Edmund Kemper, Gary Ridgway, Graham Coutts, Jeffrey Dahmer, Jerry Brudos, John Christie, John Wayne Gacy, Karen Greenlee, and Ted Bundy. Some lesser known necrophiles will be discussed with here.

Nicholas and Alexander Grunke, and Dustin Radke

In the late evening of September 2, 2006, twins Nicholas and Alexander Grunke, 20 years of age, and Dustin Radke, also 20, went to St. Charles Cemetery, in Cassville, Wisconsin, intending to remove the body of Laura Tennesen, 20, from her grave so that Nicholas Grunke could engage in sexual intercourse with the corpse. Nicholas Grunke had allegedly lusted after her—who died in a motorbike accident on August 27—since he had spotted her picture in the obituary column of a local newspaper.

The three men used shovels to reach Tennesen's grave. The police were tipped off to suspicious activity in the cemetery. When an officer arrived, he found an abandoned vehicle parked near the cemetery. Minutes later he saw Alexander Grunke walking toward the vehicle, dressed in black and sweating profusely. When questioned, Grunke told the officer his brother and Radke were trying to dig up a grave. The grave was found partially dug up; the offenders had only managed to reach the top of the grave's concrete vault. Radke told police that Nicholas Grunke had asked him to help dig up the Tennesen's body and take it to Grunke's house so that Grunke could have sex with it. He also informed that on way to the cemetery, they had stopped by a Dodgeville store to buy condoms because Nick wanted to use them when he had sex with corpse.

The defendants were charged with a number of offenses including damage to cemetery property, attempted criminal damage to property, and attempted third-degree sexual assault on a corpse, or necrophilia. The charge of necrophilia was brought under section 940.225(7).

Circuit Judge George Curry dismissed the sexual assault charges, noting that there was no law that addressed necrophilia. However, there was enough evidence to continue the case based on criminal damage to property and the alleged attempt to break into a burial vault. The State appealed the decision. The Court of appeals of Wisconsin ruled that the decision of Circuit Judge was correct and that section 940.225(7) indeed does not address necrophilia (please see below under Legal aspects; Wisconsin).

Moninder Singh Pandher and Surendra Koli

These two are the latest necrophiles who have come to world attention. During December 2006, skulls and bones of a number of missing children belonging to migrant workers were discovered in the village of Nithari. It is a small village on the outskirts of Noida City, an industrial township in Uttar Pradesh near New Delhi. Migrants come here from far away places like Bihar and West Bengal in search of better lives.

On December 26, 2006, Delhi police arrested a rich and politically connected businessman, Moninder Singh Pandher, and on the following day his cook and aide Surendra Koli (his first name is also variously spelled as Surender or Subhash, and second name may be spelled as Kohli), on the suspicion of the murder of a 19-year old girl named Payal. She was one of these missing children, and often visited Pandher's residence. Payal had gone missing after she went to Pandher's residence on May 7, 2006, and this aroused suspicion. When their house was searched, numerous pornographic CDs and pictures of naked children, mostly Indians, in company of Pandher, were found. A massive investigation followed, which the media called "the Noida serial murder investigation. " It included brain mapping and narco analysis of the offenders. On March 2, 2007, Koli reportedly to unburden his conscience, at a Delhi court and admitted raping, killing, and having sex with dead bodies of children and women. He gave a clean chit to his employer Pandher, perhaps under pressure. Subsequently, a case was registered against Koli under various sections of the Indian Penal Code, including rape, murder, kidnapping, and criminal conspiracy. Since necrophilia is not a crime in India, no case could be registered against him for having sex with the dead. In India the only section that can possibly be invoked against necrophiles is section 297 of the IPC, but to be able to invoke this section, the offender must have trespassed on burial places [please see below under Indian law].

Following statements by Koli, the Central Bureau of Investigation had no choice but to release Pandher. However, it slapped lesser charges against Pandher for bribing police officials, indulging in prostitution, procuring call girls, and destruction of evidence.

MEDICO-LEGAL INVESTIGATION

When a corpse suspected to have been sexually abused is found, the primary task is to determine if the injuries found on the body were antemortem or postmortem. It is quite possible that the victim was first tortured, raped, and killed subsequently, in which case it becomes a case of sadistic murder rather than necrophilia. In such cases, the injuries on the body and around genitalia, etc. would be antemortem in nature. Alternatively, the victim may have been killed first and sexually assaulted afterward, in which case it becomes a true case of necrophilia. Injuries would be postmortem in such cases. The determination of antemortem or postmortem nature of injuries can give a rough indication whether it necrophilia or sadistic murder (much more common than necrophilia).

Vaginal, oral, and rectal swabs from the dead bodies are taken following standard protocols for live victims (please see chapter on rape). Laboratory examination has been shown to reveal the presence of intact spermatozoa, P30 and restriction fragment length polymorphism (RFLP) typable DNA on a vaginal swab in a corpse as old as 34 days.[57] This was most certainly a case of sadistic murder rather than necrophilia, yet it demonstrates the value of collectiing trace evidence even in bodies recovered after burial.

LEGAL ASPECTS

In many nations and jurisdictions, there are no specific laws against sexual intercourse with a corpse. Thus any necrophiles who are caught have to be charged under related laws, such as "disturbing the peace of the dead," "defiling a dead body," "disturbing law and order," "hurting sentiments of relatives," etc. An interesting situation may arise, if a fresh corpse is found in possession of a necrophile and sexual intercourse is proved (e.g., by detection of culprit's semen in the dead body). In such a case, the prosecution may try to prove that sexual intercourse was performed on the woman during life, and the woman was killed later. This brings graver charges of rape and murder upon the culprit. Since having intercourse with a dead woman is not rape, the defense may try proving it was a case of sexual intercourse *after* the woman's death, making it necrophilia, and attracting a far less severe sentence. From a medical standpoint, it is a question of antemortem or postmortem sexual intercourse. This is not an entirely hypothetical situation. Similar questions have been raised in Pandher's and Koli's cases recently. The cases are still awaiting trial.

Laws relating to necrophilia in some major nations and jurisdictions are as below:

AUSTRALIA

Western Australia

The Criminal Code of Western Australia does not mention *necrophilia* explicitly, but section 214 addresses the issue of misconduct with regard to corpses, which includes acts of necrophilia. Necrophilia under this section is a misdemeanor, and the punishment is imprisonment for 2 years. It states:[58]

> Any person who, without lawful justification or excuse, the proof of which lies on him—
> (1) Neglects to perform any duty imposed upon him by law, or undertaken by him, whether for reward or otherwise, touching the burial or other disposition of a human body or human remains; or
> (2) Improperly or indecently interferes with, or offers any indignity to, any dead human body or human remains, whether buried or not; is guilty of a misdemeanor, and is liable to imprisonment for 2 years.
>
> Summary conviction penalty: Imprisonment for one year or a fine of $4,000.

Northern Territory

According to section 140 of the Criminal Code of Northern Territory (for details, please see chapter on exhibitionism), necrophilia is a crime and attracts a punishment of imprisonment up to 2 years. Section 140 states:

> Any person who, without authorization or excuse, the proof of which lies on him—
> (a) neglects to perform any duty imposed upon him by law or undertaken by him, whether for reward or otherwise, touching the burial or other disposition of a human body or human remains; or
> (b) improperly or indecently interferes with or offers any indignity to any dead human body or human remains whether buried or not, is guilty of a crime and is liable to imprisonment for 2 years.

New South Wales

The criminal law of New South Wales is governed by the Crimes Act 1900 (for details, please see chapter on frotteurism). While division 10 of Part 3 deals with most sexual offenses, necrophilia is addressed by division 11 entitled "Misconduct with regard to corpses." Section 81C states:

> Any person who:
> (a) indecently interferes with any dead human body, or
> (b) improperly interferes with, or offers any indignity to, any dead human body or human remains (whether buried or not), shall be liable to imprisonment for 2 years.

Tasmania

Necrophilia is not mentioned in the Tasmanian Criminal Code Act 1924. However, necrophilia is implicitly included in section 139 of this Act (included in chapter XIV entitled "Crimes Against Morality"). It states:[59]

> ***Misconduct in respect of human remains***
> Any person who—
> (a) neglects to perform any duty, either imposed upon him by law or undertaken by him, with reference to the burial of any dead human body or human remains; or
> (b) improperly or indecently interferes with or offers any indignity to any dead human body or human remains, whether buried or not—is guilty of a crime.
>
> Charge:
> (a) Neglecting duty as to burial.
> (b) Interfering with human remains.

Any attempt at sexual intercourse with a dead body would be covered by clause (b) of the section (indecent interference or offering any indignity to any dead human body).

Victoria

According to section 34B of the Crimes Act 1958 of Victoria, it is an offense to interfere with corpse of a human being, either sexually or otherwise. Section 34B states:[60]

> (1) A person must not intentionally—

(a) interfere sexually or commit an indecent act with a corpse of a human being; or
(b) unlawfully remove body parts from a corpse of a human being—
whether that corpse is in a public cemetery within the meaning of the Cemeteries and Crematoria Act 2003 or at any other place. Penalty: Level 6 (5 years maximum).

(2) Subsection (1) does not apply to—
(a) any person who is engaged in the preparation of a corpse of a human being for the purposes of interment or cremation within the meaning of the Cemeteries and Crematoria Act 2003; or
(b) any other lawful interference with a corpse of a human being, including a lawful interference for the purposes of a medical, scientific or hygienic procedure.

Canada

The Criminal Code of Canada is a very comprehensive document containing 849 sections divided in 28 parts. Part V deals with sexual offenses, public morals and disorderly conduct. According to Section 182[61], necrophilia is an offense.

Every one who
(a) neglects, without lawful excuse, to perform any duty that is imposed on him by law or that he undertakes with reference to the burial of a dead human body or human remains, or
(b) improperly or indecently interferes with or offers any indignity to a dead human body or human remains, whether buried or not, is guilty of an indictable offense and liable to imprisonment for a term not exceeding 5 years.

France

Article L225-17 of the French Penal Code makes necrophilia an offense. It allows the judge to punish necrophiles for "affect on the integrity of a corpse." The punishment is 1 year of prison and up to 15,000 euros.[62]

Germany

The German Criminal Code (Strafgesetzbuch, StGB) has ample provisions for punishment of necrophilia. Chapter 11 deals with "crimes which relate to religion and philosophy of life." Section 168 entitled "Disturbing the Peace of the Dead" states:[63]

(1) Whoever, without authorization, takes away the body or parts of the body of a deceased person, a dead fetus or parts thereof or the ashes of a deceased person from the custody of the person entitled thereto, or whoever commits insulting mischief thereon, shall be punished with imprisonment for not more than 3 years or a fine.
(2) Whoever destroys or damages a place for laying-in-state, burial site or public place for remembering the dead, or whoever commits insulting mischief there, shall be similarly punished.
(3) An attempt shall be punishable.

This section can be used against necrophiles. Section 211 appears aimed at class VI necrophiliacs noted above. It states:[64]

(1) The murderer shall be punished with imprisonment for life.
(2) A murderer is, whoever kills a human being out of murderous lust, to satisfy his sexual desires, from greed or otherwise base motives, treacherously or cruelly or with means dangerous to the public or in order to make another crime possible or cover it up.

Quite clearly it doesn't make much difference why the killing was done. A killing done for, greed is as heinous as a killing done to satisfy sexual desires. But the specific mention of this phrase in German Penal Code is interesting.

India

India has no explicit law regarding necrophilia. However, section 297 of the Indian Penal Code[65] addresses this perversion to some extent. It states:

> **Trespassing on burial places, etc.**—Whoever, with the intention of wounding the feelings of any person, or of insulting the religion of any person, or with the knowledge that the feelings of any person are likely to be wounded, or that the religion of any person is likely to be insulted thereby, commits any trespass in any place of worship or on any place of sculpture, or any place set apart from the performance of funeral rites or as a depository for the remains of the dead, or offers any indignity to any human corpse, or causes disturbance to any persons assembled for the performance of funeral ceremonies, shall be punished with imprisonment of either description for a term which may extend to one year, or with fine, or with both.

Gravediggers and mortuary attendants, who are most often found practicing necrophilia, engage in this activity perhaps because of their loneliness, coupled with easy access to corpses. There have been several allegations by relatives of dead women that the bodies of their kin were defiled in the night by mortuary attendants, but none have been proved. The possibility of such an act taking place on a regular basis is not impossible to imagine. Medical students have also been found occasionally to have sex with corpses for similar reasons.

This author has personally been involved as an autopsy expert in cases in which a woman was alleged to have been raped and murdered, and the autopsy surgeon failed to find any signs of rape. The relatives approached the authorities for a second postmortem (a phenomenon which is not uncommon in India). The second postmortem is invariably conducted at a different hospital, often necessitating that the body be deposited overnight at the mortuary of the second hospital. In cases where the second autopsy surgeon finds signs of rape, the defendants have been known to allege that the dead body was defiled by drunk mortuary attendants at night. No such allegations have been proved in a court of law, however.

United Kingdom

According to section 70 of the Sexual Offenses Act 2003 of UK,[66] sexual penetration of a corpse is an offense.

(1) A person commits an offense if-
  (a) he intentionally performs an act of penetration with a part of his body or anything else,
  (b) what is penetrated is a part of the body of a dead person,
  (c) he knows that, or is reckless as to whether, that is what is penetrated, and
  (d) the penetration is sexual.
(2) A person guilty of an offense under this section is liable-
  (a) on summary conviction, to imprisonment for a term not exceeding 6 months or a fine not exceeding the statutory maximum or both;

(b) on conviction on indictment, to imprisonment for a term not exceeding 2 years.

Exposing a naked corpse in public is a public nuisance (*R. v. Clark* [1883] 15 Cox 171).

United States

No federal laws cover necrophilia.[68] Laws related to necrophilia have been left up to the individual states. Section 250.10 of the Model Penal Code (MPC), a statutory text developed by the American Law Institute (ALI) in 1962 to stimulate and assist legislatures in making an effort to update and standardize the penal law, makes it a misdemeanor to treat corpse in a way that "would outrage ordinary family sensibilities."[67]

U.S. laws related to necrophilia have been discussed in great detail by Posner and Silbaugh.[68] They have included only those laws where there is a specific mention of sexual conduct with the human corpse and have chosen not to mention any law that only prohibits derogatory and offensive treatment of human remains in general, without any explicit suggestion of a sexual conduct with the corpse. It may be useful to have a look at necrophilia laws in some representative states.

Alabama

It is a misdemeanor to knowingly treat a human corpse in a way that would outrage ordinary family sensibilities.[69] Any person who willfully or maliciously desecrates, injures, defaces, removes, or destroys any tomb, monument, structure, or container of human remains, and invades or mutilates the human corpse or remains shall be guilty of a class C felony and upon conviction shall be punished as provided by law.[70] For a class C felony, the imprisonment is for more than 1 year and one day and less than 10 years.[71] The imprisonment includes hard labor. The fine is up to $15,000.[72]

Alaska

It is a class A misdemeanor to engage in sexual penetration of a corpse.[73]

Arkansas

According to section 5-60-101 of the Code of Arkansas,[74] abuse of a corpse is a class D felony. It states:

(a) A person commits abuse of a corpse if, except as authorized by law, he or she knowingly:
  (1) Disinters, removes, dissects, or mutilates a corpse; or
  (2) Physically mistreats a corpse in a manner offensive to a person of reasonable sensibilities.

(b) Abuse of a corpse is a Class D felony.

California

According to Section 7052 of the Health and Safety Code of California (as amended in 2007), necrophilia is a felony. It states:[75]

(a) Every person who willfully mutilates, disinters, removes from the place of interment, or commits an act of sexual penetration on, or has sexual contact with, any remains known to be human, without authority of law, is guilty of a felony, punishable by imprisonment in the state prison for 3, 6, or 8 years. This section does not apply to any person who, under authority of law, removes the remains for reinterment, or performs a cremation.

(b) For purposes of this section, the following definitions apply:
  (1) "Sexual penetration" means the unlawful penetration of the vagina or anus, however slight, by any part of a person's body or other object, or any act of sexual contact between the sex organs of a person and the mouth or anus of a dead body, or any oral copulation of a dead human body for the purpose of sexual arousal, gratification, or abuse.
  (2) "Sexual contact" means any willful touching by a person of an intimate part of a dead human body for the purpose of sexual arousal, gratification, or abuse.

Also according to Section 290, a person convicted of specified sex offenses has to register his or her address with the law enforcement for life. The new amendment makes an act of sexual penetration on, or having sexual contact with, any remains known to be human to the list of specified sex offenses, the conviction for which requires registration as a sex offender with law enforcement.

Connecticut

It is a misdemeanor to engage in sexual contact with a dead body.[76]

Georgia

Necrophilia is a felony in the state of Georgia. Section 16-6-7 states:[77]

(a) A person commits the offense of necrophilia when he performs any sexual act with a dead human body involving the sex organs of the one and the mouth, anus, penis, or vagina of the other.
(b) A person convicted of the offense of necrophilia shall be punished by imprisonment for not less than one nor more than 10 years.

In 2006, 54-year old Parker Ward of Georgia was sentenced to 4 years in prison to be followed by 4 years of probation for an act of necrophilia he performed on a 43-year old woman who had died of accidental drug overdose in her camper on the night of December 27, 2005. Finding her motionless, her boyfriend had asked Ward to check on her. Ward tried to give her mouth-to-mouth resuscitation. When there was no response, Ward realized she was dead. He then had sex with the corpse and afterwards called 911. It was later estimated that the victim had been dead for about 4 hours when Ward had sex with her. Her body was cold, and rigor mortis had set in. Ward presented the defense that he was drunk, as he had consumed about 6 rum drinks on that night, but the plea was not entertained.

Iowa

In Iowa, necrophilia is a class D felony. Section 709.18 of Iowa code states:[78]

709.18 Abuse of a corpse.
A person commits abuse of a human corpse if the person knowingly and intentionally engages in a sex act, as defined in section 702.17, with a human corpse. Abuse of a human corpse is a class D felony.

Section 702.17 as mentioned in the statute above defines the sex act as follows:

The term "sex act" or "sexual activity" means any sexual contact between two or more persons by: penetration of the penis into the vagina or anus; contact between the mouth and genitalia or by contact between the genitalia of one person and the genitalia or anus of another person; contact between the finger or hand of one person and the genitalia or anus of another person, except in the course of examination or treatment by a person licensed pursuant to chapter 148, 148C, 150, 150A, 151, or 152; or by use of artificial sexual organs or substitutes therefor in contact with the genitalia or anus.

Thus, even acts such as inserting a finger into the vagina of a corpse would be taken to mean as committing a sex act with the corpse, and would be punishable under section 709.18.

Indiana

Necrophilia is a class D felony in the state of Indiana. It is defined in Title 35, Article 45, Chapter 11, Sections 1 and 2 (for details of Indiana Code, please see chapter on voyeurism). Chapter 11 is entitled "Abuse of a Corpse." Section 1 states:

35-45-11-1—Applicability of chapter

Sec. 1. (a) This chapter does not apply to the use of a corpse for:

(1) scientific;
(2) medical;
(3) organ transplantation;
(4) historical;
(5) forensic; or
(6) investigative;
purposes.

(b) This chapter does not apply to:

(1) a funeral director;
(2) an embalmer; or
(3) an employee of an individual described in subdivision (1) or (2); engaged in the individual's normal scope of practice and employment.

35-45-11-2—Abuse of corpse

Sec. 2. A person who knowingly or intentionally:

(1) mutilates a corpse;
(2) has sexual intercourse or sexual deviate conduct with the corpse; or
(3) opens a casket with the intent to commit an act described in subdivision (1) or (2); commits abuse of a corpse, a Class D felony.

Washington

Chapter 9A.44 of the Revised Code of Washington (RCW) deals with sex offenses. Section 9A.44.105 provides punishment for necrophilia:

Sexually violating human remains

(1) Any person who has sexual intercourse or sexual contact with a dead human body is guilty of a class C felony.
(2) As used in this section:
    (a) "Sexual intercourse" (i) has its ordinary meaning and occurs upon any penetration, however slight; and (ii) also means any penetration of the vagina or anus however slight, by an object, when committed on a dead human body, except when such penetration is accomplished as part of a procedure authorized or required under

chapter 68.50 RCW or other law; and (iii) also means any act of sexual contact between the sex organs of a person and the mouth or anus of a dead human body.

(b) "Sexual contact" means any touching by a person of the sexual or other intimate parts of a dead human body done for the purpose of gratifying the sexual desire of the person.

Wisconsin

Section 940.225 of Wisconsin statute entitled "Sexual assault" mentions a number of sexual offenses including sexual assaults of 4 degrees and sexual contact including acts such as frotteurism. Subsection (7) of this section states:[79]

> (7) DEATH OF VICTIM. This section applies whether a victim is dead or alive at the time of the sexual contact or sexual intercourse.

This section was generally taken to refer to necrophilia.[68] But in the famous Grunke case (please see above), the court ruled that it was not so (*State v. Grunke*, 2007 WI App 198). The case was heard by justices Dykman, Vergeront, and Higginbotham. Judge Charles P. Dykman observed:

> The State asserts that the circuit court erred in concluding that §940.225(7) allows prosecution for the sexual assault of a dead body only if the defendant committed the sexual assault in a series of acts including acts that caused the death of the victim. The State argues that §940.225(7) unambiguously allows prosecution for the sexual assault of a dead body without limitation to the defendant's involvement in the death of the victim. We conclude that §940.225(7) is ambiguous because it is subject to more than one reasonable interpretation. We conclude that the more reasonable interpretation is that §940.225(7) was intended by the legislature to allow a sexual assault charge to succeed where a defendant sexually assaulted and caused the death of his victim and the sequence of events is unclear, rather than to criminalize necrophilia generally. Accordingly, we affirm... We conclude that the legislature did not enact Wis. Stat. §940.225(7) as a general necrophilia statute, which would criminalize Grunke's conduct.

Accordingly it is clear that Wisconsin currently has no specific statute against necrophilia.

Comparing Laws Regarding Necrophilia

Table 13.1 compares various laws related to necrophilia in different countries and jurisdictions.

REFERENCES

1. American Psychiatric Association. *Diagnostic and Statistical Manual of Mental Disorders*, 4th ed. Text rev. American Psychiatric Association, Washington DC, 2000.
2. Langevin, R., Bain, J., Wortzman, G., Hucker, S., Dickey, R., Wright, P. Sexual sadism: brain, blood, and behavior. *Ann N Y Acad Sci.* 1988;528:163-71.
3. Necrophilia, in *Encyclopedia of Death and Dying.* Available from: http://www.deathreference.com/Me-Nu/Necrophilia.html.
4. Longus, Parthenius, Thornley, G. (Translator), Edmonds, J.M. (Translator), Gaselee, S. (Translator). Daphnis and Chloe. *Love Romances and Poetical Fragments. Fragments of the Ninus Romance.* (Loeb Classical Library). Loeb Classical Library Volume 69. Harvard University Press, Cambridge, MA. 1916.
5. Grimal, P. *The Dictionary of Classical Mythology.* Blackwell Publishing Limited, Malden, MA, 1996.
6. Hood, J.X. *Scientific curiosities of love-sex and marriage: A survey of sex relations, beliefs and customs of mankind in different countries and ages.* Waverly Books, 1951, page 24.
7. de Selincourt, A. (trans). *Herodotus: The Histories*, Penguin, Harmondsworth, 1972, 161.

TABLE 13.1
Comparison of Laws Relating to Necrophilia in Select Nations and Jurisdictions

Country Jurisdiction	Maximum imprisonment for	Maximum fine	Relevant law regarding necrophilia
Canada	Up to 5 years		Section 182 of the Criminal Code of Canada
France	1 year	15,000 euros	Article L225-17 of French Penal Code
Germany	3 years	Any amount	Section 168 of The German Criminal Code (Strafgesetzbuch, StGB)
India	1 year	Any amount	Section 297 of Indian Penal Code
United Kingdom	Up to 6 months on summary conviction and up to 2 years on conviction on indictment	Not exceeding statutory maximum	Section 70 of the Sexual Offenses Act 2003

8. Masters, R.E.L, Lea, A.E.E. *Perverse Crimes in History: Evolving Concepts of Sadism, Lust-Murder, and Necrophilia-From Ancient to Modern Times,* The Julian Press, New York, 1963.
9. Gilman, S.L., King, H., Porter, R., Rousseau, G.S., and Showalter, E., *Hysteria Beyond Freud.* University of California Press, Berkeley, 1993. page 31.
10. Godley, A.D. (ed). Herodotus, *The Histories.* Harvard University Press, Cambridge. 1920.(3.50.1-52.4).
11. Godley, A.D. (ed). Herodotus, *The Histories.* Harvard University Press, Cambridge. 1920. (5.92g.1-4).
12. Huber, von H., Nekrophilie, *Kriminalistik,* 16, 564, 1962.
13. Herod the Great: the true story. Available from : http://www.tvthrong.co.uk/documentary/the-true-story-of-herod-the-great-tuesday-april-17.
14. The Buggery Act 1533 (25 Hen. VIII c. 6).
15. Sexual Sadism: Rape, Necrophilia, Cannibalism, Fetishism. Available from http://faculty.ncwc.edu/TOConnor/428/428lect13.htm.
16. Available at: http://dahmerdame.livejournal.com/505.html.
17. Taylor, T. The ghost of the Great Salt Lake—Or The Legend of John Baptiste, Salt Lake City, Utah, 2003. Available from: http://www.prairieghosts.com/baptiste.html.
18. Bloch, I., *Anthropological and ethnological studies in the strangest sex acts in modes of love of all races illustrated,: Oriental, occidental, savage, civilized,* Privately issued, Falstaff press, 1935.
19. Persaud, R. Blood-lust in the clinic. *The Independent (London).* February 2, 1993, Tuesday.
20. Nobus, D. Over my dead body: On the histories and cultures of necrophilia, in *Inappropriate Relationships: The unconventional, the disapproved, and the forbidden,* Goodwin, R. and Cramer, D., Eds., Lawrence Erlbaum Associates, Inc., Mahwah, NJ, 2002, pages 171–189.
21. Ollier, E. *Cassell's Illustrated History of the Russo-Turkish War.* Cassell & Company Ltd., London, 1878.
22. Long, S. Chinese Police Hold Man For Serial Necrophilia. *The Guardian (London).* January 5, 1995.
23. Lewis, M. (Director), Cane Toads: An Unnatural History (DVD-Video, NTSC, Color, running time, 65 minutes). Studio: First Run Features, 2001.
24. Bagemihl, B. *Biological Exuberance, Animal Homosexuality and Natural Diversity,* Profile Books, London, 1999.
25. Moeliker, C.W. The first case of homosexual necrophilia in the mallard *Anas platyrhynchos* (Aves: Anatidae)—Deinsea. 2001; 8: 243–247.
26. Bernardi, L. Ponti G. Un caso eccezionale di necrofilia [An exceptional case of necrophilia.] [Article in Italian]. *Minerva medicolegale.* 1957;77(2):64–8.
27. Shaffer, L. and Penn, J.A. Comprehensive Paraphilia Classification System, in *Sex crimes and paraphilia,* 1st ed. Hicky, E.W., Pearson Prentice Hall, New Jersey, 2006, chapter 8, page 87.

28. Segal, H.A. Necrophilic fantasy. *International Journal of Psychoanalysis.* 1953;**34**:98-101.
29. Rauch, H.J. Über Nekrophilie. *Arch. Psychiat. Nervenkr.* 1947;**179**:54.
30. Lazarus, A.A. A case of pseudonecrophilia treated by behavior therapy. *J Clin Psychol.* 1968 Jan;**24(1)**:113-5.
31. Rosman, J.P. and Resnick, P.J. Sexual attraction to corpses: A psychiatric review of necrophilia. *Bulletin of the American Academy of Psychiatry and the Law.* 1989; **17(2)**: 153-163.
32. Fromm, E. *The Anatomy of Human Destructiveness*, Holt, Rinehart and Winston, New York, 1973.
33. Stekel, W., Sadism and Masochism: The Psychology of Hatred and Cruelty, Grove Press, New York, 1929.
34. Gromska J., Smoczyski, S., Bardzik, S. [A case of necrophilia committed in a state of pathological alcoholic intoxication][Article in Polish]. *Psychiatr Pol.* 1969;**3(2)**:207-9.
35. Simon, R, DeVito, H. Alcohol activation of EEG abnormalities in persons with a history of violence precipitated by drinking alcoholic beverages. *Clin Electroencephalogr.* 1976;**7**:145-8.
36. Moll, A., *Handbuch der Sexualwissenschaften mit besonderer Berücksichtigung der kulturgeschichtlichen Beziehungen*, F.C.W.Vogel, Leipzig, 1912.
37. Krafft-Ebing , R.F. *Psychopathia Sexualis*, 1st ed. (1886) reprinted by Bloat Books, 1999.
38. Hucker, S., Necrophilia and other unusual philias, in *Principles and Practice of Forensic Psychiatry*, 1st edition, Bluglass R. and Bowden P., Eds., Churchill Livingstone, Edinburgh, 1990, chap. VIII.9.
39. Jones, E., *On the nightmare*. Hogarth Press and Institute of Psycho-Analysis, London, 1931.
40. Calef, V. and E. M. Weinshel. On certain neurotic equivalents of necrophilia. *Int J Psychoanal.* 1972; **53(1)**: 67-75.
41. Wulffen, E., *Enzyklopadie de modernen kriminalistik.* Langenscheidt, Berlin, 1910.
42. Bloch, I., *The Sexual Life of our time in relation to modern civilization.* Rebman, New York, 1908.
43. Allen, C., *A Textbook of Psychosexual Disorders*, 2nd Ed. Oxford University Press, London, 1969.
44. Necrophilia. In *Sex Crimes and Their Legal Aspects* by Drzazga J., Charles C. Thomas, Illinois, 1960, pages 199-204.
45. Thoinot, L. (Author), Weysse, A.W. (Translator). *Medicolegal Aspects of Moral Offenses.* Kessinger Publishing, LLC, Whitefish, MT, 2005, page 448.
46. Stekel, W. *Sadism and Masochism*, W W Norton & Co Inc, New York, 1953, p. 278.
47. Schurig, M. *Spermatologia Historico-Medica.* Johannis Beckii, Frankfort, 1720, p. 357.
48. Ellis, H.H., *Studies in the Psychology of Sex Volume V: Erotic Symbolism, The Mechanism of Detumescence, The Psychic State in Pregnancy.* F. A. Davis, 1923.
49. Rajs, J., Lundström M., Broberg M., Lidberg L., Lindquist O. Criminal mutilation of the human body in Sweden--a thirty-year medico-legal and forensic psychiatric study. *J Forensic Sci.* 1998 May;**43(3)**:563-80.
50. Setia, P., Tabin, M. An unusual case of a man having necrophilia with his own wife. Proceedings of the XXIX Annual Conference of Indian Academy of Forensic Medicine, 2008, Mumbai. Pp 17.
51. Smith, S. and Dimock, J., Necrophilia and anti-social acts, in *Sexual dynamics of antisocial behaviour*, Schlesinger, L.B. and Revitch, E., Eds., Thomas, Springfield, Illinois, 1983, chap. 13
52. Prins, H. *Dangerous behavior, the law and mental disorder.* Tavistok, London, 1986.
53. Foerster, K., Foerster, G. and Roth, E. Nekrophilie bei einem 17 jährigen Mädchen [Necrophilia in a 17 year old girl]. *Schweizer Archiv für Neurologie, Neurochirurgie und Psychiatrie.* 1976; **119(1)**: 97-107
54. Tsheryaskin, W.G. Zur frage der nekrophilie. *Zeitschrift für sexual wissenschaft-wiss.* 1929;**16**:386-392.
55. Spoerri, T. Nekrophilie: strukturanalyse enies falles. *Psychiatrica Neurologica*, 1959 (suppl 55). Karger, Basel and New York.
56. Lancaster, N.P. Necrophilia, murder and high intelligence: a case report. *Br J Psychiatry.* 1978 Jun;**132**:605-8.
57. Montagna, C.P. The recovery of seminal components and DNA from the vagina of a homicide victim 34 days postmortem. *J Forensic Sci.* 1996 Jul;41(4):700-2.
58. Criminal Code of Western Australia. Section 214 amended by No. 70 of 1988 s. 25; No. 51 of 1992 s. 16(2).
59. Section 139, Criminal Code Act 1924 (No. 69 of 1924).
60. Section 34B, Crimes Act 1958 (No. 6231 of 1958).
61. Section 182, Criminal Code of Canada (R.S., 1985, c. C-46).
62. Nécrophilie [in French]. Available from: http://fr.wikipedia.org/wiki/N%C3%A9crophilie. Retrieved May 25, 2007.

63. Section 168, German Criminal Code (Strafgesetzbuch, StGB) as promulgated on 13 November 1998 (Federal Law Gazette I, p. 945, p. 3322).
64. Section 211, German Criminal Code (Strafgesetzbuch, StGB) as promulgated on 13 November 1998 (Federal Law Gazette I, p. 945, p. 3322).
65. The Indian Penal Code, (Act No. 45 of 1860) [6th October, 1860].
66. Sexual Offenses Act 2003 [20th November 2003].
67. Schwartz, L.B. Morals Offenses and the Model Penal Code. *Columbia Law Review.* 1963;63(4):669-686.
68. Posner, R.A., and Silbaugh, K.B., *A Guide to America's Sex Laws*, The University of Chicago Press, Chicago, 1996, ch15.
69. Ala. Code §13A-11-13 (enacted 1977).
70. Ala. Code §13A-7-23.1 (enacted 1980).
71. Ala. Code §13A-5-6 (enacted 1977).
72. Ala. Code §13A-5-11 (enacted 1977).
73. Alaska Stat. §11.61.130 (enacted 1978).
74. Ark. Code Ann. §5-60-101 (enacted 1975).
75. California Codes: Health and Safety Code, §7052.
76. Conn. Gen. Stat. Ann. §53A-73A (enacted 1975).
77. Ga. Code Ann. §16.6.7 (enacted 1977).
78. Iowa Code Ann. §709.18 (enacted 1976).
79. Wis. Stat. Ann. §940.225 (enacted 1987).

14 Incest

INTRODUCTION

Incest (from Latin *in*, "not"; and *castus*, "chaste") is sexual intimacy between people who are too closely related by blood or family ties to be able to marry. Incest may occur between two consenting adults, such as grown up brother and sister, or between a mother and her adult son. More commonly, however, children below the age of consent are sexually exploited by a senior member of the family. This is known as intrafamilial childhood sexual abuse (ICSA) or incest rape. It has been considered the most prevalent and most devastating form of child sexual abuse.[1] Incest is not mentioned in DSM-IV-TR as a separate disorder, but it does recommend specifying incest in all cases of pedophilia (please see Table 2.1, from the chapter on pedophilia).

The concept of what constitutes "close relatives" is not uniform among societies, making the notion of incest somewhat fuzzy. At one extreme lie the Trobriand Islanders, who prohibit a relationship between the mother and the son, allowing all others including that between the father and the daughter. At the other extreme are the Chinese, who prohibit marriages even between people sharing the same surname, as they are considered related. Variations occur in regions within the same country, too; while as many as 50% of marriages in South India are between first cousins, the same is considered abnormal in Northern India. Levirate marriages—marriage of a widow with her husband's brother—are, however, not considered incestuous by most societies, and are even encouraged by some.[2]

INCEST TABOO

Incest taboo in human society has been explained by sociologists and anthropologists in a number of ways. According to one theory, incest taboo encourages exogamy, i.e., bonding between otherwise unrelated households; this in turn strengthens social solidarity. Another theory—advanced mainly by biologists—is that the observance of the taboo would lower the incidence of congenital birth defects. This theory has been challenged on many counts. For instance, if this were true, why would a relationship between a father and his daughter-in-law—who are genetically unrelated—be prohibited? Also if a genetically related couple decides to use contraceptives, would the society allow such unions? Finally, simple rules of genetics tell us that though initially such marriages would result in increased genetic malformations, ultimately this would tend to "cleanse the gene pool." According to the Finnish philosopher and sociologist Edward Alexander Westermarck (1862–1939), infants raised together are desensitized to later close sexual attraction and are thus unable to form sexual feelings for one another as adults.[3] This is often known as the Westermarck effect, or reverse sexual imprinting. No single theory, however, completely explains the universal prevalence of incest taboo in our society; the truth may include elements from all theories.

HISTORICAL PERSPECTIVES

References to incest can be seen in mythologies of most ancient cultures. In Greek mythology for instance, incest is not only mentioned, but it continued for generations. Gaia, the mother earth, married her son Uranus, the sky, and gave birth to 12 Titans—6 sons and 6 daughters. Continuing the tradition of incest, Cronus, the youngest of the 12 Titans, married his sister Rhea. They had 6 offspring. Two of them, Zeus and Hera, married yet again! Similar examples occur in mythologies of Egypt, Scandinavia, and the Far East. Austrian psychologist Otto Rank (1884–1939)—a student of Freud—interpreted these as symbolic fulfillment of a repressed desire.

Sometimes the incest offender was severely punished, even in the absence of intent. Oedipus was destroyed by the gods although he unknowingly violated the taboo.

The Bible

A celebrated instance of incest can be found in the Bible.

> And Cain knew his wife; and she conceived, and bare Enoch: and he builded a city, and called the name of the city, after the name of his son, Enoch.[4]

Since at that time, there were no other females except Eve, it is thought that Cain had a union with his mother, or perhaps a sister who has been unnamed.

Moses, the great leader of Israel, was himself born as a result of an incestuous relationship.

> And Amram took him Joch'ebed his father's sister to wife; and she bare him Aaron and Moses: and the years of the life of Amram were a hundred and thirty and seven years.[5]

In later references, however, incest is specifically prohibited in the Bible. Sexual intercourse with one's mother (biological or otherwise) and daughter-in-law is prohibited. The penalty is death for both parties to the incest.

> And the man that lieth with his father's wife hath uncovered his father's nakedness: both of them shall surely be put to death; their blood shall be upon them. And if a man lie with his daughter-in-law, both of them shall surely be put to death: they have wrought confusion; their blood shall be upon them.[6]

One of the most famous instances of father–daughter incest (when incidentally the initiative was taken by daughters instead of the father) is when God destroyed Sodom and Gomorrah for their perversion and sinfulness. Lot's wife was turned into a pillar of salt, and he was left only with his 2 daughters. In order to repopulate a devastated world, the daughters decided to have sexual intercourse with their father.

> And Lot went up out of Zo'ar, and dwelt in the mountain, and his two daughters with him; for he feared to dwell in Zo'ar: and he dwelt in a cave, he and his two daughters. And the firstborn said unto the younger, Our father is old, and there is not a man in the earth to come in unto us after the manner of all the earth: come, let us make our father drink wine, and we will lie with him, that we may preserve seed of our father. And they made their father drink wine that night: and the firstborn went in, and lay with her father; and he perceived not when she lay down, nor when she arose. And it came to pass on the morrow, that the firstborn said unto the younger, Behold, I lay yesternight with my father: let us make him drink wine this night also; and go thou in, and lie with him, that we may preserve seed of our father. And they made their father drink wine that night also: and the younger arose, and lay with him; and he perceived not when she lay down, nor when she arose. Thus were both the daughters of Lot with child by their father. And the firstborn bare a son, and called his name Moab: the same is the father of the Moabites unto this day. And the younger, she also bare a son, and called his name Ben–am'mi: the same is the father of the children of Ammon unto this day.[7,8]

Ancient Civilizations

In ancient Babylon, incest between father and daughter was punishable by exile; incest between mother and son was punishable by both being burned. Incestuous unions were frowned upon and considered *nefas* (against the laws of gods and man) in the Roman civilization, and were explicitly forbidden by an imperial edict in AD 295, which divided the concept of *incestus* into two categories of unequal gravity: the *incestus iuris gentium,* which applied to both Romans and non-Romans in the Empire, and the *incestus iuris civilis,* which concerned only Roman citizens. Although an Egyptian could marry an aunt, a Roman could not. Despite the act of incest being unacceptable within the Roman Empire, Emperor Caligula is rumored to have had open sexual relationships with all 3 of his sisters, Julia Livilla, Drusilla, and Agrippina the Younger.

Royal Dynasties

Incest was common in old royal dynasties, including those of the Ptolemaic and Roman periods in Egypt, Zoroastrian Iran, the Incas, and the royal families of Hawaii.[9,10] In pharaonic Egypt, brother–sister or half-sister marriages were regarded as a useful and credible way to maintain and strengthen the bloodline, although the Pharaoh also had ready access to other females who were non-relatives. Cleopatra (69–30 BC) married her younger brother Ptolemy XIII (63–47 BC). Some historians even claim that the cause of the downfall of the Egyptian empire was the growing genetic defects brought about by rampant incestuous marriages in their society; this claim has been violently contested.

Incestuous marriages were prevalent outside the ruling classes, too. During the period of Roman Egypt, from the first to the third centuries AD, the incidence of marriages between brothers and sisters in one city, Arsinoe, was as high as 19.6%; a further 3.9% were between half-siblings.[11] The rationale behind incestuous marriages varied in different communities. While the Egyptians practiced incestuous marriages in order to preserve and strengthen their bloodline, the Greeks probably resorted to this practice because of the paucity of potential marriage partners.[12] Zoroastrians of Persia, who advocated all three major types of incestuous unions, namely, father–daughter, brother–sister, and mother–son, did so out of their specific religious beliefs.

Recommendation of Incest

Surprisingly, some thinkers, most notably Augustine of Hippo (354-430), not only failed to condemn incest, but acknowledged its necessity and hence naturalness. It was argued that the children of Adam and Eve had to, if only out of necessity, resort to it.[13] St. Thomas Aquinas (c. 1225–1274) thought that incest was not as grave an offense as some others such as bestiality, masturbation, and homosexuality, because incest was procreative.[14] According to him procreative sexual offenses such as heterosexual adultery, rape, seduction, and incest were less grave than non-procreative offenses.

Modern Era

Even in the modern era, with a fairly good understanding of the phenomenon and abundant laws against the practice, incest is still much more common than has been believed till now. Even celebrities have been victims of incest. American actress Clara Bow's (1905–1965) father had sexual relations with her when she was very young.

Freud believed that all male children between ages 3 and 5 fell in love with their mother—a normal stage of psychosexual development. He called it the Oedipus complex, after the Greek mythological figure Oedipus who slayed his father Laius inadvertently and unknowingly married his mother Jocasta. Normally this stage passes uneventfully, but if the child becomes fixated at this state, it may give rise to psychological problems later in life. The counterpart of Oedipus complex in girls is the Electra complex.

ETIOLOGY

Psychoanalytic Theories

According to psychoanalysts, all children have a desire to have sexual relations with family members. *Oedipus complex* and *Electra complex*—two terms specifically appearing constantly in their writings refer to incestuous feelings among children (please see chapter 1 for details). It is theorized that eventually both boys and girls resolve this feeling by identifying with the parent of the same sex, thereby repressing the incestuous desires for the parent. Thus, the boy would identify himself with the father by adopting the morals, goals, and mannerisms of his father. Thus in an indirect fashion, by identifying with his father, he can vicariously possess his mother. Thus the child satisfies his incestuous desires, without *actually* having intercourse with his mother. He also realizes that having his mother is impossible, and thus incestuous feelings are desexualized, and fall prey to what Freud called "infantile amnesia," i.e., he eventually forgets completely that he ever desired his mother.

However, if for some reason this resolution, through identifying with the father, fails, incestuous desires for parents may continue. The desire may somehow get transferred from mother to sister, too. Psychoanalysts are, however, largely silent on how this happens.

Other Factors

Several other etiological factors have been enumerated for incest:

(i) Retaliation of the male partner against the female for actual or imagined unfaithfulness
(ii) Many men feel that their children are their sexual property
(iii) General lack of impulse control
(iv) A tradition in families, particularly in rural areas, where incest is a common practice

PREVALENCE

Judging from various reports in literature, the incidence of incest appears to be around 5%, i.e., about 5 of every 100 children living with their parents or stepparents experience sexual interactions with them. It is believed that incest between fathers and young daughters is far more common than other forms; certainly most cases of incest that come before criminal courts belong to this form. Sariola and Uutela conducted a survey on the prevalence of father–daughter incest in Finland by asking about 9,000 fifteen year olds to fill out a questionnaire anonymously. Two percent of girls reported having sexual experiences with their biological fathers, while 3.7% reported having sexual experiences with stepfathers (total 5.7% of all girls experiencing incest).[15] Kim and Kim[16] selected a total of 1,672 adolescents (1,053 student adolescents and 619 delinquent adolescents) using proportional stratified random sampling, and found that the prevalence rate of incest was 3.7% in the tested Korean population. Furthermore, families in which incest occurred were characterized by higher levels of problems, such as psychotic disorders, depression, criminal acts, and alcoholism.

The prevalence is much higher in delinquent groups. Glover and colleagues[17] conducted a survey in which they examined the prevalence of incest among adults receiving substance abuse treatment in facilities across the United States. Approximately 36% of their sample reported histories of incest: by gender, 29% of the male and 55% of the female participants reported incest histories.

VICTIM CHARACTERISTICS

Kristensen and Lau studied 385 women with histories of childhood sexual abuse (CSA) and found that more than 88% had been victims of incest[18] (for details, please refer to the chapter on pedophilia). In Kim and Kim's study,[16] adolescent incest victims were found to be significantly more dysfunctional and unhealthy in terms of family dynamics and expressed significantly higher maladaptive and problematic psychological patterns than nonvictimized adolescents.

INBREEDING COEFFICIENT

The word *incest* carries no meaning biologically. Equivalent biological terms are *inbreeding, interbreeding*, or *consanguineous mating*. When inbreeding in a community increases, the probability that both alleles at an identical locus derive from the same ancestor increase substantially, thereby increasing the possibility of genetic and hereditary disorders. The extent of inbreeding can be gauged by a mathematical quantity called *coefficient of inbreeding*. It is formally defined as a measure of how close two people are genetically. Symbolized by the letter f, it is the probability that a person received both alleles at a single locus from one ancestor.

Take a first-cousin mating. First cousins share a set of grandparents. For any particular gene in the male, the chance that his female first cousin inherited the same gene from the same source is 1/8. Further, for any gene the man passes to his child, the chance is 1/8 that the woman has the same gene and 1/2 that she transmits that gene to the child so $1/8 \times 1/2 = 1/16$. Thus, a first-cousin marriage has a coefficient of inbreeding $f = 1/16$ or 0.0625. While the average known coefficient of inbreeding in France is 0.0005, in Japan, 0.003, and in the remote village of Sibum in Arunachal Pradesh, 0.012,[19] it is as high as 0.02 in Andhra Pradesh, a coastal state of India, where there is a high percentage of first-cousin mating.[20]

ILLUSTRATIVE CASES

Muth v. Frank

This illustrative case (*Muth v. Frank,* 412 F.3d 808 [7th Cir. 2005]*)* decided whether Wisconsin's incest statute was unconstitutional insofar as it seeks to criminalize a sexual relationship between two consenting adults. The case was decided before a three-judge panel of the Seventh Circuit, in Chicago, on June 22, 2005.

Allen Muth, the petitioner-appellant, and his sister Patricia were 2 of the 14 children in a dysfunctional family. Allen was one of the oldest, and Patricia one of the youngest. During their childhood they were in and out of foster care, and along with several other siblings were involved in a cycle of sexual abuse and incest. Although they were separated for some length of time, at about the time Patricia reached the age of majority, she and Allen reunited and got married (despite the fact that in Wisconsin incest was a criminal offense). They even had 3 children without the state ever becoming aware of it.

Their incestuous relationship came to the State's attention when their middle child, Tiffany, who was disabled (perhaps as a result of being an offspring of an incestuous relationship), was abandoned by them at the home of a baby-sitter.

After a series of progressive separation procedures, the State filed a petition to terminate Patricia and Allen's parental rights to Tiffany because of their incestuous parenthood (please see Wisconsin statute below). Neither Patricia nor Allen contested the evidence of their incest, and consequently the trial court terminated their parental rights.

On appeal to the Wisconsin Court of Appeals, Patricia and Allen challenged the constitutionality of §48.415(7) which provides that incestuous parenthood is a ground for termination of parental rights. The Muths claimed that the termination of their parental rights based on their incestuous parenthood of Tiffany denied them due process of law and their rights to equal protection of the law. The court denied those claims and affirmed the trial court.

Prior to this trial, Allen moved to dismiss the criminal complaint against him, on the basis that Wisconsin's incest statute was unconstitutional insofar as it sought to criminalize a sexual relationship between two consenting adults. The trial court denied the motion and conducted a bench trial. Both Allen and Patricia were convicted on November 11, 1997. Allen was sentenced to eight years in prison and Patricia to five years. The Wisconsin Court of Appeals affirmed Allen's conviction in January 2000.

Having exhausted all state remedies, while imprisoned, on April 20, 2001, Muth filed a petition, for a writ of *habeas corpus* with the United States District Court for the Eastern District of Wisconsin. He asserted that the state anti-incest laws violated his constitutional rights and hence his imprisonment was illegal. Before the completion of briefing by the parties, the United States Supreme Court, on June 26, 2003, pronounced its decision in *Lawrence v. Texas*, 539 U.S. 558 (2003). In that landmark case, the Supreme Court held that a Texas statute prohibiting homosexual sodomy was unconstitutional insofar as it applied to the private conduct of two consenting adults (Sidebar 14.1).

Sidebar 14.1: *Lawrence v. Texas; Bowers v. Hardwick* and *Muth v. Frank*—Do incestuous couples share the same sexual privileges as homosexuals?

Between 10:30 and 11 p.m. on September 17, 1998, medical technologist John Geddes Lawrence, 60, and street-stand barbecue vendor Tyron Garner, 36, were found having consensual anal sex in Lawrence's apartment in the suburbs of Houston when Harris County sheriff's deputy Joseph Quinn entered the unlocked apartment, with his weapon drawn, arresting the two. They were held overnight in jail, and charged with violating Texas's anti-sodomy statute. Chapter 21, Sec. 21.06 of the Texas Penal Code designated it as a class C misdemeanor when someone "engages in deviant sexual intercourse with another individual of the same sex," prohibiting anal and oral sex between members of the same-sex. The case finally reached the United States Supreme Court on July 16, 2002. In a landmark 6 to 3 ruling, delivered on June 26, 2003, the justices struck down the anti-sodomy law that had criminalized homosexual sex in Texas, holding that intimate consensual sexual conduct was part of the liberty protected by substantive due process under the Fourteenth Amendment (*Lawrence v. Texas,* 539 U.S. 558 [2003]).

Seventeen years earlier, almost to date, on June 30, 1986 the court had addressed exactly the same issue in *Bowers v. Hardwick,* 478 U.S. 186 (1986), and pronounced a similar anti-sodomy law constitutional. In August, 1982, police officer Torick entered the apartment of Michael Hardwick to serve an arrest warrant for some minor offense. Hardwick had an overnight guest sleeping on the couch, who opened the door to the officer and allowed him into the apartment. After walking around, Torick observed Hardwick's bedroom door slightly opened and proceeded into the room where Hardwick and a male companion were engaged in mutual, consensual oral sex.

Torick placed both men under arrest for sodomy, which was defined in Georgia law to include both oral sex and anal sex. The local district attorney elected not to present the charge to the grand jury, which would have been a prerequisite to any trial or punishment for the offense. Hardwick then sued Michael Bowers, the attorney general of Georgia, in federal court for a declaration that the state's sodomy law was invalid. The case gained prominence, especially as the American Civil Liberties Union (ACLU) approached Hardwick and requested him to allow ACLU to pursue his cause, and he agreed.

Following a decision by the lower federal court in Hardwick's favor, the case ultimately reached the Supreme Court as the State of Georgia wished to overturn that decision. The majority opinion in *Bowers,* written by Justice Byron White, framed the legal question as whether the constitution creates "a fundamental right to engage in homosexual sodomy." Justice White's opinion for the majority answered this question in the negative, stating that "to claim that a right to engage in such conduct is 'deeply rooted in this Nation's history and tradition' or 'implicit in the concept of ordered liberty' is, at best, facetious," thus effectively upholding the constitutionality of the Georgia anti-sodomy law.

Lawrence explicitly overruled *Bowers*, holding that it had viewed the liberty interest too narrowly. The *Muth* case was going on around the same time *Lawrence* was pronounced, and Muth reasoned that he could advance *Lawrence* arguments successfully to defend his own incestuous conduct. The case ultimately reached the U.S. Court of Appeals for the Seventh Circuit, which held—on 22 June 2005—that the U.S. Supreme Court's decision in *Lawrence*, striking down anti-sodomy laws as unconstitutional *did not* extend to the conclusion that laws against consensual adult incest were similarly unconstitutional.

Muth added the reasoning of this ruling in his arguments. He argued that since their relationship—though incestuous—was also between two consenting adults, the same reasoning as in *Lawrence* should make anti-incest laws unconstitutional, too. On October 3, 2003, the district court denied Muth's petition. On June 22, 2005, the U.S. Court of Appeals for the Seventh Circuit held that the U.S. Supreme Court's decision in *Lawrence* (outlawing anti-sodomy laws), did not necessarily imply that anti-incest laws were unconstitutional, too.

Aizawa v. Japan

Aizawa v. Japan, 27 Keishu 265 [Sup. Ct, G. B., Apr. 4 1973] is important in that it brought about an important legal change in Japanese criminal code. Chiyo Aizawa (1939–), had been sexually abused by her alcoholic father Takeo Aizawa (1915–1968), ever since she was 14-years of age. Because of his deviant behavior, Takeo's wife Rika had left him, and Takeo was living with his daughter as if she were his wife. In fact, most neighbors thought Chiyo was his wife. She bore 5 children by her father—all daughters. Two of them died, so she was left with 3 daughters. In 1967, she underwent sterilization. When in 1968, she fell in love with a male colleague and wished to marry him, her father lost his temper, confined her, and threatened to kill her 3 children. She became so desperate that on October 5, 1968, she strangled her father.

According to the Japanese law, the offense of homicide was dealt with by Article 199 of the Japanese Penal Code. It stated, "A person who kills another shall be punished with death or by imprisonment at forced labor for life or for a term of not less than three years." However, there was a more severe punishment for someone killing a lineal ascendant, as Chiyo had done. This was dealt with by Article 200, which stated, "A person who kills one of his or her own or his or her spouse's direct lineal ascendants shall be punished with death or imprisonment at forced labor for life." This effectively meant that while in the case of "ordinary" murder, one's sentence could—at least theoretically— be just 3 years, in case of "special" murder, one had to undergo a minimum sentence of life imprisonment.[21]

During her trial, Aizawa insisted that her murder was in self-defense. Furthermore, continuous incest and sexual abuse had driven her almost to insanity and thus she should get the insanity defense as well. Finally, she raised the issue that Article 200, under which she was being tried, was unconstitutional, since it unreasonably discriminated between the murders of lineal and non-lineal ascendants.

The district court in Utsunomiya agreed with her reasonings and it sentenced her to a suspended sentence. However, the high court in Tokyo reversed the decision, and thus the case went to the Supreme Court of Japan in 1973. On April 4, 1973, the Supreme Court finally ruled that Article 200 was in fact unconstitutional not because the legislature was prohibited under the Constitution from differentiating between the murder of lineal and non-lineal ascendants *ipso facto*, but because the *extent* of the discrepancy of the penalty was unreasonable. Unconstitutionality arises where "the extent of the penalty is augmented to such an extent … that it loses sight of the legislative purpose." The legislative purpose of Article 200 is simply to afford greater protection to lineal ascendants, which could very well be met by having a lesser discrepancy. Aizawa received a sentence of a 2 years 6 months in prison and 3 years suspended sentence. Following this judgment, on April 19, 1973, Japanese murderers who had killed their parents were granted amnesties by the Japanese Ministry of Justice. Article 200 of the Japanese Penal Code was kept in abeyance, and finally abolished in 1995.

MEDICAL ASPECTS

It has been seen that the incidence of cervical carcinoma (caused by human papillomavirus [HPV]) is higher in consanguineous marriages. Among the hypotheses advanced to explain this peculiar phenomenon is that since consanguineous spouses have a mild sexual aversion to each other (Westermarck effect), it increases their likelihood of satisfying sexual desire outside of the marriage. Because having multiple sex partners is one of the risk factors for HPV infection, consanguineous spouses stand a higher chance of acquiring cervical carcinoma.[22]

LEGAL ASPECTS

Although incest laws vary widely among nations, civil (recognized marriage) and criminal laws (sexual intercourse) prohibiting incestuous unions even among the same jurisdiction do not necessarily coincide. Thus while marriage between two closely related persons is null and void in India, the same persons can engage in sexual union with impunity (incest is not a crime in India). Other anomalies exist, too; English law prohibits intercourse between grandfather and granddaughter but not between grandmother and grandson. The Tanach (Old Testament) contains prohibitions (primarily in Leviticus) against sexual relations between various pairs of family members such as father and daughter, mother and son, and aunts and nephews, but not between uncles and nieces.[2]

Relevant modern incest laws in some significant jurisdictions are discussed below.

AUSTRALIA

South Australia

Section 72 of the Criminal Law Consolidation Act 1935 of South Australia deals with the offense of incest:

> Any persons who, being related, either as parent and child or as brother and sister, have sexual intercourse with each other shall be guilty of incest and liable to be imprisoned for a term not exceeding seven years.

The definition of sexual intercourse is very broad in South Australian law (please see chapter on rape).

Northern Territory

According to section 134 of the Criminal Code of Northern Territory (for details, please see chapter on exhibitionism), incest is a crime with a punishment of imprisonment up to 25 years. Section 134 states:

> (1) Any person who has sexual intercourse with another person who is a close family member is guilty of a crime and is liable to imprisonment for 14 years.
> (2) If the close family member is a child of or over the age of 10 years and under the age of 16 years, the offender is liable to imprisonment for 20 years.
> (3) If the close family member is a child under the age of 10 years, the offender is liable to imprisonment for 25 years.

(4) It is a defense to a charge of the crime defined by this section to prove that the accused person was acting under the coercion of the close family member.
(5) Section 12 does not apply to the close family member with respect to whom an offense against this section is committed if that member is a child under the age of 16 years.
(6) In this section—"close family member", of a person, means any of the following persons who are members of the person's family from birth:
 (a) a parent or grandparent;
 (b) a child or other lineal descendant;
 (c) a brother, sister, half-brother or half-sister.

Section 12 mentioned in the text above refers to abettors and accessories. According to section 12, normally when an offense is committed, every person who aids another in committing the offense is an abettor, and it might appear to imply that if incest was committed on a young child, he (the child) would be an abettor to the crime. However, the text of section 134 makes it clear that this section would not apply to the offense of incest if the child was below 16 years of age.

Queensland

Queensland criminal law is governed by the Criminal Code 1899 (for details please see chapter on exhibitionism). Most sexual offenses are defined in chapter 22, entitled "offenses against morality." Incest is defined in Section 222:

(1) Any person who—
 (a) has carnal knowledge with or of the person's offspring or other lineal descendant, or sibling, parent, grandparent, uncle, aunt, nephew or niece; and
 (b) knows that the other person bears that relationship to him or her, or some relationship of that type to him or her; commits a crime.

Maximum penalty—imprisonment for life.

(2) Any person who attempts to commit the crime of incest is liable to imprisonment for 10 years.
(3) It is immaterial that the act or attempted act of carnal knowledge happened with the consent of either person.
(4) It is a defense to a charge under this section to prove that the accused person was, at the time when the act or attempted act of carnal knowledge happened, acting under the coercion of the other person.
(5) A reference in this section to an offspring or other lineal descendant, or a sibling or a parent includes a relationship of that type that is a half, adoptive or step relationship.
(6) For subsection (5), a reference to a step relationship includes a relationship corresponding to a step relationship arising because of cohabitation in a de facto relationship or because of a foster relationship or a legal arrangement.
(7) Also, for subsection (5), a reference to a step relationship does not include a step relationship that first arose after the relevant persons became adults.
(8) This section does not apply to carnal knowledge between persons who are lawfully married or entitled to be lawfully married.

New South Wales

The criminal law of New South Wales is governed by the Crimes Act 1900 (for details, please see chapter on frotteurism). Incest is defined and punished under Section 78A:

(1) Any person who has sexual intercourse with a close family member who is of or above the age of 16 years is liable to imprisonment for 8 years.
(2) For the purposes of this section, a "close family member" is a parent, son, daughter, sibling (including a half-brother or half-sister), grandparent or grandchild, being such a family member from birth.

Incest attempts are punished under Section 78B:

> Any person who attempts to commit an offense under section 78A is liable to imprisonment for 2 years.

Tasmania

According to Tasmanian Criminal Code Act 1924, incest is a crime. Section 133 states:[23]

(1) Any person who has sexual intercourse with another person knowing that other person to be his or her lineal ancestor, lineal descendant, or sibling, is guilty of a crime whether or not that other person has consented to such sexual intercourse.
Charge: Incest.
(2) Any person of or above the age of 16 years who, with consent, permits another person to have sexual intercourse with him or her knowing that other person to be his or her lineal ancestor, lineal descendant, or sibling, is guilty of a crime.
Charge: Permitting incest.
(3) This section applies whether or not the relationship between the persons is traced through lawful wedlock.
(4) In this section, "sibling" includes half-brother and half-sister.

CANADA

Section 155 of the Criminal Code of Canada defines incest and prescribes punishment for it.[24]

Incest

(1) Every one commits incest who, knowing that another person is by blood relationship his or her parent, child, brother, sister, grandparent or grandchild, as the case may be, has sexual intercourse with that person.

Punishment

(2) Every one who commits incest is guilty of an indictable offense and liable to imprisonment for a term not exceeding 14 years.

Defense

(3) No accused shall be determined by a court to be guilty of an offense under this section if the accused was under restraint, duress or fear of the person with whom the accused had the sexual intercourse at the time the sexual intercourse occurred.

Definition of "brother" and "sister"

(4) In this section, "brother" and "sister," respectively, include half-brother and half-sister.

GERMANY

Section 173 of the German Criminal Code (Strafgesetzbuch, StGB) deals with sexual intercourse between relatives. It states:[25]

(1) Whoever completes an act of sexual intercourse with a consanguine descendant shall be punished with imprisonment for not more than 3 years or a fine.

(2) Whoever completes an act of sexual intercourse with a consanguine relative in an ascending line shall be punished with imprisonment for not more than 2 years or a fine; this shall also apply if the relationship as a relative has ceased to exist. Consanguine siblings who complete an act of sexual intercourse with each other shall be similarly punished.
(3) Descendants and siblings shall not be punished pursuant to this provision if they were not yet 18 years of age at the time of the act.

Furthermore, according to Section 174, anyone who commits sexual acts on his natural or adopted child who is not yet eighteen years of age is punished with a still stricter term of 5 years (for details of this section, please see chapter on pedophilia).

Hungary

Section 203 of the Hungarian Criminal Code of 1978 makes incest a punishable offense (for more, please see chapter on exhibitionism). It states:[26]

(1) The person who has sexual intercourse or fornicates with his relative in direct line, commits a felony and shall be punishable with imprisonment from 1 year to 5 years.
(2) The descendant shall not be punishable, if he has not yet completed his eighteenth year of age on perpetration of the act.
(3) A person who has sexual intercourse with his or her sibling shall be punishable for a misdemeanor offense with imprisonment of up to 2 years.

India

Civil law

According to section 5 of the Hindu Marriage Act, 1955,[27] marriage between two Hindus is not valid if they are *sapindas* of or within "degrees of prohibited relationship" (unless the custom or usage governing each of them permits of a marriage between the two). *Sapinda*, a *Sanskrit* term, is defined in section 3(f) of the same act. It states:

(i) *sapinda* relationship with reference to any person extends as far as the third generation (inclusive) in the line of ascent through the mother, and the fifth (inclusive) in the line of ascent through the father, the line being traced upwards in each case from the person concerned, who is to be counted as the first generation;
(ii) two persons are said to be *sapindas* of each other if one is a lineal ascendant of the other within the limits of sapinda relationship, or if they have a common lineal ascendant who is within the limits of sapinda relationship with reference to each of them;

"Degrees of prohibited relationship " is defined in section 3(g) of the same act:

"degrees of prohibited relationship"—two persons are said to be within the "degrees of prohibited relationship"—
(i) if one is a lineal ascendant of the other; or
(ii) if one was the wife or husband of a lineal ascendant or descendant of the other; or
(iii) if one was the wife of the brother or of the father's or mother's brother or of the grandfather's or grandmother's brother of the other; or
(iv) if the two are brother and sister, uncle and niece, aunt and nephew or children of brother and sister or of two brothers or of two sisters;

Explanation: For the purposes of clauses (f) and (g), relationship includes—

(i) relationship by half or uterine blood as well as by full blood;

(ii) illegitimate blood relationship as well as legitimate;

(iii) relationship by adoption as well as by blood; and all terms of relationship in those clauses shall be construed accordingly.

India is a large country with many socio-religious communities. In many of these communities, marriages within families have been accepted for centuries, so much so that it has become a part of their culture and custom. The law recognizes this fact, and allows marriages within closely related individuals if "the custom or usage governing each of them permits of a marriage between them."

Marriages between closely related individuals are common in Southern India. The concept of parallel cousin and cross cousin is important to appreciate here. While the children of 2 brothers or 2 sisters are parallel cousins, children of a brother and a sister are cross cousins. In some South Indian communities, while marriages between parallel cousins are not allowed, they are allowed between cross cousins.

Criminal law

Incest is *not* a crime in India. This is perhaps due to the fact that in many communities, it is the practice to marry within relationships; they have a social sanction to commit incest. Thus theoretically, a brother (B) and sister (S) can have a live-in sexual relationship, with no criminal consequences. If the female (S) did not consent, then of course a case can be made out against the male (B) under section 376 of Indian Penal Code (please see chapter on rape). The reverse situation is not true if the male (B) did not consent and the female (S) forced a sexual relationship with him, virtually no case could be made against the female, because it is not possible for a female to sexually assault or rape a male.

If the sister (S) is married and has consensual sexual relationship with her brother, the situation becomes somewhat trickier. In this case, if the husband (H) of the female (S) does not object to sexual relationship, no case can be made out against any of the 3, but if the husband objects to this relationship, the male (B) attracts the provisions of section 497 (adultery).[28] Section 497 of the Indian Penal Code states:

> Whoever has sexual intercourse with a person who is and whom he knows or has reason to believe to be the wife of another man, without the consent or connivance of that man, such sexual intercourse not amounting to the offense of rape, is guilty of the offense of adultery, and shall be punished with imprisonment of either description for a term which may extend to 5 years, or with fine, or with both. In such case the wife shall be punishable as an abettor.

Unnatural intercourse between closely related individuals (anal intercourse), then both would be punished under section 377 of Indian Penal Code even if the act was completely consensual. It is noteworthy that unnatural intercourse is not clearly defined in the Indian Penal Code. The words used in Section 377 are "carnal intercourse against the order of nature." Thus any kind of sexual activity other than penile-vaginal intercourse (fellatio, cunnilingus, or anal intercourse) may violate this section. (For details of this section, please refer to the chapter on bestiality.)

IRELAND

In Ireland, incest is punishable under the Punishment of Incest Act 1908 as amended by the Criminal Law (Incest Proceedings) Act 1995. The maximum sentence is life imprisonment for males and

7 years for females. There are no age limits. However, a girl under 17 years cannot be prosecuted for incest.

Norway

Incest is considered a serious offense in Norway. Sections 197–199 of The General Civil Penal Code of Norway[29] address the crime of incest. No penalty is, however, imposed if the offender is below eighteen years of age. Sections 197–199 state as follows:

> Section 197. Any person who engages in sexual activity with a blood relation in the descending line shall be liable to imprisonment for a term not exceeding 5 years. Both biological and adopted descendants shall be regarded as blood relations in the descending line.
>
> Section 198. Any person who has sexual intercourse with a brother or sister shall be liable to imprisonment for a term not exceeding one year. No penalty shall, however, be imposed on persons under 18 years of age.
>
> Section 199. Any person who engages in sexual activity with a foster-child, child in his care, step-child or any other person under 18 years of age who is under his care, or subject to his authority or supervision, shall be liable to imprisonment for a term not exceeding five years.
>
> Any person who aids and abets another person to engage in sexual activity with any person with whom he himself has such a relationship shall be liable to the same penalty.

Romania

Article 222 of the Criminal Code of the Republic of Romania (for details, please see chapter on exhibitionism) outlaws incest:

> Art. 222—Sexual intercourse between persons directly related or between siblings shall be punished by strict imprisonment from 2 to 7 years.

United States

Each state has different laws regarding incest. While it would be useful to refer to the criminal codes of each state to know the details of incest law prevalent there, it might be pertinent to have a detailed look at the relevant laws in some representative states.

Alabama

According to Alabama code, incest is a class C felony. Incest is defined in the Alabama code as follows.

> (a) A person commits incest if he marries or engages in sexual intercourse with a person he knows to be, either legitimately or illegitimately:
> (1) His ancestor or descendant by blood or adoption; or
> (2) His brother or sister of the whole or half-blood or by adoption; or
> (3) His stepchild or stepparent, while the marriage creating the relationship exists; or
> (4) His aunt, uncle, nephew or niece of the whole or half-blood.
>
> (b) A person shall not be convicted of incest or of an attempt to commit incest upon the uncorroborated testimony of the person with whom the offense is alleged to have been committed.
>
> (c) Incest is a class C felony.[30]

For a class C felony, the imprisonment is more than 1 year and 1 day and less than 10 years.[31] The imprisonment includes hard labor. The fine is up to $15,000.[32]

Alaska

According to Section 11.41.450 incest is a class C felony. It defines incest as follows:[33]

(a) A person commits the crime of incest if, being 18 years of age or older, that person engages in sexual penetration with another who is related, either legitimately or illegitimately, as
 (1) an ancestor or descendant of the whole or half blood;
 (2) a brother or sister of the whole or half blood; or
 (3) an uncle, aunt, nephew, or niece by blood.
(b) Incest is a class C felony.

Louisiana

Louisiana law (Title 14, Section 78) defines incest as follows:

A. Incest is the marriage to, or sexual intercourse with, any ascendant or descendant, brother or sister, uncle or niece, aunt or nephew, with knowledge of their relationship.
B. The relationship must be by consanguinity, but it is immaterial whether the parties to the act are related to one another by the whole or half blood.
C. This Section shall not apply where one, not a resident of this state at the time of the celebration of his marriage, shall have contracted a marriage lawful at the place of celebration and shall thereafter have removed to this state.
D. (1) Whoever commits incest, where the crime is between an ascendant and descendant, or between brother and sister, shall be imprisoned at hard labor for not more than 15 years.
 (2) Whoever commits incest, where the crime is between uncle and niece, or aunt and nephew, shall be fined not more than one thousand dollars, or imprisoned, with or without hard labor, for not more than 5 years, or both.[34]

Aggravated incest is defined in Section 78.1 of Title 14, as follows.

A. Aggravated incest is the engaging in any prohibited act enumerated in Subsection B with a person who is under 18 years of age and who is known to the offender to be related to the offender as any of the following biological, step, or adoptive relatives: child, grandchild of any degree, brother, sister, half-brother, half-sister, uncle, aunt, nephew, or niece.
B. The following are prohibited acts under this Section:
 (1) Sexual intercourse, sexual battery, second degree sexual battery, carnal knowledge of a juvenile, indecent behavior with juveniles, pornography involving juveniles, molestation of a juvenile, crime against nature, cruelty to juveniles, parent enticing a child into prostitution, or any other involvement of a child in sexual activity constituting a crime under the laws of this state.
 (2) Any lewd fondling or touching of the person of either the child or the offender, done or submitted to with the intent to arouse or to satisfy the sexual desires of either the child, the offender, or both.
C. Consent is not a defense under this Section.

D. (1) A person convicted of aggravated incest shall be fined an amount not to exceed fifty thousand dollars, or imprisoned, with or without hard labor, for a term not less than five years nor more than 20 years, or both.

(2) Whoever commits the crime of aggravated incest on a victim under the age of 13 years when the offender is 17 years of age or older shall be punished by imprisonment at hard labor for not less than 25 years nor more than life imprisonment. At least 25 years of the sentence imposed shall be served without benefit of parole, probation, or suspension of sentence.

(3) Upon completion of the term of imprisonment imposed in accordance with Paragraph (2) of this Subsection, the offender shall be monitored by the Department of Public Safety and Corrections through the use of electronic monitoring equipment for the remainder of his natural life.

(4) Unless it is determined by the Department of Pubic Safety and Corrections, pursuant to rules adopted in accordance with the provisions of this Subsection, that a sexual offender is unable to pay all or any portion of such costs, each sexual offender to be electronically monitored shall pay the cost of such monitoring.

(5) The costs attributable to the electronic monitoring of an offender who has been determined unable to pay shall be borne by the department if, and only to, the degree that sufficient funds are made available for such purpose whether by appropriation of state funds or from any other source.

(6) The Department of Public Safety and Corrections shall develop, adopt, and promulgate rules in the manner provided in the Administrative Procedure Act that provide for the payment of such costs. Such rules shall contain specific guidelines which shall be used to determine the ability of the offender to pay the required costs and shall establish the reasonable costs to be charged. Such rules may provide for a sliding scale of payment so that an offender who is able to pay a portion, but not all, of such costs may be required to pay such portion.[35]

Wisconsin

Chapter 944 of Wisconsin Statutes & Annotations defines crimes against sexual morality. Section 944.06 makes incest a class F felony:

> Whoever marries or has nonmarital sexual intercourse with a person he or she knows is a blood relative and such relative is in fact related in a degree within which the marriage of the parties is prohibited by the law of this state is guilty of a class F felony.

If a couple engages in an incestuous relationship and children are borne out of that relationship, their parental rights may be terminated according to section 48.415(7). Section 48.415 provides that:

> Grounds for termination of parental rights shall be one of the following:
> ... (7) Incestuous parenthood, which shall be established by proving that the person whose parental rights are sought to be terminated is also related, either by blood or adoption, to the child's other parent in a degree of kinship closer than 2nd cousin.

REFERENCES

1. Mulhern, S. Incest: a laughing matter. *Child Abuse Negl.* 1990;**14(2)**:265-71.
2. Aggrawal, A. Incest, in *Encyclopedia Of Law And Society: American And Global Perspectives*, David S. Clark, Ed., Sage Publications, Thousand Oaks, London, 2007, Pp. 730-32 (vol. 2).

3. Westermarck, E.A. *The History of Human Marriage*, MacMillan, London, 1891.
4. Genesis 4:17. The Holy Bible. Authorized King James Version. Oxford University Press, New York, 1972.
5. Exodus 6:20. The Holy Bible. Authorized King James Version. Oxford University. Press, New York, 1972.
6. Leviticus 20.11–12. The Holy Bible. Authorized King James Version. Oxford University Press, New York, 1972.
7. Genesis 19:30–38. The Holy Bible. Authorized King James Version. Oxford University Press, New York, 1972.
8. Akerley, B.E. The *X-Rated Bible: An Irreverent Survey of Sex in the Scriptures*. Feral House, Los Angeles, 1998.
9. Middleton R. Brother-sister and father-daughter marriage in Ancient Egypt. *American Sociological Review*. 1962;27: 603–11.
10. Shaw, B.D. Explaining incest: Brother-sister marriage in Graeco-Roman Egypt. Man (N.S.). 1992;27: 267–99.
11. Scheidel, W. Brother-sister marriage in Roman Egypt. *Journal of Biosocial Science*. 1997;29:361–71.
12. Bittles, A.H. Incest, Inbreeding, and their Consequences, in *International Encyclopedia of the Social & Behavioral Sciences*, Smelser, NJ and Baltes, P.B. (Eds), Pergamon/Elsevier, Amsterdam, 2001, pages 7254-9.
13. Augustine of Hippo, Bettenson, H (Translator), *City of God*. Penguin Classics, New York, 2003, bk. 15, chap 16.
14. Aquinas, T. *Summa Theologica* (translated by Fathers of the English Dominican Province) (5 Volume Set). Christian Classics, MI, 1981.
15. Sariola, H. and Uutela, A. The prevalence and context of incest abuse in Finland. *Child Abuse Negl.* 1996 Sep;**20(9)**:843-50.
16. Kim, H.S., Kim, H.S. Incestuous experience among Korean adolescents: prevalence, family problems, perceived family dynamics, and psychological characteristics. *Public Health Nurs.* 2005 Nov-Dec;**22(6)**:472-82.
17. Glover, N.M., Janikowski, T.P., Benshoff, J.J. Substance abuse and past incest contact. A national perspective. *J Subst Abuse Treat.* 1996 May-Jun;**13(3)**:185-93.
18. Kristensen, E., Lau, M. Women with a history of childhood sexual abuse. Long-term social and psychiatric aspects. *Nord J Psychiatry.* 2007;61(2):115-20.
19. Maji, S., Krithika S., Vasulu, T.S. Genetic kinship among an isolated Adi tribe of Arunachal Pradesh: isonymy in the Adi Panggi. *Hum Biol.* 2007 Jun;**79(3)**:321-37.
20. Renshaw, D.C., *Incest—Understanding and Treatment*, 1st ed. Little, Brown and Company, Boston, 1982.
21. Williams, N. *The Right to Life in Japan (Nissan Institute Routledge Japanese Studies Series)*, Routledge, New York, 1997.
22. Denic, S. Consanguinity as risk factor for cervical carcinoma. *Med Hypotheses.* 2003 Mar;**60(3)**:321-4.
23. Section 122, Criminal Code Act 1924 (No. 69 of 1924).
24. Section 155, Criminal Code of Canada (R.S., 1985, c. C-46).
25. Section 173, German Criminal Code (S*trafgesetzbuch, StGB*) as promulgated on 13 November 1998 (Federal Law Gazette I, p. 945, p. 3322).
26. Section 203, The Hungarian Criminal Code, Act IV of 1978.
27. Hindu Marriage Act, 1955 (Act No. 25 of 1955) [18th May, 1955].
28. The Indian Penal Code, (Act No. 45 of 1860) [6th October, 1860].
29. The General Civil Penal Code (Act of 22 May 1902 No. 10), with subsequent amendments, the latest made by Act of 21 December 2005, No. 131. Norwegian Ministry of Justice, Legislation Department, 2006.
30. Ala. Code §13A-13-3 (enacted 1977).
31. Ala. Code §13A-5-6 (enacted 1977).
32. Ala. Code §13A-5-11 (enacted 1977).
33. Alaska Stat. §11-41-450 (enacted 1983).
34. La. Rev. Stat. Ann. §14:78 (enacted 1978).
35. La. Rev. Stat. Ann. §14:78.1 (enacted 1978).

15 Telephone Scatologia

INTRODUCTION

Telephone scatologia, also referred to as acoustic voyeurism, verbal exhibitionism, verbal sexual abuse, telephone scatophilia, telephonicophilia, or quite simply obscene phone calls (OPC), is a paraphilia in which the caller obtains sexual arousal or gratification by making or listening to sexual remarks. It is also considered a nonvisual analogue of exposing.[1] The *Oxford Dictionary of Psychology* defines telephone scatologia as "a paraphilia characterized by recurrent sexually arousing fantasies, sexual urges, or behavior involving making obscene telephone calls to a non-consenting recipient."[2] The term *scatologia* is derived from the Greek word, *skato*, for "dung" and *logos* for "speech"; telephone scatologia thus literally means "dirty talking through the phone." In a modern era of communication, obscenities can be conveyed through the internet, SMSs, and other means of communications. Pakhomoul asserts that though every telephone (or internet) scatologia is obscene calling (or communicating), not every obscene call is a scatologia. So-called crank calls often have nothing to do with sexual excitation and gratification and do not constitute scatologia.

The term "obscene telephone call" does not include sexually explicit phone conversations that are consensual or not anonymous. For instance, couples who are involved in a sexual relationship may call each other to engage in a sexually arousing conversation over the telephone. In another form of consensual "phone sex," a caller may dial an advertised number to hear sexual talk from someone who is hired to provide that service. The customer pays with a credit card and is usually charged by the minute. Legally speaking, this is not an obscene telephone call because it is completely consensual.

Although most surveys find exhibitionism to be the most common paraphilia, some surveys show that telephone scatologia may be the most commonly prevalent paraphilic disorder. Herold and colleagues,[3] for example, conducted a survey in which data were obtained from 103 females in two university classes. The objective was to obtain information on sexual offenses against females. As many as 84% reported having been the victims of sexual offenses. Of these, the most often experienced offense was telephone scatologia, which was reported in more than half (61%). This was followed by complaints of sexual molestation (44%), exhibitionism (27%), being followed (24%), attempted rape (16%) and rape (1%).

The revised fourth edition of the *Diagnostic and Statistical Manual of Mental Disorders* (DSM-IV-TR)[4] does not assign any specific code to telephone scatologia. Instead along with several other uncommon paraphilias (7 of which are specifically named), it is grouped under the code 302.9 (Paraphilias Not Otherwise Specified; please see chapter on zoophilia for full statement of Code 302.9).

HISTORICAL PERSPECTIVES

TELEPHONE SCATOLOGIA INVOLVING PUBLIC FIGURES

Even public figures have been involved in telephone scatologia. One of the most notorious cases is that of former president of American University in Washington, D.C., Richard E. Berendzen (1938–). Berendzen, a professor of astronomy, became its eleventh president in 1980. He worked tirelessly to quadruple its endowment from $5 million to $20 million and elevated admissions standards. However, he had to resign in 1990, because several obscene phone calls were traced to his personal phone. Berendzen targeted local women who advertised home day-care services in *The Washington Post*. The investigation began in April 1990, after Berendzen dialed "Judy," a Virginia woman, who had put up a similar advertisement and who happened to be the wife of a Fairfax County cop. She reported the call to her husband. The police put a recording device on her phone and, using computer traces, tracked calls to Berendzen's office. Berendzen resigned on April 10, after it became clear that he was the obscene phone caller.[5] Before the complaints were made public, Berendzen checked into the Sexual Disorders Clinic of Johns Hopkins Hospital in Baltimore, where he received therapy and counseling. He faced criminal misdemeanor charges that carried a jail sentence of 12 months and a $1,000 fine, but was sentenced to two 30-day suspended terms and directed to continue therapy. He also did not get his $1 million severance package from American University.[6,7]

Three years after the incident, Berendzen published a book (co-authored with Laura Palmer), revealing insights into the etiology of telephone scatologia.[8] Berendzen's early childhood was not happy. His real nightmare began at the age of 8, when his mother, summoned him to her bedroom with the words, "Come here.'' At her urging he removed his clothing and joined her and his father in bed. That occasion had been the time when his sexual abuse occurred with both parents. His sexual abuse continued with his mother alone for the next 3 years.

ETIOLOGY

Etiology of telephone scatologia is not clear, but there are many theories. One major theory is the courtship disorder theory, which is examined in detail in the chapter on exhibitionism. Other major theories are examined in brief below.

Random and Opportunistic

Matek[9] suggests that generally the calls are made at random. Even in calls that are targeted, he found that a large element of chance was involved. Therefore, one would expect to find a relatively uniform distribution of calls among the female population. Several environmental factors and those related to the offender may be involved. These factors might include (a) the availability of phones from which obscene phone calls might be made, (b) lack of social or technical monitoring in the environment, and (c) availability of potential victims. The more of these factors exist, the greater the number of obscene phone calls.[10]

Sexual Terrorism against Women

It has been argued that obscene phone calls are in fact a form of sexual terrorism against women.[11] Proponents of this view argue that when women take on "nontraditional" sex roles of career advancement and work outside the home, some men feel threatened. These threatened men use sexually oriented violence in an attempt to control the behavior of women engaging in nontraditional roles.[12] Although on the face of it the assertion does sound logical and convincing, the available data does not seem to support it. For if this contention were correct, one would expect highest OPC incidence rates among women with high occupational status, high income, or high education. Available data do not support this. Further surveys may be required before this conjecture may be rejected completely.

Displaced Aggression

This proposed etiological factor stems from a longstanding tenet in social psychology, that "frustration will often lead to aggression against a scapegoat." People who feel angry or victimized will strike out at others who are visible targets that can be safely attacked without fear of reprisal.[13]

Nadler[14] proposes that anger toward women spurs most offenders to make OPCs. Based on several case studies of men, he finds that the obscene phone caller has "severe difficulties in self-esteem" and is likely to have had a dominating, overprotective, and bossy mother. If this etiological factor is correct, the victims would usually be weaker and more vulnerable than their aggressors. This etiological factor thus predicts an exactly opposite victimology pattern from the earlier proposition (attack on socioeconomically powerful women); OPC targets in this case would likely be women who are least able to defend themselves or who have one or more of the following attributes: low education, low income, low occupational prestige, young age, or minority group status. Available data on OPC victimology tend to support this etiological factor.

Obscene Phone Calls as Aural Rape

This proposition either symbolically or analogously interprets OPCs as a form of rape, with similar victimology patterns. "Judy," the victim of Berendzen's OPCs (please see above), said, "It's not a lot different than being raped."[15] Researchers have often described OPCs in similar terms. Warner[16] describes obscene phone calls as "aural assault," and Hott[17] characterizes them as "telephone rape." This proposition would predict a victimology quite similar to that of rape, i.e., young age (16–25 years old), central city residence, never married or separated/divorced, low family income, unemployed women, and students. The available data on OPC victims is similar and thus this proposition seems well supported.[12] It is noteworthy that many of the propositions forwarded to explain the etiology of OPC can explain the etiology of rape, too.[12]

Contributory Factors

Saunders and Awad[18] assessed 19 male adolescent sexual offenders who committed exhibitionism or telephone scatologia and found that the majority were maladjusted, had committed numerous sexual offenses, and came from multi-problem families. Some contributory factors were antisocial traits, sexual deviance in the family, homosexual conflicts, and repressed sexuality.

PREVALENCE

The prevalence of obscene telephone calls is surprisingly high. In the late 1960s, the New York City telephone company received about 17,500 complaints of obscene telephone calls every year, which represented about one of five complaints directed to it.[14] In a survey of sexual offenses against female students, reported by Herold and associates in 1979, telephone scatologia was found to be most common offense.[19] In 1989, approximately 22,000 similar complaints were filed in Washington area.[20] Furthermore, it was estimated that this number represented only 7 to 20 percent of the *actual* number of obscene phone calls placed in that area. A large number of these calls were made to women. Many of them lived alone. This made victims of these calls feel very vulnerable and exposed.

OFFENDER AND VICTIM CHARACTERISTICS

The obscene telephone caller is almost always a man who calls women. He randomly chooses phone numbers from the telephone book, primarily looking for women's names. Pedophilic telephone scatologists, i.e., offenders who make obscene phone calls only to children are also known, and most children who receive such calls suffer significant psychological consequences. Those who obey the caller's demands seem to experience more serious consequences than those who do not.[21]

Leander and colleagues[22] examined 64 child victims of obscene phone calls. They found that although all children did remember the phone call per se, they tended to omit almost all of the sexual and sensitive information and about 70% of the neutral information given by the perpetrator. The children were accurate in the information they did report. Since the children did remember more of the neutral information, it was possible that they remembered the sexual information as well, but chose not to report it possibly because of shame or embarrassment. Leander extrapolated the findings to conclude that children who have been sexually abused may actually remember more than they report in an initial interview.

It would seem that the callers are a mixed group, with a variety of personal problems. As with most paraphilias, there may be an overlap with others, usually indecent exposure, frotteurism and voyeurism.[23] This co-morbidity is not surprising, if seen in the background of courtship disorder theory (please see chapter on exhibitionism for details).

The caller is not always unknown to the victim. About 25% of the British recipients of OPC believed they knew the caller's identity.[24] The obscene telephone caller enjoys the frightened response of the victim. If the caller does not think that the recipient is annoyed, then he may not call again (that is why the best choice for the victim is to hang up immediately). It is common for the caller to masturbate during or shortly after the call. Obscene telephone calling may or may not be the individual's primary mode of sexual arousal or gratification. The obscene telephone caller has doubts about his gender identity, and the calls confirm his masculine role.

TYPES OF OBSCENE CALLERS

Bullough and Bullough describe 3 types of obscene telephone callers.[25] In the most common type, the caller may breathe heavily or describe sexual activities, particularly his masturbatory action, in explicit detail. In the second type, the caller falsely informs the victim that he has held someone dear to the victim (say her husband) a hostage and that if she wants him free, she should undress, masturbate, or engage in some form of sexual behavior. In the third type, the caller tries to convince the listener to reveal intimate details of her sexual behaviors, often stating that he is conducting a survey of sexual practices for an institute, university, or research organization. This type of caller generally sounds friendly or recognizable, easily manipulating the recipient into responding or carrying on a conversation.

Other classifications have been suggested. Mead[26] has suggested 3 types, which do not exactly overlap with the typologies mentioned above: the shock caller, the ingratiating seducer, and the trickster. The shock caller typically enjoys the shock or angry reaction of the victim. As long he continues to elicit the reaction he likes, he keeps calling. Juveniles largely constitute this type of caller. The ingratiating seducer utilizes an initial false pretense to gain the victim's trust, and once this has been established, he starts using obscenity to shock the victim. The trickster roughly corresponds to the third type mentioned in the previous classification. He tricks the victim into revealing some information—most commonly relating to sexual preferences and habits —about herself. For example, the trickster may pose as a gynecologist conducting a survey and may coax the victim to remove her clothing, touch her genitalia, and reveal some information about it. The vital difference between the ingratiating seducer and the trickster is that while the seducer's victim finally discovers that she did receive an obscene phone call, the trickster's victim never discovers it even after the call is over.

Masters and colleagues[27] proposed yet another classification, in which all obscene callers have been divided into 4 types. The most frequent caller is the one who boasts significantly about his genitalia and then describes in detail his masturbatory behavior. The second type explicitly threatens the victim in some way, but he almost never follows through with his threats. The third is a kind of voyeur, who tricks the victim into revealing some personal information about herself, mostly of a sexual nature, and finally the fourth who calls phone crisis centers and while talking to the female crisis line volunteer on the phone is constantly masturbating. He is only interested in her voice, not in her advice.

The multitude of classifications can be confusing and almost all suffer from one major drawback—they do not attempt to classify the obscene phone caller from the victim's threat perception.

This is important, since it is the threat perception of the obscene caller that ultimately affects the psychological health of the victim. The following new classification is proposed in this book, which classifies all telephone scatologists in six types from type I through type VI, with type I eliciting the minimal alarm reaction and type VI eliciting the maximum. The classification is also useful since it grades the paraphilias mathematically, and is in line with classification of other paraphiliacs such as bestialists and necrophiliacs.

Class I Telephone Scatologists: Telephone Masturbators

These offenders call the telephone crisis centers and masturbate while talking to female volunteers. They do not elicit any alarm reaction because the victim never knows she has been talking to a telephone scatologist.

Class II Telephone Scatologists: Tricksters

These offenders claim they are conducting a sexual survey and glean information from the victims. They may or may not be masturbating at the time they are talking. They also do not elicit any alarm reaction in the victim.

Class III Telephone Scatologists: Ingratiating Seducers

It is only with the first 2 classes of scatologists that the victim never guesses that she had been talking to a scatologist. In the remaining 4 classes, the victim does discover that she had been talking to a scatologist. Class III scatologists gain the victim's confidence first, and only during the latter part of their conversation do they utter obscenities. Thus, while the victim is rather comfortable in the beginning, she is alarmed towards the end of the conversation. The alarm caused to the victim is minimal.

Class IV Telephone Scatologists: Shock Callers

These offenders call the victim and then remain silent, or breathe heavily or describe sexual activities, particularly their masturbatory action, in explicit detail. The victim knows from the very beginning that she has been talking to a scatologist. However, she is not alarmed enough to be psychologically paralyzed. She remains in control of the situation, and can end the call, as and when she wants.

Class V Telephone Scatologists: Annoyance Creators

These offenders simply phone their victims, speak some inanities, and quietly hang up. The offenders control the call. And since they can call again and again and speak obscenities, they are able to elicit considerable annoyance and alarm reaction from their victims.

Class VI Telephone Scatologists: Panic Creators

These are the most serious offenders. They create considerable panic and alarm in the victim. They may claim to hold someone in whom the victim is interested as a hostage and induce the victim to perform some kind of sexual activity.

ILLUSTRATIVE CASES

Gault Decision

The Gault decision (*In Re Gault,* 387 U.S. 1, 87 S.Ct. 1428, 18 L.Ed. 527 [1967]) is not specific for telephone scatologists, but for all juvenile offenders. However, since the offender here made an obscene telephone call, the case becomes important here. In this case, a young boy was sent to a detention center for 6 years for making an obscene telephone call. The final decision stressed that juvenile courts are not supposed to be run like criminal courts. They are supposed to help juvenile delinquents become lawful adults by reforming them, not punishing them.

Gerald Francis Gault, a 15-year old boy from Gila County, Arizona, was arrested in 1964 for being with a friend who stole a wallet from a woman's purse. For that offense, the juvenile court ordered probation for 6 months. On June 8, 1964, while Gault was still on probation, Mrs. Cook, his neighbor, complained to the police that Gault and a friend made an obscene telephone call to her. Police arrested Gault while his parents were at work and took him to the Children's Detention Home. When Gault's mother arrived home, she had to search to find her son in the detention home. Superintendent Flagg told Mrs. Gault that there would be a hearing the next day in juvenile court. The juvenile court held two hearings for Gault's case, one on June 9 and one on June 15. The police and the court never told Gault what law he was accused of breaking. They did not explain that he could have an attorney represent him in court. The court did not even require Mrs. Cook to testify against Gault. Instead, it relied on testimony by Superintendent Flagg that Gault admitted to making an obscene telephone call to Mrs. Cook. According to Judge McGhee, Gault even confessed during the second hearing to making obscene comments on the telephone. Gault's parents denied this, saying that Gault only dialed Mrs. Cook's number and then handed the telephone to his friend.

Based on the testimony, Judge McGhee decided that Gault was a juvenile delinquent. He ordered Gault to be confined in the State Industrial School, a juvenile detention center, until he was 21. Gault was only 15 at the time, so he faced 6 years in detention. If Gault had been an adult, his crime would have been punishable by only 2 months in prison.

Gault's parents appealed, alleging that their child was not given due process (a fair trial) and thus the Fourteenth Amendment of the U.S. Constitution was violated. Under a fair trial, the defendant has notice of the charges against him, the right to have an attorney, and the chance to face and cross-examine witnesses against him.

With an 8–1 decision, the Supreme Court ruled in favor of the Gaults, releasing their son from detention. Writing for the Court, Justice Abe Fortas said "neither the Fourteenth Amendment nor the Bill of Rights is for adults alone." Even though a juvenile case is not a criminal case, sending a juvenile to a detention center takes away his liberty and freedom: "Instead of mother and father and sisters and brothers and friends and classmates, his world is peopled by guards, custodians, state employees, and 'delinquents' confined with him for anything from waywardness to rape and homicide."

State v. Vines

An obscene telephone call made to a child may amount to child molestation, even though the child may be physically miles away from the offender. In *State v. Vines,* 487 S.E.2d 521 (Ga. Ct. App. 1997), the court held that "a sexually explicit telephone call to a child, conducted with the intent to arouse or satisfy sexual desires, was sufficient to support the charge of child molestation." It further observed that "although the language of the statute obviously applies to acts committed in the physical presence of the child, it does not require such physical presence, and the language is clearly broad enough to apply to an act committed by communication in a telephone conversation between the accused and the child." Also "the mere fact that the alleged conversation was communicated by telephone rather than in the physical presence of a child does not change the sexually exploitive and psychologically damaging nature of the act and thus does not remove it from the scope of prohibited acts."

LEGAL ASPECTS

Australia

Northern Territory

Telephone scatologia is not mentioned explicitly in the Criminal Code of the Northern Territory. However, under Section 189 of this Code (for details, please see chapter on exhibitionism), telephoning a person with the intention of causing physical or mental harm to the victim or of arousing apprehension or fear in the victim for his or her own safety is a crime and carries a punishment of up to 5 years. Section 189 covers unlawful stalking:

(1) A person ("the offender") stalks another person ("the victim") if the offender engages in conduct that includes repeated instances of or a combination of any of the following:
 (a) following the victim or any other person;
 (b) telephoning, sending electronic messages to, or otherwise contacting, the victim or another person;
 (c) entering or loitering outside or near the victim's or another person's place of residence or of business or any other place frequented by the victim or the other person;
 (d) interfering with property in the victim's or another person's possession (whether or not the offender has an interest in the property);
 (e) giving offensive material to the victim or another person or leaving it where it will be found by, given to or brought to the attention of, the victim or the other person;
 (f) keeping the victim or another person under surveillance;
 (g) acting in any other way that could reasonably be expected to arouse apprehension or fear in the victim for his or her own safety or that of another person, with the intention of causing physical or mental harm to the victim or of arousing apprehension or fear in the victim for his or her own safety or that of another person and the course of conduct engaged in actually did have that result.

(1A) For the purposes of this section, an offender has the intention to cause physical or mental harm to the victim or to arouse apprehension or fear in the victim for his or her own safety or that of another person if the offender knows, or in the particular circumstances a reasonable person would have been aware, that engaging in a course of conduct of that kind would be likely to cause such harm or arouse such apprehension or fear.

(2) A person who stalks another person is guilty of an offense and is liable—
 (a) to imprisonment for 2 years; or
 (b) where—
  (i) the person's conduct contravened a condition of bail or an injunction or order imposed by a court (either under a law of the Commonwealth, the Territory, a State or another Territory of the Commonwealth); or
  (ii) the person was, on any occasion to which the charge relates, in the possession of an offensive weapon, to imprisonment for 5 years.

India

No law in India specifically targets telephone scatologia. However, Section 507 of the Indian Penal Code can be invoked to punish acts amounting to telephone scatologia:

> **Criminal intimidation by an anonymous communication—**
> Whoever commits the offense of criminal intimidation by an anonymous communication, or having taken precaution to conceal the name or abode of the person form whom the threat comes, shall be punished with imprisonment of either description for a term which may extend to two years, in addition to the punishment provided for the offense by the last preceding section.

In India, a country with strong traditions, making sexual remarks over the telephone may amount to criminal intimidation, violating the provisions of the above section. The preceding section refers to Section 506 (entitled "punishment for criminal intimidation"). The punishment prescribed in this section is imprisonment for 2 years. Thus, telephone scatologia may carry a total punishment of 4 years.

New Zealand

Section 112 of the Telecommunications Act 2001 prescribes punishment for telephone scatologia:

> **Misuse of telephone device**
> (1) Every person commits an offense who, in using a telephone device, uses profane, indecent, or obscene language, or makes a suggestion of a profane, indecent, or obscene nature, with the intention of offending the recipient.
> (2) Every person commits an offense who—
>   (a) uses, or causes or permits to be used, any telephone device for the purpose of disturbing, annoying, or irritating any person, whether by calling up without speech or by wantonly or maliciously transmitting communications or sounds, with the intention of offending the recipient; or
>   (b) in using a telecommunications device, knowingly gives any fictitious order, instruction, or message.
> (3) Every person who commits an offense against subsection (1) or subsection (2) is liable on summary conviction to imprisonment for a term not exceeding 3 months or a fine not exceeding $2,000.

If indecent telephone calls are made for pecuniary gain, Section 113 is invoked:

> (1) Every person commits an offense against this Act who, in using a telephone device, uses or causes to be used indecent or obscene language, or makes or causes to be made a suggestion of an indecent or obscene nature, for the purpose of obtaining commercial gain.
> (2) Every person who commits an offense against subsection (1) is liable, on summary conviction,—
>   (a) in the case of an individual, to a fine not exceeding $2,000:
>   (b) in the case of a body corporate, to a fine not exceeding $5,000.

United Kingdom

Traditionally acts of telephone scatologia were prosecuted under section 43(1)(a) of the Telecommunications act 1984. This Act, however, has been repealed now by the Communications Act 2003. Section 127 states:

> **Improper use of public electronic communications network**
> (1) A person is guilty of an offense if he—

(a) sends by means of a public electronic communications network a message or other matter that is grossly offensive or of an indecent, obscene or menacing character; or

(b) causes any such message or matter to be so sent.

(2) A person is guilty of an offense if, for the purpose of causing annoyance, inconvenience or needless anxiety to another, he—

(a) sends by means of a public electronic communications network, a message that he knows to be false,

(b) causes such a message to be sent; or

(c) persistently makes use of a public electronic communications network.

(3) A person guilty of an offense under this section shall be liable, on summary conviction, to imprisonment for a term not exceeding six months or to a fine not exceeding level 5 on the standard scale, or to both.

(4) Subsections (1) and (2) do not apply to anything done in the course of providing a programme service (within the meaning of the Broadcasting Act 1990.)

The genealogy of this section may be traced back to section 10(2)(a) of the Post Office (Amendment) Act 1935, which made it an offense to send any message by telephone which is grossly offensive or of an indecent, obscene, or menacing character. That subsection was reproduced in Section 66(a) of the Post Office Act 1953. It was again reproduced in section 78 of the Post Office Act 1969, save that "by means of a public telecommunication service" was substituted for "by telephone" and "any message" was changed to "a message or other matter." Section 78 was elaborated but substantially repeated in Section 49(1)(a) of the British Telecommunications Act 1981 and was re-enacted (save for the substitution of "system" for "service") in Section 43(1)(a) of the Telecommunications Act 1984. Section 43(1)(a) was in the same terms as Section 127(1)(a) of the 2003 Act, save that it referred to "a public telecommunication system" and not (as in Section 127[1][a]) to a "public electronic communications network."

In the past telephone scatologia offenders have been charged with insulting behavior or behavior likely to cause a breach of the peace or, where relevant, with making threats to kill. They have also been prosecuted under the Theft Act 1968, when, for instance, a hoaxer put through a false call for the fire brigade, or addressed an obscene call to the telephone operator, the theft in these cases being of electricity.

United States

Each state has different laws regarding telephone scatologia or harassment through the use of the telephone. While it would be useful to refer to the criminal codes of each state to know the details of law prevalent there, it might be pertinent to have a detailed look at the relevant laws in some representative states.

Alabama

Telephone scatologia is covered under section 13A-11-8 of Alabama Code. While clause (a) entitled "harassment" is directed more to frotteurism and exhibitionism, clause (b) entitled "harassing communications" is specifically meant for obscene telephone communications:

(a)(1) A person commits the crime of harassment if, with intent to harass, annoy, or alarm another person, he or she either:

a. Strikes, shoves, kicks, or otherwise touches a person or subjects him or her to physical contact.

b. Directs abusive or obscene language or makes an obscene gesture towards another person.

(2) For purposes of this section, harassment shall include a threat, verbal or nonverbal, made with the intent to carry out the threat, that would cause a reasonable person who is the target of the threat to fear for his or her safety.

(3) Harassment is a class C misdemeanor.

(b)(1) A person commits the crime of harassing communications if, with intent to harass or alarm another person, he or she does any of the following:

a. Communicates with a person, anonymously or otherwise, by telephone, telegraph, mail, or any other form of written or electronic communication, in a manner likely to harass or cause alarm.

b. Makes a telephone call, whether or not a conversation ensues, with no purpose of legitimate communication.

c. Telephones another person and addresses to or about such other person any lewd or obscene words or language.

Nothing in this section shall apply to legitimate business telephone communications.

(2) Harassing communications is a class C misdemeanor.

Connecticut

Making obscene telephone calls is a class C misdemeanor according to Section 53a–183 Connecticut law:

Harassment in the second degree: Class C misdemeanor.

(a) A person is guilty of harassment in the second degree when: (1) By telephone, he addresses another in or uses indecent or obscene language; or (2) with intent to harass, annoy or alarm another person, he communicates with a person by telegraph or mail, by electronically transmitting a facsimile through connection with a telephone network, by computer network, as defined in section 53a-250, or by any other form of written communication, in a manner likely to cause annoyance or alarm; or (3) with intent to harass, annoy or alarm another person, he makes a telephone call, whether or not a conversation ensues, in a manner likely to cause annoyance or alarm.

(b) For purposes of this section such offense may be deemed to have been committed either at the place where the telephone call was made, or at the place where it was received.

(c) The court may order any person convicted under this section to be examined by one or more psychiatrists.

(d) Harassment in the second degree is a class C misdemeanor.

REFERENCES

1. Pakhomou, S.M. Methodological aspects of telephone scatologia: a case study. *Int J Law Psychiatry.* 29, 178, 2006.
2. Coleman, A.M. *Oxford Dictionary of Psychology.* Oxford University Press, New York, 2003.
3. Herold E.S., Mantle D., Zemitis O. A study of sexual offenses against females. *Adolescence.* 14, 65, 1979.
4. American Psychiatric Association. *Diagnostic and Statistical Manual of Mental Disorders*, 4th ed. Text rev. American Psychiatric Association, Washington DC, 2000.
5. Hammer, J., Clift, E. Obscene calls from academe. *Newsweek*, 5/7/90, Vol. 115 Issue 19, p26.
6. Scott, S., Rudulph, E. Splitsville. *Time*, 11/19/90, Vol. 136 Issue 22, p101.

7. Anon. Not $1 million, but not bad. *Time*, 12/17/90, Vol. 136 Issue 26, p65.
8. Berendzen, R. and Palmer, L., *Come Here: A Man Overcomes the Tragic Aftermath of Childhood Sexual Abuse*. Villard Books, New York, 1993.
9. Matek, O. Obscene Phone Callers. *Journal of social Work and Human Sexuality*. 1988;7:113-130.
10. Pease, K. Obscene telephone calls to women in England and Wales. *Howard Journal*. 1985;**24**:275-81.
11. Sheffield, C.J. The invisible intruder: Women's experience of obscene phone calls. *Gender & Society*. 1989;3:483-488.
12. Katz, J.E. Empirical and Theoretical Dimensions of Obscene Phone Calls to Women in the United States. *Human Communication Research*. 1994;21(2):155-182.
13. Berkowitz, L., *Aggression: A social psychological analysis*. McGraw-Hill, New York, 1962.
14. Nadler, R.P., Approach to the psychodynamics of obscene telephone calls. *New York Journal of Medicine*. 1968;**68**:521-6.
15. Carlson, P. The public nightmare of Richard Berendzen. *Washington Post Magazine*. September 23, 1990, pp.26ff.
16. Warner, P.C. Aural assault: Obscene telephone calls. *Qualitative Sociology*. 1988;**11**:302-318.
17. Hott, J.R. The Telephone Rape: Crisis intervention for an obscene phone call. *Issues in Health Care of Women*. 1985;**4**:107-13.
18. Saunders E.B., Awad, G.A. Male adolescent sexual offenders: exhibitionism and obscene phone calls. *Child Psychiatry Hum Dev*. 1991 Spring;21(3):169-78.
19. Herold E., Mantle D., and Zemitis O., A study of sexual offenses against females. Adolescence. 1979;14:65-75.
20. Price M., Gutheil T.G., Commons, M.L., Kafka, M.P., Dodd-Kimmey, S. Telephone scatologia: Co morbidity and theories of etiology. *Psychiatric Annals*. 2001;31:226-232.
21. Larsen H.B., Leth I., Maher, B.A. Obscene telephone calls to children: a retrospective field study. *J Clin Child Psychol*. 2000 Dec;**29(4)**:626-32.
22. Leander L., Granhag P.A., Christianson, S.A. Children exposed to obscene phone calls: what they remember and tell. *Child Abuse Negl*. 2005 Aug;**29(8)**: 871-88.
23. Gayford, J.J., Disorders of sexual preference, or paraphilias: a review of the literature. *Medicine, Science and the Law*. 1997;37(4):303-315.
24. Clark, R.V. Deterring obscene phone callers: Preliminary results of the New Jersey experience. *Security Journal*. 1990;**1(3)**:143-8.
25. Bullough, V.L. and Bullough, B. *Human Sexuality: An Encyclopedia*. Garland publishing. Inc. New York & London, 1994.
26. Mead, B.T. Coping with Obscene Phone Calls. *Medical Aspects of Human Sexuality*. 1975;**9**:127-8.
27. Masters, W., Johnson, V. and Kolodny, R. *Human Sexuality*. Little Brown, Boston, 1982.
28. Indian Penal Code, (Act No. 45 of 1860) [6th October, 1860].
29. Section 112, Telecommunications Act 2001 of New Zealand.
30. Section 113, Telecommunications Act 2001 of New Zealand.
31. Cordess, C., Nuisance and Obscene Telephone Calls, in *Principles and Practice of Forensic Psychiatry*, 1st edition, Bluglass R. and Bowden P., Eds., Churchill Livingstone, Edinburgh, 1990, chap. VIII.2.
32. Ala. Code §13A-11-8 (enacted 1977).
33. Conn. Stat. §53a-183 (enacted 1969).

16 Transsexualism

INTRODUCTION

A transsexual is a person who repeatedly feels—often causing great frustration—that he is a member of one gender trapped in the body of the other. He wants to live and be accepted in the society as a member of the opposite sex. A male transsexual, for example, is born with normal male genitalia and other secondary characteristics of the masculine sex, but very early in life he begins to identify with women and behaves in a manner appropriate to the female sex. Since his sexual orientation is that of a female, he can become so frustrated by male genitals on his body that he tries to castrate himself in order to give a female appearance to his external genitalia.[1] It is important to differentiate a homosexual from a transsexual. A homosexual man knows that he is a male, and is quite comfortable with his gender. He simply wants to have sex with members of his own sex. A transsexual male, on the other hand, is very uncomfortable with his biological sex; he repeatedly feels that he is a female trapped in a male body. Given a choice he would transform his body to that of a female and then engage in sex with males. Transsexualism is also not the same thing as transvestism. The chief difference between the two conditions is the same: while a transsexual wants to change his sex, a transvestite does not. Furthermore, a transvestite derives erotic pleasure from donning clothes of the opposite sex, despite being comfortable with his biological sex. A transsexual may need to don the clothes of the opposite sex, not because he gets erotic pleasure, but because he strongly feels he belongs to the opposite sex.*

Transsexualism and intersex individuals are also different. In intersex individuals, the 6 components of biological sex (chromosomes, gonads, internal genitalia, external genitalia, sex hormones, and secondary sexual characteristics) do not belong to the same sex (please see also chapter 1). In true transsexualism on the other hand, there is no incongruity among the six components of biological sex[2] (please see Table 16.1).

Benjamin[3] brings out the essence of these conditions quite beautifully (and aptly, too) in the following statement:

> The transvestite has a social problem.
> The transsexual has a gender problem.
> The homosexual has a sex problem.

Male transsexuals, or somatic males (males wanting to become females), are often designated as M/F, M-F, MTF, MtF (male to female) or transwoman. Female transsexuals similarly are designated as F/M, F-M, FTM, FtM or transman. (See Table 16.2 for transgender and transsexual vocabulary.)

* Harry Benjamin has suggested—as seen in Table 16.1—that transvestism and transsexualism must not be viewed as discrete entities. Instead they lie on a continuum.

TABLE 16.1
Comparison of Transsexualism to Similar Conditions

Transsexualism and homosexuality	There is no gender dysphoria in homosexuals. In transsexuals there is.
Transsexualism and transvestism	In transsexualism there are no erotic sensations associated with donning clothes of the opposite sex. In transvestism there are. Aside from cross-dressing, most individuals with transvestic fetishism do not have a history of childhood cross-gender behaviors (stereotypical games and pastimes of the other sex, strong preference for playmates of the other sex, etc.). In transsexualism, such behaviors are seen from childhood.
Transsexualism and intersexism	In intersexism, the 6 components of biological sex are incongruous. In transsexualism they are congruous. His sex and gender (psychosocial sex) are incongruous.

IS TRANSSEXUALISM A PARAPHILIA?

Transsexualism is *not* traditionally classified as a paraphilia, partly because of the stigma implied by this term. Money suggested that logically it (along with homosexuality, bisexuality, and transvestism) could be classified as gender transposition paraphilia.[4] Transsexualism first appeared as a psychiatric diagnosis in the third edition of the American Psychiatric Association's DSM-III, published in 1980.[5] The diagnosis was retained in DSM-III-R (Diagnostic code 302.50), which defined it as:[6]

A. Persistent discomfort and sense of inappropriateness about one's assigned sex.
B. Persistent preoccupation, for at least two years, with getting rid of one's primary and secondary sex characteristics and acquiring the sex characteristics of the other sex.
C. The person has reached puberty.

Transsexualism was subsequently subsumed in the fourth edition, DSM-IV (1994) by the term *gender identity disorder*.* This group came to include three former DSM-III-R disorders (gender identity disorder of childhood, gender identity disorder of adolescence and adulthood, nontranssexual type [GIDAANT], and transsexualism—see Tables 16.3 and 16.4). Consequently, the term *transsexualism* no longer appears in DSM-IV-TR.

According to DSM-IV-TR, there are two components of gender identity disorder, both of which must be present to make the diagnosis. There must be evidence of a strong and persistent cross-gender identification, which is the desire to be, or the insistence that one is, of the other sex (Criterion A). This cross-gender identification must not merely be a desire for any perceived cultural advantages of being the other sex. There must also be evidence of persistent discomfort about one's assigned sex or a sense of inappropriateness in the gender role of that sex (Criterion B). The diagnosis is not made if the individual has a concurrent physical intersex condition (e.g., androgen insensitivity syndrome or congenital adrenal hyperplasia) (Criterion C). To make the diagnosis, there must be evidence of clinically significant distress or impairment in social, occupational, or other important areas of functioning (Criterion D).

It is important to appreciate that there are males who meet the full criteria for gender identity disorder as well as transvestic fetishism. They are given both diagnoses.

* In DSM-IV, the term *transsexualism* appears in Appendix C (Glossary of Technical Terms), where it is defined as "severe gender dysphoria, coupled with a persistent desire for the physical characteristics and social roles that connote the opposite biological sex."

TABLE 16.2
Transgender and Transsexual Vocabulary

Androphilia —The romantic and/or sexual attraction to adult males. The term, along with *gynephilia*, is needed to overcome immense difficulties in characterizing the sexual orientation of transmen and transwomen. For instance, it is difficult to decide whether a transman erotically attracted to males is a heterosexual female or a homosexual male; or a transwoman erotically attracted to females is a heterosexual male or a lesbian female. Any attempt to classify them may not only cause confusion but arouse offense among the affected subjects. In such cases, while defining sexual attraction, it is best to focus on the object of their attraction rather than on the sex or gender of the subject.

Gynephilia —The romantic and/or sexual attraction to adult females. Also known as *gynophilia*.

Non-op transsexual —Someone who has had all the hormonal/surgical treatments, except the genital surgery, and has no desire to proceed with the surgery.

Postgenderism—A term much used by George Dvorsky, referring to a diverse social, political, and cultural movement whose adherents affirm the voluntary elimination of gender in the human species through the application of advanced biotechnology and assisted reproductive technologies. Advocates of postgenderism argue that the presence of gender roles, social stratification, and sexual dimorphisms are generally to the detriment of individuals and society. Postgenderists believe that as technology advances, sex for reproductive purposes will either eventually become a thing of the past or that all human beings will have the ability, if they so choose, to both carry a pregnancy to term and father a child, placing the entire need for gender and gender differences into question.

Post-operative transsexual —Also sometimes referred to simply as "Post-op," a post-operative transsexual is someone who has had the actual genital surgery done. It is very difficult to tell a MtF post-op transsexual from a genetic female. For FtM post-op transsexuals, there indeed are penile implants and grafts, but these are often easy to spot.

Pre-operative transsexual —Also sometimes referred to simply as "Pre-op," a pre-operative transsexual is someone who has begun the hormonal and surgical procedures and is very close to the actual sex-change operation.

Psychosexual inversion: A term often used by psychologists for transsexualism, especially in the early days of the discovery of this phenomenon. It is best to avoid this term as *inversion* has often been used as a synonym for homosexuality, too, causing much confusion.32 Other synonyms which have been used for *transsexualism* (and which should be avoided) are *psychopathia transsexualis*, *transsexism*, and *contrasexism*.

RLT —Real Life Training. It means that one lives as a member of one's preferred sex for a period of time while still having the genitalia of the former sex. This is to help the prospective transsexual determine if becoming a total member of that sex is right for him or her.

SRS —Sex Reassignment Surgery.

Transman (also spelled *trans man*, *trans-man*)—A transgender or transsexual person who was naturally born or physically assigned as female at birth but feels that this is not an accurate or complete description of him and identifies as a man. A transman should normally be erotically attracted to women (since he identifies himself as a man). However, this may not always be the case. A transman may be erotically attracted to other men, in which case he would self-identify as a homosexual male and not as a heterosexual female.

Transgenderism —A social movement seeking transgender rights and affirming transgender pride.

Transphobia —Societal discrimination and stigma of individuals who do not conform to traditional notions of gender.

Transsexual sexuality —Refers to sexual and romantic behavior of transsexual people, and is a complex interaction between self-identity and erotic attraction. Not surprisingly, it has traditionally been quite problematic to characterize a transsexual person as heterosexual or homosexual. Historically, clinicians labeled transsexual people as heterosexual or homosexual relative to their *birth sex*, but most transsexual people find this offensive and define their sexual orientation relative to self-defined gender identity. To avoid confusion and offense, the terms *gynephilia* (attraction to women) and *androphilia* (attraction to men) have been proposed.

Transwoman —(also spelled *trans woman*, *trans-woman*)—A transsexual or transgender person who was naturally born or physically assigned as male at birth but feels that this is not an accurate or complete description of him and identifies as a woman. Also known as a t-girl. A transwoman should normally be erotically attracted to men (since he identifies as a woman). However, this may not always be the case. A transwoman may be erotically attracted to other women, in which case she would self-identify as a lesbian female rather than as a heterosexual male.

TABLE 16.3
Gender Identity Disorder of Childhood, Transsexualism, and GIDAANT*

302.60 Gender Identity Disorder of Childhood

The essential features of this disorder are persistent and intense distress in a child about his or her assigned sex and the desire to be, or insistence that he or she is, of the other sex. (This disorder is not merely a child's nonconformity to stereotypic sex-role behaviors, for example, in "tomboyishness" in girls or "sissyish" behavior in boys, but rather a profound disturbance of the normal sense of maleness or femaleness.) In addition, in a girl there is either persistent marked aversion to normative feminine clothing and insistence on wearing stereotypic masculine clothing, or persistent repudiation of her female anatomic characteristics. In a boy, there is either preoccupation with female stereotypic activities, or persistent repudiation of his male anatomic characteristics. This diagnosis is not given after the onset of puberty.

302.50 Transsexualism

The essential features of this disorder are a persistent discomfort and sense of inappropriateness about one's assigned sex in a person who has reached puberty. In addition, there is persistent preoccupation, for at least two years, with getting rid of one's primary and secondary sex characteristics and acquiring the sex characteristics of the other sex.

302.85 Gender Identity Disorder of Adolescence or Adulthood, Nontranssexual Type (GIDAANT)

The essential features of this disorder are a persistent or recurrent discomfort and sense of inappropriateness about one's assigned sex, and persistent or recurrent cross-dressing in the role of the other sex, either in fantasy or in actuality, in a person who has reached puberty. This disorder differs from transvestic fetishism in that the cross-dressing is not for the purpose of sexual excitement; it differs from transsexualism in that there is no persistent preoccupation (for at least two years) with getting rid of one's primary and secondary sex characteristics and acquiring the sex characteristics of the other sex.

Some people with this disorder once had transvestic fetishism, but no longer experience sexual arousal with cross-dressing. Other people with this disorder are homosexuals who cross-dress. This disorder is common among female impersonators.

* Gender identity disorder of childhood, transsexualism, and gender identity disorder of adolescence or adulthood, non-transsexual type (GIDAANT) of DSM-III-R were subsumed by the term "Gender Identity Disorder" in DSM-IV and subsequent editions. It is useful to know what these terms meant in DSM-III-R.

TABLE 16.4
Differences between Transvestic Fetishism, GIDAANT and Transsexualism

Characteristic	Transvestic fetishism	GIDAANT	Transsexualism
Sexual excitement with cross dressing	Yes	No	No
Persistent preoccupation (for at least 2 years) with getting rid of primary and secondary sex characteristics	No	No	Yes

Source: DSM-III-R.

Some children who suffer from gender identity disorder of childhood (DSM-III-R classification) go on to acquire a homosexual orientation in adulthood. Green and colleagues[7] collected data from a group of males aged 13 to 23, who as children had exhibited extensive cross-gender behavior. In boyhood they frequently played with dress-up dolls, role-played as females, dressed in girls' clothes, stated the wish to be girls, primarily had girls as friends, and avoided rough-and-tumble play. The majority evolved into a bisexual or homosexual orientation as adults. The researchers concluded that two types of behavior were associated with later homosexual orientation—boyhood doll play and female role playing. The findings seem to suggest developmental associations between specific types of boyhood cross-gender behavior and the objects of later sexual arousal.

HISTORICAL PERSPECTIVES

Transsexualism poses special problems when one seeks out to trace its history, especially as this phenomenon was not understood properly until just a few decades ago, and was frequently confused and commingled with transvestism and even homosexuality. Yet one can deduce from the descriptions whether the earlier writers were really referring to this phenomenon.

Transsexuals and transgenders were known to ancient Hindus, and they even had an iconographic representation of Lord Shiva in androgynous form. This representation, which shows one half of his body as male and the other half as female, is called *Ardhanārī* or *Ardhanārīśvara* (half-man, half-woman). Most probably this representation had deeper philosophical meanings than just a deification of transsexuals.

The Roman emperor, Elagabalus (or Heliogabalus, ca. 203–222) was a transsexual. He married five times, thrice to women whom he divorced quickly and twice to men. In the guise of a woman, Elagabalus married Hierocles, a former slave and chariot driver, upon whom he heaped many honors. He even wished to be beaten by Hierocles as an adulterous wife. He is described as having been "delighted to be called the mistress, the wife, the Queen of Hierocles" and is said to have offered half the Roman Empire to the physician who could equip him with female genitalia.[8] He also married a man named Zoticus, an athlete from Smyrna, in a public ceremony at Rome. He often painted his eyes, epilated his hair, and wore wigs before prostituting himself in taverns and brothels, and even the imperial palace.

In 1869, Carl Westphal (1833–1890) described a phenomenon which he called "konträre Sexualempfindung " (contrary sexual feeling)* that included some aspects of transsexualism.[9,10] In 1894, Austro-German psychiatrist Richard Freiherr von Krafft-Ebing (1840–1902) described a form of cross-dressing that would today be described as transsexualism. He called it "metamorphosis sexualis paranoica."[11]

Marcuse described a psychosexual inversion in which the sufferer wanted a change of sex.[12] Abraham reported the case of the first patient on whom surgery was performed.[13] Although the term *transsexualism* was first used by Cauldwell,[14,15] it was made popular by Benjamin during the 1960s.[16]

ETIOLOGY

Why a particular person develops into a transsexual is not completely understood. However, a few explanations have been proposed.

HARD-WIRED WITHIN THE BRAIN

Harry Benjamin (1885–1986) proposed the idea that gender is hard-wired in the brain before birth.[3] Sometimes a dissociation occurs between physical and mental sexuality, although Benjamin is not very clear on how this occurs. This mismatch between physical and mental gender results in a unique type of depression, gender dysphasia, resulting sometimes even in suicide. Most transsexuals assert that because mental gender cannot be changed via psychiatric means, the only alternative left is to change the physical body to match the mind. Transsexualism is sometimes known as Harry Benjamin's syndrome (HBS).

---

* For details of cases described by Westphal, please see chapter 3.

Complex Family Dynamics

Stoller[17] presents a rather convincing scenario where the male child is "facilitated" into becoming a transsexual. The situation develops when both parents of the transsexual belong to a particular personality type. The mother (of the transsexual), in her childhood, developed a gender disorder in which a powerful masculine streak was mixed into her feminity. It happened because her own mother (the transsexual's grandmother) made the girl feel that femaleness and feminity were without value. Her father (the transsexual's grandfather), on the other hand, enjoyed her company and encouraged her to share his masculine interests. He thus encouraged her in masculine directions.

However, soon the affections of her father also disappeared, either because he left the family in separation or divorce, or turned his affections to a new child, or perhaps died. When this happened, the little girl began to develop as if she would become a female transsexual; she only wore boys' clothes, played only with boys as an equal, especially in athletics, wished she were a boy, and openly and freely stated she wanted a penis on her body. However, as opposed to a "true" female transsexual, her hopes of becoming a male were crushed, as pubertal changes begin to develop.

When the time for marriage comes, this girl deliberately chooses a man whom she can dominate and overpower. He had been dominated in his own childhood by an over-aggressive mother and did not have a firm and masculine father. After marriage, as the personalities of the two dictate, the wife takes over the power in the household, openly scorning her husband, while he, bitter and ineffective, stays away, engrossed in his own work and his hobbies.

When the child (the transsexual) is born to this couple, the mother sees in him the "perfect phallus" for which she yearned for so long. He no more remains a separate child, but becomes an extension of her body. She rewards all behavior that holds him in this same form (feminine) and discourages whatever she feels is masculine or rough. So in effect she *creates* the transsexual by subconscious operant conditioning.* Gradually the boy is "feminized" to the point of becoming a transsexual. His case is not helped by a timid father, who remains passive and distant from all this muddle.†

Why don't all children of such a couple become transsexuals? Stoller confronts this rather formidable question with the statement that for transsexualism to occur in a child "the infant must appear beautiful and graceful to his mother." Only when that happens does she develop an extremely intense, loving need for the infant, subconsciously developing him into a transsexual.

Two Special Oddities in the Male Transsexual

Stoller goes on to specify two oddities in such cases. The Oedipal conflict‡ fails to occur in such a male child, first because he does not want to possess his mother (as does a normal male child); instead he wants to be *like* his mother. Thus there is no erotic component to this relationship. Second, the father, because of his passivity, presents no threat to the child of castration.

The second oddity is that although the transsexual is detached from reality (he believes he is a female), he is not psychotic. Few claim to have a female body, which could be construed as delusional or hallucinatory, although a few exceptions have been found (see Sidebar 16.1).

---

* Please see chapter 1 for details.

† It is interesting to compare it with the proposed etiological factors of transvestism, which are very similar (please see chapter on transvestic fetishism).

‡ Please see chapter 1 for details.

Sidebar 16.1: The Curious Case of Daniel Paul Schreber—The Psychotic Transsexual

Few transsexuals are psychotic, despite their belief that they are of the opposite sex. However, a curious case has occurred in history which can be construed as a case of transsexualism due to psychotic reasons. Daniel Paul Schreber (1842–1911), a German judge, was successful and highly respected until his middle age when the onset of his psychosis occurred. He woke up one morning with the thought that it would be pleasant to "succumb" to sexual intercourse as a woman. He was alarmed and felt that this thought had come from somewhere else, not from himself. He even hypothesized that the thought had come from a doctor who had experimented with hypnosis on him; he thought that the doctor had telepathically invaded his mind. As his psychosis progressed, he believed that God was turning him into a woman, sending rays down to enact "miracles" upon him, including little men to torture him. Schreber died in 1911 in an asylum.

CLASSIFICATION

BENJAMIN'S CLASSIFICATION

As noted above, transsexualism continued to be viewed as a discrete entity until 1987. In 1966, Benjamin[3] proposed a 6-point classification system of transsexualism, which also subsumed transvestism (according to the understanding then, that the 2 conditions formed opposite ends of a broad spectrum). The scale was not only much like Kinsey's 7-point scale of homosexuality, but even used it to illustrate and clarify its own seven gradations.* Kinsey's 7-point scale is given in Table 16.5; Benjamin's scale is given in Table 16.6.

OTHER CLASSIFICATIONS

Although Benjamin's scale of transsexualism appears useful, it is instructive to go through some other classifications that have been proposed.

Stoller's Classification

Stoller proposed a simple classification dividing all transsexuals into primary and secondary groups.[18] Primary transsexuals (mostly males) have every male biological characteristic; their chromosomes are XY, gonads are histologically normal testes that produce normal male testosterone, and external and internal genitalia are male. However, from the time gender behavior appears (around 1 year of age), the child behaves in a feminine manner. As speech, fantasy life, game playing, choice of clothes, and all other manifestations of psychic development progress, this boy acts as if he were a girl. He even explicitly says that he wishes to grow up as a girl. Although he may be forced by the society to continue as a boy, he cannot do so, and soon into his adulthood starts seeking sex reassignment surgery. Stoller thought that a complex family dynamic was responsible for making a baby transsexual; the transsexual's mother, in her own childhood, developed a gender disorder in which a powerful masculine streak is mixed into her feminity. Stoller goes on to even incriminate the behavior of the transsexual's grandmother toward her daughter (the transsexual's mother) in producing the transsexual phenomenon in the child (please see etiology above for details).

Secondary transsexuals, on the other hand, do not develop opposite sex behavior from childhood, as do primary transsexuals. They lean toward being feminine, but it is never expressed overtly. In time, usually adolescence or later, manifestations of the underlying feminine urges appear. The

* Later authors added a group to Benjamin's original 6 gradations, to make them match Kinsey's scale. Group 0, which was *not* suggested by Benjamin originally, came to refer to "normal" individuals.

TABLE 16.5
Kinsey's Seven-Point Scale of Homosexuality

Heterosexual/Homosexual Rating	Description
0	Exclusively heterosexual
1	Predominantly heterosexual, only incidentally homosexual
2	Predominantly heterosexual, but more than incidentally homosexual
3	Equally heterosexual and homosexual
4	Predominantly homosexual, but more than incidentally heterosexual
5	Predominantly homosexual, only incidentally heterosexual
6	Exclusively homosexual
X	Asexual

most obvious of these is an urge to put on women's clothes. This may be a symptom of transvestism or effeminate homosexuality. Stoller asserts that the secondary transsexuals do not have the same complex family dynamics that primary transsexuals have.

Person and Ovesey's Classification

Ethel Person and Lionel Ovesey in two papers published in the 1970s defined primary and secondary transsexualism in a similar fashion.[19,20] Their primary and secondary transsexuals, however, must be viewed in the context of their etiological theory of transsexualism. They theorized that some effeminate homosexuals and transvestites develop transsexualism as a regressive phenomenon under conditions of stress. Since this type of transsexualism was "secondary" to other conditions, it was referred to as secondary transsexualism, and the transsexuals called homosexual and transvestitic transsexuals, respectively. Primary transsexualism, on the other hand, was thought to develop without the mediation of transvestism or homosexuality and to be psychodynamically distinct. Person and Ovesey's trichotomy (and to some extent Stoller's, too) was thus roughly congruent to that of DSM-III (please see below): their primary transsexuals were DSM-III's asexuals, their transvestitic transsexuals were DSM-III's heterosexuals, and their homosexual transsexuals were DSM-III's homosexuals.

Classification Proposed in DSM-III

DSM-III, published in 1980, assigned code 302.5x to transsexualism and divided it according to the predominant prior sexual history, which was coded as the fifth digit[6] (1 = asexual, 2 = homosexual [same anatomic sex], 3 = heterosexual [opposite anatomic sex], and 0 = unspecified). In the first, "asexual," the individual never had strong sexual feelings. Often there was little or no sexual activity or pleasure derived from the genitals. In the second group, "homosexual," a predominantly homosexual arousal pattern preceding the onset of the transsexualism was acknowledged, although often such individuals would deny that the behavior was homosexual because of their conviction that they were "really" of the other sex. In the third group, "heterosexual," the individuals claimed to have had active heterosexual lives. This tripartite division of transsexuals, as seen earlier, had already been employed by other workers.

EPIDEMIOLOGY

According to Roth[21] the prevalence of transsexualism in the general population is 1 in 37,000 (or about 0.00003%). According to Bodlund and Kullgren,[22] the estimates vary between 1:12,000 to

TABLE 16.6
Modified Benjamin Scale of Transsexualism

Group	Type	Description
0	—	*Normal:* No gender dysphoria. This group was not originally suggested by Benjamin.
1	I	*Pseudotransvestite:* His gender feelings are masculine. Lives as a man. May get occasional "kick" out of cross-dressing. Not a true transvestite. Leads a normal male life. Hetero-, bi-, or homosexual. Cross-dressing and sex change may occur in masturbation fantasies mainly. May enjoy transvestite literature only. May rate 0–6 on Kinsey's scale. Not at all interested in sex change operation or estrogen therapy. Interest in cross-dressing only sporadic.
	II	*Fetishistic transvestite:* His gender feelings are masculine. Lives as man. Cross-dresses periodically. Cross-dresses underneath male clothes (underdressing). Heterosexual. Rarely bisexual. May rate 0–2 on Kinsey's scale. Rejects sex change operation. Rarely interested in estrogen medication, or may occasionally use to reduce libido. May imitate double (masculine and feminine) personality with male and female names.
	III	*True transvestite:* Gender feelings masculine, but with less conviction. Cross-dresses constantly. May live and be accepted as woman. May engage in underdressing. Heterosexual, except when cross-dressed. Cross-dressing gives sexual satisfaction with relief of gender discomfort. May rate 0–2 on Kinsey's scale. Rejects sex change operation, but the idea can be attractive. Estrogen medication is attractive as an experiment, and can be helpful emotionally. May assume double personality.
2	IV	*Nonsurgical transsexual:* Gender feelings undecided. May live as a man or a woman; sometimes alternating. Cross-dresses as often as possible with insufficient relief of his gender discomfort. Libido often low. Asexual or auto-erotic. May be bisexual. May also marry and have children. May rate 1-4 on Kinsey's scale. Option of sex change attractive, but not requested or attraction not admitted. Estrogen medication needed for comfort and emotional balance.
3	V	*True transsexual, moderate intensity:* Gender feeling is opposite to biological sex, e.g., a biological male would have gender feelings of a female ("A female trapped in a male body"). Lives and works as the opposite sex if possible. Insufficient relief from cross-dressing. Libido low. Asexual, auto-erotic, or passive homosexual activity. May marry and have children. Rates 4–6 on Kinsey's scale. Requests sex change operation, which is usually indicated. Estrogen medication needed as substitute for or preliminary to operation.
	VI	*True transsexual, high intensity:* Gender feeling is opposite to biological sex. Total psycho-sexual inversion. May live and work as the other sex. Cross-dressing gives insufficient relief. Gender discomfort intense. Intensely desires relations with a person of the same sex if young. Later, libido low. Rates 6 on Kinsey's scale. May marry and have children by using fantasies in intercourse. Sex change operation urgent and usually attained. Indicated, too. Estrogen medication required for partial relief. Despises his/her sex organs. Danger of suicide or self-mutilation, if too long frustrated.

1:37,000 for male-to-female transsexuals (M/F) and 1:30,000 to 1:150,000 for female-to-male (F/M) transsexuals. According to Walinder,[23] Ross and associates,[24] and Bakker and associates,[25] the ratio of somatic males (males wanting to become females) to somatic females (females wanting to become males) is 3:1 (M/F:F/M::3:1). Roth,[22] however, estimates the ratio as 4:1 (M/F:F/M::4:1). In fact, different studies show this ratio to vary from 3:1 to 8:1,[26] but almost all studies show a greater preponderance of M/F transsexuals. Polish workers have reported an inversion of this ratio. During three consecutive observation cycles over six years, Godlewski[27] reported a ratio of M/F:F/M::1:5.5.

Again in a study of 1454 transsexuals, Dulko and Imielinski[28], using a SPSS statistical program, reported a ratio of M/F:F/M::1:4.4 (there were a total of 329 M/F and 1125 F/M transsexuals).

It is possible for persons to be sexually attracted to transsexuals. *Andromimetophilia* is a term normally applied to arousal from female partners who imitate men. However, this term is also often used for an attraction toward preoperative female to male transsexuals, or postoperative female-to-male transsexuals. Conversely, the term *gynemimetophilia* may be used for a sexual attraction toward preoperative male-to-female transsexuals, or postoperative male-to-female transsexuals.

MANAGEMENT

Modern surgical techniques and hormone therapy allow M/F and F/M transsexuals to undergo a permanent sex change operation. However, the management of M/F transsexualism is more common and satisfactory. The male transsexual's penis and testes are surgically removed, and an artificial vagina (neovagina) is created. Breast implants are inserted, although some breast development usually is promoted with the use of female hormones. Female transsexuals are required to undergo mastectomy and hormone treatments to produce the male secondary sexual characteristics. However, attempts to create an artificial penis have not been very successful.

After a successful sex change operation, the patient may suffer from normally encountered pathologies of new sex organs. For instance, a neovagina created artificially in a M/F transsexual may show bacterial vaginosis. However, there are important differences in the microbiology and pathology of these conditions as compared with non-transsexual women.[29]

LEGAL ASPECTS

Because of gender-based discrimination and gender-based victimization suffered by transsexuals, there is a high rate of suicide and attempted suicide in these individuals. In one study it was found that the prevalence of attempted suicide was as high as 32%.[30] This can have important medico-legal implications for people interacting with transsexuals, such as friends, colleagues, and employers. It has been suggested that suicide prevention interventions for transgender persons are urgently needed, particularly for young people. There is also an urgent need for increasing societal acceptance of the transgender community and decreasing gender-based prejudice. Forced sex on transsexuals is another legal problem.

Recommendations of the Council of Europe

The Council of Europe was established in 1949 by 10 western European countries, but today almost all European countries are members. The resolutions of its Parliamentary Assembly are not legally binding for the Council of Europe member states, but carry significant political weight. In 1989, the Parliamentary Assembly adopted a resolution on discrimination against transsexuals, and passed a recommendation on the condition of transsexuals. Known popularly as Recommendation 1117, it suggested that the Committee of Ministers invite member states to introduce legislation whereby, in the case of irreversible transsexualism:

(a) the reference to the sex of the person concerned is to be rectified in the register of births and in the identity papers;
(b) a change of forename is to be authorized;
(c) the person's private life is to be protected;
(d) all discrimination in the enjoyment of fundamental rights and freedoms is prohibited in accordance with Article 14 of the European Convention on Human Rights.

These recommendations have not been implemented by all member states. In Portugal, for instance, sex reassignment surgery in transsexuals is not allowed under the law.[31] This means that transsexuals turn to other countries to achieve bodily "correction." Because the surgery is done in unfamiliar surroundings, coupled with the fact that the outcome is predictable, those who undergo sex reassignment surgery experience great stress. There are further administrative difficulties, when the transsexuals return to their country after surgery and request a change of their civil status records (upgradation of data concerning sex and forename in their birth certificate and identity papers).

Illustrative Cases

X, Y, and Z v. United Kingdom (1997)

This case determined whether a transsexual has a legal right to be called the parent of a child conceived through artificial insemination by a donor (AID). X, Y, and Z, who were not named to protect their identity, were all British citizens residing in Manchester. X, was a female-to-male transsexual. He had been living in a permanent and stable relationship with Y, a woman, since 1979. In October 1992, Y gave birth to Z, who had been conceived through artificial insemination by donated sperm (AID) with the agreement of the hospital ethics committee. In February 1992, X enquired of the Registrar General whether there would be any objection to his being registered as the father of Z. On June 4 , 1992, the Minister of Health replied that, having taken legal advice, the Registrar General believed that only a biological man could be regarded as a father for the purposes of registration. However, Z could lawfully bear the first applicant's surname.

Following Z's birth, X and Y attempted to register the child in their joint names as father and mother, but X was refused permission to be registered as father and that part of the form was left blank. Z was given X's surname, however. The appellants then approached the European Commission of Human Rights. Their main contention was that Article 8 (Right to respect for private and family life) of the European Convention for the Protection of Human Rights and Fundamental Freedoms (1953) had been violated (for the statement of Article 8, please see chapter on sexual masochism). The application lodged on 6 May 1993 was declared admissible on 1 December 1994.

The court observed that that there had been no violation of Article 8 of the Convention. It said that transsexuality did raise complex scientific, legal, moral, and social issues, in respect of which there was no generally shared approach among the contracting states. However, it was opined that Article 8 could not, in this context, be taken to imply an obligation for the respondent state (UK) formally to recognize as the father of a child a person who was not the biological father. The fact that the law of the United Kingdom did not allow special legal recognition of the relationship between X and Z did not amount to a failure to respect family life within the meaning of Article 8.

The Court, however, suggested a number of steps X and Y could undertake to address their genuine concerns. For example, it was suggested that X could make out a will, which would in practice solve any problem caused by the fact that Z would not automatically inherit from him on intestacy. Similarly, unless X and Y chose to make such information public, neither the child nor any third party would know that the absence of X's name on the birth certificate was a consequence of the fact that he was a transsexual. X was not prevented in any way from acting as Z's father in the social sense, and he could, together with Y, apply for a joint residence order which would automatically confer on them full parental responsibility under English law (section 8 of the Children Act 1989).

REFERENCES

1. Nakaya, M. On background factors of male genital self-mutilation. *Psychopathology.* 1996;29(4):242-8.
2. Roth, M. Transsexualism and the sex-change operation: a contemporary medico-legal and social problem. *Med Leg* J. 1981;49 Pt 1:5-19.

3. Benjamin, H., *The Transsexual Phenomenon*, The Julian Press, New York, 1966.
4. Money, J., Paraphilias, in *Handbook of Sexology*, Money J and Musaph H., Eds., Elsevier/North-Holland Biomedical Press, Amsterdam, 1977, chap. 72.
5. American Psychiatric Association. *Diagnostic and Statistical Manual of Mental Disorders*, 3rd ed. American Psychiatric Association, Washington DC, 1980.
6. American Psychiatric Association. *Diagnostic and Statistical Manual of Mental Disorders*, 3rd ed. rev. American Psychiatric Association, Washington DC, 1987.
7. Green, R., Roberts, C.W., Williams, K., Goodman, M., Mixon, A. Specific cross-gender behavior in boyhood and later homosexual orientation. *Br J Psychiatry*. 1987 Jul;**151**:84-8.
8. Benjamin, H., and Masters, R.A. New Kind of Prostitute. *Sexology*. 1964; 30: 446-448.
9. Westphal, C. Die Conträre Sexualempfindung, Symptom eines neuropathischen (psychopathischen) Zustandes. *Archiv für Psychiatrie und Nervenkrankheiten*. 1869;**2**:73-108.
10. Bullough, V.L. Transsexualism in history. *Arch Sex Behav*. 1975 Sep;**4(5)**:561-71.
11. Krafft-Ebing, R. von. *Psychopathia Sexualis*, translated by Charles Gilbert Chaddock from the seventh German edition, F. A. Davis, Philadelphia, 1894.
12. Marcuse, M. Ein Fall von geschlechtsum Wandlungstreib. *Z. Psychother. Med. Psychol*. 1916; **6**: 176.
13. Abraham, F. Genitalumwandlung an zwei maenlichen Transvestiten. *Z. Sexualwiss*. 1931;**18**:223-226.
14. Cauldwell, D.O. *Questions and Answers on the Sex Life and Sexual Problems of Trans-Sexuals*, Haldeman-Julius Publications, Girard, KS., 1950.
15. Cauldwell, D.O. *Sex Transmutation—Can One's Sex Be Changed*?, Haldeman-Julius Publications, Girard, KS., 1951.
16. Benjamin, H. Introduction, in *Transsexualism and Sex Reassignment*, Green, R., and Money, J.(eds), Johns Hopkins University Press, Baltimore, 1969, p. 4.
17. Stoller, R.J. The Gender Disorders, in *Sexual Deviation*, 3rd edition, Rosen I., Ed., Oxford University Press, Oxford, 1996, chap. 5.
18. Stoller, R.J. *Sex and Gender*. Science House, New York, 1968.
19. Person, E., Ovesey, L. The transsexual syndrome in males. I. Primary transsexualism. *Am J Psychother*. 1974 Jan;**28(1)**:4-20.
20. Person, E., Ovesey, L. The transsexual syndrome in males. II. Secondary transsexualism. *Am J Psychother*. 1974 Apr;**28(2)**:174-93.
21. Roth, M. Transsexualism and the sex-change operation: a contemporary medico-legal and social problem. *Med Leg* J. 1981;49 Pt 1:5-19.
22. Bodlund, O., Kullgren, G. Transsexualism—General outcome and prognostic factors: A five-year follow-up Study of Nineteen Transsexuals in the Process of Changing Sex. *Archives of Sexual Behavior*. 1996; 25(3):303-16.
23. Walinder, J. Incidence and sex ratio of transsexualism in Sweden. *Br. J. Psychiat*. 1971;118:16-20.
24. Ross, M.W., Walinder, J., Lundstrom, B., and Thuve, I. Cross-cultural approaches of transsexualism. A comparison between Sweden and Australia. *Acta Psychiat. Scand*. 1981;63:75-82.
25. Bakker, A., van-Kesterer, P.J., Gooren, L.J., and Bezemer, P.D. The prevalence of transsexualism in The Netherlands. *Acta Psychiat. Scand*. 1993;87:237-8.
26. Crovitz, E. Treatment of the transsexual and medico legal issues. *Forensic Science*. 1976;7(1): 1-8
27. Godlewski, J. Transsexualism and anatomic sex ratio reversal in Poland. *Arch Sex Behav*. 1988 Dec;17(6):547-8.
28. Dulko, S., Imielinski, C. The Epidemiology of Transsexualism In Poland. *Journal of Psychosomatic Research*. 2004; 56: 637.
29. Jain, A., Bradbeer, C. A case of successful management of recurrent bacterial vaginosis of neovagina after male to female gender reassignment surgery. *Int J STD AIDS*. 2007 Feb;18(2):140-1.
30. Clements-Nolle, K., Marx, R., Katz, M. Attempted suicide among transgender persons: The influence of gender-based discrimination and victimization. *J Homosex*. 2006;51(3):53-69.
31. Costa-Santos, J., Madeira, R. Transsexualism in Portugal: the legal framework and procedure, and its consequences for transsexuals. *Med Sci Law*. 1996 Jul;36(3):221-5.
32. Benjamin, H. Transvestism and Transsexualism in the Male and Female. *The Journal of Sex Research*. 1967; **3(2)**:107-127.

17 Miscellaneous Sexual Crimes and Perversions

INTRODUCTION

Besides the major paraphilic categories that appear in DSM-IV-TR, a number of other unspecified paraphilias should be examined in forensic contexts. DSM-IV-TR labels them under the code 302.9 (paraphilia not otherwise specified; please see chapter on zoophilia for full discussion of 302.9).[1] A full listing of paraphilias appears in Appendix 1. Common unspecified paraphilias are discussed below.

ANAL EROTICISM

Erotic activity focusing on the anus is pleasurable due to the abundance of nerve endings there. Since the anus is a taboo area, it may enhance the pleasure. Sigmund Freud hypothesized that this eroticism arises during childhood during the anal stage (Please see "Freud's libido theory" in chapter 1). Anal eroticism can be enjoyed by both males and females, because unlike the vagina and the penis, an anus is part of the anatomy of both males and females. For men, pleasure may be derived from stimulation of the prostate, while for women, pleasure may be derived through indirect stimulation of the vagina, particularly the G-spot.

Unusual activities have been associated with anal eroticism. Hemandas and colleagues[2] describe a unique case, in which a patient, seeking anal sexual gratification, administered in his rectum a liquid used as masonry adhesive. The matter solidified in his rectum, became impacted, and required laparotomy for its removal.

AUTOEROTIC ASPHYXIA

Autoerotic asphyxia is a self-induced decrease in oxygenation of blood (hypoxia) leading to oxygen deprivation of the brain, in turn leading to achievement or enhancement of sexual orgasm. This is thought to occur for two reasons: (i) decreased oxygenation and increased carbon dioxide retention producing feelings of giddiness, and exhilaration, which heighten sexual response (similar conditions have been observed in deep sea divers who have reported giddiness and "highs" due to increased carbon dioxide retention); and (ii) partial asphyxia, possibly bringing about increased sympathetic arousal, which in turn heightens orgasmic pleasure. Although male erection is associated with parasympathetic arousal, orgasm is believed to be under sympathetic control. Female erection and orgasm are similarly mediated.

The hypoxia is most commonly produced by complex contraptions leading to partial hanging (which may be a variant of suspension bondage), but may also be produced in other ways such as putting plastic bags or masks over the face,[3,4,5] chest compression,[6] submerging under water (*aqua eroticum*),[7,8] inhalation of chemicals such as a volatile nitrite, nitrous oxide,[9] cocaine,[10] ketamine,[11] chloroform,[12,13] or propane,[14] or a combination of these methods. Death is not intended by the victim, but it usually results accidentally when the safety mechanisms fail or when there is an overdose of inhaled chemicals. Sometimes the subject goes to extreme lengths in the choice of contraptions used. Rothschild and Schneider[15] describe a case of a 19-year old man who used a military-jet pilots pressure-suit to compress his thorax and inflated the suit with a 12-volt compressor. Additionally, his head was covered with three masks and a motorcycle helmet; his arms and legs were also bound. The cause of death was a massive compression of the thorax.

Also known as asphyxiophilia, hypoxyphilia, kotzwarrism, and sexual asphyxia, this paraphilia is of the sacrificial/expiatory type, according to Money's classification (please see chapter 1). In DSM IV TR,[1] autoerotic asphyxia is discussed under 302.83 "Sexual Masochism", however, many feel that autoerotic asphyxia may not be a true example of sexual masochism, especially as evidence exists that hypoxyphiliacs actively seek to avoid pain and suffering (e.g., the presence of a padding between the noose and the neck to avoid rope burns).[16]

Incidence and Prevalence

Data from the United States, England, Australia, and Canada indicate that one to two hypoxyphilia-caused deaths per million population are detected and reported each year.[1]

Innala and Ernulf consider the autoerotic asphyxiation death frequency to be 0.5-1 cases per million inhabitants per year.[17] Gosink and Jumbelic state that more than 1000 fatalities occur due to this cause in the United States per year.[18]

Although earlier writers categorically stated that "women never engage in these practices,"[19] a number of cases have since been described, many with even explicit photographs.[20,18,21,22] The frequency of females engaging in this practice, however, appears much lower. According to Gosink and Jumbelic,[18] the male:female ratio is greater than 50:1.

Medico-legal Aspects

One important medico-legal aspect is to differentiate between autoerotic accident and suicide. This may have legal implications, especially where there is a clause in the insurance policy stating that no money will be paid in cases of suicide. In some cases, family members are so embarrassed they are reluctant or unwilling to provide enough data surrounding the circumstances in which the decedent was found, and the cause of death may be mislabeled as suicide.[23] Unfortunately, the differentiation is not always easy, especially when there is a strong reason for suicide. Bhardwaj and colleagues[24] report one such case (for details, please see chapter on transvestic fetishism). A case is described by Vennemann and Pollak, where a 30-year old man was found hanged in the living room of his flat. The scene matched perfectly with that of a typical autoerotic death, with the deceased facing a computer screen, where the video of an unclothed female could be seen. His left hand was inside his trousers in the genital region. The autopsy, however, showed advanced sarcoidosis, which was known to the victim, and which could have been the reason for his possible suicide. After much deliberation, the authors decided that the circumstances pointed more in the direction of an accidental autoerotic death.[25] This is in contrast to Bhardwaj and colleagues' case,[24] where the cause of death was given as suicide. Benomran and colleagues[26] describe the case of a 35-year old man who was found hanging in a relatively isolated place outdoors. At first glimpse, it looked like a case of accidental autoerotic asphyxia. A vest was wrapped over his head, neck, and lower part of the face. The hands were loosely tied in front of the body. The vest was tucked between the neck and the ligature to act as a pad. However, a thorough scene examination and post-mortem examination excluded any evidence of foul play. The authors concluded that it was a case of suicide. Jones and colleages[3] in the Forensic Medicine Unit in Edinburgh reported 30 deaths due to plastic bag asphyxia over a 15-year period (1984-1998). Three were accidental deaths (including two due to autoerotic asphyxia), and the remaining 27 deaths were suicides. These studies illustrate that all factors have to be weighed and balanced very carefully before arriving at a final conclusion.

TABLE 17.1
Tourette's Disorder and Paraphilias

Tourette's disorder (TD) or Tourette's syndrome (TS), a rather unique condition, is often classified as a neurological movement disorder. It is often associated with paraphilic behavior,[51] most commonly coprolalia.[52] Other paraphilic behaviors such as exhibitionism are also seen.[53]

The prevalence of coprolalia in Tourette's disorder varies from 8% in primary pediatric practices to over 60% in tertiary referral centers.[54] Coprolalia tends to peak in severity during adolescence and wane during adulthood. Malignant Tourette syndrome, said to be present when the patient has had two or more emergency room visits or one or more hospitalizations for TS symptoms or its associated behavioral comorbidities, is significantly more likely to be associated with coprolalia.[55]

The pathogenesis may be related to dysfunction of basal ganglionic and limbic mini-circuits.

The syndrome is characterized by abrupt movements and vocalizations, or tics, usually performed in response to compelling urges. The onset is before age eighteen years. Tourette's disorder has been identified in all major cultural and racial groups, and is three to four times more common in males than in females. It was once thought to occur in about 0.5 per 1000 population, but now this figure is thought to be higher. The genetic role is obvious, as the concordance rate for this disorder within monozygotic twin pairs is as high as 75 percent.

BATTERED WIFE SYNDROME

This is not a true paraphilia, but may be considered an unusual sexual practice, especially if the perpetrator finds sexual pleasure in beating as in sadism.

COPROLALIA

Coprolalia is a rare paraphilia where the offender gets arousal from using obscene language or writing. Obscene language is sometimes used during sex to achieve sexual arousal. About 20% of patients suffering from Tourette's disorder (Gilles de la Tourette's Syndrome) display coprolalia (this has lent a certain notoriety to Tourette's disorder). Coprolalia in Tourette sufferers is rare in Japan compared with Western countries, which suggests a significant cultural influence upon the manifestation of this complex behavior. (Please see Table 17.1 for information about Tourette's disorder and paraphilias.)

Coprolalia has been described in encephalitis lethargica syndrome,[27] hemiballismus[28] (a movement disorder, characterized by unilateral wild, large amplitude flinging movements of the arms and legs, normally causing falls and preventing postural maintenance), and in the aftermath of severe carbon monoxide intoxication[29] also.

As mentioned in chapter 4, section 294 of Indian Penal Code prescribes punishment for coprolalia (please see chapter 4 for the statement of section 294).

COPROPHILIA

Coprophilia (from Greek *kópros*, "excrement," and *filía*, "liking, fondness"), also called coprolagnia or scat, is sexual arousal by the act of defecating, and/or viewing or smelling the odor of feces. It may be seen in a curious mix with masochism (please see chapter on masochism for details). Richard Freiherr von Krafft-Ebing (1840–1902) introduced the term *stercoracism* in 1894 to include scatology and an obsession with dirtiness.[30]

The revised fourth edition of the *Diagnostic and Statistical Manual of Mental Disorders* (DSM-IV-TR)[1] does not assign any specific or unique code to coprophilia. Instead, along with several other uncommon paraphilias, it is grouped under the code 302.9 (paraphilias not otherwise specified). It is one of the only 7 paraphilias which are specifically named in this category. Some

TABLE 17.2
A Coprophilia Vocabulary

Cleveland steamer —A form of coprophilia, where a man or a woman defecates on a partner's chest. In a variant, the person defecates on a partner's chest, and then spreads the feces around with his or her buttocks in a sexual nature. Also referred to as a "Hot Karl." Health risks include bacterial infection, hepatitis, and parasitic intestinal infections.

Coprography —"To write with feces." To write obscene graffiti, poems, or stories. Also used for arousal from obscene words.

Coprophagy —The act of eating feces. Quite a popular activity up until the 1700s.

Dirty Sanchez —A term used to describe the sexual practice of smearing fecal matter under the nose of the partner in the form of a moustache. It is usually accomplished by inserting a finger into one's anus and wiping the material gathered onto the upper lip of one's partner.

common terms—slang and otherwise—used in connection with coprophilic activities are given in Table 17.2.

It has been suggested that at least some cases of encopresis (involuntary fecal soiling in children who have been toilet trained) could properly be understood in terms of anal eroticism, the usual coprophilic theme. Aruffo and associates note that the anal sensations and anal erotic feelings reported by a number of encopretic children are intense, and assert that the encopretic symptom, soiling, in these children is the result of a conscious form of anal masturbation in which the fecal mass is used for stimulation.[31] They even go on to suggest that physical treatments of those children whose encopresis is psychologically driven may be contraindicated.

A related condition is coprophagia (from the Greek *copros*, "feces," and *phagein*, "eat"), the consumption of feces. Normally it is seen in patients with mental retardation, alcoholism, depression, obsessive compulsive disorder, schizophrenia, delirium, and dementia,[32] but it can be seen as a sexual fetish where consumption of feces is associated with sexual arousal. Wise and Goldberg[33] describe the case of a 47-year old man who was nonpsychotic and of normal intelligence. He had a fetish of fecal smearing, which escalated to coprophagia in a setting of depression and alcohol abuse. His treatment was focused on the psychodynamic issues that fostered his despair and allowed his fetish to evolve into coprophagia.

Very few states in the world today have specific laws against coprophilia. One of the jurisdictions that have specific laws against coprophilia in very clearly worded phraseology is Wisconsin, where coprophilia is included in the term "Sexual contact." It is defined under clauses 2 and 3 of Section 940.225 (5) (b) of Wisconsin statute.[34] For a full statement of this section, please refer to the chapter on frotteurism.

CLINICAL VAMPIRISM

Clinical vampirism is a mental disorder where the affected person is obsessed with drinking blood (preferably of human beings, but also of animals). He is also erotically aroused by this activity. Psychologist Richard Noll suggests that the condition be renamed Renfield syndrome after Renfield, a character in Bram Stoker's *Dracula* who eats spiders and flies, believing that he will acquire miraculous life forces by doing so.[35]

Very few cases of clinical vampirism are known. People who suffer from this condition are primarily male. The craving for blood arises from the idea that it conveys life-enhancing powers. According to Noll, the condition starts with a key event in childhood which causes the experience of blood injury or the ingestion of blood to be exciting. After puberty, the excitement is experienced as sexual arousal. Throughout adolescence and adulthood, blood, its presence, and consumption can also stimulate a sense of power and control. Noll explains that the Renfield syndrome begins with autovampirism and then progresses to the consumption of the blood of other creatures.

The usefulness of this diagnostic label remains in question. Very few cases have been described, and published reports that do exist refer to what has been proposed as Renfield's syndrome through the use of official psychiatric diagnostic categories such as schizophrenia or as a variety of paraphilias. The best known cases of the Renfield syndrome were those of Richard Trenton Chase and Neville Heath.

KLISMAPHILIA

Klismaphilia is sexual stimulation achieved through the use of enemas, either taking, or giving, or both. Like coprophilia, it is one of only 7 paraphilias that have been specifically mentioned under code 302.9 (paraphilias not otherwise specified). Klismaphilia was fairly widespread in Ancient Rome and Romans did not consider it as deviant sexual behavior.[36]

MUTILOMANIA

One rare paraphilia involves arousal from mutilation. There are at least 3 conditions in which mutilation provides sexual gratification: (1) amokoscisia, arousal or sexual frenzy with desire to slash or mutilate women, (2) mazoperosis, sexual gratification received from the mutilation of female breasts and (3) necrosadism, arousal from mutilating a corpse. All these features were typically displayed by Jack the Ripper, the notorious late nineteenth century killer. Krafft-Ebing, in his 1906 edition of *Psychopathia Sexualis,* mentioned his case:

> *Case #17. Jack the Ripper* On December 1, 1887, July 7, August 8, September 30, one day in the month of October and on the 9th of November, 1888; on the 1st of June, the 17th of July and the 10th of September, 1889, the bodies of women were found in various lonely quarters of London ripped open and mutilated in a peculiar fashion. The murderer has never been found. It is probable that he first cut the throats of his victims, then ripped open the abdomen and groped among the intestines. In some instances he cut off the genitals and carried them away; in others he only tore them to pieces and left them behind. He does not seem to have had sexual intercourse with his victims, but very likely the murderous act and subsequent mutilation of the corpse were equivalents for the sexual act.

Indeed the term *Jack the Ripper syndrome* has been proposed as an alternate term for amokoscisia.

Rajs and colleagues[37] studied mutilations of corpses in Sweden from 1961 through 1990. They recorded a total of 22 deaths with criminal mutilation or dismemberment of the human body. Four types of mutilations were identified: *defensive mutilation*, which is done in order to get rid of the corpse or make its identity more difficult (ten cases), *aggressive mutilation* following rage killing, in which the killer mutilates the face and genitals following death due to pure rage (four cases), *offensive mutilation*, also known as lust murder, where the offender may have necrophilic urges for postmortem sexual activity with the victim, which may involve pre- or postmutilation (seven cases), and finally *necromanic mutilation*, where the offender has definite urges to have sex with the dead, and mutilates the body in order to use parts as trophies or to use as fetishes (one case). In the last-mentioned case the cause of death was natural, while all deaths in the first 3 groups were homicidal or homicide was strongly suspected. Of these, offensive mutilation and necromanic mutilation definitely seem to have sexual components and thus may be classified as acts of mutilomania. There were differences in mode of mutilation, depending on whether the mutilation was carried out by a layman, a butcher, or a physician. In only one case was the perpetrator convicted for the mutilation act; in the remaining instances the manslaughter, as a more serious crime, was the main charge. Defensive mutilation benefited the perpetrators, because the mutilation made it impossible to establish the cause of death and the perpetrators, despite strong circumstantial evidence indicating murder, were acquitted.

TABLE 17.3
Body Secretions Used for Sexual Arousal

Body secretion	Colloquial name for condition
Feces	Brown shower
Milk	Milk shower
Saliva	Spit shower
Semen	Semen shower
Urine	Golden shower
Vomit	Roman shower

MYSOPHILIA

Mysophilia (from Greek, *mysos*, "uncleanness," and *-philia*, "love of") is sexual arousal from soiled clothing or foul decaying odors. In order to get aroused, the paraphiliac may smell, chew, or rub against foul smelling objects such as soiled jockstraps, a pair of panties, menstrual pad, or bra. The etiology is not known, but possibly these paraphiliacs have increased sensitivity to pheromones that are produced in body excrements. Locker rooms provide abundant odors for the mysophiles, who often pilfer used jock straps (much like a fetishist who pilfers shoes, bras, and panties for masturbation). Paraphiliacs suffering from a combination of sadomasochism and mysophilia often use soiled underwear as gags in bondage practices. A related condition is sexual showers, in which the paraphiliac requests the partner to spill body fluids on his or her body for sexual arousal. Table 17.3 shows various body secretions used for sexual arousal and the colloquial names of the related conditions.

PARTIALISM

Partialism is sexual arousal by specific body parts. Like coprophilia, it is one of only 7 paraphilias mentioned by name under code 302.9 (paraphilias not otherwise specified). Like most paraphilias, this particular fetish is first seen in early adolescence and continues for most of the individual's active sex life. Individuals with partialistic fetishes use fantasies or touching of actual body parts for sexual arousal. Common fetish parts are feet (most common), breasts, legs, hair (particularly red), ears, and toes. Less common fetishes include amputees (acrotomophilia) and obese persons.

Partialism is not an uncommon paraphilia, based on the volume of the sale of related pornographic material. In 1986, the U.S. Commission on Pornography reviewed 3,050 separate magazine and book titles sold in "adults only" pornographic outlets randomly selected in several cities. Of these, 746 titles could be assigned to a DSM III-R paraphilia category, and of these 233 were devoted to partialism.[38] Scorolli and colleagues[39] examined 381 discussion groups using the Internet as a data source in an effort to estimate the relative frequency of fetishes in a large sample. About 5000 individuals were targeted. Partialism was found in 33%. Feet and objects associated with feet were the most common targets of preference.

PIQUERISM

Piquerism is a psychosexual disorder in which an individual finds pleasure in penetrating his or her body with sharp objects such as pins, razors, knives, etc. This is often used as a form of sexual pleasure derived from sadomasochistic fantasies. Notorious serial killer Albert Fish often partook in piquerism, flagellating himself constantly with a nail-studded board. After his arrest and subsequent jailing for the murder of Grace Budd, an x-ray revealed two dozen needles inserted into his groin.

PYROLAGNIA

Pyrolagnia (Gr. *pyro*, "fire"; *lagneia*, "lust"), also known as pyrophilia, is sexual gratification from witnessing, making, or extinguishing fires. This behavior is different from incendiarism, where the individual sets fires to commit a crime (homicide) or conceal a crime (burglary). The term *pyromania* includes both pyrolagnia and incendiarism.[40] It is possible that the Roman Emperor Nero (37–68) was a pyrolagniac, especially as it is claimed by several historians that it was he who ordered the fire on the night of July 18, 64 AD, and while the city of Rome burnt he sang and played his lyre. This is the typical behavior of a pyrolagniac.

Most fire setters are male; however, female pyrolagniacs are also known.[41,42] Some pyrolagniacs, besides being sexually aroused, feel empowered when setting buildings on fire. They often position themselves where they can watch from a distance and masturbate.

UROPHILIA

Urophilia is sexual arousal from the sight of urine or someone urinating. Some psychoanalysts refer to it as *urethral eroticism*. Other synonyms include urolagnia and undinism. Sometimes urophilia may be seen in a curious mix with masochism (please see chapter on masochism for details).

Like coprophilia and klismaphilia, it is one of only 7 paraphilias mentioned under code 302.9 (paraphilias not otherwise specified).

Very few jurisdictions have specific laws against urophilia. One of the jurisdictions that have specific laws against urophilia in very clearly worded phraseology is Wisconsin, where urophilia is included in the term "Sexual contact." It is defined under clauses 2 and 3 of section 940.225 (5) (b) of Wisconsin statutes.[39] For a full statement of this section, please refer to the chapter on frotteurism.

VOMEROPHILIA

Vomerophilia (from the Latin *vomere*, "vomit"; *philia*, "love"), or erotic vomiting, is sexual arousal through vomiting. Stoller describes 3 cases, all of them women.[43] The first woman was in her forties, and markedly bisexual in her erotic choices. She has been a vomiter since infancy. She said that when she began to vomit, she got a "rush," a flood of good feelings throughout her entire body. She described the feeling almost as pleasurable as when one injected a narcotic in one's vein. She was convinced she never became an addict, because she could derive the same feelings through vomiting. She said, "Vomiting for me is like sex or an orgasm in that I'm tensed, I feel the rush or intense flood of good feelings almost continually throughout the vomiting and experience relief and quiet warmth in my body when I'm finished. It is not identical to an orgasm. I do not feel it intensely in my genitals alone, but I do feel it there as well as the rest of my body and feel pleasure in my mouth."

The second case is also of a female, who began to masturbate actively when she was 11 years old. Once she was caught by her stepfather, who placed her across his lap and spanked her very hard. She could feel his erect penis against her stomach and began to vomit (with an accompanying orgasm), which she claims as her best experience. Since then she began to have sick spells (with accompanying orgasms), especially in the presence of dominant males—teacher, principal, stepfather, uncle—and twice during encounters with the police over minor traffic violations. She never felt sick prior to or after these vomiting attacks. Interestingly, she did not have orgasms during vomiting when actually ill with the flu or during various childhood illnesses. She never got any pleasure from regular sex. The only activities which gave her orgasm were manual masturbation and vomiting. During masturbation her fantasy primarily consisted of being an executioner in a men's prison, and she vomited when the prisoner was twitching in death. The prisoners were those being hung for the rape and death of a small child.

Erotic vomiting had similar origins in the third case Stoller describes. When she was 4, her grandmother balanced her on one knee and held her while she vomited and may have received vaginal stimulation from the way her grandmother was holding her. Since then she had been having spells of erotic vomiting.

Although Stoller does not offer any hypothesis for erotic vomiting, it appears quite reasonable to hypothesize that this syndrome resulted from "imprinting," a special form of classical conditioning that occurs during a critical period of development (please see chapter 1 for more on imprinting). In cases 2 and 3, the first episode of vomiting occurred at a very young age, with simultaneous sexual stimulation of genital organs, and it seems reasonable to suppose that vomiting and sexual arousal were "imprinted" together.

WIFE SWAPPING

Also known as comarital sex, group sex, mate swapping, mate trading, partner swapping, or swinging, it involves a practice where couples exchange wives or partners for some period, usually a night, to bring about a variety in their sexual experiences. It has been defined as "the agreement between husband and wife to have sexual relations with other people, in contexts in which they both engage in such behavior at the same time and usually in the same place."[44]

Choosing partners occurs in various ways. In one most common variation, men throw house keys or car keys into a pile on the floor, and wives choose a partner by selecting a key ring at random. According to most studies, the prevalence of swinging among married couples is between 1 and 2%.[45,46]

MISCELLANEOUS

There are many other paraphilias, many bordering on to the bizarre. A complete list is provided in Appendix 1. Some select bizarre paraphilias that have been reported in literature are described here.

Apotemnophilia is a paraphilia where the affected person desires to have a healthy appendage (limb, digit, or male genitals) amputated (cf. acrotomophilia, please see above).[47] A case has been described of a 49-year old man who amputated his penis following instructions that he had obtained from the Internet. The patient had a long standing amputee fetish which evolved into eroticized genital mutilation. The transformation of the preferred fetish occurred in a setting of depression due to environmental stressors.[48]

First[49] interviewed 52 subjects (mean age: 48.6 years, range 23–77 years; 47 male, 4 female, 1 intersexed) telephonically, all of whom had an intense longstanding desire to have an amputation, *without* any medical indication. Seventeen per cent (n = 9) did have an arm or leg amputated ultimately, with two-thirds (n = 6) using self-designed methods that put them at risk of death and one-third (n = 3) enlisting a surgeon. None of the subjects was delusional. For all but one subject, the age of onset of this desire was during childhood or early adolescence. Six subjects who had an amputation themselves at their desired site reported that following the amputation they felt better than they ever had and no longer had a desire for an amputation.

In another bizarre paraphilia, Lange[50] describes the case of a 75-year old man suffering from deterioration of the brain who used the coin return tray of a coin-operated telephone as a vaginal substitute for abnormal sexual gratification. This uncommon sexual deviation made him to vandalize the telephone communication system.

LEGAL ASPECTS

Most paraphilias in this chapter are considered minor and very few jurisdictions in the world today have specific laws against them.

REFERENCES

1. American Psychiatric Association. Diagnostic and Statistical Manual of Mental Disorders, 4th ed. Text rev. American Psychiatric Association, Washington DC, 2000.
2. Hemandas AK, Muller GW, Ahmed I. Rectal impaction with epoxy resin: a case report. *J Gastrointest Surg.* 2005 May-Jun;**9(5)**:747-9.
3. Jones, L.S., Wyatt, J.P., Busuttil, A. Plastic bag asphyxia in southeast Scotland. *Am J Forensic Med Pathol.* 2000 Dec;**21(4)**:401-5.
4. Nadesan K., Beng, O.B. Two cases of death due to plastic bag suffocation. *Med Sci Law.* 2001 Jan;**41(1)**:78-82.
5. Schellenberg M., Racette S., Sauvageau A. Complex autoerotic death with full body wrapping in a plastic body bag. *J Forensic Sci.* 2007 Jul;**52(4)**:954-6.
6. Janssen, W., Koops, E, Anders, S., Kuhn, S., Püschel K. Forensic aspects of 40 accidental autoerotic deaths in Northern Germany. *Forensic Sci Int.* 2005;**147 Suppl**:S61-4.
7. Sauvageau A., Racette S. Aqua-eroticum: an unusual autoerotic fatality in a lake involving a home-made diving apparatus. *J Forensic Sci.* 2006 Jan;**51(1)**:137-9.
8. Sivaloganathan S. Aqua-eroticum—a case of auto-erotic drowning. *Med Sci Law.* 1984 Oct;**24(4)**:300-2.
9. Leadbeatter S. Dental anesthetic death. An unusual autoerotic episode. *Am J Forensic Med Pathol.* 1988 Mar;**9(1)**:60-3.
10. Gowitt, G.T., Hanzlick, R.L. Atypical autoerotic deaths. *Am J Forensic Med Pathol.* 1992 Jun;**13(2)**:115-9.
11. Breitmeier, D., Passie, T., Mansouri, F., Albrecht, K., Kleemann, W.J. Autoerotic accident associated with self-applied ketamine. *Int J Legal Med.* 2002 Apr;**116(2)**:113-6.
12. Singer, P.P., Jones, G.R. An unusual autoerotic fatality associated with chloroform inhalation. *J Anal Toxicol.* 2006 Apr;**30(3)**:216-8.
13. Byard, R.W., Kostakis, C., Pigou, P.E., Gilbert, J.D. Volatile substance use in sexual asphyxia. *J Clin Forensic Med.* 2000 Mar;**7(1)**:26-28.
14. Stemberga, V., Brali⊠, M., Bosnar, A., Coklo, M. Propane-associated autoerotic asphyxiation: accident or suicide? *Coll Antropol.* 2007 Jun;**31(2)**:625-7.
15. Rothschild, M.A., Schneider, V. 2 autoerotic accidents: fatal nitrous oxide anesthesia and thoracic compression. Article in German]. *Arch Kriminol.* 1997 Sep-Oct;**200(3-4)**:65-72.
16. Milner, J.S., and Dopke, C.A., Paraphilia not otherwise specificed—Psychopathology and theory. In "*Sexual Deviance—Theory, Assessment, and Treatment*", 1st ed. Laws, D.R. and O'Donohue, W., (Eds.), The Guilford Press, New York, 1997, chapter 20, pages 394-423.
17. Innala, S.M., Ernulf, K.E. Asphyxiophilia in Scandinavia. *Arch Sex Behav.* 1989 Jun;**18(3)**:181-9.
18. Gosink, P.D., Jumbelic, M.I. Autoerotic asphyxiation in a female. *Am J Forensic Med Pathol.* 2000 Jun;**21(2)**:114-8.
19. Edmondson, J.S. A case of sexual asphyxia without fatal termination. *Br J Psychiatry.* 1972 Oct;**121(563)**:437-8.
20. Sauvageau, A., Racette, S. Female autoerotic deaths—still often overlooked: a case report. *Med Sci Law.* 2006 Oct;**46(4)**:357-9.
21. Danto, B.L. A case of female autoerotic death. *Am J Forensic Med Pathol.* 1980 Jun;**1(2)**:117-21.
22. Sass, F.A. Sexual asphyxia in the female. *J Forensic Sci.* 1975 Jan;**20(1)**:181-5.
23. Kirksey, K.M., Holt-Ashley, M., Williamson, K.L., Garza, R.O. Autoerotic asphyxia in adolescents. *J Emerg Nurs.* 1995 Feb;21(1):81-3.
24. Bhardwaj, D.N., Rautji, R., Sharma, R.K., Dogra, T.D. Suicide by a transvestite or sexual asphyxia? A case report. *Med Sci Law.* 2004 Apr;**44(2)**:173-5.
25. Vennemann, B., Pollak, S. Death by hanging while watching violent pornographic videos on the Internet—suicide or accidental autoerotic death? *Int J Legal Med.* 2006 Mar;**120(2)**:110-4.
26. Benomran, F.A., Masood, S.E., Hassan, A.I., Mohammad, A.A. Masking and bondage in suicidal hanging: a case report. *Med Sci Law.* 2007 Apr;**47(2)**:177-80.
27. Dale, R.C., Webster, R., Gill, D. Contemporary encephalitis lethargica presenting with agitated catatonia, stereotypy, and dystonia-parkinsonism. *Mov Disord.* 2007 Oct 3.
28. Martí-Massó, J.F., Obeso, J.A. Coprolalia associated with hemiballismus: response to tetrabenazine. *Clin Neuropharmacol.* 1985;**8(2)**:189-90.

29. Ali-Cherif, A., Royere, M.L., Gosset, A., Poncet, M., Salamon, G., Khalil, R. [Behavior and mental activity disorders after carbon monoxide poisoning. Bilateral pallidal lesions] [Article in French]. *Rev Neurol (Paris).* 1984;**140(6-7)**:401-5.
30. Oosterhuis, H. *Stepchildren of Nature: Krafft-Ebing, Psychiatry, and the Making of Sexual Identity* (The Chicago Series on Sexuality, History, and Society). University Of Chicago Press, Chicago, IL, 2000.
31. Aruffo, R.N., Ibarra, S., Strupp, K.R. Encopresis and anal masturbation. *J Am Psychoanal Assoc.* 2000;48(4):1327-54.
32. Beck, D.A., Frohberg, N.R. Coprophagia in an elderly man: a case report and review of the literature. *Int J Psychiatry Med.* 2005;**35(4)**:417-27.
33. Wise, T.N., Goldberg, R.L. Escalation of a fetish: coprophagia in a nonpsychotic adult of normal intelligence. *J Sex Marital Ther.* 1995 Winter;**21(4)**:272-5.
34. Wis. Stat. Ann. §940.225 (enacted 1987).
35. Noll, R. Vampires, *Werewolves, & Demons.* Twentieth Century Reports in the Psychiatric Literature. Brunner/Mazel Publishing, Inc. New York. 1992.
36. McWilliams, T. Partialism and the Sexual Offender—The Fascination with Lactation. In "*Sex crimes and paraphilia*", 1st ed. Hickey, E.W., (Ed.), Pearson Prentice Hall, New Jersey, 2006, chapter 14, pages 143-6.
37. Rajs, J., Lundström, M, Broberg, M., Lidberg, L., Lindquist, O. Criminal mutilation of the human body in Sweden: a thirty-year medico-legal and forensic psychiatric study. *J Forensic Sci.* 1998 May;**43(3)**:563-80.
38. Lebegue, B. Paraphilias in U.S. pornography titles: "Pornography made me do it" (Ted Bundy). *Bull Am Acad Psychiatry Law.* 1991;**19(1)**:43-8.
39. Scorolli, C., Ghirlanda, S., Enquist, M., Zattoni, S., Jannini, E.A. Relative prevalence of different fetishes. *Int J Impot Res.* 2007 Jul-Aug;**19(4)**:432-7.
40. Sanchez, C. Pyrolagnia—Sexual Pyromania. In "*Sex crimes and paraphilia*", 1st ed. Hickey, E.W., (Ed.), Pearson Prentice Hall, New Jersey, 2006, chapter 32, pages 293-299.
41. Saunders, E.B., Awad, G.A. Adolescent female firesetters. *Can J Psychiatry.* 1991 Aug;**36(6)**:401-4.
42. Balachandra, K., Swaminath, S. Fire fetishism in a female arsonist? *Can J Psychiatry.* 2002 Jun;**47(5)**:487-8.
43. Stoller, R.J. Erotic vomiting. *Arch Sex Behav.* 1982 Aug;**11(4)**:361-5.
44. Walshok, M.L. The Emergence of Middle-Class Deviant Subcultures: The case of Swingers. *Social Problems.* 1971;**18**:488-495.
45. Cole, C. L., and Spaniard, G. B. Comarital mate-sharing and family stability. *J. Sex Res.*1974;**10**:21-31.
46. Bartell, G.D., *Group Sex*, Wyden, New York, 1971.
47. Everaerd, W. A case of apotemnophilia: a handicap as sexual preference. *Am J Psychother.* 1983 Apr;**37(2)**:285-93.
48. Wise, T.N., Kalyanam, R.C. Amputee fetishism and genital mutilation: case report and literature review. *J Sex Marital Ther.* 2000 Oct-Dec;**26(4)**:339-44.
49. First, M.B. Desire for amputation of a limb: paraphilia, psychosis, or a new type of identity disorder. *Psychol Med.* 2005 Jun;**35(6)**:919-28.
50. Lange, E. Vandalism of public telephones according to paragraph 204 of the federal penal code. Coin slot/coin return tray of a coin-operated telephone--vaginal substitute for abnormal sexual gratification. [Article in German]. *Psychiatr Neurol Med Psychol (Leipz).* 1989 Mar;**41(3)**:170-1.
51. McDougle, C.J., Southwick, S.M., Rohrbaugh, R.M. Tourette's disorder and associated complex behaviors: a case report. *Yale J Biol Med.* 1990 May-Jun;**63(3)**:209-14.
52. Kano, Y., Ohta, M., Nagai, Y. Clinical characteristics of Tourette syndrome. *Psychiatry Clin Neurosci.* 1998 Feb;**52(1)**:51-7.
53. Comings, D.E., Comings, B.G. A case of familial exhibitionism in Tourette''s syndrome successfully treated with haloperidol. *Am J Psychiatry.* 1982 Jul;**139(7)**:913-5.
54. Singer, C. Tourette syndrome. Coprolalia and other coprophenomena. *Neurol Clin.* 1997 May; **15(2)**:299-308.
55. Cheung, M.Y., Shahed, J., Jankovic, J. Malignant Tourette syndrome. *Mov Disord.* 2007 Sep 15;**22(12)**:1743-50.

Appendix 1

A COMPREHENSIVE LIST OF PARAPHILIAS

Here is a comprehensive list of all paraphilias cited in scientific and lay literature. Not all these paraphilias have necessarily been seen in clinical setups. This may not be because they do not exist, but because they are so innocuous they are never brought to the notice of clinicians. Like allergies, sexual arousal may occur from anything under the sun, including the sun.

S.no	Paraphilia	Erotic focus/Description
1.	Abasiophilia	Love of (or sexual attraction to) people who use leg braces or other orthopedic appliances
2.	Ablutophilia	Arousal by baths or showers
3.	Acarophilia	Arousal from scratching
4.	Achluophilia	Arousal from darkness
5.	Acomoclitic	Preference for hairless genitals
6.	Acousticophilia	Arousal from certain sounds, particularly someone screaming in agony
7.	Acrophilia	Sexual arousal from heights, high altitudes or being in high places.
8.	Acrotomophilia	Sexual preference for amputees
9.	Actirasty	Arousal from exposure to the sun's rays
10.	Active scopophilia	Same as voyeurism; cf. passive scopophilia
11.	Adolescentilism	Arousal from cross-dressing or playing the role of an adolescent
12.	Aelurophilia	Deriving gratification from cats
13.	Afophilia	Sexual stimulation via touch
14.	Agalmatophilia	Attractions to statues or mannequins or immobility
15.	Agonophilia	Arousal by a partner pretending to struggle (to be free), pseudo-rape
16.	Agoraphilia	Arousal from open spaces or having sex in public
17.	Agrexophilia	Excitement from knowing that others are aware of a person's sexual activities.
18.	Aichmophilia	Arousal from needles or other pointed objects
19.	Ailurophilia	Deriving gratification from cats. Same as Aelurophilia
20.	Akophilia	Sexual stimulation through hearing
21.	Albutophilia	Arousal from water
22.	Algolagnia	Arousal from both inflicting pain and / or humiliation, as well as receiving pain and / or humiliation
23.	Algophilia	Arousal from pain and / or humiliation inflicted on oneself
24.	Allopellia	Having orgasm from watching others engaging in sex
25.	Allorgasmia	Arousal from fantasizing about someone other than one's partner
26.	Allotriorasty	Arousal from partners of other nations or races
27.	Alphamegamia	Attraction to partners of another age group
28.	Altocalciphilia	High heel fetish
29.	Alvinolagnia	Sexuoerotic arousal from a partner's stomach. Also known as stomach fetish
30.	Amatripsis	Masturbation by rubbing labia together
31.	Amaurophilia	Sexual arousal by a partner who is blind or unable to see due to artificial means, such as being blindfolded or having sex in total darkness
32.	Amaxophilia	Attraction to riding in cars and motor vehicles
33.	Amelotasis	Attraction to someone who has lost a limb

S.no	Paraphilia	Erotic focus/Description
34.	Amokoscisia	Arousal or sexual frenzy with desire to slash or mutilate women (proposed name: Jack the Ripper syndrome)
35.	Amomaxia	Sex in a parked car
36.	Amychophilia	Deriving sexual pleasure from being scratched
37.	Anaclitism	Sexual enjoyment arising from activities, or being exposed to objects, normally associated with childhood (e.g. toilet training, breast sucking, playing with dolls).
38.	Anasteemaphilia	Attraction to a person because of a difference in height
39.	Androidism	Arousal from robots with human features
40.	Andromania	Same as nymphomania
41.	Andromimetophilia	Arousal from a female partner who dresses like a male. The term is also applied to an attraction to women who imitate men in other ways, preoperative female-to-male transsexuals, or postoperative female-to-male transsexuals.
42.	Androsodomy	Anal sex with a male partner
43.	Anililagnia	Sexual desire for older women
44.	Anilingus	Oral stimulation of the anus
45.	Anocratism	Anal sex
46.	Anomeatia	Anal sex with a female partner
47.	Anolingus	Arousal from licking lizards
48.	Anonraptus	A rapist who attacks only elderly women
49.	Anophelorastia	Arousal from defiling or ravaging a partner
50.	Antholagnia	Arousal from smelling flowers
51.	Anthropophagolagnia	Rape with cannibalism
52.	Anthropophagy	Pleasure derived from the ingestion of human flesh
53.	Antiophilia	Arousal from floods
54.	Aphephilia	Deriving pleasure from being touched
55.	Apodysophilia	Feverish desire to undress
56.	Apotemnophilia	Desire to have (or sexual arousal from having) a healthy appendage (limb, digit, or male genitals) amputated
57.	Aquaphilia	Arousal from water and/or watery environments including bathtubs or swimming pools
58.	Arachnephilia	Arousal from spiders
59.	Aretifism	Sexual attraction to people who are without footwear, in contrast to retifism
60.	Asphyxiaphilia	Arousal from lack of oxygen; same as asphyxiophilia
61.	Asphyxiophilia	Same as asphyxiaphilia
62.	Asthenolagnia	Arousal from pain and / or humiliation inflicted on oneself
63.	Aulophilia	Arousal from flutes
64.	Autagonistophilia	Sexual arousal and orgasm are contingent upon displaying one's self in a live show or while being photographed
65.	Autoassassinophilia	Arousal from putting oneself in a position in which one may be killed; arousal from orchestrating one's death by the hands of another
66.	Autodermatophagia	Eating one's own flesh as a form of erotic automasochism
67.	Autoerotic asphyxiation	Arousal from oxygen deprivation
68.	Autoerotica	Self-induced arousal
69.	Autofellatio	Placing of one's penis in one's own mouth
70.	Autofetishism	Paraphilic narcissism in the extreme in which one's body becomes a sexual obsession and the stimulus for all erotosexual responses.

S.no	Paraphilia	Erotic focus/Description
71.	Autoflagellation	Arousal from self-inflicted whipping
72.	Autogynephilia	Love of oneself as a woman
73.	Autohaemofetishism	Sexual arousal by the sight of one's blood; usually seen in intravenous drug users filling a syringe
74.	Automasochism	Inflicting intense pain on one's own body; different from masochism in which a partner inflicts pain. Also sometimes referred to as autosadism
75.	Automonosexualism	A man so self-centered and narcissistic that he can achieve sexual satisfaction only by masturbation or, more rarely, autofellatio.
76.	Automysophilia	Arousal from being dirty or defiled
77.	Autonecrophilia	Imagining oneself as a corpse or becoming sexually aroused by simulated corpses
78.	Autonepiophilia	Sexual attraction from being treated like an infant; synonyms are autopaedophilia, autopedophilia and paraphilic-infantilism; see also nepiophilia
79.	Autopederasty	Attempted insertion of one's penis into one's own anus (usually by a man with an unusually long penis). Due to the position and detumescence of the penis, ejaculation is not considered possible.
80.	Autopedication	Same as autopederasty
81.	Autopedophilia	Same as autonepiophilia
82.	Autophilia	Sexual love of one's self, instead of one's partner, characterized by masturbation and, more rarely, autofellatio; narcissistic sexuality
83.	Autosadism	Generic term for paraphilias involving self-infliction of pain
84.	Autoscophilia	Arousal and gratification by looking at one's body, particularly genitalia; also known as autoscopophilia
85.	Autoscopophilia	Same as autoscophilia
86.	Autovampirism	Arousal by drinking one's own blood obtained by inducing scrapes and cuts on self.
87.	Avisodomy	Breaking the neck of a bird while penetrating it for sex
88.	Axillism	The use of the armpit for sex
89.	Asphyxiophilia	Sexual attraction to asphyxia; also called breath control play; includes autoerotic asphyxiation
90.	Bagpiping	Axillary intercourse; a man rubs his penis in another person's armpit
91.	Balloon fetishism	A sexual attraction to balloons
92.	Barosmia	Arousal from smell
93.	Barysadism	Severe sexual sadism. Individuals suffering from this disorder seriously injure or kill their victims
94.	Basoexia	Arousal from kissing
95.	Batrachophilia	Arousal from or attraction to frogs
96.	Bee stings	Use of bees, such as to sting genitalia
97.	Belonephilia	Arousal from pins or needles
98.	Bestiality	Sexual intercourse with animals
99.	Bestialsadism	Torture of animal during sexual contact
100.	Biastophilia	Arousal from raping someone or from the idea of being raped
101.	Biiest	A female who has a fetish for female feet.
102.	Blastolagnia	Arousal from young females
103.	Bondage	Physical or mental restriction of partner

S.no	Paraphilia	Erotic focus/Description
104.	Brachioproctic eroticism	Insertion of the arm into the rectum of another person for sexual pleasure; also known as brachioproctism
105.	Brachioproctism	Same as brachioproctic eroticism
106.	Breast fetishism	A pronounced fetishistic sexual interest in the female breasts, their shape, movement, and especially their size
107.	Breast partialism,	Same as breast fetishism
108.	Bromidrophilia	Arousal from bodily smells
109.	Brontophilia	Arousal from thunderstorms
110.	Buccal coitus	Coitus through mouth
111.	Buggery	Sodomy
112.	Candaulism	Spouse who watches partner have sex with someone else
113.	Canophilia	Arousal from dogs
114.	Capnolagnia	Arousal from watching others smoke
115.	Catagelophilia	Love of being ridiculed
116.	Catheterophilia	Arousal from use of catheters
117.	Celebriphilia	Pathological desire to have sex with a celebrity
118.	Chasmophilia	Attraction to nooks, crannies, crevices, and chasms
119.	Cheimaphilia	Deriving pleasure from cold or winter
120.	Chezolagnia	Masturbation while defecating
121.	Chionophilia	Arousal from snow
122.	Choreophilia	Sexual arousal from dancing
123.	Chrematistophilia	Arousal from being charged for sex or having sex partner steal from them
124.	Chronophilia	Arousal from the passage of time; arousal from an older partner
125.	Chrysophilia	Arousal from gold or golden objects
126.	Claustrophilia	Love of being confined in small places
127.	Clinical vampirism	Arousal by drinking blood of others (human or animal)
128.	Climacophilia	Deriving pleasure from falling down stairs
129.	Coitobalnism	Sexual activity in a bathtub
130.	*Coitus a cheval*	Couple having sex on the back of an animal or one acting out role of horse
131.	*Coitus a mammilla*	Penetration of penis between breasts
132.	*Coitus a unda*	Sex under water
133.	*Coitus analis*	Anal sex
134.	*Coitus intrafermoris*	Penetration between the legs
135.	*Coitus per os*	Buccal coitus (coitus through mouth)
136.	Consanguinophilia	Sexual attraction between biologically close relatives
137.	Coprolagnia	The thought or sight of excrement causing pleasurable sensation
138.	Coprolalia	Arousal from using obscene language or writing
139.	Coprophilia	Arousal from feces or being defecated on; also known as fecophilia, fecalphilia, coprolagnia, brown shower, scat fetishism, japscat and scat play
140.	Coproscopist	Arousal from watching someone defecate
141.	Cordophilia	Arousal from being bound with ropes or chains and sometimes suspended.
142.	Corephallism	Anal sex with a young girl
143.	Cratolagnia	Sexual arousal from display of strength
144.	Crurofact	Leg fetish
145.	Crurophilia	Sexual arousal from legs

S.no	Paraphilia	Erotic focus/Description
146.	Crush fetish	Sexual arousal from seeing small creatures being crushed by members of the opposite sex, or being crushed oneself
147.	Cryptoscopophilia	Desire and arousal from seeing behavior of others in privacy of their home, not necessarily sexual
148.	Cunnilalia	Arousal from talking about vaginas
149.	Cunnilingus	Oral stimulation of the female genitalia
150.	Cyesolagnia	Pregnant woman fetish
151.	Cynophilia	Arousal from sex with dogs
152.	Dacnolagnomania	Sexually sadistic murder; sexual arousal and gratification are found in the act of killing; lust murder
153.	Dacryphilia	Arousal from seeing tears in the eyes of a partner
154.	Defecolagbia	Arousal from defecating.
155.	Dendrophilia	Arousal from trees, or fertility worship of them
156.	Dermaphilia	Arousal from skin
157.	Diaper fetishism	Sexual arousal from diapers
158.	Dippoldism	Sexual arousal from abusing children
159.	Doraphilia	Love of animal fur, leather, or skins
160.	Dwarf fetishism	Sexual attraction to little people
161.	Dysmorphophilia	Arousal from deformed or physically impaired partners
162.	Dystychiphilia	Deriving pleasure from accidents
163.	Ecdemolagnia	Arousal from traveling or being away from home
164.	Ecdyosis	Arousal from removing clothes in front of others
165.	Ecorchement	Arousal from flagellation
166.	Ecouteurism	Sexual gratification by listening to stories of sexual encounters of others or to sounds of others produced during intercourse, either live or recorded
167.	Ederacinism	To tear out sex organs by the roots as in a frenzy or to punish oneself for sexual cravings
168.	Electra complex	Intended sex between father and daughter.
169.	Electrophilia	Arousal from electric stimulus
170.	Emetophilia	Arousal from vomit or vomiting, Roman shower
171.	Endytolagnia	Arousal only from partners who are clothed
172.	Endytophilia	Arousal only from partners who are clothed
173.	Entomocism	Arousal from insects or use of insects in sexual activity
174.	Entomophilia	Arousal from insects or use of insects in sexual activity
175.	Eonism	Transvestism; named for Chevalier d'Eon de Beaumont (1728-1810), who is supposed to have suffered from this condition
176.	Ephebophilia	Sexual arousal from adolescent sex partners; same as phebophilia, hebephilia, or Lolita Syndrome.
177.	Eprectolagnia	Fetish for farting
178.	Eproctophilia	Sexual attraction to flatulence
179.	Ergophilia	Love of work and labor
180.	Erotographomania	Arousal from writing love poems or letters
181.	Erotomania	An unreasonable love of a stranger or person who is not interested in them
182.	Erotophonophilia	Sexual satisfaction from murdering strangers; lust murder
183.	Erythrophilia	Becoming aroused by blushing

S.no	Paraphilia	Erotic focus/Description
184.	Exhibitionism	Sexual arousal through sexual behavior in view of third parties
185.	Exophilia	Fetish for the bizarre or unusual
186.	Faunoiphilia	Sexual arousal from watching animals mate
187.	Fecalphilia	Same as coprophilia
188.	Fecophilia	Same as coprophilia
189.	Fellatio	Oral manipulation or stimulation of the penis
190.	Fetishism	Use of nonsexual or nonliving objects or part of a person's body to gain sexual excitement
191.	Fisting	Inserting fist or hand into vagina or anus; generally considered a lesbian paraphilia
192.	Flatuphilia	Arousal from having partner pass gas
193.	Foot fetishism	A pronounced sexual interest in feet. Also known as podophilia.
194.	Formicophilia	Enjoyment of the use of ants or insects for sexual purposes
195.	Fratrilagnia	Arousal from having sex or imagining having sex with one's brother
196.	Frictation	A sexual practice in which two male partners achieve sexual satisfaction by rubbing against each other while in a face-to-face position. (The female counterpart is known as tribadism). From Latin, *frico* meaning to rub down.
197.	Frottage	Rubbing body against partner (or some object) for arousal; a consensual activity, as against frotteurism which is non-consensual
198.	Frotteurism	Sexual arousal from rubbing against of touching a non-consenting person
199.	Frottophilia	Being aroused by being touched or rubbed by strangers in a public place.
200.	Furtling	The use of fingers underneath cut-outs in genital areas of photos for arousal
201.	Galateism	Arousal from statues or mannequins
202.	Ganyphilia	Sexual interest in, and preference for adolescent boys by adolescent men
203.	Garment fetishism	Sexual interest that revolves around, or fixates on, a particular type of garment.
204.	Genuphallation	Use of the knees for sex; insertion of penis between the knees of a partner
205.	Gerontophilia	Arousal from a partner from an older generation
206.	Geusophilia	Sexual stimulation through taste
207.	Gomorrahy	Insertion of a hand, a foot, or the stump of a limb (i.e., the insertion of an extremity) into an introitus/vagina or an anus/anal canal, for sexual purpose
208.	Gomphipothic	Arousal by the sight of teeth
209.	Graophilia	Arousal from an elder female partner
210.	Graphelagnia	Maniacal interest in obscene pictures, arousal from photographs of nudity or sex
211.	Grapholagnia	An urge to look at sexually-explicit, obscene, scatological, lewd, vulgar, pornographic, or offensive pictures
212.	Gregomulcia	Arousal from being fondled in a crowd
213.	Gymnocryptosis	Females talking about the sex life of their husbands
214.	Gymnophilia	Arousal from nudity
215.	Gynelophilous	Arousal from pubic hair
216.	Gynemimetophilia	Sexual arousal from a male impersonating a female.
217.	Gynophagia	Sexual fetish involving fantasies of cooking and consumption of human females; literally "woman eating"
218.	Gynotikolobomassophilia	Sexual pleasure by nibbling on a woman's earlobe
219.	Haematophilia	Sexual attraction involving blood, either on another person or blood itself
220.	Haptephilia	Arousal by being touched
221.	Harmatophilia	Arousal from sexual incompetence or mistakes, usually in female partner
222.	Harpaxophilia	Getting pleasure by robbery or being robbed

S.no	Paraphilia	Erotic focus/Description
223.	Hebephilia	Arousal by male adolescent sexual partners
224.	Hedonophilia	Sexual arousal from engaging in pleasurable activities
225.	Hematigolagnia	Arousal from bloody sanitary pads
226.	Hermaphroditphilia	Arousal from hermaphrodites
227.	Heterophilia	Arousal from members of the opposite sex
228.	Hierophilia	Arousal from sacred objects
229.	Hircusophilism	Preference for underarm hair
230.	Hirsutophilia	Arousal from armpit hair
231.	Hodophilia	Arousal from traveling
232.	Homicidophilia	Arousal and gratification through the murder, real or imagined (stage managed and acted out), of one's partner or a stranger
233.	Homilophilia	Sexual arousal from hearing or giving sermons
234.	Homeovestism	Sexual attraction towards the clothing of one's own gender
235.	Homoeroticism	Arousal from members of the same sex
236.	Homophilia	Arousal from members of the same sex
237.	Hybristophilia	Sexual arousal due to the knowledge that one's partner has committed an act of violence
238.	Hygrophilia	Arousal from body fluids or moisture
239.	Hypephilia	Arousal by fabrics
240.	Hyperphilia	Compulsive desire for sex
241.	Hyphephilia	Arousal from touching skin, hair, leather, or fur
242.	Hypnophilia	Turned-on by the thought of sleeping
243.	Hypoxyphilia	Sexual arousal from the deprivation of oxygen
244.	Iantranudia	Arousal from exposing oneself to one's doctor, usually by faking an ailment
245.	Icolagnia	Arousal from contemplation of, or contact with, sculptures or pictures
246.	Iconolagny	Arousal from pictures or statues of nude people
247.	Idrophrodisia	Arousal from the odor of perspiration, especially from the genitals
248.	Indecent exposure	Recurrent urge or behavior to expose one's genitals, especially to an unsuspecting person
249.	Infantilism	Attraction to childhood items; cross-dressing as a young child for sex play
250.	Infantophilia	Sexual attraction towards babies and toddlers, aged from 0 to about 5 years; same as nepiophilia.
251.	Inspectionism	Voyeurism
252.	Iterandria	Arousal from persons of same sex
253.	Juvenilism	Dressing or acting out in the role of a juvenile, sometimes sexually
254.	Kainotophilia	Getting pleasure from change
255.	Kakorrhaphiophilia	Arousal from failure
256.	Katoptronophilia	Sexual arousal from having sex in front of mirrors
257.	Kenophilia	Attraction to empty or open spaces
258.	Keraunophilia	Turned on by thunder and lightning
259.	Kinesophilia	Arousal from movement and exercise
260.	Kleptolagnia	Arousal from stealing things
261.	Kleptophilia	Arousal from stealing things
262.	Klismaphilia	Sexual pleasure from enemas
263.	Knismolagnia	Arousal from tickling
264.	Knissophilia	Attraction to incense-burning
265.	Lactaphilia	Arousal from lactating breasts
266.	Lagnolalia	Arousal from the discussion of subjects which are sexual in nature.

S.no	Paraphilia	Erotic focus/Description
267.	Lagnoperissia	Same as nymphomania
268.	Laliophilia	Arousal from public speaking
269.	Leptosadism	Mild form of sadism
270.	Lesbianism	Sex between two women; also known as tribadism
271.	Ligyrophilia	Arousal from loud noises
272.	Lilapsophilia	Arousal from tornadoes
273.	Lipophilia	Sexual attraction to obese individuals
274.	Lithophilia	Attraction to stones, gravel, or mud
275.	Lolita Syndrome	Sexual arousal from adolescent sex partners; same as ephebophilia, phebophilia or hebephilia
276.	Lygerastia	Tendency to be aroused by darkness
277.	Lygophilia	Love of darkness
278.	Lyssophilia	Sexual arousal from becoming angry or upset
279.	Macrogenitalism	Arousal from large genitals
280.	Macrophilia	Attraction to giants or giant creatures
281.	Maieusiophilia	Arousal from childbirth or pregnant women
282.	Mammagymnophilia	Arousal from female breasts
283.	Maniaphilia	Attraction to insane people
284.	Maschalagnia	A fetish for armpits
285.	Maschalophilous	Arousal from armpits
286.	Masochism	Reverse of sadism; sexual arousal through getting pain inflicted on oneself through another person, usually a partner of the opposite sex; also known as passive algolagnia
287.	Mastigophilia	Arousal from pain and / or humiliation inflicted on oneself
288.	Mastigothymia	Arousal from flagellation
289.	Mastofact	Breast fetish; also known as breast partialism,
290.	Matrilagnia	Sexual arousal from real or imagined sex with one's mother
291.	Matrolagnia	Same as matrilagnia, i.e. the sexual love of a son for his mother
292.	Matronolagnia	Arousal from older female partner
293.	Matutolagnia	An increase in sexual desire felt especially in the morning
294.	Mazoperosis	Sexual gratification received from the mutilation of female breasts
295.	Mazophilia	Breast fetish
296.	Mechanophilia	Turned on by machines
297.	Medolalia	Arousal from talking about the penis
298.	Megalophilia	Arousal from large objects (not necessarily fat)
299.	Melcryptovestimentaphilia	Arousal from women's black underwear
300.	Melissophilia	Arousal from bees
301.	Melolagnia	Arousal from music
302.	*Ménage a trois*	Same as Troilism or Triolism
303.	Menophilist	Arousal from menstruating women
304.	Merinthophilia	Arousal from being bound
305.	Metopophilia	Turned on by a person's face
306.	Midget fetishism	Sexual attraction to little people
307.	Metrophilia	Arousal from poetry
308.	Mixoscopia	Arousal and sexual gratification from watching one's partner have sex with someone else
309.	Mixoscopic bestialis	Sexual delight in watching an intercourse between a person and an animal
310.	Mixoscopic zoophilia	Sexual delight in watching animals copulate

S.no	Paraphilia	Erotic focus/Description
311.	Molysmophilia	Attraction to dirt, filth, or contamination
312.	Moriaphilia	Arousal from telling dirty jokes
313.	Morphophilia	Arousal from a person with a different physique
314.	Musophilia	Arousal from mice
315.	Mysophilia	Arousal from soiled items, such as a dirty diaper or soiled undergarments
316.	Nanophilia	Sexual attraction to a short partner
317.	Naphephilia	Arousal from touching or being touched
318.	Narratophilia	Arousal from erotic conversations or discussing sex with others
319.	Nasolingus	Arousal from sucking nose of partner
320.	Nasophilia	Arousal from the touch, licking, or sucking of a partner's nose; nose fetish
321.	Nebulophilia	Arousal from fog
322.	Necroacrotomophilia	Arousal from having sex with a dead amputee
323.	Necrobestialism	Arousal from having sex with dead animals. Also known as necrobestiality
324.	Necrobiophilia	Intense arousal from having sex with a living person pretending to be dead; some authors have called this practice pseudonecrophilia
325.	Necrochlesis	Sex with a female corpse
326.	Necrocoitus	Sexual penetration of a corpse
327.	Necrophilia	Sexual gratification only by having sex with the dead
328.	Necrophiliapediobeastophile	Sexual gratification by having sex with dead baby animals
329.	Necrophagia	Sexual gratification through eating the flesh of dead people
330.	Necrophilism	Sexual gratification by having sex with the dead. Same as necrophilia
331.	Necrolagnia	Sexual gratification by having sex with the dead. Same as necrophilia
332.	Necrosadism	Arousal from mutilating a corpse
333.	Necropedophilia	Sexual attraction to the corpses of children
334.	Necrozoophilia	Sexual attraction to dead animals
335.	Nemophilia	Arousal from forests
336.	Neophilia	Arousal from novelty or change
337.	Nepiolagnia	Arousal by infants of the opposite sex
338.	Nepiophilia	Arousal by infants of the opposite sex. Also referred to a condition, where the person plays a parental role with a partner who plays the infant; see also autonepiophilia
339.	Nepirasty	Arousal from handling an infant, often experienced by childless females
340.	Normophilia	Arousal by acts considered normal by one's religion or society
341.	Nosolagnia	Arousal from knowing that partner has a terminal illness
342.	Nosophilia	Arousal from knowing that partner has a terminal illness
343.	Novercamania	Sexual attraction to one's stepmother
344.	Nudomania	Arousal from nudity
345.	Nyctophilia	Love of night
346.	Nymphomania	An excessive, insatiable sexual appetite or drive in women
347.	Nymphophilia	Arousal of adult males who are attracted to young females
348.	Ochlophilia	Arousal to crowds or being in a crowd. Also arousal from biting.
349.	Oculophilia	Arousal from eyeballs; eye fetish
350.	Odaxelagnia	Arousal from biting
351.	Odontophilia	Arousal from teeth
352.	Odynophilia	Arousal from pain and / or humiliation inflicted upon oneself
353.	Oedipus complex	Intended sex between mother and son.
354.	Oenosugia	Pouring wine over female breasts and licking it from there

S.no	Paraphilia	Erotic focus/Description
355.	Oikophilia	Attraction to one's home
356.	Olfactophilia	Sexual gratification from smells
357.	Olfactory eroticism	Sexual stimulation from the odor of vaginal secretions
358.	Ombrophilia	Turned on by rain or being rained upon
359.	Omolagnia	Arousal from nudity
360.	Omorashi	Arousal from having a full bladder or a sexual attraction to someone else experiencing the discomfort of a full bladder; a fetish subculture predominantly seen in Japan
361.	Ophidiophilia	Arousal from snakes
362.	Orasophilia	Sexual stimulation via vision
363.	Ordune	Arousal from photographs of nudes or sex
364.	Organofact	Fetish for some part of the body
365.	Ornithophilia	Arousal from birds
366.	Osculocentric	Arousal from kissing
367.	Osmolagnia	Arousal caused by bodily odors, such as sweat, urine or menses
368.	Osmophilia	Arousal caused by bodily odors, such as sweat, urine or menses
369.	Osphresiolagnia	Erotic excitement produced by odors; an inordinate love of smells.
370.	Osphresiophilia	Arousal caused by bodily odors, such as sweat, urine or menses
371.	Ozolagnia	Arousal caused by bodily odors, such as sweat, urine or menses
372.	Pantophilia	Arousal from just about everything imaginable
373.	Parthenophilia	Attraction only to virgins
374.	Partner swapping	Exchanging partners (generally married) for sex
375.	Passive algolagnia	Same as masochism
376.	Passive scopophilia	Desire to be looked at by others; a form of exhibitionism
377.	Patrolagnia	Arousal from real or imagined sex with one's father
378.	Pecattiphilia	Arousal from sinning or having committed an imaginary crime
379.	Paederasty	An abnormal sexual desire towards young children. same as Pedophilia
380.	Paraphilic infantilism	Same as autonepiophilia
381.	Partialism	Sexual interest exclusively focused on a particular body part, say breasts
382.	Parthenophilia	Sexual attraction to virgins
383.	Pecattiphilia	Sexual arousal from sinning or guilt
384.	Pediophilia	Attraction to dolls
385.	Pedohebephilia	Sexual interest in persons with the body shape of under 11-year-olds as well as pubescent persons between 11 and 14 years for females and 11-16 years for males
386.	Pedophilia	An abnormal sexual desire towards young children
387.	Peeping Tom	Observing nude individuals without their knowledge. Also known as voyeurism
388.	Peiodeiktophilia	Penile exhibitionism
389.	Peniaphilia	Erotic fascination with poverty
390.	Pentheraphilia	Sexual attraction to one's mother-in-law
391.	Phallolalia	Arousal achieved by talking about the penis
392.	Phalloorchoalgolagnia	Sexual arousal by the experiencing of painful stimuli being administered to the male genitals
393.	Phallophilia	Large penis fetish
394.	Phebophilia	Sexual arousal from adolescent sex partners; same as ephebophilia, hebephilia, or Lolita Syndrome
395.	Phletbotomy	Arousal from bloodletting
396.	Phobophilia	Arousal from fear or hate

S.no	Paraphilia	Erotic focus/Description
397.	Phronemophilia	Arousal from thinking
398.	Phthiriophilia	Attraction to lice
399.	Phygephilia	Arousal from being a fugitive
400.	Pictophilia	Arousal from looking at erotic pictures
401.	Piquerism	Arousal from penetrating one's body with sharp objects (pins, razors, knives, etc.)
402.	Placophilia	Arousal from tombstones
403.	Playing the bagpipes	Having intercourse under the armpits.
404.	Plushophilia	Sexual attraction to stuffed toys or people in animal costume, such as theme park characters
405.	Pluviophilia	Sexual stimulation from rain or being rained upon
406.	Pnigophilia	Aroused from people choking
407.	Podophilia	Arousal from feet; foot fetish
408.	Poinephilia	Arousal from pain and / or humiliation inflicted on oneself
409.	Polyiterophilia	Arousal only after having sex with a series of partners
410.	Pornolagnia	Desire for prostitutes
411.	Potamophilia	Arousal from streams and rivers
412.	Psellismophilia	Becoming aroused by stuttering
413.	Pseudonecrophilia	Arousal from having sex with someone pretending to be dead
414.	Pseudozoophilia	Arousal from partner who plays the role of an animal during sex play
415.	Psycholagny	Sexual arousal and gratification obtained from mental imagery alone.
416.	Psychrocism	Arousal by being cold or watching others freeze
417.	Psychrophilia	Arousal by being cold or watching others freeze
418.	Psychrotentiginous	Arousal from cold weather
419.	Pteridomania	An intense desire for ferns
420.	Pteronophilia	Sexual gratification from being tickled by feathers
421.	Pubephilia	Arousal from pubic hair
422.	Pygmalionism	Falling in love with one's creation (*e.g.*, "My Fair Lady")
423.	Pygophilemania	Arousal from kissing buttocks
424.	Pygophilia	Arousal from coming in contact with buttocks
425.	Pygotripsis	Arousal from rubbing buttocks
426.	Pyrolagnia	Sexual gratification from witnessing, making or extinguishing fires
427.	Pyrophilia	Arousal from fire
428.	Raptophilia	Arousal only from raping a victim; acquiescence on the part of the victim may cause the paraphiliac to lose interest or, more often, to increase the threats and violence
429.	Renfield's Syndrome	Arousal by drinking blood of others (human or animals); also known as clinical vampirism.
430.	Renifleur	Person aroused the smell of urine or by sniffing underwear
431.	Retifism	Foot and shoe fetishism
432.	Rhabdophilia	Arousal from being flagellated
433.	Rhytiphilia	Arousal from facial wrinkles
434.	Robotism	Arousal by robots or the use of robots in sexual activity
435.	Sadism	Sexual arousal through inflicting pain on another person; also known as Algolagnia
436.	Saliromania	Deriving erotic pleasure from soiling or disheveling the object of one's desire, usually an attractive person; sexual arousal or satisfaction of soiling or damaging a partner's clothing

S.no	Paraphilia	Erotic focus/Description
437.	Salirophilia	Arousal from ingesting saliva or sweat
438.	Sapphosadism	Lesbian sadism
439.	Sarmassophilia	Arousal from kneading flesh
440.	Satyriasis	Excessive, insatiable sexual appetite or drive in men
441.	Savantophilia	Sexual arousal to mentally challenged individuals
442.	Scatologia	Arousal from making obscene phone calls
443.	Scatophilia	Arousal from making obscene phone calls
444.	Scelerophilia	Attraction to bad guys or unsavory characters
445.	Schediaphilia	Love of (or sexual arousal from) cartoon characters or situations; also known as toonophilia
446.	Scopophilia	Sexual arousal from watching others engage in sex
447.	Scoptolagnia	Same as scopophilia
448.	Scoptophilia	Same as scopophilia
449.	Scotophilia	Turned on by darkness
450.	Selgolalia	Arousal from telling stories that revolve around or include sex
451.	Septophilia	Sexual attraction to decaying matter
452.	Serviphilia	Sexual arousal from being or acting as a servant. A masochistic theme
453.	Siderodromophilia	Arousal from trains
454.	Sin of Gomorrah	Buccal coitus (coitus through mouth)
455.	Sitophilia	Arousal from food; use of food in sexual activity
456.	Sleeping Princess Syndrome	Arousal from those that are sleeping or appear to be asleep
457.	Soceraphilia	Arousal from one's parents-in-law
458.	Sodomy	Anal intercourse between two men or a man and a woman; also known as buggery
459.	*Soixante-neuf*	Mutual oral sex from the supposed similarity of the bodies to the numeral 69
460.	Somnophilia	Arousal from fondling one's partner in their sleep, or having sex when partner is asleep
461.	Sophophilia	Sexual gratification from learning
462.	Sorophilia	Arousal from real or imagined sex with one's sister
463.	Sororilagnia	Arousal from real or imagined sex with one's sister
464.	Spectrophilia	Arousal from looking at oneself in a mirror; arousal from image in mirrors; coitus with spirits; sexual attraction to ghosts
465.	Statuephilia	Sexual attraction to statues or dolls
466.	Statuophilia	Arousal from statues
467.	Staurophilia	Arousal from the cross or crucifix
468.	Stercoracism	A sexually pathological obsession with dirtiness
469.	Sthenolagnia	Arousal from displaying strength or muscles
470.	Stigmatophilia	Arousal from partner who is stigmatized (i.e. tattoos, piercing, scars)
471.	Strabimus	Arousal from eyes of partner
472.	Stupprator	Male aroused only by virgins
473.	Stygiophilia	Sexual pleasure from the thought of going to hell
474.	Swinging	Exchanging partners (generally married) for sex
475.	Symphorophilia	Arousal from stage-managing or arranging a disaster, crash, or explosion; arousal by accidents or catastrophes
476.	Synegenesophilia	Sexual attraction to relatives
477.	Tamakeri	Arousal when a female kicks a man in the testicles; a variant of masochism, prevalent in Japan
478.	Tantalolagnia	Arousal from teasing

S.no	Paraphilia	Erotic focus/Description
479.	Taphephilia	Arousal from being buried alive
480.	Taphophilia	Arousal from funerals
481.	Technophilia	Arousal from computer sex (i.e. cyber sex)
482.	Teledildonics	Arousal from computer sex games
483.	Teleiophilia	Sexual interest in mature persons (as opposed to pedophilia)
484.	Teleophilia	Affinity for religious ceremonies
485.	Telephone scatologia	Arousal from making obscene phone calls
486.	Telephone scatophilia	Arousal from making obscene phone calls; same as telephone scatologia
487.	Telephonicophilia	Arousal from using phone calls for sexual conversations
488.	Teratophilia	Arousal from deformed or monstrous people
489.	Thalassophilia	Love of the sea
490.	Thalpotentiginy	Arousal from heat, or warm weather
491.	Thanatophilia	Arousal by having sex with the dead; same as necrophilia
492.	Thlipsosis	Arousal from pinching others
493.	Threpterophilia	Arousal from female nurses
494.	Thygatrilagnia	A father's sexual love for his daughter
495.	Timophilia	Arousal from gold or wealth
496.	Tithiolagnia	Sexual gratification from nursing
497.	Titillagnia	Arousal from tickling
498.	Tit torture	Sexual gratification from any of several erotic BDSM activities focusing solely on inflicting pain on the breast, nipples, and areola.
499.	Traumaphilia	Sexual arousal from wounds or trauma
500.	Tripsolagnophilia	Arousal from being massaged
501.	Tocophilia	Fondness for pregnancy and childbirth
502.	Tonitrophilia	Love of thunder
503.	Toonophilia	Love of (or sexual arousal from) cartoon characters or situations; also known as schediaphilia
504.	Toucherism	Touching a non-consenting person's intimate parts in a crowd (cf frotteurism, in which the frotteur rubs his male organ against the non-consenting person)
505.	Toxophilia	Love of archery
506.	Transformation fetish	Sexual arousal from depictions of transformations of people into objects or other beings
507.	Transvestism	Sexual arousal from dressing in the clothes of the opposite sex; also known as eonism.
508.	Transvestophilia	Same as transvestism
509.	Tribadism	Same as lesbianism
510.	Trichopathophilia	Sexual attraction to hair
511.	Trichophilia	Sexual attraction to hair
512.	Triolism	Same as Troilism
513.	Tripsolagnia	Arousal from having hair shampooed
514.	Tripsophilia	Arousal from being massaged
515.	Troilism	Arousal by being the third party in a sexual scene; desire to share sexual partner with another person; also known as *menage a trois* (household of three)
516.	Tyrannism	Sexual sadism
517.	Undinism	Arousal from water
518.	Uranism	Arousal from person of the same sex
519.	Uranophilia	Sexual arousal by heavenly thoughts
520.	Urolagnia	Sexual pleasure from urinating

S.no	Paraphilia	Erotic focus/Description
521.	Urophilia	Sexual arousal from urine
522.	Urtication	The use of nettles to create extra sensation
523.	Vernalagnia	An increase in sexual desire in the spring
524.	Vicarphilia	Arousal from other people's exciting experiences
525.	Vincilagnia	Sexual arousal from bondage
526.	Vitricophilia	Sexual attraction to one's stepfather
527.	Vomerophilia	Sexual attraction to vomit; erotic vomiting
528.	Vorarephilia	Sexual attraction to being eaten by, and/or eating, another person or creature
529.	Voyeurism	Sexual arousal by observing nude individuals without their knowledge; same as Peeping Tom
530.	Wakamezake	Sexual act involving drinking alcohol from a woman's body; also called wakame sake and seaweed sake
531.	Wind Fetish	Sexual attraction to being blown by the wind
532.	Wing Fetishism	Sexual attraction to wings (angels' or demons')
533.	Xenophilia	Arousal from strangers; an attraction to foreign customs, traditions, and foreigners
534.	Xenolimia	Arousal from strangers
535.	Xylophilia	Arousal by wooden objects
536.	Ylophilia	Arousal by forests
537.	Zelophilia	Sexual arousal from jealousy
538.	Zenolimia	Arousal from strangers; an attraction to foreign customs, traditions, and foreigners
539.	Zoolagnia	Sexual attraction towards animals; sexual bestiality, sexual desire for animals.
540.	Zoonecrophilia	Having sex with dead animals
541.	Zoophagia	Eating live animals for erotic arousal
542.	Zoophilia	Sexual arousal by contact with animals
543.	Zoophilic exhibitionism	Exposure of genitals in front of animals with concomitant masturbation
544.	Zoophilic frottage	Rubbing one's genitals on the furs of live animals
545.	Zoophilic voyeurism	Peeping through windows to gaze at animals
546.	Zoosadism	Sexual arousal by causing pain and suffering to animals
547.	Zwischenstufe	Arousal from a person of the same sex

Appendix 2

GLOSSARY

Term	Meaning
Acmegenesis	Orgasm
Adolescentilism	Cross-dressing or playing the role of an adolescent
Adultery	Sexual intercourse between two people when at least one is married
Agenobiosis	Married couple that consent to live together without sex
Aliphineur	Person using lotion or other ointment to arouse partner
Allantotrioism	A form of masturbation practiced by women by substituting a sausage for the penis
Alloerasty	Use of nudity of another person to arouse partner
Allonemia	Fantasizing during coitus about someone other than one's partner, especially someone more desirable
Amychesis	Scratching partner during sex
Ischolagny	Avoiding members of the opposite gender to avoid arousal
Lagnonector	A person who kills to have sex with the corpse
Manuxorate	A male using his hand to masturbate
Maritate	A female masturbating alone
Martymachlia	Group sex
Mastix	Female Sadist
Mazophallate	Rubbing the penis between breasts
MSM	Men who have sex with men; behavioral category referencing people at risk for HIV
Necrochlesis	Sex with a corpse
Pageism	A male submitting to a female
Philemanmania	Compulsion to kiss
Queening	Sitting on the side of a person's face as a form of bondage
Rimming	Penetration of the anus with the tongue
Sacofricosis	Cutting a hole in the pockets of trousers so that a person can masturbate (usually in public)
Sexautism	Tendency to be preoccupied with sexual thoughts
Sexual aggression	Acts of sexual behavior by one person against another without the benefit of that person's informed consent.
Siphnianize	Anal Masturbation
Sororilagnia	Sex with one's sister
Sotadism	Anal sex
Stupprator	Man aroused by virgins
Syntribate	Rubbing thighs together to masturbate
Tachorgasmia	Premature ejaculation
Thygatria	Sex between father and daughter
Tragolimia	Desire for sex regardless of attraction to partner
Wakamezake	A sexual act involving drinking alcohol from a woman's body. The woman closes her legs tight enough so that the triangle between the thighs and mons pubis form a cup, and then pours sake down her chest into this triangle. Her partner then drinks the sake from the triangle. The name comes from the idea that the woman's pubic hair in the sake resembles soft seaweed (wakame) floating in the sea. Also called wakame sake and seaweed sake.

Appendix 3

SEXUAL CRIMES AND UNUSUAL SEXUAL PRACTICES: A BRIEF CHRONOLOGY

S.No.	*Year*	*Event*
1.	Mythology	(i) Greek hero Heracles forced to serve Queen Omphale for a year, dressed in women's clothings. The very first instance of cross-dressing, albeit forced. (ii) In Hindu mythology, when Lord Hanuman goes to bring back Sita, the abducted wife of his Lord, he engages in possible voyeurism for some time, when he peeps into the abductor Ravana's harem, seeing his half clad wives and concubines. (iii) Ancient Hindus have an iconographic representation of Lord Shiva in an androgynous form (half-man, half-woman), which may refer to an attempt at deification of transsexuals. It perhaps has deeper philosophical meanings too.
2.	Prehistory	(i) Sexual contact with animals proscribed from the time of Old Testament. *Deuteronomy 27:21* states, "cursed be he that lieth with any manner of beast". *Exodus 22:19* states, "whoever lieth with a beast shall surely be put to death." (ii) *Genesis 39:1-23* tells the story of possibly the first case of sexual harassment of a man by a woman, when sexual advances were made by Potiphar's wife on Joseph, a slave who had been bought by Potiphar. (iii) Many cave paintings from 40,000 and 25,000 years BC depict humans and animals having sex. Thus bestiality could be as old as this period at least.
3.	1400 BC	First ever mention of transvestism in law. Hebrew law (Deuteronomy XXII, 5) states, "Women shall not wear that which pertains to a man, nor shall a man put on woman's garment, for all that do so are an abomination to the Lord God."
4.	1300 BC	First ever mention in legal history of punishment for bestiality. Hittite compendium of laws states that sexual acts committed by men – by not by women – with certain animals such as sheep, cattle, dogs or pigs were punishable with death.
5.	8th century BC	The first famous instance of voyeurism. Candaules, king of the ancient Kingdom of Lydia from 735 BC to 718 BC arranged so his bodyguard Gyges may appreciate the exquisite beauty of his queen. Although Gyges refused at first, he ultimately allowed himself to be coaxed into seeing Candaules naked wife. The queen discovered this as Gyges was seeing her in the nude surreptitiously. She called Gyges the next day and had her husband murdered by him. The legend lends its name – candaulism – to a paraphilia, where a husband exhibits his nude wife to others.
6.	450 BC	Greek historian Herodotus (484-425 BC) reports a disease of Scythians in which men dress and work as women (transvestism).
7.	5th century BC	(i) St. Augustine (d. 430 AD) teaches that sex should only be engaged in for the purpose of procreation, and only with the female on her back and the male on top. All nonprocreative sex was considered sinful, and thus paraphiliac in nature. (ii) Herodotus notes in his *The Histories*, that the practice of necrophilia among the Egyptians is prevalent, and that in order to discourage this practice, the dead bodies of women were made to putrefy before handing them over to the embalmers.
8.	4th century BC	Plato (427-347 BCE) contends in his *Laws* that masturbation and male-male sexual activity are unnatural because they are neither procreative nor consistent with courage and self-control.
9.	41 AD	Caligula (A.D. 12 – A.D. 41), the third Roman Emperor, and one of the most sexually perverse men in history assassinated. It is said that he was a transvestite, committed incest, and even prostituted his sisters to other men. Most likely he was a zoophile too.
10.	4th century	Indian philosopher Mallanaga Vātsyāyana (fl 4th Century AD) writes *Kama Sutra*, a widely quoted text on sexual behavior. Among other things, the treatise describes consensual erotic slapping, one of the earliest descriptions of masochism.

S.No.	Year	Event
11.	9th century	According to legend, Pope Joan, a female, managed to become a Pope only because she was a transvestite. The legend is vigorously denied by the Church though.
12.	1057	The second famous instance of voyeurism. Lady Godiva, wife of Leofric, Earl of Mercia and Lord of Coventry, rides naked through the streets of Coventry in order to compel her husband to reduce taxes. Leofric, unable to stop her from doing so, issues an edict to all citizens to remain indoors and not to look at her during her ride. A city tailor Tom is unable to control his curiosity and peeps through a hole to look at her. He is struck blind by Leofric.
13.	1285	England and Wales become the first nation in the world to introduce a statutory age limit for girls below which sexual intercourse with her will always be illegal (12 years).
14.	15th Century	A Catalan painting, *Flagellation of Christ*, of this period, depicts that the floggers are deriving sexual pleasure from flogging.
15.	1431	A major charge against Joan of Arc (1412-1431) in her trial by the Catholic Church is transvestism. She is accused of breaking both scriptural and secular law by her male attire, and executed.
16.	1453	Guillaume Edeline, a priest, burned at Evreux for committing bestiality with a sheep.
17.	1468	One Monsieur Jean Beisse convicted of copulating with a cow and a goat. Jean, the cow and the goat all burned at the stake.
18.	1495	In one of the earliest descriptions of masochism, Italian philosopher Giovanni Pico della Mirandola (1463–1494) describes a man who needed to be flogged before he could have sex. The case was published in *Disputationes*, which was published one year after his death.
19.	1533	Henry VIII (1491–1547) King of England promulgates the controversial *Buggery Act 1533* (25 Hen. VIII c. 6), an anti-sodomy law. The Act made buggery (with man or beast) punishable by hanging, a penalty not finally lifted until 1861. One of the men instrumental in passing the act through Parliament was Thomas Cromwell.
20.	1540	Sir Walter Hungerford (1503–1540) becomes the first person to be charged under the *Buggery Act 1533*, although there were other charges such as treason. Beheaded on Tower Hill on 28 July 1540.
21.	1541	Nicholas Udall (1504–1556), an English playwright and schoolmaster, becomes the first person to be solely convicted under the controversial *Buggery Act 1533*. He was charged for committing sodomy with two of his pupils. Although the felony of buggery carried a sentence of capital punishment (by hanging), his sentence was reduced to just under a year in prison.
22.	1553	Queen Mary I of England (1516–1558) repeals the *Buggery Act 1533*, earlier promulgated by Henry VIII.
23.	1563	Queen Elizabeth I (1533–1603) re-enacts the *Buggery Act*, first passed by Henry VIII in 1533.
24.	1572	Saxony introduces a statutory age limit for vaginal intercourse with girls (12 years). Sexual intercourse with a girl below 12 is made illegal by this statute. England and Wales had done it earlier in 1285.
25.	1601	16 year old Caudine de Culam convicted of intercourse with a dog. Both were hanged and their bodies burned.
26.	1607	A young boy convicted and hanged for copulating with a mare. The mare was killed at the foot of the gallows with a pole axe.
27.	1639	(i) Johann Heinrich Meibom (1590–1655) , a German physician (also known as Meibomus), introduces the first theory of masochism. He postulates that flogging the back warms the semen in the kidneys, which causes sexual excitement once it reaches the testicles. (ii) In Pilgrim Father's Plymouth Colony a divorce law enacted in 1639 mentions bestiality specifically as a ground for divorce.
28.	1649	M. Vijon burned for having sex with a bird.
29.	1663	First reported English case of indecent exposure. Sir Charles Sedley (1639–1701) and two companions get drunk, strip off their clothes, climb a balcony overlooking Covent Garden and hurl urine at the public below. He is fined 2000 marks, committed without bail for a week, and bound to his good behavior for a year

S.No.	Year	Event
30.	1682	*Venice Preserv'd*, an English Restoration play written by the English dramatist Thomas Otway (1652–1685) depicts a masochistic Venetian senator engaging in what might today be termed puppy-play or kennel-training with his mistress.
31.	1683	Denmark passes a law making homosexuality and bestiality punishable by burning.
32.	1698	Kristian Frantz Paullini modifies the theory of masochism by Meibom (propounded 1639), so that warm blood, and not semen, descended from the kidneys to induce erotic sensations upon flogging.
33.	1711	Denmark modifies its earlier law passed in 1683. Now those convicted of homosexuality or bestiality are to be strangled as well as burnt.
34.	1718	*A Treatise on the Use of Flogging*, the first overtly pornographic work on the subject of flagellation, published. With its publication, flagellation becomes a passion throughout Europe. The French dub it *le vice anglais*, or the English vice.
35.	1734	One of the earliest cases of sexual harassment occurs in the colonies, when a group of female servants allege beatings by their mistresses' husbands.
36.	1748	English novelist John Cleland (1709–1789) writes the controversial classic *Memoirs of a Woman of Pleasure*, better known as *Fanny Hill*, considered the first modern erotic novel in English, which goes on to become a byword for the battle of censorship of erotica. The work includes a detailed description of a mutual flagellation scene between Fanny and an English client.
37.	1756	French writer Charles de Brosses (1709–1777) coins the term fetishism (in an anthropological sense) and develops the concept of religious fetishism. The term fetishism in a sexual sense is adopted much later by Krafft-Ebing (1840 –1902) in 1886.
38.	1774	Chevalier d'Eon de Beaumont (1728–1810), anatomically a male, and a transvestite, demands that the French government recognize him as a woman. King Louis XVI and his court comply. The king even grants funds for a new wardrobe. Today Eonism (named after him) is a synonym for transvestism.
39.	1781	In the famous case *R. v. Hill* (1781) 1 East P.C. 434, it is decided that even minimal penetration of vagina will suffice to constitute an offense of rape.
40.	1788	French physician François Amédée Doppet (1753–1799), expands the theory of masochism, first propounded by Meibom in 1639, to include women (as masochists). He proposes that flogging induces warm blood to descend from kidneys to the female genitalia, causing erotic sensations.
41.	1791	(i) Marquis de Sâde described sexual hanging in his *Justine*, with Roland's hanging being assisted by Thérèse. Interestingly the first actual known case of sexual hanging occurred the very same year. (ii) Czeck composer Frantisek Kotzwara (1730–1791) dies from erotic asphyxiation. The first recorded case of death resulting from this paraphilia. The term *Kotzwarraism* is now sometimes used for autoerotic asphyxiation.
42.	1824	*Vagrancy Act* passed in Britain. Section 4 of the Act makes exhibitionism an offense
43.	1827	A Frenchman named Leger mutilated the genitals of a young girl and drank her blood after necrophilia.
44.	1828	British dominatrix Theresa Berkley (died September 1836) invents the *Berkley Horse*, a BDSM apparatus, used for erotic spanking.
45.	1847	Sergeant François Bertrand (1824–1850), a sergeant in the French army digs up corpses from Montparnasse, a Paris cemetery to have sex with them. His activities continue for a period of two years.
46.	1869	(i) Austrian-born Hungarian journalist, memoirist and human rights campaigner Karl-Maria Kertbeny (born Karl-Maria Benkert) (1824–1882) coins the word homosexual. (ii) Carl Westphal (1833-1890), the first physician to study alternative forms of sexual expression, publishes a case study of a young woman who was drawn to her own gender and had historically dressed as a boy. He called it Conträre Sexualempfindung.

S.No.	Year	Event
47.	1877	French physician and psychiatrist Charles Lasègue, (1809–1883) describes exhibitionism for the first time.
48.	1886	(i) Austro-German psychiatrist Richard Freiherr von Krafft-Ebing (1840–1902) coins the terms sadism, masochism, and fetichism (with a 'c') for the first time. In his *Psychopathia Sexualis*, a classic study of sexual perversity. Also adopts the term fetishism in a sexual context, which was earlier used mainly in an anthropological sense. (ii) French necrophiliac Henri Blot arrested after he exhumed and fornicated with the dead body of a recently buried dancer.
49.	1888	French psychologist Alfred Binet (1857–1911) uses the term *fetichism* to denote sexual admiration of an inanimate object. Probably borrowed from Krafft-Ebing.
50.	1894	Austro-German psychiatrist Richard Freiherr von Krafft-Ebing (1840 –1902) describes a form of cross-dressing that would today be described as transsexualism. He calls it *metamorphosis sexualis paranoica*. He also introduces the terms *zoophilia erotica* and *zooerasty* denoting various shades of human-animal sexual contact.
51.	1900	First version of *International Classification of Diseases* (ICD) appears. Intended to classify only deadly somatic diseases. Behavioral problems such as sexual deviations do not find a place here. The first time that they find a place in ICD is in its sixth edition (ICD-6) in1948.
52.	1910	The term 'transvestism' first used by the German sexologist and sexual rights activist Magnus Hirschfeld in his study, *Die Transvestiten (Transvestites).*
53.	1916	The very first case of transsexualism described by Marcuse (without referring to this term though).
54.	1924	Viennese psychotherapist Wilhelm Stekel coins the term paraphilia, from the Greek *para-* (beside) + *philos* (loving), and first used in English in Stekel's translated works.
55.	1927	The first case of autofellatio described by Bragman.
56.	1931	Abraham reports the very first case of transsexualism on which surgery was performed (the term was not used until 1950).
57.	1948	ICD-6 published by the WHO. Sexual deviation as a general classification introduced for the first time. No subdivisions delineated yet.
58.	1950	The term *transsexualism* first used by Cauldwell. Such types of behaviors had been described earlier though, without referring to this term.
59.	1952	The first edition of Diagnostic and Statistical Manual (DSM-I) published. Homosexuality listed as a sexual deviation.
60.	1962	(i) Homosexuality decriminalized in Hungary. (ii) Illinois becomes the first American state to revise its criminal code. Oral–genital contacts and anal intercourse between consenting adults in private and sexual acts with animals no longer considered criminal offenses.
61.	1964	Congress passes and President Johnson signs the *Civil Rights Act of 1964*. Title VII of this Act protects employees from sexual harassment in the work place and establishes the Equal Employment Opportunity Commission (EEOC).
62.	1965	ICD-8 published. Subdivisions of sexual deviation make their appearance for the first time.
63.	1968	(i) DSM-II published. Sexual deviations do not find a major mention. There is just one statement for the entire category, and then just a listing of each sexual deviation. (ii) Robert J. Stoller proposes a simple classification of transsexuals, dividing them in to primary and secondary.
64.	1969	Bestiality ceases to be a crime in Germany. Before this year, bestiality was punishable under section 175b of The German Criminal Code (Strafgesetzbuch, StGB).
65.	1972	(i) U.S. Congress passes the Education Act amendments prohibiting sex discrimination at schools and universities that receive federal funding. Widely construed as prohibiting sexual harassment too at schools and universities. (ii) US Congress passes the Equal Employment Opportunity Act, giving the EEOC power to enforce Title VII of Civil Rights Act 1964.

S.No.	Year	Event
66.	1973	Homosexuality removed from the DSM-II classification of mental disorders and replaced by the category sexual orientation disturbance.
67.	1974	Ethel Person and Lionel Ovesey propose a classification of transsexuals, quite similar to that of Stoller proposed 6 years earlier.
68.	1975	U.S. artist Vaughn Bodé (1941–1975) dies accidentally due to an experiment in autoerotic asphyxiation.
69.	1976	(i) On April 20, 1976, in a landmark decision in *Williams v. Saxbe,* 413 F.Supp. 654 (1976), a federal district judge in Washington recognizes quid pro quo sexual harassment as discrimination. It is found that the firing of a woman by her boss for refusing to have sex with him does indeed violate the federal law against employment discrimination based on sex. (ii) Recognition of the need to establish clearer communication between the interviewer and the child suspected of being sexually abused leads to the design of dolls with genitalia, now known as anatomical dolls (ADs).
70.	1977	(i) The ICD-9 published. (ii) The state of Georgia passes law to make necrophilia a crime. (iii) The word apotemnophilia coined by John Money to describe a new paraphilia, which showed a nexus between sexual desire and a desire to be an amputee.
71.	1980	(i) John Money popularizes the term *paraphilia.* (ii) DSM-III published. Psychodynamic view of mental disorders is abandoned and the biomedical model becomes the primary approach, introducing a clear distinction between normal and abnormal. *Paraphilia* used for the first time in DSM. Homosexuality dropped from the list of paraphilias. However a new term *ego-dystonic homosexuality* appears in the general category of psychosexual disorders. It is not till the publication of DSM III-R that this term was dropped.
72.	1982	Survivors of Incest Anonymous (SIA) started. Intended to be a resource to incest survivors.
73.	1984	Dr. S. Sivaloganathan of the University of Leeds, UK, describes for the first time, a highly unusual autoerotic death of a man using submersion as an asphyxia method. He calls this *aqua eroticum.*
74.	1986	(i) In *Bowers v. Hardwick* 478 US 186 (1986), the Supreme Court upheld the Georgia law prohibiting sodomy, reasoning that there is no fundamental right granted to homosexuals to engage in consensual sodomy. In doing so, the Supreme Court retreated from its earlier position that consensual sexual activity between same sex partners that is not obscene was protected by a constitutional right to privacy. (ii) In *Meritor Savings Bank v. Vinson,* 477 U.S. 57 (1986), the US Supreme Court broadens the definition of sexual harassment. Employers are now strictly liable for damages if sexual harassment occur at workplace, even if they were not aware of it and secondly the loss to the harassed woman need not be just economic.
75.	1987	DSM-III-R (revised) published. The term *ego-dystonic homosexuality* dropped from it.
76.	1991	(i)Anita Hill, an Oklahoma law school professor accuses Justice Clarence Thomas of having sexually harassed her. (ii) *Cline v. General Electric Capital Auto Lease, Inc.,* 757 F.Supp. 923 (N.D. Ill. 1991) creates "gender harassment" as a cause of action under Title VII.
77.	1992	(i) On September 22, 5 upper-caste men in India gang-rape a 41-year old social worker in the presence of her husband, because she tried to stop a child marriage. The incident culminates in Supreme Court of India handling down a landmark judgment, in 1997, defining sexual harassment at workplace. (ii) The World Health Organization ceases to classify homosexuality as a mental disorder. American Psychiatric Association (APA) had done it earlier in 1973.
78.	1993	The famous case *R. v Brown* [1993] 2 All ER 75, decided in UK by the House of Lords. It was opined that consent by a masochist to suffer injuries was not a legally valid defense to his sadist partner causing injuries and bodily harm to him. (January 1993).
79.	1994	(i) DSM-IV published. (ii) UK Government ceases to classify homosexuality as a mental disorder. (iii) Megan's law passed in the state of New Jersey. This law requires notification of neighbors when a convicted sex offender moves into a neighborhood. (iv) Paula Corbin Jones files a sexual harassment and eschewal suit against the then U.S. President Bill Clinton.

S.No.	Year	Event
80.	1996	(i) President Bill Clinton signs the federal version of Megan's law (June 1996). (ii) American songwriter, musician and composer Kevin Gilbert (1966–1996) dies at the young age of 29 from apparent autoerotic asphyxiation. (iii) Governor Pete Wilson of California signs into law 1996 Cal. Stat 3339 (the "Castration Law"), a bill that mandates the chemical castration or surgical castration of twice-convicted child molesters. The new law makes California the first state to impose such a controversial punishment. (September 17).
81.	1997	(i) In a landmark case in India, *Vishaka v. State of Rajasthan*, A.I.R. 1997 S.C. 3011, the Supreme Court, for the first time lays down guidelines defining what exactly is sexual harassment at the work place. (On Aug 13, 1997) (ii) Twenty-five U.S. states, the District of Columbia, and the United States Government outlaw bestiality.
82.	1998	(i) Mitisubishi Motor Company agrees to settle a claim brought against them by the Equal Employment Opportunity Commission (EEOC). Mitsubishi agrees to pay $34 million in compensation for at least 350 women who were employed at a Normal, Ill. plant since 1990. The women were allegedly subjected to a pattern of sexual harassment which led to the filing of a civil class action prior to the EEOC suit (June 10). (ii) All 50 US states enact some version of Megan's law, by the end of 1998. (iii) Susan Wilson discovers that her neighbor had been secretly videotaping her with cameras hidden in her Louisiana home. At that time, there were no laws to fit the crime. Her case partly inspired the federal law, the *Video Voyeurism Prevention Act of 2004*.
83.	2000	(i) DSM-IV-TR (Text Revision of the DSM-IV) published (in July). It remains the most recent version of DSM. (ii) Masashi Tashiro (1956–), one time Japanese television performer and the founding member of the band *Rats & Star*, sent to the prosecutor's office for filming up a woman's skirt with a camcorder in Tokyo (September 24).
84.	2001	(i) China's psychiatric association removes homosexuality from its list of mental illnesses. (ii) Iowa, Maine, and Oregon pass laws criminalizing bestiality.
85.	2003	The U.S. Supreme court rules that state sodomy laws, which criminalize homosexual behavior are discriminatory and unconstitutional.
86.	2004	(i) U.S. passes the federal law, the *Video Voyeurism Prevention Act of 2004*. (ii) Kazuhide Uekusa (1960–), Japanese economist and economic analyst arrested as he tries to peep under a high school girl's skirt using his hand mirror on the escalator of Shinagawa Station of East Japan Railway Company in Minato, Tokyo (April 8).
87.	2005	Kazuhide Uekusa sentenced to a fine of 500,000 yen (and confiscation of his hand mirror), for his crime of upskirting the previous year (March 23).
88.	2006	(i) On 13 February, a Sudanese man found copulating with a goat. Ordered by the council of elders to take the goat as his wife. (ii) ICD-9-CM (9th Revision, Clinical Modification), Sixth Edition, issued for use beginning October 1, 2006. (iii) Californian Governor Arnold Schwarzenegger settles a sexual harassment case by British television personality Anna Richardson. She had claimed that the California governor had groped her breast during a 2000 interview in London, to promote *The Sixth Day*, in which he had starred as an actor. (iv) On December 26, Moninder Singh Pandher and on the following day, his cook and aide Surendra Koli are arrested by Indian police on the charges of murdering several children, and possibly committing acts of necrophilia on them.
89.	2007	(i) Israel recalls Tsuriel Raphael, its ambassador to El Salvador, after police find him drunk, naked and tied up with sex bondage paraphernalia in the garden of his residence. Raphael, in his 50s, was single and gay, A rubber ball was also taken out of his mouth. (ii) Israeli president Moshe Katsav resigns after allegations of sexual harassment against two women who worked under him.

Index

C

D

E

G

H

I

J

K

L

M

O

P

Q

R

S

U

V

W